How to Buy & Sell ^just about Everything

Also in this series

How To Do (Just About) Everything
by Courtney Rosen

How To Fix (Just About) Everything
by Bill Marken

How To Buy & Sell *just about* Everything

Jeff Wuorio

More Than 550 Step-by-Step Instructions for Everything From Buying Life Insurance to Selling Your Screenplay to Choosing a Thoroughbred Racehorse

FREE PRESS

New York • London • Toronto • Sydney • Singapore

THE FREE PRESS
A Division of Simon & Schuster, Inc.
1230 Avenue of the Americas
New York, NY 10020

For information regarding special discounts for bulk purchases, please contact Simon & Schuster Special Sales at 1-800-456-6798 or business@simonandschuster.com

●com|press

Designed and produced by .com press
.com press is a division of Weldon Owen Inc.,
814 Montgomery Street, San Francisco, CA 94133

Printed in the United States by Phoenix Color
10 9 8 7 6 5 4 3 2 1

Library of Congress Cataloging-in-Publication Data
Wuorio, Jeff
    How to buy and sell (just about) everything : more
than 550 step-by-step instructions for everything
from buying life insurance to selling your screenplay to choosing a thoroughbred racehorse / Jeff
Wuorio.
       p. cm.
    Includes index.
    ISBN 0-7432-5043-5
    1. Negotiating in business. 2. Persuasion.
(Psychology). 3. Selling. 4. Purchasing. I. Title

HD58.6.W86 2003
640'.42—dc21   2003051432

CEO: John Owen
President: Terry Newell
COO: Larry Partington
VP, International Sales: Stuart Laurence
VP, Publisher: Roger Shaw
Creative Director: Gaye Allen
Production Manager: Chris Hemesath
Series Editor: Brynn Breuner
Managing Editor: Jennifer Block Martin
Consulting Editor: Bill Marken
Production & Layout: Joan Olson, Phoebe Bixler
Illustrator: William Laird
Copy Editors: Jacqueline Aaron, Rick Clogher,
Gail Nelson-Bonebrake
Contributing Editors: Donald Breuner,
Elizabeth Dougherty, Kevin Ireland, Jane Mason,
Sarah Stephens, Julie Thompson, Robert von Goeben,
Laurie Wertz
Editorial Assistance: Sinclair Crockett, Dave Martin,
Lindsay Powers, Juli Vendzules, Heidi Wilson
Proofreaders: Jacqueline Aaron, Andrew Alden,
Cynthia Rubin
Indexer: Ken DellaPenta

CONTENTS

FOREWORD

A NOTE TO READERS

SPLURGES & RARE EVENTS

PERSONAL FINANCE

CAREERS

REAL ESTATE

HOME & GARDEN

FOOD & DRINK

FAMILY AFFAIRS

HEALTH & BEAUTY

COLLECTIBLES

COMPUTERS & HOME ELECTRONICS

TRAVEL

SPORTS & OUTDOOR RECREATION

CLOTHING & ACCESSORIES

AUTOS & OTHER VEHICLES

INDEX

CONTRIBUTOR CREDITS

A NOTE TO READERS

When attempting to follow any of the advice in this book, please note the following:

Risky activities: Certain activities described in this book are inherently dangerous or risky. Before attempting any new activity, know your own limitations and consider all applicable risks (whether listed or not).

Professional advice: While we strive to provide complete and accurate information, this is not intended as a substitute for professional advice. You should always consult a professional whenever appropriate or if you have any questions or concerns regarding medical, legal or financial advice.

Physical or health-related activities: Be sure to consult a physician before attempting any health- or diet-related activity or any activity involving physical exertion, particularly if you have any condition that could impair or limit your ability to engage in such an activity.

Adult supervision: The activities described in this book are intended for adults only, and they should not be performed by children without responsible adult supervision.

Violations of law: The information provided in this book should not be used to violate any applicable law or regulation.

Sources and prices: Prices and sources for products and services listed in this edition were accurate at press time. Since the nature of any market is changeable, however, we cannot guarantee that any source listed in these pages will continue to carry items mentioned or even remain in business. Similarly, all prices mentioned in this book are approximate only and are subject to change.

All of the information in this book is obtained from sources that the author and publisher believe to be accurate and reliable. However, we make no warranty, expressed or implied, that the information is sufficient or appropriate for every individual, situation or purpose. Further, the information may become outdated over time. You assume the risk and full responsibility for all of your actions, and neither the author nor the publisher will be liable for any loss or damage of any sort, whether consequential, incidental, special or otherwise, that may result from the information presented. Some states do not allow the exclusion of implied warranties or the exclusion of incidental or consequential damages, so the above exclusions may not apply. The descriptions of third-party products, Web sites and services are for informational purposes only and are not intended as an endorsement of any particular product or service.

Foreword

When we set out to write the weighty buying and selling guide you hold
in your hands, we hardly knew what we were in for. Sure, we've all bought
a toothbrush before, or many pairs of athletic shoes, and certainly we've
chosen a ripe juicy peach, but have we ever really thought about what goes
into making smart choices? To make astute decisions, you need not only
the collective knowledge of past purchasing experiences, but also expert
advice, rules of thumb, shrewd insider tips, and brand comparisons. We
labored to bring this level of guidance to each one of the 556 topics covered
in *How to Buy and Sell (Just About) Everything*.

The book is simple to use. For a snapshot of each topic, check out its
What to Look For list and note the number of calculators, which indicate the
difficulty level of the buying or selling decision. To continue, read the concise
steps, useful tips and warnings, and charts. You'll get the information you
need to make better informed, more confident buying and selling decisions.

Your first tip: Start with the Savvy Strategies chapter, then sail on to the
other sections. You'll become a smarter consumer and pick up tricks of
the trade that you'll be able to apply to a wealth of other buying and selling
ventures. You'll also get an insider's edge to stretching every dollar farther.

We included such topics as Shop the Warehouse Stores (11) and Save Big Bucks on Your
Mortgage (174) to help you fatten your wallet. You'll find advice on ways to get rid of things
you're done with (and make some money in the process), like unloading your wedding
dress (76), parting company with a baseball-card collection (394), or losing that clunker in
the driveway (539). For those exalted few for whom money is no object, you'll be able to
brush up on how to Hire a Butler (102), Acquire a Television Network (105), or Buy a
Thoroughbred Racehorse (112). And who could pass up the Buy Happiness (15) or Sell
Yourself to the Devil (125) entries? Just for good measure, we have Buy a Better Mousetrap
(16) in here, too. And though you may not know when you'll be in the market for a private
island, if that day comes, rest assured you'll find out how to buy one in this book.

Thanks to all our authors for spending hours researching mountains of information and
distilling it into concise, readable topics (and for going the extra mile to find out what those
numbers on the sides of auto tires really stand for and which adhesive works with what
material). A special thank you to Derek Wilson, Marcia Layton Turner and Robert von
Goeben for their expert contributions to many chapters. (You'll find the names of all the
talented and skilled authors on the Contributors page in the back of the book.) A deep bow
to managing editor Jennifer Block Martin for her expertise, vigilance and talent, and for
going above and beyond time and time again.

Jeff Wuorio

REHOUSE STORES • BUY WHOLESALE • GET OUT OF DEBT • BUY NOTHING • BUY HAPPINESS • BUY A BETTER MOUSETRAP • BUY TIM
MEONE'S FAVOR • BUY POSTAGE STAMPS WITHOUT GOING TO THE POST OFFICE • TIP PROPERLY • BUY HEALTHY FAST FOOD • BUY S
ING SERVICE • SELL YOURSELF ON AN ONLINE DATING SERVICE • SELL YOURSELF TO YOUR GIRLFRIEND/BOYFRIEND'S FAMILY • BUY
HOOSE FILM FOR YOUR CAMERA • BUY RECHARGEABLE BATTERIES • DONATE TO A GOOD CAUSE • HOLD A PROFITABLE GARAGE SAL
STUDENT DISCOUNTS • BUY FLOWERS WHOLESALE • GET A PICTURE FRAMED • HIRE A MOVER • HIRE A PERSONAL ORGANIZER • FIN
EAT BIRTHDAY PRESENT FOR UNDER $10 • SELECT GOOD CHAMPAGNE • BUY A DIAMOND • BUY JEWELRY MADE OF PRECIOUS METAL
DESMAIDS' DRESSES • HIRE AN EVENT COORDINATOR • HIRE A BARTENDER FOR A PARTY • HIRE A PHOTOGRAPHER • HIRE A CATERE
Y AN ANNIVERSARY GIFT • ARRANGE ENTERTAINMENT FOR A PARTY • COMMISSION A FIREWORKS SHOW • BUY A MOTHER'S DAY GIFT
T • SELECT A THANKSGIVING TURKEY • BUY A HOUSEWARMING GIFT • PURCHASE HOLIDAY CARDS • BUY CHRISTMAS STOCKING STU
HIGH ROLLERS ROOM IN VEGAS, BABY • BUY SOMEONE A STAR • PAY A RANSOM • GET HOT TICKETS • HIRE A LIMOUSINE • BUY A C
M • BUY A PERSONAL JET • ACQUIRE A TELEVISION NETWORK • ACQUIRE A BODY GUARD • BOOK A LUXURY CRUISE AROUND THE W
ROUGHBRED RACEHORSE • BUY A VILLA IN TUSCANY • HIRE A PERSONAL CHEF • PURCHASE CUBAN CIGARS • HIRE A GHOSTWRITE
NESS • MAKE BAIL • DONATE YOUR BODY TO SCIENCE • HIRE YOURSELF OUT AS A MEDICAL GUINEA PIG • SELL PLASMA • SELL YOU
LLEGE EDUCATION • BUY AND SELL STOCKS • CHOOSE A STOCKBROKER • DAY-TRADE (OR NOT) • BUY ANNUITIES • BUY AND SELL M
Y PERSONAL FINANCE SOFTWARE • CHOOSE A TAX PREPARER • SET UP A LEMONADE STAND • SELL YOUR PRODUCT ON TV • HIRE A C
BINESS IDEA • BUY A SMALL BUSINESS • BUY A FRANCHISE • LEASE RETAIL SPACE • LEASE INDUSTRIAL SPACE • LEASE OFFICE SPAC
B SITE • BUY ADVERTISING ON THE WEB • SELL YOUR ART • HIRE A PERSONAL COACH • SELL ON THE CRAFT CIRCUIT • HIRE A LITER,
LING BUSINESS • BUY A HOT DOG STAND • SHOP FOR A MORTGAGE • REFINANCE YOUR HOME • SAVE BIG BUCKS ON YOUR MORTGA
L A FIXER-UPPER • SELL THE FARM • SELL MINERAL RIGHTS • SELL A HOUSE • SELL A HOUSE WITHOUT A REAL ESTATE AGENT • OBT,
OK A VACATION RENTAL • BUY A CONDOMINIUM • RENT AN APARTMENT OR HOUSE • OBTAIN RENTER'S INSURANCE • BUY A LOFT IN
RNISH YOUR STUDIO APARTMENT • BUY USED FURNITURE • BUY DOOR AND WINDOW LOCKS • CHOOSE AN ORIENTAL CARPET • BUY
RRANTIES ON APPLIANCES • FIND PERIOD FIXTURES • BUY A BED AND MATTRESS • HIRE AN INTERIOR DESIGNER • HIRE A FENG SHUI
• BUY A WHIRLPOOL TUB • BUY A SHOWERHEAD • BUY A TOILET • CHOOSE A FAUCET • BUY GLUES AND ADHESIVES • CHOOSE WIN
CHEN CABINETS • CHOOSE A KITCHEN COUNTERTOP • BUY GREEN HOUSEHOLD CLEANERS • STOCK YOUR HOME TOOL KIT • BUY A \
ENTRY DOOR • BUY A GARAGE-DOOR OPENER • BUY LUMBER FOR A DIY PROJECT • HOW TO SELECT ROOFING • HIRE A CONTRACTO
OWERS FOR YOUR GARDEN • SELECT PEST CONTROLS • BUY SOIL AMENDMENTS • BUY MULCH • BUY A COMPOSTER • BUY FERTILIZE
Y KOI FOR YOUR FISH POND • BUY A STORAGE SHED • HIRE AN ARBORIST • BUY BASIC GARDEN TOOLS • BUY SHRUBS AND TREES •
LECT KITCHEN KNIVES • DECIPHER FOOD LABELS • SELECT HERBS AND SPICES • STOCK YOUR KITCHEN WITH STAPLES • EQUIP A KIT
UNTAIN OYSTERS • PURCHASE LOCAL HONEY • CHOOSE POULTRY • SELECT FRESH FISH AND SHELLFISH • SELECT RICE • PURCHASE
EADS • BUY ARTISAN CHEESES • PURCHASE KOSHER FOOD • BUY FOOD IN BULK • CHOOSE COOKING OILS • SELECT OLIVE OIL • SEL
FFEEMAKER OR ESPRESSO MACHINE • PURCHASE A KEG OF BEER • BUY ALCOHOL IN A DRY COUNTY • CHOOSE A MICROBREW • OR
ULATION PREDICTOR KIT • PICK A PREGNANCY TEST KIT • CHOOSE BIRTH CONTROL • FIND THE RIGHT OB-GYN • HIRE A MIDWIFE OR [
OOSE DIAPERS • BUY OR RENT A BREAST PUMP • CHOOSE A CAR SEAT • BUY CHILD-PROOFING SUPPLIES • FIND FABULOUS CHILDC,
CKYARD PLAY STRUCTURE • FIND A GREAT SUMMER CAMP • SELL GIRL SCOUT COOKIES • BUY BRACES FOR YOUR KID • BUY TOYS
A MODEL • SELL USED BABY GEAR, TOYS, CLOTHES AND BOOKS • FIND A COUPLES COUNSELOR • HIRE A FAMILY LAWYER • BUY PRC
PENSES • GET VIAGRA ONLINE • PURCHASE A TOOTHBRUSH • BUY MOISTURIZERS AND ANTIWRINKLE CREAMS • SELECT PAIN RELIEF
PPLIES • SELECT HAIR-CARE PRODUCTS • BUY WAYS TO COUNTER HAIR LOSS • BUY A WIG OR HAIRPIECE • BUY A NEW BODY • GET A
NICURIST • GET WHITER TEETH • SELECT EYEGLASSES AND SUNGLASSES • HIRE A PERSONAL TRAINER • SIGN UP FOR A YOGA CLASS
EA MARKET • RENT SPACE AT AN ANTIQUE MALL • BUY AT AUCTION • KNOW WHAT YOUR COLLECTIBLES ARE WORTH • DICKER WITH D
COGNIZE THE REAL MCCOY • BUY COINS • BUY AN ANTIQUE AMERICAN QUILT • BUY AN ANTIQUE FLAG • LIQUIDATE YOUR BEANIE BAI
WNSHOP • BUY AND SELL COMIC BOOKS • BUY AND SELL SPORTS MEMORABILIA • SELL YOUR BASEBALL-CARD COLLECTIONS • CHO
MPUTER • BUY PRINTER PAPER • BUY A PRINTER • BUY COMPUTER PERIPHERALS • CHOOSE AN INTERNET SERVICE PROVIDER • GET
Y BLANK CDS • BUY AN MP PLAYER • CHOOSE A DVD PLAYER • BUY A VCR • CHOOSE A PERSONAL DIGITAL ASSISTANT • CHOOSE MOI
GITAL CAMCORDER • DECIDE ON A DIGITAL CAMERA • BUY A HOME AUTOMATION SYSTEM • BUY A STATE-OF-THE-ART SOUND SYSTEM
IVERSAL REMOTE • BUY A HOME THEATER SYSTEM • BUY VIRTUAL-REALITY FURNITURE • BUY TWO-WAY RADIOS • BUY A MOBILE ENT
INEY • GET TRAVEL INSURANCE • PICK THE IDEAL LUGGAGE • FLY FOR FREE • BID FOR A SLED RIDE ON THE ALASKAN IDITAROD TRAIL
REIGN OFFICIAL • GET A EURAIL PASS • TAKE AN ITALIAN BICYCLE VACATION • CHOOSE A CHEAP CRUISE • BOOK A HOTEL PACKAGE F
OTLAND • BUY A SAPPHIRE IN BANGKOK • HIRE A RICKSHA IN YANGON • TAKE SALSA LESSONS IN CUBA • BUY A CAMERA IN HONG KO
ST BASEBALL GLOVE • ORDER UNIFORMS FOR A SOFTBALL TEAM • BUY ANKLE AND KNEE BRACES • BUY GOLF CLUBS • JOIN AN ELIT
OWMOBILE • BUY A PERSONAL WATERCRAFT • HIRE A SCUBA INSTRUCTOR • BUY A SKATEBOARD AND PROTECTIVE GEAR • BUY SKAT
EATHER ACTIVITIES • SELL USED SKIS • BUY A SNOWBOARD, BOOTS AND BINDINGS • BUY SKI BOOTS • BUY A BICYCLE • SELL YOUR B
Y A BACKPACK • BUY A BACKPACKING STOVE • BUY A KAYAK • BUY A PERSONAL FLOTATION DEVICE • BUY A WET SUIT • BUY A SURFI
RDER CUSTOM-MADE COWBOY BOOTS • BUY CLOTHES ONLINE • FIND SPECIALTY SIZES • BUY THE PERFECT COCKTAIL DRESS • BUY [
Y A MAN'S SUIT • HIRE A TAILOR • BUY CUSTOM-TAILORED CLOTHES IN ASIA • BUY A BRIEFCASE • SHOP FOR A LEATHER JACKET • BI
TE MONITOR • SELECT A WATCH • BUY KIDS' CLOTHES • CHOOSE CHILDREN'S SHOES • PURCHASE CLOTHES AT OUTLET SHOPS • BU

QUET OF ROSES • BUY SOMEONE A DRINK • GET SOMEONE TO BUY YOU A DRINK • BUY YOUR WAY INTO HIGH SOCIETY • BUY YOUR
DER THE PERFECT BURRITO • ORDER TAKEOUT ASIAN FOOD • ORDER AT A SUSHI BAR • BUY DINNER AT A FANCY FRENCH RESTAURA
WERS FOR YOUR SWEETHEART • BUY MUSIC ONLINE • HIRE MUSICIANS • ORDER A GREAT BOTTLE OF WINE • BUY AN ERGONOMIC D
SECLEANER • HIRE A BABY SITTER • BUY A GUITAR • BUY DUCT TAPE • GET A GOOD DEAL ON A MAGAZINE SUBSCRIPTION • GET SEN
AN • BUY PET FOOD • BUY A PEDIGREED DOG OR CAT • BREED YOUR PET AND SELL THE LITTER • GET A COSTUME • BUY A PIÑATA •
ED GEMSTONES • CHOOSE THE PERFECT WEDDING DRESS • BUY OR RENT A TUXEDO • REGISTER FOR GIFTS • BUY WEDDING GIFTS •
AL WEDDING OFFICIANT • OBTAIN A MARRIAGE LICENSE • ORDER CUSTOM INVITATIONS AND ANNOUNCEMENTS • SELL YOUR WEDDIN
R'S DAY GIFT • SELECT AN APPROPRIATE COMING-OF-AGE GIFT • GET A GIFT FOR THE PERSON WHO HAS EVERYTHING • BUY A GRAD
ANUKKAH GIFTS • PURCHASE A PERFECT CHRISTMAS TREE • BUY A PRIVATE ISLAND • HIRE A SKYWRITER • HIRE A BIG-NAME BAND •
ER • RENT YOUR OWN BILLBOARD • TAKE OUT A FULL-PAGE AD IN *THE NEW YORK TIMES* • HIRE A BUTLER • ACQUIRE A PROFESSION
UR FUR COAT • BOOK A TRIP ON THE ORIENT-EXPRESS • BECOME A WINE MAKER • PURCHASE A PRIVATE/CUSTOM BOTTLING OF WIN
MEMOIRS • COMMISSION ORIGINAL ARTWORK • IMMORTALIZE YOUR SPOUSE IN A SCULPTURE • GIVE AWAY YOUR FORTUNE • HIRE A
DEVIL • NEGOTIATE A BETTER CREDIT CARD DEAL • CHOOSE A FINANCIAL PLANNER • SAVE WITH A RETIREMENT PLAN • SAVE FOR YO
BUY BONDS • SELL SHORT • INVEST IN PRECIOUS METALS • BUY DISABILITY INSURANCE • BUY LIFE INSURANCE • GET HEALTH INSUR
ELOR • HIRE A HEADHUNTER • SELL YOUR   ENT • MARKET YOUR INVENTION • FINANCE YOU
TED OFFICE EQUIPMENT • HIRE SOMEONE   IRE A GRAPHIC DESIGNER • ACQUIRE CONTENT
CH A MAGAZINE STORY • SELL A SCREEN   YOUR BOOK • START A BED-AND-BREAKFAST • S
ME OWNER'S INSURANCE • OBTAIN DISAS   OUSE AT AUCTION • BUY A FORECLOSED HOME
UITY LOAN • BUY A LOT • BUY HOUSE PLA   • PULL BUILDING PERMITS • BUY A VACATION H
UY A TENANCY IN-COMMON UNIT • BUY RE   A MOVIE OR CATALOG SHOOT • FURNISH YOUR H
HT FIXTURES • BUY A PROGRAMMABLE LIG   NCES • BUY FLOOR-CARE APPLIANCES • BUY EX
INCORPORATE FLUID ARCHITECTURE INTO   ARNISH • CHOOSE DECORATIVE TILES • CHOOSE
ITS • GET SELF-CLEANING WINDOWS • CH   SELECT FLOORING • SELECT CARPETING • CHOO
SYSTEM • BUY A HOME ALARM SYSTEM   OXIDE DETECTORS • BUY FIRE EXTINGUISHERS
INTER OR ELECTRICIAN • HIRE A GARDEN   PERFECT ROSEBUSH • BUY FLOWERING BULBS
GETABLE GARDEN • HIRE A GARDEN PROF   R SYSTEM • START A NEW LAWN • BUY A LAWN N
• BUY AN OUTDOOR LIGHTING SYSTEM •   ECT PEACH • BUY AND SELL AT FARMERS' MARK
E FRESH PRODUCE • SELECT MEAT • STOO   ASE A HOLIDAY HAM • BUY NATURAL BEEF • BUY
AND PEPPER • GET A CHEESESTEAK IN P   EATTLE • FIND CRAWDADS IN LOUISIANA • BUY A

**Savvy
Strategies**

UY ETHNIC INGREDIENTS • PURCHASE VIN   OFFEE • ORDER A GREAT CUP OF COFFEE • BUY
• CHOOSE A RESTAURANT FOR A BUSINE   TOCK YOUR BAR • BUY AND SELL SPERM • CHOO
GOOD PEDIATRICIAN • HIRE A CHILD THER   NEW CRIB • CHOOSE A STROLLER • BUY BABY
EAT NANNY • FIND THE RIGHT PRIVATE SC   RAM • SIGN YOUR CHILD UP FOR LESSONS • BU
IDEOS AND MUSIC FOR YOUR CHILDREN •   R • HIRE AN ADOPTION AGENCY • GET YOUR CH
IREMENT COMMUNITY • CHOOSE AN ASS   IVING WILL • BUY A CEMETERY PLOT • PAY FOR
ICINES • SAVE MONEY ON PRESCRIPTION   ONAL • CHOOSE A WHEELCHAIR • BUY HOME-US
DY PIERCING • OBTAIN BREAST IMPLANTS   ALTERNATIVE AND HOLISTIC PRACTITIONERS • C
SELF TO A DAY AT THE SPA • BOOK A MAS   Y AND SELL USED BOOKS • SHOP AT AN ANTIQU
N ANTIQUE APPRAISED • BUY SILVERWARE • EVALUATE DEPRESSION-ERA GLASSWARE • BUY AND SELL STAMPS • BUY ANTIQUE FURN
• SCORE AUTOGRAPHS • TRADE YU-GI-OH CARDS • SNAG STAR WARS ACTION FIGURES • SELL YOUR VINYL RECORD COLLECTION • S
COMPUTER • SHOP FOR A USED COMPUTER OR PERIPHERALS • CHOOSE A LAPTOP OR NOTEBOOK COMPUTER • SELL OR DONATE A
OMAIN NAME • BUY A HOME NETWORK • UPGRADE THE MEMORY IN YOUR COMPUTER • BUY COMPUTER SOFTWARE • CHOOSE A CD
RVICE • NEGOTIATE YOUR LONG-DISTANCE PHONE SERVICE • BUY VIDEO AND COMPUTER GAMES • CHOOSE A FILM CAMERA • CHOOS
O-VIDEO DISTRIBUTION SYSTEM • BUY A SERIOUS TV • CHOOSE BETWEEN CABLE AND SATELLITE TV • GET A DIGITAL VIDEO RECORDE
STEM • GET A PASSPORT, QUICK! • PURCHASE CHEAP AIRLINE TICKETS • FIND GREAT HOTEL DEALS • RENT THE BEST CAR FOR THE L
TY-FREE • SHIP FOREIGN PURCHASES TO THE UNITED STATES • TIP IN A FOREIGN COUNTRY • TIP PROPERLY IN NORTH AMERICA • BRI
ISLANDS • RAFT THE GRAND CANYON • BOOK A CHEAP BUT AWESOME SAFARI • RENT A CAMEL IN CAIRO • GET SINGLE-MALT SCOTCH
R WAY ONTO A MOUNT EVEREST EXPEDITION • HIRE A TREKKING COMPANY IN NEPAL • RENT OR BUY A SATELLITE PHONE • BUY YOUR
SELL FOUND GOLF BALLS • BUY ATHLETIC SHOES • BUY A RACKET • BUY A GYM MEMBERSHIP • BUY AN AEROBIC FITNESS MACHINE
FISHING • GO SKYDIVING • BUY WEIGHTLIFTING EQUIPMENT • CHOOSE A CAR RACK OR CARRIER • BUY SKIS • BUY CLOTHES FOR CO
RAGE SALE • COMMISSION A CUSTOM-BUILT BICYCLE • BUY A PROPERLY FITTED HELMET • BUY THE OPTIMAL SLEEPING BAG • BUY A
LY-FISHING GEAR • BUY ROCK-CLIMBING EQUIPMENT • BUY A CASHMERE SWEATER • PURCHASE VINTAGE CLOTHING • SELL USED CL
HES AT A DISCOUNT • CHOOSE A BASIC WARDROBE FOR A MAN • BUY A MAN'S DRESS SHIRT • PICK OUT A NECKTIE • BUY A WOMAN'
LOTHES • GET A GREAT-FITTING BRA • CHOOSE A HIGH-PERFORMANCE SWIM SUIT • HIGH PERFORMANCE WORKOUT CLOTHES • BUY
BUY THE BASICS FOR YOUR CAR • BUY A USED CAR • BUY OR SELL A CAR ONLINE • BUY A HYBRID CAR • SELL A CAR • BUY A MOTOR

1 Be a Savvy Consumer

You work hard for your money. Retailers work equally hard to separate you from it. Being a savvy consumer means looking beyond the sales pitch and assessing the true value of a product.

Steps

1 Utilize the full potential of the Internet to research price, options and product reviews before you buy. Read Consumer Reports (consumerreports.org) for product reviews and the Better Business Bureau (bbb.org) or your county Citizen and Consumer Affairs Office for complaints against a business.

2 Get feedback and recommendations from friends or family who have made similar purchases. Their first-hand experience and tips will be invaluable.

3 Know what you need as far as features and what you can spend before you enter a store.

4 Ask plenty of questions. Be wary of salespeople who are overly aggressive or evasive in answering them. If you're not getting the service and information you need, find the manager.

5 Research and read labels to determine if products are made with potentially toxic materials or pose any danger to people, pets or the environment by their use. Investigate nontoxic alternatives.

6 Always find out what the return and exchange policy is before you buy. See 4 Make Returns. If you're buying online, call the toll-free customer-service phone number with return questions.

7 Read the fine print on a warranty or contract and ask for a clarification if it's unclear. Important information is often obfuscated by legal mumbo jumbo.

8 Get a signed and dated contract that spells out particulars whenever you hire service people. Before you hire a mechanic, contractor or any service professional, get an estimate and the scope of work in writing. See 537 Hire a Reliable Mechanic.

9 Charge it, especially if you're making an online, phone or mail-order purchase. Credit card companies will not hold you liable for fraudulent charges and will charge back the merchant if you receive falsely advertised, defective or damaged merchandise.

10 Avoid layaways and rent-to-own plans in most cases. You may be better off putting the money in a savings account so that you—not the store—collect the interest, until you save enough to buy it outright.

11 Stash all receipts, warranties, owner's manuals, contracts and written estimates in a well-organized filing system. A complaint is much harder to prove without documentation. Save packaging for the first week in case you discover defects or unsatisfactory performance; returns may need to be in their original packaging.

What to Look For

- Price comparisons
- Product reviews
- Return and exchange policy
- Customer service number
- Contract and warranty

Tips

Consult your doctor before buying health-related supplies, equipment or services. That will help you avoid products with dubious health benefits.

Use a credit card that rewards you with air travel miles and other incentives to reap even more benefits from your purchases.

Don't be duped by sale signs. Ask yourself, "Am I really getting a good deal for my money?"

Check the packaging and condition of a product. If a box has been retaped, ask if the item was a return, a floor model, or a reconditioned item. If so, ask for a discount and make sure the warranty is still in full effect.

Warning

Never pay money up front for goods or services offered over the phone, and don't give your credit card number or Social Security number to anyone or any company you don't know.

2 Get Something for Nothing

There's truth behind the saying "There's no such thing as a free lunch." Some freebies require that you register your address, which may bury you in junk mail. Others require your time or energy. However, for the intrepid bargain hunter, true deals make exciting prey.

FREEBIE STRATEGY

Search the Web for "free stuff." You'll find Web sites that index online freebies from manufacturers and retailers.

Arrive at rummage sales, garage sales, flea markets, farmers markets and library book sales an hour before closing to find drastically reduced prices or freebies.

Shop the nurseries at jumbo retailers in the autumn. Some stores give away dormant perennials (if they don't know better) that will rebloom in the spring.

Become a mystery shopper or participate in survey groups to get free meals, products or services and, possibly, even a paycheck. Search online to find opportunities in your area.

Attend the grand opening of new stores for free samples and giveaways. Many stores take a loss in freebies on their first day to attract customers.

Go on factory tours. You'll often get free samples of whatever the factory makes, be it ice cream, tortillas or peanut butter.

Call customer service if you have a legitimate complaint on an item. You may get a replacement product, plus freebies to keep you happy.

When making a large purchase, such as a computer, sofa or big-screen TV, ask the salesperson, "What else will I get if I buy this here?" You may discover rebates, offers and giveaways.

Volunteer for concerts, athletic events and other fund-raisers for charities and nonprofits. You'll find plenty of free food, T-shirts and products donated by corporate sponsors.

Get free diapers, formula mix and baby food by disclosing your address to third parties when you register for baby gifts or sign up for new parent services.

Listen to radio stations that give away tickets and other prizes to listeners. Use speed-dial and multiple lines to better your chances when you call in.

WARNING   If you join grocery store savings clubs and give your address, be aware that you've volunteered your personal information, which will be used for marketing and sales purposes.

3 Buy Products and Services Online

No longer just for the techno-savvy, online shopping has been embraced wholeheartedly by the mainstream community. In fact, more than 60 percent of people worldwide have bought something online.

Steps

1 Shop retailers with a reputation for quality products and excellent customer service. Bookmark them for easy access. Pay attention to the experiences of friends and colleagues, and avoid shady or unscrupulous merchants.

2 Find out what fellow surfers think of a site. Epinions.com has customer ratings of online stores, which are helpful when deciding whether to do business with a particular site. Shop at Web sites that are quick to load and easy to navigate through so you can find what you want quickly. Look for secure and simple ordering procedures.

3 Use price comparison tools, such as DealTime.com and Bizrate.com, to compare brands, prices and product features across several sites. Consider buying an online subscription to ConsumerReports.org to get critical information on large and small purchases.

4 Read customer and media reviews to find out more about a product or service. Amazon.com lists editorial and customer reviews. Cnet.com and TechTV.com are good sources for technology reviews. Look for comments from consumers in a demographic similar to your own.

5 Read the "About Us" section if you're buying from an unfamiliar Web site to find out how long the company has been in business and whether it has third-party recommendations. Check for a toll-free customer-service number.

6 Look for enhanced shopping guides and options. For example, apparel merchant Lands' End allows you to shop by size, color, product and preference, and even has virtual mannequins that you can use to "try on" outfits (see 500 Buy Clothes Online). Other merchants allow you to listen to partial tracks from CDs or read book excerpts before you buy.

7 If you're shopping for a service, such as a plumber, look for clearly posted cancellation policies and free, instant quotes. Sites like Respond.com and Improvenet.com recommend prescreened service providers or contractors by region.

8 If you're buying a product, review the shipping and handling costs, the return policy and whether the company pays shipping on returned items (see 4 Make Returns).

9 Charge your purchases on a credit or debit card. See 1 Be a Savvy Consumer.

What to Look For

- Reputable retailer
- Easy browsing or searching
- Customer ratings
- Price and feature comparisons
- Buying guides
- Shipping costs and return policy
- Secure transactions
- Receipt or confirmation

Tips

The Better Business Bureau Online (bbbonline.org) lets you search for or file complaints against a specific online retailer. Look for the BBB stamp of approval on sites that meet its standards and pay a membership fee.

Make sure any online retailer posts its privacy policy prominently and allows you to opt out of having your information used for marketing purposes or shared with other parties.

Warnings

Make sure that any purchase transactions you conduct are secure. A URL that begins with *https://* (instead of *http://*) signals that you are sending and receiving encrypted information, for security purposes.

10 Save a copy of the receipt and confirmation number on your hard drive, or print it out and keep a record of the transaction.

11 Open an electronic wallet. Available at Yahoo! Shopping and elsewhere, this application allows you to store your credit card information in one place to avoid retyping it every time you make a purchase. American Express ID Keeper (www.american express.com/idkeeper) is a Windows-based application that lets users securely store personal data, credit card information, and Web site log-ins and passwords. Additionally, this data is stored directly on the embedded chip on the American Express Blue card.

Keep your passwords private. Never share your Social Security number or checking account number when making a purchase, and never send your credit card number via e-mail.

4 Make Returns

With a surge in retail fraud, many stores are tightening up on their return policies. Stores are not legally bound to accept returns unless a product was defective or falsely advertised. The lesson? Know the store's policy before you buy, be courteous, don't expect something you're not entitled to, and hold on to those receipts.

Steps

1 Present the item in its original packaging, with the receipt and the credit card number, if any, used in the purchase. Most stores require that returns be made within 30 days, though some allow 90 days.

2 Go to the customer service counter or to a cashier. Early mornings are a good time to make returns. Tell the person behind the counter that you'd like to make a return. Provide a short explanation if necessary.

3 Expect to receive cash or have a credit applied to your credit card account. To reduce fraud, some retailers will send a check instead of providing cash. And some will only give a store credit.

4 Suggest an exchange for a product of equal value if the salesperson refuses an outright return. Be patient with the employees. Being aggressive is unlikely to help. Most salespeople know that a happy customer is good for them and, therefore, will find a way to make you happy, if they possibly can.

5 Asking to speak to a manager or supervisor may be necessary but may anger the salesperson. As a first attempt, try something like "I understand your hands are tied. Is there someone else that I can talk to?"

6 Be prepared to give up on an attempt if you meet unreasonable resistance. Try to come back when more knowledgeable staff are on hand. Do not make insults or threats as this will prejudice future negotiations against you.

What to Look For

- Store policy
- Original packaging and receipt
- Refund or merchandise credit
- Item-for-item exchange

Tip

If a product is defective or was falsely advertised and the store refuses to take it back, file a complaint with the local branch of the Better Business Bureau or your state's consumer rights department.

Warning

If you are returning to a store that has many "seasons" and you don't have a receipt, you may only get a merchandise credit for the sale price of the item, which may be much less than you paid. This is a frequent issue with stores that have five to six seasons per year and do heavy markdowns to move merchandise.

5 Deal With an Unsatisfactory Purchase

As a consumer, you have the right to assume that a product will work as advertised. This is the product's implied warranty. It doesn't matter whether you bought something through mail order, over the phone, online or at a brick-and-mortar store. But if something does go wrong, there are a number of ways you can get satisfaction.

Steps

1 See 4 Make Returns.

2 Arm yourself with information before you buy. Make sure you know where to direct a complaint in case there's a problem. If you're getting an item delivered, be sure you know the retailer's policy on shipping and on merchandise that's lost or damaged in transit. Review the warranty on an item (see 209 Buy Extended Warranties on Appliances).

2 Visit the store with the item and receipt. For an online purchase, e-mail customer service and include your order number. In a friendly but firm tone, explain the problem and your desired solution. If this fails to remedy the situation, call customer service. Most Web sites list customer-service phone numbers (in their "About Us" or "Contact Us" section). Or, call (800) 555-1212 for the toll-free directory.

3 If a store salesperson doesn't give you adequate help, or isn't able to remedy the situation, ask to speak to a supervisor. If the supervisor won't help, ask for the name of the store manager or owner. Continue up the chain to a regional manager or the manager at the national headquarters.

4 Be persistent but polite on the phone, and get the name, title and direct number of each person you speak to. To avoid aggravating disconnections during transfers, and getting stuck in the voice mail quagmire, always ask for the number you are being transferred to. Address the salesperson by name in a friendly manner and make it clear that you are confident that, although he or she is not personally responsible for the problem, he or she will want to rectify the problem and reward your loyalty to the company.

5 Be prepared to ask for a resolution. If the company admits fault, ask how they intend "to make it right." For example, if a bank screws up your account, ask for free checking for a year. If Sears fails to deliver a washing machine in a timely manner, ask for 50 percent off the unit. If you're stumped for a specific request, ask the sales representative, "What can you do to make this right and restore my faith in your company again?"

What to Look For

- Merchandise policy
- Customer-service contact information
- Consumer protection agencies
- Better Business Bureau
- Legal options
- Public attention

Tips

If a retailer is unresponsive, contact the product's manufacturer directly either on its Web site or in resources like the *Standard & Poor's Register of Corporations*.

Document everything. Write down names, titles and phone numbers of people you speak to, plus the date and time. Record what they tell you. Keep a file of receipts, warranties, correspondence and photographs.

6 Contact your credit or debit card company, if you used it to make the purchase, and request in writing that the merchant be "charged back." Credit card companies protect consumers from unauthorized charges, incomplete orders, defective products or false advertising.

7 Write a letter if your efforts fail to get results. Get the name of the person who will handle your complaint (preferably someone in management). Go online to the Consumer Action Web site (consumeraction.gov) to see a sample letter and get tips on crafting an effective complaint. Send the letter by registered mail or by overnight delivery to confirm the company receives it.

8 If the company still fails to fix the problem, report your complaint to a local or state consumer protection agency, with a copy to the company. For interstate sales, contact the Federal Trade Commission. The Consumer Action Web site will help you find the proper government agency.

9 At the same time that you complain to a government agency, file a complaint with the Better Business Bureau (bbb.org or bbbonline.org for online purchases) and with any trade organi zation that regulates the industry or retailer.

10 Consider mediation or arbitration, small claims court, or legal action as final remedies. The Better Business Bureau will help mediate disputes. Small claims court is a do-it-yourself legal recourse. Hiring a lawyer should be considered only in extreme cases where damage or injury exceed $20,000 since your legal fees will mount quickly.

11 Let a manager or supervisor at the company in question know that you intend to go public. Almost every local television station has a consumer reporter or a "consumer rip-off" feature. Contact them with a letter detailing your grievance and asking for help in finding a resolution. Companies hate bad press— even the threat of it can whip them into behaving.

A courteous and pleasant approach will aid your efforts. Avoid becoming con-frontational or emotional.

Try to get retailers and serv-ice representatives to see your point of view. A good question to ask is "What would you do if you were in my situation?"

Sell Products and Services Online

A Montana saddlery ships boots to an urban cowboy in New York City. A Florida nursery ships exotic orchids to Alaska. The Internet has revolutionized selling for small businesses and individuals with home businesses. You no longer need a physical store to sell your wares and reach many more interested buyers. Use existing venues or set up your own online store.

Steps

Sell through existing venues

1 Go to sites like Amazon.com or Half.com to sell used books, CDs and other items at a fixed price. You can list items in exchange for a percentage of the sale. Avoid sites that charge you a fee to post an ad.

2 List items that are hard to ship (like a pool table or futon) on local sites such as Craigslist.org or in regional online classifieds, so that the buyer can pick it up.

3 Use online auction sites to sell collectibles, antiques, out-of-print books and anything else you find in the attic or garage. (See 10 Use Online Auction Sites.)

4 Get listed in local directories and on referral Web sites, such as Respond.com or Improvenet.com, if you have a professional service for hire. These sites conduct background checks and refer potential customers to you for a fee.

5 If you're selling financial, romantic, psychic or other advice, consider using a site like Keen.com. Customers get connected to you through the service, which charges the customer by the minute and keeps a percentage of the profits.

Set up cybershop

1 Set up an online store. A substantial investment is required for start-up costs, which include domain name registration, site hosting, e-commerce software, site development and maintenance, marketing, credit card transaction fees, Internet access and customer service. There's also the time spent on design, taking photos of inventory and updating the site (see 157 Hire Someone to Design and Build Your Web Site).

2 Design a sleek, professional, easy-to-navigate site that loads quickly at both dial-up and broadband speeds. Or, check out Amazon.com, eBay.com and Yahoo Shopping (shopping.yahoo .com) for turnkey solutions for building an online store—the bonus is that you tap into the heavy traffic of these popular sites and take advantage of search engines.

3 Include concise, informative copy and photographs to bring traffic to your site. Update it frequently to keep the content fresh.

What to Look For

- Existing venues
- Regional sites
- Capital investment for e-commerce
- Web-site design
- URL placement

Tip

Image is everything when you sell online. Post copy that is impeccably written and free of errors. Include high-quality, well-cropped photographs of your products.

4 Register your URL on all the major search engines (including Google.com, Yahoo.com, Lycos.com and HotBot.com) to make sure your site shows up in relevant searches. Include keywords in meta tags in HTML files to increase the chances of getting hits from search engines. You may, however, find that paying for placement results in more traffic.

5 Advertise your Web site on heavily trafficked sites and through banner swaps (see 160 Buy Advertising on the Web). See Cyberatlas.internet.com for a compilation of online marketing stats and articles.

6 Establish trust. Post your privacy policy prominently. Have customer-service information clearly displayed, including third-party recommendations, like BBBOnline.com, and provide quick response. Set up a secure server to handle credit card transactions. Answer customer queries by phone or e-mail promptly, effectively and courteously.

7 Use discretion: Obnoxious, blinking ads and spam e-mails drive away customers.

Warning

Beware of individuals or companies that offer to sell instant access to wholesale inventories for your commerce site. Finding wholesale inventories isn't easy, and anyone who says differently is misleading you.

7 Save Money with Coupons

Clipping coupons can trim your grocery bills if you have the time, discipline and patience. Keep track of the money you save, then reward yourself every now and then. You deserve it!

Steps

1 Set up an easy-to-use system to organize your coupons. Keep it near your car keys as a handy reminder before you go shopping.

2 Scour newspapers, magazines, coupon mailers, food packaging, grocery store receipts and the Internet for coupons.

3 Clip coupons only for products you'd buy anyhow (see 1 Be a Savvy Consumer). Don't let irresistible savings dupe you into buying items you don't need.

4 Know prices. Brand-name products with coupons often cost more than generics without coupons.

5 Look for hidden costs. A $3 pizza coupon may not seem as good a deal after you figure in the tip for the delivery guy.

6 Find out if your grocery store will match manufacturers' coupons to double your savings. Many stores will.

7 Look to layer savings. If a store is offering a coupon on an item and you also have a manufacturer's coupon, use both.

8 Join grocery store savings clubs and use manufacturers' coupons on club sale items.

What to Look For

- Newspaper and magazine inserts
- Manufacturers' coupons
- Savings clubs

Tip

A Web search for "coupons" will yield thousands of hits, so make your search as specific as possible.

Warning

Coupons, like produce, are perishable. Use them before they expire.

8 Negotiate

Many people hate negotiating, but with a few simple tactics, it can be rewarding and fun. The following steps relate mostly to making purchases but the overall ideas—research the market, be upbeat and positive, and know what something is worth to you—can be applied to almost any negotiation. Check out 1 Be a Savvy Consumer as well.

Steps

1 Do your research ahead of time to find the best deals. If you're looking for consumer goods, the Internet is a great place to look at prices and features. Use online comparison tools like ConsumerReports.org, Yahoo Shopping (shopping.yahoo.com), and DealTime.com. If you're negotiating a salary increase, know what other people in your profession are making. If you want to buy a pedigreed puppy, find out what they're going for.

2 Know what an item is worth to you and set an upper limit on what you're willing to spend. It's easy during negotiations for the game to shift. A salesperson might offer a price reduction on one item as long as you buy an additional one. Keep your needs and your goal well defined and stick to your limit. This also applies to salary negotiations: Securing a raise may necessitate additional responsibilities.

3 Adopt a direct but lighthearted attitude. Nobody wants to deal with a sourpuss. This applies to salary negotiations as well as purchases. Your boss will deal with you more openly if you are able to state your position clearly, including why you deserve that raise. Practice salary negotiations with a pro—see 145 Hire a Career Counselor.

4 Remain indifferent when making purchases. Hardball price negotiation requires the seller to believe that you are willing to walk away. To be convincing at this, you must indeed be willing to walk. Practice with small purchases and you'll see this is true. Remember that most consumer goods, even major purchases like cars, are not "one of a kind," "rare," or "hard to find," so don't be swayed by these claims. This tactic has limited application for salary negotiations unless you are truly ready to quit. Threatening to quit is not likely to secure your raise.

5 Make the seller (or your boss) want to say yes. Most people want to be deal makers and problem solvers. Salespeople want to sell. Your boss wants productive and loyal employees. You have a problem (the washing machine is too expensive, your salary is too small) and you want their help. They are the important decision makers and you will have a great deal of respect for them if they can solve this problem.

6 Hire professional help for complicated negotiations. Real estate transactions, for example, are too complicated for most nonprofessionals. (See 184 Sell a House Without a Real Estate Agent.)

What to Look For

- Know the market
- Be friendly
- Make the seller want to help

Tip

Friends and relatives are a great source of information about sensitive financial matters but be sure to conduct additional research. Stories involving money are always subject to exaggeration.

9 Buy Green

The environmental challenges of pollution, global warming and scarce resources are daunting. Can you make a difference through your daily purchases? Yes, if you're prepared to do a little research. Every dollar spent on environmentally friendly products encourages manufacturers to think green.

GREEN PRODUCT	HOW IT HELPS
Kitchen	
Cloth napkin/dish towel	Saves trees and reduces the use of paper.
Cloth shopping bag	Reduces the use of paper or plastic bags.
Nontoxic kitchen cleaner	Reduces the amount of phosphates and other toxins flowing down the drain.
Energy-efficient appliance	Conserves energy and natural resources. Source of the most dramatic differences are found in energy-efficient refrigerators.
CFC-free refrigerator	Reduces the emissions of chlorofluorocarbons (CFCs), which contribute to ozone depletion and global warming.
Unbleached coffee filter	Reduces use of the toxic pollutant chlorine.
Bathroom	
Unbleached toilet tissue	Reduces use of the toxic pollutant chlorine.
Tampon without plastic applicator	Reduces plastic applicators in waterways, where they pose danger to fish and birds, which mistake them for food.
Electric razor	Reduces waste.
Nonaerosol deodorant/hairspray	Eliminates aerosol release of CFCs.
Low-flow shower head	Conserves water.
General household	
Bulk-size cleaner	Reduces waste.
Nontoxic cleaner	Reduces water, air and land pollution from polishes, detergents and other cleaning agents.
Rechargeable batteries	Reduces toxic waste found in disposable batteries.
Reusable camera/lighter	Reduces waste.
Car/transportation	
Fuel-efficient vehicle (30 miles per gallon or more)	Reduces gasoline consumption and air pollution. See 526 Buy a Hybrid Car.
Bicycle	Reduces traffic through zero-emission transportation. See 482 Buy a Bicycle.
Office	
Recycled paper	Saves trees and encourages production of recycled products.
Refillable toner cartridge	Reduces toxic and excessive waste of toner cartridges.

10 Use Online Auction Sites

Imagine having a garage sale that millions of people visit. Online auctions allow you to do just that. Television sets, bean bag chairs or designer wedding dresses: If you have it or are dying to get it, an online auction is the place to go. Yahoo.com and Amazon.com have auction sites, but eBay.com is widely considered the premier site for buyers and sellers alike. For general auction tips, check out 374 Buy at Auction.

Steps

Buying

1 Sleuth out the going rate for what you're shopping for. Check final bids for similar items in archived auctions. Visit Tias.com or WorthGuide.com to see prices for collectibles. See 1 Be a Savvy Consumer and 375 Know What Your Collectibles Are Worth.

2 Check a seller's history for positive comments. Online auctions are self-policing with buyers and sellers offering feedback on each other. A seller's name will be followed by the number of auctions he or she has held and a satisfaction rating by the bidders.

3 Provide feedback on other sellers to encourage them to do the same for you. Take a deep breath before you fire off an inflammatory negative review—these reviews are permanent and may reflect poorly on you.

4 E-mail the seller with any questions, and if anything about the seller seems dubious, don't bid.

5 Read the item description carefully; some sellers bury negative information in confusing language or small print. If the size of an item isn't included and is important, e-mail the seller for it— photos can be deceiving.

6 Find out the cost of shipping beforehand. If it's not listed, ask the seller. Some sellers overcharge for shipping to make extra money.

7 Use proxy bids, which let you make an initial bid and set a maximum one. Your bid then gets automatically increased against competing bids, until you win the auction or someone outbids your maximum. Most sites let you know via e-mail when you've been outbid.

8 Add pennies to your offer to sneak above other bids. For example, if someone has a maximum bid of $75 and you bid $75.07, you'll beat them with only 7 cents.

What to Look For

- Buyer and seller history
- Item description
- Proxy bids and sniping
- Dutch auctions
- Site regulations
- E-mail communication
- Shipping and insurance

Tips

Know your limit. Avoid getting swept up in the bidding frenzy and paying more than an item is worth or that you can afford.

Be wary of shill bidders who work in cahoots with the seller to artificially drive up the auction price. If you suspect a seller is using shill bidders, report it to the Website administrator.

Both eBay.com and Amazon.com insure auctions from reputable sellers up to a certain amount. They also offer escrow services so buyer and seller can safely exchange large amounts of money.

Many auction sites have wonderful community features that allow you to network with other collectors. Take advantage of them.

9 Be a sniper. Bid at the very last minute before an auction ends to "snipe," or snatch away an item from another bidder. There are Web sites that will do the sniping for you for a fee.

10 Use a credit or debit card if possible. These cards provide protections to you as a buyer that checks and money orders don't. Never send cash.

11 Save all e-mails related to a transaction until it is completed and you are satisfied with your purchase.

Selling

1 Buy several items from an auction site before you begin selling to build up your personal profile with positive feedback.

2 Include photos that show the complete item, plus details of unique features or flaws. Compress the image files to minimize download time for people checking out your stuff.

3 Do a search before you list an item to make sure there aren't other people auctioning the same thing. Wait to list your item until the other auction ends.

4 Use so-called Dutch auctions (in which you sell more than one of the same item) only on very popular products; otherwise you'll drive down the demand and price.

5 Know the auction site's rules. For example, while you can purchase guns at other sites, many auction sites (including eBay.com) prohibit the sale of firearms, explosives, live animals and human body parts.

6 Plan your auction to end at a time when lots of people use the site, such as weeknights or weekend days. Run longer auctions so more people have time to stumble upon them.

7 Give bidders every reason to place a bid. Accept credit cards and offer guaranteed satisfaction. Respond promptly to questions from bidders.

8 E-mail the winning bidder promptly to arrange payment (many sites use PayPal). Ship the item as soon as the payment goes through. Print all e-mails related to a sale and file them until the transaction is completed.

9 Package items securely and use a shipping service that automatically insures packages up to $100. Buy insurance for packages worth more than $100.

Write (and spell-check) an attention-getting title and a thorough, accurate product description. Include condition, history, dimensions, distinct markings, shipping costs, and payment options. Glean keywords from other ads that people are likely to search for and write your item description accordingly.

Warning

Never provide your Social Security number or bank account number to sellers. If a seller asks for this information, report it to the Web administrator immediately.

11 Shop the Warehouse Stores

Stores like Costco and Sam's Club are worth going to just for the people-watching. Whether they're a good deal or not depends on if you're an educated consumer and can exercise some discipline against impulse purchases.

Steps

1 Do not expect knowledgeable salespeople. While many of these stores pride themselves on having friendly employees, there's no question that they keep their costs low by employing minimum-wage labor. If you haven't already done some comparison shopping, you probably won't be able to make an informed purchase.

2 Understand the annual fee required by most warehouse stores. If you don't plan to use the store frequently it probably isn't worth joining. With an annual fee of $35, you will need to spend about $260 before you begin to see any savings at all, compared to regular grocery stores.

3 Compare price tags. On average, the prices at a warehouse store are lower than at most other stores. But that's not a guarantee that all prices are lower. Some stores will advertise a very low price on a few items, then hope you'll assume all prices are low. Unless you've checked the prices somewhere else, you can't assume you're saving any money. And popular brand name goods at a warehouse store are frequently more expensive than generic goods at a regular grocery store.

4 Be aware that inventory may change rapidly and if you spot something you need, get it. Many items are in a one-time shipment.

5 Resist impulse buying. "The more you buy, the more you save" is a big, fat tempting lie. Buying and saving are two different things. If you buy something you don't need, you're not saving anything, you're wasting. See 1 Be a Savvy Consumer.

6 Get deep savings on big ticket items like electronics, furnishings and appliances if you know what you need. On the other hand, don't compromise on style, color or quality just to save on something that may not fit with the rest of your house.

7 Bring cash, a checkbook, a debit card or a Discover card. Most clubs don't accept credit cards.

8 Pay attention to rebates. In order to get the full benefit from a warehouse store you have to follow through with the rebate mail-ins that apply to some purchases. Know the procedure for collecting your rebate and be sure to get the proper forms.

What to Look For

- Competitors' prices
- Savings on big-ticket items
- Rebates

Tips

Warehouse stores offer film processing, pharmacies, carpet sales and installation, automotive services and other features to enhance membership benefits.

If you run a small business or plan to shop a lot, get an executive card that returns 2 percent of your expenditures at the end of the year.

Warehouse stores offer excellent deals on seasonal items like patio furniture and barbecue grills. They also have very good deals on popular books, CDs and DVDs.

Costco (costco.com) and Sam's Club (samsclub.com) both have online stores.

Some clubs offer temporary passes so you can browse the selections before you join. If you buy anything with the temporary pass, you'll need to pay an additional 5 to 10 percent.

12 Buy Wholesale

If "never pay retail" is your credo, you know that a trip to the outlet mall is just the tip of the iceberg. But how low can the prices go? Further reductions will only be possible through some effort on your part, like buying larger quantities or securing a reseller's license.

Steps

1 Work your network of colleagues, friends and family to find wholesale sources. Plumbers, contractors, landscapers, florists, interior designers and jewelers all have access to wholesale markets and/or prices. These professionals may require that you hire them to take advantage of reduced prices, so balance these expenditures against potential savings.

2 Call wholesale suppliers and ask if they have special hours for the general public. Wholesalers are listed in the Yellow Pages by category, such as "Plumbing Supplies—Wholesale." They'll charge sales tax and mark up prices a bit, but you can still find great bargains.

3 Join associations or professional groups that share your interests. Many groups, through their combined buying power, have access to lower prices. Magazines and Web sites devoted to your special interest will probably advertise groups to join.

4 Consider applying for a business license and reseller's license from your state or county if you use a lot of something. Most wholesale suppliers will sell to you once you supply this information. Of course, you have to either be in business already or establish one. This is not as difficult as it might first seem. Existing hobbies, interests or skills can be treated as a business venture. For example, if you enjoy gardening, look into getting a business license as a plant nursery. A few sales to friends will make you legitimate. Research legal requirements carefully and compare costs to expected savings.

5 Shop around to find the best prices. Warehouse clubs often have prices that are close to wholesale. See 11 Shop the Warehouse Stores.

6 Pay by credit card wherever possible for optimal buyer protection. If you have to pay COD, make sure to thoroughly inspect all merchandise before you accept goods.

What to Look For

- Wholesaler contacts
- Wholesale suppliers
- Business license

Tips

Some companies buy overstocks or discontinued items and sell them in bulk quantities at wholesale or below-wholesale prices. While these can be great bargains, there's probably a reason for this—they were unpopular to begin with.

Cosmetic seconds, items that are functionally sound but have a slight blemish, can be great deals. Usually the blemish is insignificant, but be sure to check before you buy.

Highpoint, North Carolina, is the wholesale furniture capital of the United States. Research manufacturer names, models, style numbers, color descriptions and material specifications for furniture pieces that you like. Then, during Highpoint's semiannual after-market sales, purchase clearance items and floor samples.

Warning

If it sounds too good to be true, it probably is. Web sites that offer to give you instant access to wholesale inventories are highly suspect.

13 Get Out of Debt

It's downright silly that people who bend over backwards to find bargains also pay hundreds or thousands of dollars in interest every year without thinking twice. If you really want to save money, pay off outstanding loans and credit card debt as quickly as possible. Some of these guidelines may sound harsh but the price you'll pay for ignoring them is even harsher.

Steps

1 Make a monthly budget and stick to it. Housing, food, utilities, car and insurance payments have to be made. Allocate an additional amount each month to paying off your debt. Many financial planners say this is the most effective way to manage your finances. See 141 Buy Personal Finance Software.

2 Control your spending. This is the first step toward fixing money problems. Most people who spend too much are enthralled with the act of buying, not the value of the goods. Question every purchase—what will happen if you don't buy? You might be surprised how little real value most stuff has and how easily you can do without it.

3 Keep a shopping journal of what you buy each day and how much it cost. This may seem tedious but will track each expenditure and encourage conscious spending.

4 Destroy all of your credit cards except one, with the lowest possible (long-term) interest rate. Leave this card at home and use it only for emergencies. Transfer the debt on your other cards to this remaining card. Carry a small amount of cash for daily expenses. See 126 Negotiate a Better Credit Card Deal.

5 Maintain contact with your creditors. Avoiding phone calls and letters from your creditors will make your problems worse. They want to work with you and it's in your interest to do so before they turn things over to a collection agency.

6 Refinance your mortgage at a lower rate. If your credit is already bad, this may not be possible. But if you can get a lower rate, you can apply your savings directly to pay down your debt, or pull extra cash out to take care of it at once. See 173 Refinance Your Home and 174 Save Big Bucks on Your Mortgage.

7 Investigate a home equity loan with which you can pay off other debts. The idea is to combine your debts into one payment, at the lowest possible interest rate. If you have substantial credit card debt, you're probably paying a very high interest rate, so other loan options are worth exploring. Approach your bank for information. (See 185 Obtain a Home Equity Loan.)

8 Sell valuables and use the money to pay off your debt. RVs, cars, boats, and other expensive toys should be eliminated. They won't be fun anyway, if they're dragging you into financial ruin.

What to Look For

- Mortgage options
- Liquidated assets
- Debt consolidation
- Lower interest rates
- Lower payoff amount

Tips

CheapskateMonthly.com provides further ideas about controlling your expenses and managing your money.

Pay your bills on time. Besides imposing hefty late fees, creditors bump up interest rates for late payments. Pay parking tickets and car registration swiftly to avoid late penalties.

Call the credit company if, after the above measures, you still can't tackle your debt. Ask for a "lower payoff amount." Credit companies will often work with you in severe cases so that they can recoup some of their money.

Warnings

Never use a debt consolidator that advertises aggressively or promises you a quick fix. Often, they'll plunge you deeper into debt and may even trash your credit record.

Don't apply for a zero-interest card unless you're absolutely committed to paying off your debt before the interest-free period ends. If you don't, you'll get stuck with a very high rate.

14 Buy Nothing

Ownership can be a burden. Once you buy something, you have to carry it around, fix it, remember where you put it, and keep it clean. Experiment with the freedom of buying nothing and embrace Henry David Thoreau's sentiment that "he who owns little is little owned."

Steps

1 Practice reverse snobbery. Express contempt for people who mindlessly buy things. This has two benefits: It raises the act of not buying things to a lofty moral height, from which you can denigrate others, and you get to enjoy the irony of simultaneously being a snob while making fun of other snobs.

2 Go to shopping malls and department stores and briefly let your materialistic impulses loose. Try on a bunch of sweaters and choose three or four. Add a few ties or scarves. Walk around for a few minutes enjoying your stack of loot. Then put it back on the shelf and walk out. Think about how unnecessary that stuff is. You probably already have something just like it. What a relief to not have more junk around the house.

3 Get satisfaction from money saved, not money spent. Set up direct deposit so that 10 percent or more of your paycheck goes automatically into a savings or investment account or buys United States savings bonds.

4 Become a scrounger. Old bicycles, furniture, building materials, vehicles, books and clothing are everywhere, once you start looking. Become skilled at resurrecting old stuff and finding uses for it. Take pride in being an eccentric recycler.

5 Look for barter opportunities. Swap your homegrown vegetables for repairs on your house, for example. Some cities have local barter networks where credits can be earned and exchanged for needed services. Because no money is exchanged when you barter, you avoid paying taxes, which can mean a substantial savings.

6 Consider having a "buy nothing Christmas" this year. You can find details at BuyNothingChristmas.org.

What to Look For

- Needs versus wants
- Ways to save, not spend

Tips

Studies have shown that most children want more time from their parents, not more toys.

November 29 is Buy Nothing Day, with worldwide demonstrations in support of sensible consumption.

BUY WHOLESALE • GET OUT OF DEBT • BUY NOTHING • BUY HAPPINESS • BUY A BETTER MOUSETRAP • BUY TI
H • BUY POSTAGE STAMPS WITHOUT GOING TO THE POST OFFICE • TIP PROPERLY • BUY HEALTHY FAST FOOD • BUY S
ICE • SELL YOURSELF ON AN ONLINE DATING SERVICE • SELL YOURSELF TO YOUR GIRLFRIEND/BOYFRIEND'S FAMILY • BUY
SE FILM FOR YOUR CAMERA • BUY RECHARGEABLE BATTERIES • DONATE TO A GOOD CAUSE • HOLD A PROFITABLE GARAGE SA
STUDENT DISCOUNTS • BUY FLOWERS WHOLESALE • GET A PICTURE FRAMED • HIRE A MOVER • HIRE A PERSONAL ORGANIZER • FI
EAT BIRTHDAY PRESENT FOR UNDER $10 • SELECT GOOD CHAMPAGNE • BUY A DIAMOND • BUY JEWELRY MADE OF PRECIOUS METAL
DESMAIDS' DRESSES • HIRE AN EVENT COORDINATOR • HIRE A BARTENDER FOR A PARTY • HIRE A PHOTOGRAPHER • HIRE A CATERE
Y AN ANNIVERSARY GIFT • ARRANGE ENTERTAINMENT FOR A PARTY • COMMISSION A FIREWORKS SHOW • BUY A MOTHER'S DAY GIF
T • SELECT A THANKSGIVING TURKEY • BUY A HOUSEWARMING GIFT • PURCHASE HOLIDAY CARDS • BUY CHRISTMAS STOCKING STU
E HIGH ROLLERS ROOM IN VEGAS, BABY • BUY SOMEONE A STAR • PAY A RANSOM • GET HOT TICKETS • HIRE A LIMOUSINE • BUY A C
M • BUY A PERSONAL JET • ACQUIRE A TELEVISION NETWORK • ACQUIRE A BODY GUARD • BOOK A LUXURY CRUISE AROUND THE W
DROUGHTBRED RACEHORSE • BUY A VILLA IN TUSCANY • HIRE A PERSONAL CHEF • PURCHASE CUBAN CIGARS • HIRE A GHOSTWRITE
NESS • MAKE BAIL • DONATE YOUR BODY TO SCIENCE • HIRE YOURSELF OUT AS A MEDICAL GUINEA PIG • SELL PLASMA • SELL YOU
LLEGE EDUCATION • BUY AND SELL STOCKS • CHOOSE A STOCKBROKER • DAY-TRADE (OR NOT) • BUY ANNUITIES • BUY AND SELL M
Y PERSONAL FINANCE SOFTWARE • CHOOSE A TAX PREPARER • SET UP A LEMONADE STAND • SELL YOUR PRODUCT ON TV • HIRE A
SINESS IDEA • BUY A SMALL BUSINESS • BUY A FRANCHISE • LEASE RETAIL SPACE • LEASE INDUSTRIAL SPACE • LEASE OFFICE SPAC
B SITE • BUY ADVERTISING ON THE WEB • SELL YOUR ART • HIRE A PERSONAL COACH • SELL ON THE CRAFT CIRCUIT • HIRE A LITER
LING BUSINESS • BUY A HOT DOG STAND • SHOP FOR A MORTGAGE • REFINANCE YOUR HOME • SAVE BIG BUCKS ON YOUR MORTGA
L A FIXER-UPPER • SELL THE FARM • SELL MINERAL RIGHTS • SELL A HOUSE • SELL A HOUSE WITHOUT A REAL ESTATE AGENT • OBT
OK A VACATION RENTAL • BUY A CONDOMINIUM • RENT AN APARTMENT OR HOUSE • OBTAIN RENTER'S INSURANCE • BUY A LOFT IN
RNISH YOUR STUDIO APARTMENT • BUY USED FURNITURE • BUY DOOR AND WINDOW LOCKS • CHOOSE AN ORIENTAL CARPET • BUY
RRANTIES ON APPLIANCES • FIND PERIOD FIXTURES • BUY A BED AND MATTRESS • HIRE AN INTERIOR DESIGNER • HIRE A FENG SHU
I • BUY A WHIRLPOOL TUB • BUY A SHOWERHEAD • BUY A TOILET • CHOOSE A FAUCET • BUY GLUES AND ADHESIVES • CHOOSE WIN
CHEN CABINETS • CHOOSE A KITCHEN COUNTERTOP • BUY GREEN HOUSEHOLD CLEANERS • STOCK YOUR HOME TOOL KIT • BUY A
ENTRY DOOR • BUY A GARAGE-DOOR OPENER • BUY LUMBER FOR A DIY PROJECT • HOW TO SELECT ROOFING • HIRE A CONTRACTO
OWERS FOR YOUR GARDEN • SELECT PEST CONTROLS • BUY SOIL AMENDMENTS • BUY MULCH • BUY A COMPOSTER • BUY FERTILIZ
Y KOI FOR YOUR FISH POND • BUY A STORAGE SHED • HIRE AN ARBORIST • BUY BASIC GARDEN TOOLS • BUY SHRUBS AND TREES •
LECT KITCHEN KNIVES • DECIPHER FOOD LABELS • SELECT HERBS AND SPICES • STOCK YOUR KITCHEN WITH STAPLES • EQUIP A KIT
UNTAIN OYSTERS • PURCHASE LOCAL HONEY • CHOOSE POULTRY • SELECT FRESH FISH AND SHELLFISH • SELECT RICE • PURCHAS
EADS • BUY ARTISAN CHEESES • PURCHASE KOSHER FOOD • BUY FOOD IN BULK • CHOOSE COOKING OILS • SELECT OLIVE OIL • SEL
FFEEMAKER OR ESPRESSO MACHINE • PURCHASE A KEG OF BEER • BUY ALCOHOL IN A DRY COUNTY • CHOOSE A MICROBREW • OR
ULATION PREDICTOR KIT • PICK A PREGNANCY TEST KIT • CHOOSE BIRTH CONTROL • FIND THE RIGHT OB-GYN • HIRE A MIDWIFE OR
OOSE DIAPERS • BUY OR RENT A BREAST PUMP • CHOOSE A CAR SEAT • BUY CHILD-PROOFING SUPPLIES • FIND FABULOUS CHILDCA
CKYARD PLAY STRUCTURE • FIND A GREAT SUMMER CAMP • SELL GIRL SCOUT COOKIES • BUY BRACES FOR YOUR KID • BUY TOYS
A MODEL • SELL USED BABY GEAR, TOYS, CLOTHES AND BOOKS • FIND A COUPLES COUNSELOR • HIRE A FAMILY LAWYER • BUY PRO
PENSES • GET VIAGRA ONLINE • PURCHASE A TOOTHBRUSH • BUY MOISTURIZERS AND ANTIWRINKLE CREAMS • SELECT PAIN RELIEF
PPLIES • SELECT HAIR-CARE PRODUCTS • BUY WAYS TO COUNTER HAIR LOSS • BUY A WIG OR HAIRPIECE • BUY A NEW BODY • GET
NICURIST • GET WHITER TEETH • SELECT EYEGLASSES AND SUNGLASSES • HIRE A PERSONAL TRAINER • SIGN UP FOR A YOGA CLAS
EA MARKET • RENT SPACE AT AN ANTIQUE MALL • BUY AT AUCTION • KNOW WHAT YOUR COLLECTIBLES ARE WORTH • DICKER WITH D
COGNIZE THE REAL MCCOY • BUY COINS • BUY AN ANTIQUE AMERICAN QUILT • BUY AN ANTIQUE FLAG • LIQUIDATE YOUR BEANIE BA
WNSHOP • BUY AND SELL COMIC BOOKS • BUY AND SELL SPORTS MEMORABILIA • SELL YOUR BASEBALL-CARD COLLECTIONS • CHO
MPUTER • BUY PRINTER PAPER • BUY A PRINTER • BUY COMPUTER PERIPHERALS • CHOOSE AN INTERNET SERVICE PROVIDER • GET
Y BLANK CDS • BUY AN MP PLAYER • CHOOSE A DVD PLAYER • BUY A VCR • CHOOSE A PERSONAL DIGITAL ASSISTANT • CHOOSE MO
ITAL CAMCORDER • DECIDE ON A DIGITAL CAMERA • BUY A HOME AUTOMATION SYSTEM • BUY A STATE-OF-THE-ART SOUND SYSTEM
IVERSAL REMOTE • BUY A HOME THEATER SYSTEM • BUY VIRTUAL-REALITY FURNITURE • BUY TWO-WAY RADIOS • BUY A MOBILE ENT
NEY • GET TRAVEL INSURANCE • PICK THE IDEAL LUGGAGE • FLY FOR FREE • BID FOR A SLED RIDE ON THE ALASKAN IDITAROD TRAIL
REIGN OFFICIAL • GET A EURAIL PASS • TAKE AN ITALIAN BICYCLE VACATION • CHOOSE A CHEAP CRUISE • BOOK A HOTEL PACKAGE F
OTLAND • BUY A SAPPHIRE IN BANGKOK • HIRE A RICKSHA IN YANGON • TAKE SALSA LESSONS IN CUBA • BUY A CAMERA IN HONG KO
ST BASEBALL GLOVE • ORDER UNIFORMS FOR A SOFTBALL TEAM • BUY ANKLE AND KNEE BRACES • BUY GOLF CLUBS • JOIN AN ELIT
OWMOBILE • BUY A PERSONAL WATERCRAFT • HIRE A SCUBA INSTRUCTOR • BUY A SKATEBOARD AND PROTECTIVE GEAR • BUY SKAT
ATHER ACTIVITIES • SELL USED SKIS • BUY A SNOWBOARD, BOOTS AND BINDINGS • BUY SKI BOOTS • BUY A BICYCLE • SELL YOUR B
Y A BACKPACK • BUY A BACKPACKING STOVE • BUY A KAYAK • BUY A PERSONAL FLOTATION DEVICE • BUY A WET SUIT • BUY A SURF
DER CUSTOM-MADE COWBOY BOOTS • BUY CLOTHES ONLINE • FIND SPECIALTY SIZES • BUY THE PERFECT COCKTAIL DRESS • BUY D
Y A MAN'S SUIT • HIRE A TAILOR • BUY CUSTOM-TAILORED CLOTHES IN ASIA • BUY A BRIEFCASE • SHOP FOR A LEATHER JACKET • BU
TE MONITOR • SELECT A WATCH • BUY KIDS' CLOTHES • CHOOSE CHILDREN'S SHOES • PURCHASE CLOTHES AT OUTLET SHOPS • BU

UET OF ROSES • BUY SOMEONE A DRINK • GET SOMEONE TO BUY YOU A DRINK • BUY YOUR WAY INTO HIGH SOCIETY • BUY YOUR V
DER THE PERFECT BURRITO • ORDER TAKEOUT ASIAN FOOD • ORDER AT A SUSHI BAR • BUY DINNER AT A FANCY FRENCH RESTAURA
WERS FOR YOUR SWEETHEART • BUY MUSIC ONLINE • HIRE MUSICIANS • ORDER A GREAT BOTTLE OF WINE • BUY AN ERGONOMIC D
ECLEANER • HIRE A BABY SITTER • BUY A GUITAR • BUY DUCT TAPE • GET A GOOD DEAL ON A MAGAZINE SUBSCRIPTION • GET SENI
AN • BUY PET FOOD • BUY A PEDIGREED DOG OR CAT • BREED YOUR PET AND SELL THE LITTER • GET A COSTUME • BUY A PIÑATA • I
ED GEMSTONES • CHOOSE THE PERFECT WEDDING DRESS • BUY OR RENT A TUXEDO • REGISTER FOR GIFTS • BUY WEDDING GIFTS •
AL WEDDING OFFICIANT • OBTAIN A MARRIAGE LICENSE • ORDER CUSTOM INVITATIONS AND ANNOUNCEMENTS • SELL YOUR WEDDIN
'S DAY GIFT • SELECT AN APPROPRIATE COMING-OF-AGE GIFT • GET A GIFT FOR THE PERSON WHO HAS EVERYTHING • BUY A GRADU
NUKKAH GIFTS • PURCHASE A PERFECT CHRISTMAS TREE • BUY A PRIVATE ISLAND • HIRE A SKYWRITER • HIRE A BIG-NAME BAND •
ER • RENT YOUR OWN BILLBOARD • TAKE OUT A FULL-PAGE AD IN *THE NEW YORK TIMES* • HIRE A BUTLER • ACQUIRE A PROFESSION
UR FUR COAT • BOOK A TRIP ON THE ORIENT-EXPRESS • BECOME A WINE MAKER • PURCHASE A PRIVATE/CUSTOM BOTTLING OF WIN
MEMOIRS • COMMISSION ORIGINAL ARTWORK • IMMORTALIZE YOUR SPOUSE IN A SCULPTURE • GIVE AWAY YOUR FORTUNE • HIRE A
DEVIL • NEGOTIATE A BETTER CREDIT CARD DEAL • CHOOSE A FINANCIAL PLANNER • SAVE WITH A RETIREMENT PLAN • SAVE FOR YO
BUY BONDS • SELL SHORT • INVEST IN PRECIOUS METALS • BUY DISABILITY INSURANCE • BUY LIFE INSURANCE • GET HEALTH INSUR
LOR • HIRE A HEADHUNTER • SELL YOUR   ENT • MARKET YOUR INVENTION • FINANCE YOU
ED OFFICE EQUIPMENT • HIRE SOMEONE   IRE A GRAPHIC DESIGNER • ACQUIRE CONTENT
CH A MAGAZINE STORY • SELL A SCREEN   YOUR BOOK • START A BED-AND-BREAKFAST • S
ME OWNER'S INSURANCE • OBTAIN DISAS   OUSE AT AUCTION • BUY A FORECLOSED HOME
ITY LOAN • BUY A LOT • BUY HOUSE PLA   • PULL BUILDING PERMITS • BUY A VACATION HO
Y A TENANCY-IN-COMMON UNIT • BUY RE   A MOVIE OR CATALOG SHOOT • FURNISH YOUR H
T FIXTURES • BUY A PROGRAMMABLE LIG   NCES • BUY FLOOR-CARE APPLIANCES • BUY EX
NCORPORATE FLUID ARCHITECTURE INTO   ARNISH • CHOOSE DECORATIVE TILES • CHOOSE
TS • GET SELF-CLEANING WINDOWS • CH   SELECT FLOORING • SELECT CARPETING • CHOO
SYSTEM • BUY A HOME ALARM SYSTEM   OXIDE DETECTORS • BUY FIRE EXTINGUISHERS
INTER OR ELECTRICIAN • HIRE A GARDEN   PERFECT ROSEBUSH • BUY FLOWERING BULBS
GETABLE GARDEN • HIRE A GARDEN PROF   R SYSTEM • START A NEW LAWN • BUY A LAWN M

Daily Life

• BUY AN OUTDOOR LIGHTING SYSTEM •   ECT PEACH • BUY AND SELL AT FARMERS' MARK
FRESH PRODUCE • SELECT MEAT • STOC   ASE A HOLIDAY HAM • BUY NATURAL BEEF • BUY
AND PEPPER • GET A CHEESESTEAK IN P   EATTLE • FIND CRAWDADS IN LOUISIANA • BUY A
JY ETHNIC INGREDIENTS • PURCHASE VIN   OFFEE • ORDER A GREAT CUP OF COFFEE • BUY
• CHOOSE A RESTAURANT FOR A BUSINE   OCK YOUR BAR • BUY AND SELL SPERM • CHOO
GOOD PEDIATRICIAN • HIRE A CHILD THER   NEW CRIB • CHOOSE A STROLLER • BUY BABY
EAT NANNY • FIND THE RIGHT PRIVATE SC   RAM • SIGN YOUR CHILD UP FOR LESSONS • BU
DEOS AND MUSIC FOR YOUR CHILDREN •   R • HIRE AN ADOPTION AGENCY • GET YOUR CH
IREMENT COMMUNITY • CHOOSE AN ASS   IVING WILL • BUY A CEMETERY PLOT • PAY FOR
CINES • SAVE MONEY ON PRESCRIPTION   ONAL • CHOOSE A WHEELCHAIR • BUY HOME-U
DY PIERCING • OBTAIN BREAST IMPLANTS   ALTERNATIVE AND HOLISTIC PRACTITIONERS • C
SELF TO A DAY AT THE SPA • BOOK A MAS   Y AND SELL USED BOOKS • SHOP AT AN ANTIQU
N ANTIQUE APPRAISED • BUY SILVERWARE • EVALUATE DEPRESSION-ERA GLASSWARE • BUY AND SELL STAMPS • BUY ANTIQUE FURNI
• SCORE AUTOGRAPHS • TRADE YU-GI-OH CARDS • SNAG STAR WARS ACTION FIGURES • SELL YOUR VINYL RECORD COLLECTION •
COMPUTER • SHOP FOR A USED COMPUTER OR PERIPHERALS • CHOOSE A LAPTOP OR NOTEBOOK COMPUTER • SELL OR DONATE A
OMAIN NAME • BUY A HOME NETWORK • UPGRADE THE MEMORY IN YOUR COMPUTER • BUY COMPUTER SOFTWARE • CHOOSE A CD
RVICE • NEGOTIATE YOUR LONG-DISTANCE PHONE SERVICE • BUY VIDEO AND COMPUTER GAMES • CHOOSE A FILM CAMERA • CHOOS
O-VIDEO DISTRIBUTION SYSTEM • BUY A SERIOUS TV • CHOOSE BETWEEN CABLE AND SATELLITE TV • GET A DIGITAL VIDEO RECORDE
STEM • GET A PASSPORT, QUICK! • PURCHASE CHEAP AIRLINE TICKETS • FIND GREAT HOTEL DEALS • RENT THE BEST CAR FOR THE L
TY-FREE • SHIP FOREIGN PURCHASES TO THE UNITED STATES • TIP IN A FOREIGN COUNTRY • TIP PROPERLY IN NORTH AMERICA • BR
SLANDS • RAFT THE GRAND CANYON • BOOK A CHEAP BUT AWESOME SAFARI • RENT A CAMEL IN CAIRO • GET SINGLE-MALT SCOTCH
R WAY ONTO A MOUNT EVEREST EXPEDITION • HIRE A TREKKING COMPANY IN NEPAL • RENT OR BUY A SATELLITE PHONE • BUY YOUF
SELL FOUND GOLF BALLS • BUY ATHLETIC SHOES • BUY A RACKET • BUY A GYM MEMBERSHIP • BUY AN AEROBIC FITNESS MACHINE
FISHING • GO SKYDIVING • BUY WEIGHTLIFTING EQUIPMENT • CHOOSE A CAR RACK OR CARRIER • BUY SKIS • BUY CLOTHES FOR CO
RAGE SALE • COMMISSION A CUSTOM-BUILT BICYCLE • BUY A PROPERLY FITTED HELMET • BUY THE OPTIMAL SLEEPING BAG • BUY A
Y-FISHING GEAR • BUY ROCK-CLIMBING EQUIPMENT • BUY A CASHMERE SWEATER • PURCHASE VINTAGE CLOTHING • SELL USED CL
HES AT A DISCOUNT • CHOOSE A BASIC WARDROBE FOR A MAN • BUY A MAN'S DRESS SHIRT • PICK OUT A NECKTIE • BUY A WOMAN'
LOTHES • GET A GREAT-FITTING BRA • CHOOSE A HIGH-PERFORMANCE SWIM SUIT • HIGH PERFORMANCE WORKOUT CLOTHES • BUY
BUY THE BASICS FOR YOUR CAR • BUY A USED CAR • BUY OR SELL A CAR ONLINE • BUY A HYBRID CAR • SELL A CAR • BUY A MOTOR

15 Buy Happiness

It's true that you can't literally buy happiness. In the words of Abraham Lincoln, "Most people are about as happy as they make up their minds to be." And he would know, because he was depressed and miserable most of the time. But money can at least provide an escape from drudgery and give you increased access to excitement and entertainment.

Steps

1 Move slowly. Don't throw yourself, and your money, into the first harebrained scheme that comes along. Spend time savoring the joys of contemplation.

2 Don't let laziness rule your buying decisions. Sitting in a beach chair while servants fawn over you may be fun for a short time, but it's not likely to provide long-term satisfaction. Look for goals and projects that combine fun and challenge.

3 Be wary of ventures where money and status are ends in themselves. A huge yacht is an obvious sign of wealth. But if it's not fun for you, it's no more capable of enhancing your well-being than a '72 Pinto.

4 Surprise people. Look for activities that will stun your friends and family. If all you've ever done is sit on the couch, do something bold like get in shape, hire a guide and climb Mount Rainier.

5 Indulge in a little eccentricity. The more money you have, the nuttier you're allowed to be. Wear your pajamas around town. Call the best restaurants in town and pay whatever it costs to get that duck a l'orange delivered to your door.

6 Look for new activities with heavy technical demands, such as photography, music dubbing, video editing, car racing or anything else that requires many hours of study and pricey equipment. You'll spend many satisfying hours shopping for supplies, learning arcane details, and talking with experts. Soon you'll feel like a member of an elite club.

7 Look for ways to include your friends and family in your new activities. You'll be happier if you can share your experiences with people close to you.

8 Avoid being pompous or superior when discussing your new acquisition or endeavor. Nothing will turn away listeners, or set you up for ridicule, more than acting as though you know everything. If you just took up sailing, for example, take joy in all the learning you can look forward to. Listen and apply yourself, and soon you'll be an expert.

Tips

Recognize the limitations of money. Money will get you access to things. Motivation and skill are up to you.

Don't flit from interest to interest, acquiring and discarding expensive toys as you go. This will only make you look silly without providing much satisfaction.

Drop in on worthy causes and shower them with money (see 119 Give Away Your Fortune).

16 Buy a Better Mousetrap

Maybe you'll never build a better mousetrap, but it's a cinch to buy one. If you have mice or rats, get rid of them fast. You can find most of the options listed below at hardware stores. Peanut butter, grains and cereals or cooked bacon make appetizing bait for traps. Some animals will outsmart any trap. The best approach is to constantly look for rodent activity, seal up entry holes and experiment with various methods.

TYPE OF TRAP/FEATURES	PROS AND CONS
Live Traps Catch and release rodents unharmed, a good choice for pacifists.	Reusable and safe around children and pets. However, they require relocating a scared, agitated rodent. Use every caution to avoid contact.
Snap Traps Use a spring-loaded wire to trap and kill rodents.	Theoretically reusable but should probably be thrown out after a successful trapping, due to disease concerns. Usually quick and lethal but not always; death can sometimes be slow and painful.
Glue Boards Use a shallow tray filled with glue, which attracts and holds rodents.	A single trap can catch more than one rodent. Death is very slow and some people find these unbearably creepy and cruel. On the plus side, they're nontoxic, easy to set and can't injure people.
Electronic Trap Use an electric current to dispose of rodents in a quick, nonmessy way.	Not dangerous to humans but can be difficult to use in wet environments. More expensive than other traps.
Poison Rodent poisons are available in liquid, pellet or bar forms and can be effective against many pests.	Poison does not require frequent checking but also does not allow you to monitor results like a trap. Rodents can also die before they exit the building, causing short-term odor problems.
Professional Exterminator Available as a one-time service or as periodic visits.	These require very little effort on your part but the poison is highly toxic and may require you to vacate the building for a short period. Exterminators can be expensive.
Ultrasonic Barriers Designed to ward off rodents with ultrasonic waves.	Leave no traps, corpses or poison. Evidence suggests that they're not very effective.
WARNINGS	Poison is dangerous for pets and kids. A bait station may be required to ensure safety. Snap traps can injure people and pets.

17 Buy Time

Ever stared at the microwave in frustration, thinking that 20 seconds is just too long? You might need to slow down a little. Look at the categories below and consider how many hours they consume each week. Spend a few dollars and reclaim some free time.

PRODUCTS/SERVICES	COST
Commute	
Listen to entertaining or educational CDs or cassettes in the car. They can make the most grueling commute relaxing.	$10 to $75; free at the library
Get a hands-free phone and turn car into office.	$10 to $20 (headset)/ $50 to $200 (car kit)
Hire a chauffeur.	$40 to $60 per hour
Household	
Get caller ID to avoid telemarketers.	$10 to 30 (caller ID display)/$50 to $75 (caller ID phone)
Hire a housecleaner.	$60 to $150 per visit
Use a diaper service.	$10 to $20 per week
Hire a service to care for your indoor plants.	$50 to $200 per month
Hire someone to run your errands.	$20 to $40 per hour
Hire professional contractors, plumbers or other tradespeople.	$75 to $300 per visit
Hire a personal organizer.	$40 to $200 per hour
Hire a pet groomer that comes to your house.	$30 to $60 per visit
Yard	
Rent power tools and equipment to expedite projects.	$20 to $200
Hire a neighbor's kid to rake leaves/shovel snow/mow lawn.	$5 to $10 per hour
Hire a gardener or landscaper.	$50 to $150 per visit
Hire a handyman for gutters, chimneys, roofs.	$30 to $75 per hour
Hire a pool cleaner.	$100 to $150 per month
Wardrobe	
Use a pick-up-and-deliver laundry service.	$75 to $100 per month
Hire a seamstress to do repairs.	$10 to $50 per piece
Install a closet organization system.	$100 to $1,000
Hire a personal shopper/wardrobe consultant.	Free to $60 per hour

PRODUCTS/SERVICES	COST
Diet	
Have groceries delivered to your home.	Free to 10 percent of order
Buy premade meals.	$5 to $20 each meal
Order takeout.	$15 to $35 each meal
Subscribe to a service that delivers meals to your door.	$8 to $10 fee per meal
Hire a personal chef four to five nights a week.	$200 to $400 per week
Health	
Buy a comfortable mattress.	$500 to $1,000
Consult a sleep expert to remedy sleep disorders.	$50 to $200
Hire an onsite personal trainer.	$40 and up per session
Consult a nutritionist.	$30 to $75 per visit
Finances	
Bank online.	Free
Buy a software program to streamline your books.	$80
Have a tax professional do your taxes.	$75 to $100 per hour
Hire a bookkeeper.	$75 to $100 per hour
Social Events and Holidays	
Mail-order or shop online.	Shipping and handling per order
Pay for gift-wrapping.	Free to $5
Hire caterers, party planners.	$100 to $10,000 and up
Hire a personal shopper.	Free to $60 per hour
Hire a social secretary.	$25,000 and up per year

18 Buy a Bouquet of Roses

A rose is a rose, right? Mais non: other than the classic lover's gift of a dozen long-stemmed roses, there are many varieties and a rainbow of colors guaranteed to put a bloom on anyone's cheek.

Steps

1 Look for closed buds on the brink of unfurling. Petal tops should show the first signs of opening, and the bud should be a little soft and springy, never hard. Then close your eyes and inhale their scent—some varieties are more fragrant than others.

2 Find beautiful roses for cheap at Costco. Two dozen stems run for under $15 and come in a variety of colors.

3 Visit a wholesale flower market (see 49 Buy Flowers Wholesale) either with a friend who has a badge or during public hours. You'll find an enormous selection of roses at a great price. Keep an eye peeled for fabulously fragrant garden roses.

4 Be on the lookout for sidewalk vendors hawking medium-quality but still beautiful roses. They may frequent the same spot near a restaurant, for example, and will wrap up two dozen roses in newspaper for as little as $5 to $10.

5 Buy lovely roses perfectly arranged from a local florist. You'll pay a premium but the flowers will be sensational—and delivered.

6 Shop online at FTD.com or 1800Flowers.com and send roses to a special someone far away. The flowers will be shipped with a vial of water on each stem to keep them fresh during transit. Pay with a credit card for guaranteed wilt-free delivery.

What to Look For

- Closed buds
- Fragrance
- Sidewalk vendors

Tips

Put your roses in water as soon as you get them home. Submerge each stem in a bowl of lukewarm water, and snip the end off at an angle while still underwater before transferring to a vase.

Mix in the packet of floral preservative and be sure to add more water as the roses drink it up.

Warning

Stay away from firm, tightly closed rosebuds—they've been picked too soon, won't last long and may in fact never open.

19 Buy Someone a Drink

Most people contemplating buying someone a drink either think about it until (and beyond) last call, but never get up the nerve. Or they use the shotgun technique—buying a drink for anyone they catch sitting still for two seconds—blasting away in the hopes of getting lucky. The best approach is something in between.

Steps

1 Try to enjoy the process, and accept that there are risks. Home-run leaders are frequently also strikeout leaders.

2 Avoid the wolf pack. Don't travel with a group of predators and expect to meet a nice person looking for a quiet time.

3 Be yourself. Sounds simple but apparently isn't. Most people are looking for a fun, intelligent, easygoing, levelheaded sort. Women aren't as impressed by flashy clothes, monster trucks, and sports victories as most men think.

What to Look For

- Money in your wallet
- Lack of a drink
- Wedding ring

4 Take your time. Don't rush up to your target, but don't wait around for hours either. If you've just arrived, have a seat and relax for a few minutes. Check to see if the person does, in fact, need a drink, or if he or she already has one. If you get an encouraging look, head over.

5 If there's a surefire pickup line in the world, the inventor is keeping it secret. Try "Hello." Look for a wedding ring.

6 Introduce yourself. If you don't get a response, you should probably forget it.

7 Offer to buy a drink. If the person agrees, you have the basis for a conversation about drink choices.

8 If your target is part of a group, be sure to acknowledge the rest of the group and include them in the conversation. If you don't, the group may close ranks and cut you off.

Tip

Meeting a stranger is always a long shot. Consider the billions of people in the world, and then think of the few you actually enjoy being around. From a statistical perspective, you could buy millions of drinks before meeting someone you like. So forget statistics.

20 Get Someone to Buy You a Drink

Decades of sexual equality and social progress have achieved only so much. Approaching someone in a bar can still be treacherous. Is a woman being unacceptably forward if she asks a man to buy her a drink? Is a man violating some rule if he expects a woman to buy him a drink? Who cares? Just have fun, don't be a jerk, and you'll be OK.

What to Look For

- Lighthearted conversation
- An escape route, if needed

Steps

1 Experiment. Walk up to your target and say, "How about buying me a drink?" You know you'll at least get a reaction, so be ready with some light conversation.

2 Don't be obnoxious. Your goal is not to get free alcohol, but to meet someone. Even if he or she thinks it's weird that you're asking for a drink, a show of personality or humor should be enough to move things along.

3 Employ the obvious backup position, if necessary: Offer to buy your target a drink.

4 Don't push too hard. Be lighthearted and casual. Your target may decline now, but there's a chance you'll bump into the person again in an hour or so.

5 Don't try to isolate your target from his or her friends. Be friendly to the whole group, and increase your chances of appearing desirable.

6 Plan an escape route. Some people think that if they buy you a drink, they're buying rights to you for the entire evening.

Tips

Don't worry about looking like an idiot. Everyone looks like one sometimes.

If you get a nasty reaction from someone, it probably says more about his or her attitude than your technique.

21 Buy Your Way into High Society

So you've made your millions but still lack respectability? Well, old chap, you can't purchase a blue-blood heritage, but you can clean up your image. You'll have to throw some money around, but be sure to do it with urbanity, style and grace. Anything vulgar and your plebeian roots will show.

Steps

1 Read the society pages in the newspaper and regional magazines to get to know the names of local movers and shakers.

2 Update your image with the help of a consultant. Your hair, makeup, clothes and accessories must look classy, not gaudy.

3 Observe and emulate the manners and behavior of the highborn. When in doubt, adopt a stance of mysterious understatement.

4 Buy the highest-priced season tickets to the opera, theater and ballet to be privy to exclusive events and openings. If necessary, enlist someone to brief you on the finer points of the events you'll be attending. See 65 Buy or Rent a Tuxedo.

5 Join private country clubs with steep membership fees and attend members-only social events. See 462 Join an Elite Golf Club.

6 Publicly distance yourself, if necessary, from any distasteful business dealings. If you made your money by "harvesting" baby seals, for example, slip a few subtle comments to the press about "the need for change" and a "new business era" while being vague about specifics.

7 Adopt a noncontroversial cause (preferably one that lends itself to gala events) and give, give, give from the bottom of your wallet. Better yet, host a fund-raising party at your estate. (First, buy an estate.)

8 See and be seen at exclusive restaurants, polo matches, fashion shows and the hottest parties of the season. An image consultant will know which events are the most strategic. See 104 Buy a Personal Jet.

9 Hire a public-relations expert to get your picture into the society pages.

10 Network, network, network. Befriend influential people and make yourself indispensable to them through generous favors and an utterly discreet nature.

11 Increase your social value by purchasing homes in desirable locations. Pieds-à-terre in Paris, New York, London and the Hollywood hills will make you popular and mysteriously unavailable during certain seasons.

12 Disdain riffraff. It's essential to choose your acquaintances wisely.

What to Look For

- Image consultant
- Cultural and charity events
- Exclusive clubs
- Public-relations opportunities

Tips

Take etiquette and image improvement courses if you lack the social graces needed to interact easily in high society.

Your alma mater might be a good route to high society. Alumni clubs are an excellent source for career and social networks.

Develop expensive hobbies and tastes so that you'll have plenty in common with society swells. Race sailboats. Ride horses. Collect art, wine or rare autos.

Warning

The woods are full of people eager to separate you from your money. Exercise due diligence before you hire an image consultant. Have them sign a confidentiality agreement.

22 Buy Your Way into Someone's Favor

This sounds ugly and probably is. But, if you've exhausted all the alternatives, this might be your only choice. Carefully define your goals, then perform a cost-benefit analysis: What do you want from this person and what can you expect to achieve for a given expenditure?

Steps

1 Decide if your strategy is the best approach. A botched plan could prove embarrassing.

2 Keeping your goal in mind, start small but move quickly. Take your target to happy hour and pick up the tab.

3 Don't force your position right away. As with any sales job, get the person talking. Learn as much as you can before committing yourself to anything. There's always the chance that you've miscalculated and can achieve your goal for far less.

4 Identify valuable services that you can offer. Sometimes small favors are more effective than money. Making yourself indispensable can have more of an impact—and be cheaper—than simply tossing money around. Be discreet and confident.

5 Know the timeline that affects your goal. If you need something right away, expect to pay more. Longer timelines allow you to work slowly and cheaply.

6 Recognize that this needs to be a short-term project. Arranging your life around mercenary practices will result in your being surrounded by a pack of sycophants instead of friends and family.

What to Look For

- Identify your goal
- Look for alternatives
- How much will it cost?
- What favors can you provide?

Tip

If companionship is your goal, consider a dog. They're better company and more reliable than a person whose friendship can be bought.

Warning

If you find yourself doing this often, you're either a politician, a pathetic loser or both.

23 Buy Postage Stamps Without Going to the Post Office

You're ready to send away for your Charles Atlas bodybuilding information, but you don't have a stamp. Zounds! No problem. Here are some easy ways to keep on licking while avoiding those long lines.

Steps

1 Look for the blue-and-red U.S. Postal Service logo at grocery stores, drugstores and mini-marts. Also look for stores that specialize in mail and shipping services. Swing by the ATM machine and buy stamps while you make deposits or withdrawals.

2 Log on to usps.gov or call 1-800-STAMP-24 to have stamps mailed to your home or office.

3 Check out Stamps.com, Endicia.com or PitneyBowes.com to buy stamps online and print them from your computer. The monthly fee makes this service more cost-effective for high-volume users.

What to Look For

- USPS machines
- ATM options
- Mail stores
- Online services

Tip

By shopping online, you can buy specialty stamps that aren't available at post offices or stores.

24 Tip Properly

Tipping rewards those who provide useful services that make your life easier and more enjoyable. Be discreet when you tip, and be generous—you'll be remembered long after your departure and welcomed back enthusiastically. See also 441 Tip Properly in North America and 440 Tip in a Foreign Country.

TIP UPON SERVICE RENDERED	AMOUNT
Car Washer	$2 to $5, depending on level of service
Coat Check Person	$1 per coat
Furniture Deliverer/Movers	$10 to $20 per person
Gas Station Attendant	$2 to $4
Hairstylist	15 to 20 percent of bill minus tax, extra for special service
Latte Maker	$1 into the tipping jar
Maitre d'	$5 to $25 for special efforts
Masseuse	10 to 15 percent of bill minus sales tax
Shoe Shiner	$2 to $3
Pizza Delivery Person	10 percent of bill minus sales tax, $2 minimum
ANNUAL TIPS	**AMOUNT (ENCLOSED IN A HOLIDAY CARD)**
Babysitter	One week's pay
Doorman	Bottle of wine or box of chocolates
Garbage Collector	$15 to $25
Gardener	One week's pay
Housecleaner	One week's pay
Janitor	$15 to $25
Mail Carrier	$15 to $20
Nanny	One week's pay
Newspaper Delivery Person	$15 to $25
Parking Attendant	$15 to $25
Personal Trainer	$20 to $50 gift certificate
Water Delivery Person	$15 to $25

25 Buy Healthy Fast Food

Is this really possible? To a degree, if you make careful selections. Some fast-food restaurants have responded to health concerns with revised menus, which include salads and meatless burgers. Even McDonald's recently announced a policy of moving toward beef produced without hormones and antibiotics. When you're out with the kids or on a road trip, we've got tips for quick and healthy noshing.

Steps

1 Opt for grilled, broiled or steamed entrées over fried. Chicken, turkey and fish are leaner than ground beef.

2 Say no to special sauces, cheese, mayonnaise and bacon; they'll pack on the calories, fat and cholesterol.

3 Order regular or junior meals instead of supersize meals. If you have a big appetite, include a side salad with low-cal dressing.

4 Pick up a salad. Leafy greens, veggies and beans are great but be frugal with bacon bits, cheese, mayonnaise-based salads and creamy dressings. Avoid fried tortilla shells.

5 Hold the dressing in exchange for dessert—creamy salad dressings have more calories and fat in a single serving than a large cookie.

6 Drink water, skim milk or unsweetened iced tea instead of soda.

7 Expand your definition of fast food: sub sandwiches or wraps with lean meat (no cheese, no mayo), burritos (no cheese, no sour cream), Greek kebabs or pitas, and Japanese bento boxes (ask for low-sodium soy sauce) are tasty, convenient alternatives to the usual burgers and fries.

8 Stock up on "fast food" while grocery shopping: cottage cheese, yogurt, minicarrots (peeled and washed), and fresh fruit.

What to Look For

- Grilled, broiled or steamed
- Regular or junior size
- Low- or no-fat dressings
- Fresh veggies
- Unsweetened drinks

Tips

A breakfast sandwich with an English muffin, egg and lean ham is pretty healthy. Croissants, biscuits, bacon and especially sausage patties are huge fat bombs.

Pick a baked potato (hold the sour cream) for a good nutritional choice. French fries, however, do not satisfy the nutritional requirements of a vegetable serving and are very high in fat.

A pizza with tomato sauce, veggie toppings and low-fat cheese is a relatively healthy meal.

26 Buy Sunscreen

By now, most of us know that the sun can be harmful. The best protection is to shield yourself with clothing, a hat and glasses whenever possible. Since this isn't always practical, you need to have some sun protection lotion. The trick then is buying the correct stuff, having it on hand, and remembering to apply it.

Steps

1 Know the difference between a *sunscreen* and a *sunblock*. A sunscreen is any product with a sun protection factor (SPF) of 15 or less. An SPF of 15 means it will take 15 times longer for you to burn with the sunscreen than without. A sunblock has an SPF of 30 or more.

2 Use a sunblock with SPF 30 or higher if you're fair-skinned, at high altitude, near the equator or outside on a hot, sunny day between 10 a.m. and 4 p.m. Protect your kids, too: Over the course of their life, most of the sun's damage to their skin will happen before they're 18. Lighter-skinned people need more protection.

3 Make sure that your sunscreen is labeled "broad spectrum" to protect against both UVA (ultraviolet-A) and UVB (ultraviolet-B) rays. Ultraviolet radiation at high doses increases your risk of basal-cell carcinoma and malignant melanoma.

4 Know what protection you're getting. A sunscreen with SPF 15 gives you 94 to 95 percent UVB coverage; SPF 28 bumps you up to about 96 percent coverage.

5 Buy zinc oxide or titanium oxide (or dioxide) to protect your ears, nose and lips if you're in the sun for prolonged periods daily. These opaque, chemical-free sunblocks are ideal for sensitive skin. A new product called Z-Cote offers zinc-oxide protection that's transparent, so you can avoid the white-nosed lifeguard look.

6 Get water-resistant or waterproof sunscreen if you'll be swimming or sweating.

7 Look for PABA-free, fragrance-free and hypoallergenic sunscreen if you're allergic to certain skin products. Do a test patch on your skin to confirm whether a sunscreen is truly allergy-free.

8 Select a sunscreen that is noncomedogenic, which means it won't block pores, if you're prone to breaking out.

9 Choose between lotions, gels, ointments, wax sticks and sprays based on your personal preference. Wax sticks are handy for lips. Sprays get the job done quickly on squirmy kids.

10 Apply sunscreen liberally 30 minutes prior to exposure. Most people need at least 1 oz. of sunscreen, enough to fill a shot glass, to cover their body. Reapply every two hours, or more often if you get wet or sweat profusely.

What to Look For

- SPF 15 or higher
- UVA and UVB protection
- Zinc oxide or titanium oxide
- Water-resistant or water-proof
- Allergy-free
- Noncomedogenic

Tips

UVB rays cause sunburns. UVA rays create wrinkles and premature aging. Studies suggest that both rays contribute to cancerous growths.

There is no proof that sunscreen prevents skin cancer. Your safest bet is to minimize sun exposure during peak hours (10 a.m. to 4 p.m.). Wear a wide-brimmed hat, UV-blocking sunglasses and tightly woven clothes if you are outside.

Warnings

There is no such thing as "safe tanning." Tanning salons expose your skin to harmful UV rays. If you burn easily but must have that golden look, use a sunless tanning lotion or foam.

Do not use sunscreen on infants under 6 months of age; keep them covered and out of the sun instead.

27 Order the Perfect Burrito

A burrito is a legion above ordinary fast food. A beacon of Mexican-American integration, it is native to neither culture but based on both. It's also cheap, delicious and often packed with more food than anyone should eat in a single meal. Burritos are common on the West Coast and in the Southwest, and they're gradually appearing elsewhere. Now, step up to the counter and order.

Steps

1 Start with a fresh flour tortilla. It will be warmed before your eyes after you order, often in a steamer. Some restaurants offer tortillas made with whole wheat, spinach, tomato or other ingredients.

2 Choose a filling, such as steak *(carne asada)*, pork *(carnitas)*, chicken or vegetables. You'll see them grilled up as you wait. Many restaurants offer other variations, such as mole, a sauce with hints of chocolate.

3 Pick up your frijoles. Beans are not merely a filler, but a vital and healthy ingredient. Choices usually include whole pinto, black or refried beans. Refried beans (cooked then mashed) are tasty but can create a mushy burrito.

4 Include rice: Most West Coast burritos do but in many other places, they don't. Establishments that take pride in their burritos will have succulent, flavorful rice. Careless burrito makers will have boring rice. Some flavor their rice with tomatillos, paprika, cilantro or other seasonings, while others offer basic white or brown.

5 Add cheese, fresh guacamole or sour cream if you like, but too much can create a gloppy mess and obscure the other flavors. Beware of adding calories and fat too. Tomatoes, lettuce and other vegetables are tasty add-ins.

6 Choose hot, medium or mild salsa. Many restaurants include a side of tortilla chips and salsa with your order.

7 Wash that little burro down with a great Mexican beer or craft beer (see 403 Choose a Microbrew).

What to Look For

- Fresh tortilla
- Choice of meat
- Choice of pinto, black or refried beans
- Rice
- Cheese
- Fresh guacamole
- Sour cream
- Lettuce
- Tomatoes
- Salsa

Tips

Some of the best burritos are found at inexpensive and unassuming taquerias.

Fresh cilantro is a sign of a good burrito. Avoid premade burritos.

Fancy or unusual ingredients do not necessarily result in a better burrito.

Warning

If you feel extreme fatigue or laziness after consuming an entire burrito, you have come down with a temporary case of burrito coma.

28 Order Takeout Asian Food

Asian food offers an extraordinary palette of flavors, and takeout gives you a break from the kitchen. But the breadth of choice and the foreign terms can be a bit daunting. Below are popular dishes with a guide to their spicy or savory ingredients. Read 294 Buy Ethnic Ingredients for more information.

MENU ITEM	WHAT IT IS
CHINESE	
Chinese Broccoli	Leafy green vegetable usually served with garlic or oyster sauce.
Chow Fun	Pan-fried, thick rice noodles with veggies or meat and a rich, gravylike sauce.
Chow Mein	Pan-fried noodles (crispy on the East Coast) with veggies or meat.
Egg Rolls	Veggies or pork wrapped in paper-thin noodles and deep-fried.
Fried Rice	Rice pan-fried with green onions, egg, soy sauce and meat or shrimp.
Hot and Sour Soup	Salty soup with chilies, tofu, egg and bamboo shoots. Sometimes fiery hot.
Kung Pao	Cubed beef, chicken or shrimp stir-fried with chilies, peanuts and hot sauce.
Mongolian Beef	Spicy meat with chilies and green onions atop crispy rice noodles.
Mu Shu Pork	Pork cooked with eggs and green onions, served with thin pancakes and sweet plum sauce.
Pot Stickers	Steamed or pan-fried pork dumplings.
Wonton Soup	Chicken broth with dumplings and veggies.
INDIAN	
Biryani	Savory basmati rice dishes mixed with veggies, chicken or lamb.
Curry	Combination of ground spices, including cumin and turmeric, used to flavor sauces and dishes.
Dal	Lentils, often served over basmati rice.
Naan	Flat, baked bread, available with butter, garlic or other spices.
Pakora	Veggie or meat fritter dipped in a lentil batter and deep-fried.
Sag Paneer	Farmer's white cheese with spinach and spices.
Samosa	Fried patty stuffed with meat or veggies, often potatoes and peas.
Tandoori	Chicken or seafood marinated in yogurt and spices, and charcoal-grilled.
Tikka Masala	Chicken tandoori bathed in herb-infused, creamy tomato sauce.
Vindaloo	Hot and spicy curried potatoes with chicken or lamb.

MENU ITEM	WHAT IT IS
JAPANESE	
Bento	Boxed meals that include meat or fish, salad, soup, rice or noodles.
Donburi	Meat or veggies cooked with egg and served on top of a bowl of rice with a rich, flavorful sauce.
Edamame	Steamed and salted soybeans.
Goma	Steamed spinach with a sesame sauce.
Gyoza	Steamed or deep-fried pork dumplings.
Miso Soup	Fish broth with miso (soybean paste), tofu (soybean curd) and seaweed.
Soba	Thick, white buckwheat noodles usually served hot in a broth or pan-fried with meat and veggies.
Tempura	Veggies or seafood dipped in batter and deep-fried.
Teriyaki	Charcoal-grilled chicken, beef or salmon in a sweet soy-based sauce served with rice.
Udon	Thin wheat noodles served in a hot broth with meat or veggies, or served cold with a light dipping sauce.
Yakitori	Chicken coated with a sweet-soy sauce and charcoal-grilled on skewers.
THAI	
Curry Sauces	Yellow (mellow), red (medium) or green (hot) curries contain chilies, coconut milk, herbs and spices. Red curries often have peanuts; green curries are flavored with Thai basil.
Larb	Ground meat, fresh mint, red and green onions, and lime juice on a bed of cabbage or lettuce.
Pad Thai	Traditional stir-fried rice noodles with peanuts, fresh bean sprouts, cooked egg, shrimp or tofu, green onions and fresh herbs.
Po Pia Taud	Fried spring rolls filled with veggies.
Pra Ram	Meat or tofu on a bed of spinach, topped with peanut sauce.
Satay	Chicken, beef or pork grilled on skewers and served with peanut sauce.
Thai Barbecue	Chicken, pork or beef marinated in spices and herbs, charcoal-grilled and served with a sweet-spicy sauce.
Thai Fried Rice	Rice fried with eggs, green onion and choice of meat; pineapple optional.
Tom Kha Gai	Tangy coconut milk soup with galanga, chicken, mushrooms and lemongrass.
Vegetable/Spring Rolls	Veggies, tofu and peanuts (sometimes chicken or shrimp) wrapped in a translucent rice noodle and served cold. Accompanied by dipping sauces.

29 Order at a Sushi Bar

For the uninitiated, sushi might be the most intimidating meal ever. Raw fish? Seaweed? To eat? Even for diehard fans, it can be tough remembering the various types. Bring along a knowledgeable friend, or just jump in and try your luck. Either way, you're in for a delicious meal and will be dazzled by the sushi chef's deft, lightning-fast food preparation.

Steps

1 Ask the sushi chef to recommend the catch of the day, since sushi-grade fish is especially sensitive to seasonal changes.

2 Swim with the big guys by getting the basics down. Nigiri is fish pressed onto rice mounds. Maki are sushi rolls wrapped in nori seaweed, and sliced; temaki are hand-rolled seaweed cones containing rice and fish. Sashimi is raw fish.

3 Keep in mind that an average person eats 10 to 12 pieces in one sitting. Nigiri usually comes two pieces to the order; maki is sliced into six pieces. Begin with a few dishes and order more if people are still hungry.

4 Start with edamame (steamed and salted soybeans served in the shell), marinated seaweed salad, or miso soup if you'd like.

5 Order one or two types of nigiri. Hamachi (yellowtail), maguro (tuna), unagi (broiled eel) and sake (salmon) are popular choices. Sushi is served with wasabi (a green, sinus-clearing horseradish paste) and soy sauce. Experiment to see which condiments you prefer.

6 Ask the sushi chef to make you a surprise if you're ready for further adventures in sushi.

7 Follow up with some maki favorites: spicy tuna rolls, cucumber rolls or California rolls (cooked crab and avocado). Tobiko (crunchy fish roe) is a typical accompaniment.

8 Try uni (sea urchin) topped with a raw quail egg, if you're feeling bold.

9 Cleanse your palate between bites with a sip of green tea and some pickled ginger (traditionally served with sushi).

10 End the meal with tamago, a slightly sweet egg omelette atop rice, or a refreshing bowl of green tea ice cream.

What to Look For

- Chef recommendations
- Nigiri, maki or temaki sushi
- Pickled ginger and green tea
- Soy sauce and wasabi
- Combination rolls

Tips

It's fine to use your fingers when eating sushi. Place the fish (not the rice) on your tongue to fully savor the flavor.

Sashimi (sliced raw fish) is technically not sushi. It's best to savor sashimi as an appetizer before you fill up on rice.

Tempura rolls, unagi, salmon skin rolls, California rolls and veggie rolls are good choices for those wary of raw fish.

Some folks enjoy sipping sake (hot or cold) or Japanese beer with their sushi.

Warnings

If a sushi bar smells funny or it appears less than spotless, depart immediately.

Pregnant women and people with compromised immune systems should not eat raw fish.

30 Buy Dinner at a Fancy French Restaurant

One glance at the menu at an elegant restaurant is enough to rattle non-French-speaking diners. Combine this with a smug waiter and you'll find yourself in a pricey pickle. Here's how to enjoy the finest French cuisine without being made to feel like *un imbécile.*

COMMON MENU ITEMS	DEFINITION
MEATS	
Terrine (teh-REEN)	Ground meat or seafood (pâté) shaped like a meat loaf.
Confit (kohn-FEE)	Preserved meat, such as goose or duck, or vegetable.
Tripe	Stomach lining of calves or lamb.
Sweetbreads	Calf or lamb glands that are white and soft.
Foie gras (FWAH GRAH)	Duck liver pâté.
Saucisson (soh-see-SAWN)	Sausage.
Tournedo (TOOR-nih-doh)	A small, lean cut of tenderloin.
Paillard (PI-yahrd)	A medallion-shaped piece of meat, poultry or veal.
VEGETABLES	
Pommes de terre (pom duh tehr)	Potatoes.
Haricots verts (ah-ree-koh VEHR)	Green string beans.
Mesclun (MEHS-kluhn)	Mixed baby lettuces and salad greens.
Endives (AHN-deev)	Torpedo-shaped lettuce with a bitter flavor, often served braised.
Truffle	A fungus with a rich, earthy flavor, a seasonal delicacy.
DISH TYPES	
Fricassee (FRIHK-uh-see)	Meat simmered in broth and wine topped with a white creamy sauce.
En Croûte (ahn KROOT)	Meat baked in a pastry.
Roulade (roo-LAHD)	Thin meat wrapped around a savory filling, tied with string.
À la Provençal (ah lah proh-vahn-SAHL)	Usually includes tomatoes, anchovies and olives.
À la Bordelaise (ah lah bohr-dl-AYZ)	Dishes prepared with red wine.
Gratin (gra-TAN)	Baked vegetable dish with crispy topping.
Soufflé (soo-FLAY)	A baked dish of cheese, veggies, or chocolate and egg whites.
Ratatouille (ra-tuh-TOO-ee)	Vegetable stew with tomatoes, zucchini and eggplant.
Crêpe (KRAYP)	Thin pancakes with sweet or savory fillings.
SAUCES	
Béchamel (bay-shah-MEHL)	White, creamy sauce.
Béarnaise (behr-NAYZ)	White wine sauce with tarragon often served atop beef.
Chanterelle (shan-tuh-REHL)	Sauce seasoned with mushrooms.
Beurre Blanc (burr BLAHNK)	White butter sauce.
Beurre Noisette (burr nwah-ZEHT)	Light brown butter sauce with a nutty flavor.
Beurre Noir (burr NWAR)	Dark brown butter sauce with a deep nutty flavor.
Aïoli (ay-OH-lee)	Homemade mayonnaise flavored with garlic and herbs.

31 Hire a Dating Service

You can't buy love but you sure can hire an assistant to help you find some. Check out the different types of dating services that help you cast a wide net for potential matches. These companies may charge anywhere from $20 to $20,000 for their services, so be sure that love doesn't make a fool out of you. Shop around and review prices and options with several services before you sign up for one.

TYPE OF SERVICE	PROS	CONS
Online Dating Service You post your profile online and respond to other profiles for a small membership fee.	Online services can provide a large selection (potentially any-one with a computer), you get to do the choosing, and you can easily sign up for more than one site. You can quickly search your area for people with compatible interests and lifestyles.	You may not have total control over information you put online, including your photo. There is no one to screen potential dates before you meet them so there's always a chance of meeting a psycho or your old gym teacher. Your e-mail address will proba-bly be shared with spammers.
Matchmaker A professional match-maker interviews you and sets you up with other subscribers he or she considers compatible.	A matchmaker can specialize in a specific religion or ethnicity. The services are personalized and confidential and all dates are screened for you by the matchmaker.	You're limited to the match-maker's subscriber base and are somewhat subject to the tastes and opinion of the matchmaker.
Singles Clubs These clubs organize socials events for people to meet other singles with similar interests.	You get to meet many people at once without the awkwardness of a date. The activities are usually fun and exciting, like horseback riding, wine tasting and hot air ballooning.	You still have to manage the pit-falls of meeting a potential date in a large group, a significant hurdle for many.
Profile and Video Dating These services allow you to view videos of prospective dates, while they can view your video.	You get to see your date on video beforehand, and you get to do the choosing.	Wading through files at the dat-ing service office can be a long process. Service is being sup-planted by dating Web sites.
Dating Consultants Dating headhunters introduce busy singles for a hefty fee; all-inclusive service offers dating makeovers, simulations and seminars.	These services can be intensive and hands-on. Due to the price, this is primarily a way for busy rich people to meet other busy rich people.	Service can run into the thou-sands of dollars.

32 Sell Yourself on an Online Dating Service

Millions of people are using online dating services to meet their Romeos or Juliets. If you want to give it a whirl, start with a compelling, yet truthful, profile of yourself. Many online dating sites allow you to post a profile for free but will charge you $20 to $35 per month to post photos, send e-mail or instant messages to other singles.

Steps

Before you sign up

1 Make a list of the qualities you'd like to find in a mate (or date).

2 Include important lifestyle issues in your profile. Are you looking for a serious commitment that could lead to marriage and kids or a strictly sexual relationship? Is religion important?

3 Surf various dating sites, such as Match.com and Yahoo Personals to view other profiles, making note of the things you like and dislike. This will help you not only refine your profile, but also decide which dating site to use.

Signing up

1 Gather or take a few flattering photographs of yourself. Your photo will be the first thing most people see. Select ones that show you looking relaxed and friendly. Showcase the best of what you've got. Don't post a photo of your cat or you with your ex.

2 Choose a user name that is simple and straightforward. Don't use your own name.

3 Brainstorm to come up with an appealing headline for your profile. Review other profiles to get an idea of the headline tone that you like. You don't need to be too cute or catchy, just fun.

4 Write a concise, descriptive and amusing profile of yourself. Describe who you are, what makes you unique (and desirable) and what you're looking for. Be true to yourself but don't be overearnest. Keep the tone upbeat, light and friendly.

5 Fill out the additional questions about height, weight, eye color and lifestyle preferences honestly. Resist the urge to manipulate these details in your favor. You'll be found out eventually and lying isn't a great way to start a relationship. Think twice before providing specific information about your income.

6 Check your profile for spelling and grammar before you submit it.

7 Beware of the seduction of spending time online answering letters—especially to people you have no interest in meeting. Guard your time and your privacy carefully.

8 Take it nice and slow after you meet. You'll need to catch up in person after the easy intimacy of e-mail.

What to Look For

- Your personal qualities and interests
- Lifestyle issues
- Flattering photograph

Tips

Choose a Web site that has a large selection of singles in your area. Make sure you can search the site geographically.

Sexual comments, innuendos or jokes will attract the wrong crowd if you're looking for a long-term, meaningful relationship.

Have a friend with a digital camera take a couple of great photos of you if you don't already have some. Consider hiring a photographer. It will be money well spent.

While it's good to have an idea about what you like in a mate, keep an open mind. The love of your life might be nothing like what you envision.

Warnings

Beware of the easy but limited intimacy that can rapidly develop in e-mail. Meet the person early on to see if there's any chemistry.

If you decide to meet someone in person, meet in a public area. Don't share private information until you get to know the person better.

33 Sell Yourself to Your Girlfriend/Boyfriend's Family

Some people say—and they're probably correct—that every job in the world is a sales job. No matter what your profession, you have to sell yourself, your ideas and your skills. The same is true when you meet your sweetheart's family. In a perfect world, they would instantly recognize your refined character and sincere qualities. But do you really want to chance it?

Steps

1 Wait until the time is right. Try not to meet the family too soon. Be sure you're serious about the relationship so that you can deal with them sincerely.

2 Find out whom you will be meeting. Memorize their names. Addressing people by name is absolutely vital and an easy way to make your social skills and manners visible. Know the expected form for addressing the parents ("Mr. Snodgrass," "Sir," "Buster").

3 Meet at a neutral location, if possible. This should be less stressful than going to their home. A restaurant familiar to you is a good option. However, be prepared to defer to the parents' preference. If you initiate a restaurant meeting it will probably be your obligation to pay.

4 Absolutely be on time. If you're late, it will almost certainly be viewed as disrespectful to them and your mate. If there's any chance that you will be late, notify someone as soon as possible. Be sure your cell phone is charged up and you have their number. If you can't make the appointment, and you can't notify them, plan to be either dead or on life support when they locate you.

5 Bring a small gift. Find out from your mate what would be appropriate. A bottle of wine, especially at a family dinner, is almost always a tasteful offering.

6 Dress for the occasion. Have your mate tell you exactly what to wear. Don't rely on subjective descriptions like "casual" or "dressy." If your mate tells you to wear your dark suit, shut up, put on the suit and make the most of it. You've got the rest of your life to show what a slob you are.

7 Show an interest in the family. They will probably want to know about you, but try to steer the conversation to their interests and activities as well. Avoid talking endlessly about yourself.

What to Look For

- The right time
- Neutral meeting place
- A small gift
- Safe conversation

Tips

Above all, be yourself. If you're not naturally the life of the party, don't try to be one now.

Don't put too much pressure on yourself. No one expects you to be perfect. Thoughtful and polite is good enough, no matter what else happens.

8 Tell stories that highlight the fine qualities of their son/daughter. This will elevate you to worthy status due to your ability to appreciate such quality family traits.

9 Avoid sensitive issues. Religion, politics, race relations, foreign affairs, and the behavior of kids today are all issues guaranteed to start trouble. If you initiate a discussion on one of these topics at a first meeting, you probably deserve to be single. On the other hand, if asked a direct question, you have no choice but to answer honestly. State your position once, and avoid being drawn into an argument. Remember not to swear.

34 Buy Doghouse Flowers for Your Sweetheart

Maybe if you explain, really, really carefully, what happened, she'll understand and forgive you. Hmmm . . . no. Better to just give up and apologize. Flowers may offer your best chance of success.

Steps

1 Abandon any plans to reassert your position. Now is not the time. Your objective is to repair damage and smooth things over. If you can't do this, then you're not ready for flowers.

2 Search your brain for clues about what kind of flowers she likes. Of course, you've had many chances to pay attention. Don't beat yourself up about it now. If you're not absolutely sure what she favors, get red roses or Casablanca lilies. See 18 Buy a Bouquet of Roses.

3 Have the flowers delivered to her at work or in a public place, if possible. Call a florist and place the order. Expect to pay at least $50, and maybe more. Do not forget to include a card and sweet message. Don't worry about exposing yourself—the florist has seen worse screwups than you.

4 If you can't have flowers delivered, go to the florist yourself. Give a quick outline of the situation and ask them for a suggestion. Stay away from carnations or baby's breath. They have "supermarket checkout" written all over them.

5 Deliver the flowers immediately. Do not stop off for "one quick beer" on the way.

6 Offer an unconditional apology. Your goal is to be finished with this incident. If you think more discussion is needed, wait a week and bring it up when both of you are alert, stress-free and even-tempered.

What to Look For

- Correct flowers
- Guaranteed delivery

Tip

Some supermarkets and roadside flower stands sell simple bouquets for less than $10. If you're not in too much trouble, you might be able to get away with this option.

35 Buy Music Online

You've got plenty of choices when shopping for music. In addition to what's available at your local record store and online shops like Amazon.com, CDBaby.com and CDUniverse.com, there are countless music files available. Apple's got the newest kid on the block with iTunes, where you can buy any song in their vast online database for 99 cents.

Steps

1 Learn the difference between streaming and downloading. Streamed music plays live when you're connected to the Internet. Downloaded music gets copied directly to your computer's hard disk. Then you can listen to it anytime, move it to a portable MP3 player or burn it to a CD. Streamed music generally can't be saved or burned to CD.

2 Get the software you need to listen to MP3s and streaming audio. It's probably already installed on your computer; if not, you can download these for free: RealOne, Winamp, Windows Media Player and iTunes.

3 Visit music sites to look for the musicians you want to hear. Some popular download sites are eMusic.com, Listen.com, MP3.com and PressPlay.com. Popular streaming sites include MusicMatch.com and Yahoo Launch (launch.yahoo.com).

4 Check for individual songs you want to hear. Just because a band or group appears on one service doesn't mean that all its songs are available there. Artists often appear at several sites.

5 Check out an artist's official Web site, especially if you're looking for new or obscure music. Many artists will promote songs by letting you download them directly from their own sites. Lots of radio stations stream their broadcasts on the Web for free.

6 Compare the plans and prices offered at different sites. Most offer a free trial period, and then charge a subscription fee ranging from $5 to $15 per month (with a discount if you subscribe for a year). Some also offer pay-per-download plans. This can be worth it if you only want to get a few tunes.

7 Find out what the subscription fee includes. Look for one that gives you plenty of downloads and unlimited streaming. For streaming sites, find one that allows you to create custom playlists or "radio stations" that play only your favorite music.

8 Watch out for plans in which downloaded music expires or becomes unplayable when your subscription lapses, or when you move the music around. This is usually called a secure service or digital rights management (DRM). It's better to use a service that gives you full rights to copy the music to another computer or portable player, and to burn the songs to CDs.

What to Look For

- MP3 and streaming audio software
- Free trial periods
- Subscription pricing
- Secure formats, DRM, expiration, or copy protection

Tips

You may have to provide some personal information (such as your name, age and e-mail address) to get songs for free.

Check out Audible.com for downloadable audio books in MP3 format.

You don't have to download music that you already have on CD. There's freely available software that will convert music on CDs to MP3 format.

Warnings

The advice given here concerns the legal, paid downloading of music.

Peer-to-peer (P2P) services let you swap music directly from your computer's hard drive to those of other people on the Internet. The most famous P2P service, Napster, collapsed under legal challenges, but P2P services still exist. Use them with extreme caution: They can be breeding grounds for viruses and spyware (which gives other people access to your computer), and their legality continues to be in dispute.

Play music immediately after downloading. Listen carefully for bad files.

36 Hire Musicians

Whether it's a string quartet or a rocking blues band, live music can make or break an event. Choosing your musicians carefully is crucial to a successful soirée—you don't want your event to be memorable for the wrong reasons.

Steps

1 Start your search as early as possible. Get recommendations from caterers or event coordinators. Look under "Musicians" in the Yellow Pages, and check party-planning directories for musicians' unions or entertainment brokers. Contact music schools, too.

2 Call at least three prospective bands. Ask about their availability, rates, number of musicians and instruments in the band, years of experience, song lists, references and liability insurance.

3 Ask about additional costs, such as overtime, travel or meals for band members.

4 Request a demo tape and find out if you can attend a performance to observe the band in person. Confirm that the musicians on the demo tape or onstage will be the ones at your gig.

5 Check references. Ask about promptness, reliability, performance quality, interactions with the audience and overall impressions.

6 Negotiate a fee. You may be able to reduce the number of band members or the playing time to bring down the cost.

7 Get everything in writing: the fee, deposit, cancellation and refund policies, overtime fees, the band's insurance information, number of musicians and instruments, date of event, setup time, performance time, band's attire, equipment provided by band, equipment provided by you, specific song requests, and contact information.

8 Get two signed copies of the contract. Give one to the broker or bandleader and keep one for yourself.

9 Provide a list of favorite and unwanted songs. Most bands will have a set song list to choose from, but some will learn songs if you request, but may charge extra.

10 Call the band or broker the week of the event to confirm the date and time. Provide directions, information about parking, and your contact information for last-minute emergencies.

What to Look For

- Availability
- Rates
- Hidden costs
- Demo tape
- Live performance
- References
- Promptness
- Reliability
- Written contract

Tips

If you want the bandleader to double as an emcee, make sure you approve of his or her style, tone and humor. Provide a schedule of events, such as an anniversary couple's dance, the throwing of the wedding bouquet.

Anticipate that the band will need a break every hour. Request that they play appropriate recorded music while on break.

Reputable entertainment brokers can save you some effort. They represent a variety of bands and DJs, and can handle all the logistics for you.

Budget money to tip the band at the end of the evening.

37 Order a Great Bottle of Wine

You settle into your seat, ready for a fine meal, when suddenly a leather-bound wine list is thrust into your hands. Panic no longer. Some simple considerations will help you quickly transform the process into a less intimidating, even enjoyable task.

Steps

1 Initiate a wine discussion with your dining companions but keep it simple. Find out the type of wine people prefer and what they plan to order as their entrée.

2 Let the group know that they should definitely feel free to ignore the traditional pairing of red wines with meat and white wines with seafood and poultry.

3 If you have a favorite, suggest it to the group. They're likely to accept your recommendation.

4 If the group is divided, consider a heavy white, such as a full-bodied Chardonnay, or a lighter red, such as a Syrah.

5 If you're completely lost, scan the list for a wine that fits the group's preferences and is within your budget range. Most white wine drinkers will accept a Chardonnay and most red fans are happy with Merlot or Zinfandel. Make a tentative selection and prepare to ask for advice.

6 Address the waiter with, for example, "I was thinking of this Riesling unless you have a better suggestion." If the restaurant has a sommelier—a wine expert—ask the waiter to send him or her to your table to discuss suitable pairings.

7 Check the bottle's label to confirm it's the wine you ordered. Smell and sample the wine to make sure it isn't vinegary, corky or musty. (If it is, you can send it back.) Give the server the nod to pour for the rest of the table. Sip and enjoy.

What to Look For

- Red or white
- Vineyard, grape variety and vintage
- Price

Tips

If you are uncomfortable discussing price limitations with a waiter or sommelier, subtly gesture to wines on the list that fit your budget.

Some waiters can provide excellent suggestions, while others are clueless. Most will at least know which wines are popular with other patrons.

Some restaurants will fax you the wine list ahead of time. Also, some finer restaurants have reserved wine lists of special or rare wines available upon request.

Red for red meats, pork and red sauces/white for poultry, fish and white sauces is a helpful guideline, but not an absolute rule. Your personal preference is equally important.

38 Buy an Ergonomic Desk Chair

If you spend most of your waking hours at your desk, you know you need a chair that works with your body to spare you from needless backaches and fatigue. Test drive several chairs at furniture, office supply and back-care stores before you pick the one that's right for you. Prices vary greatly: predictably, superior materials and construction carry a bigger price tag. Good deals abound online and at office furniture consignment and resale shops (see 156 Buy Liquidated Office Equipment).

FEATURE	WHAT IT DOES
Back Support	• Height adjustment: Supports the lumbar area (lower back). Look for chairs that provide mid-back and upper-back support as well. • Tilt mechanism: Maintains support as you move and recline. It's best to have your back slightly reclined while seated at your desk.
Seat Pan	• Your weight should be distributed evenly on the seat. Look for a rounded or waterfall edge at the front of the seat, which prevents the seat from catching behind the knees and cutting off circulation. Three to four fingers should fit between the seat pan's front edge and the back of the knees. • Seat should extend at least one inch from either side of the hips for optimum comfort. Insufficient hip room can make you sit too far forward and not get enough thigh support. • Some seat pans adjust for a forward or backward tilt.
Armrests	• Alleviate pressure on the back but may interfere with lower desks. Look for adjustable width and height to support various tasks, including writing and reading, to ease neck and shoulder tension and to help prevent carpal tunnel syndrome. • Should be contoured, broad, cushioned and comfortable.
Fabric	• Cloth coverings are less expensive and breathe well, but vinyl or leather upholstery is easier to keep clean. Look for a durable, permeable, ventilated material and check out the mesh Pellicle material in the Aeron chair, which also conforms to the body.
Height Adjustment	• Pneumatic levers or gas lifts adjust seating height while in chair. For optimal posture, thighs should be horizontal with the ground and both feet flat on the floor. The chair's height should allow wrists to be straight while typing.
Stability	• Look for a chair on wheels that swivels to avoid excess stretching and twisting of your spine. A five-point base won't tip over when you recline. • Choose hard casters for carpeting and rubber-coated ones for hard surfaces. A good chair can recline and lock into various positions.

39 Choose Film for Your Camera

Your primary considerations when buying film are where you'll be shooting and what you want to do with the pictures. This information allows you to choose the correct film speed, listed as ASA or ISO on the package.

Steps

1 Decide whether you want photographs or slides, color or black-and-white. Many professional photographers prefer slides because they have rich color saturation and minimal graininess. Black-and-white delivers striking images with stark textures.

2 Choose a film size that is appropriate for your camera. Most cameras use 35 mm (or 135) film, though cartridge-film cameras need 24 mm Advanced Photo System (APS) film. Roll-film cameras use 120 or 220; large-format, hooded view cameras use single sheets of film for each exposure (4 by 5 inches and up).

3 Understand how film speed works. Fast speeds pick up rapid action and work well in low-light situations. Slower speeds produce richer colors and greater contrast, but you'll need bright light and a steady hand. Film speed is indicated by an ISO number (how sensitive a film is to light compared to a standard from the International Standards Organization). The faster the film, the more sensitive.

4 Choose a slow speed (25 to 64 ASA) if you want minimal graininess and colors that punch, but only if you'll be photographing in the bright sunlight. Slow speeds are excellent for close-ups, still shots and photos you plan to enlarge. You may need a tripod to steady the camera with slow film.

5 Select a medium speed (100 to 200 ASA) if you want an all-purpose film that delivers clear colors and images outdoors, or indoors with a flash.

6 Opt for 400 speed if you'll be photographing action shots or if you'll be in low-light conditions, such as cloudy days or indoors without a flash. Zoom lenses require the use of higher-speed films (400 ASA and up).

7 Get 800-speed film if you're photographing very fast action or shots with dim light. This is ideal for a fireworks show, twilight or a candlelit dinner. Speeds above 800 (1,000 to 3,200 ASA) are considered professional speeds.

8 Use slide film for appropriate light if you prefer slides to photos: daylight for indoors, or tungsten light for flash photography.

9 Look for store-brand films to save money unless you plan on making significant enlargements or publishing your work.

10 Store film in a cool, dry place with good ventilation, such as a refrigerator, and get it developed as soon as the roll is finished. Never expose film to heat or direct sunlight.

What to Look For

- Photographic prints or slides
- Color or black-and-white
- Film size
- Film speed
- Lighting conditions

Tips

The techniques used at same-day film developers often result in grainy pictures with dull colors. Choose a store that has someone monitoring the developing process—this person can make adjustments to optimize color and contrast.

Kodak still manufactures 110 film (a size used in older cameras). Search online for companies that sell other discontinued films.

Warning

When traveling, never pack film in your checked luggage: The powerful X-rays used to scan checked luggage may destroy the film. Keep it in a mesh bag and at security checkpoints, ask personnel to hand-check your film if it is 800 speed or higher.

40 Buy Rechargeable Batteries

Rechargeable batteries are good for the environment and for your wallet. Here's a guide to purchasing the right rechargeables for your devices and appliances. Don't forget the charger: You can buy units that fit alkaline, NiMH and NiCd batteries for approximately $30. And when your rechargeables finally fall victim to the "memory effect"—crystals that form on interior plates and shorten the life of the battery—go to RBRC.org. You'll find collection sites in your area listed by ZIP code.

TYPE	GOOD FOR	PROS AND CONS
Alkaline	Devices that require a low amount of energy over a long time: remote controls, pagers, AM/FM radios, flashlights, CD and tape players.	Have a long shelf life, longer than equivalent nickel cadmium (NiCd) and nickel metal hydride (NiMH) cells. Energy drastically decreases after the first recharge (last 20 to 25 fewer cycles than NiCd and NiMH batteries). Life depends on the depth of discharge: the deeper the discharge, the fewer cycles the battery can endure. Reduced service life may offset any cost advantage over standard alkaline batteries when used in items that drain quickly.
Nickel Metal Hydride (NiMH)	Energy-intense products: digital cameras, music players and remote-control toys.	Pack a lot of power with each charge. Last longer between charges than NiCd batteries and are less toxic to the environment. Handle the memory effect much better than NiCd batteries. Lose charge quickly, in use or not. Lifetime only reaches up to 500 charge-discharge cycles.
Nickel Cadmium (NiCd)	Power tools and emergency lighting	Most common rechargeable batteries. Easy to use, cheap and last for 500 to 1,000 cycles. Prone to the memory effect; requires monthly prevention. Most problems due to overcharging or improper storage. Contain cadmium, a highly toxic heavy metal, that can damage the environment if not disposed of properly. (Batteries should be recycled, not discarded.)
Lithium Ion (Li-Ion)	Ideal for devices requiring a reliable, high-energy power source: cellular phones, PDAs, laptops, and MP3 players.	Rechargeable, powerful and light. Do not exhibit a memory problem, so can be recharged anytime without first having to be completely discharged). Li-Ion batteries produce the same energy as NiMH but weigh approximately 20 to 35 percent less. They are also environmentally friendly because they don't contain toxins such as cadmium or mercury.
TIPS		The energy capacity of the battery is measured in milliampere hours (mAh). The higher the mAh number, the longer the battery will hold and provide its rated charge. Digital cameras need AA batteries with 1,800 to 1,900 mAh. The shelf life of a battery varies depending on how you use it. An alkaline battery with 2,500 mAh might die in an hour or less if you use it in a digital camera. In a remote control it could last for several months.

41 Donate to a Good Cause

With so many worthy causes vying for your dollar, choose one or two that are near and dear to your heart. Has a loved one suffered from breast cancer? Are you a nature or animal lover? Is education or social welfare your passion? Once you've chosen a cause, there are excellent resources available to help you choose an organization that will make the most of your donation.

Steps

1 Visit Give.org, the Better Business Bureau (BBB) Web site on charitable giving, to find reports about specific charities. The BBB provides financial information about charities and evaluates them using specific accountability standards.

2 Contact your state attorney general's office or a local branch of the Better Business Bureau for information if a charity is not reviewed at Give.org.

3 Check that the charity is a tax-exempt organization and that donations made to it are tax-deductible. Donations made to tax-exempt organizations are not necessarily deductible.

4 Visit the charity's Web site or call it directly. Find out as much as you can about its history, programs and recent accomplishments.

5 Review what percentage of the charity's annual budget is spent on its actual mission versus fund-raising and administrative costs. Give.org recommends that a charity spend at least 50 percent of its budget on its mission, and no more than 35 percent on fund-raising.

6 Evaluate the mission of the charity and its effectiveness in fulfilling its mission. For those organizations that operate in other parts of the world, particularly the Third World, look for partnerships between the organization and the local population for most effective use of resources and the highest degree of success.

7 Confirm that the charity will appropriate your donation according to your wishes and not put it in a general fund.

8 Make your donation with a check. Never send cash.

9 File the canceled check and the charity's receipt as proof of your donation for tax purposes.

10 Consider other types of donations. Many organizations accept gifts of equipment, even vehicles. See 531 Donate Your Car.

What to Look For

- Tax-deductible donation status
- Written materials about the charity
- Mission statement
- Successful programs
- Donation receipt
- Annual reports
- IRS Form 990

Tips

An organization need not be a charity to receive donations. Schools, cultural programs and political groups all rely on donations of money and time.

If you want to further review the charity, ask it to provide you a copy of its recent annual reports and its Internal Revenue Service Form 990 (which details annual fund-raising and spending).

Charities are required to supply a copy of their IRS Form 990 upon request. Some may charge a photocopying fee.

If the organization is new and lacks a financial record, request information about budgets, fund-raising goals, a list of its board of directors and its mission statement.

If your gift is going to be sizable, consider forms other than a straight donation, and get legal and financial advice (see 119 Give Away Your Fortune).

42 Hold a Profitable Garage Sale

The secret to a profitable garage sale is ample preparation and a good team. Do the prep work in advance, and you can relax and be friendly on the big day to enjoy happy customers and pleasing profits.

Steps

1 Schedule your garage sale far enough in advance so that you can place a classified ad. Hold your sale on a nonholiday weekend unless you live in a resort town with lots of vacationers. Check the long-range forecast for good weather.

2 Dig through your garage, attic, basement and house for stuff to sell. Include everything you want to get rid of—one person's junk is another's treasure.

3 Spread the word among friends and family. The more you have to sell, the larger the crowd you can draw. Offer to sell their stuff for a 20 percent commission.

4 Scrub, wash, polish, dust and launder anything you plan to sell. If an item needs a simple repair that could greatly improve the price, fix it.

5 Round up volunteers if you expect large crowds. Friends and family may be willing to help for a free meal, the chance to sell their own junk, or just the fun of it.

6 Print up one-page fliers advertising your sale and put them up at local coffee shops, laundries, grocery stores or community centers.

7 Place large, neatly printed signs in your neighborhood the night before or the morning of the sale. Put signs in front of your house as well.

8 Use masking tape and a permanent marker to mark everything with a price. "$1 or less" tables or boxes save time and attract shoppers. Leave room to bargain down when pricing items. Remember that you're trying to get rid of your stuff when you price it. You may have spent a fortune on that Beta VCR, but you'll be lucky to get a quarter for it now.

9 Hang clothes on makeshift racks. Borrow portable tables to display items. Put crowd-pleasers (furniture, tools) up front to entice people. Have a "10 cents" box to encourage further browsing.

10 Set up your cash table near the entrance. Have plenty of small change, a cash box, a calculator, pencil and pen, a ledger book (to inventory commissions), bags and boxes, newspaper to wrap valuables, and a tape measure.

11 Make sure there's plenty of parking; relocate your car if necessary.

12 Be cheerful, get people talking and encourage haggling. Many people are reluctant to haggle but find it's fun once they start.

What to Look For

- Nonholiday weekend
- Long lead time
- Volunteers
- Fliers

Tips

Schedule your garage sale with payday in mind, typically the first and 15th of the month. People are more likely to splurge on a treasure with a fat paycheck in their pocket.

Make sure there's an electrical outlet or heavy-duty extension cord accessible so shoppers can test electrical appliances.

Give your neighbors a courtesy call beforehand to warn them of your sale. They'll appreciate it, and may even have some stuff to add to the sale.

Donate whatever is left to a charity that has a pick-up service.

Warnings

Some cities require permits for garage sales. Other cities prohibit signage. Check municipal rules in advance to avoid any problems on the day of the sale.

Protect yourself against theft and fraud. Display small valuables within eyesight. Keep money in a zipped fanny pack if you're bustling about. Keep large sums of money locked in the house. Do not accept personal checks.

43 Hire a Housecleaner

Weekends are too short to spend scrubbing, vacuuming and dusting and nothing beats coming home to a clean house, especially when you didn't do it. Hire a cleaning service or housecleaner to do your dirty work so you can go out to play.

Steps

1 Decide whether you want to use a cleaning service or an individual housecleaner. Using a service costs more, but saves you legwork, and the supplies and equipment are included.

2 Ask friends for recommendations. Check local newspapers, job boards, the Yellow Pages and the Internet.

3 Call several prospective cleaners. Confirm that they'll do the required tasks (some won't do laundry, windows or dishes). Ask about experience, availability and rates. Find out if they're bonded and insured.

4 Research tax laws to determine whether you're required to pay taxes. A good place to start is with the Internal Revenue Service's Publication 926, "Household Employer's Tax Guide." If you do need to pay taxes, verify that the person is willing and able to have his or her wages reported.

5 Check three references before you hold interviews to verify the person's promptness, reliability and quality of work.

6 Meet prospective cleaners with stellar references to show them the specifics of the job and to get a sense of their personality and professionalism. Some housecleaners don't speak English well but have excellent cleaning skills. Communication will be important if you have allergies to certain cleaning products, or unique instructions about antiques, handmade rugs or other fragile items.

7 Ask specific questions to test a housecleaner's methods: "What do you use to clean hardwood floors?" "How would you remove these stains from my stove top?"

8 Determine how often the housecleaner will come. Some will do periodic deep cleaning while others need a weekly or biweekly schedule. If you plan to use the person part-time or full-time, discuss issues like paid holidays and sick days.

9 Hire the most promising person or team for a trial period with the understanding that if you're satisfied, you'll use them regularly.

What to Look For

- Experience
- Availability
- Rates
- Quality references
- Promptness
- Professionalism

Tips

Individual operators usually earn more hourly than a person working for a cleaning service because there's no third party or overhead.

Housecleaning agencies are a good source for contacts. They'll refer you to experienced, prescreened housecleaners for a cut of the rate over a set time period.

Written contracts are not typically used with housecleaners. Writing your newly hired housecleaner a letter that spells out the terms of employment and any specific requests (the china should never go in the dishwasher) is a helpful gesture. It's even more helpful if you get it translated for people whose English isn't great.

Warning

Keep jewelry and large amounts of cash locked up when any hired workers visit.

44 Hire a Baby Sitter

Baby-sitting gives responsible teenagers a chance to earn money—and hiring a baby sitter can give you a well-deserved night on the town. Choose a baby sitter carefully; this person will be caring for your loved ones. If you're hiring a full-time or part-time baby sitter, go through an agency that does thorough background checks and provides training in emergency first aid and cardiopulmonary resuscitation (CPR). See 324 Find Fabulous Childcare for more information.

Steps

1 Rely on word of mouth to find a baby sitter. Does your child's friends have older siblings? Does your church have a teen group? Can a counselor at the local high school recommend someone? Consider a spry senior citizen who has lots of experience with children, or a camp counselor.

2 Contact a local childcare referral agency for a list of people who have graduated from their childcare skills class.

3 Call prospective sitters to discuss rates and availability.

4 Check two or three personal references. For a teenager who doesn't have baby-sitting clients yet, speak to a teacher or coach.

5 Have strong candidates come to your house for a few hours while you're there to take care of the kids. Stay in the background but keep your eyes peeled for how he or she interacts with your children and how they respond to the sitter. Trust your gut.

6 Review instructions for the baby sitter in person. Include guidelines about television viewing and Internet surfing, snacking, personal phone calls or visitors, disciplinary approaches and bedtime routines.

7 Leave a list of emergency phone numbers (including a neighbor's), how you can be reached, and any food allergies or health issues. Show the sitter where you keep first aid supplies.

8 Ask your children about the baby sitter the following day. Listen carefully to their responses to evaluate whether you'd hire him or her on a regular basis.

What to Look For

- Personal recommendations
- Rates and availability
- Children's reactions

Tips

Alert a watchful neighbor about the baby sitter's first visit. He or she can keep an eye out for loud music or friends sneaking by for a visit.

Make sure the baby sitter knows how to change diapers if such skills are needed.

If the baby sitter will be chauffeuring your kids to and from lessons, ask to see a driving record to check for moving violations.

Warning

Children make up the wildest stories for baby sitters about what parents allow them to eat, watch or do. Preempt those efforts with clear written guidelines.

45 Buy a Guitar

Elvis Presley and John Lennon strummed Gibson acoustic guitars. Jimi Hendrix powered through his classics on a Fender Stratocaster, while Bruce Springsteen remains steadfastly loyal to his own boss, a well-worn Fender Telecaster. If you've just picked up a guitar, or if you're a seasoned gunslinger looking to upgrade, how do you choose a new ax?

Steps

Before you buy

1 Choose between a steel-stringed acoustic guitar for folk and blues, a nylon-stringed acoustic for classical music, or an electric or electric bass guitar for good old rock and roll, to name a few.

2 Talk to follow musicians about their instrument of choice and what they love about it.

3 Research guitar brands using price guides, guitar magazines and the Internet. Some models appreciate in value as they get older.

4 Consider buying secondhand instead of new. If you know your stuff, you may be able to get more value for your dollar. See 3 Buy Products and Services Online.

At the store

1 Examine the construction. Look for a straight neck, a well-balanced body and frets that are smooth and flush.

2 Strap on the guitar and hold in playing position. Does it feel natural? Balanced? Too heavy? Does your hand fit comfortably around the neck?

3 Tune the guitar to see how smoothly the tuning keys operate and to test the sound quality of each string.

4 Play a song. Do you like the sound? Is it easy to press down the strings? Is there any buzzing or clicking that suggests problems?

5 If you are buying an electric guitar, plug it into an amp and play. Listen for crackling or humming. Test the controls for ease-of-use. (Humming might be caused by a bad cord; replace it with a new one.)

6 Try out several models before you decide on one. Before you buy, ask, "What can you offer me if I buy my guitar here?" Some stores will throw in freebies (picks, guitar straps, a set of strings) or discounted accessories (amp, effects, capo or a mike stand). Make sure the price includes a guitar case.

7 Remember that the retail price of a guitar is often negotiable. See 8 Negotiate. Also, make sure you know the return policy before you buy. See 4 Make Returns.

What to Look For

- Reputable brand and model
- Solid construction
- Comfortable to hold and play
- Easy tuning
- Excellent sound
- Fair price

Tips

Before renting a guitar, ask the salesperson about rent-to-own deals.

Bring along a guitarist friend when you shop, especially if you can't tune a guitar.

Avoid guitar stores without marked prices and aggressive salespeople unless you really know prices and are willing to haggle.

You can buy a beginner's guitar for $200 to $500, but if you want to buy a renowned model of a popular brand, such as Gibson, Fender, Rickenbacker or Guild, expect to pay $1,000 or more.

46 Buy Duct Tape

Do you ever feel like the entire world is being held together with duct tape? After you read the following chart, you'll know if it's true and keep a roll on hand at all times.

USES FOR DUCT TAPE
Repair splits in car seats (or other furniture, if you must).
Car repair, including attaching side-view mirrors and bumpers.
Patch holes in screens.
Converted a CO_2 filter on *Apollo 13,* allowing the astronauts to breathe during their return to Earth.
Remove warts.
Twist a long piece into rope.
Tape wires down on floor or out of the way.
Tape wires back together after splicing.
Fold in half and use as bookmark.
Repair heating ducts.
Seal boxes.
Create disk labels.
Repair leak in tire or inner tube.
Tape annoying people to walls, floor, ceiling or bed.
Roll into a ball for hockey practice.
Mark lines on a sporting event field.
Wrap around newspaper to make a dog chew toy.
Remove lint from clothes.
Put it on your lawn and paint it green. Say good-bye to mowing.
Retread your tennis shoes.
Wrap a soda can or bottle to keep it cold.
Stare at it and try to find new uses for it.

47 Get a Good Deal on a Magazine Subscription

The cost of magazine subscriptions can creep up on you: $15 here, another $40 there and pretty soon you're spending hundreds of dollars annually. Be a smart consumer and save money while you get the magazines you want.

Steps

1 Resist pitches from telemarketers, solicitors, Web sites and junk mail. There are usually hidden costs, and selling subscriptions is a popular ploy used by scam artists.

2 Order directly from the publisher. Check the price listed on the magazine's Web site and on insert cards in the magazine.

3 Call the publisher's customer service line to confirm that you have the lowest rate. Ask, "Do you have a special rate for first-time subscribers?" Such rates are often unadvertised. Ask if there is a special rate for students and/or professional educators, if applicable.

4 Make sure you know the annual rate; some weekly magazines advertise a per-issue price that sounds cheap but adds up quickly.

5 Find out the cancellation policy before you subscribe to any special offer.

6 Order a two-year subscription if you know that you'll want it. You'll save a few dollars and lock in the current rate.

7 Request that you be billed for the magazine; don't provide your credit card number. If they have your credit card number, some magazines will automatically renew your subscription unless you call to cancel it. Magazines encourage credit-card payments because it puts inertia on their side. People often wait months or years to cancel subscriptions they no longer want.

8 Be immediately suspicious of telemarketers offering "free introductory offers" or subscriptions for "pennies a day." Magazine subscription scams are common and costly.

What to Look For

- Publisher's offers
- First-time rates
- Student or educational rates
- Cancellation policy
- Multiyear discount
- Billing arrangement

Tips

You can find a magazine's subscription phone number online and in the small print near the magazine's table of contents or masthead.

Third-party subscription services rarely offer better deals than the publisher. The few dollars you save won't be worth the deluge of spam, junk mail and telemarketing calls that will come.

48 Get Senior Citizen or Student Discounts

You can save money merely by being the right age. Senior and student discounts apply to travel, entertainment and a host of products and services. A little digging will uncover all sorts of deals in your neighborhood, and around the world.

Steps

Senior discounts

1 Call the airlines or go online to find out about discounted tickets for seniors. Bus and rail carriers also offer discounts.

2 Enjoy the arts on the cheap. Most movie theaters, museums and cultural events offer discounts for seniors.

3 Check if department stores or other retailers have special days or hours for senior discounts. Some stores offer 10 to 15 percent off during those times.

4 Ask about early-bird specials, senior menus or senior discounts before you order a meal at a restaurant or fast-food chain.

5 Explore the outdoors. For a small fee, seniors can get a Golden Age Passport, which gives them a lifetime pass to all U.S. national parks. Go to NPS.gov and click on "Info Zone" for details.

6 Contact city hall or a senior center to find local discounts, including public transportation, salons, barbers, pharmacies and grocery stores.

7 Join the American Association of Retired Persons (AARP.org) to qualify for more senior discounts if you are 50 years old or older.

Student discounts

1 Visit InternationalStudent.com and apply for an International Student ID Card (for a fee) to get student discounts on travel, hostels, entertainment, books and more.

2 Travel by rail through Europe using a Eurail Pass exclusively for students. See 443 Get a Eurail Pass.

3 Be a culture hound. Theaters, museums, plays, opera and other cultural events usually offer student discounts.

4 Call magazines or newspapers and ask for the student rate on subscriptions.

5 Visit your school's student center to find out about other student discounts in your area. Some bookstores, restaurants and Internet service providers offer student discounts.

6 Upgrade your computer at deep discounts at university-run computer stores.

What to Look For

- Golden Age Passport
- AARP
- International Student ID
- Eurail Pass

Tips

Always ask before you buy. Contact customer service in person or by phone or e-mail before making a large purchase; salespeople aren't always aware of senior or student discounts.

Carry a photo ID with your birth date or your school ID to take advantage of discounts as you discover them.

Before you use the discount, ask the salesperson if there is a lower discount available. Better deals sometimes exist through general sales or promotions.

49 Buy Flowers Wholesale

Flower markets offer fresh-cut flowers, floral accessories and plants at wholesale prices to florists and business operators. The markets usually have hours for the general public where, even if you don't get wholesale prices, you'll get big discounts. Flower markets are especially useful if you need to buy flowers in bulk for a wedding or party.

Steps

1 Look in the Yellow Pages under "Florists—Wholesale" or search the Internet to find a wholesale flower market in your area.

2 Check your network of friends to see if they have access to wholesale prices (with a reseller's badge) and if they're willing to act as your buyer. If not, visit the market during public hours.

3 Go to bed early and set your alarm. Flower markets open as early as 2 a.m., and the best flowers disappear quickly.

4 Survey the entire market for prices and selection before you make a purchase. Vendors closest to the entrance often charge the highest prices.

5 Check that the stems are freshly cut and the leaves and buds are firm. Don't buy from a vendor who has brown or withered flowers in the mix.

6 Make your selection. The more you purchase from a single vendor, the more likely he or she will be open to negotiating price.

7 Expect to pay sales tax unless you have a resellers badge.

8 Fill a sink or bathtub with several inches of cold water when you return from the flower market. Remove the newspaper wrappings and stand the flower bunches in the water until you make the arrangements. Make fresh cuts on all stems before arranging, and make your rose cuts underwater. See 18 Buy a Bouquet of Roses.

What to Look For

- Reseller's badge
- Freshly cut stems
- Barely open buds

Tips

Flowers sold in the market are intended for resale, so many buds are closed. If you are buying flowers for a special event, allow a day or two for the buds to open.

Farmer's markets are another excellent source for affordable fresh flowers, especially if you buy directly from the grower.

Flower markets are a good source for vases, ribbons, floral wire, boutonniere pins and other flower-arranging equipment.

50 Get a Picture Framed

Whether it's a fine watercolor or your child's finger painting, your work of art deserves a customized frame to show off its beauty and prevent deterioration over time. A skilled framer is your partner in this process. Quality framers have years of experience with preservation framing using a variety of materials and methods, and should be able to work within any budget.

TERM	DESCRIPTION
Mat	Provides a spacer to protect paper art or photographs from direct contact with the glass. This is necessary, particularly in humid climates, to prevent the art from coming in contact with condensation or sticking to the glass and permanently damaging it. It also provides structural support for the artwork. Ask the framer if the picture warrants a double or triple matting with a straight or bevel cut. Also ask about archival quality matting for pieces you really care about.
Mounting	A picture can be hinged or stuck down. Hinging is the process of using acid-free linen tape at the top of the mat and letting it hang. A more permanent method is to mount the entire picture to the backing board, achieving a smooth, flat finish. For dry mounting, some framers use a vacuum-heat mounting press, which removes air by a vacuum suction pump before the art touches the heat plate, which seals and mounts the piece.
Backing	As with mats, the wrong backing can damage your work. Insist that your framer use a lightweight neutral-pH backing, called conservation-quality art-board, such as Tru Vue's UltiMat and UltiBlack. Barrier paper can be added to this as an extra precaution for works of higher value. Your picture should then be sealed to protect it from dust, air, moisture and insects.
Glass	Conservation quality picture framing glass is specially formulated to protect framed works of art from the damaging effects of ultraviolet light. For example, Tru Vue Conservation Series glass filters out over 97 percent of UV light. If you think reflection may be a problem, choose a nonglare glass. Consider using acrylic for pictures or posters larger than 36 by 48 inches, or for pictures and prints intended for a child's room. It is shatterproof and less expensive than regular glass.
Frame	The frame you choose should be strong enough to support the final weight of the glass, mounting and artwork. Styles are up to you.
TIPS	Choose a full-service framer, or save money at a DIY operation where the experts are on hand to guide you, but you do most of the work. Get a quote in writing that details the price of the frame, mat and labor, the design plan, and the due date.

51 Hire a Mover

The moving industry has generated so many complaints in recent years that Congress is considering legislation to increase consumer protection. Complaints range from carelessness to holding belongings hostage until additional money is paid. Be sure that you hire a reputable mover and that you understand the terms of your deal.

Steps

1 Call several moving companies, both national and local.

2 Contact the Better Business Bureau (bbb.org) to see if there are complaints against the company. Ask for and call all three references to corroborate the mover's professionalism and reliability. Choose a company with excellent customer service.

3 Ask about rates. Be aware of any conditions that will trigger additional costs, such as moves over a certain mileage or goods over a certain weight. Ask what happens if goods are damaged, and under what conditions is the mover responsible and for how much.

4 Understand how packing options affect the price. For example, if you pack certain goods yourself, can you save some money? Or pack everything yourself with portable containers that are delivered to your home. You pack them, and the company transports them to your new home.

5 If you are moving a long distance, inquire about tracking options so that you can find out where your belongings are. Be sure they can guarantee a delivery date.

6 Be sure you understand how materials affect costs and that it's covered in the contract. Many consumer complaints relate to add-on costs from packing materials such as bubble wrap and boxes.

7 Check into any special deals the company offers, and ask whether it gives auto club or senior discounts.

8 Schedule a free on-site estimate if you like what you hear. Bids will vary widely. Get several bids to find the best deal.

9 Discuss with the estimator any considerations unique to your move. Point out any especially large or fragile items, and ask how they will be handled. Point out issues that affect access, such as staircases, steep driveways or small attics, and be prepared to pay more for complicated moves.

What to Look For

- Quality references
- Rates
- Insurance
- Packing options
- Tracking options
- Guaranteed service
- Written contract

Tips

Rates are higher from May through September, the busy season for moving.

Storage facilities should be secure from theft and wet weather.

Get the truck driver's cell phone number so that you can keep track of his progress.

Warning

Fly-by-night movers—some using names strikingly similar to major companies—have gouged customers and even stolen property.

10 Get a signed contract that includes price, pick-up and delivery dates, packing services and mileage, plus policies regarding payment, insurance and guaranteed services. Make sure the contract has a customer-service number on it that you can call with any problems.

11 Do not make final payment until all items are received and reviewed for damage.

52 Hire a Personal Organizer

Personal organizers can help you tackle organizational nightmares like overstuffed closets or garages. They also can help set up an efficient home office or create time management systems specific to your busy life. Here's a list of questions to ask potential organizers.

Steps

1 How many years have you been working as an organizer?

2 What are your areas of expertise?

3 What did you do before becoming a personal organizer?

4 What is your educational background?

5 Are you a member of any professional guilds?

6 Can you supply three references who are former clients?

7 What is your rate?

8 What would you suggest for my stuffed filing cabinets/chaotic kitchen/magazine collection/home office?

9 Do you offer a free half-hour consultation in person so that I can assess whether we'd work well together?

10 How do you guarantee that your solution will work for me? Will you include a complimentary follow-up in three months if the system fails me?

11 Do you offer quarterly "tune-ups" to keep me on track?

12 Do you have a reliable handyman that you work with in case we need to construct or install organizational systems?

What to Look For

- Recommendations
- Compatibility

Tips

Rates vary from $40 to $200 an hour, depending on experience and geography.

The National Organization of Personal Organizers (napo.net) lists personal organizers by region.

53 Find a Veterinarian

If there's a pet in your family—or in your future—you'll need to find a trustworthy veterinarian. Tackle this just as you would to find a doctor for any other loved one.

Steps

1 Grill friends for recommendations; word-of-mouth references from impassioned pet-owners are the best way to find a good vet. Ask what it is that they like about the vet. Dog parks are also an excellent place to get information.

2 Check with specialty pet stores or breeders to find a vet who specializes in a certain pet or breed.

3 Choose a vet whose office location, days and business hours are convenient for you.

4 Call potential candidates and ask the office manager about their payment policies and what the rate is for a basic checkup. Confirm that you'll be able to see the same vet with each visit.

5 Find out what emergency services are offered during and after business hours. Which animal hospital is the vet associated with? Is it nearby?

6 Visit the office to make sure it is clean and orderly, and that the staff is helpful and knowledgeable.

7 Ask to meet with the veterinarian to discuss your pet. Are you comfortable talking to this person? Is he or she responsive to your questions?

8 Make sure the vet has no plans to retire anytime soon. You'll want a vet who's likely to stay in practice for the duration of your pet's life.

9 Choose the vet that best fits your needs and bring your pet there for an initial checkup. The vet will begin a medical file on your pet.

10 Keep the veterinarian's phone number with your emergency numbers. Share it with pet caretakers when you go out of town.

What to Look For

- Personal recommendations
- Convenient location and hours
- Affordable rates
- Good emergency services
- Clean office
- Friendly staff
- Personable vet

Tips

Ask if alternative and holistic treatments such as acupuncture, chiropractic and herbal treatments are available.

Find out what food, flea control products and medicines the vet carries for sale.

54 Buy Pet Food

Fluffy is a beloved member of your family. As his caretaker, you have the job of feeding him quality food that promotes good health and helps prevent disease due to nutritional deficiencies. But not all pet foods are equal; read the small print before you buy. In the United States, the Association of American Feed Control Officials (AAFCO) regulates the wording used on pet food labels.

Steps

1 Read the descriptive name of the food and know what it means. *Chicken cat food* means the food in the can must be at least 95 percent chicken. *Chicken dinner/feast/mix/formula* means that 25 percent of the ingredients are chicken. Cat food *with* chicken means that 3 percent of the ingredients are chicken. *With chicken flavor* means only that your pet may detect the flavor of chicken; no chicken need be in the food at all.

2 Read the actual ingredients on the can or package. Manufacturers must list ingredients by weight, with the first ingredient being the predominant one.

3 Choose food that has named meats (chicken, beef, lamb, salmon) instead of the generic term *meat.* Avoid foods that have only meat byproducts (organs, bones, tendons and other parts left over from slaughterhouses).

4 Reject foods that are made up solely of "byproduct meal" or meat- and bonemeal. Meal is what's left after a product is cooked at extremely high temperatures, a procedure called *rendering.* Rendered products are cheap and highly processed.

5 Look for a label that says "animal feeding tests using AAFCO procedures" have been conducted on the food, not merely tests for the presence of nutrients.

6 Read the nutritional analysis of protein, fat, fiber and other items with the understanding that these recommended percentages represent minimum amounts.

7 Select food that fits the nutritional needs of your pet. There are foods specially formulated for puppies, kittens, pregnant, lactating, mature or diabetic pets, or cats with hair balls.

8 Check the expiration date. An impending expiration date suggests that the food has been sitting on the shelf for a long time.

9 Make changes to a pet's food gradually by mixing a bit of the new food in with the old over the course of three to five days.

10 Observe your pet after you introduce new foods. A change in coat, scratching, appetite, weight, mood, stools or other areas could suggest a problem. Consult your veterinarian for dietary recommendations.

What to Look For

- Descriptive terms
- Ingredients by weight
- Named meats
- AAFCO feeding tests
- Special nutritional formulas
- Expiration date

Tips

Fido may love that cheap dry dog food, but that doesn't mean it's good for him. Some pet food manufacturers spray bland kibble with tasty fats. Making this your pet's staple is the equivalent of feeding hamburgers and fries daily to a child who loves fast food. Make sure the food provides the appropriate nutritional value.

Refrigerate unused portions of canned food. Keep dry food in a sealed container to prolong freshness.

A higher price may indicate higher-quality ingredients, but don't rely on price alone. Read the label.

Europe and Canada also have organizations that monitor pet food standards.

Warnings

Dessert is no treat for a pet: Little more than 2 oz. (60 g) of unsweetened chocolate can be a lethal dose for a 25-lb. (12.5 kg) dog.

Dogs and cats have different nutritional needs. Never feed a cat solely dog food, and vice versa, as this could lead to malnutrition and disease.

55 Buy a Pedigreed Dog or Cat

Assuming you've already answered the all-important questions of whether or not you really want a dog or cat, can properly care for it, and which breed you prefer, buying a pedigreed pet requires a bit more work.

Steps

1 Ask your vet to recommend breeders (see 53 Find a Veterinarian).

2 Read dog and cat magazines such as *Dog Fancy, Cat Fancy* and *Cat USA* for listings of breeders and national breed clubs.

3 Contact the American Cat Fanciers Association (acfacat.com) to find breeders' directories. For dogs, go to Breeders.net. In addition, get in touch with breeders through online bulletin boards with services such as America Online.

4 Attend dog and cat shows, and talk to the breeders who are exhibiting. Most reputable breeders will be involved in showing their animals. Talk to them about their breeding methods, philosophy and anything else that will give you an idea of how they operate.

5 Look for a breeder who has a thorough knowledge of the breed, and is committed to making sure the individual animal's personality is a good fit with your family.

6 Listen to the breeder. He or she should be as interested in you and the home you will provide to the pet as you are in owning the pet. Responsible breeders are very selective in choosing homes for their puppies. Be suspicious of a breeder who doesn't ask you a lot of questions about your suitability as a dog owner.

7 Ask to see at least one parent of the puppy or kitten. See how the animal interacts with the breeder. Is it friendly or does it shy away?

8 Inspect the animal carefully. It should be fully weaned and clearly ready to leave its mother. Signs of a happy animal are an active, friendly personality; clean ears, eyes and nose; healthy gums and teeth; thick, glossy coat; and a balanced gait.

9 Make sure the breeder provides you with authenticity (a signed document by a veterinarian) of the pet's health. Some purebreds are prone to congenital health problems; find out what they are before you bring home your pet so you know what to look for. For example, some dog breeds should be screened for hip dysplasia and you should receive certification that that was done.

10 Research fair prices for the breed. A good breeder will happily offer references.

What to Look For

- Reputable breeder or shelter
- Pedigree and registration papers
- Written medical history

Tips

Animal shelters often have purebreds that have been abandoned by their owners. It's worth checking with your local humane society or the rescue society for any specific breed.

If you plan on showing or breeding your new dog or cat, tell the breeder what your intentions are and be particularly rigorous in your examination of the animal.

You'll need dog food, food and water bowls, a dog bed, an ID tag, collar, leash, travel kennel and grooming equipment. Chewing toys are essential for teething puppies.

Warning

Avoid pet shops, which don't always take good care of animals and aren't as knowledgeable about breed, lineage and care.

56 Breed Your Pet and Sell the Litter

If you have discipline, a passion for animals, and a willingness to do extensive research, breeding can be a fascinating way to earn money and a great way to be around animals. The mother and newborns will need round-the-clock care and, in most cases, cuddling. If profit is your only goal, you may become frustrated with all the work that goes into breeding pets.

Steps

1 Confirm that there's a demand for the pet you intend to breed. Animal shelters are full of unwanted cats, dogs and other pets who will be put down if homes are not found.

2 Calculate medical, food, equipment and other breeding expenses. Factor in the time and energy it will take. Will you be able to make a profit?

3 Attend shows and join clubs or associations that specialize in your pet breed to stay abreast of news and to learn breeding guidelines. Talk to other breeders and get as much information as you can.

4 Read up on the reproductive cycle, mating habits, gestation, birthing process, newborn care and weaning process of your pet.

5 Advertise your intention to breed your bird, fish or other pet in newspapers or online before you begin the mating process. It is irresponsible to breed animals without finding prospective owners beforehand.

6 Select your mating pair. Make sure both animals are licensed and pedigreed, if applicable. A veterinarian or pet expert can help identify the sex of birds, fish, amphibians or reptiles.

7 Bring your mating pair to a vet for a prebreeding exam. The vet will check for genetic defects, sexually transmitted diseases and other health issues.

8 Mate the pair according to your research and the vet's advice. Provide attentive care to the mother and newborns.

9 Screen potential owners thoroughly. Look for caring, responsible owners.

What to Look For

- Sufficient demand
- Total expenses, time and effort
- Breeding guidelines
- Mating, birthing and weaning processes
- Prebreeding exam
- Responsible buyers

Tips

Breeding dogs and cats is a full-time job that requires professional knowledge and is not an easy way to make money.

Though you can sell puppies and kittens in advance, don't separate them from their mother until they are 8 weeks old.

It might be easy to breed prolific reproducers, such as rabbits, gerbils and guppies, but you'll have a hard time selling the offspring for a profit.

Warning

Thousands of unwanted pets are euthanized every year. Don't add to the problem with poorly planned breeding.

REHOUSE STORES • BUY WHOLESALE • GET OUT OF DEBT • BUY NOTHING • BUY HAPPINESS • BUY A BETTER MOUSETRAP • BUY TI
MEONE'S FAVOR • BUY POSTAGE STAMPS WITHOUT GOING TO THE POST OFFICE • TIP PROPERLY • BUY HEALTHY FAST FOOD • BUY S
ING SERVICE • SELL YOURSELF ON AN ONLINE DATING SERVICE • SELL YOURSELF TO YOUR GIRLFRIEND/BOYFRIEND'S FAMILY • BUY
HOOSE FILM FOR YOUR CAMERA • BUY RECHARGEABLE BATTERIES • DONATE TO A GOOD CAUSE • HOLD A PROFITABLE GARAGE SAL
STUDENT DISCOUNTS • BUY FLOWERS WHOLESALE • GET A PICTURE FRAMED • HIRE A MOVER • HIRE A PERSONAL ORGANIZER • FIN
EAT BIRTHDAY PRESENT FOR UNDER $10 • SELECT GOOD CHAMPAGNE • BUY A DIAMOND • BUY JEWELRY MADE OF PRECIOUS METAL
DESMAIDS' DRESSES • HIRE AN EVENT COORDINATOR • HIRE A BARTENDER FOR A PARTY • HIRE A PHOTOGRAPHER • HIRE A CATERE
Y AN ANNIVERSARY GIFT • ARRANGE ENTERTAINMENT FOR A PARTY • COMMISSION A FIREWORKS SHOW • BUY A MOTHER'S DAY GIF
T • SELECT A THANKSGIVING TURKEY • BUY A HOUSEWARMING GIFT • PURCHASE HOLIDAY CARDS • BUY CHRISTMAS STOCKING STU
E HIGH ROLLERS ROOM IN VEGAS, BABY • BUY SOMEONE A STAR • PAY A RANSOM • GET HOT TICKETS • HIRE A LIMOUSINE • BUY A C
AM • BUY A PERSONAL JET • ACQUIRE A TELEVISION NETWORK • ACQUIRE A BODY GUARD • BOOK A LUXURY CRUISE AROUND THE W
DROUGHBRED RACEHORSE • BUY A VILLA IN TUSCANY • HIRE A PERSONAL CHEF • PURCHASE CUBAN CIGARS • HIRE A GHOSTWRITE
'NESS • MAKE BAIL • DONATE YOUR BODY TO SCIENCE • HIRE YOURSELF OUT AS A MEDICAL GUINEA PIG • SELL PLASMA • SELL YOU
LLEGE EDUCATION • BUY AND SELL STOCKS • CHOOSE A STOCKBROKER • DAY-TRADE (OR NOT) • BUY ANNUITIES • BUY AND SELL M
Y PERSONAL FINANCE SOFTWARE • CHOOSE A TAX PREPARER • SET UP A LEMONADE STAND • SELL YOUR PRODUCT ON TV • HIRE A
SINESS IDEA • BUY A SMALL BUSINESS • BUY A FRANCHISE • LEASE RETAIL SPACE • LEASE INDUSTRIAL SPACE • LEASE OFFICE SPAC
B SITE • BUY ADVERTISING ON THE WEB • SELL YOUR ART • HIRE A PERSONAL COACH • SELL ON THE CRAFT CIRCUIT • HIRE A LITER
LING BUSINESS • BUY A HOT DOG STAND • SHOP FOR A MORTGAGE • REFINANCE YOUR HOME • SAVE BIG BUCKS ON YOUR MORTGA
L A FIXER-UPPER • SELL THE FARM • SELL MINERAL RIGHTS • SELL A HOUSE • SELL A HOUSE WITHOUT A REAL ESTATE AGENT • OB
OK A VACATION RENTAL • BUY A CONDOMINIUM • RENT AN APARTMENT OR HOUSE • OBTAIN RENTER'S INSURANCE • BUY A LOFT IN
RNISH YOUR STUDIO APARTMENT • BUY USED FURNITURE • BUY DOOR AND WINDOW LOCKS • CHOOSE AN ORIENTAL CARPET • BUY
RRANTIES ON APPLIANCES • FIND PERIOD FIXTURES • BUY A BED AND MATTRESS • HIRE AN INTERIOR DESIGNER • HIRE A FENG SHU
N • BUY A WHIRLPOOL TUB • BUY A SHOWERHEAD • BUY A TOILET • CHOOSE A FAUCET • BUY GLUES AND ADHESIVES • CHOOSE WIN
CHEN CABINETS • CHOOSE A KITCHEN COUNTERTOP • BUY GREEN HOUSEHOLD CLEANERS • STOCK YOUR HOME TOOL KIT • BUY A
ENTRY DOOR • BUY A GARAGE-DOOR OPENER • BUY LUMBER FOR A DIY PROJECT • HOW TO SELECT ROOFING • HIRE A CONTRACT
OWERS FOR YOUR GARDEN • SELECT PEST CONTROLS • BUY SOIL AMENDMENTS • BUY MULCH • BUY A COMPOSTER • BUY FERTILIZ
Y KOI FOR YOUR FISH POND • BUY A STORAGE SHED • HIRE AN ARBORIST • BUY BASIC GARDEN TOOLS • BUY SHRUBS AND TREES •
LECT KITCHEN KNIVES • DECIPHER FOOD LABELS • SELECT HERBS AND SPICES • STOCK YOUR KITCHEN WITH STAPLES • EQUIP A KI
UNTAIN OYSTERS • PURCHASE LOCAL HONEY • CHOOSE POULTRY • SELECT FRESH FISH AND SHELLFISH • SELECT RICE • PURCHAS
EADS • BUY ARTISAN CHEESES • PURCHASE KOSHER FOOD • BUY FOOD IN BULK • CHOOSE COOKING OILS • SELECT OLIVE OIL • SE
FFEEMAKER OR ESPRESSO MACHINE • PURCHASE A KEG OF BEER • BUY ALCOHOL IN A DRY COUNTY • CHOOSE A MICROBREW • DR
ULATION PREDICTOR KIT • PICK A PREGNANCY TEST KIT • CHOOSE BIRTH CONTROL • FIND THE RIGHT OB-GYN • HIRE A MIDWIFE OR
OOSE DIAPERS • BUY OR RENT A BREAST PUMP • CHOOSE A CAR SEAT • BUY CHILD-PROOFING SUPPLIES • FIND FABULOUS CHILDC
CKYARD PLAY STRUCTURE • FIND A GREAT SUMMER CAMP • SELL GIRL SCOUT COOKIES • BUY BRACES FOR YOUR KID • BUY TOYS
A MODEL • SELL USED BABY GEAR, TOYS, CLOTHES AND BOOKS • FIND A COUPLES COUNSELOR • HIRE A FAMILY LAWYER • BUY PR
PENSES • GET VIAGRA ONLINE • PURCHASE A TOOTHBRUSH • BUY MOISTURIZERS AND ANTIWRINKLE CREAMS • SELECT PAIN RELIEF
PPLIES • SELECT HAIR-CARE PRODUCTS • BUY WAYS TO COUNTER HAIR LOSS • BUY A WIG OR HAIRPIECE • BUY A NEW BODY • GET
NICURIST • GET WHITER TEETH • SELECT EYEGLASSES AND SUNGLASSES • HIRE A PERSONAL TRAINER • SIGN UP FOR A YOGA CLAS
EA MARKET • RENT SPACE AT AN ANTIQUE MALL • BUY AT AUCTION • KNOW WHAT YOUR COLLECTIBLES ARE WORTH • DICKER WITH
COGNIZE THE REAL MCCOY • BUY COINS • BUY AN ANTIQUE AMERICAN QUILT • BUY AN ANTIQUE FLAG • LIQUIDATE YOUR BEANIE BA
WNSHOP • BUY AND SELL COMIC BOOKS • BUY AND SELL SPORTS MEMORABILIA • SELL YOUR BASEBALL-CARD COLLECTIONS • CH
MPUTER • BUY PRINTER PAPER • BUY A PRINTER • BUY COMPUTER PERIPHERALS • CHOOSE AN INTERNET SERVICE PROVIDER • GET
Y BLANK CDS • BUY AN MP PLAYER • CHOOSE A DVD PLAYER • BUY A VCR • CHOOSE A PERSONAL DIGITAL ASSISTANT • CHOOSE MO
GITAL CAMCORDER • DECIDE ON A DIGITAL CAMERA • BUY A HOME AUTOMATION SYSTEM • BUY A STATE-OF-THE-ART SOUND SYSTEM
IVERSAL REMOTE • BUY A HOME THEATER SYSTEM • BUY VIRTUAL-REALITY FURNITURE • BUY TWO-WAY RADIOS • BUY A MOBILE EN
DNEY • GET TRAVEL INSURANCE • PICK THE IDEAL LUGGAGE • FLY FOR FREE • BID FOR A SLED RIDE ON THE ALASKAN IDITAROD TRAI
REIGN OFFICIAL • GET A EURAIL PASS • TAKE AN ITALIAN BICYCLE VACATION • CHOOSE A CHEAP CRUISE • BOOK A HOTEL PACKAGE
OTLAND • BUY A SAPPHIRE IN BANGKOK • HIRE A RICKSHA IN YANGON • TAKE SALSA LESSONS IN CUBA • BUY A CAMERA IN HONG K
RST BASEBALL GLOVE • ORDER UNIFORMS FOR A SOFTBALL TEAM • BUY ANKLE AND KNEE BRACES • BUY GOLF CLUBS • JOIN AN EL
OWMOBILE • BUY A PERSONAL WATERCRAFT • HIRE A SCUBA INSTRUCTOR • BUY A SKATEBOARD AND PROTECTIVE GEAR • BUY SKA
EATHER ACTIVITIES • SELL USED SKIS • BUY A SNOWBOARD, BOOTS AND BINDINGS • BUY SKI BOOTS • BUY A BICYCLE • SELL YOUR
Y A BACKPACK • BUY A BACKPACKING STOVE • BUY A KAYAK • BUY A PERSONAL FLOTATION DEVICE • BUY A WET SUIT • BUY A SUR
DER CUSTOM-MADE COWBOY BOOTS • BUY CLOTHES ONLINE • FIND SPECIALTY SIZES • BUY THE PERFECT COCKTAIL DRESS • BUY
Y A MAN'S SUIT • HIRE A TAILOR • BUY CUSTOM-TAILORED CLOTHES IN ASIA • BUY A BRIEFCASE • SHOP FOR A LEATHER JACKET •
TE MONITOR • SELECT A WATCH • BUY KIDS' CLOTHES • CHOOSE CHILDREN'S SHOES • PURCHASE CLOTHES AT OUTLET SHOPS • B

QUET OF ROSES • BUY SOMEONE A DRINK • GET SOMEONE TO BUY YOU A DRINK • BUY YOUR WAY INTO HIGH SOCIETY • BUY YOUR
RDER THE PERFECT BURRITO • ORDER TAKEOUT ASIAN FOOD • ORDER AT A SUSHI BAR • BUY DINNER AT A FANCY FRENCH RESTAURA
OWERS FOR YOUR SWEETHEART • BUY MUSIC ONLINE • HIRE MUSICIANS • ORDER A GREAT BOTTLE OF WINE • BUY AN ERGONOMIC
ISECLEANER • HIRE A BABY SITTER • BUY A GUITAR • BUY DUCT TAPE • GET A GOOD DEAL ON A MAGAZINE SUBSCRIPTION • GET SEN
IAN • BUY PET FOOD • BUY A PEDIGREED DOG OR CAT • BREED YOUR PET AND SELL THE LITTER • GET A COSTUME • BUY A PIÑATA •
ED GEMSTONES • CHOOSE THE PERFECT WEDDING DRESS • BUY OR RENT A TUXEDO • REGISTER FOR GIFTS • BUY WEDDING GIFTS
EAL WEDDING OFFICIANT • OBTAIN A MARRIAGE LICENSE • ORDER CUSTOM INVITATIONS AND ANNOUNCEMENTS • SELL YOUR WEDDI
R'S DAY GIFT • SELECT AN APPROPRIATE COMING-OF-AGE GIFT • GET A GIFT FOR THE PERSON WHO HAS EVERYTHING • BUY A GRAD
ANUKKAH GIFTS • PURCHASE A PERFECT CHRISTMAS TREE • BUY A PRIVATE ISLAND • HIRE A SKYWRITER • HIRE A BIG-NAME BAND •
3ER • RENT YOUR OWN BILLBOARD • TAKE OUT A FULL-PAGE AD IN *THE NEW YORK TIMES* • HIRE A BUTLER • ACQUIRE A PROFESSION
OUR FUR COAT • BOOK A TRIP ON THE ORIENT-EXPRESS • BECOME A WINE MAKER • PURCHASE A PRIVATE/CUSTOM BOTTLING OF WI
E MEMOIRS • COMMISSION ORIGINAL ARTWORK • IMMORTALIZE YOUR SPOUSE IN A SCULPTURE • GIVE AWAY YOUR FORTUNE • HIRE
DEVIL • NEGOTIATE A BETTER CREDIT CARD DEAL • CHOOSE A FINANCIAL PLANNER • SAVE WITH A RETIREMENT PLAN • SAVE FOR YO
BUY BONDS • SELL SHORT • INVEST IN PRECIOUS METALS • BUY DISABILITY INSURANCE • BUY LIFE INSURANCE • GET HEALTH INSU
ELOR • HIRE A HEADHUNTER • SELL YOUR ENT • MARKET YOUR INVENTION • FINANCE YO
TED OFFICE EQUIPMENT • HIRE SOMEONE IRE A GRAPHIC DESIGNER • ACQUIRE CONTENT
TCH A MAGAZINE STORY • SELL A SCREEN YOUR BOOK • START A BED-AND-BREAKFAST • S
ME OWNER'S INSURANCE • OBTAIN DISAS OUSE AT AUCTION • BUY A FORECLOSED HOME
JITY LOAN • BUY A LOT • BUY HOUSE PLA TY • PULL BUILDING PERMITS • BUY A VACATION H
JY A TENANCY-IN-COMMON UNIT • BUY RE A MOVIE OR CATALOG SHOOT • FURNISH YOUR
HT FIXTURES • BUY A PROGRAMMABLE LIC NCES • BUY FLOOR-CARE APPLIANCES • BUY E
INCORPORATE FLUID ARCHITECTURE INTO ARNISH • CHOOSE DECORATIVE TILES • CHOOSI
ITS • GET SELF-CLEANING WINDOWS • CH SELECT FLOORING • SELECT CARPETING • CHO
Y SYSTEM • BUY A HOME ALARM SYSTEM OXIDE DETECTORS • BUY FIRE EXTINGUISHERS
INTER OR ELECTRICIAN • HIRE A GARDEN PERFECT ROSEBUSH • BUY FLOWERING BULBS
GETABLE GARDEN • HIRE A GARDEN PROF R SYSTEM • START A NEW LAWN • BUY A LAWN
• BUY AN OUTDOOR LIGHTING SYSTEM • ECT PEACH • BUY AND SELL AT FARMERS' MARI
E FRESH PRODUCE • SELECT MEAT • STOC ASE A HOLIDAY HAM • BUY NATURAL BEEF • BUY
T AND PEPPER • GET A CHEESESTEAK IN P EATTLE • FIND CRAWDADS IN LOUISIANA • BUY
JY ETHNIC INGREDIENTS • PURCHASE VIN OFFEE • ORDER A GREAT CUP OF COFFEE • BUY
• CHOOSE A RESTAURANT FOR A BUSINE TOCK YOUR BAR • BUY AND SELL SPERM • CHO
GOOD PEDIATRICIAN • HIRE A CHILD THER NEW CRIB • CHOOSE A STROLLER • BUY BABY
AI NANNY • FIND THE RIGHT PRIVATE SC RAM • SIGN YOUR CHILD UP FOR LESSONS • B
IDEOS AND MUSIC FOR YOUR CHILDREN R • HIRE AN ADOPTION AGENCY • GET YOUR C
IREMENT COMMUNITY • CHOOSE AN ASS IVING WILL • BUY A CEMETERY PLOT • PAY FOR
CINES • SAVE MONEY ON PRESCRIPTION ONAL • CHOOSE A WHEELCHAIR • BUY HOME-U
DY PIERCING • OBTAIN BREAST IMPLANTS ALTERNATIVE AND HOLISTIC PRACTITIONERS • (
SELF TO A DAY AT THE SPA • BOOK A MAS Y AND SELL USED BOOKS • SHOP AT AN ANTIQ

**Special
Occasions**

N ANTIQUE APPRAISED • BUY SILVERWARE • EVALUATE DEPRESSION-ERA GLASSWARE • BUY AND SELL STAMPS • BUY ANTIQUE FUR
• SCORE AUTOGRAPHS • TRADE YU-GI-OH CARDS • SNAG STAR WARS ACTION FIGURES • SELL YOUR VINYL RECORD COLLECTION •
COMPUTER • SHOP FOR A USED COMPUTER OR PERIPHERALS • CHOOSE A LAPTOP OR NOTEBOOK COMPUTER • SELL OR DONATE A
OMAIN NAME • BUY A HOME NETWORK • UPGRADE THE MEMORY IN YOUR COMPUTER • BUY COMPUTER SOFTWARE • CHOOSE A CD
RVICE • NEGOTIATE YOUR LONG-DISTANCE PHONE SERVICE • BUY VIDEO AND COMPUTER GAMES • CHOOSE A FILM CAMERA • CHOO
D-VIDEO DISTRIBUTION SYSTEM • BUY A SERIOUS TV • CHOOSE BETWEEN CABLE AND SATELLITE TV • GET A DIGITAL VIDEO RECORDE
STEM • GET A PASSPORT, QUICK! • PURCHASE CHEAP AIRLINE TICKETS • FIND GREAT HOTEL DEALS • RENT THE BEST CAR FOR THE L
TY-FREE • SHIP FOREIGN PURCHASES TO THE UNITED STATES • TIP IN A FOREIGN COUNTRY • TIP PROPERLY IN NORTH AMERICA • BF
SLANDS • RAFT THE GRAND CANYON • BOOK A CHEAP BUT AWESOME SAFARI • RENT A CAMEL IN CAIRO • GET SINGLE-MALT SCOTC
R WAY ONTO A MOUNT EVEREST EXPEDITION • HIRE A TREKKING COMPANY IN NEPAL • RENT OR BUY A SATELLITE PHONE • BUY YOU
SELL FOUND GOLF BALLS • BUY ATHLETIC SHOES • BUY A RACKET • BUY A GYM MEMBERSHIP • BUY AN AEROBIC FITNESS MACHINE
FISHING • GO SKYDIVING • BUY WEIGHTLIFTING EQUIPMENT • CHOOSE A CAR RACK OR CARRIER • BUY SKIS • BUY CLOTHES FOR C(
RAGE SALE • COMMISSION A CUSTOM-BUILT BICYCLE • BUY A PROPERLY FITTED HELMET • BUY THE OPTIMAL SLEEPING BAG • BUY A
Y-FISHING GEAR • BUY ROCK-CLIMBING EQUIPMENT • BUY A CASHMERE SWEATER • PURCHASE VINTAGE CLOTHING • SELL USED CL
HES AT A DISCOUNT • CHOOSE A BASIC WARDROBE FOR A MAN • BUY A MAN'S DRESS SHIRT • PICK OUT A NECKTIE • BUY A WOMAN
LOTHES • GET A GREAT-FITTING BRA • CHOOSE A HIGH-PERFORMANCE SWIM SUIT • HIGH PERFORMANCE WORKOUT CLOTHES • BUY
BUY THE BASICS FOR YOUR CAR • BUY A USED CAR • BUY OR SELL A CAR ONLINE • BUY A HYBRID CAR • SELL A CAR • BUY A MOTOR

57 Get a Costume

Halloween, Mardi Gras, Carnavale—whatever the holiday or masked affair you're attending, it's an opportunity to showcase your ingenuity and creativity while having a blast.

Steps

1 Search online or in the Yellow Pages under "Costumes" for rental shops in your area. Costs vary, but expect to pay in the neighborhood of $50 to $100 for a full outfit. Prop houses and theater costume departments are a great source if you want to achieve a movie-quality look, but run $100 and up for the basics, and more for accessories. Check Hollywood-Costumes.com, MardiGrasOutlet.com and CostumeUniverse.com.

2 Scour your local thrift store (see 497 Purchase Vintage Clothing) for great accessories or even the perfect period outfit from the 1930s to the '80s.

3 Score on kids' costumes at huge discounts from used-clothing stores in the months following Halloween. Or visit online stores beforehand to find character costumes. An infant-size Tigger, Cat in the Hat, Superman or Dalmatian puppy runs around $15 to $20. Check out Disney.com for more options.

4 Fulfill your favorite fantasy. If you've always wanted to be a flamenco dancer, you'll find the right dress at a dance supply store—you can dress the part if not dance it.

What to Look For

- Costume rental shops
- Thrift stores
- Party stores
- Inventiveness

Warning

Some rental boutiques won't ship during October for Halloween, so plan ahead. Even if you're buying, delivery can take two weeks to a month.

58 Buy a Piñata

The blindfold is on, the stick is in hand, everyone runs for cover. Whacking on brightly colored, papier-mâché piñatas to get the loot inside has been a part of Latin American festivities for hundreds of years. String one up at your next birthday party and start swinging.

Steps

1 Investigate online piñata sites. Some companies will custom-make any design from a photograph or sketch.

2 Expect an empty piñata unless you order one prefilled. Fill it with toys, wrapped candies, confetti or party favors. For kids, plastic bracelets, tops, tiny water guns, and kaleidoscopes are hits.

3 Hang the piñata from a suitable branch with a strong rope, with plenty of space around it. Blindfold each child or adult in turn, gently spin them around three or four times, then give them three swings apiece with a bat or broomstick to hit the piñata. Take turns until someone finally breaks it open and watch the fun as everyone scrambles for the goodies inside.

What to Look For

- Colorful theme piñata
- Candies, trinkets and favors
- A tree to hang it from
- Room to swing safely

Warning

When children play with a piñata, section off a safe zone where they can swing without accidentally hitting anyone. Elect someone to watch that no child wanders into the danger zone.

59 Buy a Great Birthday Present for Under $10

Let's face it—the primary reason we spend more than we want to is last-minute desperation. But you can stay beneath the $10 mark and still give someone a birthday smile. Keep a stash of ready-wrapped, always-welcome gifts (and birthday cards) for both sexes and all ages on hand, and you'll never box yourself into a corner.

ITEM	DESCRIPTION
Gift Certificates	Everyone knows what you paid, but that's OK. They're great for children, most of whom are thrilled to spend a $10 voucher in a toy shop. Teenagers appreciate a gift card from the music store. Give new parents a gift certificate to BabyCenter.com.
Picture Frames	Perennially useful gift for adults or children on any occasion, available in stationers, frame shops, Target and more. Incredible bargains all year round at discount stores and sales. Place a favorite photo in the frame.
Books	Never go wrong with a selection from a favorite author or area of interest.
CDs, DVDs	An enormous online selection includes discounted offerings to make giving someone music or movies a snap. Or burn your own personalized CD filled with the birthday boy or girl's favorite tunes. See 35 Buy Music Online.
Candles	Keep a fragrant stash in your closet. Look for good-quality candles on sale with a soothing rather than overbearing fragrance. Some cheap candles don't burn well.
Lotions, Soaps	Have a bottle or two of beautiful scented lotion or handmade soap for a pleasing, simple gift.
Fingertip Towels	Embroidered or lace-embossed ones look pretty and can be tied with ribbon along with a bar of soap.
Vases	A beautiful vase is always welcome, especially when filled with flowers from your garden. A bud vase is a sweet gift. Thrift stores and occasional sales are good sources of glass, pottery, china and silverware.
Wine	Knot a colorful kitchen towel around a bottle of wine.
Mini Tool Kit	Good to tuck in the kitchen drawer or car trunk. Watch the shelves until you see a deal.
WARNING	In theory, there's nothing wrong with recycling gifts you've received that would suit someone else much better. Just remember to note on the box or bag who gave it to you before you put it in storage and forget. Avoid embarrassing moments later by recycling it in a different circle of acquaintances.

60 Select Good Champagne

Champagne instantly conjures up images of festive celebrations, but there's no need to wait for a special occasion to break out the bubbly. This sparkling wine has taken its rightful place on the dinner table as a delicious food accompaniment, with more affordable selections available than ever. Go to WineSpectator.com for insider tips on the best vintages, but keep in mind that a mid-range champagne may actually give you the best bang for your buck.

TERM	WHAT IT MEANS
Champagne	The only legitimate Champagne, according to French law, hails from France's Champagne region.
Sparkling Wine	All other products. (California's Korbel Champagne being one exception.) Called *spumante* in Italy, *sekt* in Germany, and *vin mousseux* in France.
Méthode Champenoise	A rigorous, multistep process. Indicates a top-quality sparkling wine was made exactly the same way as French champagne—"fermented in this very bottle."
Vintage Champagne	Made only on occasions. Wines from the declared year must compose at least 80 percent of the cuvée (blend of still wines), with the balance coming from reserve wines from prior years. Must be aged for three years before release.
Nonvintage Champagne (NV)	These blends of usually five to seven years make up 75 to 80 percent of those bottled. It is typically made in a definitive house style and maintained by meticulous blending. It is with this reserve that the winemaker is able to create the same style every year.
Sweetness	Determined by the winemaker during the process of fermentation with the addition of *dosage* (a secret blend of wine, sugar and sometimes brandy). Levels include *brut* (very dry), *extra brut* (extra dry, but sweeter than brut), *sec* (medium sweet), *demi-sec* (sweet, considered a dessert wine) and *doux* (very sweet, considered a dessert wine).
Rosé	Made by adding a small amount of red still wine to the cuvée, although some producers extract color by macerating the juice with red grape skins.
Blanc de Noirs	The clearer the better and more full-flavored. Made entirely from the red Pinot Noir and/or Meunier grapes.
Blanc de Blancs	Usually more delicate and the lightest in color. Made entirely from Chardonnay grapes.
Crémant	Made with only slightly more than half the pressure of standard sparkling wines. Has a creamier mouth-feel.
Grand Cru	The top ranking a French vineyard can receive. Means "great growth."
Premier Cru	Second highest ranking of French vineyards. Means "first growth."
Grande Marque	A French term for "great brand" and is used unofficially to refer to the best champagne houses.

61 Buy a Diamond

Diamond rings are priceless in terms of sentimental value—but affairs of the heart aside, the key to a diamond's commercial value is its rarity. A smaller stone can be worth more than a larger one provided it has more rarity factors—greater clarity and brilliance, and fewer inclusions, or internal flaws. Here's how to find the brilliant best.

Steps

1 Determine what you want or can afford to spend.

2 Establish a relationship with a jeweler who has expert gemological knowledge. While their qualifications are worth noting, of far more importance is the feeling you get when you're in the shop. If you don't feel good about what you're looking at or who you're dealing with, leave.

3 Study styles. The traditional solitaire—a single diamond held aloft by a six-prong setting—is still the most popular. See how bezel settings, where a slim border of platinum or gold surrounds a smallish diamond, can make the gem look bigger. Take a look at three-diamond settings. A row of diamonds or a diamond surrounded by sapphires or emeralds is called an anniversary or eternity-ring style.

4 Become fluent in the four Cs of the international language of diamonds: carat weight, color, clarity and cut.

 • Diamond weights, not sizes, are measured in metric carats. A single carat weighs about as much as a small paper clip. Carats are divided into fractions or decimal points. Jewelers should disclose precise amounts and ranges.

 • Letters represent diamond colors with D (colorless, very rare and most desirable) to Z (light yellow or brown and less desirable). Grades vary, so ask your jeweler. It's also a matter of taste. Winter-white diamonds look best with platinum, warmer shades with golds.

 • Clarity grades measure *birthmarks*—internal flaws are called *inclusions,* external ones *blemishes.* Grades include FL for flawless, VS1 for very slightly included, and I3 for included.

 • Seek out a cut that maximizes brilliance, fire and sparkle.

5 Ask for an independent grading report—your diamond's detailed genealogy. Don't buy a costly stone without one, since it's your guarantee that you're getting what you've paid for.

6 Take a valuable diamond to an independent appraiser. If necessary, buy it first, but only with a written, unconditional money-back guarantee allowing you a few days to have it appraised.

What to Look For

 • Expert advice
 • Style you'll love forever
 • The four Cs
 • Grading report

Tips

Your jeweler can have a unique report number laser-inscribed on your diamond's outer edge. If you ever have it resized or professionally cleaned, you can make sure you're getting your own diamond back. Grading reports and identification numbers also serve insurance purposes.

Ask your jeweler for a free copy of the industry's helpful diamond-buying booklet, or contact the Gemological Institute of America (gia.edu).

Warning

Don't think of the diamonds in engagement rings as an investment. You're already paying a markup of 100 percent or more when you buy retail.

62 Buy Jewelry Made of Precious Metals

Buying a silver necklace, a gold bracelet or a platinum wedding band sounds pretty straightforward, but you'll want to understand how to choose between various precious metals. There's yellow, white and rose gold; 14-, 18- and 24-karat gold; real gold; pure gold—and that's before you get to the mysterious markings for silver and platinum.

Steps

1 Shop at a jewelry store that makes you feel good. Trusting the jeweler, and subsequently the advice and jewelry he or she offers, is very important.

2 Buy only from a reputable retailer who will accept returns— preferably one affiliated with the Jewelers Association or another professional trade association. Look for a sticker or certificate.

3 Look for marked jewelry. While gold need not by law carry the karat marks that define its level of purity, virtually all reputable stores sell only marked gold. If it is karat-marked, law dictates that it also be stamped with a hallmark, which shows that the manufacturer stands behind the karat mark's accuracy. The country of origin is also often noted.

4 Check the craftsmanship. A high-quality piece should look just as good from the back as it does from the front, have no rough edges anywhere and—if it's a necklace or bracelet—come with a sturdy matching clasp.

5 Buy gold in a range of colors and levels of purity. The higher the karat rating (not to be confused with carat, the weight measurement for diamonds), the more pure gold is in a piece and the richer the color (and softer the item).

• 24-karat gold is 100 percent pure gold, so soft that it is not often used for jewelry.

• 18 karat is 75 percent gold, mixed with copper or silver. It is more "lemony" in tone and is strong enough for rings.

• 14 karat is 58.3 percent gold. Its lightly reddish hue comes from added copper alloys, which also lend it durability.

• 10 karat is 41.6 percent gold. Less than 10-karat gold can't legally be called or sold as gold in the United States.

6 Explore the intricate designs that can be created with silver jewelry. Prized for its rich luster, and almost as soft as gold, it's often alloyed with copper for strength.

7 Step up to platinum jewelry for the rarest, purest and heaviest precious metal. Almost double the weight of 14 karat gold, platinum is incredibly dense but also very soft. Why buy platinum? Think of it this way: If you have a large diamond, would you rather it be secured by gold prongs or platinum ones that are twice as dense?

What to Look For

• Marked metal
• Manufacturer's marking or hallmark
• Style you'll always love
• Timeless appeal
• Flattering color

Tips

The misleading term *solid gold* merely signifies that a piece isn't hollow; don't confuse solid gold with pure gold.

The absence of any karat markings at all may mean that a piece is less than 10 karats.

Gold-filled jewelry is 10-karat or higher gold that has been mechanically bonded to a base material. In gold-plated or electroplated items, the gold is applied eletrolytically to a base material such as copper.

Warning

A titanium ring sounds cool, but if you're in an accident and your arm or hand is injured, rescue personnel will not be able to cut the ring off to save your finger.

63 Buy Colored Gemstones

Prized for centuries for their beauty, and often used as currency, gemstones hold ageless appeal. Modern treating techniques enhance their look and improve their durability. Whatever your favorites—rubies, sapphires, emeralds or others—find a good jeweler to buy from.

Steps

1 Work with a jeweler whose character you trust. Since virtually all gemstones are treated, the opportunity for deception is great—you want to be dealing with someone you can depend on. If something about the experience is off-putting, leave.

2 Learn about lab-created and treated stones. Ask jewelers if a naturally mined stone has been treated—heated, bleached, coated or dyed to improve the look or durability. Some treatments can weaken a stone and lower its price.

3 Keep your eyes open for imitations, generally made of glass or plastic. Jewelers will tell you what's what.

4 Apply the four Cs to buying gemstones just as you would to purchasing diamonds (see 61 Buy a Diamond). Gemstones, however, don't carry letter grades for guidance; a trustworthy jeweler will show you how to be discerning.

5 Shop around. Numerous companies operate in the field of colored gems, so prices fluctuate far more widely than those of diamonds, and it pays to watch them over time. A one-carat ruby, for instance, can vary enormously in cost—and may be just as expensive as a diamond. And gems over three carats in size leap up in price because they are rare. Color—shade and saturation (whether the color is dull or intense)—also greatly affects price. Clarity is also important (the gem should have few flaws or inclusions), as is a perfect, light-reflecting faceted cut.

6 Check the store's return and refund policy before finalizing your purchase.

7 Make sure your receipt details all the stone's specifications including its weight and size. Ask for a grading report, and check that the receipt specifies whether the stone is a natural gem, lab-created or treated stone.

What to Look For

- Natural versus lab-created or imitation gems
- The four Cs (cut, color, clarity, carat)
- Detailed receipt

Tip

The Federal Trade Commission requires jewelers to inform customers if a gemstone has been lab-created or treated. Find out if the treatments is permanent or the stone requires special care.

64 Choose the Perfect Wedding Dress

You've dreamt about walking down that aisle since you were a little girl, and now the big day is approaching. Whether you're choosing a dress off the rack or having one made just for you, follow these tips and make your dream come true.

Steps

1   Start your search six to nine months ahead. Special orders can take four to six months, plus time for alterations.

2   Keep your file of photographs of dresses you like from bridal magazines, advertisements and boutique promotions handy when you shop.

3   Choose a style appropriate for the ceremony. For a formal evening wedding, a floor-length dress in ivory, white, cream or champagne, often worn with gloves and a train, is an elegant choice. Semiformal dresses can be also be pastels, a floor-brushing (ballerina) length, with a short veil and no train. At a less-formal or second wedding, the bride may choose a long or short dress, or even a two-piece suit. A short veil may be very stylish paired with a classic pillbox hat.

4   Flatter your figure with a dress that suits you. Take a trusted, honest sister or friend who has your best interests at heart for feedback. Try one of each basic shape—princess, ball gown, sheath and empire waist—to see which flatters you most. Check that you can walk, turn, sit and bend comfortably, as well as lift your arms and hug loved ones without splitting a seam. Comfort and confidence are vital on this day of days.

5   Shop at bridal boutiques or department stores for a wide array of styles. Try on a few designer gowns first so you recognize the quality, then choose a dress based on your budget.

6   Set a budget. Off-the-rack dresses can be found for $250 and up. Jessica McClintock has a large selection of moderately priced gowns. A simple custom-made dress can be had for as little as $750, and can go as high as $10,000 for a Vera Wang, with many dresses in the lower third of that range.

7   Ask when bridal stores are next having a sample sale. Be on the lookout for warehouse sales on discontinued styles, samples and overstocks.

8   Make the deposit with a credit card. Get an itemized receipt spelling out every detail (manufacturer's and design name, number, price, color and size) and stating that the deal is canceled if your dress isn't ready by a specified date.

9   Budget for alterations, which can run $300 or more. Ask if pressing is included and if they'll store your dress until the big day. Also ask for recommendations for cleaning and storing the dress.

What to Look For

- Inspiration in magazines
- Figure-flattering shape
- Sales

Tips

Scout local thrift shops for excellent buys. Bridal gowns have been worn only once, so providing they've been professionally cleaned, there's no problem. Designer castoffs cost more, but you could find a real steal for under $100.

Look for quality: beads sewn on rather than glued, satin that doesn't feel so thin it might tear, a built-in petticoat or slip, and gloriously soft lace and detailing. French lace is best; the cheap stuff is stiff.

Not particularly sentimental? See 76 Sell Your Wedding Gown.

Warning

Falling in love with a particular dress or style does not mean that it will flatter your figure. Ask for honest advice from someone who knows what they're talking about.

65 Buy or Rent a Tuxedo

Men's formal wear carries its own array of decisions, styles and accessories. You may wish to invest in a tuxedo if your lifestyle calls for debonair dress several times a year. If you're rarely coaxed out of your blue jeans—and especially if your waistline tends to expand and contract—a rented tuxedo should fit the bill. The rule of thumb is that if a lady wears a floor-length dress, the gentleman should wear formal attire, and that style is dictated by time of day and level of formality.

Steps

1 Give yourself enough lead time. Reserve rented formal wear or order a tailor-made tuxedo three months prior to an event to guarantee availability.

2 Do a search for tuxedos online. Many have a photo gallery to demystify the process of ordering a tux. Afterhours.com and Menswearhouse.com both allow you to choose the elements online, then go to a store for a fitting.

3 Consult with the salesman when considering the wide range of options. Jackets have a notch, peak or shoulder lapel. They can be ultra-formal full dress tails, a cutaway jacket suitable for formal events before 6 p.m., or a tuxedo jacket, appropriate for any formal affair. Shirt choices include a laydown, wing and cavalier collar, finished off with a bow tie, ascot or laydown tie.

4 Choose colors according to the time of day and nature of the event. Gray is traditional before 6 p.m., and black for all formal evening affairs. You may wish to consult your date for the evening, and coordinate cummerbund or vest as desired.

5 Secure a knowledgeable specialist's help when gearing up for a wedding. Tuxedo selection should be guided by the color of the bride's gown and bridesmaids' dresses. Wedding-party rental specials may include a jacket, trousers, vest or cummerbund, shirt, suspenders, cufflinks, studs and tie from $50 to $100 or more. Or with a certain number of groomsmen's tuxedos, the groom's tux may be free.

6 Ask groomsmen who don't live locally to get professionally measured and forward the details at least three weeks before the big day. Try-ons and last-minute tweaks should happen a few days ahead.

7 If you're buying a tuxedo, expect to pay at least $700—far more for a custom-made or designer brand. Prices range according to the style, options and fabric chosen.

8 Make sure everything fits by trying on your tux in advance of the event. Wedding parties in particular need to find out ahead of time if all the groomsmen received the correct sizes.

What to Look For

- Appropriate formality for venue
- Flattering cut
- Accessories
- Timeless style if you buy

Tips

Double check when to pick up and return tuxedos and accessories if you're renting. The best man in a wedding generally takes care of collecting and delivering them.

If you're buying a tuxedo, choose a style that will fit right in at weddings, gala evenings and any formal occasion. Steer toward the classics so it won't go out of style.

Warning

Have measurements taken professionally. Having your spouse or friend measure you is a recipe for disaster.

66 Register for Gifts

Gift registries aren't just for weddings anymore. Department and housewares stores, Home Depot, Target, R.E.I. and many others are getting into the game, offering registries both in stores and online for weddings, showers and birthdays, too. By registering, you help yourself and your guests by asking for what you really want.

Steps

General

1 Pore over magazines and catalogs and collect tear sheets, color swatches, and patterns. Note brands, design names, model names, patterns and numbers.

2 Phone for an appointment and allow plenty of time when you go in to register. Bring your binder of information, photos and ideas.

3 Be sensitive about prices when choosing items. Take into consideration how many people are attending and guests' financial status. Cover a wide price range so no one feels burdened.

4 Check computerized lists periodically to make sure they're being updated regularly. Keep mailing labels from gifts as proof of purchase in case you need to return anything. (See 4 Make Returns.)

Baby

1 Review 316 Gear Up for a New Baby, paying special attention to those items you can borrow.

2 Register for baby gear at BabiesRUs, Target or children's boutiques. Visit the store in person, or go to the online registry.

Wedding

1 Take inventory of what you both own and what you'd like to have in your new household. You don't need to limit yourselves to things for the house. For example, register at REI.com for a kayak for two. Or create a registry for your honeymoon (Honey-Luna.com) or home remodeling project (HomeDepot.com).

2 Register at department stores (such as Macy's), cookware specialty shops (Williams-Sonoma), bed and bath stores (Strouds, Bed, Bath & Beyond) and furnishings and housewares stores (Restoration Hardware, Pottery Barn, Crate & Barrel). RossSimons.com also has a discount bridal registry.

3 Enlist a registry consultant's assistance to help you hone your list, either in person or via their toll-free number.

What to Look For

* Store(s) with a wide variety of merchandise
* Online registry
* Registry available at all store branches
* Savvy advice

Tips

Make sure your registry can be viewed and purchased from online. Also check how long after the event date you can make returns.

There are tasteful ways to let people know where you're registered. It's fine to note where you are registered on shower invitations, but don't do it on wedding invitations. The person who arranges a baby shower will be able to tell guests where the mother-to-be is registered.

All national retailers have an online store. Type in www plus the name and ".com" to get you there.

Warning

If you register at too many different stores, you may not receive full sets of some items.

67 Buy Wedding Gifts

You've received the invitation, you know what you'll wear, now you just need to find the perfect gift. Check the couple's registry first, or select a more personal or unusual gift.

Steps

1 Send the personal touch. Have satin-covered down pillows monogrammed or engrave a pair of crystal champagne flutes with their names and the wedding date.

2 Plant the thought of a long and prosperous marriage with a tree or flowering rose if the couple is buying a new home.

3 Send the bride and groom on a hot-air balloon ride or a sunset cruise. A set of golf or tennis lessons is a fun wedding gift. Nontraditional gifts are especially appropriate for second marriages when all the household necessities are covered.

4 Give the bride a gift certificate for an afternoon of spa luxury. If money's no object, include her bridesmaids or maid of honor.

5 Make a gift of cash. It is common practice in some cultures for guests to give the bride or groom an envelope with money in it.

What to Look For

- Registry items
- Unique, memorable or personal gift
- Cash or charitable contribution

Warning

Check that any bridal registry list is up-to-date before you buy. Consider selecting an item from a category that's near completion to give the bride and groom the satisfaction of getting a full set rather than bits and pieces.

68 Select Bridesmaids' Dresses

You'll wear it again, right? More and more, today's brides are choosing a color and fabric, then letting their bridesmaids each choose a dress that flatters her figure. If you take the more traditional route, be thoughtful and choose a dress that's both attractive and affordable.

Steps

1 Get started. Fittings should begin four to six months before the big day. You may want to take a few maids shopping with you.

2 Decide on a color and length. Depending on the time of day, season and degree of formality, you may choose a floor-length, silk sheath for an evening wedding, or a tea-length pastel sheer for a warm afternoon ceremony. Rule of thumb: If a bride is wearing a floor-length dress, bridesmaid dresses should not be short.

3 Keep the figures of all of your bridesmaids in mind when selecting a style. A full-figured woman may not feel comfortable in a short, strapless cocktail-style dress, for example.

4 Send your bridesmaids shopping for different dresses in one designer's line, or choose any dress of a certain color and length.

5 Less is more. Since bridesmaids usually pay for their own dresses, keep cost in mind. About $200 is a good figure, but if you can do it for less, everyone will be happier.

What to Look For

- Flexible design range
- Figure-flattering styles
- Coordination of colors, fabrics, styles
- Sane prices

Tip

Bride's and bridesmaids' dresses should complement each other and be uniform enough to look good in pictures.

69 Hire an Event Coordinator

With a skilled event coordinator backing you up, you can throw a corporate picnic for 100 people, an intimate dinner party, or a country wedding—all without breaking a sweat. Replace panic with peace of mind and enjoy the festivities.

Steps

1 Base preliminary logistical decisions on your budget: number of guests, atmosphere, location, date and time, food (buffet, sit-down meal, cocktail party, box lunches) and degree of formality. Give yourself at least six to nine months lead time when planning a large event.

2 List those tasks you want taken off your shoulders. A pro can plan budgets; rent audio/visual and other equipment; scout venues; hire and manage live music; manage guest lists; arrange for decorations and valet parking; handle airline and hotel bookings for out-of-town events or guests—even hire portable rest rooms.

3 Remember that well-connected professionals can save you money by passing on discounts and perks they get from vendors and banquet managers. And since they're experienced with service-provider contracts, arrange for them to handle all the negotiations, notifying you of any hitches or price increases.

4 Consult local wedding and business reference guides, and ask for referrals from trusted friends, colleagues, caterers, and local hotels and businesses for event planners, consultants or coordinators.

5 Interview likely prospects. Ask how many events they've produced, what kind, for how many, and what made these events special to find out if they're experienced in the kind of event you're throwing. See what aspects of the event they will assume control over. They should also be able to offer creative ideas to suit your budget.

6 Discuss whether you will be billed by the hour, the event or as a percentage of the total budget. Ask if package prices are available. Explain in detail what you want the coordinator to do, then ask for a quote in writing. Ask what he or she can do to reassure you that costs won't run over, at least not without your prior agreement.

7 Query the coordinator to see how he or she would handle potential catastrophes such as the caterer running out of food, the DJ not showing up, or a sudden downpour drowning out a lavish outdoor event.

What to Look For

- Well-connected
- Referrals and references
- Proven performance
- Creative
- Committed
- Calm under pressure

Tips

Your coordinator should find out about local noise ordinances.

Hire a licensed, insured company for major events.

8 Ask if you can drop by one of their events in progress. Request contact details of previous clients and call them to ask about their experience with that particular event coordinator.

9 Spell out the project's scope in detail; describe the planner's responsibilities and delineate all payment information in a written, signed agreement.

70 Hire a Bartender for a Party

The ideal bartender keeps more than cocktails and wine spritzers flowing. A skilled professional can interact affably while moving at warp speed to keep up with thirsty guests and avoid a bottleneck at the bar.

Steps

1 Get recommendations from friends, caterers or party planners. If your search comes up short, go online to find a nearby agency.

2 Check that the bartender has his or her own bar kit. Pros travel with their own wine opener, pour spouts, cocktail shaker, strainer, long-handled spoon, towel and knife for cutting garnishes. You provide the blender, beverages, glasses and ice.

3 Test expertise, since good bartenders know major mixed-drink recipes by heart. Ask how many years of experience the bartender has and of what kind. A tap person used to working in pub-style establishments may not know cocktails.

4 Quiz prospective bartenders on how they set up their bars and how they cope with nonstop drink demands and empty glasses and bottles. They should be in command of their work space, trash containers, and supply of glassware and beverages.

5 If you're planning the party yourself rather than hiring a caterer (see 72 Hire a Caterer), ask the bartender's advice on what to order. An experienced bartender can help you calculate how much and what alcohol you'll need (see 307 Stock Your Bar).

6 Avoid novices or anyone fresh out of bartending school. Look for a tidy appearance and attire.

What to Look For

- Recommendations
- Good people skills
- Organized
- Tidy appearance and attire

Tip

Good bartenders ask about guests' ages and tastes, and know which drinks different groups favor. A bar mitzvah calls for a different approach than a wild crowd of 20-something revelers or a relatively sedate gathering of over-50s.

71 Hire a Photographer

Sure you take the best snapshots in the family and everyone's still asking for dupes from the last company picnic. But for those times when it really counts, nothing replaces a professional photographer who can truly do justice to those special moments.

Steps

1 Start looking for a photographer as soon as you have the time and location nailed down, six months to a year in advance of the event.

2 Choose a photographer who specializes in the type of event you're holding such as weddings, family portraits, corporate head shots and more. Ask for references and get personal recommendations whenever possible. Use the Yellow Pages as a last resort.

3 Ask to see samples of their work similar to what you want. Look for relaxed expressions and posing, and watch out for stiff, cookie-cutter staging. Great pictures look natural and easy.

4 Trust your instincts. Do you get a good feel from the photographer? Does he or she listen to what you really want?

5 Ask how long he or she has been in business and get a sense of their level of professionalism. You want someone who dresses and acts sharp to shoot your event.

6 Specify if you want color or black-and-white pictures.

7 Inquire if digital photographs are an option. If so, find out if you will view the pictures as paper proofs, contact sheets or on a CD. Some photographers set up a page on their Web site so you can proof images online.

8 Ask how long will it take to see the proofs, if you get to keep them, how reprints and enlargements will be handled and what they cost. Inquire about bulk discounts on large orders and the possibility of ordering prints online.

9 Review the contract and button down all the details. All terms should be specified including the deposit and cancellation and refund policies.

10 Touch base in the weeks prior to your event to finalize all the details. Give the photographer a list of people you definitely want photographed.

What to Look For

- Expertise in your event
- References
- Excellent photographs
- Prompt and professional
- Black-and-white, color or digital pictures
- Clearly spelled out terms

Tips

If your event will be photographed digitally, look at a printout of a sample photograph to make sure you're satisfied with the quality.

Check out the studio if you are having portraits taken. Look for a place to change clothes if you care to, as well as comfortable ambient temperature. You want to be very comfortable in the studio environment in order to take a relaxed photograph.

Warning

Try to get a read on whether the photographer is intrusive, bossy or arrogant. A wedding or other event which is dictated by the photographer can be a miserable affair for everyone.

72 Hire a Caterer

How many times have you been served a cold plate of rubber-tasting chicken at a dinner? The food can make or break any event, be it an intimate brunch, a business power lunch or a wedding banquet. That's why finding the right caterer for the occasion is crucial.

Steps

1 Start your search as soon as you have the date and event venue nailed down. Ask friends for recommendations. If you loved the food at an event, ask the host for the caterer's number. Also, your venue may also have a list of preferred caterers.

2 Create a budget based on what you want or can afford to pay per head for food and beverages, and go over this with prospective caterers. High prices don't necessarily guarantee quality. Some famed caterers resort to premade pasta sauces, while many small operators make everything from scratch and use fresh ingredients.

3 Look at the caterer's portfolio of color photographs. Look at the presentation in individual dishes, table designs and buffet spreads. Does the food look beautiful and delicious?

4 Get phone numbers of previous customers and ask them if they were satisfied with the caterer.

5 Ask for sample menus that fit your budget. The caterer will create a tasting for you of all the items. Besides evaluating the dishes' flavor, you can gauge a caterer's desire to please you with additional special requests. Do they use heavy oils and butter in their recipes, or would they be willing to switch to healthier options? Do they offer vegetarian dishes? A larger caterer may offer more dishes to sample, but this is not the most important criterion. Just make certain the company can handle the total number of guests, even if it has to outsource some tasks.

6 Expect to be charged a set fee per person for food. This ranges from $10 to $100 per head depending on the event, plus additional costs for beverages, furniture rental or other extras. Ask for an estimate on the rates for servers, bartenders and cleanup crew. A six-hour bash might last eight hours, and unless you arrange otherwise, the caterer must keep paying the staff until the last guest leaves.

7 Review the venue with your caterer, who will want to see the kitchen facilities and space where guests will mingle and dine. Make sure that the caterer surveys the space carefully and plans the positioning of food and beverage tables to optimize traffic flow. This is crucial to arranging serving and dining tables.

8 Determine who will provide or rent tables, chairs, centerpieces, tent, glassware, utensils and linens. Also confirm number of wait staff, their dress code, taxes, gratuities and payment schedule. Have all agreed-upon details written into the contract.

What to Look For

- Referrals
- Tasty food
- Clear price estimate
- Organized planning

Tips

Clarify the dress code for servers and staff. The bistro look—a neat white shirt, black tie and pants, and an apron—has overtaken the tuxedo look, although you can go formal if you wish.

Ask your caterer and the venue if you can bring in your own alcohol—this can save you a bundle. Buy from a discount beverage store that will let you return unopened bottles.

You are expected to tip the caterer after the event.

Warnings

Some function halls or hotels won't allow you to bring in outside caterers, so double-check up front.

Find out if the caterer is insured and bonded. If they're not, you're taking a big risk.

You would be right to worry if a caterer doesn't ask lots of questions about what you like, love and hate, and about your ideas and goals for the event. A lack of curiosity sends up a red flag that you're in for generic, impersonal service.

73 Find the Ideal Wedding Officiant

You need just the right person to make taking your marriage vows truly memorable—an officiant willing to create the perfect ceremony that captures your personalities and beliefs.

Steps

1 Find someone whose beliefs resonate with yours and who can speak eloquently on your behalf. You'll want to meet several times to discuss the ceremony and come to a mutual accord. Officiants can suggest vows or help you fine-tune your own.

2 Choose from a wide pool of possible religious officiants: priests, rabbis, Catholic scholars, theologians and cantors. If you hold a religious ceremony in a church or synagogue, you may need to use their officiant.

3 A judge or justice of the peace can do the honors, as can a mayor, governor, county clerk, notary, legally ordained minister or anyone who is deputized to perform a one-time ceremony.

4 Have a friend become a minister. At the Universal Life Church (ulc.com) you can fill out an online form, pay $12, and voilà! You're an ordained minister. (Check laws in your state.)

5 Budget the officiant's fees into your overall cost of the wedding. Traditionally paid for by the groom, they can run from $100 to $300 or more, with travel and facility costs extra.

What to Look For

- Ceremony you're comfortable with
- Perfect vows
- Flexible; will consider your wishes
- Willingness to create tailor-made ceremony
- Appropriate religious affiliation
- Fee and/or gratuity

Tip

Many religious officiators require couples to undergo premarital counseling. This could be just a few questions or a series of meetings to discuss your relationship, faith and commitment to one another.

74 Obtain a Marriage License

So you're ready to get hitched? You'll need a valid marriage license issued in the state—sometimes even in the precise town—where you'll tie the knot. States have jurisdiction over varying licensing requirements, so check with the relevant local marriage bureau.

Steps

1 Contact the county clerk in the state or county where you'll marry to learn about local requirements. Nonresidents must obtain a license in the town in which they will be married. Also, in most states you need to be 18 years or older to get a license.

2 Bring necessary documents with you: birth certificate, passport, driver's license or divorce decree, plus a photo ID.

3 Ask how many witnesses you need—in most states it's two— and if a physical examination or blood test is required.

4 Pony up $25 to $100. Often the license is only good for 60 to 90 days, and generally you and your betrothed must both appear in person to get it. There's usually a 24-hour to three-day waiting period before you can marry, except in Las Vegas.

What to Look For

- Local laws in county or state
- Needed documents
- Picture identification
- Wedding date

Tip

Jewish weddings require the bride, groom and two witnesses to sign a marriage contract called a *ketubah,* which the rabbi can provide. A Catholic church may ask for your certificates of baptism.

75 Order Custom Invitations and Announcements

Whether it's a new baby, a bar or bat mitzvah or a wedding, invitations and announcements run the gamut from charming homemade cards to embossed, foil-stamped pieces. What you choose will depend on personal style, number of guests and your budget, as well as how much time you would like to devote to the project.

Steps

1 Start working on wedding invitations as soon as you've nailed down the time and location, at least five months ahead of time. Invitations should be mailed four to six weeks before the event.

2 Mail "save the date" cards three to six months ahead if you're inviting guests who need to make travel arrangements.

3 Finalize your guest list to determine how many invitations you need. Plan to print 20 to 30 extra invitations and envelopes in case of late additions to the list or botched addresses.

4 Decide what you want to spend since your budget dictates your options including paper, printing method, design and calligraphy.

5 Place your order in a stationery store. Pick paper and a type style that suits the mood of the event. You'll choose color, texture and special effects like pressed flowers. Stay with standard sizes and save a bundle; otherwise envelopes have to be custom made.

6 Hire a designer to create a custom invitation or announcement if you don't find what you want at a stationer's. He or she will create a unique, fun, elegant or whimsical look to your specifications. (See 158 Hire a Graphic Designer.)

7 Explore printing effects. Traditional engraving, elegant letterpress, and relatively inexpensive thermography are all classy extras. Plain offset printing with black ink is the least expensive.

8 Proofread your piece very carefully when your printer gives you a proof to check. Have fresh eyes read it too.

9 Hire a calligrapher to address the envelopes for a stunning, formal touch. A professional may charge $6 or $7 per envelope.

10 Be judicious about the number of enclosures and envelopes your invitation includes. There is no rule that says you have to have an inner and outer envelope as well as one for the reply card. Save money by using just one outer envelope and enclosing a prestamped RSVP postcard.

What to Look For

- Order in good time
- Appropriate design
- Trustworthy stationery store
- Careful proofreading
- Envelope-addressing plan

Tips

Save even more money by having only the invitations printed, and then have a custom rubber stamp made for under $20 for the return address.

Print directions and a map if needed on your own computer and slip it into the envelope. Add gift registration information on the reverse side of the directions (but not in wedding invitations).

Order thank-you notes at the same time to match the invitations, and get enough to cover shower, engagement and wedding gifts.

Warning

Don't mail your invitation without correct postage. Take the completed envelope with all the enclosures down to the post office to be weighed.

76 Sell Your Wedding Gown

Maybe you went way over budget buying the most divine wedding gown in creation and need some cash, or you don't have space to store it for the future. Sell the dress to recoup some of its cost.

Steps

1 Send your gown to a dry cleaner that specializes in bridal wear. Do this immediately after the wedding—perspiration or a teeny splash of champagne can yellow and set quickly. Point out and identify visible stains for treating.

2 Invest in a dust-proof heirloom box if you must store your dress even briefly. Some dry cleaners can hermetically seal it. Avoid plastic bags and hangers—they seal in humidity and can damage or stretch delicate fabrics.

3 Go to a consignment store that sells once-worn and never-worn bridal wear. Expect it to turn away any dress that isn't cleaned, pressed, with buttons intact and in near-mint condition.

4 Agree on a selling price. The store will take into account its styling (a fading fad or timeless statement), condition and age.

5 Sign a contract, usually for three months. Often you will receive 50 percent of the sale price. If it remains unsold at the end of the agreed-upon time frame, you or the store can extend the arrangement or end it.

6 Advertise your dress online. You'll need a full-length color photograph that really shows it off and a full description right down to the beading, condition, price paid and size.

7 Give your gown to a charity thrift shop if you don't need the cash. You will be doing a really nice deed for a bride on a budget (some say it's good luck to pass along your happiness), and you'll get a tax write-off. See 498 Sell Used Clothing.

What to Look For

- Heirloom box
- Consignment stores
- Charity thrift shop

Tip

See 64 Choose the Perfect Wedding Dress.

Warning

While your dress waits to find its new owner, keep it in top-notch condition. Stuff the bodice and sleeves with white, acid-free tissue paper. If you must use a hanger, sew some straps inside the dress's waistline to hook around the hanger for extra support and avoid any stretching. Cover your dress in a white sheet and keep it in a dry, cool spot.

77 Buy an Anniversary Gift

The tradition of tying gifts to particular wedding anniversaries began in central Europe. Medieval German wives received silver wreaths on their 25th anniversary, gold ones on their 50th. Other traditions have added to the eight original gifts. (Diamonds, which originally marked the 60th anniversary, are now common gifts early in marriage.) Here's how to marry the old with the new.

YEAR	TRADITIONAL	MODERN
First	Paper	Frame a poem or love letter; artist sketch from a wedding photograph.
Second	Cotton	Clothing, linens, gift certificate for apparel.
Third	Leather	Briefcase, handbag, leather jacket, wallet.
Fourth	Fruit/Flowers	Plant a garden, give a fruit tree.
Fifth	Wood	Jewelry box, plant a tree.
Sixth	Iron	Wrought-iron garden gate, golf clubs.
Seventh	Wool/Copper	Sweater, cookware.
Eighth	Bronze/Pottery	Sculpture, matching coffee mugs.
Ninth	Pottery/Willow	Willow tree, wicker furniture.
Tenth	Tin/Aluminum	Metal-framed sunglasses, digital camera, tools, bicycle.
Eleventh	Steel	Kitchen knives.
Twelfth	Silk/Linen	Tablecloth, scarf, pajamas, linens.
Thirteenth	Lace	Antique tablecloth, curtains, table runner.
Fourteenth	Ivory	Piano.
Fifteenth	Crystal	Candlesticks, wineglasses, clock.
Twentieth	China	Trip to China, new place setting.
Twenty-fifth	Silver	Airline tickets wrapped in a silver bow, tray, tie clip, goblets, antique coins.
Thirtieth	Pearl	Earrings, necklace; mother-of-pearl inlaid pocketknife.
Thirty-fifth	Coral	Trip to the tropics, coral beaded necklace.
Fortieth	Ruby	Jewelry.
Forty-fifth	Sapphire	Jewelry.
Fiftieth	Gold	Watch, clock, pen, jewelry.
Fifty-fifth	Emerald	Trip to Ireland, jewelry.
Sixtieth	Diamond	Watch, jewelry.

78 Arrange Entertainment for a Party

The crowd gasps. Breathless, all eyes are on center stage. At your party? Sure! Finding and hiring just the right entertainer takes a knack and some time but is worth the effort.

Steps

1 Call an agency unless you have a strong personal referral. The fees are a little higher since they include commissions, but the performers are pros (ask for a publicity package), and if someone falls ill, a good agency will find a stand-in. Check out agencies with the Better Business Bureau (bbb.org).

2 Factor in the number of guests, their ages and the party's tone and choose appropriate entertainment.

3 Have the theme-party entertainer provide a goody bag, or plan a crafty activity and send the child home with a gift he or she makes for a tangible memory of the party.

4 Get a contract or letter of agreement that includes the scope and description of the act and itemizes payment information, cancellation policy and penalties for defaulting (by either party). Prices vary dramatically, but $150 to $300 isn't uncommon for an hour-long performance.

5 Give your event a whole different flavor (and avoid cleanup) by hosting it at an ice rink, bowling alley, ceramic-making studio, swimming pool or laser-tag emporium.

What to Look For

- References and referrals
- Crowd-appropriate acts
- Performed for similar age groups and crowds
- Contract or written agreement
- Sane prices
- Chance to test-drive or view acts

Tip

Review a video or watch an actual performance to make sure your choice of entertainment is appropriate.

FOR KIDS' PARTIES	FOR ADULTS' PARTIES
Caricature artists	Acrobats
Climbing wall	Casino night
Clowns	Elvis impersonators
Costumed cartoon characters and caped crusaders	Hypnotists
Interactive theater, storyteller	Musicians
Magician	Psychics, palm and tarot-card readers, astrologers
Petting zoo or wildlife visitors	Singing telegrams
Puppet shows	Stand-up comedians
Themes: face painters, musical games, sing-alongs, jewelry making, science demonstrations	

79 Commission a Fireworks Show

A dazzling fireworks display can add a memorable touch to a party, wedding or business event. For a safe and sizzling evening, leave the pyrotechnics to the pros, sit back and enjoy.

Steps

1 Be prepared to fork over some serious dough. Basic displays run about $1,500 a minute, more if choreographed. You'll have to cough up $5,000 to $10,000 for an outdoor show worth watching—$5,000 could get you 300 to 400 effects; $10,000 will buy an ideal display for a small community bash. Major pyrotechnic events run $30,000 to $100,000 or more.

2 Get referrals for several reputable, well-established fireworks providers or pyrotechnics companies experienced with similar-size shows. Make sure they are insured and ask what their policy covers. Check references diligently.

3 Kick back and let a full-service operation or event planner take over by pulling necessary permits and talking to fire inspectors. If you do it yourself, you'll need to contact the fire department, learn about local and technical guidelines, ask for copies of relevant codes and review them with the technicians.

4 Review local ordinances regarding safety zones. These mandatory distances between spectators and fireworks are governed by how far fireworks travel from their ignition point to the outer perimeter of flaming, falling debris. Compliance with these codes will dictate your choice of fireworks.

5 Find out if the fire department needs to issue a permit or approve the location and facilities.

6 Give your fantasies full rein when brainstorming with pyrotechnics providers. Discuss your budget and whether you're after a particular color scheme, theme or effects choreographed to music. Describe your audience.

7 Look at videos of past performances to get ideas. Ask for their advice; they are the pros. Take advantage of their creativity. They'll dream up tricks to maximize your extravaganza, like having effects reflect in a lake or light up a statue.

8 Find out how much bang you'll get for your buck. Get a fully itemized, written proposal confirming the agreed-upon display and location, and listing every shell with quantities, names, sizes and descriptions.

9 Get a "services provided" list covering all equipment and outlining insurance. This should be extensive, including the provider, crew, client and venue. If not, go elsewhere.

10 Get contractual assurance that transportation of fireworks will meet local and state regulations, and that the fee includes discharging the fireworks and cleanup.

What to Look For

- Experienced pyrotechnicians
- Established company
- Creativity within your budget
- Best mix of splash and show length
- Detailed proposal
- Itemization of responsibilities
- Comprehensive insurance
- Assurance of permits

Tip

Discuss the optimum moment to light the fuse. Fireworks most often cap off an evening, but don't leave it too late for the weary or tipsy to enjoy it.

Warnings

It's possible to commission indoor fireworks if the venue is right, but a fire marshal must conduct safety inspections.

Make sure all liability issues are fully taken care of. If the pyrotechnics company doesn't have an umbrella policy covering all possible contingencies, contact your insurance company and discuss a temporary policy.

80 Buy a Mother's Day Gift

On this day set aside to acknowledge the hard work and loving care that goes into motherhood, honor all the special mothers in your life—your sister, grandmother, spouse, friend, mother-in-law—in these unique and creative ways.

Steps

1 Offer Mom a chance to explore a new passion. If she's spoken of an unexplored interest—such as art, music, gourmet cooking, singing or golf—sign her up for lessons. Contact local community centers, teachers or clubs for references. If she's always wanted to play the drums, rent a set and locate a teacher.

2 Buy a flat of plants or flowers for her garden and plant them where she chooses; or put in a vegetable garden. (See 253 Start a Vegetable Garden.)

3 Make her sigh with a fabulous spa day or a massage certificate, or book her a professional beauty treatment.

4 Get her computer hooked up to the Internet, or buy her a cell phone with a family plan if she says, "You never call! You never write!"

5 Plant a container with a lush mini herb garden that she can snip at will while cooking.

6 Have some favorite family photographs matted and framed for her to enjoy.

7 Take her to a local gym for a sample session of yoga, tai chi or personal training sessions. Better yet, you go too.

8 Take her sewing machine in to get serviced.

9 Gather your clan and book a professional photographer to take a portrait of the whole family. Costs range widely, but expect to pay anywhere from $50 to $500 depending on the studio, and the number and size of prints you end up ordering. (See 71 Hire a Photographer.)

10 Buy a gift certificate from a favorite store where she usually wouldn't indulge herself.

11 Take a walk on the wild side and buy her a pair of snowshoes (available at stores such as REI.com).

12 Whet the appetite of a voyaging mom with a Topo! GPS software program from NationalGeographic.com. The CD-ROM works with a GPS receiver to plan her next ultimate adventure.

What to Look For

- Gift that says love
- Gift that says thanks
- Gift that says you thought about it
- Unusual, not just traditional

Tip

Create a Mother's Day gift with the kids. Ask them to draw and sign portraits of Mom or Grandma, then buy simple frames and help them prepare and wrap their gifts.

81 Buy a Father's Day Gift

Scoping out the array of men's gifts at department stores would leave you with the impression that every male in the country is not only in need of a new tie or gadget, but a golf fanatic. On the contrary, men's passions are diverse. Try these ideas for great dad gifts, whether you're buying for a grandfather, husband, first-time dad or good friend.

Steps

1   Zero in on an enduring hobby or new interest, then shop for gear and accessories he doesn't have yet. Is he a science or computer buff, a car or airplane fanatic, a fisherman, a cook, a gardener or basketball fan? Shop Discovery.com, an auto supply store, Williams-Sonoma or Sur La Table. Visit a local nursery or buy a couple of tickets to a ballgame.

2   Do something fun together. Plan a fishing or camping trip, or even a helicopter ride. Or buy tickets and popcorn, and let him choose the movie.

3   Tap into a nostalgic moment or time you shared. If you've traveled together, get a coffee-table book on a place you visited that evokes a great adventure.

4   Go high-tech with gizmos all men find irresistible. A Forever Flashlight (foreverflashlight.com, $40) works without batteries; after a good shake, it provides five minutes of light. Pick up a pair of binoculars that takes pictures (around $100), a two-way radio and wristwatch combo (around $50), or a wristwatch-camera combo. Get inspired at HammacherSchlemmer.com or TheSharperImage.com, or tour RestorationHardware.com.

5   Appeal to his practical side. Buy him jumper cables, a really good road map (such as from Thomas.com) or a Leatherman mini tool kit for his glove compartment.

6   Feed his sweet tooth with a bag of his favorite childhood candy. See's Candy (sees.com) has a variety of tasty gifts that will tempt anyone off the Atkins plan. Alternatively, pick up a savory treat like smoked salmon or a 20-lb. can of pistachios from Costco.

7   Head for a home improvement store and get him a cordless drill. These are as essential to survival as food, water and the remote.

8   Birdie, don't bogie. Buy a set of monogrammed golf towels and a pack of golf balls (real or chocolate), and spring for a guest pass for a day on the green. Better yet, go with him.

9   Add a little dazzle to his wardrobe. If he likes to go out on the town, order a pair of monogrammed silver cuff links. If he's just a regular Joe, update his bedraggled wallet or briefcase.

10 Give him the world. Find a gorgeous wall map, atlas or globe at NationalGeographic.com. Or appeal to a secret passion: a map of Civil War battlefields, for example, is $9.95.

What to Look For

- Hobbies and passions
- Nostalgia
- Shared memories

Tip

Give little ones a hand with their Father's Day gifts. They can create e-mail greetings for Dad or send him a virtual Father's Day tie. Head to Radio Shack (radioshack.com) and buy a recordable picture frame, and have the kids speak into it for a really memorable photo.

82 **Select an Appropriate Coming-of-Age Gift**

Most religions and cultures have their own unique ways of celebrating young girls' and boys' rites of passage—the coming-of-age mile-stones that mark their transition from children to young men and women. Celebrate their new status in society with a special gift.

Steps

Quinceañera

1 Celebrate coming-of-age in the Hispanic tradition when 15-year-old girls vow faithfulness to church and family, then are treated like princesses at elaborate celebrations.

2 Pick out a gold ring or buy a traditional tiara to symbolize the celebrant's entrance into womanhood.

3 Choose religious items such as a Bible with blank pages for dedications; or a rosary, cross or Lady of Guadalupe necklace.

Bar and bat mitzvah

1 Say "Mazel tov!" at Jewish coming-of-age rituals. The day marks the first time the bar mitzvah boy (age 13) or bat mitzvah girl (age 12) is called to the Torah to recite a blessing over the weekly reading. The celebration that follows usually includes a festive meal at a synagogue, restaurant or banquet hall.

2 Follow the tradition of giving cash in multiples of 18. (Each letter in the Hebrew alphabet corresponds to a number, and the two letters that form *chai*, "life" in Hebrew, add up to 18.)

3 Give a gold or silver symbol on a chain—a chai, *chamsa* (Hebrew for "the hand of God," to ward off the evil eye), or Star of David. Buy a mezuzah, a small case with a prayer scroll inside, for the boy or girl's home.

4 Buy Israel bonds (israelbonds.com) or plant a tree in Israel (jnf.org).

5 Book a memorable trip to Israel for the child. Many bar or bat mitzvah ceremonies are performed there as well.

Confirmation

1 Celebrate the conferring of the Holy Spirit to 13-year-old girls and boys. These are smaller-scale events, but still important in the Catholic church.

2 Monogram or inscribe a white prayer book, or engrave a silver rosary bracelet. Engrave a silver frame with the child's name and date and put a commemorative photograph or keepsake invitation inside.

3 For girls, treat the celebrant in her traditional white dress to a professional portrait, a manicure/pedicure or a grown-up hairdo for the big day.

What to Look For

- Religious or cultural significance
- Lifelong keepsakes

Tip

Gifts of cash can be set aside for college or a large purchase.

83 Get a Gift for the Person Who Has Everything

Even if money's no object, it takes creativity to find or buy a truly memorable gift for someone who has everything. Think of his or her personal history, memories and passions and you're on track to make a lasting impact. These starting points and strategies will help you channel inspiration, no matter what the budget.

Steps

1 Tap into the universal fascination with family roots. Buy afford-able software to help someone trace a family tree; Family Tree Maker is one of many good products (genealogy.com).

2 Name a Scottish whale or another beautiful creature after him or her. The Hebridean Whale and Dolphin Trust (whales.gn.apc.org), photo-identifies minke whales and lets you name the creature exclusively for its lifetime (20 to 30 years) for $150 and up. You'll receive a photograph, a certificate and a year's membership.

3 Get a fabulous wall map of an area your recipient is interested in at RandMcNally.com or exquisitely rendered maps or globes from NationalGeographic.com. Order topographical maps or an aerial photograph from the U.S. Geological Survey (usgs.gov). Historical maps start at $12. A 36-by-36-inch full-color aerial photograph might cost around $75.

4 Compile family memorabilia—photographs, certificates, personal notes and family documents—into a keepsake album. Get it pro-fessionally bound. Or buy an album from an archival store—ask for guidance on acid-free paper, preservation and mounting.

5 Ask a local historical society, parks organization or botanical garden in your recipient's hometown about donation options. Explain that you're looking for an item with special meaning. Maybe you can have a tree or park bench dedicated with a plaque (the likely cost is several hundred dollars and up).

6 Hire a master perfumer to create a unique scent. For around $20,000, French perfumer Oliver Creed will create one—the fee includes airfare and three nights in a top Parisian hotel.

7 Commission a local writer to write your recipient's life story and help you print a limited-edition book. Check with the Association of Personal Historians or visit its online directory (personal-historians.org) for local writers. Prices start at several thousand dollars, so consider making it a group gift. (See 116 Hire a Ghostwriter to Pen Your Memoirs.)

8 Order a special keepsake for descendants of immigrants via the Ellis Island Foundation (ellisisland.org). Track the appropriate ship's passenger manifest and order a copy, along with a depic-tion of the ship.

What to Look For

- A moment of fame
- A nod to heritage
- Unique
- Personal
- Nostalgic

Tip

See 118 Immortalize Your Spouse in a Sculpture.

84 Buy a Graduation Gift

Graduation is an exuberant milestone. Receiving the announcement isn't necessarily a call for gifts, but if you choose to give one, here are some ideas to help your grad celebrate both his or her magnificent accomplishments as well as the opportunities that lie just ahead.

Steps

1 Mat and frame the diploma. College grads may appreciate a framed photo of their campus. (See 50 Get a Picture Framed.) Have the graduate's initials and graduation date monogrammed on a picture frame.

2 Inscribe a classic hardcover book, dictionary or encyclopedia with a note of love and pride. Students graduating from grade school or junior high will enjoy a copy of Dr. Seuss's *Oh, the Places You'll Go.*

3 Buy custom stationery with a college grad's newest letters after his or her name (see 75 Order Custom Invitations and Announcements).

4 Give money or gift certificates, always appreciated by those in a cash-poor phase. For the grad entering the business world, spring for a briefcase (see 511 Buy a Briefcase), Montblanc pen, leather desk set or business card holder. Perhaps best of all, work your network for job leads and present a few key introductions, listed in a gift card.

5 Splurge on a special grad with a cell phone, personal digital assistant or even a laptop (refer to the Computers & Home Electronics chapter). Sterling silver key chains, cuff links or a money clip are other classy options.

6 Feather the nests of both high school and college graduates with essentials like comforters, lamps, clocks, microwaves, mini fridges, basic cookware, towels and bathroom necessities. High school grads will appreciate sweatshirts, hats, fleece throws and backpacks emblazoned with the insignia of their college-to-be.

7 Celebrate a new chapter in life with something fun—a bicycle, CD or DVD player, digital camera, television and VCR combo or audio system. Leather luggage tags are also keepers.

What to Look For

- Personalized
- Give meaningful message
- Help with practical needs

85 Select a Thanksgiving Turkey

The only turkey present at your Thanksgiving dinner should be the beautiful golden-brown centerpiece on the table—not the poor chef who has been sweating bullets in the kitchen. Start browsing cookbooks early in November to find the perfect cooking method and get a leg up on your holiday feast.

Steps

1 Buy a frozen bird weeks ahead and plan on thawing it out in the fridge for several days before roasting. If you're challenged for time, get a frozen bird already larded, stuffed and basted, or self-basted.

2 Choose a fresh turkey for noticeably tastier meat. Check to see that it is wrapped securely, then pack it in a separate bag to prevent leakage.

3 Pre-order an organic or free-range turkey that has been living the high life on feed free of hormones, antibiotics and pesticides. Free-range turkeys are allowed to wander around to their heart's content rather than being cooped up in a cage. Ask your grocer or butcher, or go online to find a supplier in your area. A few sites to consider are SamuelsRanch.com, Williebird.com and YoungsFarmInc.com.

4 Purchase 1 to 1½ lbs. (450 to 680 g) of turkey per person. Err on the high end to make sure you have leftovers.

5 Opt for a bird with a built-in pop-up thermometer that tells you when the turkey is cooked to perfection: 180 degrees F (82 C).

6 Buy a fresh or frozen breast, boneless if you prefer, if you are catering for a small group or for a bevy of white-meat fans. Around 4 lbs. (2 kg) serves four very nicely.

7 Buy a precooked, ready-to-slice whole turkey and serve it cold or heat it up. These birds are available baked, honey-glazed or smoked for extra flavor. Online sources include ShadyBrookFarms.com, Smokehouse.com and WisconsinMade.com.

What to Look For

- Fresh or frozen
- Free-range or organic
- Pop-up timer
- Size

Tip

Check frozen birds' packaging for any signs of damage or frost buildup—clues that it might have partially thawed out, then been refrozen. Make sure it is solidly frozen, with no areas that feel soft to the touch.

Warning

Never defrost a frozen turkey at room temperature. Bacteria begin to multiply as soon as the surface warms.

86 Buy a Housewarming Gift

Celebrate a friend or relative's new digs with a thoughtful housewarming gift and help get them set up in their new house in style. Browse through 59 Buy a Great Birthday Present for Under $10, and consider these ideas, too.

Steps

1 Bring a plant for a traditional gift. Lucky bamboo symbolizes good fortune, grows in water and lasts for years.

2 Give a bottle of wine, tea bags, cappuccino mix or a bag of flavorful ready-ground coffee. Package with a pair of wineglasses, mugs or demitasse cups.

3 Feed growling stomachs with cookies, cake, pastries or a fresh fruit basket. Or bring a savory snack of cheeses and a crusty loaf of fresh bread (see 287 Buy Artisan Breads).

4 Buy kitchen towels or a few hand towels and bars of soap.

5 Give a loaded picnic basket to dine on in their empty house then enjoy outdoors at a later date. A couple of folding beach or garden chairs can likewise serve many purposes.

6 Bring a new tool for the tool box: A cordless screw gun, 25-foot measuring tape, or a socket wrench set are all essential for projects around the house.

What to Look For

- Helpful
- Useful
- Versatile

Tip

If you're handy with a hammer, good at hanging pictures or a great organizer, ask if you can lend a hand.

87 Purchase Holiday Cards

It pays to get a jump on buying and sending out holiday cards. Make them yourself, have photo cards made or buy them new.

Steps

1 Buy cards cheap right after this year's holidays are over.

2 Buy charity cards to contribute some of the money to a deserving cause. If you donate to your favorite charities throughout the year, you'll likely receive several unsolicited batches of greeting cards from them.

3 Get tailor-made greeting cards for couples of different faiths. Check out sites such as the Interfaith Wedding Mall (interfaith-weddingmall.com). A box of 10 costs around $15.

4 Buy cards online at sites such as Sparks.com that mail either to you or directly to your recipients with personalized messages.

5 Create custom photo cards at various online sites like iPads.com. Mail-order them or print them out on your own computer. Or take your negative to Costco or Kinko's and get a gazillion cards blazingly fast and made for dirt cheap.

What to Look For

- Off-season prices
- Special sales
- Interfaith messages
- Ways to express yourself

Tip

Keep a permanent mailing list with names and addresses. Either tuck it inside your box of greeting cards or store it on your computer. Update it each year, and you'll have no excuse not to address and mail cards out early the following year.

88 Buy Christmas Stocking Stuffers

The definition of stocking stuffer has expanded from small gifts—coin-shaped chocolate, toothpaste, nuts and oranges—to include gourmet chocolates, CDs and MP3 players, and much more.

WHO	WHAT
Babies	Bath toys; washcloths, fuzzy letter cubes, rattles or small soft toys.
Small Children	Classic wooden toys, balls (larger than 2 inches in diameter), crayon and glitter-pen sets, and stickers. Scientific wonders from a well-stocked science or toy store. Age-appropriate videos and CDs. (See 334 Buy Books, Videos and Music for Your Children.)
Preteen Girls	Stickers, a locking diary, stretchy beaded or flower rings and bracelets, barrettes and hair decorations, socks in crazy colors and designs, manicure set or nail polish, walkie-talkies, books and CDs.
Preteen Boys	GameBoys, walkie-talkies, baseball, basketball, baseball cards, cap, socks, remote-control minicars, Yu-Gi-Oh cards, comic books, books and CDs.
Teenagers	CDs and cases, video games, the latest computer accessory, cell phone with a color screen, two-way radios, store gift certificates.
Grandparents	Playing card sets, luggage labels, old-time movies, scarf, coin purse, pillbox, or ready-to-water amaryllis bulb in a small pot, magnifying glass, compass or book-on-tape.
Women	Bars of handmade soap, thick wool socks, film, lavender sachets, skin-softening socks and gloves to wear overnight, gift certificates for espresso drinks, Leatherman Juice tool, CDs, airplane tickets (surprise!).
Men	Universal remote, business-card holder, stainless steel travel mug, tire gauge, glasses case, paperback, GPS device, crossword-puzzle book, socks, guidebook to a surprise destination.
Fitness Enthusiast	Pedometer or heart-rate monitor, resistance bands, dumbbells, skipping rope, workout or yoga video, running socks, instant ice packs, hip pack with pockets, electrolyte replacement drinks, energy bars.
Gardeners	New trowel or other hand tool, garden gloves, Bag Balm, emollient lotion, seed packets.
Home Owners	Decorative wine-bottle stoppers, small tools, kitchen towels, napkin rings, potholders, oven mitts, refrigerator magnets or coasters. See 86 Buy a Housewarming Gift.
Chefs	A pizza cutter, wooden spoons, a stove-top milk frother, ergonomically correct kitchen tools, barbecue tools, flexible plastic cutting boards.
WARNING	Check the labels on kids' toys to see if they're age-appropriate and safe.

89 Buy Hanukkah Gifts

Hanukkah, the eight-day celebration beloved by Jewish families, begins on the 25th day of Kislev on the Hebrew calendar (the exact dates in November or December vary each year). Families light candles each evening at sundown while reciting blessings. Today, each family has its own rituals, in some cases simple ones and in others extravagant. Strike the right note in either case.

Steps

1 Give Hanukkah gelt (chocolate shaped like coins) in keeping with a very old tradition.

2 Buy a dreidel. This four-sided top is another age-old traditional Hanukkah gift available from Judaica stores and sites. Not just a child's toy, dreidels can be found in silver or crystal.

3 Give children cash in $18 increments. Each letter in the Hebrew alphabet corresponds to a number, and the two letters of *chai* ("life") add up to 18.

4 Pick out a menorah from a museum shop or boutique, or online at JacobsLadderJudaica.com.

5 Buy a book with a Jewish theme or a piece of Jewish art or jewelry. Give a subscription to the local Jewish newspaper or the *Jerusalem Post.*

6 Order Hanukkah-themed gift baskets and dreidel-shaped candles at AllThingsJewish.com.

What to Look For

- Family activities
- Reflection of family values
- Spirit of giving

Tip

Some, although by no means most, families give small gifts on each of the eight nights. Others give one large gift on the first night.

Warning

Ask the parents what would be an appropriate gift for their children. If the family ritual is to give a couple of small gifts per child and you waltz in with an expensive computer game, they might not thank you for it.

90 Purchase a Perfect Christmas Tree

The best thing about decorating your home for Christmas is filling it with the seductive scent of pine needles. Whether you buy a cut or living tree, freshness is the key to longevity, fragrance and beauty. Here's a guide to finding—and keeping—the perfect tree.

Steps

1 Keep a live tree in a container outside during the year and move it into the living room every December.

2 Cut your own at a tree farm for the ultimate evergreen. If you're buying a cut tree, check to see how fresh it is. The fragrance should be strong. Grasp a branch and pull on the pine needles; if they pull out easily, the tree has dried out already.

3 To aid water absorption, quickly put the tree in a stand with water in it and keep it filled. A 6-foot tree will drink a gallon of water every two days. Leave the tree outside in water until you are ready to decorate.

What to Look For

- Fresh smell
- Vibrant color
- Pliable needles
- Needles that don't drop

Tip

Have the salesperson make a fresh, straight cut across the base. Try to get the tree home and into a bucket of water outside within half an hour of cutting it.

TREE	DESCRIPTION
Afghan Pine	Short needles with sturdy branches; open appearance; mild fragrance; keeps well; grown in Texas.
Balsam Fir	¾-to 1½-inch short, flat, long-lasting needles that are rounded at the tip; dark green color with silvery cast, fragrant, dense.
Blue Spruce	Dark green to powdery blue, very stiff needles, ¾ to 1½ inches long; good form; will drop needles in a warm room; symmetrical; best among species for needle retention. Branches are stiff and will support many heavy decorations.
Douglas Fir	Good fragrance; blue to dark green, holds 1 to 1½ inch needles well; needles have one of the best aromas among Christmas trees when crushed. Good, conical shape; dense. Most common Christmas tree in the Pacific Northwest.
Frasier Fir	Dark green, flattened needles; ½ to 1 inch long; good needle retention; nice scent; pyramid-shaped strong branches that turn upward; dense. Often shipped by mail-order companies.
Leyland Cypress	Foliage is dark green to gray color; upright branches with a feathery appearance; light scent; good for people with allergies to other Christmas tree types. Popular Southeastern U.S. Christmas tree.
Noble Fir	1-inch-long, bluish green needles with a silvery appearance; dense; short stiff branches; keeps well; is used to make wreaths, door swags and garlands.
Norway Spruce	Shiny, dark green needles ½ to 1 inch long. Needle retention is poor without proper care; strong fragrance; nice conical shape. Very popular in Europe.
Scotch Pine	Most popular Christmas tree; stiff branches; stiff, dark green needles 1 to 3 inches long; holds needles for four weeks; open appearance offers more room for ornaments; keeps aroma throughout the season; does not drop needles when dry.
Virginia Pine	Dark green needles are 1½ to 3 inches long in twisted pairs; strong branches enable it to hold heavy ornaments; strong aromatic pine scent; a Southern U.S. Christmas tree.
White Pine	Soft, blue-green needles, 2 to 5 inches long in bundles of five; retains needles throughout the holiday season; very full appearance; little or no fragrance; fewer allergic reactions as compared to more fragrant trees; slender branches will support fewer and smaller decorations than a Scotch Pine.
White Spruce	Needles ½ to ¾ inch long; green to bluish green needles; crushed needles have an unpleasant odor; good needle retention.

QUET OF ROSES • BUY SOMEONE A DRINK • GET SOMEONE TO BUY YOU A DRINK • BUY YOUR WAY INTO HIGH SOCIETY • BUY YOUR
RDER THE PERFECT BURRITO • ORDER TAKEOUT ASIAN FOOD • ORDER AT A SUSHI BAR • BUY DINNER AT A FANCY FRENCH RESTAURA
OWERS FOR YOUR SWEETHEART • BUY MUSIC ONLINE • HIRE MUSICIANS • ORDER A GREAT BOTTLE OF WINE • BUY AN ERGONOMIC (
SECLEANER • HIRE A BABY SITTER • BUY A GUITAR • BUY DUCT TAPE • GET A GOOD DEAL ON A MAGAZINE SUBSCRIPTION • GET SEN
AN • BUY PET FOOD • BUY A PEDIGREED DOG OR CAT • BREED YOUR PET AND SELL THE LITTER • GET A COSTUME • BUY A PIÑATA •
ED GEMSTONES • CHOOSE THE PERFECT WEDDING DRESS • BUY OR RENT A TUXEDO • REGISTER FOR GIFTS • BUY WEDDING GIFTS
EAL WEDDING OFFICIANT • OBTAIN A MARRIAGE LICENSE • ORDER CUSTOM INVITATIONS AND ANNOUNCEMENTS • SELL YOUR WEDDI
R'S DAY GIFT • SELECT AN APPROPRIATE COMING-OF-AGE GIFT • GET A GIFT FOR THE PERSON WHO HAS EVERYTHING • BUY A GRAD
ANUKKAH GIFTS • PURCHASE A PERFECT CHRISTMAS TREE • BUY A PRIVATE ISLAND • HIRE A SKYWRITER • HIRE A BIG-NAME BAND •
ER • RENT YOUR OWN BILLBOARD • TAKE OUT A FULL-PAGE AD IN *THE NEW YORK TIMES* • HIRE A BUTLER • ACQUIRE A PROFESSION
OUR FUR COAT • BOOK A TRIP ON THE ORIENT-EXPRESS • BECOME A WINE MAKER • PURCHASE A PRIVATE/CUSTOM BOTTLING OF WIN
MEMOIRS • COMMISSION ORIGINAL ARTWORK • IMMORTALIZE YOUR SPOUSE IN A SCULPTURE • GIVE AWAY YOUR FORTUNE • HIRE A
DEVIL • NEGOTIATE A BETTER CREDIT CARD DEAL • CHOOSE A FINANCIAL PLANNER • SAVE WITH A RETIREMENT PLAN • SAVE FOR YO
BUY BONDS • SELL SHORT • INVEST IN PRECIOUS METALS • BUY DISABILITY INSURANCE • BUY LIFE INSURANCE • GET HEALTH INSUR
ELOR • HIRE A HEADHUNTER • SELL YOUR ___ ENT • MARKET YOUR INVENTION • FINANCE YOU
TED OFFICE EQUIPMENT • HIRE SOMEONE ___ RE A GRAPHIC DESIGNER • ACQUIRE CONTENT
CH A MAGAZINE STORY • SELL A SCREEN ___ YOUR BOOK • START A BED-AND-BREAKFAST • S
ME OWNER'S INSURANCE • OBTAIN DISAS ___ OUSE AT AUCTION • BUY A FORECLOSED HOME
ITY LOAN • BUY A LOT • BUY HOUSE PLA ___ • PULL BUILDING PERMITS • BUY A VACATION H
Y A TENANCY-IN-COMMON UNIT • BUY RE ___ A MOVIE OR CATALOG SHOOT • FURNISH YOUR H
IT FIXTURES • BUY A PROGRAMMABLE LIG ___ NCES • BUY FLOOR-CARE APPLIANCES • BUY EX
INCORPORATE FLUID ARCHITECTURE INTO ___ ARNISH • CHOOSE DECORATIVE TILES • CHOOSE
TS • GET SELF-CLEANING WINDOWS • CH ___ SELECT FLOORING • SELECT CARPETING • CHO
SYSTEM • BUY A HOME ALARM SYSTEM ___ OXIDE DETECTORS • BUY FIRE EXTINGUISHERS
INTER OR ELECTRICIAN • HIRE A GARDEN ___ PERFECT ROSEBUSH • BUY FLOWERING BULBS
GETABLE GARDEN • HIRE A GARDEN PROF ___ R SYSTEM • START A NEW LAWN • BUY A LAWN
• BUY AN OUTDOOR LIGHTING SYSTEM • ___ ECT PEACH • BUY AND SELL AT FARMERS' MARK
FRESH PRODUCE • SELECT MEAT • STOC ___ ASE A HOLIDAY HAM • BUY NATURAL BEEF • BUY
AND PEPPER • GET A CHEESESTEAK IN P ___ EATTLE • FIND CRAWDADS IN LOUISIANA • BUY A
Y ETHNIC INGREDIENTS • PURCHASE VIN ___ OFFEE • ORDER A GREAT CUP OF COFFEE • BUY
• CHOOSE A RESTAURANT FOR A BUSINE ___ OCK YOUR BAR • BUY AND SELL SPERM • CHO
GOOD PEDIATRICIAN • HIRE A CHILD THER ___ NEW CRIB • CHOOSE A STROLLER • BUY BABY
EAT NANNY • FIND THE RIGHT PRIVATE SC ___ RAM • SIGN YOUR CHILD UP FOR LESSONS • BU
DEOS AND MUSIC FOR YOUR CHILDREN • ___ R • HIRE AN ADOPTION AGENCY • GET YOUR CH
IREMENT COMMUNITY • CHOOSE AN ASS ___ IVING WILL • BUY A CEMETERY PLOT • PAY FOR
CINES • SAVE MONEY ON PRESCRIPTION ___ ONAL • CHOOSE A WHEELCHAIR • BUY HOME-U
DY PIERCING • OBTAIN BREAST IMPLANTS ___ ALTERNATIVE AND HOLISTIC PRACTITIONERS • C
SELF TO A DAY AT THE SPA • BOOK A MAS ___ Y AND SELL USED BOOKS • SHOP AT AN ANTIQU

Splurges & Rare Events

N ANTIQUE APPRAISED • BUY SILVERWARE • EVALUATE DEPRESSION-ERA GLASSWARE • BUY AND SELL STAMPS • BUY ANTIQUE FURN
• SCORE AUTOGRAPHS • TRADE YU-GI-OH CARDS • SNAG STAR WARS ACTION FIGURES • SELL YOUR VINYL RECORD COLLECTION •
COMPUTER • SHOP FOR A USED COMPUTER OR PERIPHERALS • CHOOSE A LAPTOP OR NOTEBOOK COMPUTER • SELL OR DONATE A
OMAIN NAME • BUY A HOME NETWORK • UPGRADE THE MEMORY IN YOUR COMPUTER • BUY COMPUTER SOFTWARE • CHOOSE A CD
VICE • NEGOTIATE YOUR LONG-DISTANCE PHONE SERVICE • BUY VIDEO AND COMPUTER GAMES • CHOOSE A FILM CAMERA • CHOOS
-VIDEO DISTRIBUTION SYSTEM • BUY A SERIOUS TV • CHOOSE BETWEEN CABLE AND SATELLITE TV • GET A DIGITAL VIDEO RECORDE
STEM • GET A PASSPORT, QUICK! • PURCHASE CHEAP AIRLINE TICKETS • FIND GREAT HOTEL DEALS • RENT THE BEST CAR FOR THE L
TY-FREE • SHIP FOREIGN PURCHASES TO THE UNITED STATES • TIP IN A FOREIGN COUNTRY • TIP PROPERLY IN NORTH AMERICA • BR
ISLANDS • RAFT THE GRAND CANYON • BOOK A CHEAP BUT AWESOME SAFARI • RENT A CAMEL IN CAIRO • GET SINGLE-MALT SCOTCI
R WAY ONTO A MOUNT EVEREST EXPEDITION • HIRE A TREKKING COMPANY IN NEPAL • RENT OR BUY A SATELLITE PHONE • BUY YOUR
SELL FOUND GOLF BALLS • BUY ATHLETIC SHOES • BUY A RACKET • BUY A GYM MEMBERSHIP • BUY AN AEROBIC FITNESS MACHINE
FISHING • GO SKYDIVING • BUY WEIGHTLIFTING EQUIPMENT • CHOOSE A CAR RACK OR CARRIER • BUY SKIS • BUY CLOTHES FOR CC
RAGE SALE • COMMISSION A CUSTOM-BUILT BICYCLE • BUY A PROPERLY FITTED HELMET • BUY THE OPTIMAL SLEEPING BAG • BUY A
Y-FISHING GEAR • BUY ROCK-CLIMBING EQUIPMENT • BUY A CASHMERE SWEATER • PURCHASE VINTAGE CLOTHING • SELL USED CL
ES AT A DISCOUNT • CHOOSE A BASIC WARDROBE FOR A MAN • BUY A MAN'S DRESS SHIRT • PICK OUT A NECKTIE • BUY A WOMAN'
OTHES • GET A GREAT-FITTING BRA • CHOOSE A HIGH-PERFORMANCE SWIM SUIT • HIGH PERFORMANCE WORKOUT CLOTHES • BUY
UY THE BASICS FOR YOUR CAR • BUY A USED CAR • BUY OR SELL A CAR ONLINE • BUY A HYBRID CAR • SELL A CAR • BUY A MOTOR

91 Buy a Private Island

It used to be that only the rich and famous owned car phones and private atolls, but now everyone's got a cell phone and islands can be purchased for less than a luxury auto. It's no big deal at all—search for an island on the Internet, contact its broker, fill out the paperwork, hire Tattoo, and voilà! Your own fantasy island.

Steps

1 Decide on location. In general, the colder the climate, the cheaper the island. A misty, rocky Scottish isle can be had for a mere $20,000, whereas tropical islands typically start at $1 million. Keep in mind that although you can buy an island, you can't rule it—every island for sale is already part of a sovereign nation, and you're subject to that country's laws.

2 Investigate what islands are on the market by searching Web sites such as Private Islands Online and Vladi Private Islands. Contact the owner or broker of each island and ask lots of questions: How isolated and accessible is it? Can it be developed? How are necessities supplied? What is the status of existing facilities and infrastructure for food and water, electricity and fuel?

3 Inquire about renting the island before you decide to purchase it. You test-drive a car, so why not take the island for a spin? Many owners rent their island properties for all or part of a year, with prices ranging from $55 (Ilha do Pico, Brazil) to $1,500 (Coupon Key, Florida) a day. A brief stay may show you that your Robinson Crusoe fantasy isn't as romantic as it seemed.

4 Before finalizing the purchase, check the ownership policy and political stability of the nation that governs the island. Make sure the government keeps a registry of deeds and guarantees unrestricted ownership. You don't want to lose your investment to a banana republic.

What to Look For

- Type and location of island
- Online island brokers
- Livability factors
- Rental options
- Stable government

Tips

Canada has more islands for sale than any other nation at prices far below those of tropical isles.

An island broker can also arrange for a manager to safeguard your island while you're away.

Warning

Make sure that someone on the mainland knows where your island is and how long you intend to stay—it's not uncommon to be stranded on your own island.

92 Hire a Skywriter

If you're looking for an unusual way to make a *huge* impression on your special someone, the sky's the limit. A single skywritten letter is 2,400 feet (731 m) tall—as high as two Empire State Buildings stacked on top of each other! This is sure to score major brownie points with your sweetie.

Steps

1 Find a skywriting service in the Yellow Pages or on the Internet. Some skywriters will fly in from out of state for a bit more money if there's no skywriting service in your area.

What to Look For

- Local skywriting service
- Clear, open location
- Simple, effective message

2 Figure out your budget. Messages run approximately $800 for up to 30 letters in your local area. Out-of-town rates are normally $1,000 for up to 30 letters plus expenses. Most skywriters can write up to 35 normal-size letters per flight.

3 Plan where you and your honey will be when viewing the message so that you're able to see it clearly and without obstruction. Choose an open spot, such as a football stadium or a beach, where you can comfortably hang out while waiting for the plane's arrival.

4 Compose a touching message for optimum impact, but keep it simple. If you're proposing, this task shouldn't be too difficult.

Tip

Hiring a skywriter can be done year-round, even in cold climates. If possible, plan for September and October, which tend to be the best weather months (as well as football season) in most areas of the United States.

93 Hire a Big-Name Band

So, your boss wants to book the hottest band in the land to impress the shareholders? Be prepared to shell out some serious cash if you're lucky or clever enough to break through to the appropriate agent and swing the deal.

Steps

1 Contact Pollstar (pollstar.com), which maintains the world's largest database of international concert tour information and booking agents, and purchase the annual *Booking Agency Directory* ($90). This contains information on more than 9,500 artists and a cross-index of agency personnel. Pollstar's annual *Talent Buyers Directory* is another useful tool (also about $90).

2 Budget several hundred thousand dollars for the one-time performance. Costs include transportation for the band and crew, accommodations and security.

3 Contact the agency or management company that represents the band you'd like to hire. If you're lucky enough to reach the band's agent or manager *and* find that the band is available when you need it, be prepared to discuss all relevant details including the nature of the event, date and time, venue, transportation, security, publicity, insurance and cost.

4 Write up what the industry calls a *firm offer* based on details discussed in your phone conversation. The document (which can be considered legal) should be a one-page outline that summarizes everything you would provide the band, as well as a deadline of no more than one week for the agent to respond to your offer. Fax the document directly to the agent.

5 Wait for the agent to review the terms of your offer with the artist and hope that it will be accepted.

6 Put your dancing shoes on.

What to Look For

- Pollstar's *Booking Agency Directory* and *Talent Buyers Directory*
- Band's agent or management company

Tips

Lingo is very important here. You probably won't get past the receptionist if you don't use this exact wording: "May I speak with the responsible agent for [band]?"

A booking agent may also coordinate the hiring of the band. It's worth asking before you invest in Pollstar's directories.

Warning

Even a verbal agreement may be legally binding. Be very clear about what you plan to do.

94 Get Into the High Rollers Room in Vegas, Baby

They have a nickname for the high rollers in Las Vegas: whales. Why? Because their credit line and bets are so huge that you can't help but notice them. In fact, major casinos worldwide maintain a full-time staff just to lure these loaded leviathans to their private gaming table.

What to Look For

- Seven-figure credit line
- Minimum $100,000 bets
- No-limit baccarat experience

Steps

1 Arrive with a massive bankroll. Becoming a bona fide high roller takes much more than betting big. The true high rollers—and there are only about 500 worldwide—need to have a credit line of $4 million to $5 million.

2 Make a name for yourself. Getting into the high rollers room is by invitation only. If you're worthy, then you won't even need to ask—the casinos will already know who you are and invite you and your family to stay and play as long as you like. Private jet transportation, luxury accommodations, gourmet cuisine, free show tickets, expensive gifts, fine wines, butlers and chauffeurs are all on the house.

3 Gamble big—very big—around $100,000 per bet. Australian billionaire Kerry Packer, the world's highest-stakes gambler, bets up to $375,000 per hand while playing seven blackjack hands at a time. His losses once amounted to $20 million in a weekend. Still think you can swim with these sharks?

4 Master baccarat, the richest game in the casino and the one most often played in the private high rollers' room. These are often no-limit games as maximum bets cramp a whale's style.

Tips

If you're really trying to achieve high roller status, gamble at Bellagio (bellagiolasvegas.com), which caters specifically to whales.

About 85 percent of high rollers are Asian, and 15 percent are women.

Warning

Gambling can be addictive.

95 Buy Someone a Star

It sounds romantic, doesn't it? Naming a star after your sweetheart, knowing that people will gaze upon it for eternity. As long as you're aware that official astronomical organizations will never recognize your star's name (and will laugh if you ask), it's your money to burn.

What to Look For

- Online star-naming companies
- Your star (look hard)

Steps

1 Be aware that no matter what claims a company makes, the star name you purchase and have registered has absolutely no validity among the scientific community, and will not be recognized by anyone else on the planet. Yes, it may be copyrighted, but you can copyright your grocery list. Sorry.

2 Search online for star-naming Web sites, such as International Star Registry (starregistry.com) or Buy-A-Star (buy-a-star.com), pay about $60 to $160 and you'll get a package that includes an official-looking parchment certificate with your star's name on it, a dedication date and telescopic coordinates of the star. But

Tips

There is nothing to prevent a star-naming company from selling the same star to different people.

Do not embarrass yourself by asking an astronomer to point the telescope toward your star.

wait—act now and you'll also receive an informative booklet with charts of the constellations, plus a larger, more detailed chart with your star encircled in red.

3 Conduct your own star search. Finding your star will probably be impossible without a telescope. Worse, the coordinates given by star-naming companies are often inaccurate. Most people who buy a star never actually see it.

4 Save your money. If you really want to name a star after someone, find a nice, twinkling star together (make sure it's not a planet or satellite), plot it on a star chart, name it, and print a certificate on fancy paper. It will be just as valid as the certificate from any commercial star-registry service.

96 Pay a Ransom

Although kidnappings are a rare event in First World countries, many rebel factions in unstable regions of the Third World consider kidnapping and extortion a customary means of earning revenue to support their cause. And ransom demands can run into the millions of dollars. Organized crime also poses a potential threat, particularly to wealthy families. If you're at high risk, here's what you need to do.

Steps

1 Purchase a kidnap/ransom and extortion insurance policy to protect you, your family and your employees if you live, work or travel in a high-risk zone. Companies such as InsureCast (insurecast.com), AIG (aig.com) and Chubb Executive Risk (chubb.com) offer plans to cover ransom payment, medical and psychiatric care.

2 Insure your business as well as yourself: Both personal and corporate assets are at risk when kidnappers attempt to extort ransom money.

3 Call local police to investigate in the event of extortion or a kidnapping. They will be able to add another layer of security and surveillance to the investigation process.

4 Contact specially trained experts, familiar with the local laws and the dynamics of kidnapping, to swiftly mobilize international resources. This person may work with a private detective to analyze notes, set up a drop site for the demanded money, and protect the premises and the threatened individuals.

5 Check your policy in advance: If you have purchased kidnap or extortion insurance, a private detective and trained crisis-management experts may be covered.

What to Look For

- Kidnap/ransom and extortion insurance
- Police
- Trained experts
- Private detective

Tips

If you travel frequently to high-risk regions—Colombia and Mexico particularly have large numbers of kidnappings—insurance coverage could save your life.

Insurance companies can also assist with crisis-management teams and employee training to minimize losses due to kidnap or ransom.

Warning

Ransom demands are growing each year. Today, there are usually a number of kidnappings in which demands run as high as $10 million.

97 Get Hot Tickets

We feel your pain: John Tesh is in town and you can't find front-row tickets anywhere. Fret not, because those hard-to-get tickets—Broadway hits, NCAA playoffs, Wimbledon, even the Olympics—are almost always available if you're willing to invest the time and the money. Here's how to dance the hot ticket tango.

Steps

1 Start with the least expensive ticket source, and move up from there if you have to. Call the venue directly or search one of the two primary online ticketing sources: TicketMaster.com or Tickets.com. You might get lucky.

2 See if anybody in your town is trying to unload his or her choice seats at a reasonable price. Get today's local paper and look under "Tickets" in the classifieds section. Local online classifieds are a good source as well. Nonbroker bids on eBay.com with FedEx delivery is another possible way to go, but it's not without risk. (See 10 Use Online Auction Sites.)

3 Now it gets more expensive, because you'll probably have to go through a ticket broker—a fast-talking dealer who hires people to stand in line for prime tickets or buys them from season ticket-holders, then resells them at considerably higher rates. (Technically, this is illegal in most states, but it's rarely prosecuted.) The two major broker Web sites are WebTickets.com and TicketsNow.com. If you go to eBay.com and click on eBay Stores and then click on "Tickets," you'll find dozens of other ticket broker Web sites.

4 Check out online concierge services, a route few people know about. They specialize in obtaining premium seats for sold-out events. Expect to pay top dollar for the service. Check out such sites as ManhattanConcierge.com and Concierge Services of Atlanta (csoa.com).

5 Arrive at the event early if you're desperate, with plenty of cash in hand to buy tickets from a scalper—essentially a tax-free ticket broker sans office. If the price is too high, wait until the show is about to start: Scalpers still holding tickets at the last minute will usually unload them at very reduced rates.

What to Look For

- Primary ticket providers
- Local newspaper or online ads
- Online ticket brokers
- Online and hotel concierge services
- Scalpers

Tips

If you're staying at a hotel, ask the concierge to assist you with finding hard-to-get tickets. Be sure to tip well for the service. (See 24 Tip Properly.)

Although it's illegal in most circumstances to resell tickets at higher than their face value, it's not illegal to purchase them.

Warning

Beware of counterfeit tickets, particularly from scalpers. It's very tough to distinguish the fakes from the real thing.

98 Hire a Limousine

So you drive a '77 Gremlin. That's OK. As long as you have some money saved up for a night on the town, you can still play millionaire by hiring a limousine. In fact, due to fierce competition, you can ride in just about any type of stretch limo for a lot less than you'd expect— if you know how to drive a hard bargain.

Steps

1 Assess your finances. A standard limousine (four to six passengers) will set you back about $40 to $80 per hour; a stretch limo (six to eight passengers) runs slightly more—about $60 to $100 per hour. Both have an hourly minimum of four to five hours (although this is usually negotiable). For specialty limos such as a Mercedes, a Hummer or a superstretch (up to 22 passengers), costs can top out at $3,000 for the night.

2 Research, research, research. Be sure the limo operator is licensed and insured. Decide what type of limo you want (standard, stretch, superstretch or specialty) and for how long, based on the event and the number of people in your party. List the amenities you're looking for, whether it's a bar, stereo, TV and DVD player, video-gaming system, intercom, sunroof, Jacuzzi, or all of that and a bag of chips. Prices may or may not be posted online. You'll need to do some phone work to get the best deal.

3 Find out the year and make of the limo you'll be hiring, its condition, and the complimentary amenities before you give a deposit. Make sure the deposit is refundable if the limo doesn't meet with your satisfaction. Many limo companies will advertise one type of car and show up at your door with something entirely different. Most list photos of their limos on their Web sites. If quality is a top priority, plan a visit to the limo company and reserve the exact limo that suits your needs.

4 Hire a quality driver. This is crucial—a bad driver can ruin your evening. Make sure the drivers are experienced, professional and know the area. If possible, fax an itinerary to the company beforehand so the driver knows where he or she is going and what to expect. When the driver shows up, be sure to communicate any special needs you may have.

5 Be sure to ask whose responsibility it is to stock the limo with any necessary party favors ahead of time. Some companies will provide everything you need; others expect you to bring your own. Sometimes you can negotiate a lower rate if you offer to stock the bar yourself.

6 Find out if gratuities are included in the rate; regardless, you'll be expected to tip your driver, so try to keep it separate.

What to Look For

- Licensed operator
- Desired amenities
- Late-model limo
- Experienced, professional driver
- Ample party supplies

Tips

Make sure your limo is ample enough to fit everyone comfortably. If you have six passengers, get a car that accommodates eight.

If you want premium liquor, negotiate that up front, or plan to bring your own.

Ask if smoking (or other activities) is allowed. Even If it's not, most drivers will look the other way if the price is right.

If it's truly a special occasion, don't be cheap. Like most things in life, you get what you pay for: Most higher-end limo companies have superior drivers, vehicles and accoutrements.

Try to clear everything with your driver in advance. He or she is your captain for the evening and can be your best friend or worst nightmare.

Warning

Make sure the limo company and their drivers are properly licensed and insured when making your reservation. This will ensure you are dealing with a reputable company.

99 Buy a Cryonic Chamber

We know what you're thinking: Cryonic freezing—preserving recently deceased humans in the hope that they may be revived in the future through new, undiscovered medical technologies—is for wackos and megalomaniacs. Since you can't take your money with you, why not bet your life insurance policy on a long shot?

Steps

1 Contact the nonprofit Alcor Life Extension Foundation (alcor.org), the world's largest provider of cryonics services with more than 580 active suspension members.

2 Choose from two cryonic suspension options: Neuro-suspension, which is the head only ($50,000), or whole body suspension ($120,000). An additional $25,000 surcharge is applied for international applicants ($15,000 for United Kingdom residents).

3 Complete the membership application and pay the $150 sign-up fee and $398 for annual dues. Sign Alcor's legal membership documents in the presence of two witnesses.

4 Die on your own. There is no legal precedent anywhere in the world allowing a cryonic procedure to take place prior to death.

What to Look For

- Alcor Web site
- Cryonic suspension type
- Membership fees and dues

Tips

"Minimum time at the lowest possible temperature" is the rule of thumb for transporting a corpse to the Alcor facility for cryonic treatment.

Cryonic suspension fees are often covered by term, whole or universal life insurance policies.

100 Rent Your Own Billboard

In Los Angeles, it's common for the almost-famous to rent a billboard and advertise their silicone-and-plastic-enhanced selves to speed up the "discovery" process. Or maybe you have more business-minded needs, like promoting a company or product. Here's how to get thousands of motorists to glimpse your 6-foot-tall mug while speeding by.

Steps

1 Communicate your message in eight words or less. If the billboard is near fast-moving traffic, the lettering should be at least 3 feet (.9 m) high. Standard billboards range from 6 by 12 feet (1.8 by 3.7 m) on the small end up to 20 by 60 feet (6.1 by 18.3 m).

2 Determine your budget. Depending on size and location, expect to pay from $75 to $200 per month for rural sites, and from $900 to $2,500 per month for city and interstate signs. If you're renting more than one billboard, negotiate a discount. The billboards on Sunset Boulevard in West Hollywood run $10,000 per month, whereas the monthly tab for the billboard in Jonesboro, Arkansas, is $525 entering town and $375 on your way back out.

3 Contact the advertising company that owns the billboard (usually posted on a lower corner). Most advertising companies will work with you on your objectives, budget, concept, design, execution and monitoring of traffic that passes by your ad.

What to Look For

- Clear objective and message
- Suitable size
- Fair price
- Heavy traffic location

Tip

If your cause is sufficiently just, a billboard company may be willing to donate billboard space. You'll still have to pay for the design, printing and mounting costs.

Warning

Tests show that billboards motivate very few people to contact you unless you are giving away a gift or money.

101 Take Out a Full-Page Ad in the *New York Times*

Purchasing print media is fairly easy, especially now that most daily newspapers are hurting for advertising revenue. If you're a first-time buyer and shooting for something as grandiose as a full page in the *New York Times,* either hire a media placement agency or simply contact the *Times'* advertising department directly. Open that wallet wide—a single-page ad in the *Times* costs about $125,000 for a one-time insertion.

Steps

1 Decide in which edition of the *Times* you'd like your ad to appear. Depending on the message and your audience, you may want to place it in the Sunday edition, a special news section, or a weekly theme section in the *New York Times Magazine.*

2 Reserve space by calling the *Times's* order fulfillment department. To place an ad through customer order fulfillment (COF), contact a representative by calling (212) 556-7777. Outside the New York metropolitan area, dial (800) 698-5515. When you call COF, an advertising service representative (ASR) will handle your request. To submit an ad online, go to nytadvertising.nytimes.com.

3 Give the ASR your ad information, which must include size, date, edition and position request (if applicable). The ASR assigns a reservation number to your ad and tells you how much it will cost. Have the ASR assign your ad a contract number. Also make sure to retain the reservation number, as all materials submitted for publication *must* have a reservation number.

4 Prepare an insertion order for your advertisement, which should include the following: reservation number; contract number; your name, billing address and phone number; day and date of insertion; section or position request; size and cost of the ad; and a description of the ad.

5 Ask for detailed production specs including size, line screen, restrictions on tints or halftones, and minimal type sizes. Create the ad yourself or have a professional do it. (See 158 Hire a Graphic Designer.)

6 Submit your materials electronically in an Adobe Portable Document Format (PDF) file if your ad is black-and-white. For color requirements, call the color services department at (212) 556-7729.

7 Arrange to pay for your ad prior to the publication deadline unless you've already established credit. You may prepay with a bank wire transfer, credit card or a guaranteed check from the advertiser or agency.

8 Establish credit with the *Times* by calling (212) 556-8777 or send an e-mail to creditdepartment@nytimes.com for an application. If your request is granted, the *Times* will establish a credit limit and applicable payment terms for you.

What to Look For

- Appropriate edition and section
- Order fulfillment department
- Reservation number
- Insertion order
- Description of ad
- Adobe Acrobat software
- Publication deadline
- Prepayment

Tip

If you have any questions after placing your reservation, the COF office is available to help you with advertising reservations, material processing and billing information: (212) 556-7777 or (800) 698-5515 outside the New York metropolitan area.

Warning

The *New York Times* maintains an advertising acceptability department whose staff members examine ads before publication to make sure they meet the paper's standards. The *Times* does not accept advertising that is misleading, inaccurate or fraudulent; that makes unfair competitive claims; or that fails to comply with its standards of decency and dignity. The advertising acceptability department can be contacted directly at (212) 556-7171 for questions or for a pamphlet containing detailed information on acceptability guidelines.

102 Hire a Butler

Do you want someone named Jeeves answering the door of your "cottage" in a tuxedo, or are you just looking for a temporary butler to work a special event? Locating the right person for your butlering needs takes some time, energy and bucks, but you'll be thankful when your household runs like a well-oiled machine.

Steps

1 Be very clear what you expect your potential butler to do before you begin the search and interviewing process. Tasks include arranging dinner parties, looking after your yacht, making travel arrangements, maintaining the household budget, looking after visitors, doing the laundry, getting the kids off to school, tending the garden, and directing other workers in the household. Many butlers double as a personal assistant, handling correspondence and coordinating your calendar.

2 Estimate the time it will take to accomplish those duties. Could you hire a part-time butler or simply a personal assistant? Determine this in advance to find the appropriate person for the job and your budget.

3 Decide whether or not you want your butler to be an in-house resident. This will be determined by how much living space you have and how many hours of work you require. It's very important for the butler to fit in with your family or household. Reputable agencies coordinate extensive interviews between you and butler candidate before the butler is placed.

4 Analyze the costs. A butler's salary ranges from $50,000 to $120,000, but beware of hidden costs, which can include a search fee to the placement agency (between 15 and 35 percent of the butler's first annual gross salary); a nonrefundable retainer fee; all travel-related expenses including airline tickets, car rentals, and hotels for candidates and consultants; and all benefits and taxes of the butler you hire.

5 Contact a placement agency such as Domestic Placement Network (dpnonline.com), the International Butler Academy (butlerschool.com) or International Guild of Professional Butlers (butlersguild.com).

6 Search for a butler via local and regional newspapers and statewide publications if you decide not to use an agency. Ask your local Employment Security Commission if it can provide a list of potential candidates as well as good advice on local publications for butler listings. Consider placing your own ad with other agency Web sites.

What to Look For

- Expected duties and their duration
- Hidden costs
- Placement agency
- Local and regional newspapers
- Employment Security Commission
- Job or headhunter Web sites

Tip

Placement agencies usually offer a free consultation without obligation.

Warning

If you don't want your butler to reside on-site, it's still your responsibility to pay for his accommodations and transportation to and from your home as well as any work-related transportation.

103 Acquire a Professional Sports Team

You were always the last to be picked when the neighborhood kids chose teams, but now you're a millionaire and revenge is sweet. The owner of a pro sports team is pretty much a god, trading players at a whim and even relocating the team if the desire strikes. And all you need to get in the game is money—a lot of money.

Steps

1 Evaluate your financial situation. To purchase a controlling share (51 percent) of a major sports franchise, a prospective owner needs a minimum net worth of approximately $250 million. If you don't have it on your own, consider forming a partnership with other potential buyers.

2 Research the playing field. Look at the 131 franchises that make up the major sports leagues, and figure out which teams are for sale or need investors. Poor performers can be a great bargain— billionaire Mark Cuban bought the last-place Dallas Mavericks in 2000 for only $280 million.

3 Consider starting with a minor-league team. Minor-league sports franchises range from about $2.5 million for a Class A team to around $10 million for a AAA club.

4 Arrange to meet with the team's owner(s) or brokers. Most sports team negotiations are done at the dinner table: The prospective buyers and sellers talk sports over food, while the brokers and contract lawyers handle the fine print.

5 Hire a professional sports franchise brokerage firm, such as Game Plan (gameplanllc.com) or Bryan Cave (bryancave.com), to negotiate a selling price and finalize the acquisition.

6 Pack up and relocate your team to a competing city that offers better incentive subsidies, such as a new stadium. Pro team owners have the power to move teams, sell or trade players, and even determine ticket prices, but the political ramifications can be extreme (not to mention the damage to your popularity).

What to Look For

- Partial or full ownership
- Underachieving teams
- Informal negotiations
- Sport franchise brokerage firm
- Incentives for relocation

Warning

As the owner, like the coach, you'll find your reputation will be linked directly to your team's performance. Win the championship and you're a saint; sink into last place and you're the city's biggest burden.

104 Buy a Personal Jet

Ever since Bill Lear revolutionized the private jet market with the introduction of his Learjet 23 in 1964, corporate chief executives and wealthy travelers have been flying in style on custom jet aircraft. The business jet has become so common that most passengers are middle management types. In fact, it's now a buyer's market.

Steps

1 Do a cost-benefit analysis before you spring for a private jet. Aviation experts suggest that 350 to 400 hours of flight time per year usually justifies full ownership of a jet. Otherwise, you should consider fractional ownership (see Tips).

2 Consider the hidden costs. Along with a price tag that ranges from $6 million to $50 million for a new private jet, factor in necessities such as insurance, fuel, catering and pilots—who are in short supply. Aircraft management companies will take care of these needs for about $100,000 to $200,000 per year, depending on the size and usage of the jet.

3 Determine the size and flying range you'll need. Light jets ($3 million to $8 million) can take 5 to 8 passengers roughly 2,000 miles (3,219 km); midsize executive jets ($9 million to $16 million) can take up to 9 passengers from 2,000 to 3,000 miles (3,219 to 4,828 km); and large executive jets ($17 million to $45 million) can carry 12 passengers more than 4,000 miles (6,437 km). See the chart below for some specific models.

4 When you're ready to buy, contact private jet manufacturers and ask for aircraft specifications and pricing. Next, shop online via private jet dealers such as CharterAuction.com, which sells new and used jets, including repossessed aircraft at deep discounts.

Tips

Consider fractional ownership: You purchase a share in a jet plane from a management company (mostly as a tax deduction), then pay a monthly fee and hourly operations costs. On as little as four hours' notice, the management company sends out whichever jet is most conveniently located.

See 554 Rent an Aircraft.

Warning

A used jet may not be such a great deal. To land at many U.S. airports a jet must be compliant with Stage 3 federal aviation regulations. Converting a private jet to comply with regulations takes several hundred thousand dollars and many months of repair time, as most private jet aircraft repair centers are already backlogged.

AIRCRAFT	PRICE (millions)	RANGE (nautical miles/km)	SPEED (Mach)	LENGTH (feet/m)	CAPACITY (passengers)
Learjet 45	$9.5	2,100/3,889	.81	58/17.7	Up to 9
Boeing Business Jet	$48	6,200/11,482	.82	110/33.5	Up to 25
Cessna Citation X	$18.5	3,400/6,297	.92	72/22	Up to 10
Gulfstream V	$41	6,500/12,038	.87	96/29.3	Up to 19
Dassault Falcon 2000	$21	3,000/5,556	.85	66/20.1	Up to 12

105 Acquire a Television Network

Ted Turner, watch out. All you need to own a TV network is a whole lot of money and a good lawyer. The bad news: The Federal Communications Commission (FCC) isn't accepting applications for new television networks until the transition from analog to digital broadcasting is complete (circa 2006). The good news: Acquisitions are still possible, but you'll have to follow these FCC guidelines.

Steps

1 Contact the current owner of the network you'd like to acquire.

2 Sign and submit FCC Form 314, the Application for Consent to Assignment of Broadcast Construction Permit or License. Applicants who apply to purchase a station may not take over the operation until the FCC approves the application.

3 Submit a letter of consummation within 90 days, once Form 314 is approved. Within that same time period, you must submit the Ownership Report, using FCC Form 323 for commercial stations, or FCC Form 323-E for noncommercial educational stations.

4 File FCC Form 315, the Application for Consent to Transfer of Control of Corporation Holding Broadcast Station Construction Permit or License, when the controlling block of shares of the broadcasting company is transferred to you.

5 Mail your broadcast applications to the FCC in triplicate along with the appropriate filing fees. The application fee generally runs around $800, with an additional $240 for your license. Applications for noncommercial educational stations do not require a filing fee.

What to Look For

- A winning lottery ticket
- A good lawyer
- Television station or network for sale
- FCC guidelines
- FCC Forms 314, 323/323-E, 315 and 316
- Filing fees

Tip

Television broadcast regulations appear in Title 47, Sections 73.601 to 73.699 and 73.1001 to 73.5009 of the Code of Federal Regulations. You can access these regulations at www.gpo.gov/nara/cfr/ or obtain them from the Government Printing Office.

106 Acquire a Bodyguard

There are two reasons for hiring a bodyguard: You need protection or you want to look like someone who needs protection. If you're in the second group, simply locate a large guy with a suit, shades and one of those little ear radios. If you really need protection, read on.

Steps

1 Educate yourself about the range of available services. Bodyguards are more than big guys with guns. Top security professionals are likely to have specialized driving skills, weapons training, risk avoidance skills and medical training.

2 Look in the phone book or online for security services in your area. Verify that the companies are licensed to operate within your state and that they are committed to working within the law.

3 If you still feel unsafe, consider a new line of work—or new friends.

What to Look For

- Specific skills of security personnel
- Proper licenses

Tip

Many full-service security companies offer training courses for clients. This is a good way to understand potential risks and enhance your security.

107 Book a Luxury Cruise Around the World

Magellan led the first world cruise, and since then it's been the ultimate way to explore in luxurious comfort. Essentially you're a full-time passenger along a cruise line's entire seasonal route, staying on while most other passengers disembark after traveling a segment. On a typical four-month voyage, you may visit more than 50 seaports in dozens of countries.

Steps

1 Examine the chart at right and decide which of the five cruises currently offered best fits your desired itinerary. Visit each cruise ship company's Web site to gather more details about each world cruise. Most world cruises depart from the United States in the winter and sail to tropical regions.

2 Decide how much you're willing to spend. Prices for a 108-day trip aboard the Radisson *Seven Seas Mariner* range from $50,000 for a deluxe suite to $197,000 for a master suite. (Of course, that's per person—but if you have to ask . . .)

3 Do some research. The Cruise Critic Web site (cruisecritic.com) is also an excellent source for world cruise information.

4 Book as far in advance as possible, at least six to eight months. Unlike virtually every other cruise, world cruises are never available at a discount at the last minute because of how trip segments are sold. You can, however, earn discounts for early reservations, early payment and repeat travel.

5 Plan carefully: World cruise cancellation penalties are severe— a 100 percent loss if you cancel 74 days or less prior to selling. Trip cancellation and worldwide medical insurance are strongly recommended. See 434 Get Travel Insurance.

6 Pack appropriately. The *Queen Elizabeth 2,* for example, hosts more than 50 formal evenings during its world cruise. If you're flying to your departure port, arrange to have your excess luggage freighted to the port in advance. See 65 Buy or Rent a Tuxedo.

What to Look For

- Destination
- Early booking
- Trip insurance

Tip

Freighter travel offers the best world cruise value, with fares typically being from $70 to $130 per day lower than conventional cruise ship rates. The majority of freighter cruises range in duration from about 30 to 75 days. See 445 Choose a Cheap Cruise.

COMPANY	DEPARTURE CITY	ARRIVAL CITY	TRIP LENGTH	PORTS OF CALL
Holland America (hollandamerica.com)	Fort Lauderdale	Los Angeles	108 days	Fort-de-France, Barbados, Puerto Ordaz, Devil's Island, Fortaleza, Salvador de Bahia, Rio de Janeiro, Buenos Aires, Palmer Station, Ushuaia, Punta Arenas, Arica, General San Martin, Callao, Papeete, Bora Bora, Auckland, Wellington, Sydney, Cairns, Guam, Hong Kong, Shanghai, Osaka, Honolulu.
Peter Deilmann Cruises (deilmann-cruises.com)	Las Palmas	Venice	136 days	Dakar, Rio de Janeiro, Buenos Aires, Port Stanley, Cape Horn, Ushuaia, Valparaiso, Easter Island, Papeete, Noumea, Manila, Yokohama, Shanghai, Hong Kong, Singapore, Colombo, Muscat, Heraklion, Dubrovnik.
Queen Elizabeth 2 (cunard.com)	New York	New York	106 days	Fort Lauderdale, Cartageña, Balboa, Acapulco, Los Angeles, Honolulu, Papeete, Moorea, Auckland, Padang, Manila, Kagoshima, Taipei, Hong Kong, Laem Chabang, Singapore, Kochi, Mumbai, Victoria, Port Louis, Durban, Cape Town.
Crystal Cruises (crystalcruises.com)	Buenos Aires	Valparaiso	104 days	Montevideo, Puerto Madryn, Port Stanley, Ushuaia, Punta Arenas, Puerto Montt, Valparaiso.
Radisson *Seven Seas Mariner* (explore.rssc.com)	Los Angeles	Fort Lauderdale	108 days	Nuku Hiva, Papeete, Rarotonga, Sydney, Noumea, Port Vila, Honiara, Guam, Kobe, Hong Kong, Singapore, Penang, Cochin, Mahe, Mombasa, Durban, Cape Town, Luderitz, Jamestown, Fortaleza, St. Kitts.

108 Sell Your Fur Coat

Maybe you've just moved to Miami. Or maybe that coat you spent thousands on a few years ago is woefully out of date now. Turn to one of several fur companies that buy and sell used furs on a consignment basis—*if* it's in good condition.

Steps

1 Learn as much as you can about your fur beforehand. What kind of fur is it and how old is it? What is the coat's style and size?

2 Get your coat appraised at a fur specialist (look under "Fur Dealers" in the Yellow Pages). U.S. law requires furriers to appraise garments in person. Age has less to do with the value of a used garment than the care it has been given over the years (proper cold storage during the summer months is a huge factor).

3 Send your coat to one of three retailers that purchase or consign used fur from anyone in the United States: Henry Cowit Inc. and Ritz Furs in New York City, and Chicago Fur Outlet in Chicago. After inspection, they'll give you an estimated resale price.

4 Sell your coat through a newspaper (preferably, a cold-climate region) or an online ad on eBay.com or eFurs.com.

What to Look For

- Type and quality of fur
- Age of coat
- Size, style and condition of coat
- Professional appraisal
- Reputable fur retailer
- Advertise in cold climates
- Online auction sites

Tips

It's easier to resell a darker fur such as mink or sable.

Donate a fur coat that's in bad condition to a charity as a tax deduction. Furriers usually don't resell coats in bad condition.

109 Book a Trip on the Orient-Express

Since 1883, when this fabled train made its inaugural journey between Paris and Istanbul, the Orient-Express has been synonymous with decadence, scandal and adventure. If you've always wanted to experience the romantic era of deluxe rail travel, here's your ticket to ride.

Steps

1 Choose which continent you want to tour. The Orient-Express company operates privately owned, custom-built trains on four continents: Europe, Asia, Australia and North America.

2 Choose a route. Some routes are only one-way either direction and others, such as North America, are Grand Tours (depends on what continent you want to travel on). Meals, tea, coffee and gratuities are included. Fares are per person and based on double occupancy. Private compartments are available for an additional fee.

3 Book your trip at Orient-Express.com or through a travel agent. Since most Orient-Express routes are one-way, it's usually a good idea to have a travel agent arrange your vacation around the train ride, including airline flights and hotel accommodations.

What to Look For

- Destination
- Route
- Glamour
- Intrigue

Tip

The butler did it.

Warning

It is the passenger's responsibility to ensure that he or she complies with any necessary visa or vaccination requirements.

ROUTE	LENGTH OF TRIP	PRICES
Venice Simplon Orient-Express		
London-Paris	1 day	$1,280*
London-Paris-Venice (and vice versa)	2 days/1 night	$4,100**
London-Paris-Venice-Rome	3 days/2 nights	$5,140**
Venice-Prague-Paris-London	5 days/4 nights	$5,020**
Paris-Budapest-Bucharest-Istanbul (and vice versa)	6 days/5 nights	$11,340**
The Grand Tour of Great Britain (United Kingdom)		
London-York-Edinburgh-Chester-Bath	7 days/6 nights	$5,135
Eastern & Oriental Express (Singapore, Malaysia and Thailand)		
Singapore–Bangkok (and vice versa)	3 days/2 nights	$1,490 to $3,110
Singapore–Chiang Mai	4 days/3 nights	$1,840 to $3,570
Bangkok–Chiang Mai	2 days/1 night	$910 to $1,650
Bangkok–Chiang Mai–River Kwai–Bangkok	3 days/2 nights	$1,490 to $3,000
American Orient-Express (United States and Canada)*		
National Parks of the West	8 days/7 nights	$3,190 to $5,890
The Great Trans-Canada Rail Journey	10 days/9 nights	$3,990 to $7,209
The Great Northwest and Rockies	8 days/7 nights	$3,190 to $5,890
The Pacific Coast Explorer	8 days/7 nights	$2,590 to $4,990
The Antebellum South	8 days/7 nights	$2,590 to $4,990

* Price is per person based on Day Car (2003)

** Price is based on a Double Cabin (sharing) (2003)

***All prices are per person, double occupancy

110 Become a Wine Maker

There are many ways to make a fortune, but buying a winery isn't one of them. Those who can afford to plunk down several million dollars on a boutique winery may be more into the bucolic lifestyle and bragging rights than future profits. Buying a winery outright is the most expensive way to get into the business, but it's also the easiest.

Steps

1   Research what's involved with wine making. The University of California at Davis has a world-renowned department of viticulture and enology offering programs in all aspects of the business. Visit www.wineserver.ucdavis.edu for more information.

2   Take stock of your assets and your determination. Producing quality wines year after year takes expertise in microbiology, agronomy, marketing, enology and machine repair, or the time and money to hire experts. Wine making is hard work regardless of whether it turns a profit and requires 100 percent determination and dedication.

3   Choose a location. Wines from states other than California, Oregon and Washington will be difficult to market. Every wine-growing region has different microclimates suited to the cultivation of specific varietals. If you favor one type of wine over another, buy a winery where those grapes grow.

4   Consider buying a winery Down Under. Australia is quickly becoming one of the world's fastest-growing wine exporters by volume, and Aussie vineyards are dirt cheap compared with those in California's wine country.

5   Find out if the winery has a strong, popular public identity, up-to-date equipment and facilities, and established distribution and sales networks. If growth is important, make sure that the existing facilities have room to expand.

6   Establish an annual output. Most U.S. wineries are small, family- or individually owned businesses, and produce from 3,000 to 10,000 cases per year. Anything more and you're leaving boutique territory and venturing into the mass-market realm.

7   Retain quality personnel. If the winery is strongly associated with a well-regarded wine maker, it's important that he or she stay on. Consistency is crucial to a winery's success.

8   Determine whether you want to cultivate your own grapes or just own a wine-making facility. In the Napa Valley, an acre of prime

What to Look For

- Expertise in wine making
- Suitable location for varietal
- Strong brand image
- Boutique production quotas
- Expert wine maker
- Cultivating vineyard versus buying grapes
- Tasting room

Tip

Because of the wide range of wineries, there is no industry standard for fixing the value of any one property. However, expect to part with at least $13 million for a small Napa Valley winery.

vineyard goes for about $64,000 to $102,000, not including the additional $15,000 to $20,000 to plant, maintain and harvest each acre. If you don't have the capital to invest in starting an average boutique vineyard—which won't produce for three years—consider purchasing grapes from growers. You'll knock five years off getting your brand to market—three for the vines to bear fruit and two to age your reds.

9 Decide if you want to build a tasting room (or keep an existing one), and who will manage it while you're away. Direct sales allow you to keep 100 percent profit; sell through a distributor and your share drops to 50 percent.

111 Purchase a Private/Custom Bottling of Wine

You don't need to grow or crush a single grape to be a wine maker. Welcome to the golden age of the American wine business, where wine-making companies do all the work and you get all the credit. All you need to provide is the money.

Steps

1 Express yourself. Making your own label is the easiest way to create custom bottles of wine and champagne. Simply design a label and have a wine-making company slap it on a bottle. Voilà! *Votre Nom Ici Vineyards* is in business. Most custom bottlers have an in-house graphics department to assist you in developing your label or have your own done (see 158 Hire a Graphic Designer). You'll also have to make other tough decisions: plastic versus wood corks, and the color of the embossed foil. Prices for custom blended and labeled wines start at about $45 per bottle.

2 Immerse yourself in the process from start to finish. Making a custom crush is for serious wine enthusiasts. Experts from wine-making companies such as California's Associated Vintage Group (AVG) assist you through the entire process of creating your own wine—say a Bordeaux-style blend of Cabernet and Merlot. You'll be involved in deciding which grapes to purchase, what ratio to use in blending, which fermentation and aging techniques to use (oak barrel or stainless steel tank), and what type of bottle and label design to pick. Prices for custom crush red wines are about $60 per case, based on 3,000 cases. Expect to pay slightly less for whites.

What to Look For

- Wine-making company
- Designer label
- Personalized blend
- Custom crush

Tip

For under $100 you can purchase a home wine-making kit, which includes a 6-gallon (22.7 l) primary fermenter, a hydrometer, a 5-gallon (19 l) glass carboy, bottle brush, wing-style hand corker, racking tube, airlock adapter, and other tools of the trade.

112 Buy a Thoroughbred Racehorse

Fantasizing about seeing your colors on the next Seabiscuit or Secretariat? Chomping at the bit to make your own run for the roses? A good place to start is the racetrack. Owning a racehorse is an exhilarating, rewarding pursuit if you know how to play the game.

Steps

1 Decide if you have the knowledge to buy on your own or if you need help. If you know very little about buying racehorses, a bloodstock agent, who is paid a commission to buy and sell horses, will offer advice and recommend those that meet your budget. Horse trainers may also offer important advice.

2 Factor in all the costs before you make a purchase. Expect to spend $25,000 to $30,000 annually to keep a horse in training. Costs include $35 to $100 per day for training expenses, $150 to $500 per month for vet charges, and $100 for monthly shoeing expenses. Don't forget the hay, straw, grain and other dietary supplements to keep your horse in tip-top racing condition.

3 Decide whether you want to own a racehorse outright, share an interest in one with a partnership, or invest in multiple horses through a syndicate. Many partnerships advertise in racing trade publications and host Web sites that list their horses and track records. Shop around; contact numerous syndicate managers and prospective partnerships before you invest.

4 Buy a racehorse in one of three ways: through a claiming race, at auction or through a private purchase. See the chart (right) for details.

5 Hire a trainer. The best source for locating an experienced horse trainer is RaceHorseTrainers.com, sponsored by the United Thoroughbred Trainers of America Inc.

6 Obtain a racing license. Owners must have a license in order to participate in races. Each state has its own licensing applications, procedures and fees.

7 Register your Thoroughbred with the Jockey Club. A copy of the registration papers must be kept on file at the racetrack during the period that the horse is racing. These papers include the horse's name, pedigree and physical description.

What to Look For

- Bloodstock agent and trainer
- Total cost of ownership
- Private ownership versus partnerships
- Claiming race, auction or private sale
- Racing license, registration and colors
- Birth dates of yearlings
- Yearlings versus trainers

Tips

Thoroughbred refers to a breed of horses.

The birth date is important for a yearling because all Thoroughbreds are given a January 1 birthday by racing authorities. A foal born near that date will therefore have a developmental jump on a horse born later in the year. That edge can be crucial when they begin racing as two-year-olds.

First-time buyers should consider a horse already in training (rather than a yearling), because it can race immediately.

The average Thoroughbred races about 12 times a year.

8 Apply for colors with the Jockey Club. Brightly colored racing silks must be worn every time a jockey rides your horse; your pattern will become your trademark at the track.

9 Recoup your investment by finishing in the top five. Typically, the winning horse takes home 60 percent of the listed purse, 20 percent goes to second place, 12 percent to third, 6 percent to fourth and 2 percent to fifth place. A horse that performs consistently well will increase in claim value and can be worth millions as a breeder depending on its pedigree.

VENUE	DETAILS
Claiming Race	• Quickest and most popular way to buy affordable horses in the United States. • All horses running are for sale. Price is set before race, based on quality of horse. • Rates start at about $4,000 for low-level horses, $8,000 to $12,000 for top breeds. • Prices not negotiable, unless two buyers bid on same horse. • Horses are sold as is; cannot be inspected by veterinarian before sale. • Claimed horse is yours at end of race—owner's permit, housing and transportation are your immediate responsibility.
Auction	• Horses usually grouped by type being sold: yearlings, horses in training or brood mares. • Horses are listed in auction sales catalogs, with family tree and date of birth (if horse is a yearling). Bold-type listing means horse has won stakes race—expect to pay more. • Hire bloodstock agent to help if you're new to Thoroughbred buying. • Most popular Thoroughbred auction in United States is at Keeneland, near Lexington, Kentucky.
Private Purchase	• Easiest way to purchase a horse. • Horse sold to you directly from stud at negotiated price. • Lets you get the best possible advice from trainer or bloodstock agent before you buy. • Horse can be examined by vet before sale.
WARNING	When you buy a racehorse at a claiming race or auction, be prepared to pay for, insure, transport and house the horse immediately after the race or at the auction's fall of hammer.

113 Buy a Villa in Tuscany

So you just finished reading Frances Mayes's *Under the Tuscan Sun: At Home in Italy,* and now you want your own romantic villa in this charming region of Italy. Well, it's not that simple. Buying any home is a complicated process, but buying one in a foreign country is a recipe for disaster unless you do your homework. Here's the assignment.

Steps

1 Decide exactly where in Tuscany you want to buy your villa based on careful research over the course of many trips to the region. The most common complaint among foreign homeowners about buying a Tuscan villa is that they didn't do enough research and regret the location they chose. Where are the local airports and train stations? Is the area accessible in harsh winters? What are the locals like? Make sure that you love the locale and your neighbors just as much as the house.

2 Figure out the exact type of villa you want and how much property you're willing to take on. Consider how much land you want to maintain, who will maintain it while you're away, and how much living space you need to be comfortable.

3 If your real estate agent asks, sign the *Proposta irrevocabile d'acquisto,* once you've found your dream villa and you're ready to make an offer. Although this means *irrevocable proposal of purchase,* it's not a binding document and doesn't mean you've reserved the villa even though there's been an offer price and a written acceptance by the seller. This piece of paper is only enforceable between the seller and the real estate agent.

4 Sign the *compremesso,* the first of two binding contracts you enter with the seller once you've agreed on a price. The *compremesso* is basically a proof of intention to buy the villa and is binding in a court of law. It includes information such as the seller and the buyer, description of the property to be sold, the price, and the date of the final contract, or *rogito.* Once you and the seller have signed the *compremesso,* you are committed by law to the transfer of the property. You may still withdraw, but at the risk of losing your deposit.

5 Obtain a *codice fiscale,* or tax code, which you need in order to pay tax on the building. The *codice fiscale* works just like a tax identification number and is easy to apply for.

6 Autograph the *rogito,* pop the cork and let the *vino* flow! This final contract is a legally binding document that requires the presence of a *notaio,* or notary public, to oversee the signing of the *rogito* (describes the property and land) and collect tax on the property. The *rogito* also includes the date of the sale, name of the seller, the new buyer (that's you), and the declared value of the property.

What to Look For

- Location, location, location
- Desired type and size of villa
- *Proposta irrevocabile d'acquisto* (purchase proposal)
- *Compremesso* (preliminary contract)
- *Codice fiscale* (tax ID number)
- *Rogito* (final contract)
- *Notaio* (notary public)

Tip

If you don't speak Italian, you can have a *scrittura privata,* or simplified version of the contract, read aloud by the notary and directly interpreted by a representative.

Warnings

The cost of being a nonresident in Italy can be very high: Property tax as well as water, electricity and telephone bills are often as much as 50 percent more for nonresidents.

Within the time limit stipulated in the *proposta irrevocabile d'acquisto,* if the real estate agent is approached by another buyer who makes a better offer for the same property, the agent can make another "irrevocable proposal to buy" for the same property without your knowledge, even though doing that isn't considered respectable.

114 Hire a Personal Chef

A personal chef can be a godsend and surprisingly easy to find. You could hire one to help you eat better or lose weight, to avoid grocery shopping or simply to save time. But the best part is that you don't have to clean the kitchen, and there's always some gourmet snack in the freezer just waiting to be reheated.

Steps

1 Know the difference between a personal chef and a private chef. The former serves several clients, usually one per day, and provides multiple meals that are stored and frozen for the week. The latter is usually a live-in employee who prepares up to three meals per day.

2 Determine what your weekly budget is for your personal chef. The average price for a meal that feeds a family of four is about $40, not including groceries. Expect to pay about $275 (plus groceries) for a week of meals for two people, $250 for one person. Prices vary depending on the region and level of service that is desired.

3 Decide exactly what you'd like your chef to do. Some stock the fridge with additional meals for the week. Others bring their own pots, pans and utensils while preparing your entrées on-site.

4 Begin your search online or in your local newspaper. Contact Personal Chefs Network (personalchefsnetwork.com) and Hire a Chef (hireachef.com) for free lists of personal chefs in your area.

5 Be sure that your chef not only meets your culinary requirements but also has a disposition that fits well with you and your family, since he or she will become a regular in your home. And don't hesitate to ask for references.

6 Tell your personal chef what your likes and dislikes are as well as any individual dietary requirements, and specific requests so that he or she can plan your menu accordingly. Have your chef submit menus for your approval, and ask if packaging, labeling and storing your entrées are all features included in the agreed-upon price.

What to Look For

- Rates and services
- Packaged meals
- Cooking equipment
- Web sites listing personal chefs
- References
- Menu requests

Tip

During the interview process, ask chefs whether they are certified or working toward their Certified Personal Chef designation, which was created in 1996. Currently, only one out of five active personal chefs has obtained a CPC certificate, according to hireachef.com.

Warning

Make sure that your personal chef is insured in the unfortunate event that he or she causes injury to you or your family.

115 Purchase Cuban Cigars

So you want to want to savor the flavor of communism, eh? You may not know a Romeo y Julieta from a Swisher Sweet, but the allure of smoking smuggled goods is too tempting to pass up. Buying Cubans isn't the hard part—it's not getting duped that's difficult.

Steps

1 Know what you're getting into. Ever since the United States placed economic sanctions on the Cuban government in 1963, it has been illegal to import Cuban cigars into the United States. But there is an exception: Visitors returning from a licensed visit to Cuba can bring Cuban cigars into the United States, provided the cigars are for personal use (not resale) and that their value does not exceed $100.

2 Be aware of the risks. It's illegal to buy, sell, trade or otherwise engage in transactions involving Cuban cigars in the United States, even if they were purchased from a foreign country via the Internet. You may face civil fines of up to $55,000 per violation and criminal prosecution, but the more likely punishment will be the confiscation of your cigars.

3 Expect to pay $170 to $500 for a box of Cuban cigars; anything less is suspicious. Dozens of online retailers will express-mail boxes of "Cuban" cigars to you anywhere in the world, including the United States. However, most of those mailed to the States are fakes, regardless of guarantees. And since you were trying to make an illegal purchase, you really have no one to file a complaint with.

4 Go north. The easiest and surest way to get Cuban cigars safely past customs is to buy them in Canada and repackage them. Remove the rings and place the cigars in a different (not Cuban) box. Clerks in many Canadian cigar stores will do this for you, but watch for the bait-and-switch. Most customs agents won't bother to detain you over unidentifiable cigars (it's not like you're smuggling heroin). Replace the rings after you return home.

5 Play it safe. If you just want to smoke an authentic Cuban cigar while you're traveling abroad, purchase one at an upscale hotel. You'll pay top dollar, but you'll most likely be buying the real thing.

What to Look For

- Risk of fine and prosecution
- Fake Cubans
- Internet retailers
- Canadian cigar stores
- Upscale hotel abroad

Tips

Avoid cigar stores that advertise Cuban cigars, particularly "discounted" Cubans—you're being targeted for a reason and are probably being sold a counterfeit.

The easiest way to spot a fake is to inspect the ring. If it's loose or out of place, the cigar is either fake or dehydrated. Also, avoid Cuban cigars wrapped in plastic—a sure sign that they were made by machine.

Warning

Never smuggle Cuban cigars in from Jamaica. Customs officials routinely suspect Jamaican visitors of smuggling marijuana and inspect their bags thoroughly.

116 Hire a Ghostwriter to Pen Your Memoirs

Everyone tells you to write a book about your life because it would make a phenomenal story. You would, but your writing skills stink. Time to hire a ghostwriter to weave your stories, diaries and research into a best seller with your name on the cover. Next stop: Oprah!

Steps

1 Find a ghostwriter. Look in the classified ads of publications such as *Writer's Digest* and *Writers' Journal*, and on writer-based Web sites with message boards where ghostwriters advertise their services.

2 Get an estimate of the costs as well as how long the project will take. Your ghost will charge either a project fee (national average is $15,000 to $25,000), an hourly rate ($25 to $85 per hour), or by the page ($100 to $175 per page). The writer will charge more if he or she gets credit, or if research is involved. In either case, a share of royalties can be part of the agreement (particularly if the writer thinks your memoirs are publishable).

3 Be sure to check the credentials of the ghostwriter you're considering and ask for references. Legitimate freelancers will be happy to provide this information. Scrutinize samples of the ghostwriter's published material and check to see if it meets the quality and style that you're looking for. Talk with previous employers.

4 Realize that as you investigate ghostwriters, they will also be evaluating whether they can work with you and whether writing your memoirs is even worth the effort. If you can't relate well to a ghostwriter during initial meetings or conversations, you may be better off parting ways.

5 Make clear at the outset if you want the ghostwriter's help to create a book proposal and pitch it to an agent or a publishing house. It's usually not the ghostwriter's job to get your memoirs published—just to write them. (See 164 Hire a Literary Agent.)

6 Ask your writer to send you a table of contents and a few pages of text so you can be sure that he or she has a good grasp of the project before you sign a contract. Ghostwriters will often lay out the structure of a book and provide you with a sample chapter for a partial fee.

7 Establish in the contract if you want sole authorship (where the ghostwriter receives no credit or mention at all). This is crucial for avoiding future misunderstandings and lawsuits.

8 Have a publisher, acquisitions editor or literary lawyer examine the contract for you on *your* behalf before you sign it. Remember, what is not in the contract is as important as what is in it.

9 Give your ghost all the materials that you possess on the subject, and as many interviews as needed once the contract is signed.

What to Look For

- Writers' publications
- Writers' message boards
- Time and cost estimates
- Credentials and references
- Compatibility
- Sample table of contents and chapter
- Contract

Tips

Bringing in a ghostwriter during the early stages of a project often shortens the process.

Ghostwriters not only write, they also edit, collaborate and research on behalf of the client. Sometimes they write nothing at all and simply coach.

To help you develop your storytelling skills, see if your ghostwriter is willing to coach you in the areas where you're weakest. It may cost you more, but you'll learn faster with this type of constructive criticism.

Warning

Reimbursement of the ghostwriter's phone, postage and other minimal out-of-pocket expenses are usually your responsibility.

117 Commission Original Artwork

Although there are many artists who produce commissioned art—from family portraits to custom-made wedding rings—finding just the right artist for the job is the most important and the hardest step.

Steps

1 Determine what media you're interested in (painting, sculpture, film) and the project's budget before you begin searching for an artist. (See 118 Immortalize Your Spouse in a Sculpture.) You'll find out quickly whether you can afford a well-known and established artist or a less expensive, emerging one.

2 Search for an artist through art agencies, art dealers and galleries, the Internet and personal references. Beyond aesthetic considerations, look for an artist who will listen to your ideas, follow your direction and clearly understand what you want the finished piece to look like.

3 Once you've identified an artist who is willing and able to work with you, set a date to hold a planning session and begin to write down as many ideas and detailed descriptions about the commissioned piece as possible.

4 Create an agenda for the meeting that will ultimately become a creative brief. Include as many details as possible in your discussion. What is the piece for? How large will it be? What format? Are there specifications that need to be met? This will help guide you and the artist through the meeting and ensure that you express all of your ideas and concerns. The more successfully you and the artist communicate with each other, the more closely your expectations will be met.

5 Be sure to have a commission contract drawn up and signed before further work is done. This legally binding contract should include details regarding the following: preliminary designs, payment schedule, completion date, insurance, shipping and installation, termination agreements, ownership and copyright, alterations and maintenance, contact information, and the state in which the work is produced.

6 Schedule a review of preliminary sketches as the artist begins the project. A commissioned artist must be open and willing to follow your direction. At the same time, you're paying for his or her talent and vision: Don't consistently squelch his or her creativity merely to stay in control of the process. This is a collaborative process, not a win-or-lose proposition.

7 Review the sketches thoroughly at each review stage in the process and be honest in your assessments. Carefully examine the finished piece and give it your final approval. Remember to get the artist's certificate of authenticity and any other documentation that he or she may provide.

What to Look For

- Art agencies
- Art dealers and galleries
- Commission contract
- Preliminary sketches
- Artist's certificate of authenticity

Tips

Depending on the complexity of the work and the budget, you may ask the artist for a second, more refined series of sketches to solidify a direction or narrow the choices. The artist should not begin work on the final piece until he or she is completely clear on every aspect of the project.

If the subject can be studied in person, allow the artist to do so as much as he or she likes. This will help the artist capture nuances and contours that photographs are rarely able to convey.

Warning

If the commission is extensive, complicated and/or involves several artists, you should probably hire a professional art consultant to manage the project.

118 Immortalize Your Spouse in a Sculpture

Now here's a gift for the person who thinks he or she has everything. Nothing says "I love you" like a timeless, original, full-size bronze likeness of your beloved. The result is sure to be a conversation piece like no other. But first you need to bust a move.

Steps

1 Take the time to interview as many candidates as possible; commissioning the right artist is critical. The interviewing process will allow you and your spouse to see the differences in style and technique, and also help define what you're looking for. You may even look into hiring an outside consultant, who has far more resources, to find the perfect sculptor for the job.

2 Contact your artist of choice by e-mail or telephone to discuss your initial ideas, requirements, completion date and price. The size, materials, weight, base and a slew of other factors will affect the final price. If the price is too steep, consider emerging artists; they may not charge as much but may still produce excellent work.

3 Make an initial appointment with the artist, which usually lasts for about an hour, and ask your spouse to attend. Specify to the artist exactly what you want the sculpture to look like, including posture and attitude. The artist will take photos and measurements of your spouse, discuss the angle and mood, and may even create a mask of your spouse's head to work with.

4 Draw up a formal commission contract, which the artist will probably supply. The first payment—commonly one-third of the total fee—is usually due upon signing the contract. Details such as size, materials, base, completion date, schedule of payments and sitting sessions should be stipulated.

5 Pay the second installment before the artist creates the mold. At this point discuss color, if that's an option, and decide how the piece will be mounted. The artist will then rework the piece with wax for the fine details, finalize the patination (coloring of the bronze), then put it on its base.

6 Return to the studio when the piece is being finalized for any final touch-ups. Most sculptures take four or five sittings to perfect. The sculpture is not complete until you and the artist are completely satisfied with the likeness and mood of the piece.

What to Look For

- Consultant
- Artist
- Commission contract
- Payment schedule
- Size, materials and base
- Preliminary sitting
- Patination
- Subsequent sittings

Tips

Many sculptors are willing to travel, so if you find one with a phenomenal reputation but outside your local area, ask if the artist will come to you for the project.

In addition to bronze, take a look at stone, onyx and the many resin castings available.

119 Give Away Your Fortune

Giving away a lot of money isn't as easy as it seems. In fact, most wealthy philanthropists probably had an easier time acquiring their fortune than giving it away. Deciding who gets what is the tough part. Once you've made that decision, the following information may make the ways in which you

VEHICLE	WAYS TO GIVE	BENEFITS OF GIVING
Real Estate	If you own property that is fully paid off and has appreciated in value, you can donate it as an outright gift. It can sometimes be the simplest solution, with many tax benefits.	You get to deduct the fair market value of your gift, avoid all capital gains taxes, and remove that asset from your taxable estate. You can transfer the deed of your home or farm now and retain the right to use the property for your lifetime and that of your spouse.
Cash	The simplest way to give away your fortune is to make a cash gift to an individual or worthy cause. The tax implications are much simpler as well.	You can usually deduct a cash gift for income only in the year that you donate it—any excess can be deductible over the next five years.
Life Insurance	If you have a life insurance policy you no longer need, you can contribute it to your cause of choice. Or you can buy a new policy and name someone as the beneficiary. This makes afford-able a significant future gift, especially for younger donors.	For the gift of a paid-up policy, you'll receive an income tax deduction equal to the lesser of the cash value of the policy or the total premiums paid. If you continue paying premiums on a policy after it's gifted, you're entitled to additional tax deductions.
Stock	If the stock you purchased over a year ago is now worth more than you paid for it, you can donate it and avoid the capital gains tax on the appreciation. If you own stock that's worth less now than when you bought it, sell it and make a deductible gift of the pro-ceeds. That allows you to realize a loss that you may be able to deduct from other taxable income.	Your income tax deduction is based on the appreciated stock's full fair market value when you donate the stock, rather than your lower purchase price. The ceiling on deductibility for appreci-ated stock is around 30 percent of your adjusted gross income, with a five-year carryover for any part of the donation that exceeds 30 percent.
Life Income Plans	If you'd like to make a gift now but need the money that your assets earn, make your donation by will. You can pay yourself and others income for life in exchange for your gift of appreciat-ed assets.	You're entitled to significant tax sav-ings on this year's income tax return, and your yearly income may be taxed more favorably than the income your assets now earn. You're also free of investment con-cerns, and you get the same estate tax benefits as for charitable gifts by will.

donate your fortune a bit easier, particularly in the tax arena. Always seek the advice of an attorney, tax professional and/or investment professional when making plans for a large donation. See 127 Choose a Financial Planner.

VEHICLE	WAYS TO GIVE	BENEFITS OF GIVING
Retirement Plan Assets	The simplest way to donate the balance of a retirement account when you die is to list the beneficiary in your will.	• Funds can go directly to the primary beneficiary or be transferred so that it will pay a lifetime income to a family member, after which the remaining funds go to a worthy cause. • You might even consider a deferred gift that is designed to pay a life income to yourself.
Bequests	Charitable bequests are easy to make since there are no minimum dollar requirements or complex rules. You can name a beneficiary in your will in a variety of ways. For example, you can leave a specific dollar amount or property to a cause, or even a portion or the remainder of your estate after other bequests and taxes have been paid.	• You'll get significant tax savings on this year's income tax return.
Endowments	An endowment guarantees a perpetual flow of money to any cause you wish to support. The endowment corpus, or principal, can never be touched but spins off interest to provide funding to support medical research or the arts, provide athletic or academic scholarships, finance scientific research or fund a nonprofit foundation. The institution that benefits from the endowment has a fiduciary responsibility to invest the money wisely, maintain the long-term value of the fund, and direct the resulting funds precisely as the donor requests.	• Memorialize yourself, your spouse, dog, best friend, or hero with a financial award (the Bob Smith Trophy), a scholarship (the Bob Smith Scholarship Fund) or capital campaign contribution (the Bob Smith Aquatic Center). • You get to say exactly how you wish the funds to be used. While institutions clearly prefer broad discretion in directing the funds, you can be as specific as saying "I want all crew shells to be named *Bob Smith* from now until eternity." • Charitable donations are tax-deductible. • It's a great way to support something near and dear to your heart.
WARNING	Without a will, you are powerless over how your assets will be distributed. See 344 Write a Living Will.	

120 Hire an Expert Witness

If you're in serious trouble with the law, you'll not only need the best lawyer you can afford, you may also need to hire expert witnesses to testify on your behalf. If you're representing yourself (never a smart move) or want to be more involved in your lawyer's selection of expert witnesses, the following steps may be helpful.

Steps

1 Decide on the type of expert you need. Does the case involve medical issues? High technology? An expert witness referral service can pair you up with the right person. Typically, there's no financial or contractual obligation until the person is hired.

2 Contract the expert as a consultant and then determine whether or not you want him or her to testify at trial. Realize that as long as the expert is a consultant, his or her work is confidential.

3 Expect to pay consultants on an hourly basis. The wide range of rates from $50 to $500 an hour is determined by your needs.

4 Decide just how much information you want to provide the witness about the case, and explain in detail the exact issue or issues that you'll need addressed. An aggressive expert who asks to review any and all case materials could easily become party to facts that are potentially damaging to your case.

5 Provide the expert with the expected trial or deposition dates as early as possible and define the time commitment needed.

6 Make sure the expert understands that his or her file is completely open to review in court. Be sure that the file contains only those documents that you, your counsel and the expert would agree to provide to opposing counsel.

7 Let your expert know that you expect nothing but honest answers both before and during the trial. When the expert's name is disclosed as a potential expert in the matter, his or her prior work becomes subject to examination.

What to Look For

- A good lawyer
- Expert witness referral service
- Appropriate expert
- Fee structure
- Time commitment

Warning

Avoid experts who want to direct the case or who seem to be tailoring their answers to fit what they think you want. These experts often lack credibility.

121 Make Bail

You've seen it on TV a thousand times—someone runs afoul of the law, gets thrown in the joint, and his lawyer has to bail him out. But what exactly is the purpose of bail, and how do you post it?

Steps

1 Get arrested and charged with a crime. You will be required to post bail before the police will let you go. Bail is set by a judge to guarantee that a defendant will appear when required. The more likely it is that a person is dangerous or a flight risk, the higher the bail will be.

2 Have your lawyer try to convince the judge to release you on your own recognizance before you buy a bond or post bail.

3 Get out of jail the most economical way by posting the full amount of the bail in cash. If you can pay the full bail amount, you don't need to hire a bail bondsman and you save 10 percent of the bail amount. When the case is concluded, all of the cash is returned (minus a small administrative fee).

4 Hire a bail bonds company, or have a friend, lawyer or relative do it for you. Bail agents' phone numbers are almost always posted in the jail, and offices are probably located across the street or near the courthouse. (You can also look under "Bail Bonds" in the Yellow Pages.) A bail bond is a kind of guarantee that you'll appear in court for your trial. You pay 10 percent of your bail to the bondsman, and the bondsman pays 100 percent of your bail to the court. (If bail is set at $100,000 and you need a bond, it'll cost you $10,000.) When you appear in court the bondsman gets his or her 100 percent back and keeps your 10 percent. If you don't show up in court the bondsman loses 90 percent of the bail and sends a goon after you to break your kneecaps. Simple. (See 140 Get Health Insurance.)

5 Make sure you deal only with a licensed bail agent. Ask to see his or her license and identification prior to paying for the bond. Also, make sure you are given itemized receipts for all charges, and copies of all signed contracts and agreements.

6 Use your property, stocks, money market accounts and other assets as collateral if you don't have the cash to buy a bond. You can sometimes arrange a payment plan, depending on your credit history.

What to Look For

- Bail bonds company
- Cash or other assets to buy bond
- Licensed bail agents
- Itemized receipts and copies of contracts
- Collateral or credit payment plan

Tips

Since it can take up to five days to see a judge, most jails have standard bail schedules. These specify bail amounts for common crimes, which allows you to get out of jail as quickly as possible.

It never hurts to ask the judge at your arraignment to lower your bail, particularly if you have a good reason.

Warning

Jails and bail bond sellers usually do not take credit cards or personal checks.

122 Donate Your Body to Science

If you're just dying to get into medical school, you can always enroll later in life. Donating your body to science is the ultimate rare event—a once-in-a-lifetime opportunity to benefit medical teaching and research since the study of human anatomy does require a body.

Steps

1 Preregister your donation with a local medical school or university. You'll be given a registration packet that covers policies and procedures; read it very carefully.

2 Sign a consent form stating your desire to donate your body, and put a copy of it with your will and other personal documents. You won't be listed as a donor until a completed form has been returned and acknowledged. Cancel your decision at any time by notifying the medical school or university in writing.

3 Arrange for the medical school or university to be notified when you die, so that your body can be properly transported and prepared. When your corpse is delivered to the medical institution, it will be embalmed and refrigerated until it's needed for study.

4 Check with the school to see what its policies and procedures are regarding your body after it has been studied. Most institutions will respectfully cremate your remains at their expense and give your ashes to your loved ones. Don't expect to get paid for your donation pre- or postmortem. By law, medical schools are not permitted to purchase anyone's body.

5 Contact the United Network for Organ Sharing (unos.org), a national group that oversees organ transplantation procedures in this country, for more information on donating your body.

6 Rest in peace? Perhaps not: Your spouse, adult children, siblings, parents and guardians can arrange to have your body donated after you die by filling out an after-death donor form. In the event that your body cannot be accepted, your family needs to make alternate plans for your disposal.

What to Look For

- Medical school or university
- Registration packet
- Consent form
- Final disposition policy

Warning

The mistreatment of donated bodies is not uncommon. The Uniform Anatomical Gifts Act governs the donation of bodies for dissection, research and transplantation throughout the United States, but dead people can't file a complaint.

123 Hire Yourself Out as a Medical Guinea Pig

There are many good reasons to rent your body to science: You can help advance medical research, benefit future generations or make some cash. Before you climb on that metal table, decide just how far you're willing to go.

Steps

1 Decide what kind of experiment you'd like to be a part of. Any study will have requirements that you may or may not meet. The more specific they are, the more money you'll make. Research the qualifications to make sure you're a suitable candidate.

2 Choose a simple experiment to begin with. Some studies require you to undergo medical exams. See the chart below for details.

3 Research the more complicated types of experiments before you sign up. The pay is tempting (up to hundreds of dollars) but the experiment usually involves multiple visits or overnight stays in the hospital. While the risks do increase as the experiment becomes more involved, all regulated studies are generally safe.

4 Sign a consent form once you've found an experiment that works for you. This states the procedure and duration of the experiment, possible risks or side effects, and how much you'll be paid.

5 Listen to the doctors and do what they say. You're allowed to leave the experiment at any time if you feel sick or are in pain, but are not advised to do so against medical orders.

What to Look For

- Type of experiment
- Requirements
- Time commitment
- Consent form

Tips

For information about the safety of human subject trials, visit the Office of Human Subjects Research of the National Institutes of Health (ohsr.od.nih.gov), and the Office for Human Research Protections of the U.S. Department of Health and Human Services (ohrp.osophs.dhhs.gov).

See 124 Sell Plasma.

TYPE OF STUDY	WHAT IT INVOLVES	WHAT IT PAYS
Questionnaires and Interviews	Quick and easy commitment. Usually require you to answer interview questions or fill out questionnaire on a subject. May involve looking at images and describing your feelings toward them. Follow-up sessions sometimes required.	Lowest-paying studies. Usually pays $5 to $20, depending on time commitment.
Type I Medical Exams and Interviews	Greater time commitment. Researchers usually interested in relationship between general health and stress levels, anger management, or other mental factors. Subjects usually undergo lengthier examination, including general physical (height, weight, blood pressure), followed by interview about mental health.	Pay varies widely, but generally between $20 and $100.
Type II Medical Exams and Interviews	Same as Type I experiments, except also may involve more advanced procedures, such as blood tests, electrocardiogram (EKG), magnetic resonance imaging (MRI) tests and internal exams.	Pay ranges from $50 to $100, with low risk.

124 **Sell Plasma**

If you're looking to make some quick cash you can always donate your plasma, the clear yellowish fluid portion of the blood that transports water and nutrients to all the cells in the body and is used for transfusions to people who have suffered shock, burns or trauma. Although your body quickly replenishes its supply of plasma, there are a few precautions you should take before using yourself as an organic ATM.

Steps

1 Check with the Yellow Pages or a nearby college campus for the closest plasma collection center, blood bank or blood collection facility. There are more than 400 for-profit plasma collection centers in the United States.

2 Eat something two hours before donating plasma and drink lots of water to avoid light-headedness.

3 Plan to spend a few hours at the center the first time you go. Prospective donors are questioned about their health history and circumstances that may put them at risk for being HIV positive. You will also be asked if you've had any piercings or tattoos within the last 12 months. You'll undergo a physical exam, be screened for drugs, and be asked to sign waivers.

4 Lie down, relax and let the technician insert a needle into your vein. The blood flows into a sterilized machine that separates the plasma from the red blood cells and then pumps blood back into your bloodstream, in a process called *apheresis.*

5 Allow time for your medical history to be reviewed each time you return. After the initial visit, donating usually takes 30 minutes if there is no waiting line.

6 Expect to earn up to $35 for each donation (twice a week max). Donors who have been vaccinated for hepatitis B can earn up to $60 per week.

What to Look For

- Questionnaire
- Physical exam
- Drug test
- Payment

Tips

Every unit of plasma collected is tested for the presence of hepatitis, HIV, antibodies and antigens. The amount of plasma you can donate is based on your weight.

If you really want to help your fellow citizens, donate blood—it's in shorter supply and it's a nonprofit gesture.

Warning

It's easy to sell your plasma often, but you risk scarring your veins and depleting your iron levels if you donate too frequently.

125 Sell Your Soul to the Devil

The quickest way to sell your soul to the Devil is to join the Church of Satan (it takes a few hours). Established in 1966, the church teaches its members to take pride in having the strength and dedication to implement the tools of Satan and the wisdom to recognize the Unseen in our society.

Steps

1 Find a cold room that has not received sunlight for three days and large piece of natural parchment paper that also has been in total darkness for three days.

2 Draw a large pentagram on the parchment paper and place it on the floor in order to protect yourself. Stay inside the pentagram from beginning to end. Treading outside it will make any mistake permanent.

3 Saturate the air with incense of your choice, and conduct the ritual in solitude to maintain full powers of concentration.

4 Take a vial of goat's blood (not sheep's blood, ever!) and scatter drops within the pentagram—but not outside it, and not on your foot. After the scattering you must not tread on the blood, otherwise you will carry it with you outside the pentagram.

5 Memorize and utter the Church of Satan Invocation: "In the name of all the Lords of the Abyss, I call out to the Powers of Darkness. Come to my aid for I am helpless before my adversaries. I am thy servant. Thy will is as my own. I am ever dutiful in serving thee. Come forth from thy dark abodes and answer to your names. Hear my plea!"

6 Send $100 to the Church of Satan (churchofsatan.com). In 16 weeks, you'll receive an embossed crimson card declaring you a member of the church. This card is your means for identifying yourself as a genuine member of the Church of Satan to other members.

What to Look For

- Cold, dark room
- Parchment
- Incense
- Goat's blood
- Church of Satan invocation
- Lifetime membership fee

Tip

Since Satanism is a philosophy that holds individualism as one of its main values, the Church of Satan doesn't expect all its members to agree on everything—or even to get along with each other.

Warning

Once you complete the ritual, the adamantine Gates of Hell are thrown open. Boldly stride within and learn about the "Feared Religion," or slink away in fear and ignorance. The choice is yours.

REHOUSE STORES • BUY WHOLESALE • GET OUT OF DEBT • BUY NOTHING • BUY HAPPINESS • BUY A BETTER MOUSETRAP • BUY TIM
MEONE'S FAVOR • BUY POSTAGE STAMPS WITHOUT GOING TO THE POST OFFICE • TIP PROPERLY • BUY HEALTHY FAST FOOD • BUY S
ING SERVICE • SELL YOURSELF ON AN ONLINE DATING SERVICE • SELL YOURSELF TO YOUR GIRLFRIEND/BOYFRIEND'S FAMILY • BUY
HOOSE FILM FOR YOUR CAMERA • BUY RECHARGEABLE BATTERIES • DONATE TO A GOOD CAUSE • HOLD A PROFITABLE GARAGE SAL
STUDENT DISCOUNTS • BUY FLOWERS WHOLESALE • GET A PICTURE FRAMED • HIRE A MOVER • HIRE A PERSONAL ORGANIZER • FIN
EAT BIRTHDAY PRESENT FOR UNDER $10 • SELECT GOOD CHAMPAGNE • BUY A DIAMOND • BUY JEWELRY MADE OF PRECIOUS METAL
DESMAIDS' DRESSES • HIRE AN EVENT COORDINATOR • HIRE A BARTENDER FOR A PARTY • HIRE A PHOTOGRAPHER • HIRE A CATERER
Y AN ANNIVERSARY GIFT • ARRANGE ENTERTAINMENT FOR A PARTY • COMMISSION A FIREWORKS SHOW • BUY A MOTHER'S DAY GIFT
T • SELECT A THANKSGIVING TURKEY • BUY A HOUSEWARMING GIFT • PURCHASE HOLIDAY CARDS • BUY CHRISTMAS STOCKING STU
E HIGH ROLLERS ROOM IN VEGAS, BABY • BUY SOMEONE A STAR • PAY A RANSOM • GET HOT TICKETS • HIRE A LIMOUSINE • BUY A C
M • BUY A PERSONAL JET • ACQUIRE A TELEVISION NETWORK • ACQUIRE A BODY GUARD • BOOK A LUXURY CRUISE AROUND THE W
OROUGHBRED RACEHORSE • BUY A VILLA IN TUSCANY • HIRE A PERSONAL CHEF • PURCHASE CUBAN CIGARS • HIRE A GHOSTWRITE
NESS • MAKE BAIL • DONATE YOUR BODY TO SCIENCE • HIRE YOURSELF OUT AS A MEDICAL GUINEA PIG • SELL PLASMA • SELL YOU
LLEGE EDUCATION • BUY AND SELL STOCKS • CHOOSE A STOCKBROKER • DAY-TRADE (OR NOT) • BUY ANNUITIES • BUY AND SELL MU
Y PERSONAL FINANCE SOFTWARE • CHOOSE A TAX PREPARER • SET UP A LEMONADE STAND • SELL YOUR PRODUCT ON TV • HIRE A C
SINESS IDEA • BUY A SMALL BUSINESS • BUY A FRANCHISE • LEASE RETAIL SPACE • LEASE INDUSTRIAL SPACE • LEASE OFFICE SPAC
B SITE • BUY ADVERTISING ON THE WEB • SELL YOUR ART • HIRE A PERSONAL COACH • SELL ON THE CRAFT CIRCUIT • HIRE A LITERA
LING BUSINESS • BUY A HOT DOG STAND • SHOP FOR A MORTGAGE • REFINANCE YOUR HOME • SAVE BIG BUCKS ON YOUR MORTGA
L A FIXER-UPPER • SELL THE FARM • SELL MINERAL RIGHTS • SELL A HOUSE • SELL A HOUSE WITHOUT A REAL ESTATE AGENT • OBTA
OK A VACATION RENTAL • BUY A CONDOMINIUM • RENT AN APARTMENT OR HOUSE • OBTAIN RENTER'S INSURANCE • BUY A LOFT IN N
RNISH YOUR STUDIO APARTMENT • BUY USED FURNITURE • BUY DOOR AND WINDOW LOCKS • CHOOSE AN ORIENTAL CARPET • BUY
RRANTIES ON APPLIANCES • FIND PERIOD FIXTURES • BUY A BED AND MATTRESS • HIRE AN INTERIOR DESIGNER • HIRE A FENG SHUI
• BUY A WHIRLPOOL TUB • BUY A SHOWERHEAD • BUY A TOILET • CHOOSE A FAUCET • BUY GLUES AND ADHESIVES • CHOOSE WIN
CHEN CABINETS • CHOOSE A KITCHEN COUNTERTOP • BUY GREEN HOUSEHOLD CLEANERS • STOCK YOUR HOME TOOL KIT • BUY A
ENTRY DOOR • BUY A GARAGE-DOOR OPENER • BUY LUMBER FOR A DIY PROJECT • HOW TO SELECT ROOFING • HIRE A CONTRACTO
WERS FOR YOUR GARDEN • SELECT PEST CONTROLS • BUY SOIL AMENDMENTS • BUY MULCH • BUY A COMPOSTER • BUY FERTILIZ
Y KOI FOR YOUR FISH POND • BUY A STORAGE SHED • HIRE AN ARBORIST • BUY BASIC GARDEN TOOLS • BUY SHRUBS AND TREES •
ECT KITCHEN KNIVES • DECIPHER FOOD LABELS • SELECT HERBS AND SPICES • STOCK YOUR KITCHEN WITH STAPLES • EQUIP A KIT
UNTAIN OYSTERS • PURCHASE LOCAL HONEY • CHOOSE POULTRY • SELECT FRESH FISH AND SHELLFISH • SELECT RICE • PURCHAS
EADS • BUY ARTISAN CHEESES • PURCHASE KOSHER FOOD • BUY FOOD IN BULK • CHOOSE COOKING OILS • SELECT OLIVE OIL • SEL
FFEEMAKER OR ESPRESSO MACHINE • PURCHASE A KEG OF BEER • BUY ALCOHOL IN A DRY COUNTY • CHOOSE A MICROBREW • OR
ULATION PREDICTOR KIT • PICK A PREGNANCY TEST KIT • CHOOSE BIRTH CONTROL • FIND THE RIGHT OB-GYN • HIRE A MIDWIFE OR
OSE DIAPERS • BUY OR RENT A BREAST PUMP • CHOOSE A CAR SEAT • BUY CHILD-PROOFING SUPPLIES • FIND FABULOUS CHILDCA
CKYARD PLAY STRUCTURE • FIND A GREAT SUMMER CAMP • SELL GIRL SCOUT COOKIES • BUY BRACES FOR YOUR KID • BUY TOYS
A MODEL • SELL USED BABY GEAR, TOYS, CLOTHES AND BOOKS • FIND A COUPLES COUNSELOR • HIRE A FAMILY LAWYER • BUY PRO
PENSES • GET VIAGRA ONLINE • PURCHASE A TOOTHBRUSH • BUY MOISTURIZERS AND ANTIWRINKLE CREAMS • SELECT PAIN RELIEF
PPLIES • SELECT HAIR-CARE PRODUCTS • BUY WAYS TO COUNTER HAIR LOSS • BUY A WIG OR HAIRPIECE • BUY A NEW BODY • GET
NICURIST • GET WHITER TEETH • SELECT EYEGLASSES AND SUNGLASSES • HIRE A PERSONAL TRAINER • SIGN UP FOR A YOGA CLAS
A MARKET • RENT SPACE AT AN ANTIQUE MALL • BUY AT AUCTION • KNOW WHAT YOUR COLLECTIBLES ARE WORTH • DICKER WITH D
COGNIZE THE REAL MCCOY • BUY COINS • BUY AN ANTIQUE AMERICAN QUILT • BUY AN ANTIQUE FLAG • LIQUIDATE YOUR BEANIE BA
WNSHOP • BUY AND SELL COMIC BOOKS • BUY AND SELL SPORTS MEMORABILIA • SELL YOUR BASEBALL-CARD COLLECTIONS • CHO
MPUTER • BUY PRINTER PAPER • BUY A PRINTER • BUY COMPUTER PERIPHERALS • CHOOSE AN INTERNET SERVICE PROVIDER • GET
Y BLANK CDS • BUY AN MP PLAYER • CHOOSE A DVD PLAYER • BUY A VCR • CHOOSE A PERSONAL DIGITAL ASSISTANT • CHOOSE MO
ITAL CAMCORDER • DECIDE ON A DIGITAL CAMERA • BUY A HOME AUTOMATION SYSTEM • BUY A STATE-OF-THE-ART SOUND SYSTEM
VERSAL REMOTE • BUY A HOME THEATER SYSTEM • BUY VIRTUAL-REALITY FURNITURE • BUY TWO-WAY RADIOS • BUY A MOBILE EN
NEY • GET TRAVEL INSURANCE • PICK THE IDEAL LUGGAGE • FLY FOR FREE • BID FOR A SLED RIDE ON THE ALASKAN IDITAROD TRAIL
REIGN OFFICIAL • GET A EURAIL PASS • TAKE AN ITALIAN BICYCLE VACATION • CHOOSE A CHEAP CRUISE • BOOK A HOTEL PACKAGE
OTLAND • BUY A SAPPHIRE IN BANGKOK • HIRE A RICKSHA IN YANGON • TAKE SALSA LESSONS IN CUBA • BUY A CAMERA IN HONG K
ST BASEBALL GLOVE • ORDER UNIFORMS FOR A SOFTBALL TEAM • BUY ANKLE AND KNEE BRACES • BUY GOLF CLUBS • JOIN AN ELI
OWMOBILE • BUY A PERSONAL WATERCRAFT • HIRE A SCUBA INSTRUCTOR • BUY A SKATEBOARD AND PROTECTIVE GEAR • BUY SKA
ATHER ACTIVITIES • SELL USED SKIS • BUY A SNOWBOARD, BOOTS AND BINDINGS • BUY SKI BOOTS • BUY A BICYCLE • SELL YOUR E
Y A BACKPACK • BUY A BACKPACKING STOVE • BUY A KAYAK • BUY A PERSONAL FLOTATION DEVICE • BUY A WET SUIT • BUY A SURF
DER CUSTOM-MADE COWBOY BOOTS • BUY CLOTHES ONLINE • FIND SPECIALTY SIZES • BUY THE PERFECT COCKTAIL DRESS • BUY
Y A MAN'S SUIT • HIRE A TAILOR • BUY CUSTOM-TAILORED CLOTHES IN ASIA • BUY A BRIEFCASE • SHOP FOR A LEATHER JACKET • B
E MONITOR • SELECT A WATCH • BUY KIDS' CLOTHES • CHOOSE CHILDREN'S SHOES • PURCHASE CLOTHES AT OUTLET SHOPS • BU

QUET OF ROSES • BUY SOMEONE A DRINK • GET SOMEONE TO BUY YOU A DRINK • BUY YOUR WAY INTO HIGH SOCIETY • BUY YOUR
RDER THE PERFECT BURRITO • ORDER TAKEOUT ASIAN FOOD • ORDER AT A SUSHI BAR • BUY DINNER AT A FANCY FRENCH RESTAURA
OWERS FOR YOUR SWEETHEART • BUY MUSIC ONLINE • HIRE MUSICIANS • ORDER A GREAT BOTTLE OF WINE • BUY AN ERGONOMIC D
SECLEANER • HIRE A BABY SITTER • BUY A GUITAR • BUY DUCT TAPE • GET A GOOD DEAL ON A MAGAZINE SUBSCRIPTION • GET SENI
AN • BUY PET FOOD • BUY A PEDIGREED DOG OR CAT • BREED YOUR PET AND SELL THE LITTER • GET A COSTUME • BUY A PIÑATA •
ED GEMSTONES • CHOOSE THE PERFECT WEDDING DRESS • BUY OR RENT A TUXEDO • REGISTER FOR GIFTS • BUY WEDDING GIFTS •
EAL WEDDING OFFICIANT • OBTAIN A MARRIAGE LICENSE • ORDER CUSTOM INVITATIONS AND ANNOUNCEMENTS • SELL YOUR WEDDIN
R'S DAY GIFT • SELECT AN APPROPRIATE COMING-OF-AGE GIFT • GET A GIFT FOR THE PERSON WHO HAS EVERYTHING • BUY A GRAD
ANUKKAH GIFTS • PURCHASE A PERFECT CHRISTMAS TREE • BUY A PRIVATE ISLAND • HIRE A SKYWRITER • HIRE A BIG-NAME BAND •
ER • RENT YOUR OWN BILLBOARD • TAKE OUT A FULL-PAGE AD IN *THE NEW YORK TIMES* • HIRE A BUTLER • ACQUIRE A PROFESSION
OUR FUR COAT • BOOK A TRIP ON THE ORIENT-EXPRESS • BECOME A WINE MAKER • PURCHASE A PRIVATE/CUSTOM BOTTLING OF WIN
MEMOIRS • COMMISSION ORIGINAL ARTWORK • IMMORTALIZE YOUR SPOUSE IN A SCULPTURE • GIVE AWAY YOUR FORTUNE • HIRE A
DEVIL • NEGOTIATE A BETTER CREDIT CARD DEAL • CHOOSE A FINANCIAL PLANNER • SAVE WITH A RETIREMENT PLAN • SAVE FOR YO
BUY BONDS • SELL SHORT • INVEST IN PRECIOUS METALS • BUY DISABILITY INSURANCE • BUY LIFE INSURANCE • GET HEALTH INSUF
ELOR • HIRE A HEADHUNTER • SELL YOUR   ENT • MARKET YOUR INVENTION • FINANCE YOU
TED OFFICE EQUIPMENT • HIRE SOMEONE   RE A GRAPHIC DESIGNER • ACQUIRE CONTENT
CH A MAGAZINE STORY • SELL A SCREEN   YOUR BOOK • START A BED-AND-BREAKFAST • SI
ME OWNER'S INSURANCE • OBTAIN DISAS   OUSE AT AUCTION • BUY A FORECLOSED HOME
ITY LOAN • BUY A LOT • BUY HOUSE PLA   • PULL BUILDING PERMITS • BUY A VACATION HO
Y A TENANCY-IN-COMMON UNIT • BUY RE   A MOVIE OR CATALOG SHOOT • FURNISH YOUR H
IT FIXTURES • BUY A PROGRAMMABLE LIG   NCES • BUY FLOOR-CARE APPLIANCES • BUY EX
INCORPORATE FLUID ARCHITECTURE INTO   ARNISH • CHOOSE DECORATIVE TILES • CHOOSE
TS • GET SELF-CLEANING WINDOWS • CH   SELECT FLOORING • SELECT CARPETING • CHOC
SYSTEM • BUY A HOME ALARM SYSTEM   OXIDE DETECTORS • BUY FIRE EXTINGUISHERS •
INTER OR ELECTRICIAN • HIRE A GARDEN   PERFECT ROSEBUSH • BUY FLOWERING BULBS
GETABLE GARDEN • HIRE A GARDEN PROF   R SYSTEM • START A NEW LAWN • BUY A LAWN M
• BUY AN OUTDOOR LIGHTING SYSTEM •   ECT PEACH • BUY AND SELL AT FARMERS' MARK
FRESH PRODUCE • SELECT MEAT • STOC   ASE A HOLIDAY HAM • BUY NATURAL BEEF • BUY
AND PEPPER • GET A CHEESESTEAK IN P   EATTLE • FIND CRAWDADS IN LOUISIANA • BUY A
Y ETHNIC INGREDIENTS • PURCHASE VIN   OFFEE • ORDER A GREAT CUP OF COFFEE • BUY
• CHOOSE A RESTAURANT FOR A BUSINE   TOCK YOUR BAR • BUY AND SELL SPERM • CHOC
GOOD PEDIATRICIAN • HIRE A CHILD THER   L NEW CRIB • CHOOSE A STROLLER • BUY BABY
EAT NANNY • FIND THE RIGHT PRIVATE SC   RAM • SIGN YOUR CHILD UP FOR LESSONS • BL
DEOS AND MUSIC FOR YOUR CHILDREN •   R • HIRE AN ADOPTION AGENCY • GET YOUR CH
REMENT COMMUNITY • CHOOSE AN ASS   IVING WILL • BUY A CEMETERY PLOT • PAY FOR
CINES • SAVE MONEY ON PRESCRIPTION   ONAL • CHOOSE A WHEELCHAIR • BUY HOME US
DY PIERCING • OBTAIN BREAST IMPLANTS   ALTERNATIVE AND HOLISTIC PRACTITIONERS • C
ELF TO A DAY AT THE SPA • BOOK A MAS   Y AND SELL USED BOOKS • SHOP AT AN ANTIQU
N ANTIQUE APPRAISED • BUY SILVERWARE • EVALUATE DEPRESSION-ERA GLASSWARE • BUY AND SELL STAMPS • BUY ANTIQUE FURN
• SCORE AUTOGRAPHS • TRADE YU-GI-OH CARDS • SNAG STAR WARS ACTION FIGURES • SELL YOUR VINYL RECORD COLLECTION • S
COMPUTER • SHOP FOR A USED COMPUTER OR PERIPHERALS • CHOOSE A LAPTOP OR NOTEBOOK COMPUTER • SELL OR DONATE A
MAIN NAME • BUY A HOME NETWORK • UPGRADE THE MEMORY IN YOUR COMPUTER • BUY COMPUTER SOFTWARE • CHOOSE A CD
VICE • NEGOTIATE YOUR LONG-DISTANCE PHONE SERVICE • BUY VIDEO AND COMPUTER GAMES • CHOOSE A FILM CAMERA • CHOOS
-VIDEO DISTRIBUTION SYSTEM • BUY A SERIOUS TV • CHOOSE BETWEEN CABLE AND SATELLITE TV • GET A DIGITAL VIDEO RECORDER
STEM • GET A PASSPORT, QUICK! • PURCHASE CHEAP AIRLINE TICKETS • FIND GREAT HOTEL DEALS • RENT THE BEST CAR FOR THE L
Y-FREE • SHIP FOREIGN PURCHASES TO THE UNITED STATES • TIP IN A FOREIGN COUNTRY • TIP PROPERLY IN NORTH AMERICA • BRI
SLANDS • RAFT THE GRAND CANYON • BOOK A CHEAP BUT AWESOME SAFARI • RENT A CAMEL IN CAIRO • GET SINGLE-MALT SCOTCH
WAY ONTO A MOUNT EVEREST EXPEDITION • HIRE A TREKKING COMPANY IN NEPAL • RENT OR BUY A SATELLITE PHONE • BUY YOUF
SELL FOUND GOLF BALLS • BUY ATHLETIC SHOES • BUY A RACKET • BUY A GYM MEMBERSHIP • BUY AN AEROBIC FITNESS MACHINE •
FISHING • GO SKYDIVING • BUY WEIGHTLIFTING EQUIPMENT • CHOOSE A CAR RACK OR CARRIER • BUY SKIS • BUY CLOTHES FOR CC
AGE SALE • COMMISSION A CUSTOM-BUILT BICYCLE • BUY A PROPERLY FITTED HELMET • BUY THE OPTIMAL SLEEPING BAG • BUY A
-FISHING GEAR • BUY ROCK-CLIMBING EQUIPMENT • BUY A CASHMERE SWEATER • PURCHASE VINTAGE CLOTHING • SELL USED CL
ES AT A DISCOUNT • CHOOSE A BASIC WARDROBE FOR A MAN • BUY A MAN'S DRESS SHIRT • PICK OUT A NECKTIE • BUY A WOMAN'
OTHES • GET A GREAT-FITTING BRA • CHOOSE A HIGH-PERFORMANCE SWIM SUIT • HIGH PERFORMANCE WORKOUT CLOTHES • BUY
Y THE BASICS FOR YOUR CAR • BUY A USED CAR • BUY OR SELL A CAR ONLINE • BUY A HYBRID CAR • SELL A CAR • BUY A MOTOR

Personal Finance

126 Negotiate a Better Credit Card Deal

That plastic card in your wallet isn't the only thing flexible about your credit—your card's interest rate and annual fee are, too. Credit card offers range all across the board. That's great news for you as a consumer, because with a little effort you can get a better deal.

Steps

1 Find out which cards have lower rates than your current card. Call your credit card company and indicate that you are thinking of canceling your account and going with another card with a much lower rate. Ask for a rate that matches the other card.

2 Negotiate a reduction in your annual fee. Finance charges are not the only cost of holding a credit card. The annual fee can add up to much more than your monthly finance charges. Call your credit card company and negotiate hard to reduce or even eliminate this fee. Again, threatening to close your account usually gets their attention. Don't bother trying this with cards that are co-branded with airlines or hotels to offer rewards; these cards will never drop their fee.

3 Go to a site such as Bankrate.com to compare rates, but make sure you pay attention to all the details of the agreement. Note whether there is a grace period and how long it is; how long the introductory rate is in place; what the late fee is; whether the rate applies to new purchases, balance transfers, cash advances or only some transactions; and whether the introductory rate automatically increases if a payment is late.

4 Cite your history as a customer. If you've been with a card company for a while, play up your loyalty. Learn your FICO score (MyFICO.com) to know whether your credit rating is top-notch or not. (See 172 Shop for a Mortgage for more information.) If it is in great shape, you'll likely be able to secure a very low rate elsewhere—and you should tell your current credit card company that.

5 Arrange for a balance transfer to your new card from your old card once you line up a better rate elsewhere. Read the fine print about balance transfer interest rates: They can often be higher than the interest on purchases.

6 Factor in the perks. Many cards that give added benefits, like airline miles or cash rebates, often charge annual fees and have higher interest rates. If you use your card substantially, these benefits add up and may be more valuable than the amount of the fees. Do the math to see if you come out ahead on benefits.

7 If you pay off your balance in any one month, forget interest rate and maximize other benefits. Let's face it, if you don't carry a balance, who cares what the rate is? Go for the added benefits like miles, loyalty points, cash rebates or low or no annual fees.

What to Look For

- Lowest interest rate
- Rate and fee details
- More competitive cards
- Added benefits

Tips

If you have a good history with your credit card company, try asking for both a larger credit line *and* lower interest.

If you're looking for rock-bottom rates, check out teaser cards that offer zero percent interest for a set period of time. Be aware, though, that the rate may only apply to balance transfers, and it will inevitably spike.

Since credit card companies make more money off of customers who don't pay their balances in full, you may actually be in a better negotiating position if you've had a history of on-time payments but don't pay it off each month.

127 Choose a Financial Planner

Are you on the lookout for someone to advise you on financial issues that go beyond basic investing? The right person may be a financial planner. Planners come in all types. Some focus on investments; others work in planning insurance, budgeting, estate and related issues. But as with almost anything in the world of money, *caveat emptor.*

Steps

1 Be clear on what your life goals and objectives are when searching for a suitable planner. Do you want a comfortable retirement, a college education, a vacation home, capital to finance a career change or something else?

2 Decide whether you need the resources of a full-service national firm or if a local office will be sufficient. National firms have big-name investment researchers and analysts on board to generate their own opinions. Generally, the more services available, the higher the overhead a firm has to cover and the higher the fees charged to its clients. In many cases, access to research information more than makes up for the added fees, but be sure you'll actually take advantage of them before you pay them.

3 Ask friends and colleagues for recommendations and references. Try to interview at least three planners. Find someone who understands the debt (mortgage, car loans, etc.) side of your equation and will take that into account when creating your plan.

4 Check the planner's credentials. Certified financial planners have passed exams covering a number of financial topics. Others may have designations in certain fields such as investing and insurance. Contact American Financial Planners (american-financial-planners.com/credentials.html) for a list of financial planner credentials and the organizations that provided them.

5 Get a feel for the planner's philosophy. Some planners are flat-out aggressive when it comes to investing, while others are more conservative. But it's your money, and any decent planner should be able to map out a plan that fits your needs and comfort level.

6 Make certain you know exactly how the planner will be compensated. Some charge a flat fee for setting up a financial plan; other planners sell products on a commission basis. Be sure to negotiate if you like the planner but the fee seems high.

7 Ask the planner for references, especially from clients whose needs are similar to yours. If the planner balks or talks about confidentiality, find someone else.

8 Establish how and how often your planner will be in contact with you. Will it involve phone calls, e-mail updates or quarterly reports? And if your finances take a downturn, will your planner call with feedback and reassurance, or will you have to pursue him or her?

What to Look For

- Financial objectives
- Specific services
- Credentials and references
- Compatible philosophy
- Compensation basis

Tips

If a planner is part of a large firm, ask if you'll be handed off to someone else for things like taxes and insurance. Some people prefer one planner who'll handle all their financial dealings.

Financial planners who are paid on a commission may try and steer you to invest in products that will yield them the best compensation rather than what is in your best interests. Fee-based planners are generally preferred for their objectivity.

Ask about the charges for phone consultations and questions. It may seem like a quick question to you, but that 15-minute phone call may result in a bill. Experienced financial planners can charge up to $250 per hour or more.

Warning

Make sure your investment pot is large enough to warrant getting a planner. If you only have $1,000 to invest and a planner is going to charge you a couple hundred dollars, you'd be better off learning what you need to do on your own.

128 Save with a Retirement Plan

In a universe where sure things are almost unheard of, a retirement plans is as close to a financial slam dunk as you will likely get. The benefits are manifold and include generous contribution limits and tax advantages.

Steps

1 Know what your choices are. There are three primary kinds of retirement plans—employer-sponsored plans (401(k) and Simple IRA), personal savings plans (conventional and Roth IRA), and plans for self-employed people (SEP IRA).

   • Employer-sponsored plans: Plans like 401(k)s and Simple IRAs are retirement plans offered by the company you work for. The contributions grow, tax-free, until you withdraw them after retirement. Depending on the plan, you make regular tax-deferred contributions, and sometimes your employer may match some or even all of your contribution. In 2003, the maximum contribution for a 401(k) is $12,000 of your compensation. For a Simple IRA, it's $8,000.

   • Personal savings plans: These are plans you set up yourself in addition to the plans offered at work. Conventional IRAs let you contribute as much as $3,000 a year. The contribution may be tax-deductible, depending on your income and other factors. The Roth operates differently. Your contributions to a Roth—up to $3,000 a year—are not tax-deductible. However, you may withdraw proceeds from a Roth tax-free after you retire. Both a conventional IRA and a Roth let your deposits grow tax-free.

   • Self-employment plans: These are plans for people who work for themselves. They are self-administered, and allow you to take a portion of your income and direct it to a tax-deferred savings plan. Many participants also contribute to an IRA at the same time. For a SEP IRA, you can contribute 25 percent of your self-employment income or $40,000, whichever is less.

2 Determine your eligibility. Employer-sponsored plans may have a waiting period after your hire date. Individual plans are open to everyone, though conventional and Roth IRAs have income limits. Self-employment plans are usually open to all people.

3 Sign up. If you have a plan offered at work, specify how much of your salary you want deposited into your account. For self-directed and self-employment plans, check with large institutions like Charles Schwab (schwab.com) and Fidelity (fidelity.com). These companies let you sign up online in minutes.

4 Choose where your money goes. Most retirement plans offer a dizzying array of options to invest in. The key to long-term gains is proper diversification. Strive for a blend of stocks (including

What to Look For

• Eligibility date
• Contribution limits
• Investment options
• Company matching
• Vesting period
• Borrowing privileges

Tips

While stocks can give solid long-term gains, they may be volatile over the short term. If you've got a long time until your retirement, you can afford to be more aggressive in your investment choices. If you're closer to retirement, consider less volatile investments, like bonds or cash.

Contribution limits usually increase every year. Most savvy investors are sure to contribute the maximum amount they can, so adjust your contribution schedule at the beginning of every year to max out your plan.

For holders age 50 or older, there are catch-up provisions that allow you to contribute an amount in excess of the basic annual contribution. For 2003, the catch-up amount for a 401(k) is $2,000, $500 for a conventional IRA, and $1,000 for a Simple IRA.

small and large cap, and international), bonds and cash. Your exact mix depends on when you want to retire and your tolerance for risk. Many financial Web sites and financial planners offer portfolio diversification advice.

5 Ask about matching contributions on 401(k)s and Simple IRAs. Company matches are literally free money. Some companies are generous enough to contribute a dollar for every dollar you deposit yourself, although the most common match is 50 cents per dollar invested by an employee.

6 For employer-sponsored plans, find out how long the vesting period is, which refers to the amount of time before any company contributions become your property. It can take several years before you're fully vested, although employee contributions are 100 percent vested at the outset.

7 Understand the tax advantage. Most money that you deposit into the majority of plans is considered tax-free income by the IRS. That's an immediate payback—you're paying no taxes on money that's still yours. That money and any gains from its investment remains tax-deferred until you retire and begin to withdraw it.

8 Reexamine your tax withholdings on your paycheck. Since a retirement plan leaves a portion of your income untaxed, you may be withholding too much money from each paycheck (and giving the government an interest-free loan). Calculate your real tax liability for the entire year, divide it by the number of paychecks, and set your withholding accordingly. Talk to your accountant for more information.

9 Avoid early withdrawals. You may be liable for the tax on any money you withdraw before you reach age 59½ and also have to pay an additional penalty.

10 Use your nest egg for emergencies if you must. Many plans let you borrow against some retirement plans in situations of hardship or for a first-time home purchase, sometimes up to half the money in the account. But penalties and taxes may be extreme, so check the details before you tap into your retirement account.

11 If you have a 401(k) or other employer-sponsored retirement plan and you leave that company, roll this money into an IRA. Some companies will let you keep your funds in their plan after you leave, but you have much more control and a much greater range of investment choices in an IRA.

Warnings

Look carefully at how much of your money goes into the stock of the company you work for. As any Enron employee will tell you, having the majority of your money in one asset can leave you dangerously undiversified.

Consider commissions and fees when choosing a broker to handle your plan. Most retirement accounts will hold stocks and mutual funds, and different brokers have different trading fees. It pays to shop around.

129 Save for Your Child's College Education

Better sit down. Experts say that someone born in 2003 and entering a public college or university in 2021 can expect to shell out $95,000 for an undergraduate degree. A private college may run upwards of $240,000. Although there are several college savings plans to choose from, the 529 plan is a standout. In addition to providing a means of establishing a regular savings program for you, there are big tax advantages—namely that your investment grows tax-free until the child enters college and can then be withdrawn untaxed to pay tuition. Take steps now to ease the future shock of college costs.

Steps

1 Estimate how much you will be expected to contribute to your child's college education. Review financial aid packages for families with your income level and asset portfolio to establish a baseline savings target. Web sites like Kiplinger.com and FinAid.com provide a useful family contribution estimator.

2 Choose your college savings plan wisely. Some allow you to deposit more than $200,000 tax-free, while others limit the amount. Look into how a plan invests its money. Some managers buy mutual funds; others, certificates of deposit. Be sure to get details about how the plan has performed in the past. Here is a sampling of plans:

- State-operated 529 plans. A 529 is one of the most attractive options available to help families save for college because anyone can open one, the money deposited grows tax-free, and it can then be withdrawn to cover college costs without being taxed. (A 529 also has important estate-planning bene-fits.) You can even begin saving before your child is born. Every state now operates at least one 529 plan. First, you select the state plan that best fits your needs based on how much you can invest, how the funds are invested, and the tax ramifications, such as being able to avoid state taxes in addi-tion to federal taxes. Second, sign up using a simple form. After that, you begin to deposit as much each year as you can under the plan's guidelines. Your money is invested and grows completely tax-free, and each plan is professionally managed.

- Coverdell Education Savings Account (CESA), formerly known as an Education IRA, will allow you save up to $2,000 a year tax-deferred. The biggest advantage is that funds can be used for elementary and secondary school education, in addition to college. However, the cons far outweigh that advantage: CESA funds are considered student assets when financial aid is cal-

What to Look For

- Contribution estimator
- The right plan
- Tax advantages

Tips

If you can, keep the plan in your name, even if you're saving for your child's edu-cation. Not only do you maintain control of the money, but you may also be better positioned if you need to apply for financial aid. If the money is in your child's name, he or she may appear more wealthy and be eligible for less aid.

Funding a 529 in your state may entitle you to take a tax deduction for the amount invested. However, if you set up a 529 in another state, you lose any tax deduction your state offers.

culated, potentially reducing the amount of financial aid your child will be eligible to receive by falsely increasing their anticipated earnings. The money is also considered the student's and cannot be turned back over to the person who established the account, as with a 529. Finally, with smaller maximum contributions, administrative fees can turn out to be larger in proportion to the dollars saved.

- State prepaid tuition programs, which are a variation of a 529 plan, let you save by locking in current tuition rates for future use. Prepaid tuition plans are college savings plans that are guaranteed to increase in value at the same rate as college tuition. So by purchasing the equivalent of a year's worth of tuition today, you ensure that in 15 years your investment will still be worth a year's worth of tuition at the current rate. The tuition rate used is at an in-state public college, so if your child elects to attend a private college, you will still be responsible for paying the difference between a year at a public college versus a year at a private one.

- Uniform Gift to Minors Account/Uniform Transfer to Minors Act (UGMA/UTMA) is an old standby that allows you to give your child up to $11,000 without getting hit by gift tax, which he or she can use for any purpose. That's the good news and the bad news—it's more flexible in terms of how the funds can be used, but your child assumes complete control at age 18. Most states offer these accounts, which can be set up at a brokerage firm.

3 Shop around for a 529 plan, once you've decided what features are of greatest value to you. Even though your plan is operated by a particular state, you're not limited to choosing a school in that state. Rather, you can use the money for any college. Some plans, however, do offer tax advantages for in-state residents.

4 Compare plans. Use Fidelity's Comparison Table (fidelity.com) to evaluate the various college savings programs and to see which best suits your needs and situation. Check out Savingforcollege.com to compare 529 plans state by state.

Warnings

A 529 plan isn't perfect: No one fully knows how it will affect financial aid formulas. Also, if you use some of the money for something other than school-related expenses, you'll be hit with a 10 percent penalty on earnings.

There's a major consideration involved with UGMAs. Once your child reaches 18, he or she gets control of the money. And that might mean the money goes for a Harley instead of Harvard.

Prepaid tuition programs at specific schools can be great if your child seems destined for a particular school (he or she may be part of a legacy or the school may be close to home), but you may forfeit some of its value if you transfer your savings to a different school.

130 Buy and Sell Stocks

Stocks are a lot like sex in high school: Everyone pretends to know everything, few actually know anything, and nobody ever lets on about what they don't know. Here's what to look for, and how to build a stock portfolio that's right for you.

Steps

1 Understand how stocks operate. Stocks are a form of equity investing, because when you buy shares of stock you actually get partial ownership of that company. When a company does well, its value increases, and so does the value of the shares.

2 Join the National Association of Investors Corporation (NAIC) to gain access to a low-cost stock purchase program. Members can buy stock in a long list of companies, paying as little as $10 a month, as a way to slowly build a nest egg. The cost to join NAIC is less than $50 a year and includes a monthly subscription to a magazine on investing.

3 Get to know the stock exchanges. Stocks are traded on three major exchanges in the United States: the New York Stock Exchange, which includes some of the biggest companies in the world; the American Stock Exchange; and the NASDAQ National Market System, an electronic exchange. Each exchange trades the stocks of different companies, so once you choose a company to invest in, find out which exchange it is traded on in order to monitor it.

4 Familiarize yourself with different types of stocks. *Growth stocks* are stocks in relatively inexpensive companies that have a good chance to increase in value. *Income stocks* have less growth potential but consistently produce high dividends. Other types include *value stocks,* which are a variant of growth stocks; *cyclical stocks,* which are tied to economic ups and downs; and *international stocks,* which are stocks in foreign companies that may or may not be traded on U.S. exchanges.

5 Clarify your investment goals. Do you need to stockpile funds for your retirement or are you looking to purchase a house within two years? Or are you looking for investments that produce income? As a general rule, the longer the investment time frame, the more aggressive you can afford to be.

6 Determine how stocks fit into your overall portfolio. Stocks, like all investments, should take up a limited portion of your assets according to your master financial plan. Construct an asset allo-

What to Look For:

- Types of stocks and companies
- Solid products or services
- Good financials
- Undervalued stocks (low price-earnings ratio)
- Technical analysis

Tip

Recent laws now reduce the tax on corporate dividends, making income stocks very attractive. Consider this new tax incentive if you are purchasing stocks for income.

cation for your entire investment portfolio, decide how much of it should go to stocks, and stick to that percentage. As stocks gain and lose value, you may need to buy or sell to maintain your planned mix.

7 Start with simple parameters. Pick companies that you know and products that you're familiar with. Do you use them? Are they good?

8 Understand the underlying fundamentals of the companies whose stock you buy. These include the markets they are in, their balance sheet (which shows assets and liabilities) and their competitors. Another indicator is the company's past and present earnings and how that relates to the number of shares the company has outstanding (known as *earnings per share*). This is a closely watched number among professional investors.

9 Review stock analyses from research firms like ValueLine and Morningstar, which sell subscriptions to their reports. Local libraries typically carry recent issues.

10 Calculate the stock's price-earnings (P/E) ratio. This ratio divides the price per share of the stock by its earnings per share. This shows you how expensive a stock price is when compared with the company's actual earnings. As a rule, the higher the P/E, the more the potential of the company may already be priced into the stock.

11 Get professional help. The most traditional avenue is through a brokerage house, where you can get firsthand advice from a broker. But you'll pay a commission for any transaction (which, depending on the house, can be substantial). See 131 Choose a Stockbroker.

12 Look at online brokerages and discount houses. The commissions are low, the trades are quick, and the research resources are often extensive, but you won't get any hand-holding.

13 Match your stock to your needs and temperament: Invest in risky stocks only if you have the stomach and the time to ride out market fluctuations.

14 Diversify for greater safety. When buying several stocks, mix things up. Buy stocks from different industries, and balance aggressive stocks with more conservative choices.

Warnings

Never buy on so-called tips. Not only can the information be suspect, but tips can often circulate long after action has occurred. Trading on an old tip is like buying an umbrella after the rain has stopped.

The dot-com era has taught investors to be cautious when following analysts' recommendations. Investment banks that publish reports on companies may also do other banking or consultation work with the company. And while this may not be a conflict of interest at every bank, it has certainly raised eyebrows in recent years. Bottom line: Overly bullish recommendations need to coincide with your own independent research.

131 Choose a Stockbroker

Plenty of investors buy stocks on their own. But if you prefer not to fly solo, it pays to know what sort of broker best fits your needs. You may want someone to actively plan your investments, or you may prefer someone who's available only if you need advice.

Steps

1 Determine the services you're looking for and your investment goals. Brokers offer varying degrees of services: Some may focus purely on investing, while others may place a greater emphasis on investor education and financial planning. See 127 Choose a Financial Planner, too.

2 Compare discount and full-service firms. Discount brokers make securities purchases and sales at a lower commission, but offer little or no advice; full-service brokers will work with you on an investment strategy, but you'll pay more.

3 Ask friends and colleagues for referrals. Try to interview at least three candidates before making a choice.

4 Meet the prospective brokers in their offices and inquire about their investment philosophy and how they handle clients. Have them give you details about any special training or designations they may have. Ask how long they've been in business, and if they've ever been disciplined. (See Tip.)

5 Discuss compensation. Find out what the fee structures and minimum purchase requirements are. Ask about any special commission they might get for certain brands of mutual funds.

6 Find out how often your broker checks in with clients. If you only want to hear from a broker every few weeks, don't choose someone who prefers to strategize at every shift of the market.

7 Ask a broker for referrals to clients whose background and goals match your own. If the broker balks, look for someone else.

What to Look For

- Services you need
- Similar philosophy
- Credentials
- Appropriate fee structure
- Track record with clients

Tip

The National Association of Securities Dealers (nasd.com) has information on the required qualifications to be a broker. You can also get information about individual brokers' work history plus any disciplinary actions.

Warning

Follow your gut feeling when meeting with potential brokers. Like any salesperson, brokers run the gamut from ultrapushy and aggressive to more relaxed. Work with someone whose style you feel comfortable with.

132 Day-Trade (or Not)

For a while, it seemed that everyone was day-trading. And even though it sounds simple—buy a fast-moving stock and ride out its short-term price movement—it's a strategy that's fraught with risks. Not even professional money managers do it that often. But if skydiving is your style, at least be prepared before you take this leap.

Steps

1 Put day-trading in context with your entire financial picture. Individual equities are an asset class like any others. Construct an asset allocation for your entire investment portfolio, and

What to Look For

- Online order execution
- High-speed Internet connection

decide how much of it should be allocated to day-traded stocks. Talk to a financial adviser; most will recommend allocating only a small portion of your assets to day-trading.

2 Learn what to look for. Some traders monitor price movement in the hopes of catching an uptick; others keep an eye out for quarterly or annual reports that may impact short-term prices.

3 Do your homework on stocks. Trade in a small number of securities and understand the fundamentals of their business. Stock prices are affected by many factors, so understand what drives the price for your specific stock. Get to know the companies well, and watch them like a hawk.

4 Know the pace and the risks. Day-trading goes against the very core values of long-term investing. Rather than holding them for the long run, day-traders opt for a hit-and-run approach, often buying and selling stocks the same day.

5 Sign up for online order execution, which is critical for speedy buys and sells. Most firms that offer this service charge a monthly fee for access, plus a per-trade charge.

6 Get a DSL line or other high-speed connection for your computer. Since day-trading truly trades on speed, you must have real-time access to data, which can cost anywhere from $75 to $300 a month for the service. Although you don't have to have a special software package, buying one can help you spot trends. Ask if you can operate from your broker's office, if access to the right equipment is something you currently lack. Some firms may be willing to set you up in return for a commitment to make a certain number of trades per week.

7 Set aside enough time. Successful day-trading requires constant attention. If you have a job or some other time-consuming responsibility, that sort of focus may be hard to come by. If you are serious, treat day-trading as a job.

8 Choose one to three trading techniques you'll use and stick to them, such as watching for a three- to five-day pullback on a particular stock's price after an event or trading technique. Don't go beyond your comfort zone or knowledge base.

9 Start slow. Try day-trading just one or two stocks using only a modest investment. Watch them closely, and see what drives their price movements. You'll gain experience, and it's a cheap education if things go badly.

10 Keep a journal detailing the trades you've made, what cycles you see in the market, when you were successful and when you failed. Review your journal every few weeks to spot trends and to learn from your mistakes.

Tip

Use stop-loss orders—where you specify a price for a stock to be sold automatically—to limit the downside risks of day-trading.

Warning

Be sure you are familiar with the new rules of day-trading, instituted in September 2001. Pattern Day Traders (PDTs) must now have more money to start ($25,000 instead of just $2,000) but can buy on margin to a greater degree (4:1, up from 2:1). However, there are also rules for closing out trades and fund availability that you need to be up on before you get started as a day-trader.

133 Buy Annuities

Annuities can prove to be a valuable element in funding your retirement plans. An annuity is basically a contract for which you make an up-front payment. In return, the company selling the annuity promises to pay you regular payments in the future. But you must know how annuities function and what their key features are.

Steps

1 Start shopping. Insurance companies, banks, brokerage houses, mutual-fund companies, and even nonprofit organizations all sell annuities.

2 Learn the two basic kinds of annuities and how they differ.

- A *fixed annuity* guarantees you a certain future payment. This is a good option only for very, very conservative investors. The rate of return on your money is low, and annuities use actuarial tables based on a person living to be 100.

- With a *variable annuity*, you choose where to invest your money, and the size of your payment depends on the performance of that invested capital. They are a great way to invest money tax-deferred that is not otherwise eligible for retirement savings. You can choose to invest in stocks, mutual funds, money markets and other options.

3 Put money into the annuity during the accumulation period; receive payments during the payout period. Choose between immediate or deferred payouts.

4 Check out the tax implications: You don't pay any tax on the annuity as long as you don't withdraw any money. Once the payout begins, the money you receive is taxed as ordinary income.

5 Be aware of penalties. If you begin to take money out prior to age 59½, you may be hit with a 10 percent IRS penalty, on top of any taxes for which you may be liable. Additionally, the company may assess surrender charges if you take out money not long after you made a deposit (but that can sometimes be as long as 10 years).

6 Choose a beneficiary. Should you die before the payout period—or at some point during the payout period itself—your beneficiary gets a death benefit (either all the money in the account or a predetermined minimum).

7 Be clear on what the other fees are, such as any mortality and expense risks charges and administrative fees. And always get a complete list of all fees and charges attached to any annuity.

8 Work with your tax adviser when considering an annuity. For all the tax advantages of annuities, you may do better in the long run with an IRA or a 401(k) plan where you work.

What to Look For

- Fixed versus variable annuities
- Accumulation and payout periods
- Death benefit
- Surrender charges
- Other fees and expenses

Tips

If you're considering a variable annuity connected with a mutual fund, ask about the fund's performance, just as you would with any mutual fund.

Studies show that variable annuities only make sense for people with a longer time frame. Schwab estimates that it takes 5 to 15 years before the tax benefits outweigh the often-higher fees imposed by variable annuities.

Ask about a "free look" period to assess communication and record keeping. Many companies let you own an annuity for up to 10 days. Then, if you're dissatisfied in any way, it will return all your money without any surrender charges.

Warnings

There can be inheritance tax disadvantages to annuities. The growth of an annuity can be fully taxable as income. Some other investments have a stepped-up cost basis.

Independent ratings on annuities are hard to come by. Get advice from your financial planner before choosing an annuity.

134 Buy and Sell Mutual Funds

If you want to acquire a broad range of investments with just one purchase, mutual funds are the way to go. They're easy to buy, just as simple to sell, and rich in benefits and features. You will have to do your homework to identify which ones best fit your needs.

Steps

1 Get to know the basic makeup of mutual funds. Mutual funds are a portfolio that can contain a variety of securities, including stocks, bonds and certificates of deposit. Most funds have a specific focus or concentration.

2 Identify your investment goals. Specific objectives will help you determine the sort of mutual fund that best fits your needs. Do you need to pay for a college education? Fund your retirement? Buy a vacation home?

3 Determine how mutual funds fit into your overall portfolio. Like all investments, only a portion of your assets should be allocated to mutual funds (according to your plan). Determine that percentage and stick to it. Most mutual funds consist of stocks, which have more inherent risk than other investments. Younger people, for example, may hold a larger percentage of their assets in mutual funds, as their investing timeline is usually longer.

4 Evaluate your tolerance for risk and tailor your investments accordingly. If you're risk averse but you buy the most aggressive fund on the market, you're likely to be in for a string of sleepless nights.

5 Start your search. Most financial magazines have annual issues that rate mutual funds according to performance, risk and other parameters. Web sites such as Fidelity.com and Schwab.com have fund evaluation tools. Get a copy of the prospectus.

6 Investigate performance—in particular, a fund's long-term performance. For instance, Fidelity's well-known Magellan Fund has a 10-year average rate of return of 9.15 percent. Compare a fund's performance to an established benchmark, like the S&P 500. Also, companies like Morningstar (morningstar.com) rate mutual funds against others in their own class.

7 Check out a fund's expenses. Mutual fund costs are ultimately subtracted from proceeds to investors and are usually expressed as an expense ratio. Magellan has an expense ratio of less than 1 percent.

8 Get a sense of a fund's volatility. Compare one year's performance to the next. A stable fund will perform relatively consistently from year to year, while a fund with greater risk may go through highs and lows like a roller coaster.

9 Buy the fund through a financial adviser (you may have to pay a one-time fee) or the fund family itself, or use an online broker.

135 Buy Bonds

If stocks are a form of ownership in a company, bonds are more of a pure loan. In effect, you lend money to a company or the government with the guarantee that you'll get it back over time, in exchange for getting paid interest. In that sense, buying bonds can provide a nice mix with stocks and other investments. And you can do it yourself, although it's smarter to work with a financial planner to be sure bonds fit with your particular investment strategy.

Steps

1 Ask your financial adviser what types of bonds are available and who sells them. Companies issue *corporate bonds* to pay for various activities. These usually offer the highest rate of return (known as the yield). The federal government issues *Treasury bonds*, including Treasury bills (aka T-bills) and Treasury notes. These bonds don't yield as much as corporate bonds, but they are exempt from state and local taxes. Local governments issue *municipal bonds* to pay for community projects. These are free of federal taxes and may be exempt from other taxes.

2 Find out when the bond matures and how the interest payment is structured. A short-term bond matures in 3 years or less; an intermediate bond, in 5 to 12 years; a long-term bond, in 12 years or more. Interest can be paid monthly, quarterly or annually. You'll want to select a bond that works for your income needs; for example, if you have to make a tuition payment monthly, get a bond that pays interest monthly.

3 Pay close attention to a bond's rating to determine how safe that bond is. Agencies like Moody's or Standard and Poor's indicate how financially solid the bond's seller is. A higher rating generally means a secure bond. And the higher the rating, the lower the interest rate; junk bonds are risky but offer a much higher return (if the companies actually survive to pay back your loan). You may find a corporate bond with a lower rating and fairly good rate of return. The hard part is assessing how stable a company will be over the life of the bond so you can get your money back.

4 Know what "call" indicates. A bond's issuer, whether a company, municipality or government agency, retains the option to retire bonds early if it is in their interest to do so. This means that when interest rates go down, a bond issuer has the option of paying it off before the maturity date so that it can issue new bonds at a lower rate. You, as the investor, have your cash back, but you're faced with a lower rate of return if you reinvest the money.

5 Understand that bonds generate income through a series of prearranged payments to bondholders. But you can also make money because of interest-rate movement. For example, if you own a bond that yields 7 percent interest and interest rates go down, any new bonds being issued will pay less than the one you own. That makes your bond a more valuable commodity.

What to Look For

- Corporate, Treasury or municipal bonds
- Term to maturity
- Yield
- Rating

Tips

Shop and compare. Not all sellers may offer every available bond, nor will two sellers necessarily quote the same price for a bond. Waiting for the market to shift may also work to your advantage, but be aware that the same bond may not be available next week.

Diversify. As with stocks, it's better to mix up the sorts of bonds you own. Diversity of type, yield and maturity offers greater safety.

Issuers are developing all sorts of innovative bonds to meet specific needs. For instance, the federal government now offers an inflation-indexed Treasury bond designed to adjust to changing inflation rates.

6 Be very aware of the risks involved. Interest-rate movement can also work against bonds. If interest rates go up, the bond you're holding becomes less valuable than new bonds that get issued. In addition to call provisions, companies can also go bankrupt and default on their bonds (think Enron), leaving bondholders with no interest or principal payments during the bankruptcy, and new bonds or a combination of stocks and bonds once the company exits bankruptcy protection.

7 Buy the bonds from a full-service broker (often charging a sizable commission—be sure to ask), from a discount broker (which costs less) or online through a site like etrade.com. Just pick the bonds you want and place an order. You can buy Treasury bonds directly from the federal government at regularly scheduled auctions. Contact a nearby Federal Reserve Bank for details or go online to www.publicdebt.treas.gov/ols/olshome.htm.

8 Consider bond funds. Many financial institutions offer bond funds that pool money from many investors to buy funds of differing types and maturities. The advantages are professional management and convenience. But remember you're still buying bonds, with all the same inherent risks.

Warning

If you're buying a small number of bonds at $1,000 each, or $5,000 to $10,000 for municipal bonds, the cost of the trade may be so high as to wipe out any yield you'd earn. Look carefully at the trade fee and the APR to make sure it's worth proceeding.

136 Sell Short

You might want to think of selling short as the flip side of the traditional stock market strategy. Rather than hoping a stock does well, you're betting on it to do poorly. If it seems risky, you're right—you're essentially swimming against the tide. There's money to be made, but it's critical to know the ins and outs of this aggressive system.

What to Look For

- Margin account
- Market downturns
- At-risk stocks

Steps

1 Set up a margin account at a brokerage house. You need to put up collateral, such as cash or stocks, and the brokerage house will lend you up to 50 percent of their value.

2 Use the margin account to borrow shares of stocks from other accounts with your broker's help. You then sell them. If the price of the shares goes down, you buy the shares again at the lower price, return them to the accounts you borrowed from, and keep the difference. That's the practical definition of "shorting a stock."

3 Know the sorts of conditions that work. Selling short can be an effective strategy if the market as a whole is dropping. It can also be useful with a stock whose company has been hit by bad news or other developments that cause the stock to decrease in value.

4 Try short-selling on a very limited basis. You'll get a feel for how it works—and how it can hurt.

Warning

Selling short can leave you having to pay a huge tab if things go against you. For example, if you short a stock at $5 a share and instead it goes up to $15, you're on the hook for $10 for every share you shorted.

137 Invest in Precious Metals

Experienced investors have long known that gold, silver and platinum can be a solid investment choice. Precious metals are stable in times of worldwide uncertainty, or when the economy is bad. Used correctly, they can be an effective component of a diversified investment portfolio, but remember, they are an investment like any others, and have an element of risk (albeit more modest). It's essential to achieve the proper mix.

What to Look For

- Coins or bars
- Certificates
- Mutual funds
- Futures

Steps

1 Be familiar with the five principal ways to invest in gold and precious metals: tangible coins and bars; certificates; precious metals mutual funds; stock in mining companies; and gold and metals futures.

2 Go with coins or bars if you're interested primarily in safety and diversity.

3 Break down tangible precious metals into its subcategories: bullion and numismatics. Gold bullion (or bars) is pure or almost pure gold. Numismatics are minted coins, which often commemorate special occasions.

4 Search for both online and brick-and-mortar precious metals dealers. Find out how long the dealer has been in business, whether he or she specializes in one segment of the market, and who the typical client is.

5 Shop around. The markup on coins and bars will vary. One popular choice for coins is the 1 troy ounce size as they are easy to buy, sell and store.

6 Educate yourself about the numismatics market. The design and condition of a coin can affect its price as much as the precious metal content itself.

7 Choose certificates if you would rather not store anything. A certificate represents ownership of a certain quantity of a specific precious metal.

8 Consider stocks and funds for additional choices. Precious metals funds, because they are diversified and managed, are the most stable. Stocks are less stable, because you're buying into only one company.

9 For a higher risk/higher potential return alternative, consider precious metals futures if you feel confident of your ability to predict whether the value of metals will increase or decline. Futures are a contract to buy or sell metals at a particular price at a specific point in time. Doing well with them depends solely on what happens to the value of those metals during the contract term.

Tips

Because of their volatility, precious metals should represent only a small portion of your portfolio—10 percent at the most.

The most conservative way to go into precious metals is through a mutual fund. It's professionally managed, diversified and is particularly well-suited to new investors.

Warning

The drawback to precious metals is that they increase in value only when the price per ounce goes up. By contrast, stocks and bonds can pay dividends and offer other income sources. If conditions for gold are poor, your stash can sit for years doing virtually nothing.

138 Buy Disability Insurance

Here's a sobering thought: You're far more likely to suffer an injury and lose time from work than you are to be killed outright. Even the most systematic and aggressive savings program can be drained if you're unable to work for a year or more. That makes disability insurance—which provides an income if you're injured and unable to work—an absolute must.

Steps

1 Learn about the elements of a disability plan. The *benefits period* is how long the policy will continue to provide you an income. The *elimination period* is the time between when you're injured and when you start getting benefits. Most policies provide benefits to age 65, but offering only two years of benefits is not unheard of. Be clear on what type of coverage you have.

2 Find out if your employer offers a disability plan. It's not common, but it is out there.

3 Make sure your plan provides enough coverage. Most long-term disability plans replace only 60 percent of a base salary, up to a maximum of $5,000 per month in benefits (bonus and commission income is not covered).

4 Know what is covered. Many disability insurance policies have strict guidelines for which disabilities are covered and which are not. For example, mental disabilities and incapacitation are gray areas. Read the fine print.

5 Calculate your financial needs. If you were laid up for a year, how much would you need for you and your family to live? Be sure to factor in future expenses, like college educations. Bring your financial picture into focus and compare that to the coverage. Being underinsured can be a big financial risk.

6 Shop around for a disability plan if your employer doesn't offer one. Contact agents and search online sites that give rate quotes. Large insurance providers all offer disability packages.

7 Supplement your company's plan with individual long-term disability coverage if your employer's program won't cover all of your family's expenses. Individual coverage can go as high as $10,000 to $15,000 per month, but it's tax-free if you pay the premium.

8 Expect to pay a sizable premium. Don't be surprised if your annual premium tops $1,800.

9 Tinker with your policy so you get adequate coverage without paying too much. The less you settle for in monthly benefits, the lower your premium.

What to Look For

- Employer-provided coverage
- Adequate coverage
- Supplemental individual coverage to fill in the gap
- Affordable premium

Tips

If you can only afford limited disability coverage, try to protect yourself with as much savings as possible.

If the coverage is too expensive, increase the elimination period, say from 60 days to 90 days, to cut your costs.

You can buy optional riders that provide for cost of living and future earnings increases. If you are in your 20s or 30s, this may be a good addition to consider.

139 Buy Life Insurance

Having too little life insurance can be devastating to your family should you make an early exit. Having too much is an utter waste of money. That makes knowing how much you need—and what type of coverage is best for you—a critical decision.

Steps

1 Determine if you need life insurance. If no one, such as a spouse or a child, depends on your income, then it's pointless for you to insure yourself. Life insurance is protection against lost income—no more, no less. Similarly, if you are well-off financially, your family may not need an influx of cash when you die.

2 Calculate how much coverage you'll need. Determine how much your beneficiaries need to live on, and for how long. Losing a loved one is difficult emotionally and financially, and many dependents will want a period in which they won't have to worry about money. While two years is the average cushion, some people may want to make sure their beneficiaries are set for life. Calculate all expenses for the covered period, including big ticket items like college and mortgages, as well as living expenses like clothes and food. Then subtract the amount of money you think your beneficiaries will make from salaries and investments (remember, they may not go back to work right away). By subtracting all estimated expenses from the income you estimate your beneficiaries will earn, you get a basic idea on how much insurance coverage you need.

3 Choose what type of coverage best meets your needs. Insurance is protection, not an investment. Think of insurance in terms of decreasing responsibility as you get older. When you are younger and have kids and a mortgage, you need protection. As you get older, your kids have graduated and you likely have few or no payments left on your mortgage, so you need less protection.

- *Term* life insurance is the simplest way to go—you pay the premium and are covered for a specific benefit for the period during which you want coverage. When you stop paying, you stop being covered. Term is a much cheaper option in the long run, and you can invest the money you would have otherwise paid for whole life in mutual funds.

- *Universal* life policies allow you to adjust your premiums as well as your death benefit. *Variable* life lets you choose how to invest the policy's cash value. A portion of what you pay in premiums goes into a cash value, which could increase over time and can be redeemed before your death. Unfortunately, the mortality expense of all cash value policies goes up significantly after age 60, so that you could be in the situation where your payment goes up drastically or your investment account used to pay your premiums quickly dries up. If you die with a large

What to Look For

- Sufficient coverage
- Reasonable premiums
- Death benefit
- Term versus whole life policy
- Universal or variable life
- Cash value

Tips

Know the terminology. A *premium* is the money you pay to keep the policy in force. The *death benefit* is the payment dictated by the policy to be made upon your death. The *beneficiary* is the person or persons who will receive the death benefit.

The cost of term life insurance has been falling, so it may be worth replacing an existing term policy you have. Check current rates for term life insurance at comparison sites such as Term4Sale.com.

Evaluate whether it makes sense to get an insurance policy on someone else, such as your spouse or business partner, whose death would cause real hardship for you. Insurance policies can be purchased for just about anyone.

cash value balance, your beneficiary still gets only the face amount, not the face amount plus the cash value.

- *Whole* life insurance has significant drawbacks. First, the premiums are generally far more costly—especially in the early years of the policy, when you're mostly paying commissions rather than building cash value. Second, if you have to cash out the policy early, you may have to pay a surrender charge.

4 Check the ratings. Insurers run the gamut from shaky upstarts to household-name institutions. Most companies are rated for financial strength and claims paying ability by independent rating agencies. Ratings from A.M. Best, Moody's, and Standard and Poor's are the most often cited.

Borrow against your life insurance

1 "Borrow" money from a cash value life policy as an absolute last resort. If you own a home consider an equity line before borrowing from your cash value. With an equity line, your interest is deductible and you will most often get a better rate than the insurance company is willing to offer. (See 185 Obtain a Home Equity Loan.)

2 Contact your insurance company if you have no other options and find out how large your cash value is and how much you can borrow. The amount available to you depends on how much cash has accumulated in the policy. That, in turn, depends on how long the policy's been around, how much you've paid into it, and other factors. For example, if you have a $300,000 policy with a cash value of $50,000, your borrowing capability will be based on the $50,000 cash value.

3 Understand that when you borrow against your cash value, you must pay interest on the amount you borrow. The interest you pay does not go into your cash value, as many people think. Instead it goes back into the pockets of the insurance company.

4 Carefully check the terms and conditions of the loan. Some insurance companies restrict how much of your cash value you can borrow, and have special payback terms. Make certain that the interest rates are lower than what other loan sources, such as home equity loans, are offering.

5 Withdraw the money. There is no restriction on how you can use the money, as there is with a 401(k) withdrawal, for example. You don't ever have to pay it back, as long as you're willing to have a reduced death benefit for your beneficiaries when you do pass away. But, you'll also pay interest on it for the rest of your life. On top of that, any interest you owe on that loan will also be deducted from the payout.

Warnings

If you borrow from a policy that is characterized as a modified endowment contract, you could create a taxable event under certain circumstances.

If you stop paying premiums after 8 or 10 years when the cash value has risen enough, and take a loan against it, you may actually have to continue paying annual premiums. Find out in advance if you have this type of vanishing premium policy and under what circumstances you'd have to start paying premiums again.

140 Get Health Insurance

While you may not need life insurance, and you might be willing to risk not having earthquake insurance, don't gamble with health insurance. Just a couple of days in the hospital can drain almost anyone's savings. Health insurance can be expensive, but with a little research, you can find coverage that fits your budget.

Steps

1 Sign on with the health insurance provided by your employer: it is likely to be the cheapest option you can find. Search for your own insurance if you're self-employed, or if your company doesn't offer it.

2 Investigate coverage under COBRA (Consolidated Omnibus Reconciliation Act of 1985) if you've recently left your employer. Through COBRA you can extend your coverage for 18 months beyond your separation date, though you have to pay the premium yourself.

3 Find a health insurance broker to compare plans and costs for you. The National Association of Health Underwriters (nahu.org) can help find one in your area.

4 Purchase a fee-for-service plan. The biggest plus is that you have complete control over which doctor you see and determine for yourself when you need to see a specialist. However, there is a significant out-of-pocket cost for this kind of care, the premiums are generally higher, and if your doctor charges more than what is considered customary, you may have to shell out additionally for that care as well.

5 Sign up for a managed care plan where your insurance provider determines which doctors you can see. There are three basic kinds of managed care:

• Preferred provider organizations (PPOs) have a list of doctors to select from when choosing a physician who will be your first contact for health care. If you see doctors in your insurer's network, you pay a low co-payment. However, if you see a physician not in the network, your co-pay is higher. You also generally don't need prior approval to see a specialist—PPOs give you the most flexibility but cost more in monthly premiums and out-of-pocket costs.

What to Look For

• Employer-provided coverage
• An insurance broker
• Fee-for-service plan
• Managed care plan
• Adequate coverage
• Preexisting conditions
• Affordable premiums

Tips

One way to hold down the cost of a fee-for-service plan is by increasing your deductible. This is the amount you must pay before any coverage applies.

Make certain your policy has a guaranteed renewal clause. It ensures that you can renew your coverage as long as you like. It also prevents your insurer from dropping your policy or raising your premiums if you get sick.

- Point-of-service (POS) networks are similar to PPOs, except that your primary care physician makes decisions about which specialists you can and can't see. You can still see a physician outside the POS network, but face higher fees and more paperwork to do so.

- Health maintenance organizations (HMOs) are the most restrictive, yet least expensive managed care programs. Most require that you see a doctor in their network, but offer low or no co-pays in exchange. Many HMOs also require you to see your primary care physician before getting referred to a specialist.

6 Find out if benefits are limited for preexisting conditions, or if you have to wait for a period of time before you're fully covered. Other plans may completely exclude coverage of preexisting conditions.

7 Compare the prescription drug coverage offered by various plans. Many plans have tiered benefit systems, and usually offer a preferred list of prescriptions that have a lower co-pay. Search for any medication you are taking on this list; drugs not on the list can have a co-pay that is twice as high. Also, see if any plans limit the amounts of new prescriptions or refills on a given drug.

8 Check to make sure your regular doctors are on your plan's preferred provider list. All plans provide a database of their provider list on their Web site. Go with a plan that lists most or all of your regular doctors. Be aware that most PPOs will pay up to 20 percent less for out-of-network doctors.

9 Investigate what sorts of delays you may encounter with managed care. Some plans are notorious about keeping members waiting to see a doctor. Ask a doctor you intend to visit how long a typical wait is before you choose a plan.

10 Shop around. Call several agents and compare policies and premiums.

11 Look into other potential sources for health insurance. Alumni associations, professional groups, fraternal organizations and other associations often offer health coverage to their members.

141 Buy Personal Finance Software

Some people just aren't cut out to work with a broker or a financial planner. But they still have finances to manage. Whether you need unbiased financial advice or an efficient way to track your money, don't overlook financial software.

Steps

1 Decide what you need in a software program. Basic programs include check book balancing, online banking, investment tracking and organizing data for use in tax preparation software (such as TurboTax, purchased separately). More advanced programs, geared toward small businesses, are capable of double-entry bookkeeping, tracking accounts payable and receivable, tax strategies, printing invoices, and more. Many have online bill payment or can print checks from your printer, which is helpful when you're knee-deep in monthly bills.

2 Visit local computer software stores or check out sites that sell personal finance software, such as Amazon.com, to compile a list of available titles. Also check out sites that rate software, such as PCMagazine.com and Cnet.com. With a list of brand names and application titles, turn to the manufacturer Web sites—such as Intuit.com and MYOB.com—to gather more detailed information about hardware required to operate the software, level of complexity, and pricing. Some Web sites even offer a free trial or demo.

3 Ask around among friends and colleagues to see if they use the program and if so, how they like it.

4 Make sure the application is not too complex for you. Some are geared toward novices, while others are better suited to experienced users. Match the program's level to your own.

5 Choose a program that offers regular upgrades. This is particularly important with tax software, as the government has no doubt changed several tax codes since you started reading this book.

6 Look for Internet connectivity. Some financial programs let you download stock quotes, analysis, bank statements and other data. Others, including QuickBooks (intuit.com) and AccountEdge (myob.com), enable you to share data online between two or more users.

What to Look For

- Functions you need
- Ease of use
- Upgrades
- Internet connectivity

Tips

No matter which program you buy, use it regularly. The software is useful only if you keep your records up to date with it.

Check with your bank to see if it offers online banking and bill payment through desktop software. To save money and retain customers, many banks only offer these services through their own Web site.

Also consider Web-based financial services. Some sites offer financial management and electronic bill payment, and all you need is online access. These services usually have fewer features, but if your needs are simple, this could be the way to go. One example is Yahoo Bill Pay (billpay.yahoo.com).

142 Choose a Tax Preparer

You don't like to do your taxes? Get in line. Trying to keep up with the ongoing changes in the tax code is reason enough to want to work with a tax preparer. Not all tax pros are the same, so it's important to know what you want in a tax preparer and how to get it.

Steps

1 Make sure you really need a preparer. If your return is straightforward and simple, spending money on professional tax preparation may be a waste. You might only need the help you can get from a software program (see 141 Buy Personal Finance Software).

2 Choose a preparation service if your return isn't too complex. A chain service like H&R Block may be perfectly suitable, and chances are it's the least expensive choice. If you want continuity, however, don't go with a chain tax service. Turnover may make it difficult for you to use the same preparer from one year to the next.

3 Hire a qualified individual if your return is more involved and you need that one-on-one relationship. Your options include a public accountant, a certified public accountant (CPA) or an enrolled agent. A CPA must pass an exam (a standard public accountant has not yet) and keep up with ongoing education. An enrolled agent is licensed by the federal government to prepare taxes and, if need be, represent taxpayers in the event of a problem.

4 Know precisely what you're getting for your money. Although CPAs may have a formal designation, not every one is a tax specialist. Enrolled agents, on the other hand, specialize in taxes.

5 Make certain you and your tax preparer are a good fit philosophically. If you're conservative, steer clear of a preparer who wants to aggressively push the envelope on your deductions. You'll simply end up convinced that April is the cruelest month.

6 Check references to learn how responsive a particular accountant is. A tax preparer who is slow to respond can end up costing you money in late fees and penalties.

7 Save money on fees by giving your tax preparer organized files and receipts. The cleaner your records are, the less time a tax preparer has to spend in organizing them (and the less likely it is that you'll miss a valuable deduction).

8 Review your return carefully before filing it, even if a professional prepared it. Tax pros are human, but their mistakes can ultimately cost you money.

What to Look For

- Tax service or individual preparer
- Suitable training
- Similar philosophy

Tips

If you're unsure whether a tax pro is worth the money, bear in mind that you may get back more in tax savings than your preparer charges. After all, it's a preparer's job to stay current on any changes that can work in your favor. And the fee is tax-deductible.

Know who's going to prepare your return. In some larger tax services, subordinates do the actual preparation and company principals only look over the final product.

Warning

Tax shelters are a major red flag with the IRS, so make sure you understand any program suggested by a preparer. If it sounds too good to be true, it may be.

AREHOUSE STORES • BUY WHOLESALE • GET OUT OF DEBT • BUY NOTHING • BUY HAPPINESS • BUY A BETTER MOUSETRAP • BUY TIM
MEONE'S FAVOR • BUY POSTAGE STAMPS WITHOUT GOING TO THE POST OFFICE • TIP PROPERLY • BUY HEALTHY FAST FOOD • BUY S
TING SERVICE • SELL YOURSELF ON AN ONLINE DATING SERVICE • SELL YOURSELF TO YOUR GIRLFRIEND/BOYFRIEND'S FAMILY • BUY
CHOOSE FILM FOR YOUR CAMERA • BUY RECHARGEABLE BATTERIES • DONATE TO A GOOD CAUSE • HOLD A PROFITABLE GARAGE SAL
STUDENT DISCOUNTS • BUY FLOWERS WHOLESALE • GET A PICTURE FRAMED • HIRE A MOVER • HIRE A PERSONAL ORGANIZER • FIN
REAT BIRTHDAY PRESENT FOR UNDER $10 • SELECT GOOD CHAMPAGNE • BUY A DIAMOND • BUY JEWELRY MADE OF PRECIOUS METAL
IDESMAIDS' DRESSES • HIRE AN EVENT COORDINATOR • HIRE A BARTENDER FOR A PARTY • HIRE A PHOTOGRAPHER • HIRE A CATERE
Y AN ANNIVERSARY GIFT • ARRANGE ENTERTAINMENT FOR A PARTY • COMMISSION A FIREWORKS SHOW • BUY A MOTHER'S DAY GIF
FT • SELECT A THANKSGIVING TURKEY • BUY A HOUSEWARMING GIFT • PURCHASE HOLIDAY CARDS • BUY CHRISTMAS STOCKING ST
E HIGH ROLLERS ROOM IN VEGAS, BABY • BUY SOMEONE A STAR • PAY A RANSOM • GET HOT TICKETS • HIRE A LIMOUSINE • BUY A G
AM • BUY A PERSONAL JET • ACQUIRE A TELEVISION NETWORK • ACQUIRE A BODY GUARD • BOOK A LUXURY CRUISE AROUND THE W
OROUGHBRED RACEHORSE • BUY A VILLA IN TUSCANY • HIRE A PERSONAL CHEF • PURCHASE CUBAN CIGARS • HIRE A GHOSTWRITE
TNESS • MAKE BAIL • DONATE YOUR BODY TO SCIENCE • HIRE YOURSELF OUT AS A MEDICAL GUINEA PIG • SELL PLASMA • SELL YOU
OLLEGE EDUCATION • BUY AND SELL STOCKS • CHOOSE A STOCKBROKER • DAY-TRADE (OR NOT) • BUY ANNUITIES • BUY AND SELL M
UY PERSONAL FINANCE SOFTWARE • CHOOSE A TAX PREPARER • SET UP A LEMONADE STAND • SELL YOUR PRODUCT ON TV • HIRE A
USINESS IDEA • BUY A SMALL BUSINESS • BUY A FRANCHISE • LEASE RETAIL SPACE • LEASE INDUSTRIAL SPACE • LEASE OFFICE SPAC
EB SITE • BUY ADVERTISING ON THE WEB • SELL YOUR ART • HIRE A PERSONAL COACH • SELL ON THE CRAFT CIRCUIT • HIRE A LITER
ILING BUSINESS • BUY A HOT DOG STAND • SHOP FOR A MORTGAGE • REFINANCE YOUR HOME • SAVE BIG BUCKS ON YOUR MORTGA
LL A FIXER-UPPER • SELL THE FARM • SELL MINERAL RIGHTS • SELL A HOUSE • SELL A HOUSE WITHOUT A REAL ESTATE AGENT • OB
OOK A VACATION RENTAL • BUY A CONDOMINIUM • RENT AN APARTMENT OR HOUSE • OBTAIN RENTER'S INSURANCE • BUY A LOFT IN
RNISH YOUR STUDIO APARTMENT • BUY USED FURNITURE • BUY DOOR AND WINDOW LOCKS • CHOOSE AN ORIENTAL CARPET • BUY
ARRANTIES ON APPLIANCES • FIND PERIOD FIXTURES • BUY A BED AND MATTRESS • HIRE AN INTERIOR DESIGNER • HIRE A FENG SHU
N • BUY A WHIRLPOOL TUB • BUY A SHOWERHEAD • BUY A TOILET • CHOOSE A FAUCET • BUY GLUES AND ADHESIVES • CHOOSE WI
TCHEN CABINETS • CHOOSE A KITCHEN COUNTERTOP • BUY GREEN HOUSEHOLD CLEANERS • STOCK YOUR HOME TOOL KIT • BUY A
ENTRY DOOR • BUY A GARAGE-DOOR OPENER • BUY LUMBER FOR A DIY PROJECT • HOW TO SELECT ROOFING • HIRE A CONTRACT
OWERS FOR YOUR GARDEN • SELECT PEST CONTROLS • BUY SOIL AMENDMENTS • BUY MULCH • BUY A COMPOSTER • BUY FERTILI
UY KOI FOR YOUR FISH POND • BUY A STORAGE SHED • HIRE AN ARBORIST • BUY BASIC GARDEN TOOLS • BUY SHRUBS AND TREES
LECT KITCHEN KNIVES • DECIPHER FOOD LABELS • SELECT HERBS AND SPICES • STOCK YOUR KITCHEN WITH STAPLES • EQUIP A KI
OUNTAIN OYSTERS • PURCHASE LOCAL HONEY • CHOOSE POULTRY • SELECT FRESH FISH AND SHELLFISH • SELECT RICE • PURCHAS
READS • BUY ARTISAN CHEESES • PURCHASE KOSHER FOOD • BUY FOOD IN BULK • CHOOSE COOKING OILS • SELECT OLIVE OIL • SE
OFFEEMAKER OR ESPRESSO MACHINE • PURCHASE A KEG OF BEER • BUY ALCOHOL IN A DRY COUNTY • CHOOSE A MICROBREW • O
VULATION PREDICTOR KIT • PICK A PREGNANCY TEST KIT • CHOOSE BIRTH CONTROL • FIND THE RIGHT OB-GYN • HIRE A MIDWIFE OF
HOOSE DIAPERS • BUY OR RENT A BREAST PUMP • CHOOSE A CAR SEAT • BUY CHILD-PROOFING SUPPLIES • FIND FABULOUS CHILDC
ACKYARD PLAY STRUCTURE • FIND A GREAT SUMMER CAMP • SELL GIRL SCOUT COOKIES • BUY BRACES FOR YOUR KID • BUY TOYS
S A MODEL • SELL USED BABY GEAR, TOYS, CLOTHES AND BOOKS • FIND A COUPLES COUNSELOR • HIRE A FAMILY LAWYER • BUY PR
XPENSES • GET VIAGRA ONLINE • PURCHASE A TOOTHBRUSH • BUY MOISTURIZERS AND ANTIWRINKLE CREAMS • SELECT PAIN RELIE
UPPLIES • SELECT HAIR-CARE PRODUCTS • BUY WAYS TO COUNTER HAIR LOSS • BUY A WIG OR HAIRPIECE • BUY A NEW BODY • GE
ANICURIST • GET WHITER TEETH • SELECT EYEGLASSES AND SUNGLASSES • HIRE A PERSONAL TRAINER • SIGN UP FOR A YOGA CLA
EA MARKET • RENT SPACE AT AN ANTIQUE MALL • BUY AT AUCTION • KNOW WHAT YOUR COLLECTIBLES ARE WORTH • DICKER WITH
ECOGNIZE THE REAL MCCOY • BUY COINS • BUY AN ANTIQUE AMERICAN QUILT • BUY AN ANTIQUE FLAG • LIQUIDATE YOUR BEANIE B
AWNSHOP • BUY AND SELL COMIC BOOKS • BUY AND SELL SPORTS MEMORABILIA • SELL YOUR BASEBALL-CARD COLLECTIONS • CH
OMPUTER • BUY PRINTER PAPER • BUY A PRINTER • BUY COMPUTER PERIPHERALS • CHOOSE AN INTERNET SERVICE PROVIDER • GE
UY BLANK CDS • BUY AN MP PLAYER • CHOOSE A DVD PLAYER • BUY A VCR • CHOOSE A PERSONAL DIGITAL ASSISTANT • CHOOSE M
IGITAL CAMCORDER • DECIDE ON A DIGITAL CAMERA • BUY A HOME AUTOMATION SYSTEM • BUY A STATE-OF-THE-ART SOUND SYSTE
NIVERSAL REMOTE • BUY A HOME THEATER SYSTEM • BUY VIRTUAL-REALITY FURNITURE • BUY TWO-WAY RADIOS • BUY A MOBILE EN
ONEY • GET TRAVEL INSURANCE • PICK THE IDEAL LUGGAGE • FLY FOR FREE • BID FOR A SLED RIDE ON THE ALASKAN IDITAROD TRA
OREIGN OFFICIAL • GET A EURAIL PASS • TAKE AN ITALIAN BICYCLE VACATION • CHOOSE A CHEAP CRUISE • BOOK A HOTEL PACKAGE
COTLAND • BUY A SAPPHIRE IN BANGKOK • HIRE A RICKSHA IN YANGON • TAKE SALSA LESSONS IN CUBA • BUY A CAMERA IN HONG
RST BASEBALL GLOVE • ORDER UNIFORMS FOR A SOFTBALL TEAM • BUY ANKLE AND KNEE BRACES • BUY GOLF CLUBS • JOIN AN EL
NOWMOBILE • BUY A PERSONAL WATERCRAFT • HIRE A SCUBA INSTRUCTOR • BUY A SKATEBOARD AND PROTECTIVE GEAR • BUY SK
EATHER ACTIVITIES • SELL USED SKIS • BUY A SNOWBOARD, BOOTS AND BINDINGS • BUY SKI BOOTS • BUY A BICYCLE • SELL YOUR
UY A BACKPACK • BUY A BACKPACKING STOVE • BUY A KAYAK • BUY A PERSONAL FLOTATION DEVICE • BUY A WET SUIT • BUY A SUF
RDER CUSTOM-MADE COWBOY BOOTS • BUY CLOTHES ONLINE • FIND SPECIALTY SIZES • BUY THE PERFECT COCKTAIL DRESS • BUY
UY A MAN'S SUIT • HIRE A TAILOR • BUY CUSTOM-TAILORED CLOTHES IN ASIA • BUY A BRIEFCASE • SHOP FOR A LEATHER JACKET •
ATE MONITOR • SELECT A WATCH • BUY KIDS' CLOTHES • CHOOSE CHILDREN'S SHOES • PURCHASE CLOTHES AT OUTLET SHOPS • B

Careers

143 Set Up a Lemonade Stand

If life has handed you lemons, make lemonade. Here are a few tips if you—or a young colleague—want to go into the citrus-hawking business and hope to turn a sweet profit as a result.

Steps

1 Set up your stand at the foot of your driveway if you get lots of people walking and driving by. Or go into business with a friend who lives in a better location.

2 Determine when the busiest times of day or weekend are—those are the times when you'll sell the most lemonade.

3 Set up your stand. Make a large sign that includes the price. Have plenty of disposable cups on hand. If you're going to be out there for a while, bringing along a cooler filled with ice is a smart move, too.

4 Buy lemons and granulated sugar and make your lemonade. In a large pitcher, combine the lemon juice, granulated sugar and cold water; stir briskly to dissolve. Add ice cubes.

5 Price your lemonade to cover all your costs—such as the expense of the lemons, cups, and sugar. Add in a profit margin as well.

6 Replenish your lemonade supply as the traffic demands.

What to Look For

- Location, location, location
- Water
- Lemons
- Customers

Tip

Here's one juicy recipe:

- Lemon juice, freshly squeezed from 8 large lemons—about 1½ cups (375 ml)
- ½ cup (125 ml) of sugar, granulated—more or less to taste
- 5 cups (1.25 l) cold water

144 Sell Your Product on TV

Want to give your credit card a breather and, instead, sell something on the Home Shopping Network or QVC? It can be a long shot, but one that can pay off if you have the right product.

Steps

1 Think about the benefits your product offers. Can it be demonstrated on television? Does it solve a problem? Is it topical or timely in some way? Watch QVC and Home Shopping Network (HSN) to see what features they tout for products they represent.

2 Go to HSN.com and click on Vendor Information for an application. For QVC, go to QVC.com and click on the Frequently Asked Questions section, then on Vendor Information.

3 Complete the application and then mail it along with a catalog, brochure, picture and/or a sample of your product.

4 Wait. It may be weeks or months before you hear back from the companies about their interest level in your product. And if you do, they may need more information. For its second round of evaluation, QVC asks for a sample. HSN says to give its staff at

What to Look For

- A unique product
- A demonstrable product

Tips

The most appealing products to HSN are unique, are of limited availability or something that can be easily demonstrated on television.

least 45 days to evaluate your product. If the merchandising specialists from HSN want you, they'll contact you to set up an appointment to meet with a representative.

5   Look for an opportunity to attend a local qualifying meeting with QVC officials. The company frequently sends representatives to major cities to investigate local products, which gives you the opportunity to dazzle them with your product and personality.

6   Be prepared to pay to get your product on the air. This will vary based on feedback from HSN staff, although QVC does not require such payments.

7   Gather estimates from vendors on how quickly you can ramp up production. With large volume orders the rule at HSN and QVC, you'll need to demonstrate you can meet supply needs.

Know the audience demographics when matching a product. HSN's viewers are primarily women age 40 and up; QVC claims a broader audience, depending on the product.

145 Hire a Career Counselor

Has your career reached a turning point? Are you miserable in your job or looking for strategic routes to climb the corporate ladder? Do you need to conduct a job search? Career counselors are especially effective at providing assistance to people whose careers are in transition.

Steps

1   Ask job placement centers for recommendations and call them.

2   Find out what the fees are and what services are offered. Will you be taking any self-assessment tests? Will the counselor help you polish your job-hunting skills and build up your network? Do you need to work on communicating more effectively to be more successful in your current job?

3   Find out if the counselor specializes in a particular industry. It may be pointless to hire someone unfamiliar with your field.

4   Ask about credentials. To be called a career counselor you must have a master's degree in counseling with a specialty in career counseling. How many years of experience does yours have? What kind of clients has he or she worked with? Has the counselor published any books? Ask for and call references.

5   Develop realistic time frames to accomplish the goals you've set.

6   Take self-assessment tests and personality inventories as your counselor directs. Fill out any questionnaires that will help identify and clarify your values. Your counselor will show you how the results relate to your career and how to maximize your strengths.

7   Follow your counselor's guidance and explore career options, develop strategies, gather information, hone your communication skills, and much more.

What to Look For

*   Suitable services
*   Sound credentials
*   Proven track record
*   Good rapport

Tip

Some nonprofit organizations, such as the public library or YWCA, schedule short, low-cost career guidance seminars that can be a great way to determine if you really need to hire a counselor on your own.

Warning

If a career counselor asks you to take the Minnesota Multiphasic Personality Inventory, find someone else to work with. MMPI is used to assess personality and mental illness.

146 Hire a Headhunter

Running a business can monopolize more time than you have to recruit new talent—particularly if you're running solo. Hire a head-hunter to fill key positions and bring in qualified personnel.

Steps

1 Investigate the cost. Headhunters may charge you as much as 40 percent of your new employee's first-year salary, although 20 to 30 percent is more the norm.

2 Understand how search firms charge. A contingency search firm only charges a fee if it finds a suitable hire. A retained search firm charges a fee based on a percentage of the new hire's salary, but does a lot more legwork to narrow the list of qualified candidates. Many top-notch headhunters will not work on contingencies, and many will want a fee if you fill the position with them or without them.

3 Find a headhunter with extensive experience in your particular industry or functional area to get the type of candidate you're looking to hire.

4 Verify their success rates. Some headhunters strike out on as much as 25 percent of their searches, depending on the industry they specialize in or the type of position they try to fill.

5 Ask questions about the process they use for identifying potential candidates, whether any personality or skill-based assessments are performed, and if references are routinely verified.

6 Check the firm's references. Asking past clients about the firm's performance is an excellent way to gauge how they'll approach your hiring needs—reputation is gold in the headhunting business, so do your homework.

7 Ask who'll be doing the actual search: a principal of the headhunting firm or a lower-level staff member. Find out how long a typical recruitment search takes.

8 Ask if there are companies they can't approach. Many headhunters won't recruit from their own clients, which limits the pool of candidates they bring to you. Similarly, provide a list of companies you do want them to approach. Chances are you know your competition better than the headhunters do; spend the time to educate him or her.

9 Be very detailed in your description of job requirements. A recipe for failure is to tell a headhunter, "We need a really smart person to head up sales." A more successful description is, "We need a candidate who has served in a VP capacity with a Fortune 500 company, handling international distribution of enterprise software to value-added resellers in Europe."

What to Look For

- Fee for service
- Expertise in your field
- Familiarity with a functional area
- Proven track record
- Solid references
- Restrictions on recruiting

Tips

Good searches can take up to six months.

Be very specific on the type of company you want your hires to come from.

147 Sell Yourself in a Job Interview

How do you make someone want to hire you? Simple: Put yourself in the shoes of the interviewer and focus on his or her needs and you'll become an irresistible applicant.

Steps

1 Find out as much as you can about the company: How is it performing? What is its mission statement and who are its customers? What are the interviewer's priorities and responsibilities? The more you know, the more you'll be able to ask informed questions about the job.

2 Study the description of the job for which you have applied. Be clear on what is expected and if you have the background and skills to do it.

3 Take an inventory of your strengths and practice discussing how they complement the requirements of the job. Write down specific examples that demonstrate these strengths and be able to speak fluidly and intelligently about them.

4 Make a winning first impression at the interview. Be prompt, make eye contact and give a firm handshake. Dress one notch above what's expected for the position you're interviewing for.

5 Look for common ground between you and the interviewer to establish a positive rapport and to stand out from the crowd. You may have the same alma mater or mutual friends. Be careful not to overplay this and look desperate.

6 Turn what could be seen as potential weaknesses into strengths. You might say "I haven't worked in promotions but I coordinated getting the word out for my son's school carnival and we had twice as many people attend this year." Be calm and confident.

7 Use specific examples to describe why you're a perfect match for the job. Ask probing questions to demonstrate a genuine interest in the position. In the process, interview the interviewer to find out why the position is open. Get a sense of what the turnover rate is at the company, what the position's job track is, and how the company keeps its employees happy. You're trying to find out if you want to work for that company as much as they're trying to find out if they want you.

8 Demonstrate that you are a problem-solver. Identify an issue the company is facing or a problem you might potentially encounter in that job and discuss how you'd solve it.

9 Make the interviewer feel good about hiring you. Be enthusiastic, responsive, truthful and friendly.

10 Follow up with a thank-you note that reiterates your qualifications and mentions specific topics covered in the interview to trigger the person's memory about your winning interview.

What to Look For

- Research the company
- Practice, practice, practice
- Strengths tied to job requirements
- Confidence
- Strategic thank-you notes

Tips

By focusing on the interviewer's needs, you'll take your mind off your nervousness. The interviewer will see a confident, insightful applicant.

Always bring an extra copy of your résumé.

Warning

Questions about race, religion, gender, marital status, child care and sexual preference are against federal law. Interview questions should focus on the job, not your personal life.

148 Take Out a Patent

If you want to protect an invention, your safest bet is to get a patent. It's a lengthy, involved and expensive process, but when you come out the other end, you'll have won exclusive rights to your particular idea or invention for 20 years.

Steps

1   Be patient—you'll spend a lot of time pursuing a patent. A search can take as long as six weeks, the application can take weeks to prepare, the prosecution phase may eat up another two years, and the issue process can take as long as nine months.

2   Research your idea to make sure no one beats you to it. Go to the Web site of the U.S. Patent and Trademark Office (uspto.gov) to do a preliminary search. It's free.

3   Conduct a bona fide patent search. Go to the Patent Office in Washington, D.C., and do a search. If that's not practical, hire an attorney in Washington to do the search for you, or find a local attorney that specializes in patent issues.

4   Decide whether you need U.S. or international patent protection. If you intend to market your product outside the United States, securing a patent in other parts of the world can slow knock-offs.

5   Hire a patent attorney. Unless you have firsthand experience with patents, it's essential to the successful navigation of the patent process to work with a good attorney. The application process is usually far too involved for a layperson. Obtaining a patent personally can easily top $10,000 in attorney fees—more if you try to get overseas patents as well.

6   Be clear what information needs to be included in your application. The Patent Office requires that you provide enough detail about your invention that someone else could build it. Include any drawings or other materials that describe the invention.

7   Take an oath that it's your idea to the best of your knowledge. This is the final element to the application.

8   Write your first check. Send $355 to cover the patent application fee, and get ready for the prosecution phase. During this part of the process the Patent Office reviews your application, and you'll probably have to submit amendments and changes.

9   Prepare formal, final drawings. If the prosecution phase is successful, the Patent Office issues a Notice of Allowance.

10   Write your second check. This time you'll need to send the Patent Office about $685 to cover an issue fee. Finalize the documents as directed by the Patent Office.

11   Pay periodic maintenance fees—starting at about $900 after a couple years and eventually topping $3,000 to maintain your protection. A patent lasts 20 years from the date of the application.

What to Look For

- Patience
- Similar patents
- A patent attorney

Tips

Expect that your first application needs changes. The problem can be merely a matter of style, and you'll be given time to correct it.

Although developing a prototype, or model of your invention, is smart, it's not required for a patent application. A prototype can point out any flaws in your concept or design, however, which would be helpful to know before you go to the time and expense of patenting a process that doesn't perform as expected.

149 Market Your Invention

The best invention ever devised will remain only a fascinating trinket if people don't know about it. Even a genius would do well to know some marketing basics. Here are some ways to get the word out about your invention.

Steps

1 Fine-tune your prototype to resolve any lingering design issues. You'll need a flawless version to sign up licensees and investors or show potential clients.

2 Decide if you intend to retain full control of the concept, and all the associated marketing, or if you will license it to an established business.

3 Ask your patent attorney to help you draft a nondisclosure agreement early on, essential to protect your intellectual property when dealing with potential licensees.

4 Draw up a marketing plan, which is absolutely central to gaining attention for your Invention. Define your customers and pinpoint your competition. Even if you want to sell your idea outright, a sound marketing plan will make your pitch that much more comprehensive.

5 See 148 Take Out a Patent.

6 Budget a reasonable amount of funds to get the word out—from trips and trade shows to print and television advertising. Hire professionals to help craft the message (see 157 Hire Someone to Design and Build Your Web Site and 158 Hire a Graphic Designer). Identify and attend trade shows, speak at civic clubs, and research and get to any event where potential customers or buyers might be.

7 Set a price. Research your competition so you get a sense of what the market will bear. If you want to sell the product outright to someone else or license it in some way, call in a consultant to determine a fair market value.

8 Work with your attorney to understand licensing and what kinds of deals you can make. Be careful to define and cover derivative work, where a licensee makes a new product that extends your original concept.

9 Write a press release and start making the rounds. Contact your local paper to propose a profile of your invention, and e-mail the editor of any major trade publications that are read by your target audience. Send out a press kit with information about your product, your background and the key benefits to television stations, newspapers and magazines in your area. Get the word out to everyone you can think of.

What to Look For

- Prototype
- Nondisclosure agreement
- Marketing plan
- Legal advice
- Financial backing

Tips

Be wary of companies purporting to market your invention. As the inventor, save the money and do a better job of it yourself.

Talk about your invention at local groups such as the Rotary Club (rotary.org) or the chamber of commerce. You never know where a potential backer might be.

Find a financial angel. These are private investors who will fund business ideas, back inventions and provide manufacturing capital. Ask your accountant or attorney for referrals, and look into angel organizations located throughout the country. Read 150 Finance Your Business Idea.

150 Finance Your Business Idea

A great business idea without money is like a brand-new car with no gas: Both are sweet to look at but don't go anywhere. Fortunately, there's a wide range of sources you can tap to drum up money to fuel your new venture.

Steps

1 Write a comprehensive business plan. This document outlines your idea, including how you plan to develop it, and most important, how you see it making money. Consult the wide variety of books, or type "business plan" into a search engine for more sources to help you write a business plan.

2 Build a convincing business model for your company. This will have detailed financials that describe every aspect of your business, including costs for sourcing or manufacturing your product, projected sales, and marketing expenses as well as general and administrative overhead.

3 Determine how much money you are going to need. Include start-up funds and sufficient capital to keep the business afloat until your revenue covers your expenses. Add up all of your anticipated expenses during start-up: Salaries, building leases and equipment purchases, furniture, office supplies, telephone service and business card printing (see 158 Hire a Graphic Designer). The more specific your list of expenses, the lower your chances of running out of money.

4 Seek out help from those who have done it before. Consider offering them stock in your company for their assistance, but not before you decide if you want to retain full ownership.

5 Hire a reputable law firm to set up the legal structure of your business. Business entities come in many forms and include S or C corporations, limited liability corporations (LLC), partnerships and sole proprietorships. Set up your business correctly from the beginning to facilitate financing and shield your assets. Use a firm with experience handling companies in your field.

6 Work closely with your law firm and create a financing structure. Determining the deal you give to investors, and codifying it properly, is crucial to eliminating problems down the line. Decisions include whether to take money as debt or to give up equity, what kind of rights and privileges (if any) come with being an investor and, most important for them, how investors get paid back.

What to Look For

- Comprehensive business plan
- Overall funding needs
- Appropriate lending institutions
- Sources of collateral
- SBA loans
- Alternate sources of capital

Tips

When it comes to business financing, investigate all possibilities. Often, you can combine funding from various sources to create a suitable package.

The only grants available these days to entrepreneurs are hard to find and most require some investment on the part of the business owner in order to qualify. Call your local small business development center to find out about available grants.

7 Decide what kind of investors you want. Many companies want powerful executives or financiers as investors, but find them meddlesome and impatient. Friends and family can be an excellent source of friendly money, but investing in start-ups is risky, and relationships can go sour if people start losing money.

8 Use your savings. Any lenders or investors will expect you to fund your business to the best of your financial ability and self-financing is the best way to retain control.

9 Go to a bank or credit union that you have a relationship with, and ask about a business loan. You'll likely get a better reception from an institution you have a proven track record with than from a new lender.

10 Turn to vendors you plan to use and ask whether they would be willing to provide products or services up front, as a means of reducing your start-up costs, in return for full payment plus interest within a specified amount of time. Their ability to do so may lower or even eliminate your need for external financing.

11 Ask potential suppliers if they would help finance your company, either by providing extended payment terms or extending a loan. Since vendors have the most to gain when it comes to landing a significant contract, some may be willing to give you some starting help in return for a guarantee of business.

12 Put up collateral. Depending on the size of the loan, you might offer your car, house or other type of property.

13 Investigate the government's Small Business Administration (SBA.gov) loan programs. The SBA oversees programs that guarantee small-business loans, and encourages banks and other institutions to fund businesses they might otherwise turn down. The terms and fees are usually comparable to conventional financing.

14 Tap into your own assets. Many entrepreneurs have valuable assets they can borrow against to start their business. Home equity is the most obvious choice, with the added bonus that interest payments are tax deductible. Some 401(k) programs and life insurance policies may also be borrowed against. Entrepreneurs have to gauge the degree to which they leverage their personal assets against the risks of start-up businesses.

15 Consider using a credit card. It's relatively easy and quick to get needed funds from your credit cards through cash advances, although the interest rates are much higher than those from other sources.

Warning

Although investors provide what seems to be free money, they also want to own a portion of your business in return. Many venture capitalists and angel investors will only consider business opportunities where they can own 20 to 50 percent of the company.

151 Buy a Small Business

If you have your heart set on working for yourself, buying an existing business might be just the ticket—or it can be a nightmare if you're not prepared. Know what you want and investigate your options aggressively. First, read 150 Finance Your Business Idea. Then, do your research—the more you learn, the better your chances for success.

Steps

1 Analyze why you want to buy a business. Are you looking for greater independence or the possibility of increased income?

2 Consider your background. It's more likely you'll do well if you choose a business you're familiar with. Are you interested in a specific product, or an operation that's service-oriented?

3 Check Web sites such as BusinessesForSale.com to find interesting companies, and contact local business brokers to identify companies that may be on the block.

4 Perform a complete financial review of the business. This will typically include the company's past income statements, balance sheets, and statements of cash flow, as well as its projected financials going forward. Look closely at all liabilities; as the new owner you are inheriting the company's debt as well as its business. Work closely with an accountant familiar with businesses in the same field.

5 Get a Dun & Bradstreet (dunandbradstreet.com) credit report on the company to evaluate its track record and to double-check its reported numbers.

6 Ask for a due diligence package, which should include past tax returns, any significant contracts the company has signed (including office or store leases) and any employee or contractor agreements. It will also include legal documents, such as filings, articles of incorporation and any past or pending lawsuits the company is involved in. Work closely with a lawyer to evaluate these and other documents.

7 Ask why the business is for sale. Is the current owner retiring, or hoping to pass off some ongoing problem—or worse, a fatally flawed business or location—to an unsuspecting buyer?

8 Focus on the problems. It's easy to be blinded by the appeal of a business, but pay just as much attention to the flaws. Are they correctable or likely to be a constant headache?

What to Look For

- An appealing business
- Credit report
- Detailed financial records
- Outside financing
- A fair price

Tips

Look for a business that has real growth potential. For instance, a pizzeria with limited hours might boom if it stayed open longer.

Once you buy the business, give yourself a chance to become comfortable with it. A drop off in income during the first few months of ownership isn't a cause for panic.

9 Observe the business. If you're considering buying a restaurant, for example, watch the customer traffic for a week to see if it measures up to the revenue the current owner claims. Talk to customers to get their honest take on the product or services.

10 Use a business broker or consultant if you feel you need some help locating potential businesses for sale or determining if the asking price is reasonable.

11 Prepare a comprehensive business plan if you need to raise capital. Banks and other lenders will want to see detailed plans of how you envision future growth. Calculate what you can afford to invest. Read 150 Finance Your Business Idea.

12 Determine a valuation for the business. Most industries have a standard method and concentrate on a multiple of the previous year's revenue (the exact multiple will depend on the industry). If the business has a lot of capital equipment (a manufacturer, for example), the market value of the equipment is taken into account. Fast-growing businesses in a hot market are usually valued higher, as future potential is factored into the selling price.

13 Justify the purchase price to yourself. Once you've determined a valuation, or come to an understanding on price, run your own analysis to see if it fits your needs. Calculate a break-even on the business. If you're 10 years from retirement, does it make sense to buy a high-priced business that won't show decent returns for 15 years?

14 Ask if the current owner will consider financing part or all of the sale. That can mean a low down payment and an attractive payment schedule for you.

15 Consider proposing that the current owner stay on for a while after you buy the business if he or she is a real asset. Many owners stay on as consultants to smooth the transition. This can be an effective way to smooth over problems that may crop up during a transition of ownership.

Warning

Be wary of any business with incomplete or confusing financial records. That may hint at a poorly run operation or an owner who's not eager to share all the facts. If something seems fishy, it usually is.

152 Buy a Franchise

If you want to go out on your own, but not necessarily start a business from scratch, buying a franchise may be an option to consider. You can own your business, and get support and guidance as you start out. Franchises also have a track record you can investigate. The odds of success are actually greater with an established company rather than with a start-up, but the downside is that franchise fees, royalties and other issues can drive up overall costs of doing business.

Steps

1 Identify your skills and interest to target an appropriate franchise. If you have a design background, a sign-making franchise would match your skill set. If you don't even like to pump gas, stay away from an oil-change franchise.

2 Be aware that you'll still have a boss. Even though it's your business, franchises have tight rules and regulations.

3 Determine how much cash you have to invest up front in such a venture. Some franchises may be out of your league simply based on the required down payment. Setting up a McDonald's, for example, costs nearly $1 million, while Chem-Dry only asks for $7,950 down.

4 Choose between a larger franchise that carries more brand-name value and a smaller operation that offers more personal, hands-on support and responsiveness if you run into problems.

5 Investigate how long the business has been around. Many franchises have surprisingly short life spans. Think of all the frozen yogurt joints and muffin shops that have gone belly-up. Assess whether a franchise is riding out a short-term fad or is part of a trend, like Dunkin' Donuts, that's here to stay.

6 See 150 Finance Your Business Idea and run your own detailed financial model. Don't rely on the numbers the franchiser gives you. Create a detailed analysis of sales, cost of sales and goods, overhead and franchise fees. Determine how much you have to invest up front, and how much you will take home at the end of the day. Check out the royalties: The going royalty for a franchise is anywhere between 3 and 10 percent of what you gross. If you need help, pull in an accountant or financial planner with expertise in franchises.

7 Ask what the company expectations are: Some franchises demand quick success translated into specific sales numbers, while others will give you time to grow.

What to Look For

- Suitable business and approach
- Franchise history
- Ongoing support
- Adequate training
- Terms of royalties
- Supplies and equipment

8 Find out how you will be supported. Will the franchise help with ads, bookkeeping and personnel matters? Ask how much training the parent company offers and what it involves.

9 Hire a franchise attorney to review the documents and help negotiate a deal with the franchisor. You want someone with particular experience with franchises, rather than a general practice lawyer.

10 Review the UFOC (Uniform Franchise Offering Circular, provided by franchisors to prospective franchisees) carefully to understand how well the franchise has been doing, what its prospects for the future are, and how happy its current franchisees are.

11 Look carefully through the UFOC, which the U.S. Securities and Exchange Commission (SEC.gov) requires franchises to prepare, for any signs of franchisee discontent. Pending litigation or a class-action suit is a sign that there may be problems.

12 Put your financial affairs in order. Most franchises will want to see evidence of your financial security or business experience before selling you a franchise.

13 Talk to other franchises. Pick their brains for every bit of information and feedback you can get. Track down franchisees who have left the company to understand what went wrong for them. Their story could be yours.

14 Ask your banker or attorney if they've heard anything—positive or negative—about the franchise.

15 Find out about supplies and equipment. Some franchises require that you buy almost everything you need from them, although you may benefit from economies of scale. Be sure the rates are reasonable and competitive with other sources.

16 Ask what the franchise fee covers. Some investments pay for all start-up costs, while others don't include training and marketing, to keep the stated up-front cost low.

17 Find out if additional capital investments will be needed down the line in order to be profitable, or if the start-up costs are the only major investment.

18 Hire a general manager or operations supervisor with industry experience in order to give yourself the best chance of success.

153 Lease Retail Space

If you're selling a product, you may need a space from which to hawk your wares. Don't sign a lease on the first bargain you see—find a location that's accessible to your customers and suited to the needs of your business.

Steps

1 Make sure that any space you're considering is big enough for both your current needs and your foreseeable growth. Be realistic and don't overcommit.

2 Do your homework beforehand. Investigate traffic patterns; tour the building. Find out who the previous tenant was, and why the business left. Learn what kinds of marketing the location does in support of its tenants (if any) and whether co-operative marketing funds are available to you.

3 Weigh the benefits of guaranteed foot traffic at a mall location against premium rent. Some malls require that all tenants stay open during mall hours, and pay for common area usage as well as the store's own space and upkeep. Stores may also be asked to pay a percentage of sales to the mall.

4 Identify your closest competitors. Also check out neighboring businesses with an eye for complementary products or services. Is there an established cluster economy? If you are locating in a mall, check the lease agreement for any guaranteed protection against competition (malls may rent only to a set number of similar stores at any given time).

5 Evaluate whether the physical location and space is a good fit with your product line. Do you need a large, bright space or a charming, cozy nook?

6 Investigate any restrictions on signage. Signs are vitally important to retail businesses, yet many landlords decide on what a store can and cannot do. The rules may be even stricter in a mall, which closely monitors its physical appearance.

7 Negotiate the terms of your lease aggressively. Never accept wording that's confusing or that leaves you wondering who is liable for what. Ask for the right of first refusal on adjacent space in case you need to expand. Negotiate for free improvements and other incentives before signing your lease.

8 Hire a real estate attorney who not only specializes in lease negotiations, but knows your area and, preferably, has dealt with your kind of business before. A lease negotiation can cover tens, if not hundreds, of terms, and you want someone in your corner who's seen it all before.

9 Know who's responsible for maintaining the heating, air-conditioning and other systems, as well as keeping up the parking lot and building exterior. This can be critical in older buildings.

What to Look For

- Sufficient space
- Room to grow
- A fair lease

Tips

If negotiation isn't in your blood, have an attorney handle the transaction.

If you're unsure of whether your business can make it in a particular mall, one option is to lease a cart or kiosk for a month or two. Although you won't be able to stock much merchandise, you can get a firsthand feel for the amount of traffic, interest in your inventory, and demographics of the shoppers there.

Investigate liability insurance carefully. Since the general public will be walking through your store, be sure that you have adequate coverage in case an accident happens in your store.

Warnings

Some landlords require a percentage of sales in addition to the monthly lease payment. For such an arrangement to be worth it, get guarantees on foot traffic and low penalties for leaving your lease early.

Think twice about renting space just because it's cheap. You may find out later just why it's inexpensive—perhaps that location has a track record for failed businesses, or the layout discourages foot traffic.

154 Lease Industrial Space

Finding and renting industrial space is different from renting office space or an apartment and requires specific information to ensure you get the space you want at an affordable rate. Here's a rundown of things to bear in mind.

Steps

1 Determine the type of space you'll need. Have a good grasp on requirements for phone, broadband data service, HVAC, gas, water and electricity. You'll want enough power to provide adequate lighting and operate necessary equipment. Take all your needs into consideration when looking at space: storage for both raw materials and finished product, a production area or assembly line, ceiling height, column spacing, dock-high or drive-in truck access, signage, offices and rest rooms. Think about proximity to freeways for access, as well as public transportation, parking requirements and, possibly, rail access.

2 Try to develop a preliminary layout that takes into account all aspects of your operations. The layout should include utility connections for each piece of equipment. With this information, you can determine what type and how much space you'll need.

3 Take a drive through industrial zoned areas where you might want to locate. Look for "space available" signs with names and phone numbers to call for information. Interview brokers with signs advertising promising properties and ask to be taken on a tour of suitable spaces at terms you could afford.

4 Request a copy of the lease form for the space for your and your attorney's review.

5 Provide a viable business plan and financial statement for the landlord's review to facilitate acceptance of your lease offer. Then make a written offer on a form that can be provided by a broker.

6 Remember that commissions are generally paid by the landlord, so using a broker shouldn't cost you anything. But also remember that a landlord's broker may not represent your best interests. In such cases, you can work with your own broker, who can take you on a tour of available properties. Be sure to confirm whom the broker represents.

7 Prepare to negotiate all of the lease terms, not just lease rates. Industrial leases can be long and complex. Make sure the terms of the lease protect the interests of both you and the landlord, and yet are not unreasonable for the tenant.

What to Look For

- Appropriate zoning
- Suitable location
- Functional space
- Adequate space
- Affordable lease rates and terms

Tips

Although lease rates may be higher than in other locations, consider industrial parks, which are developed with industrial zoning, offer a prestigious atmosphere, and may have amenities that are important for your business, such as common truck docks and rail facilities, extra parking and perhaps even common office facilities.

Check out enterprise or empowerment zones in certain local jurisdictions that offer tax and employment incentives for businesses to locate there.

155 Lease Office Space

Leasing space for your company affects profit, employee satisfaction and ability to grow. Plan ahead, know what you're looking for, and be ready to shop aggressively.

Steps

1 Gauge what your space requirements are now and what they may be in years to come. A general rule of thumb is to allot 175 to 250 square feet of usable space per person.

2 Contact a commercial real estate agent for help in finding suitable rental space. Agents have the inside track on what space is coming on the market soon and can advise you on which properties are the best. Some firms specialize exclusively in office space leases.

3 Discuss needed improvements. Tenant improvements are subject to serious negotiation, particularly if vacancies are high.

4 Examine parking carefully. Will you have a number of parking spots set aside for your employees, or will they have to compete for street parking?

5 Reduce your costs considerably by sharing space with another firm, including office equipment, reception areas, meeting rooms and rest rooms. But know that sharing space brings less privacy.

6 Check out incubators—areas in which small-business entrepreneurs have access to low-cost office space. You may benefit from sharing expertise as well as office space. Do an online search, or start at the Web site of the National Business Incubation Association (nbia.org).

7 Consider all-inclusive executive office suites. Although the rate may be a bit higher, many suites come furnished and have access to office equipment and conference rooms, thereby lowering up-front costs for physical space and equipment to almost nothing. Many also provide a receptionist.

8 Read a prospective lease exhaustively. Review your monthly payment, the length of the lease, what the landlord is responsible for, any provisions for getting out of the lease early, and other standard clauses such as annual rent increases tied to inflation. Ask if the lease includes upkeep of grounds and other maintenance. Don't forget telephone lines, cable service, broadband Internet connections and other communication needs.

9 Review occupancy date, options regarding expansion, extension of the lease term, termination, contraction (the need to scale

What to Look For

- Current and future space needs
- Commercial real estate agent
- Price
- Infrastructure
- Sharing or subletting
- Incubators

Tips

Don't be afraid to negotiate terms of your lease. With rental rates dropping, landlords may be hungry to rent their space as best they can.

Large businesses often go through cycles of layoffs; you may be able to find a company with extra office space it would be willing to sublet at a bargain price.

back), and first right of refusal on adjoining space, as well as security, reception area, amenities (lunch rooms, rest rooms, snack vending), access to conference rooms, elevator usage, and HVAC issues (such as who is responsible and what is the expected response time when a problem arises).

10 Find out about any restrictions on signage.

11 Retain the services of a real estate attorney who not only specializes in lease negotiations but knows your area and, preferably, has dealt with your kind of business before. A lease negotiation can cover tens, if not hundreds, of terms, and you want someone in your corner who has seen it all before.

156 Buy Liquidated Office Equipment

Stock your office on the cheap with discontinued equipment, damaged furniture and surplus furniture. Desks, workstations and computers can all be had for a fraction of what you would pay for new. But if you see something you like, act now—it could be gone tomorrow.

Steps

1 Start by doing an Internet search. You'll find all sorts of companies offering liquidated office equipment. Key words such as "discount" and "excess inventory" should lead you to some great suppliers.

2 Get quotes on items that you're interested in. Then, compare with prices found in local brick-and-mortar stores.

3 Watch the classified ads in your local paper for notices of upcoming office furniture liquidations.

4 Contact the purchasing department at local corporations to learn of upcoming equipment sales. Some companies regularly sell off used office paraphernalia they no longer need.

5 Examine the equipment or furniture to see if it's damaged in any way. Even the slightest ding may peel more off the price.

6 Check such sites as eBay.com and CraigsList.org frequently. Read the public auction notices in the business section of your newspaper; you can get significant savings on used and discontinued furniture and equipment from bankruptcies.

What to Look For

- Internet-based companies
- Corporation sales
- Comparative price quotes
- Public auctions

Tips

Look into refurbished electronics and computers sold on manufacturers' Web sites. These are returned goods that the manufacturers restore to new condition and are sold at deep discounts, and often carry a limited warranty.

Be aggressive and thorough in your search. Discounts on new equipment of 50 percent and more are not unheard of.

157 Hire Someone to Design and Build Your Web Site

Everyone has a Web site these days (you *do*, don't you?). Some are for fun, while others are pure business. If you're planning a new site, you have to know its function before you can create its form. Then, if you don't want to build it yourself—or know better than to try—you'll be better prepared to hire someone to do it for you.

Steps

1 Decide if the Web site will be for personal use or a business tool. Do you want a purely informational site for prospective clients? Or will it be interactive, so that visitors can buy a product or service online?

2 Ask friends and business associates to recommend some Web-site designers. Identify at least three suitable contenders to compare their styles, prices and technical expertise.

3 Review the designers' Web sites to see samples of their work. Ideally, look at examples of sites that are similar to your business.

4 Ask designers to describe their approach to building a site. Some concentrate purely on getting information to visitors, while others focus more on design aesthetics or technical issues. Find out whether the individual is a designer or a programmer at heart. Technical experts typically don't have the design talent needed to make a site look great as well as work seamlessly. Likewise, a designer may not be as up-to-date on the latest Web technology and know how to engineer the site correctly. A firm with several experts may be the wisest way to get all of the expertise you need.

5 Find out what specifics they would recommend for your site including how many pages you'll need, how the content is best arranged, how to apply technical solutions to problems and other issues. Compare these recommendations and gauge how experienced the designer is. Pay attention to how well they communicate and if you could establish a good rapport.

6 Bring along a list of Web sites you like and why. Discuss with prospective designers to get feedback and be confident that they understand what you want your site to look like.

7 Discuss their fee structure. Does the cost include Web hosting, registering a domain name, or updating the Web site? (This is frequently a hidden cost, since many sites need to be updated by a trained programmer or designer.) Ask whether you will be able to maintain the site yourself.

8 Set up a schedule that details what each phase will accomplish, what materials they need to get from you, and an overall timeline for the whole project. Fees will be tied to the schedule.

What to Look For

- An experienced designer
- Prior work
- Technical skills
- Design expertise
- Appropriate fees
- Web-site management

Tips

Web sites are like advertising: You'll want to match yours to your company identity. A graphics design firm will want a flashy intro page; a mortuary might opt for something a bit more conservative.

Don't be afraid to keep shopping if a designer seems too expensive or doesn't jibe with the sort of Web site you have in mind. There are plenty of designers out there.

158 Hire a Graphic Designer

A designer's job is to communicate your vision in printed materials or often, on the Web. Graphic artists blend together typography, paper, color, illustration, photography—and pizzazz—to deliver a message to your customers on a business card, logo, brochure, poster, invitation, book or even a T-shirt. If you don't know Helvetica from a hole in the ground, it's time to find yourself a designer.

Steps

1 Decide what you need. Does your new company need business cards? Would a logo help establish your presence in the market-place? Do you need to tap into a new pool of customers? Have you got a product or service that nobody knows about? Effective graphic design lets people know who you are and what you do.

2 Ask friends and colleagues for recommendations. Ask printers if they can recommend a designer they've worked with. Or go to the American Institute of Graphic Artists (AIGA.com) and browse listings of designers in your area. Look at the designers' Web sites to see if their style is suited to what you're looking for.

3 Review the designers' portfolios. Get a sense of how similar your business is to the type and size of the clients they typically work with. When you see something particularly interesting or good, ask, What was the problem you were asked to solve, and how did you arrive at this solution?

4 If you like their work, discuss the project you need done. Expect the designer to ask you lots of questions about the project and your business.

5 Ask for a quote. Some designers will bid small jobs on the spot. Others will send you a quote later, which should include a ballpark estimate for printing. Design fees are in addition to illustration, photography and printing costs (subject to a standard 17.5 percent markup), but the designer manages all of those elements.

6 Budget according to size and complexity of the piece. Black-and-white or two-color work is cheaper than full-color. Logos are the most time-intensive and tend to command very high prices. Actual fees are based on the amount of work but also how big your company is. A new identity for Joe's Pretzel Palace will be vastly cheaper than one for the Ford Motor Company.

7 Hire the designer. Make sure the contract has all the details of the job, including a printing estimate and schedule, before you sign it. You will typically pay half of the total fee in order to begin the job, and the remaining half when it's printed.

8 Meet and review sketches to determine if the designer is going in the right direction. He or she will take your feedback and refine the concept. You'll meet several times during the process to keep tightening up the design until it's complete and printed.

What to Look For

- Good recommendations
- Clear idea of what you want
- Someone you can work with well

Tips

For Web site work, see 157 Hire Someone to Design Your Web Site. Some graphic artists work in both print design and Web design.

Designers tend to specialize in different areas, such as developing corporate identities, which involves designing a logo and applying it to business cards, stationery, brochures and the company's Web site. Others specialize in environmental graphics, signage, exhibit design or product package design, while still others are strictly book designers.

Start collecting materials that you like: business cards or logos, brochures and other printed pieces with a particular style or approach, or invitations that caught your eye.

Warning

Check final proofs with the utmost care: If there's a typo, and you've signed off on the job, fixing the error will be on your tab. Check phone numbers and ZIP codes carefully.

159 Acquire Content for Your Web Site

Unlike many other business tasks, getting good content for your Web site is an easy and inexpensive matter. And finding the right content can make your site a real eye-catcher. Whether you're trying to boost traffic or provide information, you'll find a wealth of sources.

Steps

1 Set up a Frequently Asked Questions (FAQ) section on your site and establish message boards where visitors can share information. Develop a newsletter and archive it at the site. Work up other proprietary material, such as booklets and articles.

2 Link to other sites. This connects your visitors to other sources of information and can build your traffic as well if the sites link back to yours.

3 Check out Web sites that offer articles, reports and other items for reprinting, as long as the source is credited. Be careful not to use copyrighted materials without permission.

4 Contact authors of articles in trade journals and specialty newsletters and ask if they would submit an article for your site in return for publicizing their business. Offering to post a photo of the author and a short blurb about their firm may be enough to entice experts to provide good material you can use.

5 Turn to Uncle Sam. Most of the material the government distributes is copyright free. That means Small Business Administration (SBA) content may be usable, though it always pays to double-check before you upload it to your site.

6 Place a submissions guide on your site. If you lay out the parameters of what you want and how you want it submitted, you may be surprised with the response you'll get.

7 Buy it outright if necessary. For special reports, research and stock photos the prices you pay will vary according to size or quantity of the material and whether royalties are involved.

8 Run ads in online classifieds looking for writers. CraigsList.org is a great way to reach talent in big cities. Remember, content can be submitted from anywhere.

9 Don't go overboard: Content overkill can drive a visitor away by making a site too complex to navigate and slow to load.

10 Consider a syndication service. If you have the budget, a number of Web businesses offer a wide range of information for use on your Web site. Some examples are YellowBrix.com for business information and uclick.com for comics and cartoons.

11 Be vigilant about copyright issues. If you have any doubts, contact the person or Web site whose content you want to use. They may want appropriate credit, or payment.

What to Look For

- Free content
- Modestly priced content
- Copyright issues

Tips

Don't be shy about offering links. Most other Web sites will be pleased to hook up.

Troll the Internet. There are countless Web sites that offer free content.

160 Buy Advertising on the Web

Internet-based advertising can be a boon to your business or Web site's growth. But online ads are like any other form of advertising. You need to think about your target audience and set clear objectives on what you want the ads to do. Here's the scoop on how to get started.

Steps

1 Find where to buy online ads. An ad network—one of about a hundred firms that sell ads across a number of online sites with a single purchase—is the easiest place. Other options include advertising agencies, national newspaper sites, e-mail news-letters, search engines and sites that specialize in reaching a technology audience.

2 Determine who your target audience is and where they are most likely to spend time when online. Those are the sites where you want to be seen. It is worth spending more to reach the people who will actually become customers.

3 Learn how effective each type of ad is. Banners—the advertising boxes that appear on a Web page—are the most common, but have become less and less effective. Interstitial ads pop up on a page or interrupt between pages, but can be much more expensive to produce and place. The key is targeting a specific audience like parents, home owners or dog lovers.

4 Hire an ad agency or designer (see 158 Hire a Graphic Designer) who specializes in Web advertising to design an ad for you. Pay careful attention to the wording, message and how your company or service is branded. Make sure it is consistent with your overall marketing so you reach the appropriate audience, and they don't click off of your site once they find you.

5 Shop aggressively. The market is competitive, so look around for the best prices and a deal that meets your needs. Advertising sales people expect you to negotiate prices.

6 Choose the price structure that works for you: If you choose per impression, you may pay a CPM (cost per thousand) each time your banner appears. Per click-through, you'll pay for each hit your ad gets. Per lead, you may pay each time you get an online registration or a request for a catalog. Per sale, you pay each time someone buys something you've advertised. Rates are highly variable.

7 Review your results and make adjustments as necessary. Changes can usually be completed and integrated within days. Check to see if you met your goals once the campaign is done. If not, give some thought to revamping your campaign or choosing another form of advertising.

What to Look For

- Type of ad
- Price structure
- Appropriate placement
- Cost-effective results

Tips

Consider the issue of timing. Make sure your ads will appear when your target audience is most likely to see them.

Try a test campaign first to see what results your ad brings. Once you find a winner, broaden your campaign.

161 Sell Your Art

Some artists may recoil at the notion of selling their work, but it's the best way to lose the label *starving artist.* Approaching your work as a salable commodity as much as a creation can ultimately boost your visibility and, hopefully, your sales. Put your creativity to work and get the word out in as many ways as possible.

Steps

1 Network. Join a museum or artists' group to meet other artists as well as potential customers. Ask other artists questions about how they are selling and distributing their work.

2 Develop a marketing plan to attract new business.

3 Strut your stuff: Send out press releases and propose article profiles to local newspapers and national publications to heighten awareness of you and your work. Articles that feature you and show photographs of your work garner attention and potential clients.

4 Create a Web site to introduce people to your work. (See 157 Hire Someone to Design and Build Your Web Site.) Then gather addresses and send out quarterly mailings featuring new work. Or, save time and money by sending out e-mail updates with links to new work posted on your Web site. Include links to any articles or sites that have spotlighted you.

5 Enter competitions. Use any honors and awards you receive to net publicity and greater exposure for your work.

6 Ask the owners of cafes, shops and restaurants if they'd be interested in displaying your art. Offer a small commission from any resulting sales. Also consider buying a stall at local art fairs and shows (see 163 Sell on the Craft Circuit).

7 Look for galleries that feature art complementary to yours. Offer diversity—a gallery that has 20 artists doing seascapes may not be on the lookout for another.

8 Sell yourself to the gallery owner. Be able to discuss your work convincingly and clearly, including how it's created and why it will appeal to clientele.

9 Be prepared to take a big financial hit for gallery visibility. Most take a 50 percent cut of the retail price.

10 Push for a public showing of your work at galleries, with an opening night reception. Send out invitations to clients, friends, family and high-profile community members.

11 List your work on eBay.com to appeal to consumers who don't have the time or inclination to pay gallery prices. Set a reserve price that assures you'll get a decent return on your time.

What to Look For

- Networking
- Visibility
- Galleries and alternate venues

Tips

To boost your visibility, have an open-studio sale. Invite everyone you know—most particularly gallery owners—to come and see your work firsthand.

Devote some regular time to putting down your brushes and putting on your marketing hat. That can spark creative thinking on ways to sell your work more effectively.

Warning

If you show at a gallery, beware of hidden costs. Insurance and any additional framing, presentation or marketing costs may be passed along to the artist. Check with gallery owners.

162 Hire a Personal Coach

A personal coach—sometimes called an executive coach—can be a boon to your professional and personal development. A coach can help you identify your personal and professional goals, then direct you in how to achieve them given your own strengths, personality, and ambition: He or she is more of a personal problem solver, there to help you figure out what it is you want out of life, and how to get it.

Steps

1 Ask friends or colleagues for referrals to coaches with whom they're working. Try to get a recommendation from someone with circumstances similar to yours. Calling the human resource department of corporations is another way to gather some names of reputable coaches to consider.

2 Turn to online sources to create a list of local coaches. Coach University (CoachInc.com) and the International Coach Federation (coachfederation.org) both have search functions that allow you to search for a coach by geographic area or specialty.

3 Request a list of referrals from coaches you've identified, so that you can speak with individuals they've counseled to get a sense of who is in the best position to help you.

4 Interview at least three coaches before making your selection. Ask contenders if they are accredited by any sort of professional association. Inquire about specific training and credentials, such as through Coach University, which provides coach training, and the International Coach Federation, which provides certification.

5 Ask the candidates to talk about their background and about what makes them a successful coach. Decide whether your personality meshes with theirs. Be sure you'll feel comfortable asking for help and taking direction from them. Is their approach hands-on and proactive, or is it so laid-back that you'll get feedback only when you seek it?

6 Schedule how long and how often you'll meet. Will face-to-face meetings will be augmented by phone calls, e-mails and other communication? Will there be any limits on this? How long should you commit to working together?

7 Develop realistic time frames to accomplish the goals you've set.

8 Find out what kind and how much homework will be expected. Will that fit your style and time frame?

9 Get a quote on how much the coach charges. Costs can reach $1,000 a month or more. Some provide face-to-face counseling while others are more phone- and e-mail–based.

10 Listen to your gut. No matter how great the recommendations, how many years they've been coaching or what famous clients they have, if you're not comfortable working with them, it won't be worth it.

What to Look For

- Personal recommendations
- Professional credentials
- Style of approach
- Amount and kind of feedback
- Service fees

Tip

Find out if a coach offers any alternatives to his or her regular service. Some, for instance, offer lower group rates or may provide as-needed problem-solving help.

163 Sell on the Craft Circuit

Selling crafts may seem like a small and simple business, but nothing could be further from the truth. From homemade birdhouses to hand-crafted jewelry, the craft circuit is a multibillion-dollar industry that's growing faster than you can draw a hot-glue gun.

Steps

1 Become familiar with the different types of craft fairs. One fair is a sales event tied to a specific season, such as Christmas. The other is a recurring event—flea markets or street fairs—that take place weekly. Identify those fairs best suited to your work. Some restrict entrance to artisans who have applied for and received permission to participate, while others simply require payment of an entrance fee. The American Craft Council (craftcouncil.org) is a good source for information about fairs across the country, including who attends and exhibits at each one.

2 Entrance to juried shows is tougher. Your acceptance is based on the quality of your work, the number of similar artisans, and success at previous fairs. It's not apolitical. They want successful artists who bring in good foot traffic.

3 Talk to fellow artisans to scope out which shows are worth participating in and which are not. Research major events in your region on Web sites such as ArtAndCraftShows.net.

4 Attend fairs that will attract your targeted audience. Some fairs attract buyers from gift stores looking to make large wholesale purchases, while others attract customers shopping for things for their home. Determine what type of buyer is attracted to each show, and if it coincides with your target market.

5 Apply to craft shows as early in the year as possible. The best locations generally go to the earliest to sign up, and the best shows have long waiting lists. Your wait is in direct proportion to how many other vendors are in your particular category of work, such as quilting. Your application should reflect any honors and awards you've won, as well as years of experience, to increase your chances of being accepted. If asked for preference, request a corner location in the middle of the floor, which gets more traffic, generally, than mid-aisle booths.

6 Have professional photos taken of your work to include with your application. Keep a variety of color and black-and-white prints, as well as slides available to send when requested. Set up a Web site so customers can view your work online. See 161 Sell Your Art.

7 Do a cost-benefit analysis on the entrance fee versus expected revenue. Some fairs charge vendors more than $1,000 to participate. Don't forget to include all expenses, including travel, hotels and shipping merchandise to and from the show. Can you can bring in enough cash from your sales to make the effort worth it?

What to Look For

- Recurring and seasonal fairs
- Satisfied vendors
- Vendor requirements

Tips

Craft experts say it's important to keep introducing new products. That keeps you from becoming stale to repeat customers.

Bring along help whenever possible to relieve the boredom, help serve customers and provide a break when you need one.

8 Jump-start your craft fair experience by signing up for local mall shows, which are generally easier to get into and run year-round. You'll get a feel for what customers like in your area and have a chance to polish your sales skills, which will be invaluable as you move into larger shows.

9 Do your homework for specific shows and plan your inventory carefully to know what will appeal to the people walking the aisles. You want to have a variety of products to appeal to a broad range of customers, but you need to balance that against the cost of transporting and displaying the items.

Interacting with customers is critical to your success. Let buyers know how long a particular item took to create and what inspired you. Describe any unusual techniques you've adopted. An effective, eye-catching sign can be critical to attracting customers to your wares.

10 Price your merchandise according to what other craftspeople of your skill and ability are charging, as well as the size of the piece, the amount of time you invested creating it, cost of materials and the overhead you need to cover to stay in business. Your merchandise should be priced appropriately. Some fairs are very high-end while others are more mass market.

11 Buy a booth or make arrangements to rent one from an exhibit house, which can be found in the Yellow Pages under "Trade Shows, Expositions and Fairs." Or check online at sites such as EventSupplierDirectory.com. Booths are expensive, so know what you need and shop aggressively. Outside shows generally require a covered area in order to protect your work from both sun and rain. You'll also need a table or display unit, tablecloths or covers, a chair, and packing supplies, storage boxes and carts to pack and haul your work without it getting damaged, and a space to store it between fairs.

12 Arrange for a merchant credit card account with a bank to accept credit card payments. Sometimes banks are reluctant to allow part-time or home-based businesses to hold merchant accounts, so you may have to be persistent. Some online financial services, like Intuit.com, provide small merchant credit card accounts. Shop around to get the lowest up-front investment and ongoing fees. And check out MobileArtisans.com for potential providers.

13 Do some preparation before the fair and distribute handouts with prices, product lines and contact details. Create or update your Web site (see 157 Hire Someone to Design and Build Your Web Site). Many people don't buy at the fair, but will collect your materials and order from you later.

14 Start locally to see how your merchandise moves before you branch out to fairs outside your area.

15 Be prepared to travel if you do well and want to continue to grow. Making the most of the craft circuit will likely mean traveling to fairs outside your area to find a new base of prospective customers.

164 Hire a Literary Agent

Many publishing houses won't even glance at a proposal unless it has come in through an agent. Agents with valuable connections can distribute your work and have the know-how and experience to negotiate the best deal. They can also be a generous font of guidance and advice. But it's essential to find a suitable match.

Steps

1 Start your search by asking some writerly friends for references. Ask with whom they're working and if they're satisfied.

2 Find books similar to ones you want to write and make note of the name of the literary agent who represented the author (they usually get thanked in the acknowledgments).

3 Visit agency Web sites for information on genres they specialize in, clients they represent, preferred method of communication, and any guidelines for submissions. Check if you can send in a full manuscript. Most agents don't read unsolicited manuscripts and many won't read unsolicited proposals.

4 Consider both large and small agencies. The bigger ones may have greater resources; the smaller operations may give you more personalized service. If you're taken on by a larger firm, ask who will be your agent; the agency may have a marquee name, but a newcomer, junior associate or assistant may actually handle your account.

5 Have any agent outline exactly what he or she will do for you, and what the specialty is. Some agents will help you land magazine assignments—others will work only on book projects.

6 Find out how long the prospect has actually worked as an agent. If the person is relatively new to the field, ask what he or she did before, to gauge what publishing connections can be brought to the table. An agent's greatest asset is his or her relationships with editors.

7 Get a sense of how aggressive an agent might be. Some will go to the ends of the earth to sell your project. Some won't go any farther than the end of their desks. Ask to talk to past clients to find out which category this agent falls into.

8 Ask about commissions. Most agents charge a 15 percent commission on anything they sell on your behalf, and some charge for incidentals like photocopies and postage. And since agents only earn a fee when they have generated income for you, they have a strong incentive to work on your behalf.

9 Request a written contract that confirms everything you and your new agent have agreed to.

What to Look For

- Client/agent matching services
- Large versus small agencies
- Type of clients
- Aggressive personality
- Commission

Tips

Get a personal referral wherever possible. Agents, like publishers, rarely look at unsolicited materials.

Anyone considering going the self-publishing route, such as using print-on-demand companies like XLibris, iUniverse, and Infinity Publishing, won't need an agent at the start. However, if the book does well, publishers may come calling, and you'll need an agent then to represent your interests. See 167 Sell Your Novel.

Keep in mind that it's considered advantageous to have a New York City–based literary agent. That's not to say agents in other cities won't do a good job, just that the publishing decisions are generally made in Manhattan.

Warning

Never work with an agent who charges to read a book. That's nothing but an unadulterated rip-off.

165 Pitch a Magazine Story

Many of the articles you read in magazines started with a writer pitching an idea to an editor. The field of freelancing has a few land mines, particularly for first-time writers, so you'll need to watch your step.

Steps

1 Find out if the magazines you'd like to write for accept freelance submissions. Although it's becoming more rare, some publications still are exclusively staff-produced.

2 Match your idea to the publication. Identify magazines that would publish the kind of idea you have in mind. Read several back issues of the magazine(s) or check the online archives to get a feel for the readership, the topics covered, and the general tone of the articles. Be certain that the magazine hasn't covered your idea in some fashion already. Also, look closely at the length of the articles and see if it fits your style.

3 Turn to subscription databases like Wooden Horse Publishing (woodenhorsepub.com) and Writer's Market (writersmarket.com) for more in-depth guidance regarding what the magazines are looking for and how they want to be contacted. Writer's Market costs less than $50 per year and Wooden Horse is about $150, but both are excellent information sources.

4 Review editorial calendars, which are often featured on magazine Web sites. These give advertisers, readers and writers a heads-up regarding planned issue themes. Keep upcoming topics in mind when you're pitching, and be sure to mention the particular issue to which you think your idea is particularly well suited.

5 Think at least three months ahead—the minimum time table most magazines work under. That means you'll need to pitch Mother's Day ideas in January or February and back-to-school subjects no later than May.

6 Avoid the biggest rookie mistake: sending a finished, unsolicited manuscript. Instead, find out how the magazine accepts article ideas. Ask to see a copy of its writers' guidelines and follow them to the letter.

7 Pinpoint the best editor for your idea. If need be, call the magazine and ask which editor is best to contact, and how he or she prefers submissions (via e-mail or conventional mail).

8 Craft a one-page query letter. Identify the specific audience that may find the article interesting. And cite any statistics or research that support your proposal.

9 Include three clips (photocopies of actual articles you've written as they appeared in a publication) with your query letter. If the magazine is of general interest, submit a variety of clips; if it focuses on a particular topic, include clips that show your expertise in that area.

What to Look For

- A fresh idea
- A suitable magazine
- Editorial calendars
- Writers' guidelines
- Contract details

Tips

Pay rates vary depending on the magazine, the scope of the story and your experience. As a general rule of thumb, the smaller the magazine or your clip file, the lower the rate. Some magazines offer pay in publication copies, while others offer anywhere from 1 cent a word to $5 a word, with the majority of magazines paying below $1 a word.

If you have photography skills, ask about taking your own pictures as a way to fatten your paycheck.

Think about sending in several good ideas in one query letter. You may boost your chances and, ideally, get more than one assignment.

166 Sell a Screenplay

Think you've got the next *My Big Fat Greek Wedding* on your hard drive? We've all probably felt that at one time or another—the difference is, not all of us know what to do once the last page emerges from the printer. Here are some pointers on selling your screenplay.

Steps

1 Contact production companies and film studios to find out who receives unsolicited screenplays. Find out if material needs to come through an agent. If so, take the plunge and get one; it may even help with those studios that don't insist on this.

2 Get a personal contact to hand-deliver your script. Even if it's the father of a friend's friend, any type of personal connection is better than an unsolicited submission. Work your Rolodex; you'd be surprised how many contacts you have.

3 Write a logline, which is a three- to four-sentence description of your plot line. Many producers make preliminary decisions based on a logline, so make sure it will knock their socks off.

4 Draft a synopsis, which is often requested as a second-round qualifier by a studio executive or agent. This one-page summary expands on the logline, complete with character descriptions and plot twists.

5 Make sure your screenplay is long enough but not too long. The general rule of thumb is 100 to 140 pages.

6 Check that everything's spelled correctly. Typos can sink even the most readable story. Consider hiring an editor if you want to be sure your copy flows well and is free of gaffes.

7 Send a clean, crisp copy of the screenplay. If your printer stinks, print out the script at a copy shop.

8 Keep your first page simple but informative: the title, your name and whatever contact information may be relevant.

9 Skip the artsy or colorful covers. Like resumes that come on colored paper, a script that's dolled up suggests something that doesn't warrant any attention otherwise.

10 Apply for consideration to screenwriting contests. Ben Affleck and Matt Damon's Project Greenlight (projectgreenlight.com) searches for aspiring screenwriters and directors, and Kevin Spacey's TriggerStreet (triggerstreet.com) provides a forum for screenwriters. Being chosen for participation in one of these events could move you to the front of the screenwriters' line.

11 Be a writer, not a director. Keep suggestions about lighting and camera angles to yourself.

What to Look For

• Studio contacts
• A sharp-looking script
• A compelling story

Tips

Check out scriptwriting software. It can help you with dialog, action and overall format.

The script has to be able to stand on its own. Any letter you include to justify its merits will likely give a studio enough reasons to reject it.

Send your script to as many studios as you can. The more you hit, the better your chances of a sale.

Pay rates will vary. A newcomer will obviously command far less than an established pro.

167 Sell Your Novel

Conventional wisdom holds that you have only a couple minutes to convince an editor that your novel is worth buying. That makes every second critical to presenting your work in the best light. Even Michael Chabon and Barbara Kingsolver started out this way.

Steps

1 Pay a professional editor to review your book and polish it. Editors can be a big help when it comes to identifying flaws in the plot or stilted dialog.

2 Make sure your manuscript is clean, free of mistakes and neatly bound. Although nonfiction books are generally bought based on a sample chapter, outline and proposal, fiction is only purchased after reading the entire manuscript.

3 Get an agent. Most publishing houses won't even look at a manuscript unless it comes via an agent. See 164 Hire a Literary Agent.

4 Choose publishing houses who sell the genre of book you've written. If you think you're the next Danielle Steel, don't pitch your romance novel to a house that deals exclusively in history. Do send your material to as many houses that seem a reasonable fit.

5 Write a solid cover letter to accompany your manuscript. This is absolutely critical to getting an editor's attention. Start the letter with a "hook"—something unique or provocative about the book. This makes the editor want to read the novel itself. Also include:

- Why you chose this particular editor. That shows you've done your homework.

- Any information about prior publishing experience you have. If you have none, however, don't let on that you're a beginner.

- A brief summary of the novel—no longer than three paragraphs—with an estimated word count.

- A description of the audience you think will read your novel, such as suspense fans, sci-fi junkies or teens.

6 Mail the manuscript to as many publishers as you think are potential buyers, unless your agent will market your work. Tell the publisher if you are submitting to other publishers or if they are the only one.

7 Wait. Depending on the size of the publishing house, it can take several months before you hear anything. Hold off e-mailing or phoning to ask about the status of the book. That's a sure way to turn off an editor.

8 Turn over any offers to your agent. He or she is more objective and will work to get you higher advance payments, which in turn means higher percentages for the agent.

What to Look For

- An agent
- Suitable publishing houses
- Cover letter and summary
- Patience

Tips

Check out *Writer's Market* (writersmarket.com), an excellent source of publishing house names and contacts.

Get a personal introduction to publishers. This will help you to stand out from the hordes of author wannabes. Work your network. Even if the connection is personal ("His children and my children go to school together."), if it seems appropriate, use it.

Include a self-addressed, stamped envelope in the overall package so that an editor can send back your manuscript.

Try not to get discouraged. Many great books have been through the rejection meat grinder before getting published.

If you exhaust all the possibilities at traditional houses, look at self-publishing (see 168 Self-Publish Your Book).

168 Self-Publish Your Book

Self-publishing can be a smart choice for writers. It's cost-effective, relatively fast, pays much better than standard royalty contracts, and lets you maintain control over the publishing process. But there are drawbacks to consider.

Steps

1 Decide what your goal is. Some writers want to print out just enough copies of their prized project for colleagues and friends; others think they have a book that will sell to a larger audience.

2 Examine competing titles to make sure you're not covering the same ground. Find out what sales of those books have been to see if it's really worth your while to tackle a similar topic. Call book distributor Ingram at (615) 213-6803 and punch in the ISBN of the book you want to check on; you'll hear a voice message containing the number of copies sold in the last year.

3 Determine what format you'd like to publish in: hardcover, soft-cover, or ebook, which is essentially an electronic file and requires no paper printing.

4 Check out print-on-demand publishers. If all you want to do is get a book published, these vanity presses will do the job for a price. Some vanity houses will print just a few copies for a few hundred dollars. Print-on-demand is ideal for very short runs (25 to 500 copies). Instead of printing on traditional, ink-based offset printing equipment, pages are reproduced using a high-end copier. A digital file from a page layout program links directly to a high-speed copier and then is machine-bound. Some shops offer perfect binding so it looks just like a printed book. Look at sources like Trafford.com, Xlibris.com and Iuniverse.com.

5 Print your book directly from your completed files with a direct-to-press printer. Instead of producing a different piece of film for each color of each page, the files are transferred directly to the printing plate. You'll eliminate all the film costs, and save time too.

6 Shop aggressively if you really want your book to sell. If you're an established writer considering self-publishing, look around. You can either choose to have a print-on-demand company, such as those mentioned above, handle all the layout, printing and production activities, or go to a local offset printer and oversee each of those steps in the process personally.

7 Ask potential suppliers to send you samples of their recently printed books. Don't be shocked: The quality will vary considerably with regard to paper quality, cover design, layout, and whether it was run on a sheet-fed press or a web press. Ask questions about how individual pieces were produced.

What to Look For

- An affordable publishing house
- Good-quality work
- Print run minimum
- Print-on-demand option
- Distribution capability
- Decent royalty structure

8 View competitors' books to determine what size and format you'd like your book to take. Find out if there are standard sizes you should stay with to reduce costs, or whether a different format will help your book stand out. Format sizes can affect which print-on-demand publisher you can work with.

9 Familiarize yourself with printing costs. These will vary, but you can expect to spend more than $1 per book for a minimum print run of several thousand copies. You may also be charged extra for layout help, editing, design of a book cover, and for photos. Typical fees are $3 to $6 per page for editing, $3 to $5 for production, $500 to $5,000 and more for design, plus $3 per 300-page book for printing.

10 Hire a designer with book experience (see 158 Hire a Graphic Designer). He or she will design the type, flow the pages, and create a spectacular jacket as well. This is more expensive, in some cases considerably so, but the difference in creating a quality product is significant.

11 Tally up your costs, including printing, graphic design, artwork, photography, copy editing and other expenses. A traditional publishing house that buys your book would normally absorb these costs, but then again, you lose control.

12 Request an International Standard Book Number (ISBN), which is the standard code for identifying your book, at isbn.org. The cost for 10 ISBNs is $150, plus a minimum $75 processing fee.

13 Find out how and by whom your book will be distributed. Some print-on-demand companies handle it in-house. If you do it, you'll need to have the books shipped to you, to contact book chains about stocking your book, potentially visit each bookstore individually, and handle any mail orders on your own. Some bookstores will accept a limited number of your books on consignment, which means you leave them and if they sell, you get paid; if they don't, you pick them up in a couple of months. Some companies have extensive bookstore distribution; others focus more on online sales, which will have bearing on the types of activities you'll need to perform to be successful.

14 Be prepared to sell yourself. Any real marketing of the book will have to come from you. Self-publishing also means self-promotion, or hiring a publicist to do it for you.

Tips

In general, the more copies you print, the lower the unit cost. On the other hand, you don't want a garage packed to the rafters with your books.

Self-publishing has its risks but also its rewards. Most publishing companies pay authors a royalty between 8 and 10 percent of sales; self-publishers can increase that to 50 percent or more.

The largest segment of the 125,000 books that will be published this year is the novel, at 12 percent of the total.

169 Start a Bed-and-Breakfast

For many people, running a bed-and-breakfast (B&B) may seem like a dream job. This is a business, however, that you'll need to go into with your eyes wide open. If you're not a people person committed to working 24/7, running a B&B may be more like a recurring nightmare. Do some homework to ensure your plan is not only viable but doable.

Steps

1 Evaluate whether you have the personality and interest to host guests in your house night and day, season after season. Being outgoing and friendly is part of the job whether or not you feel like it. Interview B&B owners and learn about their lives—and whether that's the life you really want.

2 Decide where you'd like to live and work. Locations close to tourist draws are generally the most popular, although out-of-the-way accommodations can be just as popular if there is something distinctive and alluring about the place or its surroundings.

3 Check local zoning codes by calling the zoning board at your town hall to ask about the process for getting approval for a B&B. Be aware that some areas prohibit them. If you plan to renovate an existing building, have a contractor confirm compliance with local building codes. Find out whether there are any restrictions on the types of food that can be served, such as a full breakfast versus just coffee and muffins.

4 Draw up a business plan. Work your numbers carefully. The profit margin for many B&Bs is modest at best. Contact national trade associations such as the American Bed and Breakfast Association (abba.com) for guidelines about setting up a B&B. Also, talk to other B&B owners; some might share financial information. See 150 Finance Your Business Idea.

5 Determine how many guests you can and want to accommodate. Some B&Bs limit themselves to just a few guests, others take in 20 and more. Investigate how this will be impacted by the building codes; B&Bs with more than five rooms must comply with the Americans with Disabilities Act (ADA.gov).

6 Survey local competitors' prices. You'll want to be competitive with others in the area.

7 Develop an effective yet realistic marketing plan and budget. How will people hear about your B&B? Effective advertising can be expensive and high-income customers may be difficult to

What to Look For

- Zoning laws
- Building code constraints
- Comprehensive business plan
- Financing

reach. Free ink is terrific marketing, and cheaper than advertising, so explore getting editorial coverage in local papers, regional publications and national travel magazines. A good PR consultant may be worth the cost if you get the right coverage.

8 Compile an e-mail list of past guests to take advantage of cheap and effective outreach. Make sure you are listed in all relevant B&B guides and directories, and both printed publications and online resources. Pay attention to your competition's advertising: What works and what doesn't? Remember that marketing can seem like a financial black hole, so spend for maximum measurable impact. Put up a Web site to attract customers from all over (see 157 Hire Someone to Design and Build Your Web Site).

9 Hire qualified staff to keep things running smoothly. A housecleaner is vital; a cook, dishwasher, bartender, waiter and groundskeeper may be helpful additions during the high season and as the business grows.

10 Subscribe to a reservation service agency in order to reach a broader market, reduce your workload, and turn over the financial dealings to the experts. Turning over reservation and payment arrangements may negate the need for a merchant credit card account, too. However, there is an annual fee and a commission to be paid for each reservation handled. B&B Midwest Reservations (bandbmidwest.com), for example, charges a $75 setup fee and takes 25 percent of each reservation made on a member's behalf.

11 Set guest policies and house rules regarding check-in and -out schedules, cancellations and late arrivals, as well as whether pets, children and smoking are permitted.

12 Cater to your guests by making their experience as wonderful as possible. Serve excellent food and build a good wine list. Make sure the rooms are spotless, cozy and inviting. Remember that it's the little things that will keep guests coming back, such as the homemade muffins, the twilight kayak paddle or the tour of the gardens.

13 Network with fellow B&B owners, visitors bureaus, tourism offices and chambers of commerce to increase awareness of your business. Join national trade associations like ABBA.

Tips

Most B&B guests are looking for personal attention and charm when they make a reservation. Be sure you deliver that in order to win loyal customers.

B&Bs in new buildings are rare. Guests generally want old-world charm, not the latest construction.

If you're renovating, be sure to set aside plenty of space for your own private quarters. At the end of the day, you'll want to retreat into your own rooms for much-needed privacy.

170 Sell a Failing Business

Businesses flourish, and businesses flounder. Companies go through good times and bad. When the bad times are bad enough, they can force the owner to put the business on the block. Here are some special considerations to ensure you and the buyer both get a fair deal.

Steps

1 Accept that you won't get top dollar for a business gone bust. The best you may be able to expect is a "fire sale" price. Recognize that the market for a struggling business is small. You may be limited to buyers with experience in turnarounds.

2 Bring in a consultant or business appraiser to determine a fair market value. Emotional involvement may restrict your ability to come up with a reasonable price tag. Produce comparable valuations of similar properties in your area.

3 Consider using a broker to sell the business. An experienced broker can put you in contact with far more buyers than you'd find on your own.

4 Disclose your business's problems, since a well-prepared buyer will uncover them, anyway. But if there is a personal reason for a recent fall-off in business, such as the owner's ill health, be sure and state it up front. If the business's troubles are a relatively recent phenomenon, you may be able to get more money for it than if the decline has been consistent and long-term. Be completely forthcoming, even if you aren't asked directly. Failing to disclose significant problems can be grounds for fraud.

5 Present facts and figures about your business at its prime to show prospective buyers what kind of money the business once generated, and could again. Amount of customer traffic, average transaction amount, and weekly or monthly receipts is all useful information.

6 Clear any pending litigation and sizable debt before you go on the market. Nothing can kill a business sale faster than a lawsuit or large debts.

7 Establish trust with a buyer by being up-front about the challenges your business faces. This will build faith in you as the seller.

8 Be patient. It may take a buyer some time to perform due diligence and create a plan to restore the business to profitability.

9 Separate assets from the business entity, such as equipment, technology or property. Sell them or license them if you can't get a buyer for the whole company. Licensing technology your company has developed will at least provide an ongoing source of income, even if you can't divest the rest of the business's assets.

What to Look For

- A reasonable price
- A business broker
- Trust with a buyer

Tips

Try to emphasize the opportunity in the business. Possibilities—rather than just problems—may sway some buyers.

Choose a broker carefully. Some won't hustle to sell a business that shows poor prospects.

Warning

Try not to shut the business down with the hope of selling to someone who will reopen it. Once a business has closed, the only real asset for sale is the property and equipment. You'll get far less from the sale if yours is not an "ongoing concern."

171 Buy a Hot Dog Stand

No matter if they're franks or brats, kielbasa or linguiça, the wiener is a winner. Owning a hot dog stand may especially appeal to the entrepreneur who can't fathom a desk job. But there's a good deal more involved than boiling the water and slathering on the mustard.

Steps

1 Check with the city to see if hot dog stands are allowed. Some communities have health ordinances that put the kibosh on them.

2 Build a financial model for your hot dog stand. Spy on other vendors to see how many hot dogs they sell, and see how much food they throw out at the end of the day. Separate your variable costs, which increase with each sale (such as hot dogs, napkins and condiments) and your fixed costs, which you have to pay even if you sell nothing (equipment, permits, electricity and gas). From this calculate the number of sales you have to make to break even. Can you do it?

3 Sign up for a course on food handling, which your county likely hosts once a month. You may be required to prove attendance before the health department will green-light your plans.

4 Find a location. Again, check with your city. Some communities require that you operate in a private location, such as on the premises of a business that allows you to be there. Identify a busy street with few food options, or a large business with hungry employees. Factor in the tastes and demographics of the neighborhood when designing your menu.

5 Look into the health code requirements. Your cart may be required to have hot and cold water and a certain number of wash sinks. Bring pictures or schematics of your hot dog stand to your local health department for approval.

6 Buy the equipment you need, including the cart, coolers, food-handling gear, cooking equipment and other necessities, at a restaurant supply store. Costs vary, but expect to pay from $6,000 to $8,000 for a new cart, half that or less for a used model. Also, look into leasing equipment, which requires less capital up front.

7 Get both a seller's permit and a reseller's permit. These are easy and inexpensive to obtain from city hall.

8 Buy your supplies (see 274 Select Meat). Shop around for the best prices and tastiest product. Check out restaurant supply stores and bulk warehouses. Don't overlook your local grocery store, particularly if your stocking needs are modest.

9 Research inventory and stock level requirements. Food businesses lose tremendous amounts of money due to bad ordering and spoilage. Plan your inventory to have a minimal amount on hand at any time (which also lowers your inventory carrying costs).

What to Look For

- Local business ordinances
- Health codes
- Good location
- Clean, functional equipment
- Seller/reseller permits
- Great-tasting dogs

Tips

Be consistent. If you feature a certain hot dog or soda, stay with it. Customers like that kind of predictability.

Don't skimp on the condiments. Offer everything from mustard to jalapeños. If there are regional tastes where you live, make sure you cover them as well.

REHOUSE STORES • BUY WHOLESALE • GET OUT OF DEBT • BUY NOTHING • BUY HAPPINESS • BUY A BETTER MOUSETRAP • BUY TIM
MEONE'S FAVOR • BUY POSTAGE STAMPS WITHOUT GOING TO THE POST OFFICE • TIP PROPERLY • BUY HEALTHY FAST FOOD • BUY S
TING SERVICE • SELL YOURSELF ON AN ONLINE DATING SERVICE • SELL YOURSELF TO YOUR GIRLFRIEND/BOYFRIEND'S FAMILY • BUY
CHOOSE FILM FOR YOUR CAMERA • BUY RECHARGEABLE BATTERIES • DONATE TO A GOOD CAUSE • HOLD A PROFITABLE GARAGE SAL
STUDENT DISCOUNTS • BUY FLOWERS WHOLESALE • GET A PICTURE FRAMED • HIRE A MOVER • HIRE A PERSONAL ORGANIZER • FIN
EAT BIRTHDAY PRESENT FOR UNDER $10 • SELECT GOOD CHAMPAGNE • BUY A DIAMOND • BUY JEWELRY MADE OF PRECIOUS METAL
IDESMAIDS' DRESSES • HIRE AN EVENT COORDINATOR • HIRE A BARTENDER FOR A PARTY • HIRE A PHOTOGRAPHER • HIRE A CATERE
Y AN ANNIVERSARY GIFT • ARRANGE ENTERTAINMENT FOR A PARTY • COMMISSION A FIREWORKS SHOW • BUY A MOTHER'S DAY GIFT
FT • SELECT A THANKSGIVING TURKEY • BUY A HOUSEWARMING GIFT • PURCHASE HOLIDAY CARDS • BUY CHRISTMAS STOCKING STU
E HIGH ROLLERS ROOM IN VEGAS, BABY • BUY SOMEONE A STAR • PAY A RANSOM • GET HOT TICKETS • HIRE A LIMOUSINE • BUY A C
AM • BUY A PERSONAL JET • ACQUIRE A TELEVISION NETWORK • ACQUIRE A BODY GUARD • BOOK A LUXURY CRUISE AROUND THE W
OROUGHBRED RACEHORSE • BUY A VILLA IN TUSCANY • HIRE A PERSONAL CHEF • PURCHASE CUBAN CIGARS • HIRE A GHOSTWRITE
TNESS • MAKE BAIL • DONATE YOUR BODY TO SCIENCE • HIRE YOURSELF OUT AS A MEDICAL GUINEA PIG • SELL PLASMA • SELL YOU
LLEGE EDUCATION • BUY AND SELL STOCKS • CHOOSE A STOCKBROKER • DAY-TRADE (OR NOT) • BUY ANNUITIES • BUY AND SELL M
Y PERSONAL FINANCE SOFTWARE • CHOOSE A TAX PREPARER • SET UP A LEMONADE STAND • SELL YOUR PRODUCT ON TV • HIRE A
SINESS IDEA • BUY A SMALL BUSINESS • BUY A FRANCHISE • LEASE RETAIL SPACE • LEASE INDUSTRIAL SPACE • LEASE OFFICE SPAC
EB SITE • BUY ADVERTISING ON THE WEB • SELL YOUR ART • HIRE A PERSONAL COACH • SELL ON THE CRAFT CIRCUIT • HIRE A LITER
LING BUSINESS • BUY A HOT DOG STAND • SHOP FOR A MORTGAGE • REFINANCE YOUR HOME • SAVE BIG BUCKS ON YOUR MORTGA
LL A FIXER-UPPER • SELL THE FARM • SELL MINERAL RIGHTS • SELL A HOUSE • SELL A HOUSE WITHOUT A REAL ESTATE AGENT • OBT
OK A VACATION RENTAL • BUY A CONDOMINIUM • RENT AN APARTMENT OR HOUSE • OBTAIN RENTER'S INSURANCE • BUY A LOFT IN
RNISH YOUR STUDIO APARTMENT • BUY USED FURNITURE • BUY DOOR AND WINDOW LOCKS • CHOOSE AN ORIENTAL CARPET • BUY
RRANTIES ON APPLIANCES • FIND PERIOD FIXTURES • BUY A BED AND MATTRESS • HIRE AN INTERIOR DESIGNER • HIRE A FENG SHU
N • BUY A WHIRLPOOL TUB • BUY A SHOWERHEAD • BUY A TOILET • CHOOSE A FAUCET • BUY GLUES AND ADHESIVES • CHOOSE WI
TCHEN CABINETS • CHOOSE A KITCHEN COUNTERTOP • BUY GREEN HOUSEHOLD CLEANERS • STOCK YOUR HOME TOOL KIT • BUY A
ENTRY DOOR • BUY A GARAGE-DOOR OPENER • BUY LUMBER FOR A DIY PROJECT • HOW TO SELECT ROOFING • HIRE A CONTRACT
OWERS FOR YOUR GARDEN • SELECT PEST CONTROLS • BUY SOIL AMENDMENTS • BUY MULCH • BUY A COMPOSTER • BUY FERTILIZ
Y KOI FOR YOUR FISH POND • BUY A STORAGE SHED • HIRE AN ARBORIST • BUY BASIC GARDEN TOOLS • BUY SHRUBS AND TREES •
LECT KITCHEN KNIVES • DECIPHER FOOD LABELS • SELECT HERBS AND SPICES • STOCK YOUR KITCHEN WITH STAPLES • EQUIP A KI
OUNTAIN OYSTERS • PURCHASE LOCAL HONEY • CHOOSE POULTRY • SELECT FRESH FISH AND SHELLFISH • SELECT RICE • PURCHAS
READS • BUY ARTISAN CHEESES • PURCHASE KOSHER FOOD • BUY FOOD IN BULK • CHOOSE COOKING OILS • SELECT OLIVE OIL • SE
OFFEEMAKER OR ESPRESSO MACHINE • PURCHASE A KEG OF BEER • BUY ALCOHOL IN A DRY COUNTY • CHOOSE A MICROBREW • O
VULATION PREDICTOR KIT • PICK A PREGNANCY TEST KIT • CHOOSE BIRTH CONTROL • FIND THE RIGHT OB-GYN • HIRE A MIDWIFE OR
HOOSE DIAPERS • BUY OR RENT A BREAST PUMP • CHOOSE A CAR SEAT • BUY CHILD-PROOFING SUPPLIES • FIND FABULOUS CHILDC
ACKYARD PLAY STRUCTURE • FIND A GREAT SUMMER CAMP • SELL GIRL SCOUT COOKIES • BUY BRACES FOR YOUR KID • BUY TOYS
A MODEL • SELL USED BABY GEAR, TOYS, CLOTHES AND BOOKS • FIND A COUPLES COUNSELOR • HIRE A FAMILY LAWYER • BUY PF
PENSES • GET VIAGRA ONLINE • PURCHASE A TOOTHBRUSH • BUY MOISTURIZERS AND ANTIWRINKLE CREAMS • SELECT PAIN RELIE
UPPLIES • SELECT HAIR-CARE PRODUCTS • BUY WAYS TO COUNTER HAIR LOSS • BUY A WIG OR HAIRPIECE • BUY A NEW BODY • GE
ANICURIST • GET WHITER TEETH • SELECT EYEGLASSES AND SUNGLASSES • HIRE A PERSONAL TRAINER • SIGN UP FOR A YOGA CLA
EA MARKET • RENT SPACE AT AN ANTIQUE MALL • BUY AT AUCTION • KNOW WHAT YOUR COLLECTIBLES ARE WORTH • DICKER WITH
ECOGNIZE THE REAL MCCOY • BUY COINS • BUY AN ANTIQUE AMERICAN QUILT • BUY AN ANTIQUE FLAG • LIQUIDATE YOUR BEANIE B
WNSHOP • BUY AND SELL COMIC BOOKS • BUY AND SELL SPORTS MEMORABILIA • SELL YOUR BASEBALL-CARD COLLECTIONS • CH
OMPUTER • BUY PRINTER PAPER • BUY A PRINTER • BUY COMPUTER PERIPHERALS • CHOOSE AN INTERNET SERVICE PROVIDER • GE
UY BLANK CDS • BUY AN MP PLAYER • CHOOSE A DVD PLAYER • BUY A VCR • CHOOSE A PERSONAL DIGITAL ASSISTANT • CHOOSE M
IGITAL CAMCORDER • DECIDE ON A DIGITAL CAMERA • BUY A HOME AUTOMATION SYSTEM • BUY A STATE-OF-THE-ART SOUND SYSTE
NIVERSAL REMOTE • BUY A HOME THEATER SYSTEM • BUY VIRTUAL-REALITY FURNITURE • BUY TWO-WAY RADIOS • BUY A MOBILE EN
ONEY • GET TRAVEL INSURANCE • PICK THE IDEAL LUGGAGE • FLY FOR FREE • BID FOR A SLED RIDE ON THE ALASKAN IDITAROD TRA
OREIGN OFFICIAL • GET A EURAIL PASS • TAKE AN ITALIAN BICYCLE VACATION • CHOOSE A CHEAP CRUISE • BOOK A HOTEL PACKAGE
COTLAND • BUY A SAPPHIRE IN BANGKOK • HIRE A RICKSHA IN YANGON • TAKE SALSA LESSONS IN CUBA • BUY A CAMERA IN HONG
RST BASEBALL GLOVE • ORDER UNIFORMS FOR A SOFTBALL TEAM • BUY ANKLE AND KNEE BRACES • BUY GOLF CLUBS • JOIN AN E
NOWMOBILE • BUY A PERSONAL WATERCRAFT • HIRE A SCUBA INSTRUCTOR • BUY A SKATEBOARD AND PROTECTIVE GEAR • BUY SK
EATHER ACTIVITIES • SELL USED SKIS • BUY A SNOWBOARD, BOOTS AND BINDINGS • BUY SKI BOOTS • BUY A BICYCLE • SELL YOUR
UY A BACKPACK • BUY A BACKPACKING STOVE • BUY A KAYAK • BUY A PERSONAL FLOTATION DEVICE • BUY A WET SUIT • BUY A SUR
RDER CUSTOM-MADE COWBOY BOOTS • BUY CLOTHES ONLINE • FIND SPECIALTY SIZES • BUY THE PERFECT COCKTAIL DRESS • BUY
UY A MAN'S SUIT • HIRE A TAILOR • BUY CUSTOM-TAILORED CLOTHES IN ASIA • BUY A BRIEFCASE • SHOP FOR A LEATHER JACKET •
ATE MONITOR • SELECT A WATCH • BUY KIDS' CLOTHES • CHOOSE CHILDREN'S SHOES • PURCHASE CLOTHES AT OUTLET SHOPS • B

QUET OF ROSES • BUY SOMEONE A DRINK • GET SOMEONE TO BUY YOU A DRINK • BUY YOUR WAY INTO HIGH SOCIETY • BUY YOUR
RDER THE PERFECT BURRITO • ORDER TAKEOUT ASIAN FOOD • ORDER AT A SUSHI BAR • BUY DINNER AT A FANCY FRENCH RESTAURA
OWERS FOR YOUR SWEETHEART • BUY MUSIC ONLINE • HIRE MUSICIANS • ORDER A GREAT BOTTLE OF WINE • BUY AN ERGONOMIC [
SECLEANER • HIRE A BABY SITTER • BUY A GUITAR • BUY DUCT TAPE • GET A GOOD DEAL ON A MAGAZINE SUBSCRIPTION • GET SEN
IAN • BUY PET FOOD • BUY A PEDIGREED DOG OR CAT • BREED YOUR PET AND SELL THE LITTER • GET A COSTUME • BUY A PIÑATA •
IED GEMSTONES • CHOOSE THE PERFECT WEDDING DRESS • BUY OR RENT A TUXEDO • REGISTER FOR GIFTS • BUY WEDDING GIFTS
EAL WEDDING OFFICIANT • OBTAIN A MARRIAGE LICENSE • ORDER CUSTOM INVITATIONS AND ANNOUNCEMENTS • SELL YOUR WEDDI
R'S DAY GIFT • SELECT AN APPROPRIATE COMING-OF-AGE GIFT • GET A GIFT FOR THE PERSON WHO HAS EVERYTHING • BUY A GRAD
ANUKKAH GIFTS • PURCHASE A PERFECT CHRISTMAS TREE • BUY A PRIVATE ISLAND • HIRE A SKYWRITER • HIRE A BIG-NAME BAND •
BER • RENT YOUR OWN BILLBOARD • TAKE OUT A FULL-PAGE AD IN *THE NEW YORK TIMES* • HIRE A BUTLER • ACQUIRE A PROFESSION
OUR FUR COAT • BOOK A TRIP ON THE ORIENT-EXPRESS • BECOME A WINE MAKER • PURCHASE A PRIVATE/CUSTOM BOTTLING OF WIN
MEMOIRS • COMMISSION ORIGINAL ARTWORK • IMMORTALIZE YOUR SPOUSE IN A SCULPTURE • GIVE AWAY YOUR FORTUNE • HIRE A
DEVIL • NEGOTIATE A BETTER CREDIT CARD DEAL • CHOOSE A FINANCIAL PLANNER • SAVE WITH A RETIREMENT PLAN • SAVE FOR YO
BUY BONDS • SELL SHORT • INVEST IN PRECIOUS METALS • BUY DISABILITY INSURANCE • BUY LIFE INSURANCE • GET HEALTH INSUR
ELOR • HIRE A HEADHUNTER • SELL YOUR ___ ENT • MARKET YOUR INVENTION • FINANCE YO
TED OFFICE EQUIPMENT • HIRE SOMEONE ___ RE A GRAPHIC DESIGNER • ACQUIRE CONTENT
CH A MAGAZINE STORY • SELL A SCREEN ___ YOUR BOOK • START A BED-AND-BREAKFAST • S
ME OWNER'S INSURANCE • OBTAIN DISAS ___ OUSE AT AUCTION • BUY A FORECLOSED HOME
JITY LOAN • BUY A LOT • BUY HOUSE PLA ___ PULL BUILDING PERMITS • BUY A VACATION H
JY A TENANCY-IN-COMMON UNIT • BUY RE ___ A MOVIE OR CATALOG SHOOT • FURNISH YOUR I
IT FIXTURES • BUY A PROGRAMMABLE LIG ___ NCES • BUY FLOOR-CARE APPLIANCES • BUY EX
INCORPORATE FLUID ARCHITECTURE INTO ___ ARNISH • CHOOSE DECORATIVE TILES • CHOOSE
TS • GET SELF-CLEANING WINDOWS • CH ___ SELECT FLOORING • SELECT CARPETING • CHOC
SYSTEM • BUY A HOME ALARM SYSTEM ___ OXIDE DETECTORS • BUY FIRE EXTINGUISHERS
INTER OR ELECTRICIAN • HIRE A GARDEN ___ PERFECT ROSEBUSH • BUY FLOWERING BULBS
GETABLE GARDEN • HIRE A GARDEN PROF ___ R SYSTEM • START A NEW LAWN • BUY A LAWN I
• BUY AN OUTDOOR LIGHTING SYSTEM • ___ ECT PEACH • BUY AND SELL AT FARMERS' MARK
FRESH PRODUCE • SELECT MEAT • STOC ___ ASE A HOLIDAY HAM • BUY NATURAL BEEF • BUY
AND PEPPER • GET A CHEESESTEAK IN P ___ EATTLE • FIND CRAWDADS IN LOUISIANA • BUY A
JY ETHNIC INGREDIENTS • PURCHASE VIN ___ OFFEE • ORDER A GREAT CUP OF COFFEE • BUY
• CHOOSE A RESTAURANT FOR A BUSINE ___ TOCK YOUR BAR • BUY AND SELL SPERM • CHOO
GOOD PEDIATRICIAN • HIRE A CHILD THER ___ L NEW CRIB • CHOOSE A STROLLER • BUY BABY
EAT NANNY • FIND THE RIGHT PRIVATE SC ___ RAM • SIGN YOUR CHILD UP FOR LESSONS • BU
DEOS AND MUSIC FOR YOUR CHILDREN • ___ R • HIRE AN ADOPTION AGENCY • GET YOUR CH
IREMENT COMMUNITY • CHOOSE AN ASS ___ IVING WILL • BUY A CEMETERY PLOT • PAY FOR
CINES • SAVE MONEY ON PRESCRIPTION ___ ONAL • CHOOSE A WHEELCHAIR • BUY HOME-US
DY PIERCING • OBTAIN BREAST IMPLANTS ___ ALTERNATIVE AND HOLISTIC PRACTITIONERS • C
SELF TO A DAY AT THE SPA • BOOK A MAS ___ Y AND SELL USED BOOKS • SHOP AT AN ANTIQU

Real Estate

N ANTIQUE APPRAISED • BUY SILVERWARE • EVALUATE DEPRESSION-ERA GLASSWARE • BUY AND SELL STAMPS • BUY ANTIQUE FURNI
• SCORE AUTOGRAPHS • TRADE YU-GI-OH CARDS • SNAG STAR WARS ACTION FIGURES • SELL YOUR VINYL RECORD COLLECTION • S
COMPUTER • SHOP FOR A USED COMPUTER OR PERIPHERALS • CHOOSE A LAPTOP OR NOTEBOOK COMPUTER • SELL OR DONATE A
MAIN NAME • BUY A HOME NETWORK • UPGRADE THE MEMORY IN YOUR COMPUTER • BUY COMPUTER SOFTWARE • CHOOSE A CD
VICE • NEGOTIATE YOUR LONG-DISTANCE PHONE SERVICE • BUY VIDEO AND COMPUTER GAMES • CHOOSE A FILM CAMERA • CHOOS
-VIDEO DISTRIBUTION SYSTEM • BUY A SERIOUS TV • CHOOSE BETWEEN CABLE AND SATELLITE TV • GET A DIGITAL VIDEO RECORDE
STEM • GET A PASSPORT, QUICK! • PURCHASE CHEAP AIRLINE TICKETS • FIND GREAT HOTEL DEALS • RENT THE BEST CAR FOR THE L
Y-FREE • SHIP FOREIGN PURCHASES TO THE UNITED STATES • TIP IN A FOREIGN COUNTRY • TIP PROPERLY IN NORTH AMERICA • BRI
SLANDS • RAFT THE GRAND CANYON • BOOK A CHEAP BUT AWESOME SAFARI • RENT A CAMEL IN CAIRO • GET SINGLE-MALT SCOTCH
WAY ONTO A MOUNT EVEREST EXPEDITION • HIRE A TREKKING COMPANY IN NEPAL • RENT OR BUY A SATELLITE PHONE • BUY YOUR
SELL FOUND GOLF BALLS • BUY ATHLETIC SHOES • BUY A RACKET • BUY A GYM MEMBERSHIP • BUY AN AEROBIC FITNESS MACHINE
ISHING • GO SKYDIVING • BUY WEIGHTLIFTING EQUIPMENT • CHOOSE A CAR RACK OR CARRIER • BUY SKIS • BUY CLOTHES FOR CC
AGE SALE • COMMISSION A CUSTOM-BUILT BICYCLE • BUY A PROPERLY FITTED HELMET • BUY THE OPTIMAL SLEEPING BAG • BUY A
-FISHING GEAR • BUY ROCK-CLIMBING EQUIPMENT • BUY A CASHMERE SWEATER • PURCHASE VINTAGE CLOTHING • SELL USED CL
ES AT A DISCOUNT • CHOOSE A BASIC WARDROBE FOR A MAN • BUY A MAN'S DRESS SHIRT • PICK OUT A NECKTIE • BUY A WOMAN'
OTHES • GET A GREAT-FITTING BRA • CHOOSE A HIGH-PERFORMANCE SWIM SUIT • HIGH PERFORMANCE WORKOUT CLOTHES • BUY
JY THE BASICS FOR YOUR CAR • BUY A USED CAR • BUY OR SELL A CAR ONLINE • BUY A HYBRID CAR • SELL A CAR • BUY A MOTOR

172 Shop for a Mortgage

Unless you have a stash of cash, you'll need to get a mortgage to buy a home. As of this writing, interest rates are at historic lows, putting home ownership within the grasp of many more people. Engage a mortgage broker to shop around for you, or dive in yourself.

Steps

1 Choose your mortgage rates and payment schedule. A *fixed* program keeps the same interest throughout. An *adjustable* rate mortgage typically starts out with a lower interest rate but can change, which generally means that it could change up or down periodically with lower rates for shorter periods, depending on the structure of the mortgage. Another option is the *balloon payment,* where early monthly mortgage payments are often lower, but then a large payment is required after a certain number of years. (These are generally chosen by people who know they'll move within five years.)

2 Calculate how much you can afford to pay every month and choose your terms. Terms may be for 15, 20, 25 or 30 years. Obviously, a 15-year program lets you buy the house outright in half the time, but the monthly payment is higher. Choosing a 15-year mortgage will save you tens of thousands of dollars in interest in the long run, but the increased monthly cost may be unaffordable. The traditional 30-year fixed mortgage may be the most popular because of the lower monthly payment. Adjustable interest-only loans are also available for certain terms with lower monthly payments.

3 "Buy down" the interest rate on a loan. For instance, paying a point on a loan—expressed as a percentage of the loan amount—may drop the rate by as much as one-quarter of a percent. Paying points makes financial sense only if you plan to remain in the house several years at least, enough time to offset the extra cost by paying lower interest. Finance the points to benefit from lower rates without paying for it out of pocket by adding such fees to the loan balance.

4 Get your credit report before you apply. This report is available from the major credit reporting agency sites, Equifax.com, Experian.com or TransUnion.com and will be used by your lender to review your mortgage application. Most charge $12.95 for this service. Make sure any defaults, mistakes, or missing or outdated information are corrected before you start shopping for a mortgage. Get changes in writing.

5 Contact the same credit reporting agencies to see your FICO score (Fair, Isaac & Co., the developer of the dominant scoring software used in the mortgage market), and to determine how much negotiating power you have with banks. The closer the score is to 800, the better. You may only get a single viewing of your magic number, which costs about $6.

What to Look For

- Interest rates and terms
- Affordable monthly payment
- Low or no loan fees

Tips

Shop aggressively. Mortgage lending currently is exceedingly competitive, so don't be shy about asking for better terms, especially if your FICO credit score is 700 or above.

Go over mortgage costs carefully. Different lenders will often call the same cost by different names.

Be aggressive. If one lender has a lower cost on a particular item, use that as leverage to reduce another lender's charges.

Watch out for points, which are finance charges that are sometimes levied in refinances. Each point is 1 percent of your mortgage balance. While points are often rolled into your loan and have a minimal effect on monthly payment, they do increase the overall cost of the loan.

Lock in a rate while you complete your mortgage application.

See 174 Save Big Bucks on Your Mortgage.

6 Start by shopping where you bank. Your bank or savings and loan may offer attractive terms for existing customers.

7 Contact a mortgage broker who has access to several lenders and can quickly compare rates to find you the best deal.

8 Shop online. Many online lenders offer low rates and quick turn-around. LendingTree.com will send your request out to four lenders for free.

9 Pay particular attention to loan closing costs, which are quoted once you are approved for a mortgage. These will differ from one lender to the next and can add considerable expense to obtaining a loan. Expect to pay anywhere from 3 to 6 percent of the overall cost of the mortgage. Credit unions often give their members great deals on closing costs.

10 Review your good faith estimate in detail before signing on for a loan. Lenders are required to provide you with a detailed breakdown of all costs associated with the mortgage.

173 Refinance Your Home

Interest rates are a moving target. If your mortgage's interest rate is considerably higher than current levels, consider refinancing to lower your monthly payments. You can also pull out cash to make a major purchase or pay for some needed remodeling.

Steps

1 See 172 Shop for a Mortgage and 185 Obtain a Home Equity Loan for a summary of the process.

2 Ask yourself how long you're going to stay in your home. Divide the cost of refinancing by 12 to find out how many months you need to stay put for a refinance to be monetarily worthwhile. Typically you need to stay put for at least three years and secure a rate at least 1 percent lower in order for refinancing to make sense.

3 Contact your current lender first if you've just purchased your home. With a recent appraisal on file, you may save closing costs and be able to move more quickly by working with the same mortgagor. Investigate online lenders as well.

4 Pay attention to fees and closing costs, as with a first mortgage. These will include the cost of getting your house reappraised and may differ a great deal from one lender to another.

5 Consider limiting the term to be no longer than what is left on your current mortgage, or you'll end up with much lower payments but a much longer mortgage.

What to Look For

- Lower interest charges
- Low loan fees

Tips

Have your tax returns, bank account statements, credit card statements, W-2s, brokerage account statements, title and purchase agreement, proof of home owner's insurance, taxes and other materials ready.

Lock in a rate while you complete your mortgage application.

Use the refinancing calculator on Bankrate.com to calculate potential savings.

174 Save Big Bucks on Your Mortgage

A home mortgage is the biggest ongoing debt most people will ever face. One of the easiest and most powerful money strategies you can employ is to pay off your mortgage early. It's a painless way to save thousands of dollars.

Steps

1 Look at the breakdown of your mortgage payment. Your monthly mortgage statement shows two elements: the principal payment, which is the portion of your debt that you're actually paying, and interest on the principal.

2 Pay off your mortgage early just by adding more to your monthly payment. Calculate whatever you can afford, and simply add that each month.

3 Make the equivalent of an extra payment each year. This requires simply adding an additional $\frac{1}{12}$ of your payment to each mortgage check you write. Indicate on your mortgage payment slip that you're paying additional principal. For example, by paying an extra $50 a month on a 30-year, $100,000 mortgage at 6 percent interest, you slice six years off the life of the mortgage, and you save almost $25,000 in interest.

4 Sending in biweekly payments, rather than one monthly check, is another strategy for more quickly reducing your debt, if your lender allows it. Signing up for an official biweekly mortgage may not be worth the fee, however.

5 Renegotiate your mortgage rate by refinancing it if interest rates drop considerably. Typically it's not worth doing unless you can secure a rate at least 1 percent lower. See 173 Refinance Your Mortgage.

6 Consider variable interest or shorter term loans. A 30-year fixed interest loan is not your only choice. Many lenders offer variable loans, or loans that have a short-term "teaser rate" that keeps the interest low for a set period. If you're thinking of selling soon, there are also interest-only loans for different periods, as well as loans that are fixed for 5 or 10 years, then go variable.

What to Look For

- Affordable extra payments
- Refinancing

Tips

If you've had your mortgage for a while and interest rates have dropped, consider refinancing. This will reduce your monthly payment and free up even more cash that can go directly toward the principal.

Every extra dollar you add goes directly toward reducing the principal that you owe on your home.

See 172 Shop for a Mortgage and 173 Refinance Your Home.

Warning

Avoid paying the fee that some lenders charge to set up a biweekly mortgage (in which you pay a half-payment every two weeks). Adding one extra monthly amount every year does the same thing, and you can do that on your own.

175 Obtain Home Owner's Insurance

If you own a home, home owner's insurance is an absolute must. Not only is it essential to protecting your investment, no lender is going to finance you even a penny without it.

Steps

1 Calculate how much it would cost to rebuild your home. Many home owners mistakenly look at how much their home is worth. Insurance companies use guidelines for estimating replacement costs and the resulting premiums for total replacement policies.

2 Investigate different types of coverage. For instance, HO-1 is basic coverage that protects you from 11 different risks, including theft, fire and major breakage; by contrast, HO-5 covers everything except earthquakes, flood and war. (See 176 Obtain Disaster Insurance.)

3 Compare different providers. Premiums differ depending on where you live, the value of your home, and other factors such as how long you've lived there and whether there have been past claims at that address. AllQuotesInsurance.com and InsuranceFinder.com are among several sites that can provide you with a number of quotes.

4 Find out what steps you can take to lower your premium cost, such as installing a security system. Some insurance providers will also offer lower rates for existing customers, so turn to your auto insurer for a home owner's quote first.

5 Save money by raising or lowering your deductible depending on your needs. A high deductible lowers your premiums but means greater out-of-pocket costs if something happens. For instance, increasing your deductible from $100 to $1,000 can save 20 percent or more on premiums.

6 Find out what the policy covers for your home's contents. If necessary, buy a floater for artwork, computers, jewelry, expensive photography equipment and other valuable items. Look into adding a rider for living expenses. This can help pay for your having to live somewhere else while your home is being rebuilt or repaired.

7 Make sure you're covered for liability in case a neighbor trips on your stairs and breaks a leg. Some home owner's policies also cover you when you are away from your home and are liable for someone else's misfortune; double-check under what circumstances your coverage kicks in.

8 Scrutinize your home owner's policy if your lender has attached it to your mortgage or refinance.

What to Look For

- Rebuilding cost coverage guidelines
- Disaster coverage
- Coverage for contents
- Replacement cost coverage

Tip

Do a complete inventory of everything you own to verify what's missing in case of theft or fire. Videotape all your belongings from clothes to jewelry to computers and home electronics and keep the tape in a safe deposit box.

Warnings

You'll have to shell out more money when something is damaged or stolen to supplement what your insurance company pays you, unless you have replacement value coverage. Some policies have inflation protection that covers the increasing cost of rebuilding your home.

Read through your policy carefully to see what is and isn't covered. Then pay extra to get the coverage you've determined that you need.

176 Obtain Disaster Insurance

Hurricanes, floods and earthquakes: If you're a home owner, these calamitous events are justifiably unnerving. The good news is your insurance probably already covers you for hurricanes. You'll have to add protection against earthquakes and floods on your own. And if you live in shaky territory or near a river, that can be costly.

Steps

1 Check your home owner's insurance to see precisely what it covers. It's likely you won't need to add anything for hurricane protection, since policies usually cover damage from wind and rain. In hurricane-prone areas of Florida, however, it can cost nearly $3,000 to protect a home worth $300,000. It all depends on the location and the corresponding risk.

2 Buy flood insurance if you live in an area prone to flooding. Obtained through the National Flood Insurance Program (www.fema.gov/nfip), flood insurance covers up to $250,000 for a single-family home and up to $100,000 for its contents. You may not have a choice in the matter. If you have a mortgage and live in a designated Special Flood Hazard Area, federal regulations require you to have flood insurance.

3 Evaluate whether you need earthquake insurance. Few home owner's policies cover earthquakes, which means it's up to you to get it.

• Don't assume you're safe outside of California. It's no surprise that California leads the list in earthquakes, followed by Washington, Oregon, Nevada and Arizona. But 39 states have a medium to high potential for quakes, and roughly 90 percent of all Americans live in areas considered seismically active.

• Contact your state. For instance, the California Earthquake Authority (CEA, earthquakeauthority.com) sells earthquake insurance to state residents. Get details on what the earthquake insurance covers. A solid policy covers the cost of replacing or repairing any property damaged in a quake.

• Be prepared to pay a sizable premium, depending on where you live. For instance, the CEA offers $75,000 of earthquake coverage on a $500,000 house for more than $2,000 per year.

4 Check out other options, including the protection of nonattached garages, coverage of the contents of your home, and the size of the deductible you pay before coverage applies.

5 Consider full replacement coverage. Depending on where you live, this could add a couple hundred dollars to your premium.

What to Look For

• Existing home owners' coverage
• Local insurance requirements
• State-provided earthquake insurance
• Replacement coverage

Tips

The cost of earthquake coverage varies greatly, and you can expect to pay more for a brick house (they don't handle earthquake stress as well as wood structures). Also, the older your home, the more expensive your coverage will be.

Ask your insurance agent for recommended actions you can take to reduce the damage from a natural disaster, such as reinforcing the roof, adding storm shutters, or retrofitting the foundation.

Factor in federal assistance from federal agencies like FEMA, which provide disaster relief.

Warning

Floods and storms can cause sewer, septic and drain backups, which are not covered by most home owner's policies. Get an extra rider if you believe your home is at risk. At a cost of approximately $20 to $40 a year, it could be well worth it if a particularly rainy season causes costly backups.

177 **Buy a House**

Home ownership is still very much a part of the American dream but one that mandates homework, legwork and considerable effort on your part to ensure that the process goes as smoothly as possible. Here's how to make your dream a reality.

Steps

1 Decide if it makes sense for you to buy a house or keep renting. If your job keeps you on the move, it may not be worth it. You may need to stay put for at least three years to recoup your closing costs. If your desire to own a home is based on wanting to create stability, keeping control over your living situation, building equity and investing in your future, go for it.

2 Strengthen your credit: Pay off credit cards, resolve any credit disputes or delinquencies, and cancel unused cards. Your credit rating takes into account both how you use the credit you have available and whether your available credit is too high for your income. Call a credit reporting agency and request a copy of your credit report, which may cost $10 to $15.

3 Decide what sort of home you want. A single-family home in good condition offers instant livability. While it's more work than a condominium, and likely more expensive up front (see 193 Buy a Condominium), you don't have to share ownership. Or build equity quickly if you have the skills and ample time by purchasing a fixer-upper and making it livable (see 180 Buy and Sell a Fixer-Upper). Spec homes (new homes constructed by a builder that don't have a buyer yet) can also be a good deal if the builder is eager to get its money out of the project. Duplexes can be an excellent way to generate income, by owning one half and renting the other. TIC units are another option (see 197 Buy a Tenancy-In-Common Unit).

4 Simplify your search by defining the area you'd like to live in. Scout out what's available in the vicinity. Look at prices, home design, proximity to shopping, schools and other amenities.

5 Visit a few open houses to gauge what's on the market and to see firsthand what you want, such as overall layout, number of bedrooms and bathrooms, kitchen amenities, and storage.

6 Use a mortgage calculator (such as one at Quicken.com) to determine how much house you can afford, whether renting or buying is more advantageous for you right now, and how much you'll likely be able to borrow. However, take these figures with a grain of salt; some are inaccurate. Get prequalified to get the

(continued)

What to Look For

- A suitable house
- A good location
- An affordable mortgage
- Appraisal
- Inspection reports
- Preliminary title report

Tip

If you qualify, check out first-time buyers' programs, which often have much lower down payment requirements. These are offered by various states and local governments, such as nyhomes.org/sony/sonyma.html in New York. You may also be able to access up to $10,000 from your 401(k) or Roth IRA without penalty. Ask your broker or employer's human resources department for specifics regarding borrowing against those assets.

actual amount you can pay (see 172 Shop for a Mortgage). Most lenders allow you to put up to 28 percent of your gross income or 36 percent of your net toward a house payment.

7 Be ready to hand over a substantial down payment. Most mortgages are based on the buyer putting down 10 to 20 percent of the purchase price. Putting down less up front often requires you to pay private mortgage insurance (PMI), which increases your monthly housing cost.

8 Shop for a home on your own only if you understand the trade-offs. Most homes are listed with agents to ensure that other agents will have easy access to information about the home. (See 184 Sell a House Without a Real Estate Agent.)

9 Shop for a real estate agent who will search for suitable properties, represent your interests and negotiate on your behalf. A buyer's representative can evaluate the properties you view, do a market analysis to determine its value in the marketplace, select an appropriate price to begin negotiations and advise you in writing the contract.

10 Go into exhaustive detail when describing to your agent what you want in a home: number of bathrooms and bedrooms, attached garage, land and anything else that may be important, like good light or a big enough yard for the kids. If your agent shows you homes that aren't what you want, find another one who listens more attentively.

11 Shop aggressively. Unless you're under the gun time-wise, look at as many homes as possible to get a sense of what's available. Don't rush into buying if you don't have to.

12 Look beyond the home to the neighborhood and the condition of nearby homes to make sure you aren't buying the only gem in sight. The area in which your home is located is sometimes a bigger consideration than the home itself, since it has a major impact on your home's resale value. Buying a fixer-upper in the right neighborhood can be a great investment, and being able to identify up-and-coming communities—where more people want to live—can lead you to a bargain property that will only appreciate in value.

13 Visit properties you're seriously interested in at various times of the day to check traffic and congestion, available parking, noise levels and general activities. What may seem like a peaceful neighborhood at lunch can become a loud shortcut during rush hour, and you'd never know it if you drove by only once.

14 Determine whether you need to sell your current home in order to afford a new one (see 183 Sell a House). If so, any offer to buy that you make will be contingent on that sale. Contingent

Tips

Find out your credit rating early on to assess how strong your mortgage application is. The higher your FICO score, which ranges from 300 to 800, the better rate you'll qualify for. Go to MyFICO.com and for a fee request a report, or request a complete credit report from a major credit reporting agency and ask that your FICO score be revealed on it.

Get a firm estimate of how much you can expect to pay in closing costs (charges that the lender levies connected to the purchase of the house). These take in various charges that generally run between 3 to 6 percent of the money you're borrowing. Credit unions often offer lower closing costs to their members.

offers are more risky and less desirable for the seller, since the sale can't be completed until the buyer's house is sold. You may want to put your current house on the market first.

15 Try not to fall in love with one particular property. It's great to find exactly what you need, but if you get your heart set on one home, you may end up paying more than it's worth because you're emotionally invested. The deal may also fall apart.

16 Work with your agent to present an offer. In many areas multiple offers are commonplace; your agent should help you craft a competitive bid that makes the most of your financial assets. He or she can help you determine how close to the asking price you should be and, if your offer's turned down, how to counteroffer. Make sure final acceptance is predicated on a suitable home inspection.

17 Include earnest money with your offer. Your agent can assist in arriving at a suitable amount—usually $1,000 to $5,000. Once you sign an offer, you are officially *in escrow*, which means you are committed to buy the house or lose your deposit, unless you do not get final mortgage approval. During escrow (typically 30 to 90 days), your lender arranges for purchase financing and finalizes your mortgage. This is also when all inspections must be completed.

18 Request the following surveys and reports: inspection, pests, dry rot, radon, hazardous materials, landslides, flood plains, earthquake faults and crime statistics.

19 Close escrow. This final step in buying a home, usually conducted in a title office, involves signing documents related to the property and your mortgage arrangements. The packet of papers includes the deed, proving you now own the house, and the title, which shows that no one else has any claim to it or lien against it. If any issues remain, money may be set aside in escrow until they are resolved, which acts as an incentive for the seller to quickly remedy any problem areas in order to receive all that is owed.

Warning

Make sure to order a home inspection while you're in escrow. Those few hundred dollars are money in the bank when it comes to identifying potentially serious problems such as leaks, roof problems, drainage, radon, pest damage, structural issues and other potential problems.

178 Buy a House at Auction

"Sold to the highest bidder!" Buying a home through an auction can mean incredible deals. In most cases, the seller is either the government, which has taken possession of the property due to unpaid taxes, or the lender, when the former owner stopped paying the mortgage. Despite the sad circumstances, competition for homes can be keen.

Steps

1 See 374 Buy at Auction, 177 Buy a House, 180 Buy and Sell a Fixer-Upper and 179 Buy a Foreclosed Home for more information.

2 Get preapproved for a mortgage. Have your financial package ready to go before the bidding begins.

3 Look in the newspaper classifieds or under "Home Auctions" in the Yellow Pages and on Internet search engines. Call nearby real estate agents to see if they're aware of any scheduled auctions. Add your name to mailing lists from local auction houses to be alerted to upcoming opportunities.

4 Get a list of the properties up for auction. Get as much information as possible beforehand from the auctioneer to get a feel for which properties may interest you.

5 Visit the properties on the block. Auctioneers generally have a preview date during which tours of the house will be given, although this isn't guaranteed.

6 Have any home in which you're interested inspected by a professional inspector. This can cost several hundred dollars but will identify any significant problems that affect the value of the home, such as pest damage, faulty foundations or leaks. You may get approval to have the home inspected as a contingency, but bear in mind that contingencies of any kind reduce the probability of the bid being accepted at the lowest price. Other auctioneers only sell properties as-is.

7 Decide how high you're willing to go. Mentally setting your maximum bid can stop you from spending more money than might be reasonable for a property, or losing a deposit.

8 Realize that buying at auction involves some risks. In some cases, you can't withdraw a winning bid, even if you're not able to secure financing later. Penalties for backing out of a winning bid can be steep, often as high as 25 percent of the bid amount or whatever the bid deposit may have been.

9 Finalize your mortgage if yours is the winning bid. Contact your lender as soon as possible after the auction to wrap up your financing and paperwork.

10 Close escrow. Typically, you will have two weeks to 30 days to do this.

What to Look For

- Preapproved mortgage
- Inspection reports
- Free and clear title

Tips

Some auctioneers, at the home owner's request, will set a reserve price that guarantees a minimum price will be received. This means that even if you're the winning bidder, you may not get the house if your highest bid isn't over the reserve price, which should be disclosed in advance of sale.

Auctioneers may add a buyer's premium of 5 to 10 percent of the winning bid as their cut. Be sure and take this into account when you're calculating the maximum price you're willing to pay. Confirm who pays the auctioneer's fee.

Check with the auction company to make sure the property has a free and clear title. You don't want to buy something only to learn after the fact that you may be liable for unpaid taxes or other bills attached to the property.

Warning

If you're buying a property as an investment, rather than a residence, the mortgage approval process may require a much larger chunk of change up front.

179 Buy a Foreclosed Home

When you buy a foreclosed home, you're cashing in on a home some-one was no longer able to pay for. Foreclosures are difficult—both to locate and to execute the transactions—but the potential to turn them over for a tidy profit may be there.

Steps

1 See 177 Buy a House and 180 Buy and Sell a Fixer-Upper.

2 Understand that foreclosure means that because a home owner has become unable to pay the mortgage, the lender takes back the property. The legal steps involved differ from state to state.

3 Investigate the advantages. Since a bank or other lender wants to recover as much of its investment as quickly as possible, fore-closed homes are often unloaded at significant discounts—upwards of 30 percent or more.

4 Find an agent experienced in foreclosures. Some sellers won't accept offers from unrepresented buyers.

5 Search for foreclosure listings in real estate magazines, news-letters, newspapers and Internet search engines. Call lenders for real estate owned (REO) properties lists of foreclosures. Government agencies such as Fannie Mae (fanniemae.com) and the Department of Housing and Urban Development (hud.gov) also advertise foreclosed homes for sale. Check public records for other leads. A lender deciding to foreclose must file a notice of default in the local county clerk's office.

6 Tour the property and inspect it as closely as possible. Some foreclosures—unlike fixer-uppers—are in fairly good shape. Others may be behind in maintenance.

7 Have your agent check nearby or comparable homes to see if the asking price for a foreclosed home is, in fact, a bargain.

8 Check your credit report and correct any defaults or outdated information. Get prequalified for a mortgage (see 172 Shop for a Mortgage). Depending on the agency handling the sale, it may be required.

9 Find out if there is a listing broker and make an offer.

10 Check to see if a foreclosed home has any liens on it, such as unpaid property taxes. Find out who is liable for those costs.

11 Have the home inspected if the seller allows. Some sellers include this as part of the sales agreement, but the buyer still pays for it.

12 Be prepared to deal with more paperwork with a foreclosure than you would with a conventional purchase, particularly when a government agency is involved.

What to Look For

- Experienced agent
- Suitable properties
- Outstanding lien issues
- Lots of paperwork

Tips

Find out how foreclosure works in your state. Procedures and legal requirements differ, so get a sense of how soon you can go after a home that appeals to you.

Be particularly aggressive in negotiating with a bank. They're very keen to sell a foreclosed home fast, as it's just sitting on their books doing nothing.

HUD and other agencies often auction foreclosed homes. However, buyers are frequently unable to inspect any property before making an offer. With so little infor-mation, the higher the bid for the property, the higher the risk that you may end up with a money pit. See 178 Buy a House at Auction.

Warning

Beware that buying fore-closed property has a very low probability of success for all of the above condi-tions and because many people try to do it.

180 Buy and Sell a Fixer-Upper

It just needs a little TLC, right? If you're willing to put some elbow grease into it, buying and selling a fixer-upper can be a profitable endeavor. But there's a level of risk involved, not to mention a substantial commitment of time and effort on your part, and long periods of time when you will be living in chaos and sawdust. If you're still up for the challenge, it can be a rewarding experience.

Steps

1 Decide on the geographic area in which you want a property. Whether you intend to live in a home or not will impact where you'll want to buy. Remember that your ideal place to live may not be the best place to invest in property.

2 Be prepared for an extensive search. Many fixer-uppers—particularly those in especially bad shape—don't command much attention, so you may have to hunt around. Drive through desirable neighborhoods to spot "For Sale" signs.

3 Keep in mind that "location, location, location" is still the mantra of real estate purchases, whether for a fixer-upper or a single family home. Steer away from properties in areas that are going downhill, because you'll have trouble recouping your investment no matter how beautiful the structure. Find out if the asking price of that fixer-upper is comparable with the prices of other homes on the block. Make sure the fixer-upper is in an area of appreciating house values. That way, your house will be worth even more when your repairs are completed, rather than less because of worsening market conditions in the neighborhood. Try to meet some of the neighbors who might give you some information on what's been going on in their block.

4 Look in the classifieds, and at community bulletin boards or other public spots for the magic words "fixer-upper," "needs TLC," "handyman special" or "diamond in the rough."

5 Review local listings of foreclosed properties in your city. When banks or municipalities have had to take ownership of a property, they're generally very motivated to hand it off to a private buyer like you (See 179 Buy a Foreclosed Home). Contact real estate agents to see if they are listing a fixer-upper.

6 Keep an eye out for properties that need only cosmetic improvements. Houses that could use new paint, carpeting or flooring are the least expensive and offer the fastest potential turnaround. Larger problems such as bad roofs or faulty foundations are often prohibitively expensive and undermine eventual profit, depending on what you got the house for and how much you think you can sell it for.

7 Watch for vacant homes that have not been kept up by the owner. These forgotten houses can often have the most motivated seller you could hope to find.

What to Look For

- Decent location
- Profit potential
- Reasonable repair requirements
- Inspection reports

Tips

Be patient. Unlike the folks on Home and Garden Television's "Weekend Warriors" who make it sound as though renovations happen within a few weekends, fixer-uppers can take a long time to find and much longer to spruce up, particularly if you're holding down a day job.

Timing is often more important than the state of the house. If you sell during a hot market, price appreciation can help offset the cost of your improvements.

Don't be taken aback by properties that have been on the market for a long time. It's not unusual for some fixer-uppers to be up for sale for a year or more, depending on market conditions.

8 If you find an appealing property with seemingly reasonable repair needs, confirm. Have the home professionally inspected. Specify that the final sale is contingent on a satisfactory complete inspection.

9 Accompany the inspector when he or she goes through the house for a blow-by-blow account. Then review the report in detail to see what's wrong. You may also need to get additional inspections including soil, pest, roof and seismic. Be sure the inspector generates a narrative report rather than a checklist.

10 Get a formal appraisal ($200 to $400) of the home's value and have your agent work up comparables. If possible, have the appraiser estimate how much the home should sell for after it is restored to good condition.

11 Set your target purchase price. Pros suggest bidding at least 20 percent below its potential fixed-up value.

12 Get several bids from contractors of how much it will cost to fix what needs to be fixed (see 242 Hire a Contractor, Plumber, Painter or Electrician). Be sure to check zoning requirements and include permit fees. The house's value should increase at least $2 for every dollar you spend on improvements. Calculate the potential value of the house after renovations and be sure that it isn't higher than comparable houses on the block. Be realistic about repair costs.

13 Make the final sale contingent on obtaining a satisfactory bid for improvements. That way, if the bids you receive are simply too expensive, you can back out of the deal. Keep in mind that contingencies of any kind could make it hard to negotiate a lower price or even make a deal in a seller's market when competition among buyers can be intense.

14 See 172 Shop for a Mortgage, and pursue a mortgage that includes funds for home renovation, such as the Federal Housing Authority 203(k) program.

15 Make whatever repairs and renovations are necessary and then sell the property. (See 183 Sell a House.)

As a general rule of thumb, improvements that are invisible to the average home buyer or merely bring the home in line with expected minimum standards don't add to the resale value. If you make the wrong improvements, such as enlarging a closet or converting two bedrooms into a master suite when you only had two bedrooms to begin with, you won't see much, if any, return on your investment. Another potential pitfall is over-improving the home compared to other homes in the neighborhood.

Warnings

Conditions that your home inspector finds that can warrant backing out of a deal include pest infestation, radon, significant water damage to the structure, or other major fixes. Be aware that naturally occurring threats, such as mud slides or floods, if you're located in a flood plain, may be equally dangerous. Properties should be investigated by a structural engineer as well.

It's a conflict of interest if your home inspector also offers to do the work he or she has stated needs to be done.

181 Sell the Farm

Selling a farm is often as emotional a process as it is financial. Your property may have been in your family for generations, making the sale a wrenching, difficult decision. Here are some thoughts to bear in mind that may lessen the strain a bit.

Steps

1 Keep the land and retain ownership. Lease the property to a fellow farmer, who will work it and pay an agreed-on price for the use. You'll receive revenue without having to do anything but pay the taxes. Of course, rental income fluctuates with market demand for whatever crops are grown.

2 Have your farm's value appraised by an experienced farm appraiser and contact the local Cooperative Extension Service for assistance in valuing your property or determining how best to sell it. Appraisal should include "highest and best use," which suggests the property could be rezoned from agricultural to more valuable development now or in the future if property is "in the path of growth." Also check plans for freeway expansion in the area. Make certain the appraiser's specialty is farm properties, since residences and other properties are very different in terms of land value, use and other considerations. The operation's overall income potential is an important factor in estimating the farm's value, as is the value of livestock, equipment and machinery, and the age and condition of any outbuildings, such as barns and pens.

3 Contact neighboring landowners first to see if they're interested in expanding their holdings, or ask them to put the word out. Place classified ads in the local newspaper, as well as in farm publications that have a good circulation where the land is located.

4 Finance the sale yourself by offering a contract sale option where the buyer makes a down payment and then agrees to pay you a set amount each month or year. There's a risk if the buyer defaults, but the advantage is being able to charge a reasonable interest rate on the loan you've made, as well as spreading out the taxes owed on the sale. Also, title doesn't transfer in a contract of sale until it's paid off, making default less of a problem.

5 Exchange your farm land for property elsewhere to potentially reduce your tax bill. Research your options.

6 Hire a real estate agent with prior experience selling farms to broker the property. You'll pay a commission but you will broaden your exposure to prospective buyers. Commissions may even be negotiable but usually run from 2.5 to 3 percent.

7 Auction your land. While it may yield a price below market value, you can set a reserve price below which you will not agree to sell. In some cases, auctions can result in a purchase price far

What to Look For

- Fellow farmers
- An appraisal
- Interested neighbors
- An agent
- An auctioneer

Tips

Be sure to work with a qualified tax professional to make certain that every tax ramification of selling the property is taken into account. For further information, have a look at IRS Publication #225 (Farmers Tax Guide, available at irs.gov).

If you intend to bequeath part of your farm to your heirs, save them some money by selling assets that you've recently acquired, which would be considered *high basis* assets because their market value is close to what you paid for them. Then you can pass along *low basis* assets, which were purchased long ago or have appreciated considerably, on your death and significantly reduce or eliminate any capital gains taxes to be paid. That's because when property is passed down through an estate, the recipients receive a *stepped-up* basis that equals the fair market value on the date of your death. Your heirs will pay less in taxes and the farm will stay in the family.

above what you might have expected, if competition is fierce. Ask auctioneers what time of year is best for selling off farmland. (See 374 Buy at Auction.)

8 Value assets such as grain, barns and other improvements separately at the time of sale to establish a basis for depreciation for the new owner. (See Tips.)

9 Be sure to separate the value of the cropland from that of the personal residence. Keep it out of the equation when calculating the basis for the business property, which is subject to capital gains. (The capital gain on a business property is determined by subtracting the selling price minus the initial purchase price.)

10 Donate the farm to a nature preserve or nonprofit organization if you can find no takers, wish to preserve the land and prevent it from being developed, and can afford to accept a tax break instead of income. Look into organizations such as the Nature Conservancy (nature.org) or the Trust for Public Lands (tpl.org).

182 Sell Mineral Rights

Think you've got gold in them thar hills? Or oil, gas, coal, copper or other minerals? Sell the mineral rights while you hang on to the property. Depending on the particulars, mineral rights may produce a steady stream of income.

Steps

1 Have your property surveyed for mineral content. Look under Natural Resources in the U.S. Government Offices section of your phone book for a geologic survey.

2 Separate the various types of minerals evident on your property. Instead of leasing the rights to all minerals to one company, specify which minerals they can claim. Have an experienced attorney help you. Also determine the length of the lease—two years, three years, five years.

3 Ask the local Environmental Protection Agency office about the need for an environmental impact report before proceeding with the lease of the property. A damaging report might force cancellation of the lease.

4 Ask about a signing bonus. Weigh the size of the bonus against proposed royalty payments. Getting money up front is an advantage if no minerals are found; a higher royalty rate is best when minerals are actually located.

5 Become acquainted with other ways to handle mineral rights. For example, you can sell the property but retain the mineral rights for yourself.

What to Look For

- Geologic survey
- Legal expertise
- Lease term
- Signing bonus
- Royalty rate

Tip

When transferred, mineral rights generally include everything underground, starting at a certain depth and proceeding downward.

183 Sell a House

Like buying a home, selling one is a significant project. Even if you plan to use an agent, it's in your best interest to understand all the various elements that contribute to a successful sale. The more you know, the more cash you'll pocket in the end. Think of your preparation as money in the bank.

Steps

Get prepared

1 Decide if you want to use a real estate agent or not. A selling agent generally receives 2.5 to 3 percent of the sale price. In return, he or she should work aggressively to sell your home and list it in the Multiple Listings Services (MLS) where it can be seen by other agents. On the other hand, you may be able to save several thousand by handling the marketing of your home on your own. Read 184 Sell a House Without a Real Estate Agent and pay particular attention to the time involved.

2 Get recommendations from satisfied friends and acquaintances and interview several agents who specialize in your geographic area. Get a feel for their approach and how proactive they'll be in marketing your home. Have them outline their strategy for making your home as attractive as possible.

3 Review current listings in your area and set a strategic asking price. Your agent should get comparative prices on nearby homes and do a market analysis taking into account the size, location, condition and other elements to price it accurately. Ask to see the analysis so you understand how the agent established the asking price.

4 Confirm that the house will be listed in the MLS, that it will have an online presence, and that a professional-looking fact sheet will be prepared to help market the house.

5 Alert your neighbors that your house is going on the market. Hold a pre-open house, give a tour and ask for their help in finding a suitable buyer. Many homes are sold by word-of-mouth through friends and neighbors, so make use of your contacts.

Get ready to show

1 Perform any needed repairs on the interior and exterior of your home and fix, paint or otherwise repair anything that may hinder a sale.

2 Increase curb appeal. Try to ensure that your home makes the best first impression possible. Clean the windows, cut the grass and weed the flowerbeds.

3 Remove any extra furniture, wall hangings, tchotchkes and trinkets that can be distracting to potential buyers—many homes suffer from "too much good taste." Remember, less is more. Give

What to Look For

- A suitable agent
- Realistic asking price
- An aggressive marketing plan

Tips

Ask how long your contract with an agent runs. Most are for 90 days, but can often be negotiated. If the house sits for too long unsold, find yourself a new agent.

Research how fast homes are selling in your area. That will give you an idea of how long you may have to wait to sell your home.

If you're buying another home, you can make that purchase contingent on the successful sale of your current home.

Bake cookies or bread before the open house to take your marketing strategies to a subliminal level. If it's nice outside, open the windows to get a nice breeze blowing through and eliminate household odors.

any walls that need it a fresh coat of neutral paint. Think about having your home professionally staged (see sites such as StagedHomes.com). This will cost you, but you can both shorten the sales time and boost the bidding with a well-staged home.

4 Place a "For Sale" sign in your front yard and have fact sheets readily available.

5 Hold an open house, instead of just showing the house by appointment only. This is standard practice for real estate agents, and they are the ones who set it up and handle it. It's not only great for attracting buyers, but agents will also see your home and, in turn, mention it to other buyers. If you are present during the open house, refer any questions to your agent.

6 Keep your house spic-and-span. Prospective buyers often appear with as little as a half hour's notice. Your agent will put a lockbox on your door to gain entrance without your presence.

7 Board your pets while the house is being shown. You love them, but they may cause an allergic reaction in some people, or distract, irritate or scare off potential buyers.

Make the deal

1 Establish your flexibility. Decide ahead of time how much, if any, you're willing to trim from the asking price to make a sale. Or, in a hot market, be prepared to deal with multiple offers. Consider financing the sale yourself.

2 Get psyched up to dicker. Depending on local market conditions, many buyers may not offer the full asking price the first time around. In a buyer's market, you'll need to determine what is most important to you—price, moving date, keeping the appliances—and get the best deal possible. That said, the first offer is frequently the best offer, so don't be unreasonable. In a seller's market, expect to get close to your asking price or over in a very short period of time. But be careful: Pricing your home too high could keep it on the market longer than you wanted, causing you to have to drop the price later anyway (see Step 4 below).

3 Weigh the pros and cons of multiple offers, if you're lucky enough to have them. Consider the offering price, how solid the buyer's financing is, whether the sale is contingent on the sale of the buyer's house, and the move-out date. Your real rstate agent should be able to advise you.

4 Reduce the asking price if your home doesn't attract any offers. Start with a 5 percent drop and see if that boosts interest.

Be prepared to pay for various reports including pests, flood and insurability. They range from $30 to $300 each.

Warning

Create a paper trail of all improvements. Not only will they increase the value of your house, but you may be sued if you fail to make a full disclosure of them during a sale. Take the disclosure process very seriously.

184 Sell a House Without a Real Estate Agent

If the notion of handing over a commission to a real estate agent irks you, sell your house on your own. Before you go this route, factor in everything that's involved: You'll not only put out that sign on your lawn, but take phone calls and schedule appointments, buy classified ads, hold open houses, and conduct negotiations—all on your own.

Steps

1 Read 183 Sell a House for the basic rundown.

2 Figure out whether it makes sense financially to go to the trouble and expense of marketing and selling your house yourself, based on the commission you're saving. On a $100,000 home, you'll save half of the 6 to 7 percent real estate commission ($3,000 to $3,500), assuming that your buyer uses an agent. If neither of you uses an agent, you'll save $6,000 to $7,000 per $100,000. But you'll incur additional marketing expenses that you wouldn't have with an agent, such as newspaper listings, flyers, signs, Web sites, and anything else you to do promote it.

3 Be aware that serving as your own agent means that you'll need to be available at all times to take phone calls from potential buyers, schedule walk-throughs, and be at the house when folks want to tour. If your schedule doesn't allow for this level of flexibility, using an agent may make more sense.

4 Consider other options for selling your home. For instance, For Sale By Owner organizations offer ways to market your home for much less than what a real estate agent would charge—usually a flat fee upwards of a couple thousand dollars—while giving you step-by-step instructions on how to complete a sale.

5 Research what other houses in your neighborhood have sold for in the last couple of years to determine a reasonable asking price. Your county tax department has records of such comparable sales. Before you set the asking price, take into account closing fees, other selling expenses, and the amount of cash you want after the sale. Your home will sell faster if it is priced appropriately.

6 See "Get Ready to Show" steps under 183 Sell a House. Prepare a professional-looking letter-size fact sheet that contains a full-color photo of the house, the asking price, a list of features and amenities, utilities figures, property taxes and your contact information.

7 Get the word out. Pass out fact sheets to local real estate agents. Place an ad in the real estate section of your newspaper. Put up signs advertising your property for sale on your front lawn

What to Look For

- Clean, attractive property
- Time to prepare, show and negotiate
- Help from your neighbors
- Comparable listings
- Appropriate asking price
- Widespread advertising
- Open homes
- Final negotiations

Tips

In most states, the seller traditionally pays fees associated with the buyer getting a real estate mortgage. These fees include hiring a mortgage broker and are typically 1 to 1.5 percent of the mortgage amount (for example, $900 to $1,350 on a $90,000 mortgage).

Be careful not to schedule your open house to conflict with a major event, such as the World Series, or holidays. Early in the year, the housing market starts to heat up with families wanting to get settled in their new home before school starts in the fall.

Ask open house visitors to sign a guest book so that you have their names and addresses for follow-up. Give them a call within a week to find out whether they're still considering your house or are still looking.

One way to smooth any prospective problems before they crop up is to only consider offers from buyers who are prequalified for a mortgage.

or in a front window. Post fliers describing the house in public areas and in apartment complexes that may be teeming with prospective home buyers.

8 Practice showing the home with some astute friends, then schedule your open house on a Sunday. Be there to answer questions.

9 See "Make the Deal" Steps under 183 Sell a House.

185 Obtain a Home Equity Loan

Need to pay taxes or college expenses, or make home improvements? If you need cash, the source could be right under your feet. Look at a home equity loan for very low interest rates and flexible terms. Shop around and nail down the best deal possible.

Steps

1 Understand that a home equity loan is based on the equity in your house—the value of the property less what you owe on your first mortgage. For example, a $200,000 home with a $125,000 mortgage has $75,000 in equity.

2 Investigate lines of credit. A home equity loan is a pure loan with established payback terms. A line of credit can be used as you wish and offers greater payback flexibility—usually a minimum payment based on how much of the credit you have accessed. If you don't know how much that wedding is ultimately going to cost, for instance, a line of credit based on a high estimate may work out best. Or if your expenses will occur over several months, as in a remodeling project, a line of credit to draw on will end up costing less than a major loan at the start.

3 Find out how much you can borrow. Most home equity packages will let you borrow up to the point that your total debt—mortgage and home equity loan—reaches between 70 and 90 percent of the home's value.

4 Watch interest rates. Although home equity loans are less expensive than regular mortgages, interest rates will vary. Sites such as Bankrate.com display rates.

5 Keep an eye on costs. Compared to mortgages, home equity loans and lines of credit are currently dirt cheap. Many let you set up one at no cost at all and may offer low "teaser" interest rates for as long as one year.

6 Apply. Bring tax returns and proof of income.

Make sure that any valuables are safely stored before any open house.

What to Look For

- Maximum loan available on your home
- Low interest rate to start
- Inexpensive or free setup

Tips

Home equity is a great way to consolidate other debt, such as credit card. One big plus: The interest is tax deductible on your primary residence; credit card interest is not.

Home equity loans are currently exceedingly competitive, so ask at least two lenders for rates and terms.

Warning

Beware of quickie home equity loans that are promised in days instead of the typical two-week time frame. Although these loans are legit, they cost more in higher interest rates. Unless you absolutely need the money in a week, be patient and save yourself some cash.

186 Buy a Lot

Have you fantasized about living by a wooded stream or on a mountaintop? Can you simply not find the house you want from what's available on the market? Buying a lot to build on has its own set of considerations. The most important one is still location.

Steps

1 Check your local newspaper for listings of lots for sale. Or hire an agent who specializes in lots to help you find one that's a good value and suitable for the home you want to put on it.

2 Consider the location carefully, as well as proximity to shopping districts and parks, quality of the schools, traffic and congestion, public transit and the crime rate. Look at the lay of the land.

3 Features such as steep drop-offs, drainage problems or poor access roads may increase costs. Find out if utilities such as gas, electricity, sewer, garbage and water are available, especially if you are buying a lot off the beaten path, and how much it will cost to access them.

4 Define in general terms the structure you'd like to build, including square footage, number of floors, number and types of rooms, architectural style, as well as any specific features you want, such as a pool or large deck. Depending on the size and design of your home, a particular lot may or may not work. Consult an architect (see 188 Hire an Architect) or buy a plan (see 187 Buy House Plans) to rough out some designs and assess feasibility.

5 Investigate what the future holds for neighboring properties. Will other houses be built? How many? Are they zoned for residential or could commercial buildings be put in? How will this affect parking and traffic? Is there a possibility of additional buildings or roads being added in the future? How will your view be impacted? Look into potential environmental disputes such as water rights or endangered species habitats that could affect your property's value or ability to be sold or developed.

6 Hire a surveyor to map out the specifics of the property. A title company can order this or refer you to a suitable surveyor. Costs will vary according to the time needed for the survey and how difficult the job is. Ask for estimates.

7 Find out if the lot is in a flood plain. If it is, you'll not only need flood insurance (see 176 Obtain Disaster Insurance), but will need to have a soil engineer conduct a survey to spot potential sliding problems.

8 Buy owner's title insurance. This coverage lets you gain clear title to the property. The cost will depend on the value of the land.

9 Put down earnest money to hold the property while you close the deal—a small percentage of the overall value. See 172 Shop for a Mortgage, and complete your financing.

What to Look For

- Location
- Utilities and services
- Lay of the land
- Ideal structure
- Zoning issues
- Surveyor
- Insurance
- Financing

Tips

Call local builders to learn more about housing developments they are building and lots that are still available. Finding a builder (see 189 Hire a Builder) who owns land that you're interested in generally simplifies the process of purchasing the land and building a home, which can be done in a single transaction.

Visit the lot several times at different times of the day to get a complete feel for sun and shade patterns, as well as traffic and parking issues.

Warning

If you buy an odd-shaped lot or one that's difficult to build on, be prepared for extra expenses such as house plan modifications.

187 Buy House Plans

Having trouble finding an existing house that you want to buy? Consider buying plans and building your own home. That set of blueprints, with or without minor modifications, may well be the first step you take to create your dream home.

Steps

1 Determine the size of the house you can afford to build. The National Association of Home Builders (nahb.org) has information on the average cost per square foot for new homes in any area. Multiply the square footage of the home you want by the average cost per square foot to determine a ballpark cost.

2 Draw up a detailed, prioritized list of what you want your home to include in terms of number of bedrooms and baths, and garage size. What are must-haves and what can you live without? Include outdoor features such as porches, decks and a pool.

3 Ask yourself how you want to use the house now and in the future. Do you like to entertain? Do you want a casual great room or formal dining and living rooms? Will your home eventually need to accommodate aging parents, returning adult children or grandchildren? Do you need a separate entrance for an au pair?

4 Consider your lot requirements, such as sloping, corner or zero-lot line (where one side of the house sits on one lot line). Foundation options (basement, crawlspace or slab) will be dependent on what the lot will allow, based on the grade and other factors. If you've found plans for your ideal home, buy them and then look for a lot on which that particular layout will work. Otherwise, if you find the perfect lot (see 186 Buy a Lot), you'll need to be pickier as you choose your home plans in order to be sure that they'll fit on your land.

5 Browse house plan catalogs and magazines found at home improvement stores or bookstores. Many architects offer plans for sale online. Some sites let you specify exactly what features you want, such as a certain size kitchen or number of bedrooms.

6 Evaluate the plan for overall size, traffic patterns, appealing exterior materials, efficient use of space and materials, and well-planned work and storage areas. Ask a contractor to review the blueprints as well.

7 Expect to spend anywhere from $400 to $1,300 for plans depending on the project size and level of complexity. Buy up to eight nonreproducible sets—enough to distribute to tradespeople, contractors and lenders, or one reproducible master set.

8 Hire an architect to review your plans. He or she can make any modifications you think are necessary. See 188 Hire an Architect.

What to Look For

- Plans that suit your needs
- Architect to modify plans
- Lot requirements

Tips

Chances are good that plans will need to be adapted to meet your family's specific needs, so don't be afraid to make modifications with the help of an architect. Seismic and local building requirements will also likely mandate changes.

188 Hire an Architect

Architects go beyond strict functionality to create spaces that actually enrich the quality of life. They think holistically to create a home that truly works with the land it sits on. Chemistry is key when choosing an architect since you'll not only be spending a lot of time together, but sharing a great deal of personal information during the process.

Steps

1 Visit AIA.org and review the material the American Institute of Architects provides on hiring an architect.

2 Follow this rule of thumb: If you're tearing down or moving any walls, or if the job involves any plans or new construction, hire an architect. Or, think of it this way: The minute you have second thoughts, or start to question your solution, hire an architect.

3 Ask friends and colleagues for referrals. Identify someone with a project similar to yours, and visit the job site or finished home if possible. Find out if there are any issues to be aware of.

4 Consult your contractor for guidance if you're building a custom home or have purchased a lot as part of a package deal. Contracting firms sometimes keep an architect on staff, or will suggest one based on your project's needs.

5 Interview several candidates. Review academic and professional credentials and awards. You're assessing whether the architect listens to your ideas and is able to offer plausible, creative but financially doable solutions to your requests, but as importantly, if the two of you click. Ask for and call provided references.

6 Bring the architect into the picture when you know basically what you want, but before you decide on a course of action. As trained problem solvers, architects can provide solutions at the front end of the process on all aspects of design and cost-effective use of building materials. Architects are familiar with all building codes and disability requirements. They also understand the importance of intangible elements such as natural light.

7 Work up a sketch or provide photos of buildings you like from magazines and other sources. The architect will accommodate your lifestyle and specific space requirements.

8 Ask how fees are structured. Your job may be priced as a fixed figure, a percentage of total construction costs, or on an hourly time and materials basis. You'll pay more for overtime and making changes to the plans; you'll also be asked for a retainer before work begins.

9 Make sure all elements of the contract are clearly spelled out in writing and that you agree to the terms. Required by law in California and other states, the contract should include a detailed description of the job, total budget and architect's fee, and schedule of completion.

What to Look For

- An experienced architect
- Personalities that mesh
- Projects similar to yours

Tips

Ask when the architect will be able to do your job. Depending on how busy he or she is, some architects may have to put you on the back burner for a while.

Be sure to ask about any issues that are important to you such as using environmentally friendly and energy efficient materials or incorporating solar power.

Architects provide a wide range of services: programming (coming up with a wish list), preliminary (schematic) design, design development, preparation of construction documents, managing the job together with the general contractor and securing permits and zoning approvals.

Warning

Discuss what mechanisms are in place to stay within budget and what protections you as a consumer have in the event that actual costs exceed the budget.

189 Hire a Builder

Find a custom builder to build a one-of-a-kind dream house on either your land or the builder's. Specializing in single-family, high-end homes, custom builders generally build 25 homes (or fewer) a year.

Steps

1 Read 242 Hire a Contractor, Plumber, Painter or Electrician for background on licensing and other specifics. Get referrals from friends and neighbors who are satisfied with their builder's work. Calling your town engineers for recommendations is also a smart move, since they have to approve any additions or new homes.

2 Retain an architect (see 188 Hire an Architect) whether you're drawing up plans for new home construction or using an existing set of blueprints (see 187 Buy House Plans). Make sure builders you interview are capable of handling the type of construction you're looking for.

3 Get at least two but preferably three competitive bids for every job. Compare the bids to make certain they cover the same scope of work, use the same quality of materials, provide the same warranties, and have the same completion date.

4 Ask if the builder has done any projects similar to yours. If so, do your best to check them out as that will give you a first-hand view of a comparable project. Call the home owners and ask how the work went and if they have any positive or negative comments about the builder.

5 Get the builder's license information. Ask how long they've been in business and how large their staff is. Finally, find out all you can about their level of insurance and whether their workers are bonded.

6 Check out the builder's record with local home building organizations, contractor associations or your state's licensing board. Contact your local Better Business Bureau (bbb.org) to learn if any complaints have been lodged against the builder.

7 Get all guarantees and warranties in writing. It's essential to have an attorney draw up a contract or review any the builder supplies. The contract should be as detailed as possible, specifying materials used, brands, colors, and more.

8 Make certain your contract specifies a payment schedule and finance charges, if they apply. It should include a start and completion date, set penalties for any delays as well as specify how any cost overruns will be handled.

9 Hold a percentage of the purchase price in escrow until any disputes have been resolved. Most construction contracts include a clause that states how much will be put aside until you're fully satisfied, but if not, add it to cover the value of whatever work has not yet been resolved. This can be enough incentive for the builder to resolve any problems quickly and painlessly.

What to Look For

- A licensed builder
- A home plan you like
- Good references
- A clean BBB record
- Similar projects

Tips

Production builders specialize in higher volume projects.

If you decide to build a home with a builder and negotiate the deal yourself without a real estate agent, be sure to ask for a credit of 3 percent to cover the commission the builder would have had to pay an agent. The builder probably won't offer it, but you're entitled to it.

If the interest rate the builder offers for a series of payments is too high on a remodeling project, consider getting a home equity loan. The interest rate will likely be a good deal less expensive than builder financing. (See 185 Obtain a Home Equity Loan.)

Warning

Any changes you decide to make to your plans along the way need to be documented in order to ensure your contractor takes care of them, typically called a *change order*. Whenever you make a decision, be sure either you or your contractor puts it in writing and signs it. Oral agreements to fix something offer no protections or proof that the request was ever made.

190 Pull Building Permits

If you're considering a construction or remodeling project of any size, chances are good you'll have to request, or pull, a building permit from the city you live in. Specifics vary, but a permit is essentially a license that grants you permission to do the job, and at the same time serves as a mechanism to ensure that new or renovated structures comply with current local building codes.

Steps

1 Find out if you need a permit. Small jobs—such as interior painting—don't require one. On the other hand, projects involving construction, repair, improvement, modification or demolition usually mandate a permit. You may also need separate electrical, plumbing and mechanical permits. Call your city's building inspection office if you have any doubts.

2 Ask what you need to do to get the permit. Simple projects— adding an outdoor light, for instance—may only require an over-the-counter permit if any at all. However, if the job calls for any addition, alteration or construction of a new structure, you may be required to have an architect submit formal plans before a building permit is issued. The architect will pull the permits for you (or at least help). See 188 Hire an Architect.

3 Head down to your city's building department for the appropriate paperwork. Some will have forms available on their sites for download that you can fax or mail in.

4 When you're ready to officially apply for the permit, bring along blueprints, architectural drawings, necessary installation literature from manufacturers, and the license number of the contractor doing the work. Most building departments will want to verify that the contractor has general liability insurance and proof of worker's compensation coverage, so get copies of those in advance to speed the approval process. See 189 Hire a Builder.

5 Pay up. Rates will vary according to the community but fees are pegged to the total value of the project. For example, expect to pay a few hundred dollars for a project costing $20,000.

6 Post the permit in the front window of your home or job site.

7 Depending on the size of the project, you may need to schedule interim inspections with the building department. Smaller projects, such as installing a wood stove, generally require one inspection on completion, but larger projects may have three or four progress inspections.

What to Look For

- A simple permit
- Architectural drawings
- Appropriate paperwork
- Scheduled inspections

Tip

It pays to check. For instance, although painting is a simple project, if you're in a historic district, you may have to pull a permit.

Warning

Don't try to skirt the law. A building permit may seem expensive, but it's a lot cheaper than getting caught without one. Again, penalties vary but, in the example described in Step 5, the fine can be nine times the cost of the building permit. Plus, most insurance companies will refuse to pay a claim if there's a problem down the line and you didn't have the project inspected. You may also need to disclose permits for remodeling projects when you sell the house.

191 Buy a Vacation Home

Buying a vacation home—that haven away from it all—is an enticing thought, but the process is subject to the same practical considerations as any other financial decision you may make. Know what you're looking for, shop aggressively and pay attention to the numbers to ensure you walk away with the best deal possible.

Steps

1 Look where you've vacationed before, or if you're looking in a new geographic region, rent a home for a season to make sure you love it.

2 Get preapproved for a mortgage. This is a critical step, particularly if you already have a home loan and will add to your debt level. Depending on what you owe on your primary residence, you may be limited by what a lender is willing to give you for a vacation home mortgage. Alternatively, look into refinancing your primary residence at a lower rate for cash to buy a second home. See 172 Shop for a Mortgage and 173 Refinance Your Home.

3 Think about what sort of vacation home you want: a cabin, a house or a condo? Condos come with additional issues, such as home owners associations (HOA). See 193 Buy a Condominium.

4 Is proximity to water important? As a rule, the closer you are to desirable attractions of a given area, the more you're going to pay for that convenience.

5 Interview several local real estate agents before selecting one. Ask how many vacation home listings they have, how many years they've worked in the business, and whether they have a particular specialty. Make sure you're comfortable trusting the person you choose with your search.

6 View various homes in different settings. Get a sense of how location, size of the homes and other factors affect price differences.

7 Consider ongoing maintenance. How will you keep the house up if you're not there all the time, particularly if it's subject to a wide variety of weather conditions? Factor in the cost of hiring a local individual or service to look after the property in your absence.

8 Review 177 Buy a House for the rest of the house-buying process.

9 Check with the HOA, if there is one, for any restrictions on renting out your property. You may be limited in the amount of time the property can be occupied by someone else.

10 Look out for Uncle Sam, who gets into the act too: If you make a vacation home available for rent for more than 14 days in a year, the IRS categorizes it as an income property rather than a residence. You'll be paying taxes on the net rental income after expenses, which could bump you into the next tax bracket.

What to Look For

- Mortgage prequalification
- Price
- Location

Tips

Shop for lower prices during the off season.

In some parts of the country a dock is worth as much as 25 percent of the total property value. If a dock doesn't already exist, find out if there are restrictions on adding a new one.

Consider homes that may need some fixing up. "Sweat equity" can mean a lower price and, ultimately, a better investment, as long as you don't mind spending your vacation time renovating the property.

192 Book a Vacation Rental

Would your family enjoy a week in a cozy beach cottage? Or is your ideal getaway a condo overlooking the golf course? Start by deciding what you want, whether it's a house, villa, chalet, hotel or cabana.

Steps

1 Plan ahead—up to a year in advance. If you frequently vacation in a particular spot, set time aside to check out the rental market and get a jump on next year's reservations.

2 Find out when the peak rental season is. Save some money by vacationing off-season, but be aware that the weather, and snow or water conditions, may not be as agreeable.

3 Check local classifieds and Web sites frequently to see what's available. Contact the chamber of commerce or a real estate agent for leads listing available rentals.

4 Tour the properties for a firsthand look. If you can't go in person, make sure you can see clear photos of the home and facilities.

5 Inquire about pool, beachfront or lake access, hot tub, kitchen, laundry facilities and other amenities that are important to you.

6 Read any lease or rental agreement completely before signing. Be clear about all elements of the contract, including the security and cleaning deposits, liability issues and extra costs such as pool fees or sailboat rentals. If you have any questions, have an attorney review the agreement before signing.

What to Look For

- Sufficient space
- Affordability
- Convenient location
- Amenities and activities

Tip

Travel abroad on the cheap by swapping houses with someone from another country (homelink.org is one such site).

Warning

Don't get saddled with a hefty cleaning fee. Before you sign the contract, ask if cleaning is included or if you'll need to hire a service.

193 Buy a Condominium

If your version of the American dream doesn't include mowing the lawn, think about buying a condo. Good options for both first-time home buyers and older folks who are ready to downsize, condos are typically smaller and less expensive than a single family home, and can include attractive amenities as part of a home owners association (HOA), such as pools and fitness facilities. Bone up on both the pluses and the minuses.

Steps

1 Think about how long you're going to stay in one place. Buying a condo is no different than buying a single-family home—you need to live there at least a couple of years to recoup closing costs, assuming the property will appreciate.

2 Give some thought to what you want. If you're not interested in the pool or sauna, understand that the condo's price and ongoing monthly association fees will reflect their use regardless of your interest in swimming or sweating.

What to Look For

- Amenities of interest
- Appraisal (or comparable sales from broker)
- Good reputation
- Good construction
- Assessments and dues

3 Visit various condominium or townhouse communities and multi-unit buildings so you know what's available where you live. Get a sense of prevailing prices.

4 Request a market analysis from a real estate agent regarding the selling prices of condos in the building or area. Check the price appreciation on the market analysis to evaluate how quickly the condos are increasing in value; subtract the selling price from the purchase price and divide by the number of years the property has been held by the previous owner for a ballpark estimate of annual appreciation, if any (varies from state to state and place to place), in the neighborhood.

5 Get prequalified for a mortgage (see 172 Shop for a Mortgage).

6 Find out if the building has a good reputation. Ask current residents how often repairs and maintenance are required, and how good the soundproofing is between units.

7 Check out parking, storage, security and other amenities.

8 Ask to see the minutes from a recent meeting of the home owners association (HOA). Find out what the hot issues are and if members are fighting tooth and nail. You may want to keep looking—nobody wants to live where neighbors are at each other's throats.

9 Ask how large the HOA's reserve funds (used to pay for maintenance and emergency repairs on the building) are. The larger the reserve, the less a chance of an assessment or one-time payment to chip in for an unexpected expense. The smaller the reserve, the greater the chance you'll be billed for an assessment in the near future. Some states require periodic updates of reserves to be published to HOA members.

10 Check the HOA's history of assessments to see how many have been made in the past 10 years and how large they have been. This information will help you gauge how likely it is that you'll be assessed in the near future, and indicate how well-managed the building is. Better managed buildings make fewer assessments.

11 Talk to other members and find out how restrictive your HOA is. For instance, some buildings even dictate what sort of holiday lighting you can put up. Request the same information as you would for buying a house. Read the CC&Rs (covenants, conditions and restrictions).

12 Budget in association dues, which are above and beyond your monthly mortgage payment. To assist in long-term financial planning, ask the condo association whether association fees have increased in recent years. Also estimate monthly maintenance costs that you're responsible for in addition to the association fees.

13 Make an offer and close on the deal. See 177 Buy a House for more specifics.

Tip

Count how many common walls you may have with neighbors for a feel for how much noise you may hear (or transmit).

Warning

Some apartment buildings are converted to condos, giving you the opportunity as an apartment dweller to buy into the building and own your own place. Just because you live in a building now doesn't necessarily mean it's a good deal as a long-term investment, however. If your own building converts to a condo, evaluate it just as carefully as you would if you were looking at a building across town. You may find it makes more sense to move.

194 Rent an Apartment or House

The rental markets in many cities are cyclical: a few boom years with renters scrambling for any available studio followed by a glut in availability. In either scenario, the most desirable rental units are snapped up the quickest. Do your homework, then hit the pavement.

Steps

Conduct the search

1 Be prepared: Create a renter's résumé with your current and previous five addresses and landlord phone numbers, your employer and length of employment, your current salary and other income, personal references, among other information. Include a copy of your credit report (see 172 Shop for a Mortgage, Step 5). You want to look as good on paper as possible to stand out from other applicants.

2 Look in the newspaper classifieds, apartment hunter publications, college campus bulletin boards, and online for available units to investigate. Ask friends about openings in their buildings.

3 Consider how much you can afford to pay. A good rule of thumb is no more than 30 percent of your take-home monthly income.

4 Enlist a rental agent to narrow your search. Depending on the market, this service may be free (paid for by landlords) or cost you a percentage of your rent when you land the apartment.

5 Turn to a roommate service if you're looking for cheaper space to share. Be clear what qualities you desire in a roommate, as well as types of people or habits you'd prefer to avoid, such as smokers.

Case the joint

1 Inspect the property carefully. If there's any damage, you not only want to ask that it be fixed, but don't want to be blamed for it later. Make sure such problem areas are addressed in a lease, either by your agreeing to live with it, or the landlord agreeing to fix it by a certain date.

2 Check out common walls (walls shared with adjoining apartments). The more walls in common, the greater the chance of noise from next door. Also consider a common entrance in terms of how much privacy you may want.

3 Ask about amenities such as enclosed parking or a garage, a yard, storage, laundry facilities, pool, tennis, gym or concierge services.

Negotiate the deal

1 If you find an apartment you love but is a stretch financially, ask if there are responsibilities you can take on to lower your rent, such as cutting the lawn, sweeping common areas or taking deliveries. Or if you find a great apartment but it lacks services such as utilities, laundry facilities, cable TV and Internet access,

What to Look For

- Sufficient space
- Privacy
- Any prior damage

Tips

If the building allows pets, don't be surprised if you have to pay additional damage security deposit.

Get in writing how soon after you move out you will receive your security deposit. Some landlords drag their feet.

If it's a large complex or a hot rental market, you may have to pay an application fee to be considered as a tenant.

If you are relocating temporarily for business, investigate corporate housing, which is paid for by your employer. Check SpringStreet.com/corporate and similar sites for listings.

See 195 Obtain Renter's Insurance.

Ask if your security deposit can be placed in an interest-bearing account so that you're at least earning money while your landlord holds it. Many states have specific laws about how security deposits are treated.

In some cases, you can negotiate to have a percentage of your rental payment applied to a future down payment.

ask the landlord to throw some in at no charge. Many newer buildings will. Or offer to sign a longer-term lease or give a higher security deposit in exchange for more services.

2 Examine your lease in detail: How much notice is required prior to moving, how large a deposit you have to make, how much cleaning is required upon leaving to get your deposit back, and other provisions. Some agreements require first and last months' rent plus a security deposit—a significant chunk of change. Is the lease month to month, or a 6- or 12-month period?

3 Find out what kinds of cosmetic changes you can make, such as painting walls, or structural changes, such as adding shelving.

4 Ask for a lease with an option to buy if you'd be interested in purchasing the property down the line.

Warning

If you feel a landlord is refusing to rent to you because of your age, ethnicity, sexual preference, or physical handicap, report it to the local housing office.

195 Obtain Renter's Insurance

Just because your landlord owns the building doesn't mean he or she is responsible for covering your belongings in the event of a fire, theft or other nasty event. Even if you think all your worldly possessions don't amount to much, don't overlook this critical form of protection.

Steps

1 Shop around, starting with the auto insurance company—you may be able to tap into volume discounts if you have more than one policy with a company. Then check other agents and online insurance services. As a rule, renter's insurance is cheap—a couple hundred dollars a year should easily buy upwards of $15,000 in personal belonging protection and several hundred thousand dollars of liability coverage. Get your landlord's requirement in the lease or rental agreement for minimum coverage.

2 Investigate what the renter's insurance policy covers. Beyond protecting you if your property is stolen or lost in a fire, or suffers water damage, it must also offer liability coverage if, for instance, you leave the iron on and cause a fire.

3 Think you don't have much stuff? The average renter has more than $20,000 worth of belongings which may include expensive electronic equipment, bikes and small appliances. Photograph or videotape each item, list when you acquired it and its purchase price or current value. Keep your list in a safe deposit box along with the photos and videotape.

4 Spend a little more and get replacement coverage. This guarantees that your property will be replaced at current value, not what you bought it for originally.

What to Look For

- Adequate protection for belongings
- Adequate liability protection
- Replacement coverage

Tips

You may qualify for a discounted premium for having fire or smoke detectors or burglar alarms. (See 237 Buy Fire Extinguishers and 235 Buy Smoke Alarms.)

Check to see if your policy covers computer equipment, cell phones and other electronic gear. If not, you'll have to buy separate floater policies to cover them. Make sure you frequently back up computer files you can't afford to lose and store them in a separate location.

196 Buy a Loft in Manhattan

Imagine being able to look out the window of your spacious loft to see the hustle and bustle of the Big Apple. If you've always dreamed of living in the heart of the city, a loft might suit you perfectly. You can often find a good-size live/work loft for the same price as apartments in many cities.

Steps

1 See 177 Buy a House.

2 Investigate what kind of loft you can get for your budget. Lofts are generally wide open spaces, with high ceilings. Some need a fair amount of work to be livable, including, perhaps, the addition of walls or partitions, and interior finish.

3 Investigate cooperatives (which is what most apartments and lofts are in New York). You won't actually own the loft, but will be a shareholder in a corporation that owns the entire building, which entitles you to a long-term proprietary lease. A co-op carries a monthly maintenance fee in addition to the lease cost that covers the mortgage expense of the building, as well as heat, hot water, taxes and other costs. Ask about how much debt the building has, and therefore, how much each unit must pay if it's a co-op. Typical prorated debt ranges between $25,000 and $40,000.

4 Check out lofts that are condominiums (see 193 Buy a Condominium). You will actually own the property, but pay a monthly home owners association fee. The advantage is that you buy the unit up front with a monthly fee that is almost always lower than for a comparable co-op since you're not paying a pro rata share of the building's mortgage.

5 Compare prices. The bigger the loft, the more you'll pay, as with a more desirable neighborhood. To illustrate, a 1,300-square-foot loft in SoHo listed in 2003 for $1.3 million; in the up-and-coming North Chelsea neighborhood, prices range from $400 to $550 per square foot, versus $600 to $750 per square foot in TriBeCa.

6 Explore neighborhoods, which differ in price according to access to good schools and other amenities, and traffic. Pay attention to what's happening, such as new shops coming in or restaurants closing, as they may be a sign of what's to come.

7 Expect to pay more—much more—in trendy new buildings, such as Richard Meier's glass towers in Greenwich Village, which sold for $1,000 to $1,800 per square foot before they were even built. Stick with existing buildings without doormen for lower prices, although they're difficult to find no matter what.

8 Find an attorney who specializes in New York real estate. If you're not familiar with the legal wrinkles of buying a loft, it's important to have a pro on hand who does.

What to Look For

- Type of ownership
- Good location
- Legal help

Tips

As in other real estate ventures, get preapproved for a mortgage before you shop to give you a good idea of how much you can afford.

The difference between a co-op and a condo will show up in the price. As a rule, condos are more expensive. Also, many boards that oversee co-ops have much more muscle to reject prospective buyers than do condo management boards.

Contact the New York City Loft Board (nyc.gov/html/loft/home.html) with any issues regarding the legalization and regulation of loft buildings converted to residential use.

197 Buy a Tenancy-in-Common Unit

This old English common law arrangement applied to a group of non-spouses who owned and used the same property. These days, tenancy-in-common (TIC) is a complex legal arrangement where multiple owners buy a building together which has not been split into condos. If you think that means a special set of considerations, you couldn't be more right.

Steps

1 Explore the benefits of this unique arrangement. Individual owners have the ability to sell. Also, if the TIC is an income-producing property, an individual owner can do a tax-deferred exchange into another "like-kind" income-producing property and avoid paying capital gains.

2 Take a hard look what's involved. You have to identify a suitable property, find a group of people you get along with well enough to be successful co-owners, and deal with a lot of paperwork.

3 Understand the three methods of getting into a TIC.
• Buy into an existing partnership.
• Form a TIC from the outset.
• Convert a partnership or limited liability corporation (LLC) into a TIC.

4 Take inventory of each potential co-owner's finances. Since all TIC members share the debt and will be listed on the mortgage, everyone will need to be prequalified.

5 Locate a property. In some cases, TICs in search of additional owners advertise an open unit in the local newspaper or with a real estate agent. Conversely, a group could look together for a suitable property to buy.

6 Split ownership according to each party's wishes. Say you and someone else want to buy a home or building together—that doesn't mean that the property or ownership has to be divided into equal shares. Or, you may want to buy into a TIC property for investment purposes. Many options are acceptable so long as they're clearly stated in all documentation.

7 Have an attorney draw up papers outlining the TIC agreement (even if your state doesn't require it) which clearly stipulates varying percentages of ownership, defines common and private areas and shared expenses and establishes a mutually agreed-upon course of action if a co-owner fails to abide by the agreement.

8 Investigate all possible mechanisms for breaking up a TIC. One owner may simply agree to sell his or her share to another. Partners can also file for a court action for partition. The court may order that the property be sold and each owner receive a proportionate share of the money. Another vehicle for dissolution is to convert the building into condominiums, with each resident owning his or her own unit (see 193 Buy a Condominium).

What to Look For

• Partners for ownership
• An attorney

Tip

Have your attorney draft or review tenancy-in-common papers to prevent nasty misunderstandings down the line. Even if you use a sample TIC agreement from a Web site, verify that nothing important has been left out inadvertently.

Warning

Bear in mind that a partner upon his or her death can transfer ownership to anyone they choose. None of the other partners has any say in the choice. It's something to consider if you get along with a partner fine but know you won't work well with his or her heirs.

198 Buy Rental Property

Stocks and bonds aren't the only money-making investment in town. Consider rental property if you're prepared for extensive research, a fair amount of financial commitment and, depending on how you set things up, a significant role in maintaining the property.

Steps

1 Assess your financial requirements and goals. Do you need a steady stream of income from your rental or do you plan on selling it for a profit in a couple of years? If it's the latter, look for lower priced property that you can fix up as you rent it out.

2 Consider being a resident landlord by purchasing a multiunit property and living in one apartment. In many cases, the income from the other unit(s) will cover your mortgage payment, allowing you to effectively live for free. Being on-site has other advantages, including ensuring that the property is well-maintained.

3 Decide if you want to do maintenance yourself. If you have the skills, equipment and temperament to deal with upset tenants and a backed up toilet at 2 a.m., fine. If you plan on hiring a property manager, add about 5 percent of gross income into your calculations.

4 Choose the kind of property you want. Single-family houses are generally less expensive than apartment complexes because of pure size, but generate less income. Apartments, on the other hand, can require more upkeep.

5 Get preapproved for a mortgage (see 172 Shop for a Mortgage). Financing investment property is different from residential property in that it requires a much larger down payment.

6 Start shopping: Check out classified ads in the newspaper and online. Find a real estate agent who specializes in commercial or income-generating properties.

7 Choose property where people want to live, close to shops, parks and decent schools, and in a well-kept neighborhood. There's nothing worse than owning a rental property without any renters. In addition, check out any restrictions on renting with the home owners association, which, if there is one, can have a say in any rental agreements.

8 Consider what improvements, if any, you may be willing to make. Buying a fixer-upper will be less expensive than a property in pristine condition, but you can go broke bringing a property up to rentable condition. Before you buy, get cost estimates for all necessary fixes. See 180 Buy and Sell a Fixer-Upper.

9 Have the property inspected. You may also want to order an appraisal to get a fair market value.

10 Search past records for vacancy rates over the last five to ten years as well as at present. If the building is occupied, find out

What to Look For

- Income produced meets financial goals
- Suitable property
- Appealing location
- Vacancy rates
- Neighborhood rental rates

Tips

Check to see whether the value of other area properties have increased or decreased in the past five years. Try to buy in an area that's on the way up.

Pay attention to when improvements were made to a property, which aids in the estimate of the building's value. Recent renovations are worth more than upgrades done a decade or more ago.

Be on the lookout for any hazards common to older properties, such as asbestos, lead-based paint and electrical systems that are not up to code. Budget in reconciling these problems.

how long the tenants have lived at the property. Long-term residents are valuable, but may also have been signed on at a lower rental rate.

11 Plan on spending time and money advertising for and interviewing potential renters. Have a contingency plan in place if a unit remains vacant for a few months.

12 Determine what a competitive rental rate is for your property by asking rental agents what they would expect to charge, by reviewing area apartment listings, and by personally visiting units available in the neighborhood.

13 Run the numbers. Make certain that whatever income you derive covers your costs of owning the property, plus a profit.

14 Work with an attorney to draw up and review any necessary papers relevant to the purchase.

15 Negotiate the terms of the sale. Some sellers may be willing to pick up a share of closing costs and other expenses. The eventual price will also be affected by prevailing market conditions—keep these in mind when negotiating.

Some cities offer low interest financing to property owners needing to make renovations. Look into such programs if you know you'll need to have the property painted, windows replaced or similar exterior repairs made.

Discuss any tax benefits with a tax specialist. There may be local tax incentives for renovating your property as well as advantageous approaches to declaring your expenses.

199 Rent Your Home for a Movie or Catalog Shoot

Lights, camera, paycheck! Getting your home in a movie, on TV or in the next glitzy housewares catalog can be fun and pull in some cash to boot. But there are issues to bear in mind, not only to increase the chances of making your home a star, but to protect it in the process.

Steps

1 Submit your home as a possible location with film studios, production companies and advertising firms, which maintain lists of properties available for shooting purposes.

2 Ask what the rate is. Depending on how long they'll be in your home and the scope of the project, pay ranges from a couple hundred to more than a thousand dollars per diem. If the location is in a television series, they could come back year after year.

3 Expect your home to be taken over by people setting up shop in all parts of the house, including the bathrooms. Find out whether you should remove your furniture or make any changes before they come in or whether the production crews will. Ask if they plan to make any temporary changes and what they'll be.

4 Ask for a written policy outlining what the company does in case anything is damaged. The contract should include a provision to "return the house back to its original state," which may involve repainting or carpet cleaning, and the time frame for doing so.

What to Look For

- Studio and production company property lists
- A contract

Warnings

Don't expect to make gobs of money renting out your house. Keep in mind that while the production crew is filming, you'll likely have to pay to live somewhere else.

Production companies use trucks to haul cameras, and tracks and cranes that need off-site parking locations, which could significantly inconvenience you and your neighbors.

EHOUSE STORES • BUY WHOLESALE • GET OUT OF DEBT • BUY NOTHING • BUY HAPPINESS • BUY A BETTER MOUSETRAP • BUY TIME
EONE'S FAVOR • BUY POSTAGE STAMPS WITHOUT GOING TO THE POST OFFICE • TIP PROPERLY • BUY HEALTHY FAST FOOD • BUY SUN
NG SERVICE • SELL YOURSELF ON AN ONLINE DATING SERVICE • SELL YOURSELF TO YOUR GIRLFRIEND/BOYFRIEND'S FAMILY • BUY DC
OSE FILM FOR YOUR CAMERA • BUY RECHARGEABLE BATTERIES • DONATE TO A GOOD CAUSE • HOLD A PROFITABLE GARAGE SALE •
DENT DISCOUNTS • BUY FLOWERS WHOLESALE • GET A PICTURE FRAMED • HIRE A MOVER • HIRE A PERSONAL ORGANIZER • FIND A V
HDAY PRESENT FOR UNDER $10 • SELECT GOOD CHAMPAGNE • BUY A DIAMOND • BUY JEWELRY MADE OF PRECIOUS METALS • BUY C
ESMAIDS' DRESSES • HIRE AN EVENT COORDINATOR • HIRE A BARTENDER FOR A PARTY • HIRE A PHOTOGRAPHER • HIRE A CATERER •
AN ANNIVERSARY GIFT • ARRANGE ENTERTAINMENT FOR A PARTY • COMMISSION A FIREWORKS SHOW • BUY A MOTHER'S DAY GIFT •
CT A THANKSGIVING TURKEY • BUY A HOUSEWARMING GIFT • PURCHASE HOLIDAY CARDS • BUY CHRISTMAS STOCKING STUFFERS •
LERS ROOM IN VEGAS, BABY • BUY SOMEONE A STAR • PAY A RANSOM • GET HOT TICKETS • HIRE A LIMOUSINE • BUY A CRYONIC CHA
RSONAL JET • ACQUIRE A TELEVISION NETWORK • ACQUIRE A BODY GUARD • BOOK A LUXURY CRUISE AROUND THE WORLD • SELL Y
ROUGHBRED RACEHORSE • BUY A VILLA IN TUSCANY • HIRE A PERSONAL CHEF • PURCHASE CUBAN CIGARS • HIRE A GHOSTWRITER
NESS • MAKE BAIL • DONATE YOUR BODY TO SCIENCE • HIRE YOURSELF OUT AS A MEDICAL GUINEA PIG • SELL PLASMA • SELL YOUR
LEGE EDUCATION • BUY AND SELL STOCKS • CHOOSE A STOCKBROKER • DAY-TRADE (OR NOT) • BUY ANNUITIES • BUY AND SELL MUT
SONAL FINANCE SOFTWARE • CHOOSE A TAX PREPARER • SET UP A LEMONADE STAND • SELL YOUR PRODUCT ON TV • HIRE A CAREER
Y A SMALL BUSINESS • BUY A FRANCHISE • LEASE RETAIL SPACE • LEASE INDUSTRIAL SPACE • LEASE OFFICE SPACE • BUY LIQUIDATE
ERTISING ON THE WEB • SELL YOUR ART • HIRE A PERSONAL COACH • SELL ON THE CRAFT CIRCUIT • HIRE A LITERARY AGENT • PITCH
A HOT DOG STAND • SHOP FOR A MORTGAGE • REFINANCE YOUR HOME • SAVE BIG BUCKS ON YOUR MORTGAGE • OBTAIN HOME OV
THE FARM • SELL MINERAL RIGHTS • SELL A HOUSE • SELL A HOUSE WITHOUT A REAL ESTATE AGENT • OBTAIN A HOME EQUITY LOAI
A CONDOMINIUM • RENT AN APARTMENT OR HOUSE • OBTAIN RENTER'S INSURANCE • BUY A LOFT IN MANHATTAN • BUY A TENANCY-
RTMENT • BUY USED FURNITURE • BUY DOOR AND WINDOW LOCKS • CHOOSE AN ORIENTAL CARPET • BUY LAMPS AND LIGHT FIXTUR
LIANCES • FIND PERIOD FIXTURES • BUY A BED AND MATTRESS • HIRE AN INTERIOR DESIGNER • HIRE A FENG SHUI CONSULTANT • INC
RLPOOL TUB • BUY A SHOWERHEAD • BUY A TOILET • CHOOSE A FAUCET • BUY GLUES AND ADHESIVES • CHOOSE WINDOW TREATME
OSE A KITCHEN COUNTERTOP • BUY GREEN HOUSEHOLD CLEANERS • STOCK YOUR HOME TOOL KIT • BUY A VIDEO SECURITY SYSTE
RAGE-DOOR OPENER • BUY LUMBER FOR A DIY PROJECT • HOW TO SELECT ROOFING • HIRE A CONTRACTOR, PLUMBER, PAINTER OF
LECT PEST CONTROLS • BUY SOIL AMENDMENTS • BUY MULCH • BUY A COMPOSTER • BUY FERTILIZER • START A VEGETABLE GARDE
A STORAGE SHED • HIRE AN ARBORIST • BUY BASIC GARDEN TOOLS • BUY SHRUBS AND TREES • BUY A HOT TUB • BUY AN OUTDOC
D LABELS • SELECT HERBS AND SPICES • STOCK YOUR KITCHEN WITH STAPLES • EQUIP A KITCHEN • CHOOSE FRESH PRODUCE • SE
EY • CHOOSE POULTRY • SELECT FRESH FISH AND SHELLFISH • SELECT RICE • PURCHASE PREMIUM SALT AND PEPPER • GET A CHEE
CHASE KOSHER FOOD • BUY FOOD IN BULK • CHOOSE COOKING OILS • SELECT OLIVE OIL • SELECT OLIVES • BUY ETHNIC INGREDIEN
CHASE A KEG OF BEER • BUY ALCOHOL IN A DRY COUNTY • CHOOSE A MICROBREW • ORDER A COCKTAIL • CHOOSE A RESTAURANT
GNANCY TEST KIT • CHOOSE BIRTH CONTROL • FIND THE RIGHT OB-GYN • HIRE A MIDWIFE OR DOULA • FIND A GOOD PEDIATRICIAN •
AST PUMP • CHOOSE A CAR SEAT • BUY CHILD-PROOFING SUPPLIES • FIND FABULOUS CHILDCARE • FIND A GREAT NANNY • FIND THE
MER CAMP • SELL GIRL SCOUT COOKIES • BUY BRACES FOR YOUR KID • BUY TOYS • BUY BOOKS, VIDEOS AND MUSIC FOR YOUR C
THES AND BOOKS • FIND A COUPLES COUNSELOR • HIRE A FAMILY LAWYER • BUY PROPERTY IN A RETIREMENT COMMUNITY • CHOO
THBRUSH • BUY MOISTURIZERS AND ANTIWRINKLE CREAMS • SELECT PAIN RELIEF AND COLD MEDICINES • SAVE MONEY ON PRESCF
S TO COUNTER HAIR LOSS • BUY A WIG OR HAIRPIECE • BUY A NEW BODY • GET A TATTOO OR BODY PIERCING • OBTAIN BREAST IMP
GLASSES AND SUNGLASSES • HIRE A PERSONAL TRAINER • SIGN UP FOR A YOGA CLASS • TREAT YOURSELF TO A DAY AT THE SPA • E
• BUY AT AUCTION • KNOW WHAT YOUR COLLECTIBLES ARE WORTH • DICKER WITH DEALERS • GET AN ANTIQUE APPRAISED • BUY
AN ANTIQUE AMERICAN QUILT • BUY AN ANTIQUE FLAG • LIQUIDATE YOUR BEANIE BABY COLLECTION • SCORE AUTOGRAPHS • TRAD
AND SELL SPORTS MEMORABILIA • SELL YOUR BASEBALL-CARD COLLECTIONS • CHOOSE A DESKTOP COMPUTER • SHOP FOR A USE
PUTER PERIPHERALS • CHOOSE AN INTERNET SERVICE PROVIDER • GET AN INTERNET DOMAIN NAME • BUY A HOME NETWORK • UPC
ER • BUY A VCR • CHOOSE A PERSONAL DIGITAL ASSISTANT • CHOOSE MOBILE PHONE SERVICE • NEGOTIATE YOUR LONG-DISTANCE
E AUTOMATION SYSTEM • BUY A STATE-OF-THE-ART SOUND SYSTEM • BUY AN AUDIO-VIDEO DISTRIBUTION SYSTEM • BUY A SERIOU
UAL-REALITY FURNITURE • BUY TWO-WAY RADIOS • BUY A MOBILE ENTERTAINMENT SYSTEM • GET A PASSPORT, QUICK! • PURCHASE
FREE • BID FOR A SLED RIDE ON THE ALASKAN IDITAROD TRAIL RACE • BUY DUTY-FREE • SHIP FOREIGN PURCHASES TO THE UNITED
ATION • CHOOSE A CHEAP CRUISE • BOOK A HOTEL PACKAGE FOR THE GREEK ISLANDS • RAFT THE GRAND CANYON • BOOK A CHEA
E SALSA LESSONS IN CUBA • BUY A CAMERA IN HONG KONG • BUY YOUR WAY ONTO A MOUNT EVEREST EXPEDITION • HIRE A TREKK
LE AND KNEE BRACES • BUY GOLF CLUBS • JOIN AN ELITE GOLF CLUB • SELL FOUND GOLF BALLS • BUY ATHLETIC SHOES • BUY A P
A SKATEBOARD AND PROTECTIVE GEAR • BUY SKATES • GO SPORT FISHING • GO SKYDIVING • BUY WEIGHTLIFTING EQUIPMENT • CH
SKI BOOTS • BUY A BICYCLE • SELL YOUR BICYCLE AT A GARAGE SALE • COMMISSION A CUSTOM-BUILT BICYCLE • BUY A PROPERL
ATION DEVICE • BUY A WET SUIT • BUY A SURFBOARD • BUY FLY-FISHING GEAR • BUY ROCK-CLIMBING EQUIPMENT • BUY A CASHM
S • BUY THE PERFECT COCKTAIL DRESS • BUY DESIGNER CLOTHES AT A DISCOUNT • CHOOSE A BASIC WARDROBE FOR A MAN • BU
FCASE • SHOP FOR A LEATHER JACKET • BUY MATERNITY CLOTHES • GET A GREAT-FITTING BRA • CHOOSE A HIGH-PERFORMANCE S
CHASE CLOTHES AT OUTLET SHOPS • BUY A NEW CAR • BUY THE BASICS FOR YOUR CAR • BUY A USED CAR • BUY OR SELL A CAR C

Home & Garden

200 Furnish Your Home

Today's home is where you go to relax and refresh yourself, attend to the details of your life and share the company of others. An extension of your personality and lifestyle, a carefully furnished home is a true haven. Shop with style, versatility and easy care in mind to ensure that your space will be functional as well as attractive.

Steps

1 Window-shop first. Visit a variety of stores, and pore over catalogs before making a choice you'll live with every day.

2 Make a style file. Collect photos not just of interiors, but also of patterns, graphics and shapes you like. Carry a swatch envelope with fabric snippets, paint-color chips and other color samples. Found a peach nail polish that's just the right shade for a rug? Brush some on a piece of paper.

3 Assess your lifestyle. Do you give elegant dinner parties or invite friends over for potlucks? Do you need a sofa long enough for a nap? Your furnishings should accommodate your activities.

4 Measure rooms carefully, then sketch floor plans, rooms and furniture arrangements on graph paper. Even better, make cutouts of furniture you can move around. Or, look for room-layout software. Keep traffic flow in mind: You don't need a straight shot through each room, but avoid obstacle courses.

5 Prowl auctions, yard sales and your family's houses for used furniture (see 202 Buy Used Furniture). Buy new pieces that complement old favorites. Before you toss an older piece, consider refinishing or painting to help it blend with your new furniture. Make sure it suits your needs for appearance, comfort, function and durability.

6 Pick colors that work for the long term. Don't tie yourself to this season's "in" colors, but realize they may dominate choices in many furniture products. Neutral upholstery is easy to work with, but pass on all-white if you have kids or pets.

7 Opt for practical, easy-to-live-with fabrics. Save bright, trendy patterns for replaceable slipcovers. If you have a cat, avoid open-weave fabrics and leather, and look for upholstery that's more likely to stand up to claws.

8 Buy the best quality you can afford when choosing a major piece such as a sofa. It's likely to get constant use and it needs to last. If your budget allows, invest in features such as a hardwood frame and hand-tied springs. Stain-resistant fabrics may cost more up front, but they'll quickly earn their keep.

9 Don't feel restricted to the styles of the store's floor samples. You can order many pieces in different woods, finishes and fabrics, and each one creates a different look. Leg, skirt and pillow options can customize your choice.

What to Look For

- Versatility
- Four-point test: appearance, comfort, function, durability
- Practical colors and fabrics
- Quality
- Free delivery

Tips

Take advantage of free decorating advice. Most furniture stores have in-house experts ready to help.

Measure doorways and stairways to be sure furniture can reach its intended spot. Always carry a tape measure when shopping (store-tag dimensions can be wrong).

It's important to size your furnishings to the room. A high-ceiling great room needs large, even oversize furniture. Standard pieces will look lost.

Keep your eyes peeled. Glean ideas from friends' homes, house tours, TV and movies, and home decor books and magazines.

10 Shop at stores that have earned a reputation for excellent quality and good customer service. Free delivery—including unpacking and placing in the room—is a plus.

11 Don't buy all the furnishings you need at once, even if you can afford to. Choose a few good pieces and enjoy adding to the ensemble gradually while giving yourself room to change your mind and allow your taste to expand and develop.

Consider a sectional sofa, especially if you anticipate moving often. You can rearrange the pieces to adapt to different room dimensions.

201 **Furnish Your Studio Apartment**

Small is beautiful—and even comfortable if you're a shrewd decorator. Furnishings must work harder; clever storage is essential. With a little imagination and ingenuity, one-room living won't drive you up the walls.

What to Look For

- Mobile room dividers
- One great focal point
- Multipurpose furniture
- Inventive storage

Steps

1 Create rooms within the room to better manage the space. Hang fabric, blinds or curtains from ceiling rods or tracks, and define zones with area rugs. Partition areas with a folding screen or use chests and shelves on casters. Low bookshelves can cordon off a space while providing needed storage.

2 Give a dramatic bed or sofa a starring role. Even when space is compact, you need a few large-scale focal points.

3 Put multipurpose pieces to work. Use a trunk, chest or ottoman as a coffee table and storage unit; configure wood storage cubes to any height or width; treat a tailored daybed as extra seating.

4 Buy high-quality, versatile furnishings you can use later in a larger home. Today's TV cart is tomorrow's entertaining trolley. A sectional sofa will become separate chairs. An armoire adds function to almost any room.

5 Keep the scale light to avoid overwhelming your space. Choose see-through and reflective furniture with glass or plastic shelves and tabletops, as well as tubular or wire legs.

6 Maximize storage by building a window seat or platform bed over drawers. Install an efficient closet system and you may not need a bureau. Create storage space on the walls, doors and even the ceiling using shelves, bins and hooks. Collect baskets, hatboxes and funky vintage suitcases for stackable storage that can double as side tables and nightstands.

7 Enhance room volume with mirrors. Lean a tall mirror against a wall to expand perspective. Hang a group of small mirrors across from a window to bounce light around.

Tips

Use paint and slipcovers to unify secondhand or mismatched items. Paint pieces the same color as walls for a light, airy look.

Arrange furniture on the diagonal to make the room look wider.

202 Buy Used Furniture

No longer just for student apartments, vintage furniture is now chic. Thank trends such as cottage and eclectic decorating, as well as rising interest in comfortable weekend homes. Shop for versatility and timeless design, and each piece will hold up for years.

Steps

1 Carry a list of what you're looking for, noting the ideal and maximum dimensions for each piece. Remember to measure the clearance of doorways and stairs. Keep a measuring tape with you. You never know when you'll see something.

2 Visit secondhand, charity and consignment shops regularly. Ask them to call you when something you want comes in.

3 Attend auctions and get on the mailing list. Older furniture is often well constructed, but use auction previews to inspect for damage. Sit on the chair to test for comfort, loose joints or wobbly legs. Open doors and drawers to check for any sticking, broken parts or damaged or missing hardware. See 374 Buy at Auction and 375 Know What Your Collectibles Are Worth.

4 Shop flea markets, yard sales and estate sales. While the best selection is on the first day, the best deals are on the last half day—sellers don't want to haul furniture home or store it over the winter. See 372 Shop at an Antique Fair or Flea Market.

5 Think versatility. Value design above finish or upholstery, which can be changed. How would a piece work if you shortened its legs or removed its drawers? If it's not an antique, imagine how paint or a slipcover can create a fresh personality.

6 Add repair costs to an item's selling price if you don't know how to refinish or refurbish yourself. Steam-cleaning stained fabric is affordable, but reupholstering can eat up any savings unless the piece is top quality and will hold its value.

7 Drive a vehicle roomy enough to get your furniture home from the flea market or yard sale. Stores in a permanent location usually allow a few days' grace for pickup, but most items are auctioned on the spot. The auctioneer might help you arrange for professional delivery, but that boosts your purchase price.

8 Request an exchange or money-back guarantee in case you find that a piece is badly damaged or just doesn't fit.

What to Look For

- Sturdy construction
- End-of-sale bargains
- Versatile design
- Minimal need for repair

Tips

Mention your used-furniture needs to friends. You might be able to swap pieces so both find happy new homes.

It's easy to replace door and drawer hardware on vintage (not antique) pieces. An old pull will tell you the screw size and thread, but the length is determined by the thickness of the door or drawer.

See 381 Buy Antique Furniture.

203 Buy Door and Window Locks

"Locks only keep honest people out," the saying goes, but high-quality door and window hardware make your house or apartment less attractive to burglars. If you survey your home as a potential target and don't try to cut corners, you'll find security devices you can trust.

Steps

1 Ask your police department for a home security inspection. Or, have a locksmith evaluate your home, explain all security options, and install professional-quality devices. Call members of the Associated Locksmiths of America (aloa.org).

2 Replace hollow-core entry doors with solid hardwood at least 1¾ inches (4.5 cm) thick, steel-clad or insulated fiberglass doors. The frame should not have gaps wide enough for a pry bar.

3 Install exterior doors with hinges on the inside. Burglars can pop out exterior hinges and remove a locked door. Install a 180-degree peephole rather than a door chain. Make sure you can't put a hand through your mail slot and reach the lock.

4 Upgrade key-in-knob locks (thieves can jimmy their spring-action latches with a credit card) to ones with hardened steel pins or a dead bolt ($10 to $35). If you like the convenience of a key-in-knob lock, add a deadbolt above it.

5 Invest in grade 1 or 2 dead bolts (under $65), which withstand kicking, prying, wrenching, hammering, sawing and drilling. A single-cylinder deadbolt is key-operated from the outside; a double-cylinder is key-operated from both sides. If your door has a glass pane or is near a window, install a double-cylinder model so a burglar can't break the glass and unlock the door. Keep a key for emergencies near the door, not in the lock.

6 Shop for dead bolts that have a steel bolt with a 1-inch (2.5 cm) throw (the bolt extends that far into the door frame), strike plates secured with 2½- to 3-inch (6 to 7.5 cm) screws, five- or six-pin cylinders and a free-spinning solid-metal cylinder collar. Screws must be long enough to penetrate the framing around the door.

7 Install a steel door pin near each hinge to secure swing-out doors, preventing the door from being pried out.

8 Secure double-hung windows with a nail or bolt. Drill the hole through both sashes at a downward angle to prevent a burglar from jiggling the pin loose. Keyed sash stops ($6) are also available. Be aware that crescent or butterfly latches are easily picked with a knife.

9 Install retractable window grates for worry-free ventilation on basement and ground-floor windows.

10 Prevent sliding doors from being lifted off their tracks by using vertical bolts or antilift plates between the doors and their top tracks. Heavy-duty keyed locks mount on the inside edge of the frame.

What to Look For

- Police or locksmith's advice
- Solid door and sturdy frame
- Upgraded key-in-knob locks
- Dead bolts
- Sliding- and swinging-door locks
- Window-sash stops
- Window grates

Tips

Basement and back doors, as well as the interior door to an attached garage, should have the same level of security as entry doors.

Give only car keys—no house keys—to mechanics and parking valets. Most high-security lock keys can only be copied with your permission at dealers and locksmiths.

When you move to a new home, change its locks—or at least the cylinders. You never know who has keys to the old hardware.

Warning

Some building codes prohibit locks that are key-operated on both sides because someone could get trapped inside without the key during an emergency.

204 Choose an Oriental Carpet

Oriental rugs bring a richness to a room not easily matched by any other floor covering. For thousands of years, Asian artisans have woven rugs in distinctive patterns from individually knotted strands. Careful shopping involves knowledge and scrutiny of pattern, material and craftsmanship.

Steps

1 Measure your space carefully so you know what size rug will fit. For stair runners, measure and count the number of risers.

2 Bring a photograph of the room where the rug will go so you can choose the colors and pattern. Patterns include geometric, floral, pictorial and decorative.

3 Opt for wool for warmth, softness and resilience. Consider less-rugged but sensuous silk for luxury, low-traffic areas and warm climates. If a rug is labeled as *art silk,* it's actually rayon.

4 Ask what the country of origin is. Traditionally, Persia (now Iran) produced the finest rugs. Genuine Oriental rugs come from Afghanistan, China, India, Iran, Nepal, Pakistan, Tibet, Turkey, Azerbaijan, Armenia, Romania, Albania, Morocco and Egypt. True Oriental carpets are not made in Western countries. Also find out in what area of the country the rugs were woven or by what people. For example, while Turkish rugs run the gamut in quality, the city of Hereke is known for its exceptional silk carpets.

5 Inspect the rug carefully. Turn it over to examine its color and weave. Artificially aged (called washed and painted) rugs are usually lighter on the back than on the front. This contradicts normal fading, in which the back would never be exposed to daylight, and the face of the rug might fade. Washed and painted isn't necessarily a bad thing; just know that you are not getting a naturally aged rug.

6 Check knot count. A higher count creates more detail and usually adds durability, but the count can vary by design and country of origin. A higher knot count usually equals a higher price per square foot.

7 Test for colorfastness by rubbing a damp cloth over a dark area of the rug. If the color comes off, keep shopping.

8 Ask the salesperson to "do a little better." Bargaining is expected. Depending on their country of origin, quality, age and condition, contemporary rugs sell for $20 to $75 per square foot.

9 Arrange to take the rug home as a trial run on approval. Get a due-back date in writing.

10 Insist on a receipt with a detailed description, including age, country of origin, and materials, such as silk or wool. Based on this, many stores will accept the rug as a trade-in later.

What to Look For

- Suitable color and pattern
- Wool or silk
- Country of origin
- Naturally or artificially aged
- High knot count
- Price based on quality, origin, age and condition
- In-home trial
- Trade-in and trade-up policies

Tips

Find a reputable store with knowledgeable salespeople. Beware of perpetual going-out-of-business sales and traveling hotel-room sales.

Avoid stores with no price tags on rugs and buy only from reputable auction houses.

Wilton, Karistan and Couristan brand rugs are made by machine in Oriental rug designs, but they are not considered Oriental rugs. No genuine Oriental rugs are made of nylon or polypropylene.

Buy abroad to get extraordinary deals. Be prepared to bargain. See 439 Ship Foreign Purchases to the United States.

Warning

Discounts exceeding 20 percent usually indicate the original price has been inflated.

205 Buy Lamps and Light Fixtures

Just as jewelry accessorizes a dress, decorative light fixtures accessorize a room and create a mood. More than beauty, however, effective lighting adds safety, comfort and drama. Use illumination from three sources of light: general (or ambient), task and accent.

Steps

1 Choose lighting according to its application. General, or ambient, lighting brightens an entire room indirectly; task lighting helps you read, sew, cook or do paperwork under focused illumination; accent lighting spotlights decorative objects.

2 Experiment with different bulbs to achieve the brightness, warmth of tone or clarity of light you're looking for. Warm incandescent, color-true halogen or super-efficient compact fluorescent bulbs are new on the market. The final type lasts up to 10 times longer but uses only one-third of the energy—for example, a 25-watt compact fluorescent is as bright as a 75-watt incandescent bulb.

3 Use recessed lights, floor lamps and soffit uplights for entertaining and watching television instead of a harsh, single ceiling light. Add table lamps for reading or sewing, and track lights to accent art and architectural features.

4 Create dining-room intimacy with a low pendant or a candle-style chandelier (both on dimmer switches). Use twin lamps on a sideboard for soft background light.

5 Cook up an efficiently lit kitchen. Under-cabinet lights brighten countertops so you don't work in your own shadow. Halogen bulbs render food colors accurately. Position recessed, track and pendant lights to illuminate work centers. Install low-voltage strip lights inside cabinets with glass doors.

6 Furnish the bedroom with general and task lighting for a relaxing atmosphere. Flank the bed with mounted sconces or swing-arm lamps to free up nightstand surfaces. Recessed can lights are inconspicuous and ideal for low-ceiling rooms.

7 Focus on function in the home office. To avoid eyestrain, use at least 100 watts of incandescent or 40 watts of fluorescent task lighting for reading, writing and computer work. Supplement table and floor lamps with uplights and wall washers that spotlight plants or bookshelves.

8 Shop for style and construction as well as price. Fixtures sold at lighting showrooms may cost more, but usually are higher quality, and lighting consultants can offer design advice. Custom finishes, blown-glass shades and halogen bulbs also add to the cost of fixtures.

What to Look For

- General, task and accent lighting
- Several light sources
- Focus on room function
- Suitable bulbs

Tips

Use dimmers to adjust the brightness of almost any fixture to suit different moods.

Check that lights are safety-approved by Underwriters Laboratories (UL.com).

Contact the American Lighting Association (americanlightingassoc.com) to locate member showrooms that offer a broad selection of fixtures, as well as design assistance from certified lighting consultants.

Arrange lamps at the correct height. When you're sitting, the bottom of a table lamp's shade should be at eye level, 38 to 42 inches (97 to 107 cm) above the floor.

The height of standing lamps is flexible—they can beam light up to add a soft glow to a dim corner or focus down with a shade for reading.

Lamps can be customized with new shades. You can also change the adapters on track lighting to accommodate many types of hanging fixtures.

206 Buy a Programmable Lighting System

Imagine being able to call out "Let there be light!" and have all the lamps in your house respond immediately. Sophisticated whole-house lighting systems are now available to both create moods and offer increased convenience and security. Costs range from $200 for simple functions to several thousand dollars for full-house systems.

Steps

1 Focus on wireless systems if you're retrofitting this technology to an existing home. Wireless systems use infrared or radio frequency (RF) signals instead of behind-the-walls wiring. For new construction, install wireless or hardwired systems.

2 Decide what to connect. Integrate lighting devices with entertainment—lights dim and shades lower automatically when you start a movie. Or link safety and security devices: As alarm sensors are tripped, they activate flashing lights; if fire alarms sound, the whole house lights up.

3 Place control pads in convenient locations. With some hardware variations, each system's central control unit connects to wall-mounted keypads, from which you command lights and devices. Install keypads at entry doors, bedsides or wherever they're desired. Keypads hold up to nine buttons, linked to receivers in outlets, sockets and wall switches.

4 Program lighting scenes: custom, dimmable lighting combinations designed for the moods or activities you enjoy in each room. Different light levels work better for entertaining, reading, dining and home theaters. In addition, there are sleep, vacation and emergency modes. Once you've programmed key settings, they can be stored for easy access.

5 Control your environment. Timers and remote controls are favorites to access your system. Some feature an in-car option. As you reach your driveway, you can turn on interior and exterior lights. Others allow you to connect to the central control—and the home itself—through a computer or Web-enabled personal digital assistant to access your system from almost anywhere.

6 Find dealers and installers through manufacturer Web sites. Look for manufacturer-trained personnel especially for hardwired systems. Programmable lighting sources include GE Lighting (gelighting.com), Lightolier Controls (lolcontrols.com), LiteTouch (litetouch.com), Lutron (lutron.com) and Vantage Controls (vantagecontrols.com) and others. These firms also offer design and programming, integration with other electrical systems, and user training. Whole-house systems start at about $1,600 plus installation.

What to Look For

- Wireless or hardwired systems
- Functions beyond lighting
- Lighting scenes
- Helpful extensions
- Trained dealers and installers

Tip

Before buying, check the method of programming. Some systems must be programmed by professional installers, some you set up with a personal computer, and others you program from the keypads themselves.

207 Buy Household Appliances

The best appliances are the ones that do the job well and also save time and energy. Would a jumbo oven (or two) or a fridge-door ice dispenser make your life easier? Prioritize your architectural and space needs, budget and then consider style.

APPLIANCE	PRICE RANGE	DESIGN OPTIONS AND FEATURES
Refrigerator and Freezer	$500 to $7,000	Built-in models fit flush with cabinets. Ice and water dispenser; water filter. Trim-kit option disguises front panel as cabinet. Spillproof shelves. Separate temperature and humidity controls. Energy Star label. Color, stainless-steel or glass doors.
Range	$350 to $9,000	Built-in or freestanding. Spillproof elements or glass cooktop. Warming drawer. Gas burners with electric oven. Infinite heat source (provides continuous heat front-to-rear, left-to-right for easy movement of large cookware). Infinitely adjustable heat electronic controls. Built-in grill or griddle. Large oven window. Simmer and high-Btu burners on commercial-grade models.
Cooktop	$250 to $4,500	Glass or electric (coil, radiant, halogen or induction). Various widths. Glass smooth-top surface. Built-in ventilator. Flexible element configuration. Built-in grill or griddle. Digital displays. Hot-burner indicator. Sealed gas burners. Electric bridge to small burners for larger cooking area and keep-warm elements. Very low- and very high-commercial-grade models.
Wall Oven	$500 to $5,000	Single or double oven. Thermal, convection or speed-cook system. Enamel or stainless-steel finish. Delay start. Larger interior. Glass door; side-opening door. Steam option (for baking). Temperature probe.
Microwave	$80 to $1,500	Countertop, built-in or mounted under the counter models. Dial or electronic controls. Programmable settings. Microwave-convection combo. Built-in exhaust fan for over-the-range models.
Dishwasher	$350 to $2,000	Smart loading pattern to fit maximum number of dishes safely. Front or top controls. Dish drawers available for small loads. Extra sound insulation. Soil sensor. Dual spray heads. Delay start. Trim option to disguise front. Stainless-steel interior. Energy Star label.
Clothes Washer	$300 to $2,000	Top or front loader; freestanding, stacking or combination. Dial or electronic controls. Load sensors. Favorite cycle settings. Built-in water heater. High-efficiency (Energy Star–rated) models. Quiet operation. Stainless-steel interior. Extra-large capacity.
Clothes Dryer	$300 to $900	Top or front loader; freestanding, stacking or combination. Hamper-style door. Extra-large capacity. Variety of cycles. Moisture sensor. Extended tumbling. Quiet operation. Adjustable end-of-cycle alert sound. Electronic controls. Removable drying racks. Stainless-steel interior.

208 Buy Floor-Care Appliances

Could you eat off of your floor? Although you probably wouldn't want to even if they were squeaky-clean, regular cleaning will increase the life of your floors and help you breathe easier by removing allergens. Because no single appliance cleans all floors—carpet, wood, tile, linoleum or vinyl—look for one that fits your particular needs with features that make the job easier.

Steps

1 Know what kind of vacuum power to look for. Cleaning effectiveness is determined by suction, not horsepower. Instead of motor sizes, compare the cubic feet per minute of the airflow.

2 Buy a full-size vacuum for overall performance. Uprights ($95 to $1,300) require less bending, but they're heavy to hoist up stairs. Look at light and self-propelled models. Features like carpet-pile selectors, bag-change signals, attachments, and retractable or extra-long cords add convenience.

3 Choose a canister vacuum ($180 to $1,200) if most of your cleaning is on bare floors, on stairs and in furniture-crowded rooms. Canisters with a powered head have a separate motor that turns a brush to deep-clean carpet. Look for different cleaning attachments and an easy-to-empty dirt container.

4 Clean floors quickly with a stick vacuum or electric broom ($40 to $90). Some use suction only; others add a brush to loosen dirt. Convertible stick vacuums convert to handheld units for stairs. You can also tackle stairs and small messes with a handheld-only vacuum ($20 to $100).

5 Install a central vacuum during new construction or remodeling. This built-in system is clean and quiet with the motor installed in the garage or basement, and only has one cleaning hose to lug around and plug into outlets in each room. It's also a better choice if you're allergy-prone.

6 Banish allergens with a high-efficiency particulate air (HEPA) vacuum filter system. These workhorses remove 99 percent of the dust, pollen and mites captured with a specially sealed bag or filter. (Bagless vacuums also can be HEPA models.)

7 Sanitize hard-surface floors and relieve allergies with steam mops ($90 to $180), which turn tap water into 240-degree steam that loosens dirt and grease from tile, hardwood, laminate and vinyl. A cleaning cloth traps dirt and protects surfaces.

8 Deep-clean carpets when needed with a do-it-yourself hot-water extractor ($300 to $400). Note: For Oriental rugs and noncolorfast fabrics, dry shampooers are safer.

What to Look For

- Maneuverable uprights
- Powerful canister vacuums
- Handy stick vacuums
- Handheld vacuums or manual carpet sweepers
- Central vacuum system
- Safe deep-cleaners
- Sanitizing steam mops

Tips

Make sure that any attachments are easy to use, the dirt container is easy to empty and the unit is easy to maneuver.

A green CRI label indicates that a vacuum has undergone voluntary testing by the Carpet and Rug Institute and meets performance and air-quality standards.

Bag or bagless? Bagless vacuums confine allergens, but emptying the dust cup puts some of it back in the environment. They do save you the job of buying and changing bags.

Occasionally turn area rugs over and vacuum the back side to remove gritty dirt.

Warning

If you have pets, seal and discard vacuum cleaner bags at least once a week. Be aware that fleas can continue to develop inside vacuum cleaner bags and re-infest the house.

209 Buy Extended Warranties on Appliances

An extended warranty or service contract is like an insurance policy —your investment pays off only when the worst happens. But do you really need one? These days, the majority of brand-name appliances are well-built and will last their normal life span with few or no repairs, rendering extended warranties unnecessary. If you do choose to get one, make sure you do your homework.

Steps

1 Research the brand's repair history via independent consumer agencies, such as ConsumerReports.org. Most appliances include a one-year warranty—five years for major parts—and you should have few problems during that time.

2 Consider who is offering the warranty. You'll get the best service from the manufacturer, which is most concerned with your satisfaction. Second choice is a dealer's warranty. Be cautious about third-party warranties sold by the dealer but independently serviced. Should that company disappear, you might be out of luck. Extended Warranty Buyer's Guide (extendedwarranty.info) offers links to independent companies.

3 Read the actual contract, not just the brochure that markets it. Understand what is covered and excluded. Compare the extend-ed warranty to the original equipment warranty to make sure the extended one isn't just repeating coverage offered in the original warranty. Find out what the deductibles are and if you must get estimates or second opinions before repair. Ask what the standard minimum repair charge is.

4 Ask questions. What maintenance must you perform to validate the contract? Can you renew it annually? Do you get reimbursed for expenses such as for clothes ruined by a faulty washer or dryer, or food lost if the freezer fails?

What to Look For

- Brand and model repair history
- Preferred manufacturer coverage
- Thorough contract
- Terms that fit your needs

Tips

Can't decide at purchase time? Return the registration card; many manufacturers will contact you with an extended-warranty offer when the original warranty nears expiration.

Many credit-card companies automatically extend a man-ufacturer's warranty by one year when you use their card.

Warning

Warranties can often set you back more than half the cost of replacing the insured item.

210 Find Period Fixtures

From doorknob to dado, finding appropriate fixtures is key to the restoration of a period home. Booming interest in vintage decor has spread from purists to home owners who wish to retain the original spirit of their home. Do your research and pay attention to the details.

Steps

1 Contact your local library, historical society and similar organizations for photographs, artifacts and other research materials from nearby houses of the same period as yours. Those buildings probably share similar features that may remain even if your house's are gone.

2 Visit museums and tour historic sites until you learn to recognize the proportions and details of pieces appropriate to your house's period. Browse vintage books and magazines.

3 Subscribe to magazines that focus on restoring and decorating older homes. Their advertising is your direct route to period-sensitive new products, such as cabinets inspired by the Colonial, Victorian or Arts and Crafts eras.

4 Look for catalogs and Web sites related to settlements such as colonial Williamsburg and groups such as the Frank Lloyd Wright Foundation. Products licensed by such sources must meet strict standards of authenticity.

5 Join historic preservation organizations to meet like-minded home owners who have faced similar shopping challenges.

6 Attend home shows to identify craftspeople and repair shops you can hire to duplicate or re-create custom items.

7 Shop at estate auctions and antique shops for early chandeliers, sconces and ceiling-light fixtures. Take a magnet with you to determine the metal finishes. It will stick to steel or iron but not bronze or copper.

8 Find period-looking knobs, pulls, latches, hinges, house numbers and other hardware from many catalog sources and at boutique shops.

9 Play detective in your own home to find traces of old paint and wallpaper, covered-up flooring and structural clues partially hidden by previous remodeling work. Explore your attic and basement for dismantled house parts. Be careful when dealing with lead-based paint and avoid contact with asbestos insulation.

10 Explore salvage yards for vintage plumbing fixtures. Sinks and tubs are easy to find, and most are in remarkably good shape. If they're not, porcelain reglazing services can repair dings and scratches to make surfaces look good as new.

11 Work with a lumberyard or woodworking shop to locate period-style millwork, wainscoting, doors, windows and mantels.

What to Look For

* Historical accuracy
* Period-inspired design
* Licensed reproductions
* Usable antiques

Tips

Need a fresh background for your period finds? Several paint companies have created well-researched historic palettes of appropriate hues.

To replace or supplement damaged tile or wallpaper, contact firms that specialize in matching existing materials. If they can't find more, they may reproduce your originals.

Examine flea-market buys carefully for repairs and signs of wear. Beware of reproductions being advertised as antiques. Get written documentation of an item's age and provenance.

Warning

Update wiring on old lamps and light fixtures for safe operation.

211 Buy a Bed and Mattress

Do you really have a bad back—or just a bad bed? Buying a new mattress set can be confusing and expensive—a queen set can cost $400 or $4,000. Most of us spend one-third of our lives in bed, though, so it's worth it to find one that's just right for your body.

Steps

1 Look at construction, not price. A $400 mattress and box spring may be as good as a $700 set. In more-expensive pocket-spring mattresses, each spring rests in its own fabric pocket and responds independently to the weight above. In less-expensive continuous-spring mattresses, a single length of wire forms the springs.

2 Test mattress support by lying beside your sleeping partner; you shouldn't roll toward each other and one person shouldn't feel motion as the other leaves the bed.

3 Consider coil count and the gauge of the wire in the coils as indicators of firmness (and often quality). Generally, the more coils, the firmer the mattress, although thicker wires can compensate for fewer coils. Lower gauge means the wire is thicker.

4 Consider a waterbed—helpful for some back problems—or an airbed, where electronically controlled air pockets adjust firmness for each person. Make sure your floor can accommodate a waterbed's weight.

5 Check out latex rubber and viscoelastic mattresses ($900 to $3,000) by brands such as TrueSleep and Tempurpedic. The dense foam is energy absorbing, heat sensitive and self-adjusts to body mass and temperature. Allergy and dust-mite resistant, this mattress doesn't need to be turned.

6 Take a test nap on a polyurethane foam mattress ($150 to $400). They also self-adjust and come in various thicknesses and firmnesses. Place on a platform bed or box spring.

MATTRESS	DIMENSIONS
Twin/Single	39 by 75 inches (99 by 190 cm).
Twin Extra-long	39 by 80 inches (99 by 203 cm).
Full/Double	54 by 75 inches (137 by 190 cm).
Queen	60 by 80 inches (152 by 203 cm).
Eastern King	76 by 80 inches (193 by 203 cm).
California King	72 by 84 inches (183 by 213 cm).

What to Look For

- Correct dimensions
- Sleeping support
- Quality and firmness
- Top comfort

Tips

Before investing in a new bed, try it out: Ask to sleep on a friend's bed for a night.

Choose a bed 4 to 6 inches (10 to 15 cm) longer than the tallest person sleeping in it.

Why buy a mattress and box spring set? A new mattress on an old box spring will last only one-third as long as it should.

If a queen or king box spring won't fit up your stairs, ask about a split box spring.

Warnings

When you're in the store for a mattress sale, be on guard for the salesperson's nudge toward fancier models. What's more, you'll find the same mattress labeled differently at different stores. This makes comparison shopping practically impossible.

If you buy a super thick pillow-top mattress, your old sheets may no longer fit.

212 Hire an Interior Designer

You don't have to be rich to hire an interior designer. In fact, professional advice can stretch your budget and help you avoid mistakes, saving money in the long run. Let a designer find just what you need—or didn't know you needed—to bring your dream home to life.

Steps

1 Collect magazine clippings of the style, color, fabrics and furnishings you like and decide which existing furnishings you wish to keep. Sketch a simple floor plan.

2 Visit show houses and model homes or read local publications to find designers whose work you like. The American Society of Interior Designers (interiors.org) has a free referral service to locate members near you.

3 Interview each designer to assess compatibility—you'll need to work well together. Review portfolios and ask for references.

4 Determine each designer's fees. He or she might charge for a consultation, a flat project fee, an hourly fee, a percentage of the project cost, or cost plus (wholesale plus markup). Fees vary widely by location, reputation and experience.

5 Set the project's scope and budget. Ask about ways to save money to cut the overall cost of the job. Maybe you can do some of the painting yourself. Find out if you can spread out a big project and do just one or two rooms at a time.

6 Sign a contract before work begins. Clarify what services the designer will provide, when he or she will be on site, whether the designer or someone else will oversee the work, all budget details, how you will be billed, and the projected time frame. Clarify in your contract how cost overruns will be handled.

What to Look For

- Compatibility
- Relevant experience
- Fees to match your budget
- A clear contract

Tips

If all you need is basic advice on furnishings and color or pattern schemes, try in-house decorators at furniture showrooms and high-end paint or wallpaper stores.

Finding an interior designer is like finding a hairdresser: At first you must show or explain the style you're after, but later he or she will understand what makes you happy.

213 Hire a Feng Shui Consultant

Feng Shui literally means "wind and water" in Chinese. Both an art and a science, this ancient philosophy is based on principles rooted in an extraordinary sensitivity to nature. Feng shui maintains that a balanced environment positively affects the health and success of those who live there. How do you find a good consultant? Read these tips.

Steps

1 Study the principles behind both Eastern and Western feng shui methods to understand the various theories. Delve into books, browse the Internet or take short courses to gain knowledge.

What to Look For

- Classical versus Western approach
- Training and professionalism
- Trustworthy practices
- Acceptable fees and results

2 Focus on classical feng shui for assessments based on ancient disciplines such as yin and yang, Flying Stars, Five Elements and the I Ching, which relies on astronomy, mathematics and Oriental astrology. Consultations require thorough readings of the living environment, people, time and energy.

3 Consider practices such as Black Hat and Eight Life Aspirations. They are complementary mixtures of ancient and modern practice developed over the last 20 years.

4 Ascertain credentials; ask for and call references. When and where was the consultant trained? How many consultations has he or she done? What affiliations does he or she hold? Try to get a sense of how well you would work together.

5 Find out how the consultant works. Ask which feng shui tradition is he or she a practitioner of? How are fees structured? What consultation services are included—for example, is there a report or follow-up? Are repeat visits necessary?

Tip

Some consultants sell cures or other products. Don't feel pressured to purchase these; in fact, hard-sell techniques contradict a professional approach.

Warning

Some consultants may be only slightly better informed than you, having only attended a one-day workshop.

214 Incorporate Fluid Architecture Into Your Home

Most people remodel because their home no longer fits their needs. They like the location but need more—or a different—living space. Fluid architecture hinges (pardon the pun) on walls that rotate, pivot and slide to reshape rooms to your needs with the push of a button.

Steps

1 Analyze whether your home does what you need it to do. What activities does your family enjoy? Which rooms or spaces work for you and which don't?

2 Evaluate your home's natural setting. Do you want better visual access to any landscape features? Do you enjoy great views only at certain times of the day or year? Would you like greater access to the outdoors?

3 Investigate fluid architecture, a system patented by FutureSpace (fs-c.com). Movable walls multiply the function of the same square footage. The same wall can rotate from home theater equipment on one side to a home office on the other.

4 Move a bedroom outdoors on remote-controlled motorized tracks that draw only ⅛ horsepower; if it starts to rain, sensors tell the room to slide back inside. Making a movable 12-by-14-foot (3.6 by 4.3 m) room costs at least $45,000.

5 Remodel your house using fluid architecture concepts in about four months. Depending on its features, a rotating wall designed and installed by professional engineers and architects costs about $11,500.

What to Look For

- Lifestyle needs
- Same-space adaptability
- Indoor-outdoor living

Tip

Alfresco rooms make the most sense in a relatively bug-free Southwestern climate, but translucent screens are available for insect control in other areas.

215 Select Paint, Stain and Varnish

What's the easiest way to update a room? Paint! How do you protect wood against the elements (or your child)? Stain or varnish! If you're drowning in a sea of options at the paint store, your enthusiasm may wane. Relax. Your ideal finish starts here.

Steps

1 Choose acrylic latex formulas for wet conditions or climates. These adhere better and resist peeling and mildew. Latex (water-base) paint ($12 to $30 per gallon) resists cracking and yellowing, emits less odor and dries quickly—and lets you clean up tools with water. Alkyd (oil-base) paints ($20 to $30 per gallon) can cover in one coat and adhere to difficult surfaces. Because alkyd paints dry slowly, brush strokes level out.

2 Decide how much sheen you want. Flat paint minimizes irregularities, but its dull finish can trap dirt. Satin or eggshell finishes resist dirt and stains on high-contact walls. Paint kitchens, bathrooms and trim with semigloss to repel dirt and mildew. Once sold only as alkyd, hard-gloss finishes now also come in latex.

3 Use water- or oil-base enamel to paint and protect wood in one step. Enamel hides blemishes and its durable surface wipes clean, making it a popular choice for bathrooms, kitchens and moldings. Spray enamel is handy for irregular surfaces.

4 Buy exterior paints ($20 to $25 per gallon), which are blended for color retention, mildew resistance and flexibility during temperature changes. It stays glossy and resists chalking, cracking and peeling. Acrylic latex paints absorb less water and minimize mildew growth. Oil-base paints offer one-coat covering and better durability if you're painting in temperatures below 50 degrees F (10 C). Every major manufacturer has several sheens and formulas, and good-better-best lines.

5 Follow sheen guidelines for exterior paints. Flat finishes hide imperfections on older wood siding. Use semigloss paint for trim or for smooth aluminum or vinyl siding. Satin and semigloss boost washability and stain resistance.

6 Highlight wood grain or harmonize different varieties of wood with either stock or custom-mixed stain ($5 to $10 per quart). Penetrating oil stains sink into pores, sealing and slightly darkening wood. Pigmented oil or wiping stains are easier to control. Powder-in-water stains clean up easily but can raise wood grain.

7 Stain wood siding for long-lasting coverage that breathes, which prevents blistering, cracking, or peeling. Solid stains cover like paint but let texture show through. Semitransparent stains impart subtle color without hiding grain. (Both run $8 to $19 per gallon.)

8 Protect high-traffic areas from scratches and spills with polyurethane varnish. Solvent-base varnish ($20-plus per gallon) contains more solids than water-base does, so it requires fewer

What to Look For

- Water- or oil-base paint
- Suitable sheens
- Easy-clean enamel
- Durable exterior formulas
- Even-tone stains
- Protective varnishes
- Appropriate primer

Tips

More expensive paint contains more of the pigments and binders that help the paint flow better, are easier to apply, hide better, and produce uniform color and sheen. Top-quality paint can last twice as long. Because of all this, your overall project cost is less if you buy better quality paint.

Seal wood knots and block stains with a layer of primer so they don't bleed through the finish. Latex primers ($12 to $13 per gallon) dry quickly and clean up with soap and water. Alkyd primers are good on raw wood, but require paint thinner for cleanup and may take overnight to dry.

Tint primer to match finish coat for better coverage.

New for interiors: chalkboard paint, faux-finishing glazes and low-odor paint. New for exteriors: UV-resistant dark colors and formulas that can be applied down to 35 degrees F (2 C).

coats—but as it slowly dries, it generates fumes and traps dust specks. Water-base varnishes ($30-plus per gallon) contain fewer irritating chemicals, are less affected by UV light and dry in under 2 hours—versus 5 hours to overnight.

9 Buy a high-quality paintbrush to make the job go faster and smoother. Premium brushes have hardwood handles and flagged or split-bristle tips that hold more paint. Use natural-bristle brushes with oil-base paints; they absorb the water in latex paints and become limp. Nylon or polyester brushes are better for water-base paints. Buy a 3- to 4-inch-wide (7.5 to 10 cm) wall brush for broad, flat surfaces; a 3-inch (7.5 cm), straight-edge trim brush for doors, wainscoting, and window frames; an angled-bristle sash brush for edging and painting windows. Single-use foam applicators are fine for touch-ups but deteriorate during big jobs.

Buy top-quality paint for smoother flow, better coverage and up to twice the durability. Over time you'll save money and labor.

Warning

Wear a respirator with organic filter cartridges ($20 to $40) while applying varnish.

216 Choose Decorative Tiles

Decorative tiles make any room or small space memorable. These durable, practical works of art add personality and an upscale look for $5 to $50 each. The hard part of choosing accent, border, mural and mosaic tiles is narrowing it down to your favorites.

Steps

1 Imagine what colors or designs will reinforce your room's decorative theme—you'll have thousands of options. Handmade artisan tiles offer rich glazes, strong textures and whimsical pictorial designs, but cost more than mass-produced tiles.

2 Contact kitchen design stores, interior designers and ceramic supply shops to find a tile artist in your area.

3 Mix field tiles and accent tiles for a striking and less-expensive effect. Repeated across a large area, plain or solid-color field tiles are sold by the square foot; accent tiles, which are added to trim or decorate field tiles, are priced per piece based on size, design, glaze and how they're made.

4 Use border tiles to emphasize a horizontal plane, frame a mirror or window, define where different surfaces meet or cap an area of related field tiles.

5 Repeat a wallpaper, china or fabric motif with a tile mural. Mass-produced murals using stock decals cost less.

6 Re-create old-world texture and detail with mosaics, now available preassembled on mesh backings for easy installation. Glass and metal are the hot materials in this category. Their reflective and translucent qualities wake up bland kitchens and bathrooms.

What to Look For

- Color and design
- Artisan or handmade options
- Function plus decoration
- Easy installation

Tips

Install pricey tiles strategically for budget-conscious pizzazz at eye level or in locations where the design attracts notice.

Ask an interior designer for advice if you're unsure about mixing tile shapes and proportions.

217 Choose a Ceiling Fan

Call it good wind chill. Since the breeze a ceiling fan generates makes you feel 2 to 6 degrees cooler, you can raise your thermostat that amount and save 16 to 48 percent on air-conditioning. What makes some fans sell for $50 and others for $500 or more? It's all in the range of styles, features and construction.

Steps

1 Find a fan that fits the room. For up to 100 square feet (9.3 square m), you'll need a blade span of 36 inches (91 cm); spaces up to 150 square feet (13.9 square m) requires 42 inches (107 cm); up to 225 square feet (20.9 square m) requires 48 inches (122 cm); up to 375 square feet (34.8 square m) requires 52 inches (132 cm).

2 Attach flush-mount or hugger fans to low ceilings. On a high ceiling, downrods bring the cooling action into the living space. Sloped ceilings require a special angled mount. For safety, all blades must be at least 7 feet (213 cm) above the floor.

3 Shop for quality components. Die-cast (not stamped) motor housings and blade holders reduce motor noise and add stability. Permanently lubricated bearings and a sealed oil reservoir provide maintenance-free operation.

4 Compare blade performance. Blade pitch (angle) ranges from 8 to 15 degrees; the higher the pitch, the more air the fan moves.

5 Select a finish to match your decor. Motor housings come in brass, steel, nickel, iron, verdigris (greenish-blue), copper, bronze and painted looks. Blades are made from plastic, metal, cloth, palm and bamboo, as well as wood finishes. Reversible blades offer two different looks.

6 Consider how the room's lighting will work with the fan. Ceiling fans generally replace existing light fixtures. Do you want built-in fan lights, or will you customize with a decorative light kit? To ensure the fan and light finishes match, buy both through the same fan company.

7 Boost convenience with a wireless remote or hardwired wall control to adjust fan speed, lights and other features.

8 Shop for options. A dimmer switch adjusts lighting to fit your mood. Programmable controls can automatically adjust fan speed to compensate for cooler night air, or can turn off lights and the fan after a certain number of hours.

What to Look For

- Sufficient blade span
- Appropriate mount style
- Die-cast construction
- Sealed oil reservoir
- Warp-resistant blades
- Finish and light options
- Convenient controls

Tips

Choose fans rated for damp or wet environments if you're buying for a bathroom, kitchen or covered porch.

Look for fans bearing the Energy Star label, which indicates that they move air up to 20 percent more efficiently than typical models.

Unusual blade and housing finishes are striking, but a white fan will nicely blend into your white ceiling.

Warnings

Most ceilings require bracing to support the extra weight of a ceiling fan. Consult with an electrician or a home center.

Solid-wood blades can warp over time.

218 Buy a Whirlpool Tub

Up to your neck in hot water with all this confusion about jets and pumps? Not to worry. Once you choose between an air-jet bathtub and a whirlpool system, your cares will bubble away.

Steps

1 Choose a tub system. In air-jet tubs, air is propelled through dozens of small holes for an all-over bubbling action. In whirlpool tubs, air and water is forced through four to eight large jets for a vigorous massaging action. These powerful jets open, close and swivel to adjust pressure and flow. Smaller jets may cycle along the backrest or target the feet or neck.

2 Figure out where the tub will go. Easiest to install are 5-foot (1.5 m)-long models that slide into your existing tub alcove. Recess-mount tubs fits between walls, which butt against the tub rim. Deck-mount tubs drop into the floor or a platform, requiring a tiled surround. Corner tubs maximize floor space.

3 Make sure your water heater is large enough to fill about two-thirds of your tub with warm water. Whirlpool tubs vary in size, holding 25 to 150 gallons (95 to 560 liters) of water.

4 Test size, back support and comfort in showroom models. To accommodate short and tall people, compromise on a tub about 5½ feet (1.7 m) long by 33 to 42 inches (84 to 107 cm) wide. Before buying a giant tub for two, think how often you'll share it, since you'll be paying to heat a lot of water.

5 Weigh your tub options. Enameled cast iron is durable but heavy— make sure your floor can support it. As for lightweight plastic, molded acrylic resists stains better than sprayed-on gel-coated fiberglass tubs. Easy-care enameled steel tubs come in just a few sizes and shapes.

6 Make sure you have access to the components. All mechanical tubs require maintenance access via an apron or a panel in the tub surround. Whirlpool tubs may require a large opening to reach pipes; air-jet systems need motor access only.

7 Pay attention to the details: Look for protected jets, and sensors that cut the motor if the water is low, so the motor won't burn out. Built-in grab bars and slip-resistant floors add safety. Units with internal water heaters maintain a consistent temperature.

8 Determine if you want a self-cleaning system. Because whirlpool tubs recirculate water, their systems need frequent cleaning. Some air-jet systems automatically purge bacteria-causing residue after each use.

9 Consider your budget. Whirlpool and air-jet tubs sell for anywhere from less than $1,000 to more than $20,000, depending on system, size, materials used and other options.

What to Look For

- Air-jet versus whirlpool
- Number and location of jets
- Size and shape
- Preferred material
- Safe and hygienic system

Tips

Jacuzzi is the best-known whirlpool brand, not a generic term.

Because air-jet baths don't recirculate, users can add aromatherapy salts or oils. In whirlpool tubs, these products can leave residue in the pipes.

Ask if the motor must go next to the tub. Installing the motor up to 15 feet (4.5 m) away will reduce noise and vibration.

Opt for a 2-horsepower variable-flow pump over a 1-horsepower one for more power and less energy consumption.

See 263 Buy a Hot Tub.

Warnings

Keep young children away from tubs unless there is constant adult supervision. The suction action may catch long hair, causing the person's head to be trapped under water.

The tub must be connected to an electrical supply circuit that is protected by a ground fault circuit interrupter (GFCI). The GFCI should be tested periodically to ensure that it is working properly.

219 Buy a Showerhead

Today's showers feature multiple sprays, antiscald valves, and artistic styles and finishes. Height-adjustable models fit any budget, and other options raise the price from $40 to upwards of $3,000.

Steps

1 Choose a handheld nozzle ($50 and up) with a controlled spray to bathe children, wash pets or help those who need to shower sitting down. Some mount on a vertical slide bar for versatility.

2 Pamper yourself with a unit that offers adjustable force and aerated, massaging, and drenching rain-shower spray patterns.

3 Select a finish to match your faucets. Nontarnishing surfaces— also known as PVD (physical vapor deposition) finishes—mean easier upkeep but cost more.

4 Switch to a low-flow model to save up to 17,000 gallons (65,000 liters) of water per year—and $60 to $120 off your annual utility bill.

5 Protect against scalding with pressure-balance and maximum temperature controls. Showerhead water filters (about $25) reduce skin-drying chlorine.

What to Look For

- Spray patterns
- Practical finish
- Water-saving features
- Safety options

Tips

If you have hard water, look for self-cleaning spray holes that shed mineral buildup.

Compensate for low pressure with a model designed to concentrate water flow. Or replace standard ½-inch (1.2 cm) pipes with ¾-inch (2 cm) ones.

220 Buy a Toilet

Although it's one of the most used fixtures in the bathroom, most of us never think about what makes one toilet different from another— until it's time to buy one. Models range from very basic equipment to a truly royal flush.

Steps

1 Choose from traditional two-piece toilets (from $80) that have tank and bowl bolted together, low-profile one-piece toilets (from $200), and easy-to-clean wall-mount tankless ones (from $250).

2 Pick your throne with comfort and space in mind. Narrow spaces favor round bowls, but elongated bowls provide another 2 inches of support. Seat heights range from 10 inches (25 cm) for kids to the standard 14 to 15 inches (35 to 38 cm) for adults and the wheelchair-accessible 17 inches (43 cm).

3 Choose a flush action. All new toilets use 1.6 gallons (6 liters) of water to flush. Affordable gravity-fed toilets run water from the tank into the bowl to create a siphon that drains waste. Pressure-assisted toilets (add $100) use compressed air to propel water and expel waste with noisy turbolike force.

4 Look for extras like a built-in pump to boost water pressure, and a 3-inch (7.5 cm) flush valve and 2-inch (5 cm) trapway to clear the bowl quicker.

What to Look For

- Easy-to-clean design
- Comfortable height
- Efficient flushing action

Tips

Treat yourself to heated seats, deodorizer fans and bidet-style spray-and-dry devices. Self-closing lids reduce noise and arguments.

Most toilets bolt to the floor 12 inches (30 cm) from the wall, but some require 10 or 14 inches (25 or 35 cm).

221 Choose a Faucet

A well-made, well-designed kitchen or bath faucet combines function and style, and makes life easier. Better valve mechanisms and tougher finishes boost durability and looks. See what's on tap these days.

Steps

1 Get a handle—or two—on design. Two-handle models (from as little as $50) let you adjust water temperature more precisely with independent hot and cold controls. Large wing levers and cross-shaped handles are popular styles. Single-handle faucets, also called post-mount or center-set (generally $75 to $200), operate from a top- or side-mount lever or knob. Most models with pull-out spouts are single-handle. One of today's trends is the modular approach: choose from different handles for the same faucet body. Mix and match for a custom look.

2 Start with the finish if style is important. Chrome-finish faucets are the least expensive (from $60) and often carry long warranties against scratches. Colorful enamel or epoxy coatings (add $20 to $200) are vulnerable to chips, scratches and damage from solvents. Stainless steel costs 25 to 40 percent more than coated faucets.

3 Check out physical vapor deposition (PVD) finishes, made by vaporizing pure metals and glazes into a nontarnishing, scratch-resistant film. These outperform conventional plated finishes, but cost $150 to $750 or more. Explore finishes such as brushed chrome, satin nickel and oil-rubbed bronze for vintage appeal. Brushed or satin finishes disguise scratches, too.

4 Choose a spout. Beyond the standard, straight-spout faucets, you'll find high-arching goosenecks, handy for filling tall pots. A splurge-worthy pull-out faucet reaches anywhere in a three-bowl sink, fills pots outside the sink and replaces a separate sprayer. Switch from stream to spray at a fingertip's touch. Restaurant-style models boast the longest hoses.

5 Remember that the simpler the works, the less there is to break or wear out. There are four types of faucets. *Compression valves* using rubber washers may eventually drip, but are easy to fix. *Ball valves*, which regulate flow and temperature via a steel ball, are washerless, require less maintenance and are inexpensive to replace. *Ceramic-disk* and *cartridge faucets* are nearly maintenance free and are generally guaranteed not to wear out, but carry higher price tags. Whichever you choose, look for a lifetime warranty on the valve as well as the finish.

6 Deliver purified water on demand with filtering faucets ($200 and up). Some filters are housed under the sink; others fit inside the spout. Antiscald faucets let you set the maximum water temperature. Electronic faucets use infrared sensors to turn the water off, which results in cleaner faucet handles and less water wasted.

What to Look For

- Practical handles and controls
- Durable, appealing finish
- Lifetime warranty
- Special options and accessories

Tips

You don't have to pay top money for good quality. Many faucets share the same basic parts—and even finishes—across several price lines.

For a streamlined, modern look, choose a wall-mounted faucet, often used with above-counter vanity bowls.

Warning

Make sure your faucet connections match your sink holes; if they don't, you'll have to drill more holes or cover unused holes with an escutcheon plate.

When it comes to do-it-yourself projects or crafts, choosing the appropriate glue or adhesive will provide stability and strength. It gets a little sticky: Glues are based on natural polymers, such as starch and protein from flour, milk and animal parts, while adhesives come from synthesized polymers.

FOR WOOD	DESCRIPTION	USES, PROS AND CONS
Clear Cement	Clear liquid in tubes (1 oz., $2)	Use for lighter wood and porous materials. Somewhat water-resistant.
Contact Cement	Gel in bottles or cans (1 qt., $7.70)	Used for craft projects. Bonds veneers or plastic laminates to wood. Apply with paintbrush or roller. Once tacky, it bonds on contact and permanently. Use in well-ventilated area.
Epoxy	Two-part: catalyst and hardener; often in twin syringes (8 oz., $10)	Very strong and resistant to water and solvents. Setting times vary. Fills gaps.
Hide Glue	One-part liquid (4 oz., $5)	Common glue for assembling and repairing antique furniture. (Not as common for modern furniture.) Not as waterproof as white or yellow glue and takes longer to set up.
Hot-Melt Glue	Sticks (6 for $2.50) used in electric glue gun	Excellent adhesive for crafts and household repairs. Fast-setting; needs little clamping.
Plastic Resin (urea resin or urea-formaldehyde)	Powder; mixes with water (16 oz., $7)	Use on any interior wood. Water-resistant.
Waterproof Adhesive (resorcinol)	Brown powder or liquid mixed with water just before use (1 pt., $21)	For indoor wood; good for bowls and trays. Resists chemicals. Must be used at temperatures over 70 degrees F (21 C). Stains light-color wood.
White Glue (polyvinylacetate or PVA; Elmer's brand)	Creamy white standby we all know and love (8 oz., $2.75)	Used for craft projects. Sets in an hour. Dries clear and won't stain. Not moisture- or heat-resistant. Tends to run.
Woodworker's Glue (yellow glue, carpenter's glue, aliphatic glue)	Yellowish glue in plastic squeeze bottles (8 oz., $3.50)	General indoor woodworking jobs. Relatively thick; easy to use. Medium heat and moisture resistance. Excellent at filling gaps.
Polyurethane Glue (Gorilla Glue brand)	One-part adhesive (8 oz., $7.80)	Used for woodworking. Multipurpose but expensive. Use like epoxy. Needs at least 24 hours to set. Waterproof, stainable, slightly elastic. Foams up and fills gaps. Hard to remove if it dries on your hands.

FOR OTHER MATERIALS	DESCRIPTION	USES, PROS AND CONS
Acrylic Resin	Two-part adhesive	For interior or exterior use. Sets in less than a minute without clamping. Good at filling gaps. Waterproof; cleans up with acetone.
Contact Cement	Gel in bottles or cans (1 qt., $7.80)	Used to bond wood or to bond plastic laminate to counters and tabletops. Apply with paintbrush or roller. Once tacky, bonds on contact and permanently.
Cyanoacrylate (instant glue, Super Glue and Krazy Glue brands)	Single glue tube (.07 oz., $1.50)	Used to repair ceramics, eyeglasses and more. Bonds instantly with drop or two. Use with caution; can seal eyelids, skin together.
Epoxy	Two-part catalyst and hardener; often sold in two-tube syringe set (25 ml, $3.50)	Excellent for china repairs. Bonds dissimilar materials. Strong and waterproof. Cleans up with acetone.
Construction Adhesive (mastic, panel adhesive, Liquid Nails brand)	Thick; asphalt, rubber tubes, or caulking-gun cartridges (10.5-oz. cartridge, $2.70)	Resin based; sold in cans. Bonds paneling, drywall, flooring to wood, metal, masonry. Strong.
Wall-Covering Adhesives	Wheat (8-oz. $4.50), premixed polymer-base ($19 per gallon)	Mix powdered type to make clear adhesive for paper that is not prepasted; use vinyl-over-vinyl adhesive to adhere new over existing wall covering.
Glue Sticks	Chapstick-like tubes in various sizes	Great for paper and light fabrics where see-through isn't an issue. Can be lumpy.
Adhesive Cartridges (Xyron brand)	Available in repositionable, acid-free and permanent adhesive, laminating and magnetic cartridges. Machines and cartridges vary in width from a few inches to 18 inches ($50 to more than $100)	Excellent for crafts, memory books, photo albums, school projects, handmade cards and stickers. Glue is carried on a rolling paper in the cartridge, so never gets on your hands. Low tech, hand crank delivery system offers superb, fume-free performance.
Spray Adhesive (3M Spray Mount, Krylon brands)	Aerosol spray (various sizes under $15)	Permanent or repositionable adhesives good for paper, scrapbooking, photo albums. Messy to use; toxic fumes.
WARNINGS	Glues and adhesives are often toxic. Be sure to use in a well-ventilated area, or wear a respirator. Keep all adhesives and glues away from children.	

Change a room's mood, maximize privacy and accent your view—all with the right window treatments. A wide range of styles, fabrics and materials add functionality and flair to any room.

TREATMENT	MATERIALS	WHERE AND WHY TO USE
Blinds • Horizontal	Aluminum, plastic, wood and faux wood.	Achieve contemporary, linear look where wall space is minimal. Durable and easy to clean; control light and privacy with quick lift or tilt.
• Vertical	Aluminum, vinyl or reinforced fabric.	Practical and minimal treatment diffuses glare through large windows, or sliding or French doors. Overlapping vanes rotate for light control.
Curtains and Drapes	Fabric in many colors, patterns, fibers and textures from lace to velvet; effects from flowing or gauzy to fun, formal and elegant.	Suit many decorating styles; heading treatments (how curtain hangs from rod) direct look. Fabric adds visual warmth; optional foam lining insulates. Couple with gauzy inner curtains for different quality of light, or lightweight liners to protect fabric from fading.
Swags	Soft or sheer fabric.	Simple, no-sew treatment. Drape over another treatment or use alone to soften window frame without reducing light. Portable.
Shades • Cellular	Sheer or opaque paper or fabric.	Can be mounted inside or outside window frame. Variety of opening mechanisms. Cells come in different widths (½ inch, one inch, etc.). For privacy and light, some pull from bottom up. Motorized shades are ideal for skylights. Can be custom fit to unusual window shapes and sizes.
• Roller	Vinyl, canvas or bonded fabric.	Inexpensive, versatile. Create consistent exterior view under varied curtains. Provide moderate to blackout privacy. Variety of fabrics, trims.
• Roman	Choice of fabric determines appearance.	Controlled by cords and pulleys; boast casual, unfussy lines. Panels lift, stack and almost disappear when shade is raised. Add some insulation.
Shutters	Wood or polymer panels or louvers; fabric, glass or metal inserts.	Add traditional or cottage charm to many window styles. Install to play up architectural elements or when there is no room to extend treatment beyond window frame. Shutters adjust easily for light and privacy. Measure precisely to fit frame dimensions.
Cornices and Valances	Anything from wood to silk-flower garland.	Top window with shelf, panel or decorative accent that suits treatment below or stands alone. Can hide drapery hardware or make window and ceiling look taller.

224 Get Self-Cleaning Windows

If you could banish one home maintenance chore, would it be washing windows? Wishes do come true: A new type of glass actually breaks down and loosens dirt, minimizing spots and streaks with very little help from you.

Steps

1 Determine whether self-cleaning windows are right for your climate. They work better in wet regions than dry ones because they require water to wash away dirt and grime.

2 Understand the chemical make-up of the glass:

- The sun's ultraviolet light activates a durable, transparent titanium dioxide coating that is chemically fused to the glass. Even on cloudy days, the resulting *photocatalytic action* oxidizes organic dirt and loosens it from the surface.

- Normal glass panes are *hydrophobic* (water repellent): Raindrops slide down, leaving behind dirt streaks and evaporated spots. Self-cleaning glass is *hydrophilic*: It forces water to spread out evenly in a sheet, washing away dirt loosened by the photocatalytic action. The sheeting action allows the window to dry quickly with minimal spotting and streaking. At night, the glass remains hydrophilic but loses its photocatalytic action.

3 Research self-cleaning glass through glass contractors and home improvement centers. Two manufacturers now offer self-cleaning glass: Pilkington North America (activglass.com) and PPG Industries' SunClean brand (ppg.com).

4 Do a cost-benefit analysis. Windows equipped with self-cleaning glass cost 10 to 20 percent more than windows with ordinary glass. Factor in the elbow grease and Windex, and you may have yourself a deal.

5 Plan when and where to install self-cleaning windows. When you're buying new or replacement windows, upgrade to self-cleaning glass particularly where access is difficult or dangerous: huge plate-glass or second-story windows, skylights, sunrooms and glass roofs.

6 Consider combining self-cleaning glass with low-emissivity (insulating) and solar-control glazing to save energy costs as well as cleaning time.

What to Look For

- Appropriate climate
- Cost-effectiveness for your situation
- Low-emissivity and solar control glazing

Tip

During dry spells, you'll need to give a light spray with the hose to rinse the exterior of self-cleaning windows. Also, the glass won't shed any inorganic matter—paint spatters, for example.

225 Choose Wallpaper

You've decided to be adventurous and wallpaper your walls, but the choices are overwhelming. What look are you after? How do you find the best wallpaper to meet your decorating style, needs and budget?

Steps

1 Chart a decorating course based on your furniture, carpet, curtains, art and collections. Decide which colors, motifs or other elements you want to enhance or unify.

2 Measure your room and sketch a detailed floor plan, including doors, windows and other permanent features. Plot wall height minus baseboards and moldings, then measure the length of each wall segment. Round up measurements to the next foot. To find square footage, multiply room height by circumference, then subtract openings you won't be papering. (It's always better to buy too much than too little and be stuck in the middle of your project.)

3 Take your notes, along with paint, carpet and fabric samples, to wallpaper dealers, home centers or home decor retailers. Sign out sample books to see how the paper looks in your home.

4 Take the stress out of blending paper and border designs with manufacturer's swatch books. Pick bold patterns for large rooms full of activity or for rooms used briefly or only occasionally—a hall, powder room or formal dining room. Select neutral, smaller patterns for a family room, bedroom or home office.

5 Diminish architectural flaws. Stripes accentuate crooked walls. Choose a forgiving floral or intricate pattern to disguise cracked or uneven walls or mask an awkward room shape. Apply liner paper first over bricks, concrete blocks or paneling.

6 Pay attention to the repeat (the vertical match between adjoining sheets of paper). Large repeats require that you cut larger pieces to match patterns when hanging. If walls are fragmented—in a kitchen, say—opt for a smaller repeat.

7 Choose vinyl or vinyl-coated paper for a kitchen, bathroom, child's room or anywhere you need a durable, easy-to-clean surface. Vinyls tend to cost less than papers, generally $9 to $35 per single roll or spool.

8 Choose paper wallpaper for a living room, dining room or other light-use area. More delicate than vinyl, paper adheres well but can tear when wet. Prices vary for machine-printed, decorator hand-blocked and silk-screened types (up to $90 per single roll).

9 Place your order. Paper is priced by the single roll but sold in double rolls (about 56 square feet or 5 square meters); most borders are sold in 5-yard (4.6 m) spools. Using your measurements, a salesperson will calculate how much to order. Buy all the rolls you need at once to assure uniform run or dye-lot numbers.

What to Look For

- Detailed floor plan
- Coordinated patterns
- Pattern repeat
- Durability and cleanability

Tips

Wallpaper displays can be daunting, but you'll often find books sorted by style or room via a colored-dot or other marking system. Some books contain only borders.

Buy an extra roll to repair damaged areas in the future. Use trimmings to line drawers and decorate lamp shades or storage boxes.

Choose foil-faced paper, paintable embossed paper or grass cloth for dramatic effects. Hang wallpaper of *trompe l'oeil* moldings or columns for instant architectural elements.

Warnings

Make sure the adhesion method required is suitable for your skill level. Most papers arrive prepasted—just wetting them makes them stick—but you must paste some papers (often imported or designer brands) before hanging. Some borders and wall decals are self-sticking.

If you do not have solid wallpapering skills, hire a professional to do the work for you. You'll save money (no botched up rooms to redo), frustration and time.

Beyond their romantic glow and homey crackle, modern wood stoves produce low-cost heat, and burn cleanly and efficiently, producing minimal ash and smoke. You pick the technology and choose the ideal-size stove to match your heating needs. Buy the most efficient stove you can afford. It'll pay for itself in the long run.

Steps

1 Evaluate your home's floor plan to determine where you should install a wood stove. Some stoves can heat an entire house; others work best as zone heaters for the most-used areas. A stove placed in one room will heat adjacent rooms if there's good airflow at the ceiling and floor.

2 Show a dealer a sketch of your home, the area that needs heat, and a description of the insulation surrounding that area. The dealer will help you calculate the proper stove size, expressed in British thermal units (Btus). You'll waste money if you buy too big a stove, and it will either create a smoky fire or use more fuel than necessary.

3 Talk to one or more professional chimney sweeps (csia.org) about the brands you're interested in, and get their recommendations.

4 Understand the technology in catalytic stoves ($1,000 to $2,000). A catalytic combustor cuts normal burn temperatures in half for a slow, controlled fire with the fewest emissions. Look for a cast-iron or plate-steel stove body ¼ inch (6 mm) thick and a tight-closing bypass plate ⁵⁄₁₆ inch (8 mm) thick. Also look for a design that protects the combustor from direct flame.

5 Consider noncatalytic (recirculating) stoves ($500 to $2,200) for their two-chamber combustion, which injects jets of preheated air into the fire to boost heat and reduce emissions. Look for a cast-iron or plate-steel body ¼ inch (6 mm) thick. To resist warping, the fire chamber's baffle should be ⁵⁄₁₆-inch (8 mm) plate steel with V-shaped supports. These models have no combustor to maintain, but their smaller fireboxes mean you'll have to use shorter logs and load them more frequently.

6 Buy a super-efficient pellet stoves ($1,700 to $3,000) for the cleanest-burning option. They burn easy-to-handle pellets formed from wood waste. A thermostat-controlled auger delivers fuel from a hopper to the firebox. Fans pull air in and exhaust gases out through a house-warming heat exchanger. Pellet stoves need battery backup during power outages.

7 Get toasty warm beside stylish stoves in steel or soapstone. Design options to consider include legs or a pedestal base, colorful porcelain finishes and tile accents. Check out well-known brands such as Vermont Castings (vermontcastings.com) and Hearthstone (hearthstonestoves.com).

What to Look For

- Best location
- Desired heat output
- Catalytic or non-catalytic stove
- Pellet stove
- Decorator details
- Convenient features

Tips

Look for two labels. One certifies that the stove meets Environmental Protection Agency emissions standards; the other lists efficiency range and heat output in Btus.

Look for standard features including self-cleaning glass, hidden hinges and reversible flues, as well as optional accessories such as fans, gold-plated accents and heat shields for walls.

Warnings

Your home's air will become very dry when heated with a wood stove. Combat this with a humidifier or by placing a kettle of water on the stove.

Ordinances regulating wood stove use vary by city and sometimes within cities. Check the back of the stove for the EPA certification label to see if you comply with local ordinances.

Dirty chimneys can cause catastrophic chimney fires. Hire a chimney sweep for regular cleanings.

Select Flooring

The materials you choose for flooring anchor each room's style and function. All materials aren't suitable for all situations, though; check the chart below to see what fits your budget, lifestyle and expectations. Prices are for materials only; variable installation costs can balance total price.

MATERIAL; PRICE; FORMAT; FEATURES

Solid Wood

$3.50 to $7 per square foot

Strips, planks, parquet; unfinished or prefinished.

Many species, styles; natural character; can be refinished several times (long life). Adds to home's value.

Should be sealed or finished in moist locations; not suitable for installation below grade.

Laminate

$2 to $7 per square foot

Planks and tiles.

Realistic look-alike for wood and stone; durable and stain-resistant; easy to install, even below grade.

Hollow sound; surface cannot be refinished. Makers of some brands discourage bathroom installation.

Cork

$3 to $6 per square foot

Sheets and tiles, unfinished or prefinished.

Natural insulator; environmentally friendly; long-wearing and self-healing; hypoallergenic; comfortable.

Shades vary; professional installation preferred.

Engineered Wood

$4 to $7 per square foot

Strips and planks, usually prefinished.

Looks and feels like solid wood but easier and less expensive to install; laminated construction adds stability below grade.

May be professionally refinished at least once.

Vinyl

$1 to $4 per square foot

Sheets and tiles.

Many colors and patterns; water-resistant in sheet form; resilient. Hard-wearing, warm underfoot, low maintenance, hygienic (pore-free) and fire resistant.

Lower grades can tear, dent and discolor.

Ceramic

$1 to $6 per square foot

Tiles.

Many styles and colors; easy to clean; impervious to moisture and stains (glazed tile).

Cold; noisy; requires perfect subfloor; grout needs periodic sealing.

Bamboo

$5 to $8 per square foot

Strips and planks, finished or unfinished.

Hard, stable, readily renewable resource; wear- and stain-resistant; can be refinished; single texture option.

Darkens in sunlight.

Linoleum

$3 to $4 up per square foot

Sheets and tiles.

Environmentally friendly composition; wide color range goes all the way through; durable; self-healing; antistatic. Requires professional installation.

Stone

$3 to $10 up per square foot

Slabs and tiles.

Natural material; earthy look and texture; durable; adds value to home.

Some stone is brittle, slippery; porous types need sealing against stains.

TIP Wide-plank flooring is available from several sources. Reclaimed lumber from old wine vats or even torn-down stadiums and factories can add character and history. Look at sources such as Terramai.com, which reclaims and mills hardwood railroad ties from Thailand.

Wall-to-wall carpet can make or break the way your living spaces look. Carpeting is warm, quiet and comfortable, and offers more colors and textures than any other flooring. Compare fiber and pile to make sure the look you love is also durable and easy to keep clean.

Steps

1 Pick pile length and type. In cut-pile carpets, the yarn stands up straight from the backing. In loop-pile construction, the yarn loops over and returns to the backing. Level (same-height) and multilevel loops are casual and durable. Cut-and-loop or sculptured carpets combine both types, and both hide footprints and trap soil.

2 Narrow your texture choices. Saxony, plush and velvet styles boast smooth, uniform surfaces suitable for formal rooms, although they show footprints and vacuum marks. Frieze types have an extreme amount of twist (see Step 3), making them durable in high-activity spaces. Berbers weave fat yarns into a nubby, sometimes multicolored texture.

3 Compare the pros and cons of each type of carpet fiber, keeping in mind your preferences for resilience, stain resistance, wear and cleanability. Understand twist's role in quality and performance. During carpet construction, fine strands—filaments—are spun into a tightly twisted yarn and heat-set for shape. Higher (tighter) twist creates stronger yarn and more durable carpet.

4 Consider nylon ($10 to $35 per square yard), the most popular synthetic fiber. Hard-wearing nylon provides brilliant colors and hides soil and traffic well. Thanks to its resilience, wear resistance and cleanability, nylon works almost anywhere.

5 Look to olefin (polypropylene) carpeting ($8 to $25 per square yard) when you need high stain, static and mildew resistance, but resilience isn't a priority.

6 Choose polyester ($8 to $18 per square yard) for its soft feel and color clarity. Less durable than nylon, polyester stands up moderately well to wear and stains, but its cleanability is only fair. Best for use in low-traffic areas.

7 Pay a premium for wool ($24 to $60 or more per square yard), the oldest carpet fiber. Naturally soft and hard-wearing, wool has excellent resilience but low stain resistance (unless it's treated); it wears and cleans well compared with all other fibers.

8 Check density by folding back the carpet and examining its backing. Carpet with more yarn tufts per square inch is more crush resistant. The less backing you see, the denser the carpet.

9 Evaluate the number of ounces of fiber in a square yard of carpet (face weights). Generally, the heavier the carpet, the better it holds up. The same carpet might be sold in 28-, 34- and 40-oz. weights. Choose heavier weights for high-traffic areas.

What to Look For

- Suitable pile and texture
- Fiber pros and cons
- High twist, density and face weight
- Quality carpet pad

Tips

A firm and resilient cushion or pad acts as a shock absorber and extends the life of any carpet, regardless of its quality. Use a minimum 8-lb. pad when installing over concrete.

Remember to budget the cost of installation—typically $3 to $4 per square yard.

If you're sensitive to new-carpet fumes, seek out a green label certifying reduced volatile organic compounds; ask that the carpet be aired before installation.

Have a remnant's cut edges bound to create a room-size area rug you can take with you when you move.

See 204 Choose an Oriental Carpet.

Choose Kitchen Cabinets

Picking out cabinets for your new or remodeled kitchen is not an open and shut matter. The choices for door style, wood, finish and options are endless. Cabinets can add up to 70 percent of a kitchen's cost, so research your options for the best return on your investment.

Steps

1 Analyze your kitchen layout and your family's lifestyle and cooking habits. Plot what you need to store and display, as well as accessories that will simplify and organize your kitchen activities.

2 Get professional guidance—from an architect, a kitchen designer, at a store or on the Internet—to narrow your style and component choices and make the most of your space.

3 Choose stock cabinets when controlling costs is your priority. Mass-produced in standard sizes, stock cabinets leave room in your budget for upgrades elsewhere. You'll find fewer finish options but many popular styles, woods and accessories.

4 Spring for custom units if you need to fit exact dimensions. Top-quality materials and craftsmanship increase both the cost and turnaround. Semicustom cabinets are also made to order, but their set widths may require inserts for a perfect fit.

5 Select the wood you want and desired finish. Maple, oak and cherry are favorite hardwoods. Signs of quality cabinets are grain that matches from piece to piece and furniture-quality finishes.

6 Investigate manufactured finishes such as laminate or thermofoil. Both are easy to clean and less expensive than wood, but also less durable. Ask about typical repairs and what the warranty covers. Examine a showroom sample that has been in use for a while to see how it wears.

7 Insist on construction that can support heavy cookware and withstand countless openings, bumps and spills. Drawers with dovetailed joints are stronger than stapled ones. Doors with fitted mortised corners are sturdier than noninterlocking butt joints. Also look for ¾-inch-thick (2 cm) face frames.

8 Peek inside cabinets. Most stock and semicustom units use solid wood only for the exposed frame, doors and drawers. Even high-end cabinets may contain particleboard or veneer-covered plywood inside. Both are less likely to warp than solid wood, and can be stained or painted.

9 Look for drawers that extend completely and are equipped with self-closing glides rated to hold 75 lb. (35 kg). Well-made drawers boast ½- to ¾-inch (1.2 to 2 cm) sides with dovetailed or doweled joints and a strong bottom that's glued into grooves. The strongest shelves are ¾-inch (2 cm) plywood.

What to Look For

- Stock, semicustom or custom options
- Wood and finish choices
- Sturdy construction
- Furniture-quality details

Tips

Look at other kitchens to fine tune your layout ideas and get a sense of the color and wood you like.

For more information on cabinets, contact the National Kitchen and Bath Association (nkba.org). Also visit manufacturer and home center Web sites such as Lowes.com and HomeDepot.com. Some have interactive showrooms where you can mix and match door styles, woods and finishes.

If your old cabinets are in good shape but dated, refinish them. The next step is refacing, which involves recovering or replacing just the doors and drawers.

If you love the look of an expensive hardwood, keep in mind that less expensive woods can be stained to look like your choice. For example, you can order a cherry finish on pine.

Warning

Although you can save up to 40 percent with ready-to-assemble cabinets, these are not of high enough quality for a kitchen. They are OK for laundry rooms and garage storage, though.

Countertops have an enormous impact on the look and feel of your kitchen. The many choices available offer varying cost, weight, durability, upkeep and aesthetics. Consider customizing each work zone with the most appropriate surface. Install luxury materials only where you need them to save money.

MATERIAL/PRICE	PROS	CONS
Laminate $10 to $40	Easy to install; many colors, patterns and textures; resists stains and impact; inexpensive.	Has visible seams; you can't cut on it; difficult to repair if scratched. Not advised for wet environments.
Ceramic Tile $4 to $80	Easy to install and repair; wide range of design options; glazes fight off moisture, scratches, heat, stains.	Grout between tiles can stain or mildew; sharp impact can crack tiles; can be tough to clean grout.
Rock Maple $16 to $40	Also called butcher block. User-friendly surface; easy on knife edges; takes on character; can be renewed by sanding and oiling.	Vulnerable to water, cuts and burns; requires thorough cleaning when exposed to raw meat or fish; needs regular treatment with mineral oil or beeswax.
Solid Surfacing $40 to $75 and up	Dozens of colors and stonelike patterns; near-invisible seams blend with integral sinks and edge.	Requires professional installation; damaged by hot pans; expensive (solid-surface veneer may be a good alternative).
Engineered Stone $50 and up	Granite look but more uniform; never needs sealing; resists stains, heat, scratches.	Requires professional installation and repair. Stone heavy; poor impact resistance compared with real granite; visible seams.
Granite $50 to $300	Toughest and least porous material; highly scratch- and stain-resistant if sealed. Gorgeous natural colors, patterns.	Requires professional installation and repair, periodic sealing; expensive to buy and install; visible seams; heavy.
Marble $50 to $75	Traditional, old-world look; cool, nonstick surface ideal for baking.	Porous and prone to stains, scratches, discoloration; needs regular sealing and professional installation.
Limestone $50 and up	Heat-, impact- and stain-resistant; limited color palette; requires periodic sealing and polishing.	Softer than granite and marble; soapstone and slate alternatives have rustic character.
Concrete $60 and up	Once sealed resists stains, burns, scratches; pigments add color choices.	Heavy; needs periodic sealing; abrasive (protect knife edges from surface). Requires professional installation.
Stainless Steel $50 to $65	Commercial look; resists heat; sanitary and easy to clean.	Requires professional installation; shows scratches and fingerprints.
TIP	All prices are per installed square foot.	

231 Buy Green Household Cleaners

Synthetic and solvent-laden, today's cleaners, brighteners and bleaches fight dirt with less effort than ever before. But many of these products get their strength from chemicals that pollute your household air and water runoff and threaten your health during normal use. You can be clean and green, though, if you're alert to product contents.

Steps

1 Read labels and packaging to determine each product's ingredients. Environmentally friendly cleaners contain nontoxic, biodegradable ingredients and non-petroleum based surfactants. They don't create fumes or leave residues and are never tested on animals. Don't be fooled by the terms *natural* or *nontoxic*. These are not regulated and can be used as the manufacturer wishes.

2 Keep household products in their original containers so that safety information and directions for use always remain with the product.

3 Choose cleaners that do not contain toxic ingredients. Formaldehyde and ammonia irritate the skin, eyes and lungs. Benzene is classified as a carcinogen. Lye fumes almost instantly corrode respiratory passages. Even minimal exposure to bleach and hydrochloric and sulfuric acids cause coughs or headaches; further contact can easily damage lungs.

4 Reduce allergies and skin or eye irritation by buying products without artificial fragrances and colors. Many of these additives do not degrade in the environment and may have toxic effects on fish and mammals.

5 Shop green at food cooperatives, farmers' markets and natural foods stores. Look for the natural products aisle in your supermarket. Check online at sites such as SeventhGeneration.com and PlanetInc.com.

6 Make your own cleaner recipes from lemon juice, Borax, baking soda and white vinegar. Label these mixtures so they're not mistaken for a beverage.

What to Look For

- Clear labeling
- No toxic ingredients
- No artificial colors and fragrances

Tips

Use any cleaner in a well-ventilated area.

Practice prevention first. Wipe spills quickly to avoid stains. Line the oven bottom to catch spills. Use screens over drains and don't pour grease down them.

See 9 Buy Green.

Warnings

Reject any product that does not list ingredients and anything labeled with Caution, Warning, Danger or Poison.

Some common household cleaners are extremely dangerous when combined: Never mix chlorine bleach and ammonia—the result is toxic chloramine gas.

Install childproof locks on your supplies cabinet.

With a basic set of tools, you can often take care of small jobs around the house yourself. Buy the best quality tools you can afford and gradually add more. Look for brands such as Sears' Craftsman that offer lifetime warranties.

TOOL	WHAT TO LOOK FOR
Claw Hammer	Comfortable but forceful size, 16 oz. ($5 to $13) with curved claw can pry out nails without gouging drywall. Drop-forged, steel head, smooth or textured for framing.
Screwdrivers	Buy a kit with multiples or individually ($2 to $6.50 each). Get both standard (slotted) heads, and Phillips (+-shaped head) for in several different sizes.
Putty Knives	Get stiffer blades for scraping; flexible ones for applying putty, glazing and spackle and for mixing materials ($1 to $6). Different widths available.
Tape Measure	Retractable, spring-loaded metal tape; ¾-inch-wide by 16-foot-long ($7 to $12) or 25- to 35-foot-long ($15).
Levels	Use 9-inch torpedo level ($7 and up) for installing appliances, hanging pictures or doing basic carpentry. Keep a 3-foot level ($15) on hand for larger projects.
Plumb Bob	Pointed weight ($8 to $13) hangs from line and uses gravity to demonstrate plumbness (exactly vertical); useful for hanging wallpaper, building fences.
Locking Pliers (Vice Grips)	8 to 10 inches long ($12) with serrated, straight jaws. Locking pliers can grab with tremendous force. Look for sets with multiple types.
Crescent Wrench	8- to 10-inch size ($13 to $20). Used for turning nuts, bolts and plumbing fittings. Adjustable; useful when you don't know the exact size of the nut.
Socket Wrench Kit	Available in standard and metric sizes. Look for medium to small-size ratchet wrench, plus extension attachments ($20).
Utility Knife	Cuts cardboard, sheetrock, carpets and more. Replaceable, retractable blades.
Handsaw	15- or 20-inch-long handsaw ($9 to $25) is quiet, portable and safe. For fine woodwork, treat yourself to a Japanese back saw ($25 to $300).
Clamps	Pull together pieces of wood and hold them tight until glue sets. C-clamps ($2 to $20) or larger bar clamps ($5 to $25) suit most jobs. Pistol-action quick-grip clamps are easier to use but not as powerful; good for small projects.
Electric Drill	Drills holes and drives screws quickly and easily. Get variable-speed, reversible model with ⅜-inch keyless chuck to hold bits in place (from about $35). Cordless drills cost more but let you work anywhere. Get one with enough power to get the job done.
Circular Saw (Skill Saw)	Cuts boards up to 2 inches thick. 7¼-inch blade and power rating of 12 or 13 amps. Smaller and battery operated versions available. Saws with cord run $50 to $150; cordless, $100 to $300.

233 Buy a Video Security System

Somewhere between a baby monitor and commercial video surveillance, installing a video security system in your home offers peace of mind beyond what mechanical locks and wireless sensors can provide. Answer the front door without opening it, or watch your children play in their rooms or the backyard—all from the TV screen or anywhere in the world via the Internet.

Steps

1 Plan which areas you want to have monitored. Exterior doors are a logical spot, as well as landscaped areas where intruders can lurk. Inside the house, consider monitors for rooms occupied by children or elderly residents.

2 Monitor entries with a video door phone system. Most include a weatherproof camera with an infrared lens for night vision. Look for cameras that tilt or pan to show a broader area than a door peephole can. Many systems have two-way microphones.

3 Consider extra features such as motion sensors, dome (overhead) cameras and a device that automatically takes time- and date-stamped snapshots when a visitor presses the doorbell— creating a record of who comes while you're not home.

4 Decide how you'll view images. Basic systems (from about $230) include a 4-inch (10 cm) black-and-white monitor and two cameras; upgrade ($350 and up, depending on extensions) to get larger and/or color monitors and more cameras.

5 Link the system to one or more televisions so you can see who's at the door without leaving your couch. Connect a VCR to record what the camera sees; network with a personal computer to view images from one or more cameras at the same time. An Internet connection lets you view the images from any Web-enabled device. Password systems let you open your front door remotely to let in guests or repairmen.

6 Create an intercom system with closed-circuit TV access by adding Web cams and monitors. Each system—wired or wireless—has a few transmission limitations. Some only receive signals within a limited distance. Signals generally travel farther when they're in the line of sight instead of traveling through walls.

7 Choose auxiliary indoor cameras according to their purpose. In a baby's room, for example, look for an infrared lens and a directional microphone that activates the camera only when the baby coos or cries. Web cams start as low as $20; basic indoor systems range from $70 to $100.

What to Look For

- Video door phone with adjustable lens
- Optional security features
- Connection to TV, VCR or Internet
- Auxiliary indoor cameras

Tips

View monitor reception in person to make sure the image is acceptable. If you buy online, check the return policy first.

Make sure outdoor cameras have weatherproof housings and will operate in very cold temperatures.

You can conceal miniature wireless cameras as small as 2 inches (5 cm) tall almost anywhere. Distance and barriers, however, will restrict their ability to transmit.

See 419 Buy a Home Automation System.

234 Buy a Home Alarm System

Each year more than 2 million American homes are burglarized, according to the National Burglar and Fire Alarm Association (alarm.org). Most of them have no alarm system. Electronic security devices provide affordable peace of mind, and recognizes and reacts instantly to unauthorized entry.

Steps

1 Survey your home and determine how many windows and doors you want integrated into the system.

2 Contact your insurance agent, a security system adviser, the NBFAA or your police department's crime prevention department for names of security system companies. Ask each company for an inspection, a recommendation and a quote in writing.

3 Decide whether you want to contract with a 24-hour central monitoring station for a monthly fee. If your system detects a break-in, it alerts security professionals to dispatch local police. Less expensive dialer accessories can link sensors to your phone lines and call preselected numbers if security is breached.

4 Consider your family's lifestyle. Do people or pets sometimes roam the house at night? Select appropriate sensors and locations.

5 Choose a system with a control panel that can monitor all the zones in your home. Each window or door integrated into the system is considered a zone. A basic system (about $400 without monitoring) can control eight zones, but many can be expanded to watch up to 32.

6 Determine locations for the control panel and keypads. The control panel commands the system and the keypads allow you to program the system and turn it or its components on and off. A typical setup puts one keypad near the front door and another keypad—and perhaps a panic button—close to the bedrooms.

7 Look for systems that connect to lighting controls, smoke and carbon monoxide sensors, and flood detectors. Also make sure system switches won't freeze in cold climates. (See 419 Buy a Home Automation System.)

8 Choose a user-friendly code that everyone in the family can remember in an emergency. Try the keypad to assure that it's easy to use.

9 Realize that it's difficult to retrofit a hardwired security system. With a wired system, you'll have to drill holes in walls so wires can be routed. If you want to avoid this expense and inconvenience, choose a wireless system.

What to Look For

- Sensor, control panel and keypad locations
- Some form of system monitoring
- Reputable security firm
- Hardwired or wireless system
- Add-on alarm options
- User-friendly system

Tips

The monitoring service you choose may be limited based on what system you buy. Choose the service before the system.

With a key-chain remote, you can disarm the security system, turn on lights and unlock the door—all from your car in the driveway.

Check that your system has a battery for backup power.

Ask how often you have to perform maintenance tests.

Warnings

More and more false alarms are forcing police to change their priorities on answering alarm calls. Contact your police department to find out what their policy is.

If any alarm or security system representatives come to your home, ask to see company identification to make sure they are legitimate.

235 Buy Smoke Alarms

Your home most likely has at least one smoke alarm, but is it enough? Smoke alarms provide an early warning that can save lives, but different fires call for different alarm types.

Steps

1 Protect your home right now with easy-to-install battery-powered alarms. Some use lithium batteries which last 10 years.

2 Hardwire new homes with alarms powered by alternating current (AC). AC models built into bedroom and other ceilings are linked; if one senses a fire, it triggers all others through the wiring. Retrofitting older homes can cost $1,000. AC alarms in new homes must include a battery backup in case of power outages.

3 Detect fires fed by paper, electricity and flammable fluids with ionization alarms ($10 to $50), which use a harmless amount of radioactive material. Two-battery ionization models also detect carbon monoxide gas.

4 Get photoelectric alarms ($20 to $100), which have sensors and light beams that react quickly to smoldering fires such as bedding and upholstery fires, which often kill from smoke inhalation.

5 Play it safe. For full protection, buy dual-detection alarms (about $30), which combine both fire-sensing technologies. Because these run on batteries, hybrid units work independently and are not wired to other alarms.

6 Buy alarms with a hush button that silences the horn while you clear away smoke. Buttons big enough to push with a broom handle are easiest to activate.

What to Look For

- Battery or AC power
- Ionization, photoelectric or hybrid type
- Large hush button

Tips

All alarms must meet the test standards established by Underwriters Laboratories (UL.com). Check the date stamp on the back to make sure it's a fresh unit.

Some fire departments offer smoke alarms for little or no cost, and may even install them for you.

Warning

Many fires occur in homes with smoke alarms that have been disconnected because cooking fumes set them off. Don't play Russian roulette: Get a kitchen alarm with a "hush" button.

236 Buy Carbon Monoxide Detectors

Called "the silent killer," odorless, tasteless carbon monoxide (CO) gas results from faulty combustion in a furnace, fireplace or gas range, or a car (in an garage). A CO detector is your only means of protection.

Steps

1 Shop for a CO detector. There are only three types; they're all affordable ($30 to $50) and easy to install:

  • A biometric CO detector has a gel cell of synthetic hemoglobin that absorbs CO. The combination battery and sensor module must be replaced every two to three years, but the detector should last about 10 years. After an alarm, the sensor should clear itself within 2 to 48 hours when left in fresh air. If it is not cleared, it will sound again when put back in the detector. Sensors that don't clear must be replaced.

What to Look For

- Electric or battery power
- Digital display
- Indicator light

Tips

Whichever type of alarm you choose, buy the freshest one available. Open the package to find the date of manufacture stamped on the back.

- A semiconductor detector is a plug-in device with an electronic sensor, and lasts from 5 to 10 years.

- An electrochemical detector responds differently to different levels of CO exposure. Its self-powered battery doesn't need to be replaced, and the detector will last for at least five years.

2 Look for the Peak CO Memory feature on higher-end models. These displays remember the highest level of CO registered over a given time, which helps emergency personnel determine the severity of the problem, and can tell you if the detector sensed high CO levels while you were away.

3 Buy a detector with special light features if someone in your family is hard of hearing. During an alarm, an indicator light flashes as the horn sounds. Although many alarms have a liquid crystal display (LCD), it's easier to read a light-emitting diode (LED) display in dim light.

4 Listen for a continuous siren that indicates a full alarm. A repetition of loud pulsating beeps means there is some CO buildup; a chirp every minute alerts you to an alarm or battery problem.

Look for Underwriters Laboratories (UL.com) certification.

Many building codes now require CO detectors if a house is heated by gas or oil or has a fireplace.

237 Buy Fire Extinguishers

You never want to have to use them, but it's wise to own several fire extinguishers. Used correctly, they'll reduce flame and smoke damage and may save your home—or your life. But not all fires are alike and using the wrong type of extinguisher will actually make things worse.

Steps

1 Look for symbols or the letters A, B and C to determine which fire class(es) the extinguisher will put out. Class A extinguishers put out fires fueled by wood, paper, cloth, rubber and most plastics. Class B extinguishes flammable liquids, such as gasoline, oil and grease. Class C is for wiring, appliance and electrical fires.

2 Buy the most suitable extinguisher for each room. Keep one in the garage, and another near the furnace. In the kitchen, get a combination B-C extinguisher for grease and gas fires.

3 Check each extinguisher's number rating. The higher the number, the larger a fire the extinguisher can put out. (A 4-A unit will put out twice as much Class A fire as a 2-A one.) A high number usually means a big, heavy unit.

4 Select disposable or rechargeable models. Disposable units ($10 to $20) are typically made of plastic and lose pressure after about 12 years. Rechargeable extinguishers (up to $50) can be refilled after use and if they lose pressure. They should be serviced annually by the manufacturer.

What to Look For

- Relevant fire-class rating
- High number rating
- Manageable size and weight
- Disposable or rechargeable

Tips

Whatever class or size you choose, the extinguisher must be approved by Underwriters Laboratories (UL.com) or Factory Mutual (FMglobal.com).

Make sure you and other family members understand how to operate your home's fire extinguishers.

238 Choose an Entry Door

In homes as in personal relationships, nothing beats a great first impression. A high-quality door sets a welcoming tone and raises the perceived value of your entire home as well as provides added security.

Steps

1 Complement your home's architecture with an appropriate door style—moldings and raised panels for a traditional house, sleek lines for contemporary style, ornate carving for a Victorian.

2 Simplify installation with a prehung door, already framed and weather-stripped. Door-replacement kits include steel frame inserts, but are available in fewer sizes than prehung doors.

3 Get out your measurement tape and choose between a standard single door, 32 to 36 inches (81 to 91 cm) wide; an extra-wide door, typically 42 inches (107 cm) wide; or double doors. New homes with higher ceilings look better with 8-foot (2.4 m)-tall entry doors. Keep in mind that changing your existing door size will require costly structural work.

4 Choose a wood door for natural warmth and beauty, but expect it to require maintenance. Wood doors used to warp and crack over time, but today's engineered-wood cores, laminated construction and vapor barriers help keep doors weathertight.

5 Buy a steel door for strength and security. Most new models feature heavy galvanized steel around a wood or steel frame, with a dense polyurethane foam core that insulates almost five times better than wood. Choose standard steel, steel embossed with wood grain or vinyl-clad steel.

6 Select fiberglass composite for the look of wood without its upkeep. These models wrap tough, compression-molded fiberglass around an energy-efficient polyurethane foam core. Paintable and stainable, fiberglass won't rust and resists shrinking and swelling.

7 Brighten your foyer with a glass door panel, transom or sidelights. Frosted, beveled and leaded patterns range from simple to ornate, private to unobstructed. For security and noise reduction, order laminated glass.

8 Complement your door's style and scale with solid brass or bronze handle sets and locks. Pick tarnish-free metal finishes with lifetime guarantees if the door is exposed to weather.

9 Invest in quality materials that will last for decades. Prices vary between manufacturers and according to style, size, material and options. Insulated fiberglass costs more than steel but carries a longer warranty. A 36-by-80-inch (.9 by 2 m) wood door can cost $275 to $3,500, depending on the type of wood, construction, finish and glazing. Paneled single fiberglass doors start at about $600, steel at about $200.

What to Look For

- Appropriate style
- Easy installation
- Suitable size and scale
- Durable materials
- Decorative glass inserts
- High-quality hardware
- Energy saving features

Tips

Save energy with features such as compression weather-stripping, a thermal-break threshold, an extended sill plate, a triple bottom sweep and a moisture-resistant bottom rail.

To decide what color, take a picture of your home from across the street. Print several black-and-white copies and use colored pencils to plan different door styles. Or, take a picture with a digital camera, then try out different colors in any graphic editing program.

Order wood and veneer doors prefinished. Finishes applied on site (paint, varnish and polyurethane) are difficult to maintain on solid-wood doors.

239 Buy a Garage-Door Opener

Sure you could operate a garage door manually, but why would you? Each year 3 million of us buy a remote opener. Beyond dependability, compare cost, safety, security and noise—important for garages that contain workshops or have bedrooms or offices overhead.

Steps

1 Compare mechanisms.

- Chain drives ($130 to $180) are noisy because they use a metal chain along a metal trolley.

- Screw drives ($150 to $250) lift the door with a threaded steel rod. Look for the latest models that use a plastic-lined track to reduce noisy metal-to-metal contact and to increase opening speed.

- Belt drives ($170 to $350) are the quietest. Their flexible rubber belts dampen vibrations and eliminate the noisy metal-to-metal contact of chain or screw drives.

2 Evaluate the openers' motors.

- Some high-quality, efficient openers use a direct current (DC) motor instead of standard alternating current (AC) motor. A DC motor uses less electricity and its speed can easily be controlled, allowing a simpler drive mechanism to be used for reliability and less noise. It also allows for a soft start and stop cycle to eliminate loud clank sounds. The door starts closing slowly, reaches full speed and then slows down again just before it touches the floor.

- Select a ½- or ¾-horsepower opener instead of the basic ⅓ if you have a large or heavy door.

- Compare models' lift speed, typically 7 inches (18 cm) per second.

3 Take safety concerns into account. An automatic reverse feature stops and reverses the door if it touches something—a child playing underneath, for example. For heightened security, get a remote control that uses rolling codes to transmit a different opening signal each time. Models with multifunctional controls may have one button for opening the door, another that switches on just the garage light, and a third that can switch on lights or appliances inside the house. Some wall panels let you turn the opener off if you're going to be gone for an extended period of time. (See 419 Buy a Home Automation System.)

4 Buy an opener at a store or from a dealer and put it in yourself, or pay $125 to $175 plus for the unit for professional installation. Most openers include two remotes; a third adds about $30. A wireless outdoor keypad comes in handy if you forget the remote or its battery is dead. An indoor keypad adds convenience.

What to Look For

- Quiet, dependable action
- Power and speed
- Automatic reverse
- Rolling codes
- Wireless keypads

Tips

If you often forget whether you've closed the door, get the Chamberlain Garage Door Monitor (chamberlain-diy.com), which shows the garage door's status from anywhere inside the house.

Only two manufacturers make most garage-door openers, which explains why models sold under different brand names may look similar.

Look for a model with magnetic stop sensors for precise opening and closing.

Mechanisms with fewer parts require less maintenance.

240 Buy Lumber for a DIY Project

A successful do-it-yourself project starts with good wood. At first you may think there's a secret lumberyard code when you confront the many types and dimensions of wood. But once you take time to learn how the industry assigns grades and determines sizes, it's easy to choose and order the lumber best suited for your purpose—and maybe save money, too.

Steps

1 Using a plan or sketch of your project, take a cutting list of all the pieces you need in each length to a lumberyard. You'll find a broader selection, better quality and more expertise there than at a home center.

2 Choose softwood or hardwood. Most construction lumber is softwood and is milled from fast-growing evergreens—pine, fir, cedar, redwood—in 2-foot increments from 6 to 20 feet in length. Hardwood comes from dense-grained deciduous trees such as maple, cherry and oak. Used for fine woodworking, it's available in more thicknesses and in random widths and lengths.

3 Match grade to purpose. To guarantee uniformity, lumber is graded by the quality of its surface. Terms differ for softwoods and hardwoods, but all describe appearance rather than strength. Look for clear- or select-grade boards for visible projects like shelves or decks. Select grade has few knotholes or discolorations. Common grade, which has more defects and is usually cheapest, is fine for items you plan to paint.

4 Decipher lumber sizes. Sawmills cut wood into standard sizes, from 1 to 8 or more inches thick and 4 to 12 or more inches wide. When this rough lumber is planed, it loses ⅛ inch or more from each dimension, so a 2-by-4 is actually 1.5 by 3.5 inches.

5 Buy precut wood for popular uses—stair treads, window trim, shelving and pieces such as spindles and furniture legs. These save time and take the guesswork out of choosing species and grade, but cost more.

6 Order lumber by the linear foot or the board foot. Use the former to order moldings, trim and same-dimension lumber (30 linear feet of 1-by-6 boards, for example). Use the latter to order random-width hardwood by volume for building furniture. As an example, 1 board foot equals 144 cubic inches.

7 Select pine or fir for rough-cut projects and framing. Pick hardwood for fine furniture and projects that will get a clear finish. Pine cuts easily and takes paint and varnish well. In hardwoods,

What to Look For

- Lumberyard versus home center
- Wood choice
- Suitable grade for purpose
- Precut wood
- No defects
- Moisture content

Tips

The only way to ensure that you get high-quality wood is to pick out the boards yourself—or at least approve their selection.

Lumber describes milled wood more than 2 inches thick. Thinner wood is technically a board. Wood thicker than 5 by 5 inches is timber. Now you know.

Lumber prices vary by season, region, availability and demand.

Once you've calculated how much wood your project requires, get 10 percent extra to allow for mistakes and to match grain. Don't buy more than that. Wood can warp if it's not stored in ideal conditions.

Countries outside the United States have different systems for sizing lumber.

ash and poplar are typically painted because they stain unevenly. Stain maple and oak to highlight their grain. Walnut is strong and stains nicely; beech looks great varnished or stained but is hard on saws.

8 Inspect for defects. Knots are a cosmetic flaw (unless they're large or about to pop out), but splits often get wider. To check for warping, lift one end of a board and sight down its edge to see if it bends in either direction. To check for bowing or arching, lay the wood on a level surface. A seriously bowed, cupped or crooked board is seldom workable, although minor bows will flatten out as you nail.

9 Check moisture content, or seasoning. Lumber is kiln-dried (KD) or air-dried (AD). KD wood has about 8 percent moisture content; AD, 15 to 25 percent. For indoor furniture, KD lumber is preferable because the wood shouldn't dry out any further.

10 Choose plywood for its strength and stability, the result of gluing several thin layers of wood together at right angles. Plywood used for sheathing, subfloors and rough carpentry typically has a veneer of Douglas fir, graded on each side. If both sides will show in your finished project, buy A-A or A-B grade. Plywood comes in 4-by-8-foot panels ¼, ⅜, ½, ⅝ or ¾ inch thick ($14 to $40 for Douglas fir, according to grade and thickness).

11 Use hardwood-veneer plywood for furniture and cabinetry. It also comes in 4-by-8-foot sheets, but most dealers will sell a partial sheet. Thicknesses range from ⅛ to ¾ inch; the latter costs $65 to $105 per sheet. Be sure to ask for *cabinet-grade plywood,* which is typically 9-ply birch coming from Denmark and other sources, and available through plywood distributors. Use finish-grade plywood for built-in projects, combined with more costly solid woods for exposed areas. You can get plywood with a veneer of virtually any kind of wood in the world.

12 Shop for alternatives to old-formula pressure-treated lumber (see Warning) for building decks, picnic tables and play structures. Heartwood grades of redwood and cedar are naturally rot- and insect-resistant; prices vary widely by season and location. Consider composite (wood-plastic) lumber for durable, splinter-free decking. Engineered lumber products come from small-diameter and fast growing plantation trees. They use wood fiber more efficiently than conventional lumber, reducing pressure on old-growth forests and resulting in stronger structures. Choose exterior plywood—made with waterproof glue—for other outdoor projects.

241 Select Roofing

Protect your largest investment—your home—with a roof that looks great and lasts a long time. Compare the materials' pros and cons to decide which one meets your needs and budget. Contact the National Roofing Contractors Association (nrca.net) for a licensed contractor to help you calculate your

MATERIAL	WARRANTY; COST PER SQUARE FOOT	WEIGHT PER SQUARE	PROS AND CONS
Composition, Organic or Fiberglass Base	20 to 30 years, $25 to $35	200 to 300 lbs.	Most common and affordable choice with asphalt coating. Fiberglass is stronger and more flexible than organic (cellulose). Variety of colors, styles, brands. Very good fire protection. Low maintenance. Can be walked on. Can be installed over a previous layer. Flat look, except for top grades. Brittle when cold.
Dimensional	20 to 30 years, $60	300 to 450 lbs.	Better wind resistance than lighter composition shingles. Same materials but thicker for attractive appearance. Have shadow lines (to simulate a thicker material with more character) and are longer.
Wood Shingles, Shakes	15 to 20 years (depending on climate), $100 to $200	300 to 350 lbs.	Typically rot-resistant Western red cedar. Natural character and variation blends with environment, weathers evenly with age. Good insulation. Requires ongoing maintenance. Little variation in color. Good installation depends on experience.
Clay or Concrete Tile	30 to 75 years, $130 to $500	560 to 1,030 lbs.	Ideal for Southwestern, Italian or Spanish Mission architecture. Many colors in flat, barrel or S shapes. Very good fire protection. Long life span. Low maintenance. No problem with moisture or insects. Heavy; may require reinforced roof framing (although synthetic concrete is much lighter). May break if walked on.
Steel or Aluminum	40 to 50 years, $150 to $240	50 to 90 lbs.	Standing-seam, wavy or faux-shake styles. Many enamel finishes. Lightweight; can be installed on almost flat roofs and over existing asphalt shingles. Long life. Interlocking panels install quickly, shed snow easily. Fire resistant. Recyclable. Lower grades can dent. Conducts heat; look for coatings that deflect the sun.

roof's area and installation costs. Note: Roofing is sold by the square (100 square feet of coverage). Keep in mind that a more expensive roof should carry a longer warranty.

MATERIAL	WARRANTY; COST PER SQUARE FOOT	WEIGHT PER SQUARE	PROS AND CONS
Copper	50 years, $250 to $500	100 to 150 lbs.	Adds to home's value. Recycled and recyclable. Shingle or standing-seam styles. Low or no maintenance; develops attractive patina over time. Noncombustible. Lightweight but wind-resistant. Will not mildew. Expensive. Limited number of suppliers.
Natural Slate	100-plus years, $300 to $600	700 to 2,000 lbs.	Classic, beautiful appearance. Moderate range of color choices, depends on where quarried. Very good fire protection. Rot- and insect-proof. Long life span. Low maintenance. Heavy; may require additional roof support. Difficult to install. May crack if walked on. Expensive up-front cost.
Synthetic Slate	50 years, $250 to $400	170 to 280 lbs.	Molded from vinyl or rubber composites. Lighter, more flexible, easier to install than real slate. Strong enough to walk on. Fire resistant; impervious to moisture, insects. Traditional color choices. New product; limited supplier network.
Thatched	10 to 70 (even 100) years depending on material. Cost N/A	N/A	No need for a sub-roof. Fixed directly to the rafters so offers storm protection. Not many companies offer this material. May take 3 to 4 weeks to complete. High insurance rates. Requires treatment for fire and insect resistance (check local building codes for suitability).
WARNING	Before you choose slate or clay tiles, have an architect or structural engineer make sure your home can carry the added weight.		

When you're hiring a home improvement professional, you're buying that person's ability to bring your concept to life. It's of critical importance to find a trustworthy, licensed professional for any work that includes carpentry, drywall, concrete, insulation, plumbing, painting, flooring and tile.

Steps

General Contractor

1 Talk to people you trust who have hired general contractors. Gather leads from lumberyards, architects, home inspectors and real estate agents. Contact online services, such as ImproveNet.com and the National Association of Home Builders' Remodelers Council (nahb.net/remodeler_working), or trade groups like your local Remodelers Council branch.

2 Go online or telephone your state's contractor licensing board to verify credentials and confirm that a contractor's license is up to date. You'll be able to type in their license number and get information directly. Note that there are several sub-categories of licenses for various specialties; requirements vary by state. Also call the local building inspection department and ask what they think of a contractor's work. Contact your local or state consumer protection office or Better Business Bureau (bbb.org) to find out if the contractor has any unresolved complaints on file.

3 Identify several contractors. Confirm that they and their subcontractors are licensed and bonded. Describe your project and ask if they've handled comparable jobs in the past year. Check their availability for your intended time frame. Discuss your budget. Narrow the field to those available contractors who impressed you most.

4 Ask for names and numbers of current and former customers. Interview them about each contractor's strengths and weaknesses, and ask how the job went. Was the quality of the work and materials what you expected? Was the project completed on time and within budget? During work, did the contractor keep you informed? Did the crew and subcontractors treat your property and family respectfully? Would you hire him or her again? Ask a customer from four or five years ago how the job held up.

5 Solicit competitive bids from at least three contractors. Contractors will use the architect's blueprints or construction documents to make an accurate bid. (See 188 Hire an Architect.) If there are significant differences between bids, ask why. A low-ball bid won't end up costing the least if you soon have to replace poor-quality materials or shoddy workmanship.

6 Hire a licensed contractor for any job over $500 in value (laws vary by state). Contractors know the building codes; only they can give bids and are liable for the work they do. If an unlicensed

What to Look For

- Satisfied past clients
- Relevant experience
- Insured and licensed workers
- Personal attention
- Low but realistic bid
- Detailed contract

Contractors' Tips

Review sample bids and contracts and compare them to those you receive to see if the contractor puts schedule details, product selections and change orders in writing.

For a sample contract, contact the American Institute of Architects (aia.org) or the Associated General Contractors of America (agc.org). Have a lawyer review your contract before signing.

Look for a good fit. Ask if you will be treated as a partner in the project. A strong rapport and close communication with your contractor helps make any job go well.

A permit is required for most work costing more than $300 (see 190 Pull Building Permits).

Call a contractor's suppliers and subcontractors to make sure he or she pays their bills on time.

contractor is hired, you accept responsibility for any damage. Discuss the contractor's guarantee or warranty programs. If something seems amiss, go elsewhere.

7 Ask for the payment schedule. Execute a written contract specifying the work to be done, estimated start and finish dates, total cost and payment schedule. A detailed contract protects both you and the contractor. Accept informal letters of agreement for jobs costing $1,000 or less.

Plumber

1 Follow the steps for contractors.

2 Confirm that the bid includes removal of any fixtures that need replacing, such as an old tub.

3 Ask what their minimum and hourly charge is. Also ask if 24-hour emergency service is available, and about additional costs.

4 Contact the Plumbing-Heating-Cooling Contractors-National Association (phccweb.org) to find a master plumber, who will have the most expertise and experience.

Painter

1 Follow the steps for contractors.

2 Have the painter inspect the site before submitting a bid. Make sure multiple quotes cover the same specifications—all preparation including lead paint removal, areas to paint, number of coats, and paint brands and colors.

3 Discuss the painter's preferred methods of paint application—spraying or hand painting—as well as paint removal: torching, sanding, or using chemicals.

4 Make sure your contract holds the painter responsible for cleaning paint spatters from all surfaces and that both your property and adjacent property (such as your neighbor's car) is protected. Unlicensed painters are not liable for damage—you are.

Electrician

1 Follow the steps for contractors.

2 Tell the electrician what you need done. Electrical contractors don't necessarily handle all kinds of jobs.

3 Hire an electrician affiliated with the International Brotherhood of Electrical Workers (ibew.org), which has one of the longest apprenticeships of the trade. Licensed electricians must follow all electrical codes and use only materials certified by Underwriters Laboratories (UL.com). Only licensed electricians can obtain necessary permits. By law, they are responsible for the work and for fixing any problems the building inspector finds.

Plumbers' Tips

If you need a gas line put in for a new stove or dryer, call a plumber.

Comparison shop and buy your own fixtures to save the plumber's markup (see 221 Choose a Faucet).

Painters' Tips

If you're hiring a painter to do stenciling or other decorator techniques, confirm that he or she has relevant experience.

Find out if your painter belongs to the Painting and Decorating Contractors of America (PDCA).

Warnings

Make sure the contractor provides you with a certificate of insurance before you make any payments or work begins.

Be leery of contractors who ask for more than 30 percent up front.

243 **Hire a Gardener**

If you just don't have the time, skill or patience to cultivate your dream garden, hire a gardener to transform your yard into an oasis. Or you can just hire someone for the basic upkeep—mowing the lawn, raking leaves and hauling away debris—and take care of the more creative work yourself.

Steps

1   Decide if you'd like garden help on a regular or occasional basis. Typically, a standard-size suburban garden requires at least several hours of work each week during the growing season.

2   Ask neighbors and friends for recommendations. Ask why they like their gardener and what specialties that person might have. Or ask for names at a local nursery.

3   Schedule tasks seasonally. Some tasks like cutting the grass and weeding need to be done weekly; others like fertilizing happen a few times a year; and still others, such as pruning and planting bulbs, are required annually. Gardening services can give you estimates that run from an hourly rate to a seasonal fee. If all you need is someone to mow the lawn and clean up debris, a weekly "mow and blow" service should suffice.

4   Tell the gardener how you want your garden treated and what materials can and can't be used. If you want the weeding done by hand instead of with an herbicide, for instance, make this clear.

5   Choose a gardener whose gardening style fits yours. If you like a natural look, then don't hire someone who tries to turn every shrub into a poodle.

6   Determine the gardener's skill level if you need special services, such as sprinkler maintenance or repair.

7   Decide if you or the gardener will choose, buy or put in plants. The gardener will usually bill you separately for plants and other supplies such as fertilizer or soil amendments.

8   Make sure you agree on work schedule details, such as what happens on rainy days, holidays and vacations.

What to Look For

- Recommendations
- Chores required
- Matching styles
- Type of garden
- Skill level

Tips

Keep tabs on what your gardener is doing, or you may end up paying for regular chemical spraying or herbicide lawn applications that do more harm than good.

Remember a good gardener on special occasions with a gift or bonus. See 24 Tip Properly.

Warning

Be wary of gardening businesses that stop by your house and tell you what problems your garden has and how they will fix them. A reputable business won't do this.

244 **Buy Outdoor Furniture**

When the weather turns warm and inviting, you want to take it outside. Create enticing outdoor rooms with furniture that not only reflects your style, but stands up to the elements and your family's activities. Different materials require different care and maintenance.

Steps

1 Match the furniture to your style, just as you would do indoors. Many styles are available, including traditional English cottage, Italian piazza, French café and modern.

2 Be realistic about your price range. A teak table, for instance, can range from $200 to $2,000 and up.

3 Look at different materials and how they suit your garden and your style. (See chart below.)

4 Look for made-for-outdoors seat cushions that resist mildew, sun fading and tearing; filling should be a polyester material that does not absorb water and dries quickly.

5 Try out the furniture before buying. Make sure chairs and benches are comfortable to sit in.

6 Get a large enough table for your needs and space. A 4-foot (1.2 m) round table seats five people comfortably.

7 Add a comfortable seat or two, such as a pair of Adirondack chairs for lounging.

8 Include a classy-looking umbrella for protection against sun and rain, and to string lights in for evening parties.

What to Look For

- Style
- Price
- Material
- Comfort
- Appropriate table size
- Umbrella

Tips

Count on your furniture lasting for many years as long as you take care of it, bringing it indoors during freezing weather (or covering with a tarp) and using wood preservatives if required.

Buy teak only from sources that use sustainable harvesting methods. This information should be indicated clearly in the description of the furniture. This ensures that the wood was grown on a plantation, not harvested from depleted natural sites.

MATERIAL	FEATURES
Plastic resin	Inexpensive, ubiquitous. Sheds rain. Store indoors during cold winters.
Cedar	Moderately priced. Durable, naturally rot- and insect-resistant. Weathers to gray; can be finished or painted.
Teak	Classic look, available in wide range of quality and prices. Turns silver-gray if unfinished; to retain original color, keep indoors or refinish frequently.
Wicker	Nice for porches or patios—works well indoors or outdoors. Move indoors during the winter. Needs cushions for comfort. Squeaks.
Aluminum	Lightweight, rustproof, usually most expensive of metal furniture. Powder-coated finish is resistant to moisture and bad weather.
Wrought Iron	Heavy and strong, needs cushions for comfort. Epoxy primer provides best rust resistance.

245 Buy the Perfect Rosebush

A rose is a rose is a rose, until you come face to face with the thousands of different varieties on the market. Choose a rose to please your nose and eyes, but also make sure it suits your climate's demands—whether you're seeking a climber for an arbor or fence, a shrub rose for a flower garden, or a landscape rose for ground cover.

Steps

1 Shop for bare-root roses from late fall to early spring depending on your climate. Dormant, leafless roses sold with roots bare of soil offer the broadest selection. Planting at the bare-root stage gets plants off to a great start and is the least expensive way to buy roses.

2 Look for the best selection of bare-root roses in mail-order catalogs or on the Internet, but make sure you can get your money back if the plant is dead on arrival.

3 Buy container-grown roses during their growing season (spring to fall, or year-round in mild-winter climates). These mature plants are more expensive, but will give the garden an established look much faster.

4 See and smell rose varieties in person at nurseries starting in April in mild climates. Or visit local rose gardens to see established plants in bloom, and note your favorite varieties.

5 Choose a rose that suits your climate. Although some varieties, such as 'Iceberg' and 'Peace,' do well almost anywhere, most roses prefer particular climates. Talk to a local expert from the American Rose Society (ars.org), which also has rose ratings. Or look in the phone book for your county's cooperative extension office and ask for a master gardener.

6 Decide on the type of rose you want based on where you will plant it in the garden. Hybrid tea roses—the most familiar type, with long stems and big buds for cut flowers—grow as upright shrubs. Other types of roses are designed to grow as climbers (such as the 'Cécile Brünner') or ground covers.

7 Save money by choosing older rose varieties (meaning those that have been available for some time). New varieties come out every year, generally at higher prices.

8 Look into antique or heirloom (as opposed to merely old) varieties for their fragrance and nostalgic qualities. They tend to be expensive. These types include moss, cabbage and rugosa. Some have very short blooming seasons.

9 Read catalog descriptions or nursery tags to make sure the rose you buy is disease resistant. The most common diseases, powdery mildew and black spot, affect the leaves, reduce the plant's beauty and life and are costly to treat. In most climates, it's not worth the risk to grow roses that are not disease resistant.

What to Look For

- Bare-root plants
- Container-grown plants
- Fragrance
- Older varieties
- Antique or heirloom varieties
- Disease resistance

Tips

Bare-root roses usually come packed in damp sawdust or wood shavings inside a plastic bag. Look for healthy roots—white and firm, not brown and slimy looking.

Make sure container-grown plants are not root-bound, with circling roots crowding out of the container.

Look for rose-planting advice at Web sites such as Jackson & Perkins (jacksonandperkins.com).

246 Buy Flowering Bulbs

Classic spring-blooming bulbs include daffodils and tulips, but other seasons also boast impressive performers, such as summertime's lilies and gladiolus. None are for procrastinators—or for limited thinkers who can't imagine the glory that comes from a brown knob five or six months after you plant it.

Steps

1 Shop for bulbs at nurseries or home improvement stores during the planting season. The earlier in the season you buy, the better the selection. Order bulbs by mail or online ahead of the season (June and July for fall planting), when many catalog companies offer discounts. Mail-order sources will take your order early, and then send the bulbs to you at planting time.

2 Buy and plant spring-flowering bulbs, such as crocuses, daffodils, hyacinths and tulips, in the fall (September through November).

3 Buy and plant summer-flowering bulbs, such as gladiolus, lilies and ornamental onions, in the spring (generally February through April).

4 Search the Web for online sources, such as White Flower Farm (whiteflowerfarm.com), John Scheepers (johnscheepers.com) and Brent and Becky's Bulbs (brentandbeckysbulbs.com).

5 Note that bulbs are graded by size, with different sizes for top grades of various types of bulbs. For best results choose top-size bulbs. If you are planting a big area, you can save money by buying smaller sizes. Choose bulbs that are firm to the touch and do not have any mold on them.

6 Save money on prepackaged bags of bulbs, or spend more and buy individual bulbs in special varieties.

7 Plant enough bulbs for a showy display. You can group tulips close together, as long as they aren't touching (which promotes rot). Space other bulbs about two or three times their diameter apart. You can fit about seven tulip bulbs in a pot that's 12 inches (30 cm) across.

8 Extend the blooming season by planting bulbs with different blooming times. Tulips and daffodils, among others, are labeled as early, mid or late season.

9 Look for spring-blooming bulbs that can be forced in the fall. These include hyacinths and certain narcissus, usually labeled for forcing.

What to Look For

- Blooming and planting seasons
- Wide range of blooming times
- Firm bulbs with no mold
- Bulk deals

Tips

Don't remove the papery coating on bulbs that have them, such as tulips, but don't worry if it slips off.

In the right climates, many bulbs will bloom year after year. Others—particularly tulips in warm climates—are one-year performers.

In mild climates, including much of California and the Southwest, buy tulip bulbs early enough so you can chill them in your refrigerator's vegetable crisper for six weeks before planting. This extra chilling will make up for the cold weather that tulips need in order to bloom well.

Buy Flowers for Your Garden

A flower garden can offer a romantic and fragrant feast for the senses, a renewable source for fresh bouquets, or simple color to brighten a patio or deck. The key is understanding what annuals and perennials are, knowing your planting seasons, and matching a plant's light and water requirements to what your garden offers.

Steps

Annuals

1 Remember that annuals are plants that grow, bloom, set seed and then die in one growing season, typically from spring to fall. In mild climates, some annuals grow and bloom through winter. Popular examples are petunias, marigolds and zinnias. Annuals generally produce maximum bang for the buck, but require seasonal replacement.

2 Choose cool-season annuals, such as pansies and Iceland poppies, for spring and fall displays (and winter in mild climates).

3 Select warm-season annuals, such as marigolds and impatiens, for flowering from late spring into fall.

4 Purchase seeds from catalogs or nursery racks, or buy seedlings sold in flats or small packs at nurseries. Starting from seed is less expensive but takes longer and is more labor intensive. Some annuals grow better when sown as seeds directly in the ground; others, such as begonias and petunias, take a discouragingly long time to grow from seed. Start your own seedlings at home for inexpensive and satisfying garden additions. Seed-starting kits are available at garden centers or from online dealers such as Gardener's Supply Company (gardeners.com).

5 Give a plant what it needs in terms of sun or shade. Most annuals prefer full sun. A few, such as impatiens and begonias, do well in shade.

6 Make sure you choose vigorous nursery seedlings. Examine them for healthy green leaves just coming out, and avoid seedlings with many yellow leaves. Select plants with mostly unopened flowers. Avoid any that are root-bound, with wads of brown roots coming out the bottom of the container.

Perennials

1 Choose perennials if you want plants that live for several years or more. Some die back to the ground in winter and reappear in the spring. Some may remain green all year in mild climates.

2 Shop for perennials nearly year-round, generally in nursery containers or small pots. Starting perennials from seed takes time, and some seeds germinate only with special care, so this is an advanced project. During late fall, winter and early spring, many

What to Look For

- Annuals sold as seedlings in small packs
- Perennials sold in small pots or gallon-size containers
- Vigorous growth, no root-bound signs

Tips

Easy-to-grow annuals include impatiens, marigolds, zinnias and sunflowers.

Save money by sowing nasturtium, sunflower, cosmos and California poppy seeds directly in the garden in spring. Make sure to keep them moist until they're established.

For a quick colorful effect in summer, look for sales on annuals potted in gallon-size containers.

perennials, such as phlox, display no top growth, so it looks like you're buying a pot full of soil.

3   Try to plant most perennials in early spring or early fall. The earlier in the growing season, the smaller the container and the less expensive the plant will be. Perennials in 4-inch (10 cm) pots may look small, but they are actually easier to establish in the garden than larger plants.

4   Neighborhood nurseries and garden centers may offer limited variety. Check out specialty perennial dealers with mail-order or direct-mail catalogs; specialties include daylilies, geraniums and salvias.

5   Look for signs of vigor in a nursery plant: healthy green leaves just coming out, either right by the soil or on a branch. Avoid plants with yellow, limp leaves or those that are root-bound.

6   Buy perennials in bloom if you want to be sure of the color.

Fail-safe perennials for sunny spots include yarrow, coneflower, daylily, and Shasta daisy. For shade, try bleeding heart, hellebore, hosta, and Japanese anemone.

You can increase your supply of perennials by dividing and transplanting existing plantings. The best timing depends on the type of plant, but generally you'd do this in fall and spring.

SEASON	ANNUALS	PERENNIALS
Early Spring	• Plant cool-season types: stock, Iceland poppy, pansy, snapdragon, larkspur, calendula. • Look for short, stocky plants in four- or six-packs; choose plants with or without flower buds, but with few or no open flowers.	• In bloom: forget-me-not, bellflower, corydalis, columbine. • Look for 4-inch or 1-gallon containers; at this time of year, some plants don't show above soil in pot.
Midspring to Midsummer	• Plant warm-season types: impatiens, petunia, marigold, salvia, lobelia. • Look for 1-gallon containers, good for quickly assembled patio displays.	• In bloom: delphinium, penstemon, daylily, peony, Shasta daisy. • Look for 4-inch or 1-gallon containers; plants should have leaves and some will have flowers; cut off dead flower stems.
Late Summer to Early Fall	• Plant selected warm-season types: salvia, zinnia. • In hot climates, take short break before planting more annuals.	• In bloom: salvia, black-eyed Susan, joe-pye weed. • Look for unwilted plants; it's OK if they aren't blooming—they will next year.
Fall	• Plant cool-season types in mild climates: pansy, calendula. • Start with seedlings or small pots only in mild-weather climates where you can garden year-round.	• In bloom: aster, chrysanthemum. • Watch for sales at nurseries.

In the dog-eat-dog, aphid-eat-rose world of gardening, it's just about impossible to eliminate all pests. Here are a few tips to keep pests under control in ways that are safe for you and the environment.

Steps

1 Match plants to the right location. A plant under stress because it's in the wrong place will be vulnerable to pests. Poor soil that drains slowly can lead to disease problems. Some plants need good air circulation to keep problems at bay—powdery mildew will plague roses planted where air circulates poorly.

2 Seek out lists of pest-resistant plants for your area.

3 Know the good bugs from the bad. Go to the library or search online to find gardening resources on pests, identifying good insects, such as ladybugs, that eat bad ones, such as aphids. Top sources are local extension agencies; for a national overview, check the U.S. National Arboretum (usna.usda.gov).

4 Investigate which pests are causing damage to your garden. Some signs are easy: a silvery trail indicates a slug or snail, for example. If petunia blossoms look chewed up, look for pepper-size droppings—signs of budworms.

5 Diversify your garden by growing a wide variety of flowers, shrubs and trees. This provides both food and a haven for birds and beneficial insects that will dine on harmful insects.

6 If deer are a problem, check with your county's cooperative extension service for a list of plants that deer won't eat. If you get desperate, an 8- to 10-foot (2.4 to 3.0 m) fence around your garden will keep Bambi and his friends out.

7 Cage the trunks of new trees to prevent grazing by deer, squirrels and rabbits.

8 Experiment with low-tech control methods. Use the hose to spray aphids off roses in the morning so the leaves have all day to dry. Put a wet, rolled-up newspaper among dahlias at night, and in the morning shake out all the earwigs into soapy water. Use insecticidal soaps for aphids. Inspect tomato plants daily for hornworms as big as your finger and camouflaged; pick them off and dispose of them.

9 Buy yellow sticky traps to control whiteflies around tomatoes, or other pests such as aphids, leafhoppers, leaf miners and wasps. The bugs are attracted to the color and get stuck. You can buy a pack of five traps for less than $5.

10 Use the widely available biological control *Bacillus thuringiensis* (Bt), sold under the trade names Biotrol, Dipel or Thuricide. This affects caterpillars that eat plants. There are different strains of Bt for different caterpillars.

What to Look For

- Ways to encourage good insects
- Low-tech solutions
- Bt

Tips

Expect a little plant damage. It's inevitable, and you'll live a happier, less stressful life if you accept this.

Invest in an insect identification book with a garden emphasis. This will help you learn which bugs help and which ones damage plants.

Integrated Pest Management (IPM) is a system for dealing with pests in ways that use chemicals as the last resort. Ask your county's cooperative extension about the program, or check online sources such as University of California at Davis's site (ipm.ucdavis.edu), or Cornell's New York State Integrated Pest Management Program (nysipm.cornell.edu/).

249 Buy Soil Amendments

Improve heavy (clay) or sandy soil with organic material such as compost. Amendments can help soil drain more effectively or retain water better, but don't provide as many nutrients as fertilizer does.

Steps

1 Get soil amendments for a flower or vegetable garden before planting in spring, or anytime you're doing much planting.

2 Choose from a local array of amendments, such as ground bark, rice hulls and mushroom compost. A good all-purpose choice is composted manure, which consists of manure and wood chips, wood shavings or sawdust.

3 Before planting a bed, add a 2- or 3-inch (5 to 7.5 cm) layer of soil amendment, and dig it in to a depth of 6 inches (15 cm).

4 For small areas of 100 square feet or so (9 square meters), buy amendments by the bag, typically 1 to 1.5 cubic feet (.03 to .04 cubic m). A bag this size will cover 18 square feet (1.7 square meters) to a depth of 1 inch (2.5 cm). For larger areas, buy in bulk at a soil, garden or building supply center. You can have the supplier deliver bulk material, or pick it up yourself.

What to Look For

- Type of amendment
- Bags for small areas
- Bulk for larger areas

Tips

Products sold as potting mixes are not intended for use as soil amendments. Fill containers directly from the bag for growing bulbs, flowers and other plants.

Choose composted material rather than fresh manure to guard against diseases that may be passed to humans through contact with animal feces.

250 Buy Mulch

Mulch is a blanket for your soil, holding water in, keeping weeds at bay and making the garden easier to care for. There's a wide variety of mulching material available; here's how to weed through the choices.

Steps

1 Choose an organic mulch, including wood chips, compost, hazelnut shells, cocoa hulls and pine needles, for your planting beds. What you choose is a matter of taste.

2 Figure out how much coverage you need. For example, to cover an area to a depth of 3 inches, multiply that by the area's width and length in feet; then divide this number by 27 to convert the measurement to cubic yards (how mulch is sold). 1 cubic yard will cover a 324-square-foot area with 1 inch of mulch.

3 Layer organic mulches (compost) to a depth of 1 to 2 inches (2.5 to 5 cm) around flowers, vegetables and shrubs; coarser mulches (shredded bark) can be applied 3 inches (7.5 cm) deep. Apply inorganic mulch such as stones of various sizes as a ground cover or for areas under trees where soil improvement isn't a consideration. Apply in layers of 1 to 3 inches (2.5 to 7.5 cm).

4 Save money by buying material in bulk. Bagged mulch costs $2 per cubic foot, while bulk material can be $12 per cubic yard.

What to Look For

- Organic or inorganic mulch
- Bags or bulk

Tips

Keep mulch 6 inches (15 cm) away from the trunks of shrubs and trees for plant health. This prevents excessive moisture from damaging the plants.

Various types of plastic sheeting are available as mulch for vegetable gardens and other spaces where looks aren't much of a consideration. They can also be used under stone or bark mulch to control weeds.

251 Buy a Composter

Turn kitchen scraps and garden debris into black gold—compost! This nutrient-rich organic matter is like giving your garden a boost of Popeye's spinach and can even decrease plant disease. Compost is made of vegetable kitchen waste and decomposed plant parts, including leaves, twigs and branches raked up and pruned from plants. There are many ways to make compost and various products to help with the process.

Steps

1 Make compost by combining green material, such as grass clippings, with brown material, such as dried leaves, stems and even shredded newspaper. Buy a covered bucket to keep kitchen scraps in until you take them to the compost pile.

2 Jump-start the process with a system that makes it easy to turn compost to speed decomposition.

3 You can choose a tumbler attached to a metal frame, which allows the bin to be turned, or one you can roll around the garden. This process usually takes five weeks. Most tumbling composters cost less than $100.

4 Save your back with a three-bin system. One bin holds new material; as that ages you turn it into the next bin to mix and aerate it, then into the third bin for finishing. Three-bin systems can cost up to $200; take a look at the Biostack composter at SmithandHawken.com.

5 Buy a worm bin to produce even better compost with less mess and no odors. Red worms, which multiply quickly, immediately get to work, breaking down kitchen scraps and bedding material such as newspaper into compost within six months. Available from catalogs such as Gardener's Supply (gardeners.com), a worm bin costs about $100, while the creepy crawlies will run you an extra $35.

6 Buy a compost thermometer to make sure the compost is hot enough to kill weed seeds. They're available for about $30 from online sources such as VermiCo.com.

What to Look For

- Tumbler
- Three-bin composter
- Worm-bin compost system

Tips

Weeds can be composted only in hot systems (which the tumbler creates).

Find out if your city or county offers free or discounted composting systems.

Warning

Discourage rats by making sure there are no animal by-products in your compost pile.

252 Buy Fertilizer

Plants grow best in fertile soil, and that means you must often help out nature by adding fertilizer. If you grow plants in containers, you have no choice: Healthy plant growth demands regular feeding. First you'll need a quick chemistry lesson.

Steps

1 Understand that plants require a basic diet of three main nutrients: nitrogen (N), phosphorus (P) and potassium or potash (K). Secondary nutrients, such as calcium, are necessary to a lesser degree.

2 Read a fertilizer label to determine its ingredients. The percentages of the three main nutrients—N, P and K—are listed, often in an abbreviated form, such as 6-2-4. You'll also see any trace elements included in the mixture.

3 Use a combination of N-P-K suited to the plants you're treating. All-purpose fertilizer (5-5-5 or 10-10-10) is good for general garden use, including flower and vegetable gardens. High-nitrogen lawn food (29-3-4, for instance) is designed to encourage quick green growth.

4 Consider specialty fertilizers for plants with special needs. For instance, azalea food is formulated for plants requiring acidic soil conditions.

5 Decide whether you want a chemical fertilizer or an organic fertilizer, derived from plant and animal sources such as kelp meal, cottonseed meal or blood meal. Chemical fertilizers generally provide more nitrogen and work more quickly; they can also burn plants more readily if directions are not followed carefully.

6 Choose a dry fertilizer to sprinkle on the ground for established areas of the garden containing trees, shrubs and flowers. The instructions will tell you if you have to work the fertilizer into the soil and water it in. Dry fertilizers also work well in a vegetable garden, where you can mix them into the soil before planting.

7 Use a liquid fertilizer for container plants (mix with water in a watering can for small applications) or if you want to spray the garden with fertilizer; some labels point out the value of applying liquid food to foliage.

8 Consider slow-release fertilizers to apply nutrients over a long season. The soil must stay moist for the fertilizer to work.

9 Always follow directions carefully. Excessive fertilizing can hurt your plants and the environment.

What to Look For

- N-P-K percentages
- Specialty plant foods
- Organic or chemical fertilizers
- Dry or liquid fertilizers
- Slow-release fertilizers

Tips

Test your soil to determine its nutrient levels. Kits are available at gardening stores and nurseries.

Feed plants according to the package instructions. Applying too much fertilizer is wasteful and can actually harm plants instead of helping them.

253 Start a Vegetable Garden

Eating fresh-picked corn or vine-ripened tomatoes is a life-altering experience. But where do you start? How do you choose from racks of seeds, catalog after catalog and rows upon rows of nursery seedlings? Successful small-scale farmers know what and when to plant, and how to start the crops.

Steps

1 Grow only those vegetables you enjoy eating. Give priority to those prized for incredible flavor when eaten fresh from the garden: sweet corn, beans and peas, tomatoes and young spinach, among others.

2 Prepare a plot of flat ground that gets full sun nearly all day. Break up and turn the soil and add compost or other organic material (See 249 Buy Soil Amendments). A full day of blazing sunshine is especially important if you grow vegetables in the cool weather of early spring, early fall or winter.

3 Figure out how much growing space you have and plant accordingly. Lettuce, for example, can be grown in a solid mat, but tomatoes need to be spaced about 2 feet (60 cm) apart. Give pumpkins at least 4 feet (120 cm) of growing room. Growing requirements are provided on seed packets, in catalogs, and on nursery tags, as well as in books on growing vegetables.

4 Choose crops that require less room if you have a small garden or grow vegetables in a container. Lettuce is a great pot plant, and 'Patio' or 'Tumbler' tomatoes will grow well in a hanging basket. Plants that climb and vine, such as cucumbers and pole beans, can be trained up a trellis to take up less room horizontally. Tuck herbs and parsley into flower beds.

5 Schedule plantings around the two main growing seasons which vary by region: cool (spring and fall) and warm (summer). Common cool-season vegetables include beets, broccoli, cabbage, carrots, cauliflower, lettuce, peas, potatoes, radishes, spinach and turnips. Warm-season crops include beans, corn, cucumbers, eggplant, melons, peppers, pumpkins, squash and tomatoes.

6 Sow some seeds directly in the ground as they grow best that way: beans, beets, carrots, chard, corn, lettuce, melons, peas, pumpkins, squash and turnips. Starting seeds is, of course, much less expensive than planting seedlings sold in flats, packs and pots.

7 Start with nursery seedlings of certain other crops unless you are an experienced vegetable grower. These plants tend to do better when set out in the garden as seedlings: eggplant, peppers,

What to Look For

- Sunny spot and good soil
- Seed packets marked with current year
- Vigorous seedlings

Tips

Shop for all kinds of seeds in early spring to mid-spring—when selection is best—even if you don't plant them right away.

Plant cool-season seedlings during late winter if you live in a warm climate, such as the Southwest, Southern California or the South.

Keep extra seeds in an envelope in a dry, cool place, such as a plastic storage box in the basement. Many vegetable seeds can still sprout after a year or more in storage.

tomatoes, broccoli, cabbage and cauliflower. Squash and cucumbers are among a few you can plant just as effectively as either seeds or seedlings.

8 Buy seeds at nurseries or by mail order starting just after the New Year, when the selection is freshest. Look for seed packets marked as having been packed for the current year.

9 Buy vegetables online and from mail-order seed companies for a far greater selection than you'll find at neighborhood nurseries. Burpee (burpee.com), Johnny's Selected Seeds (johnnyseeds .com), Park Seed Company (parkseed.com) and Thompson and Morgan (thompson-morgan.com) are a few long-established sources.

10 Shop for seedlings when your soil is prepared and you are ready to plant. Keep them moist and don't let them sit around for more than three days. Buy healthy and vigorous seedlings. They should stand up straight and be stocky, not lanky, with no yellow leaves or bug holes.

11 Save money and get truly involved with your garden by starting seeds indoors in winter and transplanting them into the garden in spring. It's simplest to start with complete kits, sold at garden centers and through catalogs, containing fluorescent lights, soil mix, containers and watering devices.

12 Sow seeds of colorful radishes or giant sunflowers to introduce children to the satisfaction and fun of growing their own food. Or lean 3 stakes together, tie them together at the top, and train pole beans up the stakes. Voilà! A bean teepee.

Warning

Just because you can grow zucchini doesn't mean you should.

WHEN TO PLANT	SOW SEEDS	SET OUT SEEDLINGS
Early to Mid-Spring	Lettuce, spinach, beet, turnips, peas, radishes, carrots, chard.	Onions, lettuce, broccoli, cabbage, celery, cauliflower, brussels sprouts, potatoes, kale.
Late Spring	Beans, corn, cucumbers, squash, melons, pumpkins, radishes.	Squash, tomatoes, eggplant, peppers, onions.
Late Summer	Lettuce, spinach, greens for fall harvest, beets, carrots, radishes, peas.	Broccoli, cabbage, kale, cauliflower.

254 Hire a Garden Professional

Maybe you need a plan for your whole garden, or perhaps you just want a classy border. Do you have special challenges such as complex drainage systems or retaining walls? It's time to call on the services of a professional designer.

Steps

1 Call nurseries and garden centers that offer design services or ask for recommendations. Ask friends and neighbors with beautiful gardens who did their work; a well-conceived, well-laid-out and beautiful garden is its own recommendation. Contact professional designers and design firms.

2 Look into employing a landscape architect—especially if your project is high-end, complex, or involves structures and landscaping. This is a licensed professional with a college degree in the field, who is trained to work with contractors, draw architectural plans and get permits from cities for work projects. For more information, including local contacts, see the Web site of the American Society of Landscape Architects (asla.org).

3 Consider a landscape designer, who may be certified and may have a college degree in the field. Check with the Association of Professional Landscape Designers (apld.org).

4 Ask to see a portfolio of the designer's work. View actual gardens he or she has designed.

5 Determine your budget. Landscaping projects can bloom into tens of thousands of dollars depending on construction requirements.

6 Decide what the scope of work will be, both beforehand and in consultation with the designer or landscaper. You can ask the designer to draw up complete plans or to suggest plants and landscaping ideas for only some parts of the garden.

7 Find out how you will be billed: by the hour, a flat fee for a plan (a modest plan may range from $200 to $1,500), as a percentage of the project's total cost, or for the whole project. Ask what the fee schedule is. How involved will the designer be during construction and planting? Will the designer supervise installation or will it be turned over to a contractor?

8 Start early in the year. The winter season is the best time to consult with a designer. You'll be ready to go when spring weather arrives.

9 Check your municipal landscaping codes. Certain cities have design-review procedures for landscape improvements, as well as requirements for water-conservation planting and irrigation.

What to Look For

- Recommendations
- Skill
- Budget
- Scope of work
- Municipal codes

Tips

If you are an experienced gardener, save money after your professional draws up the plan by buying and planting your own landscaping.

Contact local colleges with horticulture or landscaping programs. Students working toward certification or degrees may offer garden design services for much less. However, be aware that they're still learning.

Landscape contractors who also offer design services are called a design-build firm.

See 190 Pull Building Permits and 188 Hire an Architect.

255 Buy an Automatic Sprinkler System

Depending on your climate, an automatic sprinkler system for some or all of your garden is either a nice luxury or a near necessity. While a well-designed system can save you time, energy and water, it can also be expensive, often up to $5,500 for an average-size yard. Planning and installing it is complex and best left to the experts.

Steps

1 Decide how much of your yard needs irrigation beyond normal rainfall. Lawns are probably the biggest water hogs. Vegetables and flowers need constant moisture during the growing season. Shrubs and trees with deeper roots can get by with less frequent watering. You can irrigate all of these plants with the same system, set at different intervals and employing various types of sprinkler heads.

2 Consider an underground system for the parts of your yard whose basic layout won't change every year—lawns and large planted areas of trees, shrubs and flowers. These systems are constructed of pipes installed several inches underground, with sprinkler heads placed at intervals. Divide the system into different zones, depending on varying water needs.

3 Sketch the whole area, indicating planted spaces and existing watering systems.

4 Hire a pro by checking online or in the Yellow Pages under "Irrigation Systems and Equipment." Home improvement centers can provide design and installation as well as parts. Talk to landscape contractors, plumbing-supply stores, and experienced residential gardeners.

5 Study online tutorials even if you have turned the project over to a professional. One good source of information is Lowes.com.

6 Make sure you understand the automatic timer. You'll be the one adjusting and changing it with the seasons. Timers cost $50 and up, with cost determined by quality as well as the number of zones the timer serves.

7 Consider low-tech solutions such as soaker hoses to supplement underground sprinklers.

8 Look into drip or micro-irrigation systems (low volume, low pressure), which work very effectively in flower and vegetable beds that change from year to year. Drip-system kits, starting at $25 or so, are easy to install; use underground emitters that drip slowly or aboveground emitters that drip, mist or spray at a low-pressure rate.

9 Use drip lines and emitters to water container plants, especially if you are often away from home during the growing season. You'll find inexpensive kits designed for just this purpose.

What to Look For

- Professional help
- Low-tech soaker hoses
- Drip kit
- Smart timer

Tips

Check sprinkler heads and emitters at the beginning of every spring to make sure they are not clogged.

Select a drip system with an inline emitter for the most trouble-free operation.

256 Start a New Lawn

As American as apple pie, a lush lawn serves as both a verdant welcome mat to visitors and a soft playground for kids. You've got two
basic choices for installing a lawn. Planting sod—rolls of grass plus
roots and soil sliced off at a sod farm—offers instant lawn gratifica-
tion, but requires a higher initial dollar investment. Sowing seeds
saves money if you're willing to keep everyone and everything off,
nurse along the seedlings and wait for the finished product.

Steps

Getting ready

1 Measure the lawn area to determine how many square feet of
   coverage you need.

2 Find out which grasses are best for your lawn by talking with
   experts at a local nursery or calling your county's cooperative
   extension service. Bluegrass, the traditional lawn grass, does
   not perform well in all parts of the country. Consider drought-
   resistant varieties if you live where water is scarce—lawns are
   typically a garden's main water user.

3 Decide if you want to plant seed or sod. You can start cool-
   season grasses (Kentucky bluegrass, fescue and bent) from
   either. Many warm-climate grasses (Saint Augustine and hybrid
   Bermuda) are typically started from sod (or from pieces of
   vegetation called *sprigs* or *stolons*)—not from seeds.

4 Prepare the ground thoroughly for seed or sod. Weed carefully,
   then use a rotary tiller to dig in compost or a mix of topsoil and
   compost to a depth of 6 inches (15 cm). Rake out rocks and
   smooth the soil. Use a roller filled halfway with water to tamp
   down the soil for optimal germination and root growth.

Starting with seeds

1 Determine the amount of seed mix you need. This varies depending on the mix, so check the package. Seed to cover 1,500
   square feet (140 square m) costs about $50.

2 Seed the lawn in the spring, fall or early winter.

3 Plant your lawn where it gets at least six hours of sun a day,
   spring through fall—even mixes designed for shade need some
   sun to grow. If your yard doesn't have enough sun, consider
   other ground-cover choices, including gravel.

Rolling out sod

1 Purchase sod directly from sod farms (find sources in the Yellow
   Pages under "Sod," "Sodding Service" or "Lawn Supply") or
   from a local garden center. For an average-size lawn of 1,500
   square feet (140 square m), you'll spend about $420 for sod.

What to Look For

- Well-prepared soil
- Appropriate grass variety
  for your climate
- Healthy sod

Tips

Use a seed spreader to sow
at the most efficient recommended rate—a far more
precise way than scattering
seeds by hand.

Keep newly seeded areas
constantly wet until the
seedlings emerge, then
switch to twice-weekly
watering. Water newly laid
sod twice weekly. Make sure
the soil stays moist between
waterings.

2 Make sure the delivered sod is in good, healthy shape: moist roots, no yellow or brown grass, sod hanging together firmly.

3 Have sod delivered the morning you plan to lay it so that it doesn't dry out. You can lay it in spring or summer, or in mild climates during fall and winter. If you don't lay sod right away, water enough to keep roots moist. Don't saturate sod rolls with water; they'll become too heavy and muddy to roll out easily.

257 Buy a Lawn Mower

Weekly chore or blissful escape? Maybe it depends on what's going on in your house while you mow the lawn. Which mower you choose depends on lawn size and type, budget and the features you need.

Steps

1 Choose between two basic mower types: rotary and reel. Reel mowers cut with spinning blades passing over a fixed blade. Rotary mowers cut with a circulating blade underneath a sturdy housing of metal, plastic or fiberglass. Both types are available in gasoline or electric models.

2 Consider a manual reel mower for a lawn that is 1,000 square feet (100 square m) or less and is a soft-bladed type (not Bermuda or Saint Augustine)—or because you enjoy the exercise.

3 If you want a power mower, decide if you want a reel or rotary type. Reel mowers can cut the grass shorter (down to putting green height) and give a nice clean look. Rotary types are generally less expensive, easy to operate and to sharpen.

4 Choose between gas and electric. Gas mowers pollute and are noisy. With quieter, electric mowers, find out if the cord length, typically 100 feet (30 m), is long enough for your lawn. For cordless models, check to see how long the battery is good for—you'll want it to last through one mowing at least.

5 Choose between push or self-propelled (motor turns wheels, good for slopes) mowers. Front-propelled types are easy to operate. For a very large lawn, hop on board a riding mower that cuts a wider swath, or a lawn tractor.

6 Select a mulching mower and you won't be left with bags of clippings. It cuts the grass into small pieces, then blows them back down into the lawn, where they turn into fertile compost.

7 Keep these considerations in mind: Is the mower too heavy for you? Is it maneuverable enough, especially if you mow around trees? How easy is it to raise or lower the cutting height? How easy to start the motor? Is there a blade shut-off switch? Where do you put your iced-tea?

What to Look For

- Reel or rotary mower
- Hand or power operated
- Cutting swath

Tips

Collect grass clippings, discharge them to the side, or leave them on the lawn—these are the options different mowers offer.

Check with your city for rebates on electric mowers that may be available with gas-mower trade-ins.

With manual reel mowers, remember to keep blades sharp, which is best done professionally.

258 Buy Koi for Your Fish Pond

Koi, Japanese-bred ornamental carp, are prized for their beauty and magnificent coloring. You should be committed to caring for the fish before investing in them, as koi can live for 20 years or longer, reaching lengths of 3 feet (.9 m) and more. Many koi owners cherish their pets with a passion.

Steps

1 Read up on koi, how they live and what care they require, before you buy. Search online for koi Web sites and clubs in your area. *Koi USA* is a magazine for enthusiasts (koiusa.com). Call local nurseries for a referral to a local fish expert.

2 Prepare your pond before you buy the fish. It should be filtered and can be as shallow as 18 inches (45 cm), although koi stay healthier in deeper water. Moving water (a waterfall, for example) will help oxygenate the water, but make sure the pond is big enough so that the koi can retreat to a quiet corner.

3 Shop for healthy fish. Visit a specialty store and look for specimens with clear eyes, erect fins and no missing scales.

4 Note that fish are priced according to their size, shape, color pattern and availability. Young koi 3 to 4 inches (7.5 to 10 cm) long may cost less than $10, but older fish 22 to 24 inches (56 to 61 cm) long can cost $1,200 and more (and $10,000 is not out of the question for large, rare koi). Butterfly koi, named for their long, flowing fins, are more expensive than regular koi.

5 Buy koi during cool weather if possible; it's easier to move them at that time as their metabolisms have slowed for the winter. Koi do fine in cold water, but it's best to avoid widely fluctuating temperatures. In deep ponds, koi can survive even when the water is frozen over.

6 Feed your fish koi pellets, sold at fish and pet shops and by online pet suppliers, once or twice a day.

7 Plan to brush up on chemistry (water quality) and fish anatomy if you are serious about koi. For health information, check out KoiVet.com.

What to Look For

- Koi clubs, Web sites, books, magazines
- Well-prepared pond
- Healthy fish

Tip

Protect your fish from raccoons and other predators by providing hiding places in the pond (spaces under rocks) or a pond cover.

259 Buy a Storage Shed

For people without a garage or basement to store their garden necessities, a prefabricated shed can be a lifesaver. Sheds and shed kits for every budget are available at home and garden centers, and online at sites such as Gardensheds.com. Choose a size and material that works with your space, and you can keep your tools, bags of soil, lawn mower and assorted junk out of sight and safe from the elements.

Steps

1 Decide how much storage space you need. A lean-to shed 6 feet (1.8 m) long and 3 to 4 feet (.9 to 1.2 m) wide is big enough for tools and might cost a few hundred dollars. If you'll be storing a lawn mower and more, look for a freestanding shed measuring 6 by 8 feet (1.8 by 2.4 m), which will cost $1,000 or more.

2 Consider the material not only for looks but for what you need to store. Cedar siding is long lasting, readily available and weathers to a gray color, or you can paint or stain it with wood preservative to keep it brown. Vinyl siding that looks like wood is a less-expensive and even longer-lasting alternative. Metal sheds heat up quickly to high temperatures in the summer, so they're not recommended for storing gasoline or other volatile liquids and fertilizers.

3 Make sure the entrance is wide enough to get a cart, wheelbarrow and other equipment comfortably through the door— say, 3 feet (.9 m).

4 Choose a combination greenhouse and storage shed to maximize the pace. One measuring 8 by 10 feet (2.4 by 3 m) can accommodate both tools and plants, with special shelves for setting seedlings out.

5 Take advantage of features to help you work: windows and skylights for natural light, benches for work space, ramps for easier wheeled entry.

6 Visualize how the shed will look in your yard. Even a small one can seem large. Landscaping around it with shrubs and trees can make it blend into the garden.

What to Look For

- Appropriate size
- Type of material
- Special features

Tips

Do-it-yourselfers can pick up a shed kit or buy plans and build one on their own.

If you're willing to pay twice the money for the convenience, you can have a pre-built shed delivered and installed by one of the large home-improvement stores.

Consider turning your shed into a potting room come springtime. You can pot up seedlings or sit down with a cup of coffee while you plan your next harvest.

260 Hire an Arborist

Tree pruning is dangerous and requires real skill to avoid harming not only yourself, but your tree. If it has pest or disease problems that may compromise its health or if it has suffered storm damage, hire an arborist. If your trees require annual pruning or pest control, you'll want to find someone on an ongoing basis.

Steps

1 Check with neighbors or local parks and nurseries for recommendations of reputable tree services. An arborist is trained to plant, maintain and prune trees.

2 Contact the International Society of Arboriculture (champaign. isaarbor.com) or the National Arborist Association (natlarb.com) for an arborist in your area.

3 Ask for proof of insurance. A reputable arborist will have personal and property damage insurance as well as workers' compensation insurance.

4 Check with your city to see if you need a permit for tree removal, or if the arborist needs to be licensed with the municipality.

5 Ask for references to find out where the tree service has done work similar to what you are requesting. Call or better yet drive by to see how it looks.

6 Get more than one estimate.

What to Look For

- Recommendations and references
- Professional certification or license
- Insurance
- Permits
- Estimates

Tips

Make sure any pruning bid specifies which branches will be cut and removed.

Tree topping—cutting off the top—may improve a view, but could damage the tree, ultimately turning it into a hazard, in danger of falling on houses, fences or cars in its path.

261 Buy Basic Garden Tools

There's a tool for every garden purpose—a dandelion popper, a bulb dibber, a watering can for seedlings. Stock your shed with well-built, high-quality essentials—the classic tools you'll use year after year.

Steps

1 Check for a comfortable, balanced weight. Too heavy a tool will wear you out quickly, as will a poorly balanced tool. Too light, and you will have to compensate with your own energy.

2 Feel the handle. High-quality wood, usually ash, should be smooth, with an even, straight grain. Longer handles provide more leverage.

3 Make sure the head's on straight. Carbon steel is the highest quality. Consider stainless-steel tools if you're willing to pay the price. They're durable, rust-resistant and easy to clean.

4 Look closely where the head joins the handle. The strongest connections are forged sockets or steel strapped, riveted with

What to Look For

- Good feel and balance
- High-quality handles and blades
- Durable, strong materials
- Tools that meet your needs

Tips

Short-handled tools may make tall people stoop, but shorter people may find them more comfortable. Try both short and long handles to see which kind you like.

several rivets. Less-expensive tools often employ a metal sleeve that extends from the head and wraps around the handle.

5 Test for sharpness. A tool's edge will hold up better if the steel is tempered, heat-treated or solid-forged.

6 Buy your tools at hardware stores and nurseries. Or shop online at sites such as A. M. Leonard (mleo.com) and Smith & Hawken (smithandhawken.com).

Keep your tools in good shape by cleaning off dirt after every use; scrape with a wooden spoon or a stiff brush. Swipe the heads with linseed-oiled cloth at the beginning and end of every season.

ESSENTIAL TOOLS	WHAT THEY DO	PRICE
Shovel	A round-point shovel is indispensable, useful for both digging and throwing soil. A square-point type is more of a scoop.	$20 to $60
Spade	Spades have flat blades and are mainly for digging holes and turning beds.	$20 to $60
Digging Fork	Flat tines break up the soil and loosen compost; good for preparing vegetable beds. (A hay fork is only useful if you grow hay.)	$20 to $30
Weeder-cultivator	Useful hand tool digs out tap-rooted weeds such as dandelions without leaving a big hole.	$10 to $30
Hoe	Use to cut off weeds at surface level, in paths and around established plants. Not for heavy-duty ground-breaking (instead use a pick or mattock).	$10 to $35
Edger	Look for a low-tech, easy-to-use blade that can cut a neat edge between grass and pathway.	$15 to $35
Leaf Rake	Springy and flexible, cleans up leaves from lawn and paths. Expandable model helps you clean up debris between and under shrubs at its narrowest setting and rakes up loads of leaves when fully expanded.	$10 to $15
Garden Rake	Sturdy, spiked teeth make the garden rake indispensable for leveling and smoothing beds. Must be tough.	$20
Hand Pruners	For cleaner, more precise cuts, look for hand shears with bypass blades, which slip past each other when closed and cut the branch cleanly. Use on branches of 1 inch (2.5 cm) and smaller diameter. (Avoid anvil blades, which strike one another and crush the stem of the plant you're pruning.)	$13 to $28 and up
Loppers	Long-handled shears with more leverage for cutting branches up to 2 inches (5 cm) thick. Use a pole pruner with extensions for high branches.	$25 to $90
Pruning Saw	Tote a fold-up model in your pocket. The protected blade stays sharp, and the tool is small enough so you can get into the middle of a shrub to cut a branch.	$20

262 Buy Shrubs and Trees

Whether you're transforming a stark, bare-dirt yard into a lush refuge or just filling in some bare spots in an established landscape, you first need to know a bit about how plants are sold and when and how to buy them. Here's an introduction to what you'll encounter at your neighborhood nursery, as well as online and in mail-order catalogs.

Steps

1 Learn the basics about shrubs and trees, called *woody plants,* as opposed to soft-tissued annual and perennial flowers, vegetables, ferns and such. Shrubs and trees form the foundation of any garden, whether blooming or not.

2 Distinguish between deciduous and evergreen plants. The former lose their leaves every year in the fall. This category includes most oaks, maples and forsythias. Southern magnolias, camellias and other evergreens keep their leaves year-round. Evergreens with needles and cones (pines, spruces and firs) are called *conifers.*

3 Understand your climate. Find out your climate zone on the USDA's Plant Hardiness Zone Map at the U.S. National Arboretum Web site (usna.usda.gov/Hardzone/ushzmap.html). In the Western states, refer to the climate zones in *Sunset's Western Garden Book.*

4 Select plants that will flourish in your climate zone. Look for this information on nursery tags, in garden books, on Web sites, or from experts at nurseries and county extension agencies. Ask about the particular demands of your garden, based on it's sun exposure and soil (clay, loamy, sandy and so on).

5 Start shopping in early spring or early fall, just ahead of the two best planting seasons. Fall is an excellent planting time except in the coldest climates.

6 Shop for plants while they are performing (blooming or displaying fall foliage) if you're landscaping with specific colors in mind, as long as the timing is not poor for planting (for example, in the heat of the summer).

7 Select plants sold in 1-gallon, 5-gallon and 15-gallon containers throughout the growing season or year-round in mild climates. Prices will depend not only on the plant's maturity, but on market factors including scarcity, difficulty of growing and transportation costs. The range can be huge: A common 1-gallon lavender may be only $5 or $6, while a magnificent 1-gallon rhododendron may cost $25 and up.

What to Look For

- Climate zone
- Container-grown plants year-round
- Balled-and-burlapped shrubs and trees in large sizes
- Bare-root plants in winter and spring

Tips

The younger and smaller the plant, the lower the cost, but the longer you'll have to wait for it to become large.

Mail-order and online catalogs offer great selections and good values, and prices may be half the nursery's, but shipping and handling costs (10 to 25 percent of the total shipment's price) can offset the savings.

Mail-order container sizes tend to be smaller than what you find at neighborhood nurseries. The catalog listing should indicate container size.

Home centers and warehouse stores offer bargains. Shop frequently so you can buy when new shipments come in.

8 Check out container-grown plants for signs of healthy, vigorous growth: new growth, no yellow leaves, compact shape, no leggy branches.

9 Inspect the roots to make sure they're not constricted (root-bound), which retards development after planting. Look for tell-tale roots poking through the container's drain holes or emerging above the soil. If you're not sure, ask a nursery worker to help you gently pull the tree or shrub out of the pot so you can take a look.

10 Shop for balled-and-burlapped plants mainly in spring and summer. B-and-B plants have been grown in fields, then dug up and wrapped in burlap. This growing method is used for large specimens, and is often the best way to buy trees. Cut away the burlap once the plant is sitting in the hole, and have someone let you know if the trunk is straight before you fill the hole.

11 Shop for bare-root trees and shrubs in winter and early spring. Mail-order and online suppliers often specialize in bare-root plants because of the ease of shipping them. Bare-root is usually the least expensive way to buy deciduous plants, especially roses and fruit trees, and is also a good way to get plants started (see 245 Buy the Perfect Rosebush). Bare-root plants are small—only 2 or 3 feet (60 to 90 cm) high—and the roots, stripped of soil, are protected in moist wood chips or sawdust and packed in a plastic bag.

12 Look for bare-root plants without broken branches. Avoid trees with crossing branches that form an X and rub against each other.

13 Pass over bare-root plants that are beginning to leaf out—a sign that the plant is breaking out of dormancy and will have greater demands for water and light.

14 Prune bare-root trees or shrubs before transplanting if the nursery has not already done so. Both tops and roots need to be cut back a bit to keep them in balance (this is best done by someone with expertise).

15 Get bare-root plants into the ground as soon as possible so they don't dry out. Before planting, bury the root mass in a pile of damp ground bark or other organic matter to protect it.

Become acquainted with the delivery patterns of local nurseries and garden centers. For the best selection, shop on Thursday or Friday before the weekend shoppers descend.

Warning

Take a pass on trees or shrubs that have been sitting around, particularly in a supermarket or other nontraditional plant source. High temperatures and artificial or insufficient light may have stressed these plants.

263 Buy a Hot Tub

What could possibly be better than climbing into steaming hot water at the end of the day and gazing over your garden while your cares soak away? Before you peel those clothes off, however, you'll need to make several decisions about your hot tub—chiefly regarding its size, cost, safety features and installation.

Steps

1 Decide where to place the hot tub. Take privacy, accessibility and aesthetics into consideration. Don't put the tub under overhanging trees or bushes that drop a lot of leaves.

2 Make sure the site can withstand 100 to 150 pounds per square foot (500 to 750 kg per square m). You'll want the strength and security of a sturdy deck or concrete slab.

3 Choose the size of a hot tub according to how many people will use it. The rule of thumb is to multiply 75 gallons (284 l) of water by the number of people for the total water capacity.

4 Determine your budget. Two-person hot tubs start at about $4,000 and six-person hot tubs start at $8,000 to $10,000. Ask for an estimate of monthly operating costs. Full insulation will save energy.

5 Consider what material you want. Today most hot tubs are made of acrylic, which is easier to take care of and longer lasting than fiberglass. Hot tubs made out of wood, most commonly redwood, are handsome but are likely to require more cleaning and upkeep, and they don't offer contoured seating as acrylic does. For a smaller investment, consider portable hot tubs made of vinyl (about $2,500).

6 Try before you buy. A good company will let you test hot tubs in the showroom. (You'll want to dress for the occasion.) Pay attention to the jets' noise level, how easy it is to use the control, and the seating arrangement (especially with premolded seats). Can you move around comfortably? Do you want a flexible seating arrangement?

7 Look for features and amenities to add to your pleasure and reduce any worries. Covers that lock with a key keep children safe and also help keep the tub clean. Thermostats keep the temperature under control. Safety switches, such as automatic shutoffs, are available.

8 Get the specifics about the dealer's delivery and installation service. Do you want the tub left in the driveway or brought right to its new location? Installation may add 5 to 10 percent to the cost, but you may find it worthwhile, especially given electrical and plumbing factors.

What to Look For

- Location
- Size
- Budget
- Materials
- Comfort
- Safety features
- Installation help

Tips

These days the terms *hot tub* and *spa* are used interchangeably for the typical acrylic tub, usually equipped with jets to circulate the water.

Look for a spa with a skim filter—located on the side of the pool just at the water's surface—instead of an underwater filter, which can catch hair and clothing when it pulls in water.

264 Buy an Outdoor Lighting System

Outdoor lighting can create dramatic moods as well as illuminate steps and walkways for nighttime safety. It's also a project most home owners feel comfortable tackling. Low-voltage lighting is safe, easy to install and relatively inexpensive, with eight-light kits available for less than $100 at home improvement or garden centers.

Steps

1 Decide what purpose the lighting system will serve. Do you want to highlight trees or statues dramatically, or brighten a path or entry? Do you want creative or purely functional lighting, or both?

2 Choose the style of fixture you want to use. Path lights can be hidden or visible, in styles that range from flower shapes (such as tulips) to colonial lanterns, while spotlights on trees or artwork may consist of bulbs only.

3 Choose the materials and finish for fixtures. Materials include aluminum, wood and copper. Black and verdigris finishes help the fixtures blend into the garden. Or match the finish to your home's color and style.

4 Consider dramatic touches such as highlighting the form of a tree by placing a light at its base (uplighting), great for illuminating trees with interesting forms, such as Japanese maples or oaks, and statues and water fountains. A lamp positioned above a gate or arbor can spill its light on the ground like moonlight.

5 Choose a low-voltage system designed for outdoor use. You can install or move such a system easily, because the wires are buried only a few inches underground, and it uses 12 volts instead of the household-standard 120 volts (transformers reduce the current).

6 Select the bulb wattage you want to use. Common choices range in brightness from 4 to 50 watts, typically from 18 to 24 watts. You decide how bright a bulb you want for its specific use—lighting the steps may be more important than lighting a tree.

7 Determine the size of transformer needed. Multiply the bulb wattage times the number of bulbs you need. Buy a transformer with the wattage that most closely matches this total. Don't go over that amount; if necessary, divide the bulbs into two groups and use two transformers. An automatic timer allows you to set lights to go on and off at specific times.

8 Arrange lights in a line, a T-shape or a circle, but remember that the farther the last bulb is from the transformer, the dimmer its light will be.

9 Consider a motion-sensor light for safety; it turns on the lights for a few minutes whenever it detects motion.

10 Check with a hardware store or an electrician for additional information.

What to Look For

- Style of lantern
- Bulb wattage
- Transformer load

Tips

For the most effective lighting, place fewer lights close together (within a 10-foot or 3 m area) rather than more lights farther apart.

For an exotic look, light ponds underwater with waterproof fixtures.

A solar lighting system is a good alternative wherever electricity is hard to come by or expensive, and sunshine is plentiful.

Consult a professional lighting designer or landscape architect for extensive lighting schemes.

REHOUSE STORES • BUY WHOLESALE • GET OUT OF DEBT • BUY NOTHING • BUY HAPPINESS • BUY A BETTER MOUSETRAP • BUY TIM
MEONE'S FAVOR • BUY POSTAGE STAMPS WITHOUT GOING TO THE POST OFFICE • TIP PROPERLY • BUY HEALTHY FAST FOOD • BUY SU
TING SERVICE • SELL YOURSELF ON AN ONLINE DATING SERVICE • SELL YOURSELF TO YOUR GIRLFRIEND/BOYFRIEND'S FAMILY • BUY L
HOOSE FILM FOR YOUR CAMERA • BUY RECHARGEABLE BATTERIES • DONATE TO A GOOD CAUSE • HOLD A PROFITABLE GARAGE SALE
STUDENT DISCOUNTS • BUY FLOWERS WHOLESALE • GET A PICTURE FRAMED • HIRE A MOVER • HIRE A PERSONAL ORGANIZER • FIN
EAT BIRTHDAY PRESENT FOR UNDER $10 • SELECT GOOD CHAMPAGNE • BUY A DIAMOND • BUY JEWELRY MADE OF PRECIOUS METALS
IDESMAIDS' DRESSES • HIRE AN EVENT COORDINATOR • HIRE A BARTENDER FOR A PARTY • HIRE A PHOTOGRAPHER • HIRE A CATERER
Y AN ANNIVERSARY GIFT • ARRANGE ENTERTAINMENT FOR A PARTY • COMMISSION A FIREWORKS SHOW • BUY A MOTHER'S DAY GIFT
T • SELECT A THANKSGIVING TURKEY • BUY A HOUSEWARMING GIFT • PURCHASE HOLIDAY CARDS • BUY CHRISTMAS STOCKING STU
E HIGH ROLLERS ROOM IN VEGAS, BABY • BUY SOMEONE A STAR • PAY A RANSOM • GET HOT TICKETS • HIRE A LIMOUSINE • BUY A C
AM • BUY A PERSONAL JET • ACQUIRE A TELEVISION NETWORK • ACQUIRE A BODY GUARD • BOOK A LUXURY CRUISE AROUND THE WO
OROUGHBRED RACEHORSE • BUY A VILLA IN TUSCANY • HIRE A PERSONAL CHEF • PURCHASE CUBAN CIGARS • HIRE A GHOSTWRITER
TNESS • MAKE BAIL • DONATE YOUR BODY TO SCIENCE • HIRE YOURSELF OUT AS A MEDICAL GUINEA PIG • SELL PLASMA • SELL YOUR
LLEGE EDUCATION • BUY AND SELL STOCKS • CHOOSE A STOCKBROKER • DAY-TRADE (OR NOT) • BUY ANNUITIES • BUY AND SELL MU
Y PERSONAL FINANCE SOFTWARE • CHOOSE A TAX PREPARER • SET UP A LEMONADE STAND • SELL YOUR PRODUCT ON TV • HIRE A C
SINESS IDEA • BUY A SMALL BUSINESS • BUY A FRANCHISE • LEASE RETAIL SPACE • LEASE INDUSTRIAL SPACE • LEASE OFFICE SPACE
B-SITE • BUY ADVERTISING ON THE WEB • SELL YOUR ART • HIRE A PERSONAL COACH • SELL ON THE CRAFT CIRCUIT • HIRE A LITERA
LING BUSINESS • BUY A HOT DOG STAND • SHOP FOR A MORTGAGE • REFINANCE YOUR HOME • SAVE BIG BUCKS ON YOUR MORTGA
LL A FIXER-UPPER • SELL THE FARM • SELL MINERAL RIGHTS • SELL A HOUSE • SELL A HOUSE WITHOUT A REAL ESTATE AGENT • OBTA
OK A VACATION RENTAL • BUY A CONDOMINIUM • RENT AN APARTMENT OR HOUSE • OBTAIN RENTER'S INSURANCE • BUY A LOFT IN M
RNISH YOUR STUDIO APARTMENT • BUY USED FURNITURE • BUY DOOR AND WINDOW LOCKS • CHOOSE AN ORIENTAL CARPET • BUY
RRANTIES ON APPLIANCES • FIND PERIOD FIXTURES • BUY A BED AND MATTRESS • HIRE AN INTERIOR DESIGNER • HIRE A FENG SHUI
N • BUY A WHIRLPOOL TUB • BUY A SHOWERHEAD • BUY A TOILET • CHOOSE A FAUCET • BUY GLUES AND ADHESIVES • CHOOSE WIN
CHEN CABINETS • CHOOSE A KITCHEN COUNTERTOP • BUY GREEN HOUSEHOLD CLEANERS • STOCK YOUR HOME TOOL KIT • BUY A
ENTRY DOOR • BUY A GARAGE-DOOR OPENER • BUY LUMBER FOR A DIY PROJECT • HOW TO SELECT ROOFING • HIRE A CONTRACTO
OWERS FOR YOUR GARDEN • SELECT PEST CONTROLS • BUY SOIL AMENDMENTS • BUY MULCH • BUY A COMPOSTER • BUY FERTILIZ
Y KOI FOR YOUR FISH POND • BUY A STORAGE SHED • HIRE AN ARBORIST • BUY BASIC GARDEN TOOLS • BUY SHRUBS AND TREES •
LECT KITCHEN KNIVES • DECIPHER FOOD LABELS • SELECT HERBS AND SPICES • STOCK YOUR KITCHEN WITH STAPLES • EQUIP A KIT
OUNTAIN OYSTERS • PURCHASE LOCAL HONEY • CHOOSE POULTRY • SELECT FRESH FISH AND SHELLFISH • SELECT RICE • PURCHAS
EADS • BUY ARTISAN CHEESES • PURCHASE KOSHER FOOD • BUY FOOD IN BULK • CHOOSE COOKING OILS • SELECT OLIVE OIL • SEL
FFEEMAKER OR ESPRESSO MACHINE • PURCHASE A KEG OF BEER • BUY ALCOHOL IN A DRY COUNTY • CHOOSE A MICROBREW • OR
ULATION PREDICTOR KIT • PICK A PREGNANCY TEST KIT • CHOOSE BIRTH CONTROL • FIND THE RIGHT OB-GYN • HIRE A MIDWIFE OR
OOSE DIAPERS • BUY OR RENT A BREAST PUMP • CHOOSE A CAR SEAT • BUY CHILD-PROOFING SUPPLIES • FIND FABULOUS CHILDC
CKYARD PLAY STRUCTURE • FIND A GREAT SUMMER CAMP • SELL GIRL SCOUT COOKIES • BUY BRACES FOR YOUR KID • BUY TOYS
A MODEL • SELL USED BABY GEAR, TOYS, CLOTHES AND BOOKS • FIND A COUPLES COUNSELOR • HIRE A FAMILY LAWYER • BUY PR
PENSES • GET VIAGRA ONLINE • PURCHASE A TOOTHBRUSH • BUY MOISTURIZERS AND ANTIWRINKLE CREAMS • SELECT PAIN RELIEF
PPLIES • SELECT HAIR-CARE PRODUCTS • BUY WAYS TO COUNTER HAIR LOSS • BUY A WIG OR HAIRPIECE • BUY A NEW BODY • GET
NICURIST • GET WHITER TEETH • SELECT EYEGLASSES AND SUNGLASSES • HIRE A PERSONAL TRAINER • SIGN UP FOR A YOGA CLAS
EA MARKET • RENT SPACE AT AN ANTIQUE MALL • BUY AT AUCTION • KNOW WHAT YOUR COLLECTIBLES ARE WORTH • DICKER WITH
COGNIZE THE REAL MCCOY • BUY COINS • BUY AN ANTIQUE AMERICAN QUILT • BUY AN ANTIQUE FLAG • LIQUIDATE YOUR BEANIE BA
WNSHOP • BUY AND SELL COMIC BOOKS • BUY AND SELL SPORTS MEMORABILIA • SELL YOUR BASEBALL-CARD COLLECTIONS • CHO
MPUTER • BUY PRINTER PAPER • BUY A PRINTER • BUY COMPUTER PERIPHERALS • CHOOSE AN INTERNET SERVICE PROVIDER • GET
Y BLANK CDS • BUY AN MP PLAYER • CHOOSE A DVD PLAYER • BUY A VCR • CHOOSE A PERSONAL DIGITAL ASSISTANT • CHOOSE MO
GITAL CAMCORDER • DECIDE ON A DIGITAL CAMERA • BUY A HOME AUTOMATION SYSTEM • BUY A STATE-OF-THE-ART SOUND SYSTEM
IVERSAL REMOTE • BUY A HOME THEATER SYSTEM • BUY VIRTUAL-REALITY FURNITURE • BUY TWO-WAY RADIOS • BUY A MOBILE EN
ONEY • GET TRAVEL INSURANCE • PICK THE IDEAL LUGGAGE • FLY FOR FREE • BID FOR A SLED RIDE ON THE ALASKAN IDITAROD TRAI
REIGN OFFICIAL • GET A EURAIL PASS • TAKE AN ITALIAN BICYCLE VACATION • CHOOSE A CHEAP CRUISE • BOOK A HOTEL PACKAGE
OTLAND • BUY A SAPPHIRE IN BANGKOK • HIRE A RICKSHA IN YANGON • TAKE SALSA LESSONS IN CUBA • BUY A CAMERA IN HONG K
ST BASEBALL GLOVE • ORDER UNIFORMS FOR A SOFTBALL TEAM • BUY ANKLE AND KNEE BRACES • BUY GOLF CLUBS • JOIN AN EL
OWMOBILE • BUY A PERSONAL WATERCRAFT • HIRE A SCUBA INSTRUCTOR • BUY A SKATEBOARD AND PROTECTIVE GEAR • BUY SKA
EATHER ACTIVITIES • SELL USED SKIS • BUY A SNOWBOARD, BOOTS AND BINDINGS • BUY SKI BOOTS • BUY A BICYCLE • SELL YOUR
Y A BACKPACK • BUY A BACKPACKING STOVE • BUY A KAYAK • BUY A PERSONAL FLOTATION DEVICE • BUY A WET SUIT • BUY A SUR
DER CUSTOM-MADE COWBOY BOOTS • BUY CLOTHES ONLINE • FIND SPECIALTY SIZES • BUY THE PERFECT COCKTAIL DRESS • BUY
Y A MAN'S SUIT • HIRE A TAILOR • BUY CUSTOM-TAILORED CLOTHES IN ASIA • BUY A BRIEFCASE • SHOP FOR A LEATHER JACKET •
TE MONITOR • SELECT A WATCH • BUY KIDS' CLOTHES • CHOOSE CHILDREN'S SHOES • PURCHASE CLOTHES AT OUTLET SHOPS • BU

Food & Drink

265 Buy Organic Produce

Buying organic food is a good idea—for both your own health and the environment—but it's more important with some produce than with others. Strawberries, for instance, tend to soak up toxins from pesticides, while grapefruit is protected by its thick skin. Many grocery stores and farmers' markets have a broad selection of organic foods.

MORE LIKELY TO BE CONTAMINATED Important to Buy Organic		LESS LIKELY TO BE CONTAMINATED Buy Organic When Available; Conventionally Grown Is OK	
Apples	Peaches	Asparagus	Grapefruit
Apricots	Peppers	Avocados	Kiwi
Celery	Red raspberries	Bananas	Mangoes
Cherries	Spinach	Blueberries	Okra
Grapes	Strawberries	Broccoli	Onions
Green beans		Brussels sprouts	Papayas
Nectarines		Cabbage	Pineapples
		Cauliflower	Plums
		Eggplants	Radishes
			Watermelons

Tips

Farms must meet strict growing laws and practices to qualify as organic grade. Farmers pay yearly for the title, which is one reason organic produce can be more expensive.

Join a community-supported agricultural farm (see LocalHarvest.org), which sends you a weekly box of organic, seasonal goodies.

Warning

Always wash your fruits and vegetables. Even organic produce can carry residual pesticides or waste from animals that share the fields.

266 Choose a Perfect Peach

Juicy, succulent peaches are best when left to ripen in the sun, then plucked from a tree and eaten on the spot. If you can't find your way to an orchard to pick your own, keep these tips in mind when shopping for ripe peaches.

Steps

1 Shop at a farmers' market for the ripest and fleshiest peaches possible. Most likely the fruit was handpicked a day or so earlier. Talk to the farmer about the different characteristics.

2 Smell the peach. Is it perfumey and sweet-scented?

3 Inspect the peach's surface. The skin shouldn't be bruised in any way; it should have a soft, downy covering of white fuzz; and it should be streaked with both pink and yellow.

4 Taste both white and yellow peaches. Most say the spectacular flavor of white peaches is where it's at, but your definition of perfection will depend on your own taste buds.

5 Eat that exquisite peach as soon as you get it home. Or savor peaches throughout the year, by bottling into preserves or chutney.

What to Look For

- Farmers' markets
- Fragrance
- Unblemished skin
- Flavor
- Varieties

Tip

Keep peaches at the top of your grocery bag and handle with care. Ripe peaches blemish and tear easily.

267 Buy and Sell at Farmers' Markets

You can't find fresher food unless you grow it yourself. Farmers' markets are a fabulous place to hunt down fresh produce, artisan breads and cheeses, nuts, oils and preserves. Plus, you're supporting small farms. For a nationwide directory of farmers' markets, contact the U.S. Department of Agriculture (www.ams.usda.gov/farmersmarkets).

Steps

Selling

1 Go to the market and browse the stalls. You'll want to find out the prices and stock of any direct competitors.

2 Inquire with the executive director or market manager about setting up a stand. Some markets require potential sellers to fill out an application and purchase a permanent space; others rent stalls for a nominal week-to-week fee, usually $5 to $15.

3 Ask about the market's traffic to determine how much merchandise to bring. You can also query experienced vendors and the market manager to get their recommendation on how much of your olallieberry jam you can expect to spread around.

4 Make your stall inviting with colorful tablecloths and umbrellas for shade. Only put out 10 to 12 of each type of produce in a way that shoppers can pick out the ones they want without toppling piles. Keep your supply cool to stay fresh.

5 Give out samples of your wares. Free food attracts a crowd; tasty food makes a sale.

Buying

1 Don't make a list for the farmers' market as you would for the grocery store. Instead, shop with your eyes and nose, smelling and squeezing produce to find the season's best. Taste samples to choose between offerings.

2 Make the full rounds of the market before you throw down any cash. Find out who has the best crop of tomatoes or the choicest summer melons.

3 Live on the edge and buy something you've never tried before. Ask the farmer how to prepare it; many will share recipes.

4 Don't succumb to temptation and overbuy. The reason to shop at a farmers' market is to get fresh, ripe food. If it hides in your refrigerator and goes bad, you might as well go to a supermarket.

What to Look For

- USDA-listed markets
- Competition's stock and prices
- Market managers
- Inventory to sell
- Sights and smells
- New ingredients
- The right amount

Tips

Bring lots of cash. Most sellers do not take checks or credit cards—or if they do, you may pay more for that just-picked flavor.

Bring a large bag to take produce home. These markets don't usually pack your goods in paper or plastic.

268 Select Kitchen Knives

Any way you slice it, knives are the most important tool in the kitchen. A sharp blade and sturdy handle will help you slice and chop more efficiently. Invest in quality knives such as Wustoff, Henkel or Global to take your culinary clout to the next level. *Iron Chef,* watch out!

Steps

1 Look for knives made from one piece of metal, meaning that the metal blade extends down into the handle. They'll be more durable and sturdy.

2 Get a handle on materials: Do you like the sleek feel of synthetic materials, the cool grip of metal or the warmth of wood? Hold the knives as if you were chopping to get a feel for their heft and balance.

3 Invest in an all-purpose 8- or 10-inch (20- or 25-cm) chef's knife, considered the workhorse of the kitchen, and a 2-inch (5-cm) paring knife. Individual knives run between $20 and $100.

4 Add a 6-inch (15-cm) chopping knife and a 4-inch (10-cm) boning knife, and a serrated bread knife to round out your collection.

5 Opt for an eight- or ten-piece knife set if you can afford it (they run from $300 to $700). The set comes with all the crucial pieces along with extras like a meat slicer, kitchen shears or a sharpener.

What to Look For

- Solid metal blades
- Metal or wood handles
- Chef and paring knife
- Additional knives
- Knife sets

Tips

A sharp blade prevents accidents because it slices easily and effectively. A dull blade can cause clumsy slips that nick your hand or fingers.

Swipe blades on a steel or stone before each use; you'll only need to pay for professional sharpening yearly.

Dry blades completely to avoid bacteria growth in your knife block.

269 Decipher Food Labels

Food labels are a table of contents for prepared foods such as breads, cereals, canned and frozen foods, and those sodas we guzzle to excess. Labels are based on a diet of 2,000 calories a day, but requirements vary for each person depending on age, weight, gender and activity level. Read on to be an educated consumer and a healthy eater.

Steps

1 Read the ingredients. Items appear in descending order from largest to smallest amount. For example, if water is listed first on a bottle of juice, it is the primary ingredient.

2 Be aware of serving sizes. If a package contains five servings, the food label's calorie content is for *one* of those servings.

3 Examine *Calories* and *Calories from Fat.* Read on to *Total Fat,* an indication of how much fat (in grams) is in a single serving. Below that, the fats are broken down into saturated fats (which are solid at room temperature, come from animal products and contribute to heart disease) and unsaturated fats (which may be broken down further into monounsaturated and polyunsaturated fats,

What to Look For

- Order of ingredients
- Serving size
- Calories from fat
- Saturated fats
- Cholesterol and sodium
- Calorie-free, fat-free and sugar-free

Tip

If you're looking for low-fat foods, a good test is to divide a serving's total number of calories by its total grams of fat. You should end up with roughly 3 g of fat per 100 calories.

and are less associated with heart problems because they don't raise cholesterol levels as saturated fats do).

4 Stay on top of cholesterol and sodium content, especially if you have high cholesterol, heart disease or other health concerns.

5 Be skeptical of the terms *light or lite,* which can refer to the color or texture of a food. However, by law the term *free* indicates minuscule amounts of fats, cholesterol, sugar, sodium or calories. *Calorie-free* means fewer than 5 calories per serving, and *sugar-free* and *fat-free* both mean less than 0.5 g per serving. *Light* can indicate either 50 percent or less of the fat than the comparison food or ⅓ fewer calories than the comparison food.

270 Select Herbs and Spices

Herbs are fragrant and tender leaves of plants that don't have woody stems, such as chives, basil and parsley. Spices come from the bark, seeds, fruit, roots or stems of various plants and trees—for example, from cinnamon bark, saffron strands or cayenne pepper. Used well, both herbs and spices enhance flavor, but they can easily overpower a dish in too-large amounts.

Steps

1 Grow your own herbs, or buy fresh herbs only as you need them. (Mint and basil should almost always be bought fresh—there's really no substitute.) Submerge stems in a small glass of water (as you would a bouquet of flowers) to keep them fresh for up to 10 days.

2 Choose fresh herbs that have a clean fragrance and a bright color without any browning or wilting.

3 Stock up on dried herbs to have on hand for impromptu cooking: oregano, thyme and tarragon (see 271 Stock Your Kitchen with Staples).

4 Look at the color of dried herbs. They should retain some of their original color and not be too brown.

5 Smell spices before buying them. They should be aromatic and pungent.

6 Buy dried herbs and spices from a busy market with a high turnaround so you know they haven't been sitting on the shelves for six months.

7 Browse farmers' markets for fresh seasonal herbs. You can also find vendors selling bunches of dried herbs, sometimes with more exotic offerings than the grocery store carries. See 294 Buy Ethnic Ingredients and 267 Buy and Sell at Farmers' Markets.

What to Look For

- Fresh herbs
- Dried herbs
- Clean scent
- Bright color
- Aromatic smell
- High turnaround
- Farmers' markets

Tips

The more airtight your storage container, the longer your spices will last. Date spices when you buy them and don't keep them for more than six months, after which their flavor fades.

Grind whole spices, like cumin and mustard, at home in a clean coffee grinder.

Mix it up with barbecue spice blends and rubs, curry spice blends, and herbes de Provençe, made from a variety of ingredients.

Have you ever opened your fridge and in a fit of self-pity groaned, "There's nothing to eat!"? If you fill your pantry and refrigerator with the basics below, you can throw together a darn good dinner. Create a simple and savory white bean soup from canned cannellini beans, garlic and chicken stock. Or throw together cooked penne with leftover cheeses, milk and a pinch of dried mustard, cover with bread crumbs and pop it under the broiler for a real treat.

DRY GOODS

- Baking powder, double acting
- Beans, canned: cannellini, kidney, chickpeas
- Beans, fresh: black, Great Northern or navy, limas, pintos, lentils, split peas, black-eyed peas
- Canned low-sodium chicken and beef broth
- Canned tomatoes: chopped, whole and puréed
- Chocolate: bittersweet, unsweetened, semisweet; cocoa powder
- Cornstarch
- Cream of tartar
- Dried fruits: apricots, raisins, currants, cranberries, cherries

- Flour: all-purpose and cornmeal
- Garlic
- Gelatin, powdered, unflavored
- Honey
- Instant espresso for baking
- Liquor: Cognac or brandy, Grand Marnier, port, Calvados, framboise
- Oils: virgin and/or extra-virgin olive oil and safflower
- Onions
- Pasta, dried: angel hair (capellini), spaghetti, linguine, fettuccine, macaroni, penne and rigatoni
- Peanut butter
- Polenta, dry
- Rice: arborio, basmati and wild

- Shallots
- Soy sauce
- Sugar: granulated, confectioners', brown, superfine
- Syrups: corn (light and dark), maple, molasses
- Tabasco sauce
- Tea: black and herbal
- Vanilla extract
- Vinegar: sherry, red, white and rice wine, cider, champagne, balsamic
- Wines: dry sherry, Madeira, Marsala, dry Burgundy, dry Chardonnay
- Worcestershire sauce

HERBS AND SPICES

- Allspice: ground or whole
- Aniseed
- Basil
- Bay leaves
- Caraway seeds
- Cardamom
- Celery seeds
- Chili powder
- Cinnamon: ground and sticks

- Cloves: ground and whole
- Cumin: seeds and ground
- Curry powder
- Dill
- Fennel
- Ginger: ground and crystallized
- Marjoram
- Mustard: seed and powdered
- Nutmeg: whole and ground
- Oregano

- Paprika: sweet and hot
- Pepper: cayenne, red-pepper flakes
- Poppy seeds
- Sage
- Salt: kosher and sea salt
- Sesame seeds
- Thyme
- Turmeric
- Whole peppercorns

REFRIGERATOR

- Butter, unsalted
- Capers
- Cheese: Parmesan, cream
- Coffee, ground
- Eggs
- Ketchup

- Mayonnaise
- Milk
- Mustard: Dijon and whole-grain
- Preserves: jellies and jams
- Sesame oil
- Tomato paste tube

FREEZER

- Bread crumbs
- Chicken and/or beef broth
- Coffee beans, whole
- Frozen blueberries, raspberries
- Nuts: almonds, pecans, peanuts, pine nuts, pistachios, walnuts

272 Equip a Kitchen

It can take years to assemble the perfect array of nifty gadgets, trophy appliances and disaster-proof cookware. Equipping a kitchen is a truly personal undertaking. Depending on whether you intend to become a gourmet cook or pastry chef, you'll need different pieces of equipment. Here are the basics for a broad range of cooking interests. See 207 Buy Household Appliances.

LARGE APPLIANCES	SMALL APPLIANCES	POTS AND PANS
Dishwasher	° Coffeemaker	2 or 3 saucepans
Gas or electric oven and range (*gas ranges* are best overall for well-regulated heat, *gas ovens* for roasting and baking bread, and *electric* and *convection ovens* for baking)	° Blender	2 or 3 skillets
	° Electric hand mixer	Dutch oven with lid
	° Food processor	Nonstick omelette pan
	° Knife set	Roasting pan and rack
	° Standing mixer	Stockpot
	° Teakettle	Optional: wok, fish poacher, crêpe pan, grill pan, double boiler, steamer
Refrigerator and freezer	° Toaster or toaster oven	
Optional: microwave, outdoor barbecue, wine refrigerator	° Optional: immersion blender, crock pot, espresso machine, rice cooker, ice cream maker	

BAKING DISHES AND EQUIPMENT	GADGETS AND TOOLS	
2 muffin tins	° 2 large wooden cutting boards	° Slotted spoons
3 or 4 flexible rubber spatulas	° Baster	° Soup ladle
3 or 4 long-handled wooden spoons	° Bottle opener	° Strainers
8 to 12 ovenproof ramekins	° Can opener	° Tongs
Bundt pan	° Citrus zester	° Vegetable peeler
Casserole dishes	° Coffee grinder	° Wine opener
Flour sifter	° Colander	° Optional: waffle iron, kitchen scale, pasta maker, spice grinder
Half-sheet or jelly-roll pan	° Four-sided grater	
Measuring cups	° Funnel	
Measuring spoons	° Garlic press	
Pastry brush	° Juicer	
Rolling pin	° Lemon reamer	
Sauce and balloon whisks	° Long-handled fork or carving fork	
Soufflé dish	° Meat pounder	
Springform pan	° Meat thermometer	
Stacking mixing bowls	° Metal skewers for kebabs or trussing meats	
Wire rack	° Metal spatulas	
Optional: cookie cutters, pastry bag with decorating tips, palette knife for icing cakes, 3 cake pans (square and round), 2 fluted tart pans	° Nutmeg grater	
	° Pepper grinder	
	° Potato masher or ricer	
	° Salad spinner	

Choose Fresh Produce

There's nothing like eating the season's first crop of fruits and vegetables—biting into sweet, fleshy strawberries in the spring or tasting summer's succulent melons. Choosing the freshest produce possible is mostly a matter of eating in season—something we supermarket shoppers have lost sight of.

SPRING	WHAT TO LOOK FOR	HOW TO STORE	THE DISH
Apricots	Color should be uniform.	Store at room temperature, or in refrigerator if fully ripe.	Apricot tart with frangipane cream.
Artichokes	Should be tightly closed, feel firm and heavy, with no discoloration.	Keep in a closed plastic or brown bag in the refrigerator.	Steamed with fresh caper-lemon aioli for dipping.
Asparagus	Spears should be firm and bright green (except white or purple asparagus).	Refrigerate in open plastic bag.	Grilled asparagus with balsamic vinegar and salt.
Avocados	Squeeze gently for softness (for immediate use); will ripen uncut at home. Too soft means going bad.	Store at room temperature.	Mashed in guacamole or diced with mangos and red onions for fish topping.
Beets	Fresh and unwilted greens. Use beets quickly, before sugars turn to starch.	Store in open plastic bags in refrigerator.	Roast beets, slice and layer with goat cheese.
Carrots	Bright green tops, crisp, deep orange color.	Store in closed plastic bag with tops removed.	Glaze with honey and bourbon.
Cauliflower	Tightly packed florets without discoloration.	Store in closed plastic bag in refrigerator.	Blanch and cook with cream and parmesan.
Cherries	Shiny, firm, not squishy. Deep scarlet or yellow.	Refrigerate. Don't wash until you're about to eat.	In trifle with kirsch, custard and cake.
English (Garden) Peas	Pods filled but not bursting.	Refrigerate in open plastic bag.	In salad, as side dish or in risotto.
Fava Beans	Slightly fuzzy to the touch. Unblemished pods.	Best cooked and eaten immediately.	Purée for crostini.
Radishes	Firm and smooth. Small radishes tend to be milder.	Refrigerate in open plastic bag.	Shave over spinach salad with goat cheese.
Rhubarb	Crisp stalks in red, pink, green or speckled color.	Remove greens. Chill up to four days.	With strawberry in tarts.
Spinach	Bright green leaves (flat or crinkled).	Wrap stalks in damp paper towel and refrigerate in crisper.	Use in salads, wilted in pasta or as side dish.

SUMMER	WHAT TO LOOK FOR	HOW TO STORE	THE DISH
Berries	Smell for aroma. Check underside of carton to make sure it isn't berry-stained or moldy.	Store at room temperature if using same day. Store in refrigerator on paper towel–lined plate.	Best eaten fresh or in compote with ice cream.
Corn	Silk should look fresh with unwilted leaves. Kernels should be plump, filled out.	Store in crisper. Cook as soon as possible.	Barbecue, then shave off kernels to toss in tomato salad.
Cucumbers	Firm skins, not limp or shriveled. English have smooth skin; Japanese have wrinkled skin.	Store in refrigerator away from apples and tomatoes for up to one week.	Dice and add with garlic and lemon juice to plain yogurt for vegetable dip.
Eggplant	Shiny skin with firm, even texture. Small to medium are younger and sweeter.	Store in crisper.	Marinate in balsamic and olive oil and grill.
Figs	Best when ripe and soft, almost shriveled. No mold.	Store in paper towel–lined closed plastic bag in the refrigerator for two to three days.	Stuff with goat cheese, wrap with pancetta (Italian bacon) and grill.
Garlic	Firm, plump heads with no shoots.	Store in cool, dark, dry place.	Cut off top, drizzle with olive oil, wrap in foil and roast at 400 degrees F (200 degrees C) for one hour. Spread on crostini.
Green Beans	Crisp and bright.	Store in crisper.	Add to pasta and salads.
Melons	Cantaloupes: tan skin (not green). Honeydews: creamy yellow skin. All, except watermelons, smell sweet at stem end. Shouldn't hear seeds rattling when shaken.	Store unripened at room temperature. Store ripe in refrigerator.	Slice and enjoy.
Nectarines	Avoid fruit with green tinge. Flesh gives slightly to pressure.	Keep at room temperature.	Cut in half and grill, then fill pit with mascarpone.
Onions	Sweet summer onions should be firm.	Store spring onions in refrigerator and sweet onions in cool, dry place.	Caramelize for sweet pizza topping.
Plums	Uniform color and some spring when pressed.	Store in refrigerator.	Slice in fruit compote or use as tart filling.

SUMMER	WHAT TO LOOK FOR	HOW TO STORE	THE DISH
Potatoes	Avoid sprouts. Small have better flavor.	Keep in cool, dark place.	Roast with sea salt, herbs and olive oil.
Strawberries	Full red berries with some shine. No trace of mold.	Use as soon as possible; store in crisper.	Slice in spinach salad.
Summer Squash	Not too scratched or limp; look for juice coming out of stem to tell if truly fresh.	Keep in crisper or at room temperature.	Slice and grill with olive oil and salt.
Tomatoes	Firm but not hard, aromatic, full color. Cracking on skin doesn't matter.	Store at room temperature out of sun.	Steam, slice and layer with buffalo mozzarella and fresh basil, sprinkle with olive oil.

FALL	WHAT TO LOOK FOR	HOW TO STORE	THE DISH
Apples	No bruising or mushy, soft skin. Should be firm—best test is taste.	Refrigerate or keep at room temperature.	Gravenstein, Jonathan, pippin or Rome Beauty for baking. Fuji, Pink Lady or Granny Smith for eating.
Arugula	Deep green; avoid yellow leaves.	Paper towel–lined open plastic bags in refrigerator.	Use in salads, wilted in pastas or to make pesto.
Broccoli	Completely green with no yellowing; should smell sweet, not like cabbage.	Refrigerate in open plastic bag.	Braise in chicken stock with red-pepper flakes.
Brussels Sprouts	Buy on stalk. Avoid yellow or brown leaves.	Refrigerate.	Slice thin and sauté in olive oil with pancetta.
Fennel	Smooth white bulbs, firm to touch.	Keep stalk attached.	Slice thin and marinate in olive oil and lemon.
Hard-shelled Squash	Butternut, pumpkin or kabocha; no soft spots.	Store in cool, dark place.	Roasted for side dishes or puréed in soups.
Pears	Color and texture varies; best when firm with some give at stem end.	Room temperature or in crisper.	On gorgonzola crostini.
Persimmons	Hachiya: squishy when ripe. Fuyu: firm and orange.	Keep at room temperature.	Bake in cookies and bread pudding.

FALL	WHAT TO LOOK FOR	HOW TO STORE	THE DISH
Pomegranates	Should feel heavy; with a few cracks.	Store at room temperature.	Crush kernels and add juice to champagne for apéritif.
Sweet Peppers	Firm and crisp with glossy skins.	Store at room temperature.	Roast and purée for pasta sauce.
Sweet Potatoes	Firm, smooth skin with no soft spots.	Store in cool, dark place.	Roast with coarse salt and olive oil.

WINTER	WHAT TO LOOK FOR	HOW TO STORE	THE DISH
Broccoli Rabe	Green color with no yellow tinge.	Store in closed plastic bag in refrigerator.	Braise for side dish or sauté for pasta.
Cabbage	Firm, somewhat shiny, bright color.	Store in crisper.	Use in soups, or as wrapping for meat fillings.
Celery Root	Look for fresh tops; trim off hairy stems and skin.	Store in open plastic bag lined with damp paper towel.	Grate and toss with mustard-caper dressing.
Citrus	Should feel heavy.	In crisper for up to two weeks.	Enjoy alone; use juice in salad dressings, or slice in salads.
Greens: Chard, Kale, Mustard	Rich, dark leaves with no yellowing.	Store in damp towel–lined open plastic bag.	Cook in soups, or braise with olive oil, garlic and chili pepper.
Leeks	White stalk; fresh, well-hydrated top.	Store in crisper.	Slice for gratins or sauté with pancetta and peas for pasta.
Parsnips	Whiter means fresher.	Store in crisper.	Roast with other root vegetables.
Rutabagas	Smooth, firm skin.	Store in cool, dark place.	Cook in soup or roast with other root vegetables and herbs.
Turnips	Greens fresh and unwilted; keep for some time.	Wash when ready to use; store at room temperature.	Add to last 40 minutes of pot roast baking.

There are really only two cuts of meat: tough and tender. Tough cuts of meat contain the muscle, which requires braising or stewing to become tender; tender cuts demand quick cooking to retain their texture and seal in their flavor. Look for high-quality cuts of whatever type of meat you are buying.

Steps

1 Choose a grade of meat.

- Beef is divided into five grades based on fat content, marbling and quality. Look for *select* (the least amount of fat; sold in grocery stores), *choice* (fattier than select, leaner than prime), and *prime* (the well-marbled cuts high-end restaurants serve, fattier but also more flavorful). The lowest two grades of inferior meat, *commercial* and *utility*, aren't typically sold in grocery stores, and home cooks and aspiring chefs should avoid them.

- Lamb is usually sold as choice in grocery stores and has a purple U.S. Department of Agriculture inspection stamp to signify that it came from a healthy animal.

- Pork is graded as "USDA government inspected."

- Veal is graded either prime (milk fed for 60 days before slaughter) or choice, which is found at many grocery stores.

2 Choose beef with minimal outer fat. The fat should be creamy in color, and bones should be soft-looking with a reddish color. The meat should be firm, fine-textured and a light cherry red. Cook it to an internal temperature of 130 degrees F (54 C) for rare and 140 degrees F (60 C) for medium.

3 Look for lamb that's been butchered at five to seven months or younger. It has a more delicate flavor and texture than older lamb or mutton, which takes on a rich gamy flavor. Meat from high-quality young lambs is fine-textured, firm and lean. It's pink in color, and the cross sections of bones are red, moist and porous. The external fat should be firm, white and not too thick. Cook lamb to an internal temperature of 135 degrees F (57 C) for legs and 140 degrees F (60 C) for ribs.

4 Select pork that's pinkish-white to pink in color (loin meat is whiter than shoulder meat) and firm to the touch. Well-marbled pork produces tenderer results. Cook pork to an internal temperature of 150 degrees F (65 C).

5 Ask for prime-quality veal, with almost white to very light pink, firm, velvety and moist flesh. Veal is butchered young, so most of its meat is tender. Bones should be bright red, small and fairly soft to the touch. The fat covering the meat should be slight and whitish in color. Cook veal to an internal temperature of 175 degrees F (80 C).

Tips

Large cuts of meat will generally keep in the refrigerator four to five days.

See 277 Buy Natural Beef.

Warning

Avoid beef with yellowish or gray fat, absolutely no marbling, a deep red color, two-tone coloration, coarse texture or excessive moisture. You'll be able to tell excess moisture by a mushy or wet-looking piece of meat, or if the shrink-wrap is filled with condensation.

MEAT CUT	TOUGH OR TENDER	HOW TO PREPARE
Beef		
Brisket	Tough	Braise
Rib	Tender	Grill, broil
Rib eye (or Delmonico steak)	Tender	Grill, broil
Loin or sirloin (or strip steak)	Tender	Grill, broil, pan-fry
Filet (center cut filet is Châteaubriand; near the end of the filet is filet mignon and tournedos)	Tough	Marinate and grill or broil
Flank (London broil)	Tender	Sear, then braise and roast
Roasts	Tough	Roast
Skirt and plate (can include short ribs)	Tender	Grill or broil steaks; braise ribs
Steaks (T-bone, porterhouse, sirloin)	Tough	Grill, broil
Stew meat	Tender	Braise, stew
Chops	Tough	Grill, broil, roast, sauté, pan-fry
Shoulder and chuck	Tough	Braise
Rump and round	Tough	Braise
Lamb		
Chops	Tender	Grill, broil, roast, sauté, pan-fry
Rack of lamb (ribs)	Tender	Broil, roast
Shank (leg)	Tough	Braise, stew
Shoulder	Tough	Braise, roast, stew
Stew meat	Tough	Braise, stew
Pork		
Loin (center cut, sirloin roasts, chops, cutlets, crown roast and tenderloin)	Tender	Grill, broil, roast, sauté, pan-fry
Steaks	Tender	Braise
Ribs (spareribs, baby back ribs)	Tough	Braise or stew
Roasts	Tough	Braise
Shoulder (Boston butt and picnic shoulder)	Tough	Braise, roast, stew
Veal		
Loin or saddle (loin chop)	Tender	Roasted
Round roast (top round and sirloin tip)	Tender	Roasted
Rump	Tender	Boned and roasted
Sirloin	Tender	Boned and roasted

275 Stock Up for the Perfect Burger

The ultimate barbecuer's pride and joy, the humble hamburger is raised to lofty heights by choosing your ground beef well. Fat is our friend—health concerns notwithstanding, feisty butchers everywhere say it imparts flavor, and it helps the hamburger patty stay together.

Steps

1 Order ground beef from your butcher for the freshest meat possible. Specify the cut of meat: sirloin, roast, stew meat, brisket and shank, among others. Cut determines the price per pound.

2 Look for meat that's red to red-brown (sometimes the top layer of the meat will oxidize and turn slightly brown). The meat shouldn't be gray or green-gray in color and should be cold to the touch.

3 Go for the fat. The higher the fat content, the cheaper the beef. Regular ground beef and hamburger top the list at 30 percent.

4 Choose chuck if you want less fat. It usually contains 15 to 20 percent, so it's still moist and flavorful, but not as dry as ground sirloin and ground round or as juicy as regular ground beef.

5 Wrap meat in a plastic bag and buy at the end of your grocery trip so it stays in the refrigerated section as long as possible.

What to Look For

- As fresh as possible
- Desired cut
- Red to red-brown meat
- Ground to order
- Fat content

Warning

Refrigerate at 40 degrees F (4 C) or below and use within two days. Don't leave out for more than 4 hours—including time spent in the cart or car, and on your counter—it could develop bacteria.

276 Purchase a Holiday Ham

Ham can take on myriad flavors, including honey, bourbon, pepper, apple and maple. No mere pork leg, ham is either wet-brined in a mix of salt, water and sugar or dry-cured with salt, herbs and sugar, then aged for several weeks and smoked. Dry-cured hams require 48 hours of soaking to remove the salt, hours of poaching, and finally baking.

Steps

1 Tally up your guest list. A bone-in ham will provide three to four servings per pound, while a boneless ham will yield four to five. Factor in extra for leftovers; there's nothing like a honey-baked-ham sandwich or country-fried ham and eggs.

2 Order as far as three weeks in advance. Ask your butcher or grocer's meat department how to place an order for holiday ham.

3 Browse Web sites and gourmet catalogs, but factor in extra time and money for shipping. Savor a Honey Baked Ham (honeybaked.com), the Starbucks of the ham business. Presliced, these hams range from about $50 to $120. The Holiday Ham Company (holidayham.com), Williams-Sonoma (williams-sonoma.com), Neiman Marcus (neimanmarcus.com) and Harry and David (harryanddavid.com) all offer a variety of high-quality hams.

What to Look For

- Flavored hams
- Number of servings
- Butcher or grocery store
- Web sites
- Catalogs

Tip

Premium hams have less water added to the meat to plump it up.

Warning

To kill potentially harmful trichinosis, heat the inside of an uncooked ham to at least 155 degrees F (68 C).

277 Buy Natural Beef

The hottest trend among the carnivore cognoscenti is organic and grass-fed beef. Certified organic cows eat pesticide- and herbicide-free feed. Grass-fed cows (as opposed to industry-standard corn-fed) are free of hormones and chemicals, but not always organic. The beef is leaner and filled with heart-friendly omega-3 fatty acids.

Steps

1 Inquire with your local butcher, or ask your favorite steak house if it uses natural beef. If it does, ask for the farm's information.

2 Call cattle farms. Grass-fed beef is usually sold directly through small ranchers. A quarter includes steaks, short ribs, pot roast, ground beef and stew meat for $200 to $350.

3 Shop for beef online. Prather Ranch (pratherranch.com) is a great source for all-natural organic beef, or try grass-fed beef from Chileno Ranch (chilenobeef.com).

4 Look for grass-fed beef seasonally, in late spring and early summer.

5 Buy meat that's grown on a lot inspected by the U.S. Department of Agriculture, and dry-aged, vacuum-packed, frozen and shipped in insulated boxes with adequate refrigeration.

What to Look For

- Hormone- and antibiotic-free or grass-fed beef
- Butchers and steak houses
- Cattle farms
- Seasonal availability
- USDA-inspected

Tip

Line up a friend who's willing to share. When you order from a farm, you'll need to buy between a quarter and a whole side of beef.

Warning

Make sure shipments will arrive frozen to ensure they're safe to consume.

278 Buy Rocky Mountain Oysters

Take the bull by the horn: Instead of the tenderloin, why not try the tendergroin? Also known as calf fries, Rocky Mountain oysters are the testicles of cows, buffalo, pigs, lamb, sheep or turkey. They can certainly humble even the brawniest group of guys.

Steps

1 Ask your butcher a week in advance if he or she can order Rocky Mountain oysters. In the ranching communities of the West and Midwest (especially Montana, Wyoming and Colorado), tender-groin is easy to procure from butchers and meat shops.

2 Try specialty meat producers. One company that sells Rocky Mountain oysters to restaurants all over the country is Exotic Meats (exoticmeats.com), for $10.95 per lb. Or try Fairbury Lockers (fairburylockers.com) in Nebraska.

3 Look for pale, whitish-tan oysters that have been shipped frozen and vacuum-packed or stored cold at your butcher.

4 Remove the thick muscle surrounding the oyster with a sharp paring knife. Cut larger portions in half or quarters, and keep them wrapped in the refrigerator until you're ready to fry them up.

What to Look For

- Butcher
- Specialty meat retailers
- Vacuum packed and shipped frozen

Tip

To prepare Rocky Mountain oysters, batter them in flour, cornmeal, salt and pepper, then fry in a hot skillet with oil. Drain on paper towels and sprinkle generously with Louisiana Hot Sauce or Tabasco. Eat while hot.

279 Purchase Local Honey

Bees work hard for the honey: They may travel as far as 55,000 miles and visit more than 2 million flowers to gather enough nectar to make just a pound of honey. Honey's flavor comes from the source (thyme, heather, clover, eucalyptus or sunflower, to name a few), not the bee.

Steps

1 Check out BackYardBeekeepers.com and other sites. Bee-keepers are the best source for locally produced honey. If they don't sell honey themselves, they'll know where to find it.

2 Shop the farmers' markets and state fairs to find various local varieties of the sweet nectar.

3 Browse the shelves of gourmet food shops to find a wide variety of honey flavors, colors and textures.

What to Look For

- Beekeepers
- Farmers' markets or fairs
- Gourmet food shops

Tip

If your honey crystallizes, place the opened jar in a pan of hot water over low heat for 15 minutes. Stir to dissolve the sugar granules.

280 Choose Poultry

Fly away from flavorless plastic-wrapped birds and head for the free range. Uncaged, organic chickens are more flavorful than traditional chicks. Buy your bird either whole for roasting or cut into legs, thighs, wings and breasts. Removing the skin before cooking decreases the fat by 25 to 30 percent, but decreases the flavor as well.

TYPE OF BIRD	AGE AND WEIGHT	BEST USE
Broilers-Fryers	Typically 45 days old, weighing 3 to 4.5 lbs. (1.4 to 1.8 kg)	Good broiled and fried. Roast whole with lemon and olive oil or cut up for grilling or poaching.
Capon	10-week-old cocks, castrated young; weighing 8 to 10 lbs. (3.6 to 4.5 kg)	Couch potatoes of the poultry world, capon are allowed to grow old and fat in comfort. Their meat is mild and their size makes them perfect for a holiday meal. Order ahead from a butcher or specialty market. Expect to pay slightly more than for other birds.
Roasters	10 weeks old, weighing 4.5 to 8 lbs. (1.8 to 3.6 kg)	Big-breasted, with more meat per pound than most birds. Stuff ricotta, minced garlic and spinach directly under the skin before sprinkling with kosher salt and roasting.
Rock Cornish Hens	5 to 6 weeks old, weighing 1 to 2 lbs. (.5 to .8 kg)	Wonderful roasted for an elegant dinner party or split open to grill or broil.

Consider these health and environmental issues before selecting your swimmers: The chart's "best choice" fish were caught or farmed in environmentally friendly ways. Mercury threat is also noted. According to the EPA, the typical U.S. consumer eating fish from restaurants and groceries is not in danger of consuming harmful levels of methylmercury from fish and is not advised to limit fish consumption. Because the developing fetus may be the most sensitive to the effects from methylmercury, women of child-bearing age are warned to avoid fish that may have high mercury levels.

FISH (SOURCE)	ECO-FRIENDLY	MERCURY THREAT
Catfish (U.S.-Farmed)	Best choice	Low
Clams (Farmed)	Best choice	Low
Clams (Wild-Caught)	Caution	Low
Cod (Atlantic)	Avoid	Low
Cod (Pacific)	Caution	Low
Crab, Dungeness	Best choice	Low
Crab, Snow and King (Imported)	Caution	Low
Halibut (Pacific)	Best choice	High
Lobster, Rock (California, Australia)	Best choice	Low
Lobster, American	Caution	Low
Mahimahi (Wild-Caught)	Caution	Low
Mussels (Farmed)	Best choice	Low
Orange Roughy	Avoid	Low
Oysters (Farmed)	Best choice	Low
Rockfish, Rock Cod, Pacific Red Snapper	Avoid	Low
Salmon, Pacific (Wild-Caught)	Best choice	Low
Salmon, Atlantic (Farmed)	Avoid	Low
Scallops, Bay or Sea	Caution	Low
Sea Bass, White	Best choice	Low
Sea Bass, Chilean	Avoid	Low
Shark (Except U.S. West Coast Thresher)	Best choice	High
Shrimp or Prawns (Trap-Caught)	Best choice	Low
Shrimp (U.S.-Farmed or Wild-Caught)	Caution	Low
Sole, Petrale, English, Dover	Caution	Low
Squid (California)	Best choice	Low
Striped Bass (Farmed)	Best choice	Low
Sturgeon (Wild-Caught)	Avoid	Low
Swordfish (U.S. West Coast)	Caution	High
Swordfish (Atlantic)	Avoid	High
Trout, Rainbow (Farmed)	Best choice	Low
Tuna, Albacore/Yellowfin/Bigeye (Troll- or Pole-Caught)	Best choice	High
Tuna, Albacore/Yellowfin/Bigeye (Purse Seines-Caught)	Caution	High

Rice, a staple of diets around the world, is grown in beautiful marshy tiers in Asia and India, while wild rice is found in the American Midwest, and forbidden black rice comes from China. Texas has started to cultivate basmati rice, called Texmati, although purists swear by Indian basmati. Review this chart to help you put the many varieties of this precious grain to good use.

RICE	DESCRIPTION	COOKING METHOD	BEST USE
Arborio	Short-grain, polished white kernels with bland taste and soft texture.	Don't rinse; simmer 1 part rice to 2 parts liquid for 20 minutes; add the liquid gradually while stirring.	Risotto.
Basmati	Aromatic long-grain.	Rinse and simmer 1 part rice to 1½ parts liquid for 20 to 25 minutes.	Side dish with saffron, curries or Indian flavors.
Black Rice	Short-grain black rice, fragrant and nutty.	Simmer 1 part rice to 2 parts liquid for 45 minutes.	Delicious as side dish or as bed for fish dish.
Brown Rice	Long-grain with nutty flavor and firm texture.	Simmer 1 part rice in 2 parts liquid, adding a little butter to keep grains separate, for 35 to 50 minutes.	Casseroles, pilaf and salads.
Lundberg Royal	Aromatic long-grain.	Rinse and simmer 1 part rice to 1½ parts liquid for 20 to 25 minutes.	Side dish for meat and fish dishes.
Sushi Rice	Polished rice shorter than arborio; can be sweet, waxy or sticky.	Soak overnight and simmer 1 part rice to 1 part water, or following rice cooker's instructions.	Dim sum, sushi and dessert puddings
Wehani	Aromatic California long-grain hybrid that turns russet when cooked.	Rinse and simmer 1 part rice to 1½ parts liquid for 20 to 25 minutes.	Side dish or rice salads.
Wild Rice	Not rice at all, but the seed of native grass found in Midwest and California. Earthy and nutty, with firm to chewy texture.	Boil 1 part rice to 3 parts water, 45 to 60 minutes.	Delicious with nuts and dried fruits for stuffing, and in salads and side dishes.
TIP	Visit ChefShop.com to buy more than a dozen varieties of rice, including Bhutanese red rice, Spanish baldo rice, estate-grown arborio rice and organic brown rice.		

283 Purchase Premium Salt and Pepper

The most versatile spicing and flavoring agents are anything but bland. Used well, salt and pepper greatly enhance the flavor and overall outcome of your cooking. Most of today's table salt is mined from large deposits left by dried salt lakes. Common black pepper is made from ground-dried, unripened berries of the pepper plant.

Steps

Salt

1 Swap your iodized salt for kosher. Many chefs prefer kosher salt because of its coarse texture, lack of additives and less astringent flavor (2.5 lbs. for $4).

2 Keep sea salt on hand for finishing dishes just before serving. Coarser than kosher salt, sea salt is made from evaporated seawater. The result—especially the ultra-premium, hand-raked fleur de sel of Normandy—is delicious. Prices range from a few dollars for 26 oz. to $40 for 2.2 lbs. (1 kilo).

3 Experiment with out-of-the-ordinary salts. Try black salt (4 oz. for $3), a mineral compound with a sulfur taste that dissipates, in Indian masalas or seafood dishes. Hawaiian pink salt (16 oz. for $4), made from sea salt that oxidizes from contact with the iron into red clay, is tasty sprinkled over mahimahi on the grill.

Pepper

1 Start with premium whole black peppercorns. Invest in a pepper mill to grind pepper at home. Hand-grinding your pepper will keep it fresh longer, as ground pepper loses its flavor very quickly. Throw out that powdery pepper that makes you sneeze.

2 Broaden your taste horizons with white or green peppercorns. Mild white peppercorns are best for light-colored sauces, and green peppercorns, with their fresh and pungent flavor, are often used in brines and marinades.

3 Put pink peppercorns on your shopping list. These are actually dried berries from the Baies rose plant. Pungent and slightly sweet, they appear in gourmet stores either freeze-dried or packed in brine. They are often used along with white and black peppercorns for a splash of color and as a dusting over finished dishes.

4 Look for gourmet mixes of whole black, white, pink and green peppercorns.

What to Look For

- Kosher salt
- Sea salt
- Black or pink salt
- Whole black peppercorns
- Pepper mill
- White or green peppercorns
- Pink peppercorns
- Peppercorn mixtures

Tips

Whole peppercorns stored in a cool dry place will last about a year; however, pink peppercorns only last about six months.

It's good etiquette to taste a dish before you add salt and pepper—you'll be giving the chef a chance before seasoning his or her creation.

Check ChefShop (chefshop.com) for black and pink salt, and Dean & DeLuca (deandeluca.com) for a variety of coarse salt and sea salt.

Warning

Ask your doctor about regulating your sodium intake if you are at risk for heart problems or high blood pressure.

284 Get a Cheesesteak in Philadelphia

A true Philly cheesesteak, which gives locals a bigger dose of civic pride than the Liberty Bell, is a mouthwatering combination of spongy roll, heart-stopping chopped steak, cheese and toppings of your choice. In recent years the chicken cheesesteak has gained legitimacy, even for purists.

Steps

1 Find a legitimate shop. Ask locals for recommendations, read reviews in the *Philadelphia Daily News* or *Philadelphia* magazine and Web sites like Citysearch (philadelphia.citysearch.com). Best bets are Geno's, Jim's Steaks, Pat's King of Steaks and Larry's Steaks and Hoagies.

2 Know what you want before you reach the counter. Decide on meat, cheese (provolone, American, cheddar or Cheese Whiz) and toppings (pizza sauce, ketchup, fried onions, pickles, sweet or hot peppers, mushrooms and pepperoni).

3 Don't get offended or frazzled if the person taking your order acts like the Soup Nazi. This is protocol. Keep ordering—no small talk! Be confident and get the job done.

What to Look For

- The best shops
- The menu
- No small talk

Tips

For a true Philly experience, wash down your cheese-steak with a Yuengling beer while watching an Eagles game.

Bring cash. Many shops don't accept checks or credit cards.

285 Order Fresh Salmon in Seattle

Seattle's Puget Sound is a gateway for wild chinook salmon. Some salmon populations are threatened by overfishing and, while their fate is not known, one thing's for sure—the fish swimming the waters of the West taste darn good. Read on to ensure that the fish you eat has taken an environmentally friendly trip from waterways to restaurant.

Steps

1 Visit the source. Pike Place Market is a vast farmers' market, fish market, meat market (in more ways than one) and shopping cen-ter for Seattle foodies. City Fish Market at 1535 Pike Place sells delicious, environmentally friendly local salmon.

2 Ask around. Locals have a list of their favorite seafood restau-rants, many of which might be in lesser-known neighborhoods or off the beaten track.

3 Read the menu. Local salmon that run the waters of the Pacific may be labeled as chinook, chum, coho, pink, sockeye, red, Pacific or Alaskan salmon. Avoid farmed Atlantic salmon. It doesn't taste nearly as good as rich wild salmon.

4 Ask the server how your fish was caught. Look for wild or line-caught fish. Depending on the waters and time of year, be wary even when ordering wild salmon.

What to Look For

- Pike Place Market
- Locals
- Wild or line-caught

Tip

Before visiting a restaurant, call ahead and ask if it serves local wild salmon.

Warning

Don't order the endangered chinook salmon from the Puget Sound. Reputable restaurants and suppliers won't serve this endangered species.

286 Find Crawdads in Louisiana

Since 1983, the state crustacean of Louisiana has been the crawfish, aka the crawdad or crayfish. With a production of more than 100 million lbs. of the 3- to 6-inch shellfish a year, it'll be easy enough to find a fried or buttered basket on your next trip to the bayou.

Steps

1 Stop by the grocery store to pick up some crawfish. Most seafood counters in New Orleans and outlying areas carry them.

2 Keep your eyes peeled for seafood shacks selling crawdads (along with shrimp and other fish) to go. Douse 'em with some Louisiana Hot Sauce and you're good to go.

3 Visit Breaux Bridge, Louisiana, during the annual crawdad festival, held the first weekend in May. For more details, go to BreauxBridgeLive.com.

4 If you're far from the Mississippi Delta and craving some crustaceans, contact the Louisiana Crawfish Company (lacrawfish.com) to have fresh and frozen crawfish sent to your door by overnight mail. Prepare as you would lobster.

What to Look For

- Grocery stores
- Seafood shacks
- Crawfish festivals
- Web sites

Tips

Buy more crawfish than you think you'll need or want: They don't contain much meat, and some fans can eat dozens before they're full.

Resembling tiny lobsters, crawfish live in fresh water instead of seawater like their lobster relatives.

287 Buy Artisan Breads

Handcrafted loaves of crunchy, hearty artisan breads are a world away from factory-made assembly line breads. These breads range in flavor from sweet and mild to pungent and rustic. Each loaf has its own distinct shape, texture and taste.

Steps

1 Read the ingredients. You'll easily recognize the short list of often organic, unbleached wheat flour, water, salt and yeast. If the bread is made with a sourdough starter, you may not see yeast.

2 Look for golden, ridged and crusty loaves. This is the telltale crust of bread baked in an artisan's wood-fired oven or hearth, which radiates high-temperature heat around the entire loaf.

3 Tap the crust. Listen for a hollow sound that means the bread is not dense and doughy. Inside, look for uneven webbed texture with lots of nooks and crannies of different shapes and sizes. This provides the unmistakable "mouth feel" of artisan bread.

4 Taste some samples. How the bread feels is secondary to the wonderful range of flavors available.

5 Eat promptly. Artisan loaves don't stay fresh as long as chemically preserved commercial breads do. Freeze stale portions to make French toast, bread pudding, croutons or bread crumbs.

What to Look For

- Flour, water, salt and yeast
- Golden crust
- Hollow sound
- Good texture
- Distinct taste

Tip

Besides the ubiquitous sourdough bread, look for many shapes and sizes of artisan breads, such as baguettes, challah, pugliese, bâtarde, ciabatta, focaccia, raisin-walnut bread and handcrafted bagels.

Instead of buying a waxy yellow block without much taste, why not indulge in handcrafted, high-flavor cheeses? Though many of the best cheeses are made in Europe, artisans everywhere are using the time-tested techniques of France and Italy to produce wonderful cheeses for cooking and tasting. Explore texture and taste, fresh to aged, as well as a variety of milk sources.

TYPE OF CHEESE	TEXTURE; TASTE; ANIMAL'S MILK	SUGGESTED USE
Fresh Cheeses		
Feta (Greece)	Soft, crumbly; traditionally salty, tangy; sheep, goat or cow, originally from ewe's milk.	Crumble on Greek salad, mix with orzo or bake in filo.
Ricotta (Italy)	Unripened firm mass of moist cheese; unsalted, milky; cow or sheep.	Ravioli or cannelloni filling.
Mozzarella di Bufala (Italy)	Moist, milky, delicate and stringy; sweet, fresh and nutty (not like American mass-produced mozzarella used on pizza); buffalo.	Caprese salad (layers of mozzarella, ripe tomato, basil, extra-virgin olive oil and salt).
Chèvre (France: Loire)	Soft, but not completely smooth; nutty, tangy and aromatic; goat.	Spread on crostini as appetizer; serve lightly breaded and baked, with green salad.
Crescenza (Italy: Lombardy)	Wet and soft; rich, clean acidity; cow.	Sprinkled with herbs and spread on crusty bread.
Paneer (India)	Slightly firm, pale yellow; mild; cow or goat.	Deep-fried, barbecued in a tandoori, simmered with spinach.
Queso Fresco (Mexico)	Soft, crumbly; mild, tangy, salty; cow.	Crumbled on fresh black beans or enchiladas.
Natural Rind		
Crottin de Chavignol (France: Loire)	Deeply wrinkled, almost brittle interior; distinctly goaty, intense and sharp; goat.	Best enjoyed on cheese board.
Perail (France)	Thin, crusty rind with pale ivory interior; moist, young, milky and nutty; sheep.	Best enjoyed on cheese board.
Chèvrefeuille (France: Perigord)	Shiny white interior; herb-infused, often wrapped in chestnut leaves; goat.	Best enjoyed on cheese board.
Soft-white Rind		
Brie (France)	Slightly dry, edible white rind, with creamy, golden interior; buttery and rich; cow.	Best enjoyed at end of meal.
Camembert (France: Normandy)	Supple, creamy and smooth interior; buttery and rich; cow.	Best enjoyed at end of meal.

TYPE OF CHEESE	TEXTURE; TASTE; ANIMAL'S MILK	SUGGESTED USE
Semisoft		
Reblochon (France)	Dark golden rind with creamy-soft interior; delicate flavor; cow.	Delicious paired with fruit for dessert.
Gouda and Edam (Holland)	Yellow or red wax rind, semisoft interior; mellow and savory; cow.	Perfect paired with dark beer.
Taleggio (Italy: Lombardy)	Pale yellow with wax coating or thin mold; rich, buttery and runny when aged; cow.	Thinly sliced on salads.
Blue		
Stilton (England)	Slightly crumbly pale-yellow interior with blue-green veins and crusty brown rind; rich and creamy, slightly pungent and sharp; cow.	Best on cheese board or at end of meal.
Gorgonzola (Italy)	Ivory-colored interior predominantly streaked with blue vein; savory, creamy and salty; cow.	Pair with pears and walnuts on salads or sprinkle on thin-crust pizza.
Roquefort (France)	Creamy white interior with round blue veins and white rind; pungent, strong, salty; sheep.	Creamy salad dressings or at end of meal with slightly sweet dessert wine.
Hard		
Parmigiano (Italy)	Brittle and granular; salty, nutty and sharp; cow.	Thinly sliced on grilled asparagus or grated into pastas, soups and sauces.
Cheddar (England)	Firm, dry and brittle; ranging from mild and sweet to tangy and sharp; cow.	With crisp apples on cheese board.
Pecorino (Italy)	Smooth to brittle and granular; salty, fruity and nutty; sheep; Romano type is aged 8 to 12 months, Sardo 1 to 12 months and Toscano 1 to 3 months.	Shave all three on pastas or salads.
Manchego (Spain)	Firm, smooth and golden; mellow, nutty and peppery; sheep.	Best served on cheese board.
Gruyère (Switzerland)	Golden rind and firm, golden interior; sweet, nutty and rich; cow.	Grated as topping for gratins.
WARNINGS	Cheeses that have passed their prime may smell strongly of ammonia.	
	Pregnant women shouldn't eat unpasteurized imported cheeses because of the harmful bacteria they may carry, which can cause fetal distress or miscarriage. Cheeses made in the United States must be pasteurized, and so are considered safe.	

289 Purchase Kosher Food

Keeping kosher means far more than swearing off bacon. The Jewish dietary laws, called *kashruth,* require that food be grown, harvested and cooked in adherence with the kosher way. For instance, strict butchering laws demand that the animal be killed swiftly and humanely in a prescribed way that immediately cuts off blood pressure to the brain. Non-Jews also benefit. For example, vegetarians can be assured that an item designated *pareve* will not be made with any meat products.

Steps

1 Shop at a certified kosher market, meat shop or bakery. These are easier to find in some cities than others.

2 Find the kosher food aisle in your supermarket, which offers a stash of kosher diet staples.

3 Call ahead to markets, butchers and restaurants, and ask about the type of products they carry or serve.

4 Do your homework on Web sites like Kashrut.com and KosherConsumer.org to find out which products are kosher. Many well-known companies have manufactured their products in accordance with kosher laws. These include Thomas' English muffins, Lenders bagels, most Kellogg's cereals, Philadelphia cream cheese, Vlasic pickles, Pepperidge Farm, Coca-Cola, Heinz, Starbucks, Kikkoman soy sauce and Near East grains. Indicators such as KSA (Kosher Supervision of America) or OU (Union of Orthodox Jewish Congregations of America) will be on the package.

5 Shop online and have foods delivered. You can also order kosher wine online; Kosher.com and MyKosherMarket.com are good sources.

6 If you're looking for a kosher meal while traveling, search for restaurants in databases like mail-jewish.org/krestquery.html. Chicago, Los Angeles and New York are known for their kosher restaurants. Disneyland and Disney World also have many kosher products available.

What to Look For

- Kosher markets
- Kosher food aisle
- Mainstream products
- Symbols
- Web sites
- Urban areas
- Kosher restaurants

Tip

You can specify a kosher meal on an airline—and usually you'll get a better quality of meat or luck out with bagels and lox.

290 Buy Food in Bulk

Buying in bulk goes beyond just cruising by the bulk bins at your grocery store and joining a members-only warehouse chain. You can also fatten your wallet. Buy in bulk strategically so all that food doesn't spoil before you can eat it. Split quantities (and shopping runs) with a friend.

Steps

Bulk foods

1 Frequent health-food stores, coops and grocery stores that stock bulk bins. Ensure that the food is fresh. Ask the store how often it refills bins or whether you can taste samples of items such as nuts or pretzels.

2 Bring a cup or teaspoon measures for bulk bins if you don't want to buy more than you need.

3 When shopping for bulk items with expiration dates, grab from the back of the shelf.

4 Store dry goods in airtight plastic containers or glass jars with screw-top lids in a cool, dry place.

Warehouse chains

1 Head to the perishables (milk, cheese, meats) for the best deals. For example, a 16-oz. log of goat cheese at Costco costs $4.89, while a 4-oz. package from a grocery store is about $4—three times as much for the quantity, yet the quality is comparable.

2 Shop in the midafternoon when the rotisserie meats are freshly cooked and wrapped for the evening rush.

3 Save big on luxury items. Sam's Club sells 4-oz. tins of caviar for $142, compared to 1.75-oz. tins for $250 at Dean & DeLuca.

4 Find great deals on gifts at Costco. You can buy a 40-oz. tin of chocolate-covered almonds for $12.87, a 32-oz. glass jar of mixed nuts for $14.26 or a pound of smoked salmon for $9.37.

Special occasions

1 Throwing a party? A keg of beer is more economical than a stack of 12-packs. Or, buy a case of wine through a winery and save 10 to 20 percent. Pick up a party platter of cold cuts or crudités from the warehouse stores and save yourself time and money.

2 Order a whole or half pig from your butcher to roast over banana leaves in a coal-lined fire pit for luaus: Your guests will happily take any leftovers home.

3 Buy a whole chicken at the meat counter and cut it at home— freeze the legs and thighs if you're only using the breasts.

4 Stop at a roadside produce stand for great deals on fresh fruits and vegetables, such as a whole flat of strawberries or cherries.

What to Look For

- Health-food stores
- Freshness
- Warehouse stores
- Luxury items

Tips

See 265 Buy Organic Produce to find out how to get boxes of seasonal fruits and vegetables delivered to your door.

See 277 Buy Natural Beef to find out how you can buy meat in bulk.

Paper products, diapers, party supplies and cleaning agents are all prime for bulk buying because they're much costlier in small quantities and they never go sour.

Warning

Dry foods from bulk bins can go stale faster than vacuum-packed foods. But they also tend to be healthier because they're not packed with preservatives.

291 Choose Cooking Oils

Some oils have a low smoking point, meaning they'll burn at lower temperatures. Others, like canola or vegetable oils, can reach high temperatures without smoking, so they're great for deep-frying and sautéing. After you decide which oil is best for your cooking method, consider how much flavor you'd like to add to your dish: Grapeseed oil will lend the least amount of flavor to your deep-fried asparagus, while peanut oil imbues foods with a rich, nutty, roasted taste. (See 269 Decipher Food Labels and 292 Select Olive Oil.)

OIL	RECOMMENDED USE	FLAVOR LEVEL	SMOKING POINT
Canola	Deep-frying, pan-frying, sautéing, baking	Low to medium	High
Corn	Pan-frying, deep-frying	High	High
Grapeseed	Deep-frying, pan-frying, sautéing	Low	Very High
Peanut	Stir-frying, wok cooking, deep-frying	High	High
Safflower	Deep-frying, pan-frying, sautéing, baking	Low to medium	High
Sesame	Wok cooking, dressings, finishing flavor	High	Low
Sunflower	Deep-frying, pan-frying, sautéing	Low to medium	High
Vegetable	Deep-frying, pan-frying, sautéing, baking	Low	High

292 Select Olive Oil

In Mediterranean countries, olive groves grow on nearly every countryside property, and families meet in collectives to press and bottle the combined fruits of their labor. As with wine, the characteristics of olive oil depend on the soil and climate where the trees are grown, the type of olives pressed (see 293 Select Olives) and the method of pressing.

Steps

1 Look at the color. Green oils, made from early-harvested olives, are fruity, peppery and ripe. Yellow-gold oils taste buttery and smooth. You'll benefit from the increased polyphenols and other antioxidants in green oil, but it's mostly a matter of preference.

2 Taste olive oils at a gourmet grocery store or specialty shop's tasting station to find a flavor you like.

3 Buy locally pressed oils in California, Oregon and Texas soon after bottling for the freshest and most flavorful products. The pressing season runs from October to late January.

What to Look For

- Color
- Taste
- Local oils
- Extra-virgin and virgin
- Filtered and unfiltered
- Price
- Web sites and catalogs

Tips

Avoid light olive oil; it's diluted and flavorless, and the term *light* is meaningless. It has the same number of calories as other olive oils, about 125 per tablespoon.

4 Choose extra-virgin olive oil for most of your cooking needs. For frying, use virgin olive oil, which will impart less flavor, is less expensive and won't burn as easily as extra-virgin olive oil.

5 Find a filtered olive oil for sautéing and roasting, and an unfiltered olive oil for salad dressings and to drizzle on soups or pastas.

6 Cruise the Web. ChefShop (chefshop.com) has a wide variety of oils, or try Dean & DeLuca (deandeluca.com). Order the Corti Brothers catalog at (800) 509-3663 for an even greater variety of high-quality domestic and imported olive oils.

7 Store oils in a cool, dark place. Olive oils are a fresh food and can go rancid. Life span can be as little as three months for an unfiltered, late-harvest olive oil bottled in clear glass, to four years for an early-harvest, filtered oil packaged in a well-sealed tin or dark bottle and properly stored.

Make your own infused olive oils by simply putting herbs, truffle shavings or lemon zest in a bottle and fill with a mild-flavored olive oil.

Warning

Buyer beware: In Europe, fine olive oils have a label that indicates the country and region of production; no such system currently exists in the United States.

293 Select Olives

Cultivated in arid grape-growing regions, olives vary greatly in color and flavor depending on how ripe they are when picked and the method of processing. Olives can be a part of a charcuterie board and enliven innumerable cooked dishes. They're also a natural finger-food pairing with a glass of wine.

SOURCE	VARIETY	CHARACTERISTICS	FLAVOR
Italy	Calabrese	Dull green and cracked.	Similar to Sicilian type, but mellower.
	Gaeta	Dark, small and wilted.	Earthy and milky-oily, with herbal note.
	Ligurian	Dark brown to black.	Deep and flavorful.
	Sicilian	Cracked and green.	Sharp and bitter with flavorful punch.
France	Lucques	Small and dark.	Flavorful and distinct.
	Niçoise	Shiny, small, dense pit.	Provençal herbal flavor.
	Picholine	Medium green.	Bright, salty and crisp.
Greece	Kalamata	Fleshy, dark and shiny.	Rich and salty.
	Nafplion	Dark green.	Fruity and dense.
Lebanon	Lebanese Black	Smooth, medium-size, glossy brown and black.	Pleasant, intense earthy taste.
Morocco	Moroccan	Black dry-cured, salt-cured or oil-cured.	Earthy and acidic.
Spain	Gordal	Large, green.	Pleasantly meaty texture.

Why do Indian dal and Thai tom kha gai taste so much better at ethnic restaurants? Because of the quality and authenticity of the ingredients. If you want to re-create the flavors of your favorite cuisine, buy authentic condiments, grains and spices. The real thing makes all the difference in the world.

INGREDIENT	SOURCE	COMMON USES	WHERE TO FIND
Banana Leaves	Mexico, Thailand	Wrap around seasoned fish or meat, and grill or steam.	Grocer's frozen section; Pacific Rim Gourmet (i-clipse.com).
Cardamom	Africa, India	Used in chai tea. The world's second most expensive spice after saffron, black cardamom is used to spice meat or rice, while green cardamom is often used in desserts.	Premium black and green: Indian grocers; regular whole and ground green: grocer's spice aisle.
Chili Paste	Thailand, China	A spicy condiment in Thai soups and noodle dishes.	Grocery store's Asian ingredients aisle; Chinese markets.
Coconut Milk	Africa, Thailand, Philippines	Used in lemongrass and chicken soup, coconut rice and to braise shrimp. Low-fat coconut milk also available.	Grocery store's Asian ingredients aisle, or with canned foods.
Cumin	Africa, India, Middle East, Mexico	White (or ordinary) cumin, or black, which is smaller and sweeter. Whole seeds provide better flavor. Roast in a skillet and grind in a spice grinder or clean coffee grinder. Part of typical curry blend.	Black cumin seeds at Indian groceries; lighter Mexican seeds (can substitute in Indian and Middle Eastern cooking) in grocery spice aisles.
Dal	India	*Channa* is split and husked chickpeas with a sweet aroma and flavor. *Masoor* is tiny pink lentils, but red or brown lentils may be substituted. *Toor* is pale yellow husked and split Indian lentils; don't buy the oily variety, which is treated with castor oil.	Yellow, pink, red and brown lentils widely available in larger grocery stores; *channa* and *toor dal* found at Indian markets.
Fish Sauce, Thai Fish Oil	China, Thailand, Philippines, Vietnam	Used extensively in Southeast Asian soups, dressing or sauces. Made from salted, fermented fish.	Asian ingredients aisle or sold as *nam pla* (Thai) or *nuoc nam* (Vietnamese) at Asian markets.
Five-Spice Powder	China	An aromatic blend consisting of cinnamon, fennel seed, cloves, star anise and Szechuan peppercorns. Used as marinade or spice for meats and fish.	Most grocery stores and Asian markets.

INGREDIENT	SOURCE	COMMON USES	WHERE TO FIND
Garam Masala	India	Widely used Indian spice blend contains cardamom, cumin, cinnamon, cloves and black pepper. Add to soups, curries and lentil dishes.	Indian markets or grocer's spice aisle; online at EthnicGrocer.com.
Hoisin Sauce	China	Sweet, syrupy sauce used in marinades and sauces for meat, poultry and seafood dishes. Refrigerate bottled hoisin.	Larger grocery stores and Asian markets.
Kaffir Lime Leaves	Thailand, Burma, Laos	Aromatic essential for Thai soups and curries. Refrigerate leaves stored in a plastic bag for weeks, or freeze them for two to three months.	Asian markets.
Lemongrass	Thailand	Crucial for Thai soups and curries. Lemongrass has all the bright flavor of lemon without the bite. Look for stalks with plump bases.	With grocery store's fresh herbs or at Asian markets.
Oyster Sauce	China	A syrupy dark-brown sauce consisting of oysters, brine and soy sauce cooked until thick and concentrated. Popular condiment and seasoning for vegetable stir-fries and fried rice.	Grocery stores and Asian markets.
Tahini	Middle East	A ground sesame-seed paste used in hummus and baba ghanoush.	Grocery store (with peanut butter, oils or ethnic ingredients).
Tamarind	India, Middle East	Seed pod of tamarind tree. Extremely sour pulp is popular in marinades, curries and chutneys.	Found in Indian markets and some Asian markets, as well as larger grocery stores.
Turmeric	Africa, India, Indonesia, Thailand	Fresh turmeric is used in Thai yellow curries. Dried turmeric is found in many Indian dishes, from lentils to vegetables and meats.	Fresh turmeric at Asian markets; dried turmeric at Indian markets and in grocery store's spice aisle.
Udon Noodles	Japan	A thick wheat noodle used in vegetable and meat broth soups.	Fresh or dried in Asian markets.
Wasabi	Japan	A sharp, spicy condiment for sushi. Also called *Japanese horseradish*.	Asian markets in both paste and powder.
TIP	Shop at ethnic grocery stores and farmers' markets for the freshest ingredients. See 267 Buy and Sell at Farmers' Markets.		

295 Purchase Vinegar

From mildly acidic to mouth-puckeringly pungent, there's a vast array of vinegars: apple cider, wine, champagne, rice and balsamic, to name a few. Most varieties cost just $2 to $10 for a 16-oz. bottle, but aged balsamic vinegar can get pricey—$75 to $250 for about 3.5 oz.

Steps

1 Stock your larder with workhorse vinegars such as champagne, cider, sherry and balsamic vinegar (see 271 Stock Your Kitchen with Staples).

2 Shop at a large grocery store for a variety of cooking vinegars and less-expensive balsamic vinegars.

3 Find a selection of fruit and herb-infused vinegars, and high-quality aged balsamic vinegars by shopping at gourmet food and specialty stores such as Williams-Sonoma or Sur La Table.

4 Browse Asian markets for a variety of rice-wine vinegars, sometimes blended with sake vinegar for a nice edge.

5 Let your taste buds convince you of the value of aged balsamic vinegar from Italy. Made from Trebbiano grapes, it gets its sweet rich flavor from aging 5 to 20 years in wood barrels. Just a tiny bit imparts incredible flavor.

What to Look For

- Versatile vinegars
- Grocery stores
- Specialty stores
- Asian markets
- Aged balsamic vinegar

Tips

For a dessert treat, roast ripe strawberries with a drizzle of balsamic vinegar. The vinegar caramelizes the berries into a syrupy liquid, delicious over vanilla ice cream.

Mix together equal parts of salt and white vinegar to remove coffee and tea stains from cups and mugs.

296 Choose Pasta

Holding a place of honor on any pre-race dinner table, pasta makes a quick, delicious meal that you can serve with an endless list of healthy toppings.

Steps

1 Find fresh pastas in a range of flavors in your grocery store's refrigerator section or at a local farmers' market or specialty store. You can also buy them online at sites like FreshPasta.com.

2 Enjoy high-quality artisanal pastas. Sold at specialty stores or gourmet markets, these pastas are dried over several days.

3 Choose from a variety of surface textures as well as shapes. Sauces stick more to ridged pastas.

4 Stash several boxes of dried pasta in the cupboard for super fast meals. It's typically made with durum wheat or semolina flour, giving it a firmer texture, but may have less flavor due to its fast, high-temperature drying process (140 to 160 degrees F; 60 to 71 C).

5 Try your hand at cranking out homemade pasta. All-purpose flour gives it a tender texture and lets it cook quickly. Knead the dough with beets, lemons, saffron and spinach to infuse flavor.

What to Look For

- Fresh
- Artisanal
- Textured
- Boxed
- Homemade

Tip

The size of the vegetable or meat chunks in your sauce should roughly match the pasta size.

Warning

Store fresh pasta in the refrigerator—it can go rancid.

297 Buy Tea

Tea has moved beyond the white-gloved pinky-high party scene. With one-half to one-third less caffeine than coffee, it's steeped with cancer-fighting antioxidants and is the beverage of choice for much of the world. Look for loose and bagged tea in grocery stores, tea shops and specialty stores, ranging from $5 to $35 or more for a quarter of a pound. Here are the teas you are most likely to encounter; many more regional varieties exist.

TEA	VARIETY	COUNTRY	CHARACTERISTICS
Black Tea	Assam	India	Rich, dark and malty. A good alternative for morning coffee drinkers.
	Ceylon	Sri Lanka	Less flowery than Darjeeling. Rich enough to be a morning wake-up cup.
	Chai	India	Prepared tea drink of brewed black tea with cinnamon, nutmeg and cardamom, mixed with milk.
	Darjeeling	India	One of the clearest-brewing black teas; delicate and floral. Often called the champagne of teas because of its high quality.
	Earl Grey	China, India, Sri Lanka	Slightly bitter orange; scented with bergamot oil.
	English Breakfast	China, India, Sri Lanka	Full-bodied blend of black teas.
Oolong Tea	Baochong	China (Taiwan)	Floral and elegant.
	Formosa Oolong	China (Taiwan)	Between black and green tea, fruity without being sweet.
Green Tea	Anemone	China	Green peony blossoms yield a fragrant, sweet and nutty brew.
	Jasmine	China	Jasmine-blossom scent.
	Pearl Tea	China (Taiwan)	Strong, dark.
	Sencha	Japan	Herbal yellow-green tea with slightly rich flavor.
White Tea	Silver Needle	China	Delicate and light.
	White Peony	China	Deeper-colored than silver-needle tea; smooth flavor and subtle fragrance.

298 Buy Coffee

Coffee is one of our favorite legal addictions— the rich scent, full-bodied flavor and jolt of caffeine that everyone from paralegals to poets relies on to kick start their morning. Follow this guide to find a daily grind that suits you best.

Steps

1 Select a grind that is suitable for your brewing method or coffee maker (See 300 Buy a Coffeemaker or Espresso Machine). Whole beans retain their flavor better during storage but you will need to have a coffee grinder in your home.

2 Experiment with different roasting techniques. Coffee beans are roasted to remove moisture and add flavor, and different roasts produce different flavors. French roast results in a full-flavored, dark bean. Italian roast is usually medium dark. Anything lighter is usually identified simply as medium or light roast.

3 Decipher labels. Estate beans are grown and processed on a single farm. Some brands achieve a consistent flavor by blending beans from various sources. Flavored coffees are infused with liquid agents, such as chocolate, vanilla or nuts, but typically don't start with the highest-quality beans. Look for 100 percent Colombian or Hawaiian-blend beans for the best quality if you're buying canned coffee in a grocery store.

4 Buy coffee from a knowledgeable source. Premium roasters, like winemakers, are very proud of their blends. A pound of beans from a gourmet shop ranges from $8 to $30 but is of unbeatable quality. Peet's Coffee and Tea (peets.com), Tully's (tullys.com) and Starbucks (starbucks.com) are all good sources, as are countless local businesses.

5 Turn your coffee drinking into an entertaining research project by studying the general characteristics of different coffee producing regions. Coffee comes from many countries and coffee-growing regions. While it's true that soil and geography matters, any bean can be roasted in different ways, resulting in many possible flavor and blend combinations. Also, pay attention to prices, which are subject to fluctuation. For example, strong demand for Hawaiian beans may drive the price up while similar beans from another region may be available for much less.

- Arabian: Often called *mocha,* this coffee is one of the most ancient, with a medium to full body, rich flavor and dry aftertaste, and chocolate tones.

- Brazilian: A medium to moderately dark roast that goes down sweet and smooth.

- Colombian: Full-bodied, fruity and acidic, with a dark roast.

- Costa Rican: Dry and medium-bodied, with a dark roast.

- Ethiopian: Sweet, medium-bodied and fruity, with a dark roast.

What to Look For

- Suitable grind
- The right roast
- Estate beans
- Blends
- Specialty coffee beans
- Coffee beans grown in different regions

Tips

"Fair-trade coffee" is a new term and describes the effort to raise the incomes of coffee growers in developing countries. Peet's Coffee prides itself on using this program to share revenue with suppliers. If this is important to you, check out Peets.com for more information.

Organic coffees are increasingly available.

- Hawaiian: Delicate, dry, slightly sweet and subtle, with a medium to moderately dark roast.

- Kenyan: Dry and acidic, with a moderately dark to dark roast.

- Sumatran: Full-bodied and slightly fermented, with a dark roast.

- Light roast: Many areas produce beans suitable for light roasting, although Central American coffees frequently show up in light roasts.

299 Order a Great Cup of Coffee

A "tall, skinny single" might sound like a supermodel, but it's actually just a cup of joe. Brush up on the latest latte lingo and in no time you'll be speaking like an experienced coffee connoisseur, whether you stick to a straight-up cup of black coffee or dabble in flavored and foamed concoctions.

TERM	TRANSLATION
Drip	Brewed coffee.
Espresso	Powerful brew resulting from steam forced through packed ground coffee. Look for rich brown "crema" on top.
Café au Lait	Equal parts brewed coffee and hot milk.
Café Latte	Espresso with steamed milk.
Cappuccino	Latte with milk foam on top.
Café Macchlato	Espresso with a hint of milk foam.
Café con Panna	Espresso topped with whipped cream.
Cafe Americano	Espresso with a dash of hot water.
Half-caff	Espresso made with half regular and half decaffeinated beans.
Mocha Latte	Latte with cocoa, topped with whipped cream.
Skinny	Any coffee drink with nonfat milk instead of regular milk.
Single, Double, Triple or Quad	The number of espresso shots (one, two, three or four) in a drink.
Short, Tall, Grande	Small, medium, large cups (respectively).
Vanilla, Caramel, Hazelnut	Flavored syrups, usually made by Torani, that can be added to a coffee drink.
Irish Coffee	Coffee with a shot of whiskey, heavy whipping cream and three sugar cubes.

300 Buy a Coffeemaker or Espresso Machine

Brewing the perfect cup can start your morning off right, while downing a burned cup can make you walk sideways for hours. What type of machine is right for you depends on how rich you like your coffee, how much kitchen counter space you have and how much you consume.

Steps

1 Consider how much coffee you drink to determine whether you want a 4-cup or as big as a 12-cup machine. The price of coffeemakers varies greatly—anywhere from $75 for a basic model to $1,000 for one that grinds your beans, makes both coffee and espresso, and has a timer.

2 Want the best flavor? Go for a Moka pot, which makes black espresso on your stovetop (without foam or froth), or a French press, which makes thick and sometimes grainy coffee by hand. Drip coffeemakers are becoming more refined as well.

3 Determine if you have the space and cash for a big, gleaming piston-style espresso machine, or should you buy a compact and economical Krups espresso maker? Espresso machines can run from $100 to $500, and upward of $1,000 for professional and European stainless-steel piston types.

What to Look For

- Cup size
- Timer
- Two-in-one machine
- Flavor
- Pro and basic models
- Space savers

Tip

A good cup of coffee or espresso has as much to do with the quality of water, beans and grind, and the fineness of the grind, as it does with the machine. If the espresso is too fine, you won't get a topping of rich, brown "crema" in your cup. How to grind beans depends on the filter's shape and size.

301 Purchase a Keg of Beer

Ahhh, a delicious cold one, by the gallon. Just right for a large group, or one seriously misguided overachiever. Know the basics and you'll be all set for the big event.

Steps

1 Locate a liquor store, beer store or brewery in your area that sells kegs, and find out what's available. Do this one week in advance, in case they need to special order.

2 Decide how much beer you need. A pony (half) keg is 7.5 gallons and serves 83 people three 12-ounce servings each, and a full-size keg is 15.5 gallons and serves 165 people three 12-oz. servings each.

3 Choose between the less-expensive hand pump or the Cadillac-grade carbon dioxide pump.

4 Bring your driver's license, a credit card and a deposit to pay for the keg. You'll get your deposit back as long as you return the tank and tap.

5 Schlepp your keg home. Some stores deliver; otherwise, get some heavy-lifters to help you hoist it to the party.

What to Look For

- Store or brewery
- Type of beer
- Keg size
- Pump
- ID and credit card
- Delivery

Tip

For a nominal fee or deposit, the store that sold you the keg may loan you a plastic tub to chill the beer. Ask them to throw in plastic cups, too.

302 **Buy Alcohol in a Dry County**

Back in 1920 when the United States went on the wagon, alcohol was hard to come by. Now it's almost ubiquitous. But in 17 states, they're still toeing the line. Beer, wine and hard liquor are sold by law only in designated outlets, such as liquor stores, bars, hotels and restaurants. Here's how to quench that thirst and stay on the right side of the law.

Steps

1 Crack open the Yellow Pages and look up "Liquor Stores." Some states confine the purchase of bottles and kegs to these outlets. Some restaurants may also sell six-packs for carry-out.

2 Head to a bar or pub. Most states allow alcohol to be sold and taken off the premises because of reasonable-access laws.

3 Fill 'er up. In some semidry states, gas stations or grocers can sell beer, while only liquor stores may sell distilled spirits and wine.

4 Check out the Clubs of America site (greatclubs.com) to find a beer- or wine-of-the-month club that suits your palette. Or order directly from a winery or a distillery. Wine clubs managed by vineyards or other retailers won't send you alcohol if you live in states where its shipment is illegal or questionable, however.

What to Look For

- Liquor stores
- Restaurant and bars
- Gas stations or grocers
- Beer or wine clubs

Warnings

Buying alcohol from a bootlegger in a dry county is illegal. Shipping alcohol directly to Florida, Indiana, Kentucky, Maryland, North Carolina and Tennessee is a felony punishable by law.

It's against the law to purchase or consume alcohol if you are under 21 in the United States or under 19 in Canada.

303 **Choose a Microbrew**

After the demise of the leisure suit, the best thing to happen to American culture is the rise of the microbrewery. Fans can now find handcrafted beer in every supermarket, a unique brewery in every city. Before you hoist that next pint, research the many varieties out there. Sure, it's a tough job, but someone has to do it.

Steps

1 Ask the bartender to describe the brewery's offerings. From lightest to darkest, look for pilsner, lager, ale, porter and stout. Most major American beers are pilsners.

2 Start out with a lager or ale if you're new to microbrews. Then move on to experience the wide variety of flavors that are available. Heavily hopped beers tend to be slightly bitter. Seasonal special brews (such as Christmas ale) often have a higher percentage of alcohol.

3 Slog through the naming variations. A pale ale may not be all that pale, for example. Some English beers are designated as bitter (roughly equivalent to an ale) but may not be bitter at all.

4 Keep in mind that most microbrews contain slightly more alcohol than major American beer brands. Some very heavy brews contain much more.

What to Look For

- Type of beer
- Seasonal beer
- Exotic variatons

Tips

Join a beer-of-the-month club (such as beermonth-club.com). You'll sample from 6 to 24 beers each month. Prices range from $60 for three months to $300 for the entire year.

Many microbreweries produce exotic flavors, such as raspberry, apricot or peach ales.

304 Order a Cocktail

Whether you prefer yours shaken, not stirred, classic cocktails from the 1920s, '30s and '40s have made a comeback. Order up a dry martini or a sidecar next time you're out on the town and enjoy.

What to Look For

- Correct terminology
- Top-shelf or well
- Seasonal or specialty drinks

Steps

1 Familiarize yourself with the vocabulary. *Neat* means served with no ice and not mixed; *on the rocks* means poured over ice. *Shaken* means the ingredients are poured into a shaker with ice, mixed vigorously and poured into a glass. In a *stirred* drink, the ice and ingredients are put in a mixing glass and stirred for 10 seconds before they're poured into a glass. Drinks served *straight up* have no ice.

2 Call your drink. If you don't designate what type of alcohol you want in your cocktail, you'll get the bottom-shelf, least expensive brands, called *well*. You can designate top-shelf brands, such as Grey Goose vodka or Bombay Sapphire gin. For example, order a Grey Goose Greyhound or a Grey Goose and grapefruit juice for a top-shelf, and more expensive, cocktail.

Tip

Tip about a dollar a drink. It's easy to calculate when you're well irrigated, and a happy bartender is a generous bartender.

TERM	DESCRIPTION
Aperitif	A beverage, usually alcohol based, drunk prior to a meal to stimulate the appetite.
Collins	A drink made with a base spirit, lime or lemon juice, simple syrup, and club soda. Always served in Collins glasses, usually garnished with fresh fruit.
Fizz	A drink made with a base spirit, lime or lemon juice, simple syrup and club soda. Served straight up in a wine goblet.
Highball	A simple mixed drink consisting of two ingredients (such as gin and tonic water) combined directly in the serving glass, typically a highball glass.
Liqueur	An alcoholic beverage, sometimes called a cordial, made from a spirit, a sweetening agent such as sugar or honey (or both) and additional flavorings.
Rickey	A drink made with a base spirit, fresh lime juice and club soda. Traditionally served over ice in a highball glass, garnished with a wedge of lime.
Sour	A drink composed of a base spirit, lemon juice, and simple syrup. Served straight up in a Sour glass, garnished with a maraschino cherry and an orange wheel.
Spirit	An alcoholic beverage made by distilling a fermented mash of grains or fruits to a potency of at least 40 percent alcohol by volume. Examples include brandy, gin, rum, tequila, vodka and whiskey.
Toddy	A drink made with a base spirit, hot water and various spices. Served in Irish Coffee glasses, often garnished with a lemon twist or cinnamon stick.

305 **Choose a Restaurant for a Business Function**

When you're wining and dining clients at a business lunch or dinner, match the venue and food to the style of your business function. Is it a brainstorming lunch with colleagues, a yearly review with an employee or a dinner with an important client? Pick the right venue and menu, and get the job done right.

Steps

1 Set your budget. Most businesses have a cap on event expenditures. Look at the price range of each restaurant that's in the running, and factor in beverages and tip.

2 Have the restaurants send you a menu so that you can evaluate your options. Choose one that serves a variety of choices or traditional favorites (chicken, meat, fish and vegetarian dishes such as pasta), where all of your guests will find something they enjoy.

3 Visit the restaurants where you're considering holding the event. Look for appropriate space to mingle before the meal starts (for evening affairs), take the noise level into consideration, check out the bathrooms, read the wine list and scope out seating arrangements.

4 Note how far the restaurant is from your office and figure out how everyone will get there. Is there a parking lot or a valet? Convenience is key if you need to maximize available time, particularly for lunch.

5 Make a reservation. Request a special area of the restaurant, or better yet, ask for a private room or banquet hall if you have a large group.

6 Consider setting up seating ahead of time. Decide who sits where: Pair dining partners strategically, facilitate access between key people, and show respect to the top dogs.

7 Decide whether you'll have a prix fixe meal served or have guests order off the regular menu. If you're putting together a special menu, you may want to ask clients or business colleagues if they have any food allergies or dietary restrictions.

What to Look For

- Price
- Food
- Amenities
- Location
- Parking
- Reservations
- Private rooms
- Menu

Tip

Never order for everyone in the group, unless it's a prix fixe meal you've set up prior to the event. Otherwise, let everyone order for himself or herself.

306 Stock a Wine Cellar

Wines can be collected like rare books and enjoyed after they've acquired some age, or enjoyed immediately. If you're starting a wine collection, formulate a strategy based on how much you drink, what type of wine you enjoy and how much you're prepared to spend.

Steps

1 Start with a small inventory of 50 to 100 bottles, including two cases (12 bottles each) of wine for aging and a case of your favorite drinking wine, either white or red.

2 Taste, taste, taste! Tasting wines will help you discover your personal preference. Avoid buying wines just because they received a high rating from professionals or friends. See if you like them before you make an investment.

3 Balance your inventory. Indulge in one or two wines you particularly enjoy, and mix in bottles of other varietals and regions to suit guests' palates.

4 Save by stocking up on aging wines in their youth when prices are lower. Talk to someone at a reputable wine shop and get suggestions on particular wines that would benefit from aging. Bordeaux, Barolo and Brunello usually take up to 10 years of aging and can be purchased for a song ($15 to $20 a bottle) in their infancy. Some whites, such as grand cru and premier cru white Burgundy, high-quality white Bordeaux, German Riesling, Sauternes and Gewürztraminer, can benefit from aging as well.

5 Add several bottles of aperitifs and dessert wines. Dry sherry, champagne and sparkling wine suit late-afternoon sipping. Sauternes, vintage port and late-harvest Rieslings offer an after-dinner treat. See 60 Select Good Champagne.

6 Draw the line on buying more than a case of wine if it's a new vintage or blend with no proven track record for aging; the merchant won't be able to give you an accurate estimate of how long to hold onto it before drinking.

7 Know what you own and be able to find it quickly. Make a database of your cellar's inventory. Give each wine a location number and listing, and include the wine's name, vintage, producer, appellation, vineyard name, region, country, type (red, white, rosé, sparkling and so forth), quantity owned, price paid per bottle, value (latest estimated worth), and size of bottle (half-bottle, magnum and so on).

8 Keep the temperature of your wine closet, refrigerator or cellar between 50 and 65 degrees F (10 and 18 C) for reds, and 45 to 60 degrees F (7 to 15 C) for whites, or as directed by the vintner or wine merchant.

What to Look For

- Taste
- Balance inventory
- Deals
- Aging-worthy whites
- Aperitif and dessert wines
- Track record
- Cellar log
- Storage temperature

Tips

Buy quarter- or half-bottles of champagne and dessert wine if you're not likely to finish them off in one sitting—they don't keep well.

Nice, everyday white wines include Sauvignon Blanc, simple white Burgundy, Chardonnay and Pinot Gris; everyday reds include Zinfandel, Pinot Noir, and Barbera, Beaujolais, Merlot and simple Bordeaux.

Red wines particularly benefit from a few years of aging: Bordeaux, grand cru or premier cru Burgundy, big Italian reds like Barbaresco and Brunello di Montalcino, Rioja, Cabernet Sauvignon and Côte Rôtie.

Warning

Wines left to age for too long can go rancid, causing the wine to slowly turn to vinegar and the cork to dry out. That's what is meant by the term "corked."

Shaken, stirred, on the rocks or straight up with a twist, the cocktails you mix and serve will depend on your mood and the event (casual get-together or elegant soiree). With a few recipes and a fully stocked bar, you can become the mixologist of the moment, from lemon drops to bourbon on the rocks.

LIQUOR

Essentials	Extras
Amaretto	Apricot brandy
Anisette	Chambord
Bourbon	Crème de cacao
Brandy	Crème de cassis
Gin	Crème de menthe
Grand Marnier	Midori
Irish cream liqueur	Peach schnapps
Kahlúa	Peppermint schnapps
Rum, dark or spiced	Sambuca
Scotch	
Tequila	
Triple sec	
Vermouth, sweet and dry	
Vodka	
Whiskey, Canadian and Irish	

MIXERS

Essentials	Extras
Bitters	7-Up
Club soda	Grenadine
Coffee	Ice cream
Cola	Half and half
Cranberry juice	Milk
Ginger ale	Sweet-and-sour mix
Grapefruit juice	Sweetened lime juice (Rose's brand)
Lemon juice (fresh)	
Lime juice (fresh)	
Orange juice	
Pineapple juice	
Sugar	
Tabasco	
Tomato juice	
Tonic	
Water	
Worcestershire sauce	

GARNISHES

Essentials	Extras
Celery	Crystallized sugar
Cocktail onions	Maraschino cherries
Cocoa powder	Mint (fresh)
Horseradish	Pineapple
Lemons	Raspberries
Limes	Strawberries
Martini olives	Whipped cream
Nutmeg	
Oranges	
Pepper	
Salt, coarse and fine	

GADGETS

Essentials	Extras
Bar towels	Coasters
Blender	Cocktail picks
Bottle opener	Cocktail napkins
Cocktail shaker	Cocktail umbrellas
Corkscrew	Stirrers
Glasses (highball, cocktail, martini, margarita)	
Ice bucket and tongs	
Jigger	
Lemon reamer and zester	
Margarita pitcher	
Strainer	

REHOUSE STORES • BUY WHOLESALE • GET OUT OF DEBT • BUY NOTHING • BUY HAPPINESS • BUY A BETTER MOUSETRAP • BUY TIME
MEONE'S FAVOR • BUY POSTAGE STAMPS WITHOUT GOING TO THE POST OFFICE • TIP PROPERLY • BUY HEALTHY FAST FOOD • BUY SU
TING SERVICE • SELL YOURSELF ON AN ONLINE DATING SERVICE • SELL YOURSELF TO YOUR GIRLFRIEND/BOYFRIEND'S FAMILY • BUY D
HOOSE FILM FOR YOUR CAMERA • BUY RECHARGEABLE BATTERIES • DONATE TO A GOOD CAUSE • HOLD A PROFITABLE GARAGE SALE
STUDENT DISCOUNTS • BUY FLOWERS WHOLESALE • GET A PICTURE FRAMED • HIRE A MOVER • HIRE A PERSONAL ORGANIZER • FIND
EAT BIRTHDAY PRESENT FOR UNDER $10 • SELECT GOOD CHAMPAGNE • BUY A DIAMOND • BUY JEWELRY MADE OF PRECIOUS METALS
DESMAIDS' DRESSES • HIRE AN EVENT COORDINATOR • HIRE A BARTENDER FOR A PARTY • HIRE A PHOTOGRAPHER • HIRE A CATERER
Y AN ANNIVERSARY GIFT • ARRANGE ENTERTAINMENT FOR A PARTY • COMMISSION A FIREWORKS SHOW • BUY A MOTHER'S DAY GIFT
T • SELECT A THANKSGIVING TURKEY • BUY A HOUSEWARMING GIFT • PURCHASE HOLIDAY CARDS • BUY CHRISTMAS STOCKING STUF
E HIGH ROLLERS ROOM IN VEGAS, BABY • BUY SOMEONE A STAR • PAY A RANSOM • GET HOT TICKETS • HIRE A LIMOUSINE • BUY A CF
AM • BUY A PERSONAL JET • ACQUIRE A TELEVISION NETWORK • ACQUIRE A BODY GUARD • BOOK A LUXURY CRUISE AROUND THE WO
DROUGHTBRED RACEHORSE • BUY A VILLA IN TUSCANY • HIRE A PERSONAL CHEF • PURCHASE CUBAN CIGARS • HIRE A GHOSTWRITER
TNESS • MAKE BAIL • DONATE YOUR BODY TO SCIENCE • HIRE YOURSELF OUT AS A MEDICAL GUINEA PIG • SELL PLASMA • SELL YOUR
LLEGE EDUCATION • BUY AND SELL STOCKS • CHOOSE A STOCKBROKER • DAY-TRADE (OR NOT) • BUY ANNUITIES • BUY AND SELL MU
Y PERSONAL FINANCE SOFTWARE • CHOOSE A TAX PREPARER • SET UP A LEMONADE STAND • SELL YOUR PRODUCT ON TV • HIRE A C
SINESS IDEA • BUY A SMALL BUSINESS • BUY A FRANCHISE • LEASE RETAIL SPACE • LEASE INDUSTRIAL SPACE • LEASE OFFICE SPACE
B SITE • BUY ADVERTISING ON THE WEB • SELL YOUR ART • HIRE A PERSONAL COACH • SELL ON THE CRAFT CIRCUIT • HIRE A LITERA
LING BUSINESS • BUY A HOT DOG STAND • SHOP FOR A MORTGAGE • REFINANCE YOUR HOME • SAVE BIG BUCKS ON YOUR MORTGAG
LL A FIXER-UPPER • SELL THE FARM • SELL MINERAL RIGHTS • SELL A HOUSE • SELL A HOUSE WITHOUT A REAL ESTATE AGENT • OBTA
OK A VACATION RENTAL • BUY A CONDOMINIUM • RENT AN APARTMENT OR HOUSE • OBTAIN RENTER'S INSURANCE • BUY A LOFT IN M
RNISH YOUR STUDIO APARTMENT • BUY USED FURNITURE • BUY DOOR AND WINDOW LOCKS • CHOOSE AN ORIENTAL CARPET • BUY L
RRANTIES ON APPLIANCES • FIND PERIOD FIXTURES • BUY A BED AND MATTRESS • HIRE AN INTERIOR DESIGNER • HIRE A FENG SHUI
N • BUY A WHIRLPOOL TUB • BUY A SHOWERHEAD • BUY A TOILET • CHOOSE A FAUCET • BUY GLUES AND ADHESIVES • CHOOSE WIN
CHEN CABINETS • CHOOSE A KITCHEN COUNTERTOP • BUY GREEN HOUSEHOLD CLEANERS • STOCK YOUR HOME TOOL KIT • BUY A V
ENTRY DOOR • BUY A GARAGE-DOOR OPENER • BUY LUMBER FOR A DIY PROJECT • HOW TO SELECT ROOFING • HIRE A CONTRACTO
OWERS FOR YOUR GARDEN • SELECT PEST CONTROLS • BUY SOIL AMENDMENTS • BUY MULCH • BUY A COMPOSTER • BUY FERTILIZE
Y KOI FOR YOUR FISH POND • BUY A STORAGE SHED • HIRE AN ARBORIST • BUY BASIC GARDEN TOOLS • BUY SHRUBS AND TREES •
LECT KITCHEN KNIVES • DECIPHER FOOD LABELS • SELECT HERBS AND SPICES • STOCK YOUR KITCHEN WITH STAPLES • EQUIP A KIT
UNTAIN OYSTERS • PURCHASE LOCAL HONEY • CHOOSE POULTRY • SELECT FRESH FISH AND SHELLFISH • SELECT RICE • PURCHASE
EADS • BUY ARTISAN CHEESES • PURCHASE KOSHER FOOD • BUY FOOD IN BULK • CHOOSE COOKING OILS • SELECT OLIVE OIL • SEL
FFEEMAKER OR ESPRESSO MACHINE • PURCHASE A KEG OF BEER • BUY ALCOHOL IN A DRY COUNTY • CHOOSE A MICROBREW • OR
ULATION PREDICTOR KIT • PICK A PREGNANCY TEST KIT • CHOOSE BIRTH CONTROL • FIND THE RIGHT OB-GYN • HIRE A MIDWIFE OR
OOSE DIAPERS • BUY OR RENT A BREAST PUMP • CHOOSE A CAR SEAT • BUY CHILD-PROOFING SUPPLIES • FIND FABULOUS CHILDCA
CKYARD PLAY STRUCTURE • FIND A GREAT SUMMER CAMP • SELL GIRL SCOUT COOKIES • BUY BRACES FOR YOUR KID • BUY TOYS
A MODEL • SELL USED BABY GEAR, TOYS, CLOTHES AND BOOKS • FIND A COUPLES COUNSELOR • HIRE A FAMILY LAWYER • BUY PRO
PENSES • GET VIAGRA ONLINE • PURCHASE A TOOTHBRUSH • BUY MOISTURIZERS AND ANTIWRINKLE CREAMS • SELECT PAIN RELIEF
PPLIES • SELECT HAIR-CARE PRODUCTS • BUY WAYS TO COUNTER HAIR LOSS • BUY A WIG OR HAIRPIECE • BUY A NEW BODY • GET
NICURIST • GET WHITER TEETH • SELECT EYEGLASSES AND SUNGLASSES • HIRE A PERSONAL TRAINER • SIGN UP FOR A YOGA CLAS
EA MARKET • RENT SPACE AT AN ANTIQUE MALL • BUY AT AUCTION • KNOW WHAT YOUR COLLECTIBLES ARE WORTH • DICKER WITH D
COGNIZE THE REAL MCCOY • BUY COINS • BUY AN ANTIQUE AMERICAN QUILT • BUY AN ANTIQUE FLAG • LIQUIDATE YOUR BEANIE BA
WNSHOP • BUY AND SELL COMIC BOOKS • BUY AND SELL SPORTS MEMORABILIA • SELL YOUR BASEBALL-CARD COLLECTIONS • CHO
MPUTER • BUY PRINTER PAPER • BUY A PRINTER • BUY COMPUTER PERIPHERALS • CHOOSE AN INTERNET SERVICE PROVIDER • GET
Y BLANK CDS • BUY AN MP PLAYER • CHOOSE A DVD PLAYER • BUY A VCR • CHOOSE A PERSONAL DIGITAL ASSISTANT • CHOOSE MO
GITAL CAMCORDER • DECIDE ON A DIGITAL CAMERA • BUY A HOME AUTOMATION SYSTEM • BUY A STATE-OF-THE-ART SOUND SYSTEM
IVERSAL REMOTE • BUY A HOME THEATER SYSTEM • BUY VIRTUAL-REALITY FURNITURE • BUY TWO-WAY RADIOS • BUY A MOBILE ENT
NEY • GET TRAVEL INSURANCE • PICK THE IDEAL LUGGAGE • FLY FOR FREE • BID FOR A SLED RIDE ON THE ALASKAN IDITAROD TRAIL
REIGN OFFICIAL • GET A EURAIL PASS • TAKE AN ITALIAN BICYCLE VACATION • CHOOSE A CHEAP CRUISE • BOOK A HOTEL PACKAGE
OTLAND • BUY A SAPPHIRE IN BANGKOK • HIRE A RICKSHA IN YANGON • TAKE SALSA LESSONS IN CUBA • BUY A CAMERA IN HONG K
ST BASEBALL GLOVE • ORDER UNIFORMS FOR A SOFTBALL TEAM • BUY ANKLE AND KNEE BRACES • BUY GOLF CLUBS • JOIN AN EL
OWMOBILE • BUY A PERSONAL WATERCRAFT • HIRE A SCUBA INSTRUCTOR • BUY A SKATEBOARD AND PROTECTIVE GEAR • BUY SKA
ATHER ACTIVITIES • SELL USED SKIS • BUY A SNOWBOARD, BOOTS AND BINDINGS • BUY SKI BOOTS • BUY A BICYCLE • SELL YOUR
Y A BACKPACK • BUY A BACKPACKING STOVE • BUY A KAYAK • BUY A PERSONAL FLOTATION DEVICE • BUY A WET SUIT • BUY A SURF
DER CUSTOM-MADE COWBOY BOOTS • BUY CLOTHES ONLINE • FIND SPECIALTY SIZES • BUY THE PERFECT COCKTAIL DRESS • BUY
Y A MAN'S SUIT • HIRE A TAILOR • BUY CUSTOM-TAILORED CLOTHES IN ASIA • BUY A BRIEFCASE • SHOP FOR A LEATHER JACKET • B
TE MONITOR • SELECT A WATCH • BUY KIDS' CLOTHES • CHOOSE CHILDREN'S SHOES • PURCHASE CLOTHES AT OUTLET SHOPS • BL

Family Affairs

308 Buy and Sell Sperm

It's not like anyone grows up thinking, "Gee, someday I'll buy sperm and raise a beautiful family!" But for infertile couples and women who choose to raise a child without a male partner, a sperm bank is a tremendous resource. And for those gentlemen who want to take a hands-on approach to helping someone conceive—or just need the extra money—these tips will help the process go swimmingly.

Steps

Buy

1 Ask your OB-GYN for a sperm bank recommendation, or ask others who have been through the insemination process which bank they used.

2 Read the bank's Web site carefully. Examine its policies on anonymity, the donor screening process and genetic testing. If you have questions or concerns, give them a call.

3 Review the menu of fees. A wide range of services is available, from genetic testing to photo matching, shipping to storage, cord banking to sperm washing. Sperm samples themselves run from $100 to $250 depending on the processing involved. Washed sperm, for example, has the semen removed in preparation for an intrauterine insemination (IUI).

4 Start shopping: Review donor profiles and order complete medical history of those you're interested in.

5 Choose your guy, call the bank and order your sperm. Have it shipped directly to your doctor's office, or to your home if your partner or a midwife will be doing the honors.

Sell

1 Contact a reputable bank via e-mail or phone. They will conduct a brief interview, then ask you to come in.

2 Provide a sample for preliminary screening. It will be frozen, then thawed a week later to check for cryosurvival. Semen must meet minimum requirements for motility, morphology and sperm count. Most potential donors—up to 95 percent—are disqualified.

3 Complete more testing and give full medical history of your whole family, which is evaluated for potential birth defects or genetic conditions. After eight weeks to three months of testing, freezing and testing your sperm again, you are a fully qualified donor.

4 Bank the cash. Fees paid range from $35 per donation to $900 per month for three samples a week. Donors qualify for bonuses for successful referrals and when they exit the program.

5 Hands off: You are asked not to ejaculate for 48 hours prior to donating to ensure that your sperm count is high enough.

What to Look For

- Good recommendations from customers
- Health care provider's recommendation
- Thorough donor screening
- Impeccable medical standards

Tips

Most banks guarantee complete anonymity of both donor and recipient. Some, such as Cryobank.com, have an openness policy whereby if the child at age 18 or older wants to know the identity of the donor—and the donor agrees—a meeting can be arranged. Still other banks, like RainbowFlag.com, disclose the identity of the donor by mutual consent when the child is 3 months old.

Donors must commit to staying in the program for a minimum of nine months to a year due to the rigorous testing involved. Donors will be "retired" after a certain number of successful births, usually 10.

309 Choose an Ovulation Predictor Kit

You've made that big decision—you want to get pregnant. Many couples conceive within a year simply by putting away the birth control. Help pinpoint the 24- to 48-hour stretch in your cycle where you are most fertile (right before you ovulate) with an ovulation predictor kit.

Steps

1 Buy a box of test sticks. They work by detecting the surge of lutenizing hormone present in your urine, which in turn triggers ovulation within 24 hours. Each box contains five to seven sticks, since it may take several days for the lutenizing hormone to build up to a detectible amount. An average kit runs between $20 and $40 and is good for one cycle, checking once a day. Some popular brands are Answer ($20) and First Response ($30).

2 Try a reusable electronic test kit. Though more expensive, this test has been found to be more sensitive in consumer testing. One kit is the Clear Plan Easy Fertility Monitor. It utilizes disposable test sticks that you place into the unit, which analyzes and stores the data for you. The basic unit itself is just under $200, and refill sticks run $1.50 to $2 each.

What to Look For

- Test sticks
- Electronic kit

Tip

The tests are convenient, easy to use and accurate if you follow the directions. Some even come with a free pregnancy test as an added bonus.

310 Pick a Pregnancy Test Kit

Think you might be expecting? An in-home test kit will provide a prompt—and private—answer. These kits detect with 97 percent accuracy whether the "pregnancy" hormone, human chorionic gonadotropin (hGC), is present in a woman's urine. Most tests work in much the same way, but vary in sensitivity.

Steps

1 Buy an early-response kit to test on or before the first day of your missed period. The First Response Early Result Pregnancy Test is highly rated in consumer trials and gives an accurate result three days before your period is due. However, no test will pick up all pregnancies that early. You can expect a more reliable result a few days or even a week later, when the rapidly increasing hormone level is easier to detect.

2 Read the instructions. Some tests have you pass the stick through the urine stream, while with others you collect urine in a cup, then dip the stick. Many kits allow both and take five minutes or less—but they're the longest minutes of your life!

3 Make sure the result is easy to understand. Any line that appears on the absorbent wick inside the test stick should be strong and clear. If it's not, you'll need to wait a day or two and test again. Twin-packs are cheaper than buying two kits individually.

What to Look For

- Accuracy
- Ease of use
- Clear, easy-to-understand results

Warning

It's possible to get a false negative result when you're actually pregnant (positive). If your period does not start within a week, test yourself again. If pregnancy symptoms persist despite a second negative test, see your doctor.

311 Choose Birth Control

Not ready for a visit from the stork? While only abstinence is 100 percent effective at preventing pregnancy, most types of birth control are very reliable when used correctly. You'll need to discuss the options with your health care provider, but these guidelines will help you narrow your choices to find a method that works for you and your lifestyle.

TYPE (BRAND)	HOW IT WORKS	FEATURES
Male Condom	Blocks the sperm from reaching the egg. 86 to 98 percent effective.	Only latex and polyurethane condoms are proven to help protect against STDs, including HIV. Buy at drugstore. Can only be used once.
Female Condom (Reality)	Keeps sperm from entering the body. Made of polyurethane, is packaged with a lubricant. 79 to 95 percent effective.	Protects against STDs, including HIV. Can be inserted up to 24 hours prior to sexual intercourse. Buy at drugstore or at GoodVibes.com. Visible, noisy, may be difficult to insert and remove.
Oral Contraceptives	Taken daily, the Pill's hormones (estrogen and progestin) block the release of eggs from the ovaries. 95 to 99.9 percent effective.	Lightens menstrual flow and protects against pelvic inflammatory disease (PID), ovarian cancer and endometrial cancer. Does not protect against STDs or HIV. May add to risk of heart disease, including high blood pressure, blood clots and blockage of the arteries. Women who are over age 35 and smoke, or have a history of blood clots or breast or endometrial cancer may be advised not to take the Pill. Requires a prescription.
Mini-pill	Only has progestin, unlike the Pill, which also has estrogen. Taken daily, prevents sperm from reaching the egg. Prevents a fertilized egg from implanting. 95 to 99.9 percent effective.	Can decrease period flow and protect against PID, and ovarian and endometrial cancer. OK for breastfeeding women. Good option for women who can't take estrogen or who have a risk of blood clots. Does not protect against STDs or HIV. Requires a prescription.
Copper T IUD	T-shaped intrauterine device placed inside the uterus. Releases a small amount of a hormone that blocks pregnancy. Contains copper, which stops sperm. If fertilization does occur, IUD prevents implantation. 99 percent effective.	Can stay in the uterus for up to 10 years. Does not protect against STDs or HIV. Requires visit to a health care provider for insertion.
Progestasert IUD	Plastic T-shaped intrauterine device placed inside the uterus. Contains progesterone, which prevents sperm from reaching the egg. 98 percent effective.	Can stay in the uterus for one year. Requires fitting and follow-up visits with health care provider.

TYPE (BRAND)	HOW IT WORKS	FEATURES
Intrauterine System (Mirena)	T-shaped device placed inside the uterus. Releases hormone that blocks pregnancy. 99 percent effective.	Stays in the uterus for up to five years. Does not protect against STDs or HIV. Not all health care providers insert the IUS. Requires follow-up with health care provider.
Injections (Lunelle)	Pregnancy-preventing hormone shots given once a month in the arm, buttocks or thigh. 99 percent effective.	Does not interfere with spontaneity. Does not protect against STDs or HIV. Requires follow-up with health care provider.
Injections (Depo-Provera)	Shots of the hormone progestin in the buttocks or arm every three months. 99.7 percent effective.	Does not require daily use. Does not protect against STDs or HIV. Requires follow-up with health care provider.
Diaphragm or Cervical Cap	Diaphragm blocks sperm from reaching the egg; inserted inside vagina before intercourse. 80 to 94 percent effective. Cervical cap is 80 to 90 percent effective for women who have not given birth, 60 to 80 percent for women who have.	Spermicides with nonoxynol-9 (available at drugstores) will help protect from the STDs gonorrhea and chlamydia. Some women can be sensitive to nonoxynol-9 and need to use spermicides that do not contain it. Requires proper fitting by health care provider.
Patch (Ortho Evra)	A patch worn on the skin that releases progestin and estrogen into the bloodstream. 99 percent effective.	Does not require daily use. Appears to be less effective in women who weigh more than 198 lbs. Does not protect against STDs or HIV. Requires a prescription.
Hormonal Vaginal Contraceptive Ring (NuvaRing)	Self-inserted ring releases progestin and estrogen. 98 to 99 percent effective.	Does not require daily use. Requires a prescription.
Surgical Sterilization	Tubal ligation or "tube tying" prevents eggs from leaving the fallopian tubes. Male vasectomy prevents sperm from entering ejaculate. 99 to 99.5 percent effective.	Requires surgery.
Nonsurgical Sterilization (Essure Permanent Birth Control System)	A thin tube is used to thread a tiny spring-like device through the vagina and uterus into each fallopian tube and to cause scar tissue to grow and eventually plug the tubes. 100 percent effective when successfully implanted.	It can take about three months for the scar tissue to grow, so it is important to use another form of birth control during this time. Follow-up visits required.
WARNING	Norplant and Norplant 2 were taken off the market in July 2002. If you are using the Norplant system, you should contact your health care provider about what your contraceptive options will be after the five-year expiration date of your system.	

312 Find the Right OB-GYN

You'll see a lot of your gynecologist during your life—and vice versa. Whether you're planning on getting pregnant or just looking for quality care, finding an OB-GYN you can trust to respect your views is absolutely critical.

Steps

1 Ask a trustworthy medical professional to recommend a board-certified doctor. You can also search for doctors by ZIP code on the American College of Obstetricians and Gynecologists' Web site (acog.org). Ask friends and family for a recommendation.

2 Consult your insurance company. You'll likely want a doctor who is on your health care plan's network of providers.

3 Ask your physician how often you need to schedule pap smears, breast exams and other procedures. You can also discuss birth control options (see 311 Choose Birth Control).

4 Schedule an appointment to discuss prenatal care if you're pregnant or plan to become pregnant soon.

   • Write down any specific concerns you have about your pregnancy. Talk about your views on the labor process including natural childbirth, epidurals, fetal monitoring, circumcision and episiotomies. Get specific. Find out under what circumstances labor would be induced, or when a cesarean section would be advised.

   • Discuss your birth plan, particularly if it includes a home birth. Some doctors or groups will not take a patient who wants a home birth.

   • Find out if your doctor will be at your labor. Often another doctor from the group is on call; if so, you'll want to meet the other physicians.

   • Ask where your doctor delivers babies. Make sure that you are comfortable with the facility and it is covered by your insurance.

5 Chat with the physician's office manager and find out what the policies are on emergency phone calls and appointments. Talk about the doctor's fees and find out what your insurance covers.

What to Look For

- Board certification
- Shared views of pregnancy, labor and delivery
- Your insurance company's preferred practitioner
- A practice near your home or workplace

Tips

If you have an underlying condition that might shift your pregnancy into a higher-risk category (diabetes, high blood pressure, epilepsy), ask the doctor if he or she recommends specialized care.

To improve the chance that your doctor will actually be there when you give birth, look for a small practice where he or she is most likely to be on call on the big day.

If you're sticking with your regular gynecologist and are planning to become pregnant, schedule a preconception exam. You'll get some good information about your baseline health and a sense of whether your doctor is really the right person to deliver your baby.

313 Hire a Midwife or Doula

Being pregnant is a life-altering transition. Your questions and concerns will grow right along with the new life in your belly. Many women are finding the answers and reassurance they need with nurse-midwives and doulas (labor coaches).

Steps

Finding a midwife

1 Decide if you want a midwife instead of a physician to provide prenatal care and attend your birth. Check out MidwifeInfo.com to explore the differences between the two. Midwives generally approach birth with a holistic, natural, no-intervention-unless-necessary policy. Midwives deliver babies at home as well as in hospitals.

2 Find a certified nurse-midwife in your area by contacting the American College of Nurse-Midwives (midwife.org). You can also check with your local women's health center, or contact the hospital where you plan to give birth and ask for a list of midwives who have privileges there.

3 If you plan to give birth at home, you need to find a direct-entry midwife. Licensing and regulation vary from state to state; ask your obstetrician or your local women's health center, or search online for a midwife certified to practice in your area.

4 Schedule preliminary appointments with various midwives until you find one with whom you feel truly comfortable. Ask about her experience and training, her attitudes toward pregnancy and birth, how she handles complications, and if her services are covered by your health plan (see 140 Get Health Insurance).

Finding a doula

1 Hire a doula if you want a well-trained person to coach you alongside the obstetrician and/or want round-the-clock care during labor and birth. Doulas advocate for the mother and provide vigilant emotional, physical and educational support to her with specific assistance with positioning, massage and other pain-management techniques. Doulas are also available after the birth. This "fourth-trimester" care is geared specifically for the mother so that she can take care of the baby. A doula comes to your home, answers any questions you have about your baby, helps you learn to breast-feed successfully, makes sure you get food and rest, and may even do light housekeeping.

2 Ask your doctor, friends or co-workers for recommendations, or contact Doulas of North America (dona.org) for a referral.

3 Interview your choices carefully, following the same guidelines as for a midwife. Look for someone you trust to back up your choices while making you feel comfortable and secure.

What to Look For

- Shared views about pregnancy and birth
- Professional certification
- Personalized care
- Insurance coverage

Tips

Studies have shown that healthy women with no pregnancy complications are in equally good hands with an OB-GYN or a certified midwife. Other studies find that women who use doulas have shorter labors with fewer complications.

All midwives work with an obstetrician for consultations and backup. It's a good idea to meet the obstetrician before your due date.

Interested in delivering your baby at a birth center? Contact the National Association of Childbearing Centers (birthcenters.org) for a location near you.

If complications develop for you or your baby, you'll be placed in the care of an OB-GYN.

314 Find a Good Pediatrician

Picking a pediatrician can be an anxiety-inducing job. This person will be not only your child's doctor, but your guide through sleepless nights of fever, earaches and croup. You want to find someone you trust, respect and see eye to eye with, and who your child feels good about. After all, their doc will care for them (and you) from the day you first bring them home until they graduate from high school.

Steps

1 Begin your search while you're pregnant. Ask everyone—family, friends, co-workers, neighbors and medical professionals—to recommend a pediatrician. You'll want to find someone who truly enjoys working with children and their parents, responds appropriately to your concerns, and both respects and listens to you and your child.

2 Check with your health insurance company about which pediatricians in your area are covered by your plan, and to what degree. Many companies publish a provider listing that includes all doctors in a given plan. See 140 Get Health Insurance.

3 Narrow it down to three or four doctors and schedule office visits. Ask if there are fees for these informational interviews. Bring a list of questions and concerns along, and don't be shy about asking them. Are you on the same page about parenting? Are you given enough time to truly explore your concerns? How comfortable would you feel entrusting your child's health to this person? Note how the doctor responds to you.

4 Discuss the health issues that are important to you. If you're not sure whether you want to immunize your child, bring that up. Some physicians will not accept patients who do not want to be immunized. Ask about the doctor's thoughts on use of antibiotics, and how and when they should be prescribed.

5 Ask the pediatrician or the administrative staff about billing and scheduling, after-hours care, house calls and same-day or drop-in appointments for sick children. Find out how insurance claims and/or co-payments are handled. Ask if the pediatrician (or group) is affiliated with a nearby hospital, and if they have coordinated after-hours care with that facility. Ask when the doctor is available to return phone calls and respond to sick-child concerns. Will you often or always be referred to an after-hours nursing call center?

6 If possible, meet the other doctors in the group so they are not strangers if you bring your child in when his or her doctor is not on-call. If that's not possible, ask about their medical philosophies and credentials.

What to Look For

- Recommendations
- Warmth and responsiveness
- Insurance coverage
- Shared views on parenting and medical issues

Tips

Consider geographic location. You will make many trips to your pediatrician's office, so choosing someone near your home can be a big plus.

Make sure the doctor is board certified and hasn't been charged in any medical malpractice suits.

Warning

Follow your instincts: If you feel like something is wrong with your child and the doctor shrugs it off, get a second opinion or get another doctor.

315 Hire a Child Therapist

You know it's not just a phase that your child is going to grow out of. However, you don't have to go it alone: Seek the professional assistance of a therapist. You'll need to devote a great deal of time and care to finding the right person. It's important that you and your child hit it off with the therapist; otherwise, little will be accomplished.

Steps

1 Identify your child's needs. Really listen to your child's teachers and understand that he or she may behave differently at home. Try to grasp the full dimension of what's going on.

2 Get personal referrals from people you trust. Check with your pediatrician, family doctor, school teachers and counselors, and other parents who've undertaken a similar search.

3 Contact your pediatrician and school psychologist if you suspect your child has special needs that should be addressed. For example, regional centers should be contacted for mental retardation or autism. For attention deficit hyperactivity disorder, contact the Children and Adults with Attention Deficit Hyperactivity Disorder organization (chadd.org). If learning disabilities are suspected, talk to your child's principal and request a learning assessment.

4 Contact several therapists to ask about their approach. Ask about their qualifications. The therapist must have a master's degree in psychology, counseling or social work, or a doctorate in psychology (see 352 Hire a Mental Health Professional).

5 Find out about fees and office hours. Check with your insurance company; many insurers offer limited coverage for therapy.

6 Discuss your child's issues with the therapist and find out what experience he or she has in dealing with similar problems. Discuss the treatment plan. Find out how the therapist establishes trust with a potentially defiant patient—will he or she take the child for a walk? Play ball? Talk sports or Britney Spears for a while? Play therapy and art therapy are common modalities used with children. A therapist's approach is key to the success of the relationship and will vary with the age of the child.

7 Learn what happens in a typical session. Some therapists offer a trial session for a reduced fee or allow parents to sit in on one session. Whether this is advisable depends on the child's age.

8 Use your intuition above all. You are your child's best advocate and should feel confident and supported throughout treatment.

What to Look For

- Your child's needs
- Referrals
- Professional qualifications
- Insurance coverage
- Appropriate experience and approach

Tips

Most counties offer a referral line to help you find a therapist—a good place to begin your search if you can't get personal referrals.

If your child needs medication, ask the therapist or your pediatrician to refer you to a child psychiatrist.

316 Gear Up for a New Baby

Most expectant parents want to buy their new baby the world—and there is a whole world of gear out there for little ones. But you don't need to spend a bundle on your little bundle. Before you blow the budget on all-new gear, consider borrowing as much as possible or buying much of it used. Check out online sources for reviews and recommendations and then selectively purchase new items with safety, durability and adaptability in mind.

Steps

1 Talk to people about what baby items they've used, and what they like or don't like about them. Other parents who have been in your boat are your best source of information. This is also a great way to find out if someone has something (like a portable crib) that they'll lend you or let you test drive.

2 Read up: Browse the bargain hunter's guides like *Baby Bargains* and *Bargain Buys For Baby's First Year* for comparisons of major baby products by brand and price. Consult ConsumerReports.org and DrSpock.com. Shop the sales at BabyCenter.com and have gear shipped direct to you.

3 Go online to local parent sites and hit yard sales for access to ever-available used gear. You'll be able to find almost everything you need in good condition from other parents whose child has outgrown it. Usability on most of these items is counted in months, not years.

4 Have a friend who is a parent make a list of those items you should borrow or buy used and those you definitely want to buy new. You'll want to borrow or find used such items as a Baby Björn (which retails for $80 and is grown out of in less than 9 months), a portable crib, activity saucer, doorway jumper and temporary changing table.

5 Make sure any used gear is safe and in good working order. Check for recalls at BabyCenter.com and give it a good scrub with disinfectant before using. Make the Web site of the Juvenile Products Manufacturers Association (jpma.org) your first stop when shopping for nursery furniture. It provides up-to-the-minute information on recalls and safety tips as well as links to approved furniture manufacturers.

6 Invest in a crib if you plan on having more than one child, and a changing table that eventually converts to a dresser.

7 Follow safety instructions for all items. Similarly, adjust swings, jumpers, packs and activity saucers as needed as your child grows. As a rule of thumb keep in mind that your baby's legs should never fully extend while jumping—he or she should always have slightly bent knees.

What to Look For

- Other parents' advice
- Bargains
- Used items
- Solid construction
- Up-to-date safety features
- Compliance with the latest safety standards

Tips

To get the most for your money, don't restrict your search to baby stores—check out regular furniture stores (especially during seasonal sales). You might find top-quality goods at reduced prices, and a few modifications (adding drawer stops or replacing protruding drawer pulls) will keep your baby safe.

Crib alternatives—bassinets, cradles and Moses baskets—can keep a newborn snug and make it easier to move him or her from room to room. But because a baby outgrows them within six months—and you'll need that crib eventually—borrow or buy these items second-hand.

Always mail in your product registration card in case of recalls.

See 318 Choose a Stroller.

ITEM	FEATURES	PRICE, POPULAR BRANDS
Changing Table	Look for a sturdy table with handy storage space. Some have extra drawers. Concave pads and straps keep babies from rolling off. Bureaus with removable pad revert to a dresser later.	Simple open-shelf tables, start at $80. Deluxe dresser models, $250 to $1,000.
Diaper Pail	A plain pail with a tight-fitting lid works OK for a diaper disposal if it is emptied frequently.	$20 to $40; refill, $4 to $16. Diaper Genie, Diaper Champ
Baby Monitor	Get a model with two receivers to leave them in different areas of the house. Sound indicator lights allow you to do noisy things (like vacuum). Most plug in as well as use batteries; make sure reception is clear in either mode.	$35 to $90. Video monitors, $300 Fisher-Price, Graco
Front Packs and Slings	Indispensable from birth until too heavy. Allows you to "wear your baby" while doing other things. Some let baby face in or out. Look for adjustable straps. Slings are favored by some parents even into the toddling years.	Slings, start at $40. Front packs, $25 to $80. Baby Björn, Koala Sling
Backpack	For babies who can hold their head up. Test drive with baby inside to check fit. Make sure you can get the weight off your shoulders and onto your hips with the belly band. Look for adjustability, secure baby harness and sturdy support stand.	$50 to $70 Madden, Kelty
Movers and Shakers	For babies who can sit up comfortably. Bouncers, doorway jumpers and activity saucers run the gamut from stripped down to decked out. Choose sturdy swing and bouncer models with adjustable heights. Check for safety restraints that are easy to use and don't pinch.	Swings, $70 to $100. Saucers, $50 to $80. Jumpers, $40. Graco, ExerSaucer by Evenflo
Portable Cribs and Playpens	Look for a safe, sturdy model that is easy to set up and take down. Some have bassinet that insert.	$50 to $150. Graco Pac'n'Play
Swings	Birth to 2 or 3 months. Look for variable speeds, and sturdy crotch belt so baby doesn't slip under tray.	$50 to $100. Graco
Highchairs	For babies who can sit up comfortably. Get a tray that releases with one hand. Make sure crotch strap is securely tethered and that there are no parts that pinch. Upscale models have wheels and adjustable heights. Space saver option is a booster seat plus tray that belts securely to a chair.	$35 to $200. Graco, Peg Perego, Chicco Mamma Booster seat with tray, $20. Safety 1st
WARNING	Quilts, comforters, blankets, pillows and stuffed animals do not belong in your baby's bed. Any of these items are suffocation hazards since babies do not have the strength to move their head or body out of harm's way. The ties that attach some bumpers pose a strangulation risk.	

317 Buy a New Crib

Cribs run the gamut from Civics to Ferraris in looks, materials and sticker price. Shop for a crib that's built to last. It will be shaken, rattled and rolled (and sometimes slept in) for years.

Steps

1 Make sure a used or new crib carries a sticker indicating a certified manufacturer. Verify that the manufacturer complies with federal safety regulations on crib construction.

2 Buy a reputable brand, such as Pali or Ragazzi, for safe, beautiful hardwood cribs in sizes and styles that range from simple ($200) to completely over the top ($1,000).

3 Check that the frame and headboard are strong. Jiggle the bars to make sure they don't twist or move. Make sure the mattress support frame is snug and doesn't easily pull apart from the corners.

4 If you're buying a used crib or inheriting a hand-me-down, be sure to get a model that is only a few years old so it meets safety standards and its components are not worn. Make sure the entire hardware package is present and in good condition. Don't get a crib with split or loosened wood joints, missing or cracked bars or slats, cracked or flaking paint, or splinters. Top rails should have plastic gum protectors.

5 On older cribs, check that spaces between slats are no more than 2⅜ inches (6 cm) apart as required by law. Go to the National Safety Council (www.nsc.org/library/facts/cribtips.htm) for more information on crib safety guidelines.

6 Test the drop-side mechanism (on one or both sides) to make sure you can lower it easily with only one hand. When lowered, the top rail should be at least 9 inches (23 cm) above the mattress.

7 Look for a crib with at least 26 inches (66 cm) between the top of the side rail and the mattress support frame. Many cribs let you adjust the height of the mattress frame to keep a growing child safely inside. Your baby will no doubt attempt a daring crib escape at some point, and tall sides make it tougher.

8 Explore cribs with special features. Cribs you can convert into toddler or child beds are costly up front, but may save money in the long run since you can skip the intermediate bed down the line and go right into a twin.

9 Buy the best crib mattress you can afford ($80 to $140). Look for firm support, fire retardancy, and a good-quality waterproof cover. Most mattresses come in a standard size, but check the fit: If you can put more than two fingers between the mattress and the crib frame, it is not safe.

What to Look For

- Compliance with all safety standards
- Solid construction
- Style
- Sung-fitting mattress

Tip

Before buying, look at BabyCenter.com for news of product recalls. Never compromise safety.

318 **Choose a Stroller**

A stroller will be one of your most-used items, so buy the best quality you can afford or request one as a shower gift. Most parents use it several times a day, loading it in and out of the car, cruising with baby from the zoo to the mall. Most manufacturers offer a variety of styles, from standard to travel to jogging; comparison shop in *Baby Bargains* and talk to other parents about their recommendations.

TYPE	DESCRIPTION	PRICES
Standard	More comfortable than lightweight strollers. Most recline for infants. Weigh over 12 lbs. (5.4 kg). If you have an older child and a baby, consider investing in a stroller with a step for your big kid to stand on.	$30 to $400
Infant	Allow infants to recline. Many convert from car seat to stroller so baby can stay asleep.	$30 to $2,100 (prams)
Travel/Lightweight	Usually the second stroller. Lightweight and compact (usually under 12 lbs. or 5.4 kg). Few recline for infants.	$30 to $150
Jogging	Designed to absorb the shock of running, jogging and going over rough terrain.	$60 to $650 (triple)
Multiple	Carry two or more children.	$90 to $900 (quad)
Accessories	Infant insert	$25 to $50
	Fleece	$35 to $90
	Rainshield	$25 to $70
	Stroller bag	$25 to $75
	Helmet (for jogging strollers)	$15 to $20
	Flashing lights	$8 to $10
	Carrying bag (for travel)	$70 to $80
	Handlebar extension for taller parents	$30 to $35
TIPS	Save your back by buying a stroller with wheels that navigate easily and handlebars that fit properly. Buy a handlebar extension if necessary.	
	Ask if you can test drive the stroller, with child inside, to see how the stroller handles the reality factor.	
	Think about what makes the most sense for your lifestyle. Active? A jogging stroller or one that converts to a backpack may be just the ticket.	

319 Buy Baby Clothes

Let's face it—babies are messy. They spring leaks in all sorts of places. You'll be changing your newborn's clothes several times a day, so put together a basic and inexpensive baby wardrobe, and be ready for anything. Also check out 519 Buy Kids' Clothes.

ITEM	HOW MANY TO BUY	FEATURES
One-Piece Outfits	Five to seven	Onesies make dressing and layering a snap. Look for easy-entry head openings with shoulder snaps, and leg and sleeve cuffs that aren't too tight.
One-Piece Pajamas	Five to seven	Soft, cotton-footed pajamas keep your baby toasty. Gowns with drawstring hems keep infant feet covered and allow quick diaper changes, especially for newborns.
Undershirts	Five to seven	Shoulder snaps or bateau openings at the neck make it easy to slip on and off. Crotch snaps keep shirts from riding up.
Sweaters or Jackets	One or two	A button-up or zipper garment is best, as many babies hate anything pulled over their head, especially something tight. Fleece is a great choice for lightweight protection from the elements.
Cap, Sun Hat	Two or three caps, one sun hat	Soft caps hug baby's head to keep warmth in. Wide-brimmed sun hats protect tender skin. Look for hats with neck flaps (FlapHappy.com) for extra protection, and a chin tie to keep on when tiny hands discover what they can do.
Socks	Seven pairs	Pick socks with enough of a cuff to keep them on without gripping too tightly. Choose a few heavier pairs (or slipper socks) for colder days. For babies that are pulling up, look for socks with rubberized grips on the soles.
Crib Shoes	One pair	Since very young babies' feet hardly touch the ground, they don't really need shoes (and shouldn't have "real" shoes until after they start to walk). Padders slippers or leather booties (like from Robeez.com) with elastic are great for crawlers. (See 520 Choose Children's Shoes.)
Special Outfits	One or two	Indulge yourself with an adorable outfit. Don't buy more than a couple, since the next growth spurt is right around the corner. Avoid tough-to-manage one-piece outfits that fasten in the back.
WARNING		Check that any sleepwear you buy is flame retardant. Do not put your baby to bed in any other type of clothing.

320 **Choose Diapers**

Before your child is potty trained, you'll have changed about 6,000 diapers. So think long and hard about whether you'd rather be dealing with cloth or disposables at 3 a.m. Cloth diaper advocates are concerned about the rate at which disposable diapers are filling our landfills. Disposable fans argue that the water, energy and chlorine it takes to clean cloth diapers have an equally harsh impact on our environment. Even the costs are comparable.

Steps

Disposable diapers

1 Get at least one small package of diapers in newborn size, and one larger package In the next size. Some newborns are already too big for newborn-size diapers when they come home.

2 Test drive store or generic brands on your baby for comfort and leak protection. Many have the same features (like expandable sides) as premium diapers such as Huggies and Pampers. Don't stock up on any one brand until you know what works for you and yours.

3 If you have the available storage space, join a warehouse club for prices that have nonmembers drooling. Or, order in bulk online. Many sites offer free shipping for large purchases, so you won't have to sohlepp jumbo packs around. Disposable diapers and wipes can run $50 a month. See 11 Shop the Warehouse Stores.

Cloth diapers

1 Get three-dozen prefolded diapers plus four or five snap-on or Velcro waterproof covers, and pins or plastic clips, if you choose the type of diaper without sewn-on attachments. Look online for service-quality diapers; store brand cloth diapers are usually less absorbent. Many parents love the newer, all-in-one cloth diapers, which combine a diaper with a cover and don't require pins. These look and perform like disposables, although they can take a long time to dry completely.

2 Avoid the hassle of washing and drying diapers by getting a professional diaper service. These services pick up soiled diapers and drop off clean ones once a week. They provide the diapers so you don't have to buy them (you will still need covers). Call several services in your area to compare rates and start-up specials. You'll pay more for a service, but your washing machine will thank you.

3 Budget about $40 a month for a diaper service (depending on where you live). Using cloth diapers requires an investment of about $75 for three-dozen diapers and covers (for each growth stage), plus energy costs.

What to Look For

- Correct size
- Leak-proof design
- Good price

Tips

Day-care centers usually insist on disposables.

Eco-friendly disposables (like EcoBoyAndGirl.com) are available, though often expensive.

One type of diaper is no more likely than another to cause a rash, as long as you change your baby promptly. However, if your baby suffers from chronic rashes, you may want to rethink your diaper brand and talk to your doctor.

Even the most die-hard disposable fans need a few cloth diapers as emergency backups, burp cloths or spill catchers. Fans of cloth diapers should have a pack of disposables on hand for trips or emergencies.

Warning

If you choose cloth diapers, while you are out and about, you will be schlepping around dirty diapers until you get home. Many parents keep a stash of disposables for on-the-go convenience.

321 Buy or Rent a Breast Pump

If you're a nursing mom, you have milk on demand for your baby. But what happens when you are in demand somewhere else? For a back-up milk supply, you need a breast pump. All pumps, whether manual or mechanical, use suction to pull milk into a container for later feedings. The basic difference between models is how quickly, comfortably and conveniently they work—and at what price.

Steps

1 Consider how often you will be using the pump. Will you be expressing milk only occasionally, or do you want to give your baby a bottle regularly or continue to provide breast milk while you go back to work? If you will only be pumping occasionally, consider an inexpensive ($30) manual pump. Manual pumps are compact but can be slow—and sometimes painful—to use. Many models require both hands, tying you up completely. Still, for occasional at-home use, these do the trick.

2 Rent top-of-the-line equipment at a low cost. Fees average $10 to $15 a week. Keep in mind that a security deposit is required. You'll also need to buy a personal accessory kit for about $50. If something goes wrong with a rental, you can get another. Rental machines can be bulky, making them a poor choice if you're short on space or on the move.

3 Consider buying your own pump if you'll be using it for a long time or plan to have more children. You get what you pay for in terms of motor quality. Some machines let you pump both breasts at once so you're done in half the time. Pumps run from $40 for a simple battery-powered model to $300 for a powerful double-pumper like the Medela Pump In Style. (The Bailey Nurture III has all the same power but for only $125.)

4 Look for a model that suits your needs, like a pump that packs neatly into its own carry case and comes with an ice pack to get your "white gold" home safely. Choose a double-pumper if you will be using it at work; you'll be done in half the time. If you're in the car a lot, look for a pump with a car-lighter adapter.

5 Pull the pump out and get comfortable with its parts and operation a few weeks after the baby's born. Choose a time when you're not overwhelmed, or have a friend give you a hand.

What to Look For

- Manual pump
- Rental options
- Battery operated
- Portability

Tips

Although you don't need to buy a pump before your baby is born, you do need to get used to handling the pump well before you start using it.

Talk to your pediatrician about the right time to start pumping and offering your baby a daily "acclimatizing" bottle. Too early and he or she may develop "nipple confusion" and stop breast-feeding. Too late and the baby may refuse a bottle altogether.

A lactation consultant at the hospital or a representative of La Leche League International (lalecheleague.org) can help you figure out which pump is right for you and suggest places to buy or rent them.

322 Choose a Car Seat

Choosing the right car seat can be an agonizing process for nervous new parents, and a significant expense as well. Research, talk to other parents, and buy the best seat you can afford to keep your child as safe and comfortable as possible.

Steps

1 Thank Uncle Sam for seats that are easy to put in. The National Highway and Transportation and Safety Board, recognizing that 80 percent of car seats are installed incorrectly, designed the LATCH (lower anchors and tethers for children) system to make installing a seat safely and properly a cinch. LATCH technology is required in all new cars built after September 2002.

2 Research. Car seats come in many categories with a lot of over-lap. Decide if you want an infant car seat or an infant/toddler combo, which is installed rear-facing for an infant and turned around when the child is 20 lbs. (9.1 kg) and one year old.

3 Read Consumer Reports (consumerreports.org) for in-depth comparisons of various seats in each category. Confirm that any seat you're considering has passed the Federal Motor Vehicle Safety Standards (FMVSS) test.

4 Read the parent comments on Web sites such as BabyCenter.com. You'll find solid information from real users about what works (easy to install, comfy armrests) and what doesn't (hard to adjust, poor padding). If a parent says his or her child can unbuckle a particular seat, and you have a little monkey, keep looking.

5 Get an infant seat before your baby is born. Designed to hold children up to 20 lbs. (9.1 kg), infant car seats are installed rear-facing to cradle the baby's head and back as securely as possi-ble. Many seats, such as Graco and Snap-N-Go, snap into a car-mounted base, allowing smooth liftoffs for sleeping babies. Expect to pay $60 or more or borrow one.

6 After the first year, graduate to a seat designed for passengers up to 40 lbs (18.1 kg). A forward-facing seat with a 5-point harness will keep your child safe and comfortable for several years. It should be easy to install and have a locking mechanism your child can't unfasten. The straps should not get twisted or jammed. There's a wide range of seats available, and many good ones (such as Graco, Evenflo and Eddie Bauer) in the $100 range. Many parents buy a Britax (britaxchildcare.com), the creme de la creme of car seats, which is safe, well-designed, comfortable and easy to install securely.

7 Give a child over 40 lbs. (18.1 kg) a boost. Required by law in many states for children up to 60 lbs. (27.2 kg), booster seats generally thread the standard seatbelt through a back or head-rest at a height suitable for small bodies. Research and shop around for the best booster for your youngster.

What to Look For

- LATCH compatibility, if needed
- Approval by FMVSS
- Appropriate for your child's age and weight
- Safety harnesses
- Adaptability to grow with child

Tips

Try to borrow an infant car seat from a friend or family member who is no longer using it. Babies grow fast and most infant seats can withstand several years of use. Just make sure the seat is still compliant with safety regulations.

Your child is more likely to fall asleep in a car seat that's comfortable.

Local police and fire depart-ments often provide infor-mation and demonstrations on car seat safety and installation.

Ask if you can install a car seat before you buy it to make sure it fits your car and is easy to install correctly.

Warnings

Don't buy a second-hand car seat. If it has been in an accident, it is illegal to use since its ability to keep your child safe in another wreck could be greatly compro-mised.

If you get into an accident with a car seat in your car, the law prohibits using that seat any longer.

323 **Buy Child-Proofing Supplies**

Your baby's job is to explore every inch of his or her world. Your job: Make sure that the terrain is safe for the intrepid explorer. It isn't too early to start infant-proofing your home before your baby arrives. You'll need to reassess the safety of your home and outdoor areas regularly, as your little Houdini grows and becomes more mobile.

Steps

1 Review the manufacturer's guidelines for your newborn's equipment (cribs, strollers, car seats, portable cribs, baths and monitors) to make sure you're using everything safely and correctly. If you purchased an item secondhand, contact its manufacturer to obtain a copy of the guidelines or check online.

2 Move items above the crib out of baby's reach as soon as he or she learns to roll over or push himself up on his hands (typically between 3 and 6 months).

3 Make sure that by the time your baby is crawling (around 7 months), you've made your home as safe as possible. Strap tall, heavy furniture to the wall. Place fragile items out of reach. Crawl around yourself and see what looks dangerous (or enticing) from that vantage point.

4 Count outlets, cupboards, doors and openings that need to be made safe before going to the store. You can find baby-proofing supplies at children's boutiques, Babies R Us and Target, or online at BabyProof.com.

5 Install wall-mounted safety gates at the top and bottom of staircases. You may want to create baby-safe zones with additional gates. Bathrooms and kitchens pose the most hazards. Avoid finger-pinching accordion-fold gates.

6 Keep purses out of reach—especially when Grandma comes to visit. They're full of fascinating dangers, from coins and medications to nail files and makeup.

7 Look on parent Web sites for recommendations or in the Yellow Pages under "Baby Proofing" for a full-service consultant. Call for an appointment. They will come to your home and do a complete safety inspection and install all necessary equipment. They will even sell you the equipment on the spot, and while it won't be cheap, it may well be worth the peace of mind knowing it was done correctly.

8 Stay current and reassess dangers at each developmental milestone. Every time your child is able to do something new and fabulous—roll over, sit up, grasp, crawl, cruise, climb, walk, run, bolt into the street—hazards that were previously out of reach suddenly come into play. Stay one leap ahead and don't be lulled into a false sense of complacency.

What to Look For

- Safety guidelines
- Age-specific hazards
- Appropriate equipment
- Professional consultant

Tips

Take a fresh look at your safety measures when your child starts to walk. He or she is picking up speed and can reach much higher than a baby on all fours.

Keep an eye out for older children who can disable safety gates and locks. Tell them you need their help to keep the baby safe.

Warnings

Lock away medicines, toiletries, cleaning materials, matches and anything else that could pose a hazard to your baby. Post the local poison control number next to your phone. To find yours, go to aapcc.org.

Protect your child from wandering into the pool. Drowning is the leading cause of accidental death in the home of children under 5 years old. Install locks at the tops of all interior doors leading to the pool area. Buy a detector that emits a shrill warning if the surface of the water is broken, or consider an automatic pool cover. Many cities and states require pools to be surrounded by fences whether or not there is a child living in the home.

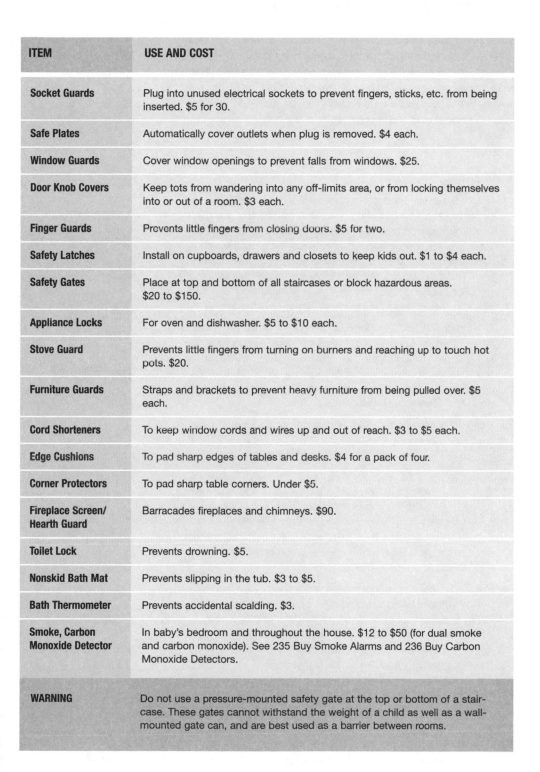

ITEM	USE AND COST
Socket Guards	Plug into unused electrical sockets to prevent fingers, sticks, etc. from being inserted. $5 for 30.
Safe Plates	Automatically cover outlets when plug is removed. $4 each.
Window Guards	Cover window openings to prevent falls from windows. $25.
Door Knob Covers	Keep tots from wandering into any off-limits area, or from locking themselves into or out of a room. $3 each.
Finger Guards	Prevents little fingers from closing doors. $5 for two.
Safety Latches	Install on cupboards, drawers and closets to keep kids out. $1 to $4 each.
Safety Gates	Place at top and bottom of all staircases or block hazardous areas. $20 to $150.
Appliance Locks	For oven and dishwasher. $5 to $10 each.
Stove Guard	Prevents little fingers from turning on burners and reaching up to touch hot pots. $20.
Furniture Guards	Straps and brackets to prevent heavy furniture from being pulled over. $5 each.
Cord Shorteners	To keep window cords and wires up and out of reach. $3 to $5 each.
Edge Cushions	To pad sharp edges of tables and desks. $4 for a pack of four.
Corner Protectors	To pad sharp table corners. Under $5.
Fireplace Screen/ Hearth Guard	Barracades fireplaces and chimneys. $90.
Toilet Lock	Prevents drowning. $5.
Nonskid Bath Mat	Prevents slipping in the tub. $3 to $5.
Bath Thermometer	Prevents accidental scalding. $3.
Smoke, Carbon Monoxide Detector	In baby's bedroom and throughout the house. $12 to $50 (for dual smoke and carbon monoxide). See 235 Buy Smoke Alarms and 236 Buy Carbon Monoxide Detectors.
WARNING	Do not use a pressure-mounted safety gate at the top or bottom of a staircase. These gates cannot withstand the weight of a child as well as a wall-mounted gate can, and are best used as a barrier between rooms.

324 Find Fabulous Childcare

There's no doubt about it—leaving your child in someone else's care can be agonizing. Quality childcare is available in most areas if you're willing to look for it, and there are many choices for parents to choose from. Some programs are so popular that parents put their kids on a waiting list as soon as the child is conceived. Do your ABCs to find a great fit for your child and your family.

Steps

General tips

1 Decide when you want to put your child in care. Some parents prefer to keep their kids at home as long as possible, and don't enroll them in a program until they are around 3 years of age. Other parents choose to put their children in a childcare setting much earlier. Still others prefer mixing time at home with time in care. Lifestyle and your child's personality will play a role in this decision—social, active children benefit greatly from the stimulation and activity offered in structured group environment.

2 Ask friends with children, family and mothers' group members for recommendations. Find out what their experiences have been like. Listen to what excites them and see if your gut tells you those same things would work well for your child. You can also search local parenting Web sites or childcare referral centers, or go to ChildCareAware.org for advice.

3 Consider the available options and decide which type of childcare best meets your needs.

Home-based care

1 Check out family daycare in your area. Typically, one adult cares for up to six children in his or her home; the number is determined by state law. These situations tend to offer the most flexibility in scheduling, but you'll need a backup if the care provider becomes ill. Family daycare is often a good opportunity to expose your child to another language.

2 Get the best of both worlds with a nanny share. Your child will get one-on-one loving care and one or two playmates. If a solo nanny is out of your price range, splitting the cost with one or two other families can make it affordable. The parents decide whose home will host the children each day—it may always be the same home, or you can switch back and forth.

Centers and preschools

1 Draw up a short list of potential care providers and contact them. Ask for brochures or visit their Web site. Find out if there is space available when you need to enroll or if there is a waiting list. Make appointments to visit providers and show up promptly.

What to Look For

- Good fit for your child
- Clean, safe space
- Sufficient play materials
- Responsive, trained staff
- Secure, nurturing environment
- Proper license or accredation

Tips

The National Association for the Education of Young Children (naeyc.org) accredit programs. Contact them for a list of standards as well as recommended teacher-to-child ratios.

There is no perfect program. Focus on what you feel is most important to you and your child.

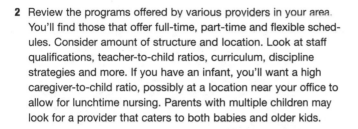

2 Review the programs offered by various providers in your area. You'll find those that offer full-time, part-time and flexible schedules. Consider amount of structure and location. Look at staff qualifications, teacher-to-child ratios, curriculum, discipline strategies and more. If you have an infant, you'll want a high caregiver-to-child ratio, possibly at a location near your office to allow for lunchtime nursing. Parents with multiple children may look for a provider that caters to both babies and older kids.

3 If possible, leave your child at home for the first visit so you can focus on learning about the program. Bring a list of questions: What is a typical day like? How are behavioral issues dealt with? Are children divided by age? Does my child have to be potty-trained to gain admission?

4 Take a good look at the space. It should be safe, well maintained and cheerful, with separate areas for quiet play and group activities and plenty of toys. Check the outdoor space. Is there room to run around? Are there climbing structures, a sand box and lots more toys?

5 Observe how the director and teachers interact with the kids. Are they approachable, flexible and respectful? How do the children respond to them? Is there a lively, engaged atmosphere that doesn't seem out of control? Do they seem happy?

6 Use your instincts as a parent and look for a fit. Some programs have an extended family feeling, while others are more businesslike. Make sure the structure of the program and its philosophy are suited to the temperament of your child. A situation may be great for one child but not for another.

7 Review details with the director. Find out what the fees are, what they cover, and how they are paid, including fees for late pick-ups. Confirm the hours of operation and what days throughout the year that school is closed. Ask how teachers are qualified, what the turnover is, and what the minimum requirements are. Inquire about enrichment such as art, music and field trips. Find out if and how often parents are required to volunteer. Ask if there is a board of directors or other parents you can contact for more information. Call them; they're usually happy to talk to prospective parents.

8 Take your child for a short visit after you've narrowed down your choices. How does he or she respond to the environment?

9 Complete the application process, pay the deposit, and set up a plan for entry into the program that will be most effective for your child. Some programs have a well-planned transition both for entering and moving from one age group to another.

10 Build an alliance with all of your childcare providers. Stay in constant communication to keep abreast of how your child is doing.

Warnings

Schools and centers should have all employees finger-printed. Search online under "community care licensing" in your area for more information.

Background check requirements vary by law from state to state.

325 Find a Great Nanny

Hiring a nanny harkens back to the times when children had a governess. Choose wisely: Not only will this person be responsible for your child's safety and happiness, but he or she will likely become an integral part of your family.

Steps

1 Decide if you want your nanny to live with you or not—there are potential benefits and drawbacks to both choices.

2 Contact local nanny agencies. Discuss your requirements and find out what's involved in the placement process. Ask how background checks are done and how applicants are screened. Find out what the fee schedule is and what the cancellation fees are.

3 Read up on prospective candidates. Ask for résumés, references and evidence of background checks.

4 Schedule in-person interviews. Go over your job description, air any concerns you have, and ask each applicant to do the same. Discuss potential behavioral and discipline issues to get a feel for how various situations would be handled and how each potential nanny would respond to your child's disposition. Watch how each candidate interacts with your child, and how your child responds to him or her. Discuss a few hypothetical situations that require good judgment and see how each applicant responds.

5 Call the references provided and have an honest conversation about the prospective nanny. Most parents have similar concerns for their children and are happy to discuss their experiences.

6 If you've met your match, call the agency to arrange for a contract and pay your final fee. Most agencies have a trial period of five days or so before finalizing the contract.

7 Alternatively, advertise for a nanny yourself to avoid agency fees. You'll save money, but you'll have to deal with the phone calls, background checks, interviews and contract issues yourself, which requires considerable time and effort. Agencies have procedures in place in the event a nanny doesn't work out; find out what they are.

8 Consider a nanny-share if footing the costs alone is too difficult and you don't require a live-in nanny. See 324 Find Fabulous Childcare.

What to Look For

- Qualified agency
- References
- Great fit with your family
- Provisions if it doesn't work out

Tips

Check each reference thoroughly, even if the agency has already done so. You will be trusting this person with the physical and emotional care of your child.

Use an agency that belongs to a professional trade association, such as the International Nanny Association (nanny.org) or the Alliance of Professional Nanny Agencies (apnaonline.org).

326 Find the Right Private School

Families choose a private education for their children for many reasons, but finding the right school takes a lot of homework (and legwork). Bottom line: The process can be grueling and requires considerable time and effort. But if you research carefully and involve your child in the process, you're likely to find a program that meets his or her goals and your expectations.

Steps

1 Decide between day and boarding school options. Decide if a particular focus suits you and your child best, such as college preparation, religious, military, athletic, artistic, linguistic or musical. Do you need a school that serves students with special needs or specific populations, such as gifted students?

2 Gather information. Ask for brochures, videos and application information. Visit school fairs. Get recommendations from teachers and other parents. Browse school Web sites to compare curricula and programs. If you're looking for an independent secondary school, consult a guidebook such as Petersons.com to get information about how selective various schools are and what kinds of testing is required for admission consideration.

3 Match your child's abilities and accomplishments to particular schools. For example, if you're looking at elite prep schools, a very strong academic record in middle school, strong SSAT or ISEE scores and solid extracurricular interests will form the foundation of the application. Essays and teacher recommendations are also required. Elementary school applications are less stringent, but require a parent application and at least one interview.

4 Schedule visits and interviews during school hours so you can get a feel for the student population and the structure of a typical day. Are the students happy, engaged and lively? Do the teachers seem approachable and professional? Is there a wide range of facilities for the students to enjoy?

5 Take into consideration teacher-student ratio, staff qualifications, counseling services and standardized test scores. Examine the curriculum to determine if it meets your child's needs. Interview the director or headmaster to get a sense of the school's philosophy and vision for its students. Find out if the school is accredited and/or affiliated with any universities. Ask about the success ratio of the graduating classes in entering secondary schools, colleges or the job market.

6 Discuss tuition. Some schools cost $20,000 or more per year, with add-ons for inclusions in sports, art programs and more. Ask about additional financial obligations such as fundraising; before- and after-school care; and coverage during holidays and summer break. Get a copy of the school calendar and note school closures. Ask how much parent involvement is required.

What to Look For

- Good fit for your child
- Curriculum meets interests
- Application requirements
- School's mission and philosophy
- School accreditation or affiliation
- Affordable tuition

Tips

Consider hiring an educational consultant to help you narrow down your search. Check the Yellow Pages under "Educational Consulting and Services."

Start looking in April so you'll be ready to submit applications the following January for that year's fall admittance.

If footing the bill is a hardship, apply for financial aid. Many schools provide partial funding for qualified families who cannot afford tuition.

327 Find a Good After-School Program

School's out, but you need to be at work for another three hours every day. The challenge is finding a convenient program that offers your kids a stimulating environment for playing, relaxing and doing homework.

Steps

1 Research programs available in your area. Visit Afterschool.gov. Contact your child's school about available programs. Inquire at community organizations such as Boys and Girls Clubs (bgca.org), the YMCA, worship centers, or parks and recreation centers. Ask friends and neighbors with school-aged children for recommendations.

2 Visit a few programs while they are operating so you can see firsthand what goes on. Do the kids seem well supervised, happy and engaged? Is there positive interaction with the staff? Are the activities age-appropriate, safe and fun? Note the space itself. Is the environment safe and clean?

3 Find out exactly what the fees are. Do you have to pay extra fees for field trips or tutoring? Are meals and snacks included?

4 Get the list of program policies regarding pickup time, attendance and holiday hours.

What to Look For

- Recommendations
- Good supervision
- Secure and nurturing environment
- Affordable fees

Tip

Some day-care centers open their doors to school-age children for after-school care.

328 Sign Your Child Up for Lessons

Is your child a tiny dancer or a karate kid? A diva, a diver or a go-cart driver? Sign her or him up for classes. Your child will have fun, make friends outside school, and maybe even discover a lifelong passion.

Steps

1 Follow your child's lead. More than anyone, he or she can tell you what interests him or her the most. You might be dying to see your daughter in a tutu, while she would rather suit up for T-ball.

2 Start the search as early as possible. Spaces fill up quickly, especially in the summer months.

3 Ask other parents and your child's teachers for recommendations. Check listings at the local library, in parenting newspapers, at the parks and recreation office, and online.

4 Determine how much various lessons cost. Will you also have to spring for uniforms or expensive equipment?

5 Make sure the classes are offered by a reputable organization and that they're held in a safe, secure environment. Instructors should have experience with kids and medical emergencies.

What to Look For

- Fun and appropriate for your child
- Reasonable price
- Excellent safety standards
- Trained instructors

Tips

Encourage other families you know to enroll a child in the same class. A friendly face will reassure your child, and you can carpool.

Ask if your child can attend a trial session for free or for a reduced rate before you commit.

329 Buy a Backyard Play Structure

Shopping for a play structure? It's a jungle out there. A well-chosen set can provide years of stimulating fun for your monkeys, but the price range and variety of choices can make anyone's head spin. And with over 200,000 playground injuries treated in the hospital each year, safety is a top concern.

Steps

1 Evaluate how much space you have before you shop. You'll need a level area at least 6 feet (1.8 m) away from your house or garage and clear of hazards such as trees, electrical wires, fences and standing water.

2 Make safety your first priority. Inspect the structure: Climb on it, shake it, stomp on it and look closely at the construction. Browse KidSource Online (kidsource.com/CPSC/playground .safety.news.html) and other such sites for more information.

3 Reduce the risk of serious injury with an appropriate surface material. Dirt and grass don't offer enough padding for falls; instead look into pea gravel, wood chips or rubberized mats. Keep in mind that the "fall zone" extends 6 feet (1.8 m) beyond the structure itself.

4 Set your budget while keeping in mind that you get what you pay for. First consideration is materials, and while you can find a metal play set for a few hundred dollars, don't expect it to last—either your child will outgrow it or it will fall apart.

5 Step up to a wooden set if you're willing to invest in long-lasting durability. Make sure the wood used is not prone to splintering or treated with toxic chemicals. The well-built Cedarworks sets (cedarworks.com, $1,000 to $5,000) are made of rot-resistant, splinter-free Northern White cedar. Accessories (curly slides, tire swings and climbing walls) will add to the ticket price.

6 Climb all over maintenance-free, sturdy plastic play structures. Relatively inexpensive ($60 to $500), they're great for toddler adventures. Check out LittleTikes.com or visit ToysRUs.

7 Choose a set your children can grow into. Adjustable-height swings, for example, offer a few extra years' use. Pay attention to the different climbing options since kids spend a significant amount of playtime scrambling up the structure.

8 Keep an eye out for hidden costs, such as delivery and setup charges. Ask about payment plans for more expensive sets.

9 Read the fine print: Ask how long and how difficult it is to assemble the set. What tools are required? Some sets are so hard to put together that it's no fun for anyone. Line up skilled and willing hands to help you set up your kid's new dream-come-true.

What to Look For

- Safety features
- Durability
- Play options
- Can grow with your child

Tips

Reeling from sticker shock? Remember that the play structure can go with you when you move, and know that it adds to the value of your property. Smaller structures, particularly plastic ones, are always in demand from other parents looking for used bargains.

Go for broke with custom play sets for $30,000 to $150,000. Once you scrape your jaw off the floor, check out BarbaraButler.com and see what people are willing to pay for their kids to play in.

Warning

Structures made from pressure-treated wood can leach toxic chemicals, including arsenic.

330 Find a Great Summer Camp

Is your child's desire to go to summer camp making her or him itch worse than a bad case of poison ivy? Picking the right camp can take more legwork than a three-legged race.

Steps

1 Begin looking in late winter or early spring. Attend camp fairs, get recommendations from other parents, ask at the library, and check sites such as KidsCamps.com.

2 Involve your child in the search. Ask if he or she would like to go to day camp or sleep away. Where are his or her friends going? Consider program length, coed versus single-sex camps, and specific-focus camps such as sports, music or the arts.

3 Verify a camp's accreditation with an organization such as the American Camping Association (acacamps.org).

4 Call the director and ask lots of questions: What is the background and experience of the camp director? How old are the counselors and how many are returning? What training do they go through? How are behavioral issues handled? What about medical emergencies?

5 Find out exactly what the camp tuition includes. If the cost is too steep, inquire about scholarships or financial aid.

6 Arrange a visit with your child. Inspect housing and activity facilities closely. Does the camp look safe and well maintained?

What to Look For

- Good recommendations
- Proper accreditation
- Well-trained staff
- Affordability
- An atmosphere that suits your child

Tips

The American Camping Association recommends a staff-to-camper ratio of one counselor for every seven or eight campers, depending on age and abilities.

Ask the camp to provide phone numbers of other parents whose children have attended the camp. Contact them and ask about their experiences with the camp.

331 Sell Girl Scout Cookies

The annual Girl Scout cookie sale happens just once a year: Stacks of colorful boxes, a freezer full of Thin Mints and happy little capitalists in green and brown uniforms bloom like May flowers. Here's how the cookie crumbles. (Sorry, only Girl Scouts need apply.)

Steps

1 Follow the guidelines set by your troop and local Girl Scout council (girlscoutcookiesabc.com). Pay particular attention to the safety tips when setting up teams and cookie spots.

2 Encourage your sales force to set goals for themselves ("I will sell more boxes than last year and win a badge.") and their troop ("Together we will make enough money to go on a field trip.").

What to Look For

- Guidelines
- High-traffic area

Tips

There are songs about every variety of Girl Scout cookie on the Internet. Learn a few and liven up your cookie sale.

E-mail everyone you know and tell them about the sale.

3 Find a high-traffic area (a grocery store's parking lot, a library, a popular park or community center, a mall, a bank on Friday) and get permission to set up a cookie stop there. Make posters to advertise and place them in highly visible locations the week preceding your sale.

4 Schedule girls and parents to work the cookie stop in shifts. Make sure everyone is clear about how to handle money and when to transfer funds to a parent so there's not a brimming cash box in full sight.

5 Be innovative. Some troops set up cookie hotlines to take phone orders (later confirmed by an adult), others set up a drive-through cookie sale by erecting a canopy tent. Challenge your troop to come up with a great sales plan, and work together to make it happen.

332 Buy Braces for Your Kid

Is orthodonture in your child's future? You'd better brace yourself for the bill. While orthodontic work is a great investment in overall dental health, the final bill bites: A jaw-dropping $3,000 to $7,000.

Steps

1 Start early. The American Association of Orthodontists (aaorthos.org) recommends that children get a screening no later than age 7. Problems detected early are generally easier and cheaper to fix.

2 Ask other parents and your family dentist to recommend an orthodontist. Since you'll be making a lot of trips to his or her office, find an accredited orthodontist who is close to your home or your child's school.

3 Consult with your insurance company to find out what is and isn't covered.

4 Call the orthodontist's office manager and ask about payment plans. Some doctors offer a reduced fee if you pay for treatment up front. Others can arrange relatively inexpensive financing (often with no money down) through a third-party lender.

5 Talk with your child about which features are important to him or her when choosing braces. The clunky metal models are no more—modern braces almost disappear on the wearer's teeth, while designer braces can sparkle in school colors. While designer features can add to the total bill, they may be important to your child and result in him or her cooperating more fully with the treatment program.

What to Look For

- Recommended, accredited orthodontist
- Location
- Health coverage
- Payment plans

Tip

Often doctors are happy to accept a large initial down payment, then arrange monthly payments until the balance is paid in full.

333 Buy Toys

Nothing is more exciting—and potentially overwhelming—than a trip to the toy store with your child. The aisles of tempting toys seem to stretch for miles. So how do you choose developmentally appropriate toys that do not break the bank?

Steps

1 Review the list of toys (see chart) recommended by the American Academy of Pediatrics (aap.org). These guidelines will help you select toys that appeal to your child's current developmental stage. See also 334 Buy Books, Videos and Music for Your Children.

2 Put safety first. Packaging is labeled with a suggested age range, to use as a guideline when buying a gift. If the toy is for your own child, use your judgment about what is appropriate, but remember that the age guidelines are generally well researched.

3 Go to a big retailer for good prices and selection but don't overlook independent toy shops. Although prices can be higher in boutiques than at large retailers, the atmosphere is less frantic and it is easier to find a knowledgable staff member who can make recommendations. You can find unique items in boutiques.

4 Shop on the Internet, especially during holiday times. Major sites such as BabyCenter.com are well organized, provide buying guides by age and advice from other parents, have frequent sales—and you don't have to wait in line. Internet shopping works especially well for gifts, since you usually don't pay sales tax, and shipping is often included in the price. See 3 Buy Products and Services Online.

5 Cruise garage sales and second-hand stores for used toys. Make sure they don't have any broken or missing parts before you buy.

6 Choose toys that are well made and can handle lots of wear and tear. Also remember that the best toys can be used over and over for many different types of play. These toys allow the chid's imagination to take over, versus the child feeling there is only one thing to do with it and becoming bored. Good examples are blocks, Play-Doh, art supplies and train sets.

What to Look For

- Age-appropriateness
- Safety
- Quality

Tips

Try before you buy, at a friend's house or a store that provides toys to play with. Some libraries lend out toys as well as books. Check with your children's librarian.

If your child doesn't seem interested in a toy, or if he or she is overwhelmed after receiving many toys at a holiday or birthday, stash the toy away and re-introduce it after a few months. More than likely, your child will be excited about the "new" toy.

AGE	DEVELOPMENTAL STAGE	RECOMMENDED TOYS
Birth to 1 year	Babies are developing their motor skills and hand-eye coordination. Choose toys that appeal to sight, hearing and touch.	Big blocks of plastic or wood; teethers with different textures; mobiles; play pots and pans; soft, washable animals and dolls; books with fun textures; busy boards; easy-to-grab squeeze toys and rattles; baby-safe mirror.
1 to 2 years	Young toddlers like to imitate and explore. They are developing language, rhythm and motor skills. Pick toys that stimulate curiosity, satisfy building urges and can take a beating.	Sturdy board books; musical tops; push and pull toys (no long strings); stacking toys; musical instruments; train sets; nesting blocks; toy telephones; large cars; sandbox with lid; sturdy dolls; play keys; bath toys; balls.
3 to 5 years	Imagination starts to develop. Focus on toys that foster creativity and imaginative play.	Books; crayons, nontoxic clay, washable markers; blackboard and chalk; building blocks; housekeeping toys; puzzles; train sets; dress-up clothes and hats; slide, swing set, playhouse; musical instruments; tricycle, mini-car or wagon; play kitchens and dishes; pretend tools. Storybooks are also a big hit.
6 to 9 years	Bigger kids are on the move, perfecting fine motor skills by doing more involved crafts. Find toys that help your child develop skills and creativity.	Puppets; sports equipment; bicycles; craft kits; skateboards; Itó or Lionel train sets; jump ropes; roller skates; board and card games.
10 to 14 years	Teens and pre-teens have definite preferences. Pick toys that expand on their interests.	Computer games; hobby kits; science sets; microscopes/telescopes; sports gear; more complex craft kits or science experiments.
WARNING	Choking, strangulation and suffocation are major causes of death among children under 3. Do not buy toys with small parts or balls that are loose or can break off and end up in your child's mouth. Use a toilet paper tube to test the size: If any loose parts fit inside the tube they are potentially lethal. Strings and balloons also pose a significant hazard. Make sure strings are not long enough to encircle your child's neck and never let children play with uninflated balloons.	

Every parent knows that exposing your kids to books and music fosters a lifelong appreciation for both. Not only that, but it's so much fun to see your daughter enjoy reading her own stories, or watch your son rockin' his 2-year-old booty. Movies can also be great learning tools. But how to select from so many choices? Talk to your local librarian or bookseller, browse the age-appropriate recommendations at online stores, and preview all movies first at ScreenIt.com before handing over the remote.

AGE	BOOKS	VIDEOS	MUSIC
Birth to 1 year	*Jamberry*; *I Am a Bunny*; any touch and feel book; nursery rhymes; *Goodnight Moon*.	The *Baby Einstein Series*; *So Smart*; Gymboree series; *Babymugs!*	Raffi; classical music of all kinds; *Music For Very Little People*.
1 to 3 years	Dorling Kindersley board books; *Guess How Much I Love You*; *The Little Engine That Could*; *The Itsy Bitsy Spider*; *Thomas the Tank Engine*; Dr. Seuss titles; *My First Farm*; *Mother Goose*; *The Very Hungry Caterpillar* and other Eric Carle titles; ABCs, numbers, shapes, colors primers; Richard Scarry books; public television character stories.	Public television character videos (Caillou, Clifford, Dora the Explorer, Sagwa); The Wiggles; Barney; *Bob the Builder*; *There Goes a. . .* series; *Thomas the Tank Engine* series; *Winnie-the-Pooh*; *Vegi Tales* (Christian angle); *Peter Rabbit*; Teletubbies; Sesame Street videos.	Raffi; Barney; *Country Bears*; *Mommy & Me* series; traditional children's song collections; Sesame Street songs; kids' compilation of adult music; *Ralph's World* series; *Wild Things*.
4 to 5 years	*Bread and Jam for Frances*; *Make Way for Ducklings*; *Blueberries for Sal*; Maurice Sendak titles; *Blue's Clues*; Berenstain Bears; public television character stories; *Madeline*; *The Giving Tree*; Dr. Seuss titles; *Where the Sidewalk Ends*; Disney stories; *Stuart Little*; *Grimm's Fairy Tales*; Hans Christian Andersen folktales; *The Miss Bindergarten* series.	Public television character videos; *Balto*; *The Wiggles*; *The Great Mouse Detective*; *Pinocchio*; *The Little Princess*; Disney movies (with discretion); *Thumbelina*; *Toy Story*, *Toy Story II*; *Bugs*; *Antz*.	*The Sound of Music* soundtrack; *Wee Sing and Play*; Peter, Paul & Mary; Bob Marley; *Peter and the Wolf*; *The Nutcracker*; Terry A La Berry.

AGE	BOOKS	VIDEOS	MUSIC
6 to 9 years	*American Girl*; *Harry Potter* series; Lemony Snicket titles; *Scooby Doo*; *Junie B. Jones*; *Animal Ark*; *Captain Underpants*; *Trumpet of the Swan*; *Madeline*; *Amelia Bedelia*; *Ramona the Pest* and other Beverly Cleary titles; *Encyclopedia Brown* series; *Jewel Kingdom* series; *Charlotte's Web*; *Stuart Little*; *Little House on the Prairie* series; *The Mouse and the Motorcycle*; *The Littles*; *Pippi Longstocking*.	*Fly Away Home*; Shirley Temple movies; *Pollyanna*; *The Parent Trap*; Disney movies; *Finding Nemo*; *The Sound of Music*; *Ice Age*; *Snow Dogs*; *The Princess Diaries*; *Scooby Doo*; *Pokemon*; *Rug Rats*; *Gigi*; *Mulan*; *Charlie and the Chocolate Factory*; *Charlotte's Web*; *The Rookie*; *Like Mike*; *Harry Potter* series; *Spy Kids*.	Pop music with age-appropriate lyrics, soundtracks from their favorite movies. Kids at this age are curious but still open, so it's a good time to expose them to world music, jazz and other favorites if you haven't already.
10 years and up	Above titles plus Judy Blume titles, *Holes*, *Wizard of Oz* series, *A Wrinkle in Time,* The *Redwall* series, J.R.R. Tolkien books; *The Chronicles of Narnia*; *Sign of the Beaver*; *Julie of the Wolves*; Sport bios; *7th Grade Weirdo*; *Little Women*; *101 Balloons*.	Above titles plus *Holes*; *Shrek*; *James and the Giant Peach*; *What a Girl Wants*; *Wizard of Oz*; *Cool Runnings*; *Drumline* (PG-13); *Mr. Bean*; *E.T. the Extra-Terrestrial*; *Grease*.	Find versions of popular music that have been edited for younger listeners. It is important to preview these, however, as it is not only the language that is inappropriate, but often the subject matter.
WARNING	Be very cautious about movie content. Disney movies, for example, are too intense for kids under 4 or 5 years of age even though many grownups think they're benign.		

335 Buy a Video Game System

Are you shopping for a console-based video-game system, but don't know an Xbox from a mailbox? For a primer, take a look at 415 Buy Video and Computer Games. The popular systems all offer spectacular graphics and special effects, and run from $150 to $300. Before you go to the next level, check out the special features.

Steps

1 Start by doing your homework. Check online (at Amazon.com and ConsumerSearch.com) and in gaming magazines (*GamePro* and *Electronic Gaming Monthly*) for product reviews, or ask video-game fanatics you know which system they prefer.

2 Stick with one of the big brand names: Sony, Microsoft and Nintendo. The system will require updates, upgrades and support in the future—and a company that is still around to provide them.

3 Shop at a retailer that stocks different systems and compare them. Ask a salesperson to define the differences between them and describe any additional features like Internet connectivity, expandability and CD/DVD capability.

4 Give each system a test run. Is it easy to use?

5 Ask about the library of game titles available for each system. Make sure you can play the games you want. If you are upgrading from an older system, find out if you can play your old games on the new machine.

6 Find out what the basic price includes. Peripherals can bump up costs considerably, but many new systems have starter packs that include several options like a second controller.

7 Compare in-store prices at a site like BizRate.com.

What to Look For

- Positive reviews
- Reliable manufacturer
- Ease of use
- Large game library
- Compatibility with your existing system
- Pricing

Tip

Look for special offers that bundle a few games with a console purchase.

336 Hire a Tutor

Tutoring benefits all kinds of students, whether they are performing above, below or at expected levels for their age group. A trained tutor can provide one-on-one attention, an individualized approach and a big boost for your child's self-esteem.

Steps

1 Determine your goals. They may be very specific, such as raising a math grade from a C to a B, or more general, such as getting your child more excited about learning.

2 Talk to your child about why you feel tutoring is so important. He or she may be resistant to the idea of needing extra help, or be embarrassed about it. Taking the time to be supportive and encouraging can make a big difference.

What to Look For

- Relevant education and experience
- Shared expectations
- Encouraging results

3 Ask for recommendations from your child's school, other parents, or local colleges and universities.

4 Interview prospective tutors about their qualifications, experience, areas of expertise and teaching style. After a first meeting with the tutor, ask your child what he or she thinks. Without a connection between the two of them, your efforts may be in vain. Be clear with the tutor about your expectations.

5 Discuss the hourly fee, which can start at $25 an hour. Choose a location that works for both your child and the tutor. Get references from the tutor's other clients and contact them. Talk to the students themselves if it's appropriate.

6 Check in with your child, the child's teacher at school, and the tutor as lessons progress. Find out if they feel tutoring is making a difference and how you can help.

7 Ask for regular updates about your child's progress.

Tip

Match your child's personal style with his or her tutor's. Would your child benefit from lots of structure or a more flexible approach? Will cracking jokes help your child crack the books?

337 Hire an Adoption Agency

Adopting a child is a long and emotional process that can take several years and costs upwards of $25,000. While you will encounter obstacles, disappointment and frustrating delays along the way, with the support of a good adoption agency, your heart and hands will soon be full.

Steps

1 Decide what type of agency is best suited to the child you're looking for. A public agency generally deals with special-needs and older children; private agencies handle a broader range of adoptions. To adopt a child from another country, you will need a licensed agency with experience in intercountry adoption.

2 Get a copy of the *National Adoption Directory* from the National Adoption Information Clearinghouse (calib.com/naic).

3 Select a short list of agencies. Check that they are licensed, and ask for references. Get information about payment schedules. Follow up on the references you receive. Weed out any agencies involved in pending or past legal action. (Contact your state's attorney general office to find out if the agencies you are considering have faced legal action in the past.)

4 Meet with a few agencies. Ask how they approach the adoption process, if they offer post-adoption support services and what fees are involved. Look for a positive attitude and an experienced staff.

5 Move forward by completing an application and participating in the home study.

What to Look For

- State licensing
- Strong referrals from adoptive parents
- A positive attitude
- No past or pending legal action
- Experienced staff

Tips

You can adopt without an agency, but you must comply with state laws. An attorney's assistance is essential.

Find out more about adopting kids with special needs at DeBolts.com and AdoptASpecialKid.org.

Join a support group of adoptive parents. Their word-of-mouth referrals will be invaluable (and you may need extra support during the arduous process of adoption).

338 Get Your Child Hired as a Model

Can't you just see your gorgeous child in a magazine ad—once you get that frosting off his or her face? Modeling is not a piece of cake. It's tough, demanding work for you and your child, and involves dealing with tight schedules, rejection and impatient art directors. But if your child is patient, easy going and comfortable in front of strangers, it may be worth a shot.

Steps

1 Be realistic. Child models must live in or very near a city where work is routinely available. The current top markets are New York, Los Angeles, Chicago and Miami.

2 Contact reputable modeling agencies (check the Internet or Yellow Pages for "Modeling Agencies") with a brief letter stating your interest. Include two or three clear photos of your child (both head shots and full body). Write your contact details and your child's name, age, hair and eye color, and clothing and shoe sizes on the back of each picture (not with a ball point).

3 Visit the agencies that offer you and your child appointments. Show up promptly, come armed with questions, and trust your instincts. If you don't like what you see or hear, try another agency.

4 Review contract offers carefully, and understand the fees and how they're paid. Agencies generally expect a commission of about 20 percent. Be aware that most contracts require you to release control of all photographs; read all provisions and make sure you consent to them.

5 Hit the pavement once you've signed the contract. The agency will send you and your child on go-sees (short meetings with prospective clients). You may face countless go-sees without ever seeing a job. Ask how you should dress your child and bring several changes of clothing, hairbrush, wipes, snacks, drinks and toys to keep your child happy through all the hurry up and wait.

6 Prepare yourself and your child for rejection. Agencies usually have a very specific look in mind, and not even a child as adorable as yours may sway them.

7 Help your child be comfortable throughout the process. Try not to get stressed. Be as natural with him or her as you can, as you are the anchor in a chaotic situation. Listen to the director at the shoot and do what she says. Help your child succeed under the lights by translating the director's instructions into words he or she better understands. Photo shoots can be long, hot and tedious. If you see that your child needs a break, tell the crew.

What to Look For

- Reputable agency
- Reasonable contract

Tips

Check out any agency you are considering with the Better Business Bureau (bbb.org). If it has any outstanding or unresolved complaints, go elsewhere. Same thing if an agency asks for money up front. A reputable agency won't earn any money until your child is hired.

You don't need to spend money on professional photos. Your own regularly updated pictures are fine. Your child will build up a pro portfolio over time.

339 Sell Used Baby Gear, Toys, Clothes and Books

Is a tsunami of gear, toys and books taking over your house? It's time to clear out. Most kids don't play with the majority of their toys and books, and they certainly can't wear clothes that no longer fit. If you can't bear to give away those expensive new sandals your kid refuses to wear, it's time for eBay, baby!

Steps

1 Sort baby gear, toys, clothes and books into categories—the discard pile, the pass-on-to-someone-else pile and the sell pile. Dole out the "pass on" items to family and friends. Sort toys by age and/or category: blocks, cars, dolls, electronic toys.

2 Sort books by age. Repair torn pages as much as possible. Wipe down board and plastic books.

3 Sort clothing by gender and size. Wash clothes, removing stains if possible. Fold neatly or hang on hangers.

4 Hold a yard sale with other families who also have gear to sell. Place large items like climbing structures, strollers, and Cozy Coupes near the curb for drive-by visibility. Make grab bags of smaller items and sell them for a dollar or two. Organize items by category. (See 42 Hold a Profitable Garage Sale.)

5 Take the "sell" pile to a kids' resale shop. Call the stores in your area to find out what they accept, what their buying hours are and how they pay (see 498 Sell Used Clothing).

6 Sell expensive or nearly new items online. Go to parent Web sites and hawk your loot to a perfectly targeted local audience. Browse eBay.com to see what is selling and for how much. Sell by the lot if you have a group of smaller toys or bags of clothes. You can make a decent return on items like individual Thomas the Tank Engine pieces and sets, bicycles, and upscale clothing and shoes. See 6 Sell Products and Services Online, spiff your goods up, post quality digital photos and get ready to haul in some cash.

7 Donate whatever doesn't sell or seem salesworthy to a local children's shelter, thrift store or preschool. Get a receipt for tax time.

What to Look For

- Sorted piles—toss, give-away, sell
- Clean items
- Go in with other families
- Online auctions

Tip

Fresh, clean toys and clothes in particular are more appealing to buyers and will fetch a higher price. Wash or wipe down everything that's plastic or wood with a disinfectant.

340 Find a Couples Counselor

Let's face it, being in a relationship can be tricky. Almost every couple can benefit from a little objective help now and then, to put the "rela-tion" back in the "ship." A skilled couples or family counselor can offer new approaches to making things work. The key is to find someone you and your partner both feel comfortable with.

Steps

1 Sit down with your partner, if possible, and talk about what each of you expects to get out of counseling. Try to be specific about your goals and be considerate of each other's wishes. Write them down if you feel it's helpful.

2 Get a professional referral or follow up on personal leads. (See 352 Hire a Mental-Health Professional.) Use the Yellow Pages as a last resort.

3 Contact therapists and ask about their qualifications, licensing, experience and education. If you have special issues (such as substance abuse, depression or anger management), ask about their experience in those areas.

4 At your first meeting with the counselor, discuss what you and your partner hope to accomplish. You'll also need to talk about scheduling and fees.

5 Consider working with someone still in training or in school if finances are an issue—they often offer reduced rates and will be supervised by a trained professional.

6 Ask a potential counselor how long it may take to work on your issues. If you cannot afford in-depth work, a shorter solution-based approach may be helpful.

7 Trust your instincts and respect your partner's point of view. A wall covered in diplomas and professional awards can't substi-tute for the right fit for you and your situation.

What to Look For

- Qualifications
- Specific experience
- Good fit

Tips

Think carefully before asking relatives or friends for refer-rals. It may prove helpful, or it may compromise your security and privacy, making an already tough task harder.

A sense of trust and security with your therapist is critical. Therapy often raises difficult issues, and working through them will be easier if you feel comfortable with your counselor.

If you are assigned a thera-pist by a court, a health maintenance organization (HMO) or an employer, find out what your options are if you do not see eye to eye with the therapist.

341 Hire a Family Lawyer

They say death and taxes are certain, but these days, so is the need for a good lawyer. Through the years, there will be times you might require legal assistance: adopting a baby, resolving divorce and custody issues, preparing a will or settling an estate.

Steps

1 Ask family, friends and co-workers to recommend an honest and dependable lawyer. Have they crossed paths with a not-so-honest lawyer? Find out who to avoid.

2 Hit the shelves at your county law library or the main branch of your public library. Look for the Martindale-Hubbell Law Directory (martindale.com), which lists and rates attorneys.

3 Put together a short list of candidates. Call them and ask for references. Then call their references. Were they happy with their services?

4 Use a lawyer referral service if you don't have time to search yourself. For a minimal fee, it will match you with someone who meets your specific needs.

5 Establish your price range. Hourly rates run from free (for lower-income families that qualify for legal aid) to thousands of dollars (for a top trial attorney).

6 Set up initial meetings with your candidates, but ask first if they will charge for these. Be prepared to ask about fees (hourly as well as for phone calls), the lawyer's track record, and his or her education and experience.

7 Make a smart choice. A trustworthy, quick-to-respond lawyer is like an honest mechanic; once you've found one, you'll rely on that person for years to come.

What to Look For

- Excellent track record
- References
- Reasonable fees
- Quick response

Tips

Many people don't look for a lawyer until a time of stress—when they're facing a lawsuit or getting divorced. Choose a lawyer for the long run, not for a quick fix.

In some states, consumer attorney organizations conduct valuable peer reviews. Check online for what's available in your state.

342 **Buy Property in a Retirement Community**

Seniors at all levels of independence may choose to buy property in a continuing-care retirement community. These communities can offer a vibrant social environment, a packed schedule of activities, help when needed, and the opportunity for transition into a more assisted living environment should needs change. They're also a good choice for people who simply want to live in an adults-only community.

Steps

1 Consider your present needs, and think about what lies ahead. Your goal may be to hold on to your independence for as long as possible.

2 Be aware of the costs beyond the cost of the home or apartment purchase (which may start at $150,000). Monthly maintenance fees can run into the low thousands.

3 Ask for referrals from your doctor, a social worker or a senior support group. You can also get lists of nearby communities online or in your phone book.

4 Tour as many properties as possible. Investigate the upkeep and safety of the facility. Find out about special amenities, from sports facilities to dining options.

5 Ask for a typical schedule. Does it offer activities both on and off the site? Does it reflect your interests?

6 Talk with the director about the staff. Is the facility properly staffed with well-trained and -screened people? What's the turnover? Talk to the employees, too. Are they happy? Do they enjoy working there?

7 Find out exactly what the fees include. If you have special meal requirements, ask if they can be met. Inquire whether the fees will change as residents find they need more assistance.

8 Chat with residents and ask for their honest opinions about the facility. If everyone is hiding in their home or apartment, that's not a good sign. Also, what is the average age of the people you see? Is that the stage you're at?

What to Look For

- Affordability
- Great facilities
- Well-trained staff
- A good fit with your lifestyle

Tips

Check your contract to establish what happens if you decide to sell your home. In some cases, you may forfeit your entrance fee, which can be $10,000 and up.

The monthly fees for some retirement communities are higher than for other types of assisted living. Get financial advice before signing on the dotted line.

343 Choose an Assisted Care or Nursing Home

At some time in our lives, you may have a parent, spouse or relative who needs around-the-clock care. Choosing an assisted care or nursing home is a truly difficult but often necessary choice. You'll want the best medical care possible, in a setting that retains the comforts of home, for a price that doesn't drain all reserves.

Steps

1 Consider an assisted care facility (a cross between a full-service apartment building and a nursing home) if your spouse or relative needs help with day-to-day activities. When the person can no longer take care of himself or herself, look at nursing homes.

2 Gather recommendations from your family doctor, friends, co-workers and social workers. Contact the American Association of Homes and Services for the Aging (aahsa.org) or the Eldercare Locator (eldercare.gov) for a list of local accredited facilities.

3 Make sure the facility has a current state license. Get reports from state inspection surveys, and find out if it is on a consumer watch list for any reason.

4 Focus on these basics: dignified care, quality medical care, good food, meaningful interactions with staff, stimulation, and a pleasant and secure environment. Be specific about the special needs of the potential resident, and make sure the staff is qualified to meet them.

5 Make as many visits and see as many people as you can. You need to feel positive about this difficult and emotion-laced decision. Don't stop searching until you do. Tour facilities with an eagle eye. You'll want to make at least three visits—one unannounced, if possible—at different times during the week and day, and once during a meal.

6 Chat with residents to find out what the brochures may not cover. Are they getting the assistance they need? Do they appear to be well cared for?

7 Ask what is included in their social and recreational programs. Look for exercise, art and music classes, movie or theater nights, social hour, and excursions. Find out if transportation to doctors' appointments, shopping and religious services is provided.

8 Look at different rooms to see how the floor plan would work for your relative or spouse. Ask if adjustable beds and other mobility-enhancing equipment are available. Find out if your relative may furnish the living quarters with his or her own furniture.

9 Ask for information about admissions procedures and contracts. Don't be shy about asking questions. Ask about fees and find out exactly what they cover. Find out if Medicare or Medicaid will cover any of the costs, which typically run around $4,000 a month.

What to Look For

- A good (and realistic) fit
- State licensing
- Excellent medical care
- Safe and well-maintained environment
- Caring staff

Tips

Start your search long before you need to, if possible.

Contact your state or local ombudsmen (get his or her number from the facility) to get a frank assessment of the place. If any doubts are raised, go elsewhere.

Spot anything worrying on a visit? Mention your concerns to the facility's administrator.

Get a sense of the level of basic kindness and compassion that the staff demonstrates to and for its residents.

344 Write a Living Will

You've chosen how to live; you can also make choices about dying.
An advance medical directive, or living will, spells out your preferences regarding the use of medical treatment to delay an inevitable
death. It also spares your family the anguish of making a heart-
wrenching decision as well as guarantees that your wishes are
followed should you be unable to communicate them.

Steps

1 Discuss your beliefs and wishes with your partner or spouse,
   family members, friends, clergy and your doctor.

2 Obtain your state's living will form from your state health department, local hospital, doctor, or the local area agency on aging.
   You may also find forms on the Internet (at no cost), or you can
   work with a lawyer.

3 Review the forms carefully. You may need the advice of your
   doctor when specifying which types of treatment you do not
   want. You can differentiate between life-prolonging procedures
   and those that alleviate pain. Detail specific wishes you have
   about your care that the form doesn't cover.

4 Sign the living will form and get it witnessed according to your
   state's laws. An improperly signed or witnessed will may be ruled
   invalid.

5 Give copies to your family members, doctor and lawyer. Put
   a copy in your home medical file.

What to Look For

- Compliance with state
  laws
- Accurate reflection of your
  wishes
- Legally signed and
  witnessed

Tip

You'll need to appoint someone to speak on your behalf
if you cannot communicate.
This person will ensure that
informed decisions are
made.

Warning

Don't put off writing a living
will until you're a senior, particularly if you have a family.

345 Buy a Cemetery Plot

Some people find peace in knowing where they will eventually rest in
peace. Work with a funeral home to prearrange a purchase; expect to
spend between $350 and $3,000 for a plot. As with buying other property, it's all about location, which can significantly affect the cost.

Steps

1 Pick a cemetery. Consider family preferences, but look for a
   reasonable price. Military cemeteries as well as some connected
   with a specific place of worship may restrict entry to people who
   meet specific criteria.

2 Tour the grounds and ask for a map of available plots. Find out
   what the price differences are. (A view adds to the cost.) If
   necessary, inquire about less expensive options at the same
   cemetery. A mausoleum or niche generally costs less than a plot.

What to Look For

- Family wishes
- Reasonable fees
- Clear rules and guidelines
- Ability to transfer owner-
  ship

Tips

Buying your own final resting
place? Make sure you have
left clear instructions in your
will regarding your intentions

3 Add up the total cost of the plot. Are there opening and closing fees, and how much are they? How will payments be made?

4 Find out what happens if you change your mind. Can you sell the plot or transfer ownership to someone else?

5 Ask about the cost for adjacent plots if several family members want to be buried together. (If you don't want to lie next Uncle Ray for eternity, speak up or forever rest in peace.)

(see 346 Pay for Funeral Expenses).

Some cemeteries have restrictions about grave markers and decorations.

346 **Pay for Funeral Expenses**

It's difficult to arrange a dignified and appropriate service for someone you love when you're suffering their loss. Take a steady friend or relative with you to help sort it all out.

Steps

1 Find out from a close family member or a lawyer if the deceased left special requests regarding funeral arrangements.

2 Set a budget. Prices for caskets and services vary hugely. Expect to spend $5,000 for the viewing, funeral ceremonies and an average casket, excluding charges for a burial plot. Consider less expensive options such as a graveside service only or cremation, which costs between $1,000 and $2,000.

3 Contact funeral homes. Family members may have their preferences. Ask about payment plans. Consumer advocates say prepaid funerals are generally a poor choice for everyone but the funeral home. And the fees (from $5,000 to $10,000) can really burn you up.

4 Ask for an itemized price list (required by federal law), and make sure you understand exactly what it includes.

5 Cut casket costs (which range from $375 to $8,500) by buying one online at sites such as FuneralDepot.com. You will avoid the funeral home's markup, and caskets can be shipped there in a matter of hours, if necessary. Or ask about rental coffins, used for viewing purposes only (the body is buried in a basic casket).

6 Find out what fees members of the clergy charge for their services, if applicable.

What to Look For

• Wishes of the deceased
• Price within budget
• No hidden charges

Tips

Prepayers spend the same amount of money, but the funeral home has their money longer. Check with ConsumersUnion.org and make sure the payments are transferable if you move.

You may be eligible for assistance with funeral costs from Social Security, the Veteran's Administration, or your state's health and human services department. Telephone the appropriate agency to obtain application forms.

REHOUSE STORES • BUY WHOLESALE • GET OUT OF DEBT • BUY NOTHING • BUY HAPPINESS • BUY A BETTER MOUSETRAP • BUY TIME
MEONE'S FAVOR • BUY POSTAGE STAMPS WITHOUT GOING TO THE POST OFFICE • TIP PROPERLY • BUY HEALTHY FAST FOOD • BUY SUN
ING SERVICE • SELL YOURSELF ON AN ONLINE DATING SERVICE • SELL YOURSELF TO YOUR GIRLFRIEND/BOYFRIEND'S FAMILY • BUY DO
HOOSE FILM FOR YOUR CAMERA • BUY RECHARGEABLE BATTERIES • DONATE TO A GOOD CAUSE • HOLD A PROFITABLE GARAGE SALE
STUDENT DISCOUNTS • BUY FLOWERS WHOLESALE • GET A PICTURE FRAMED • HIRE A MOVER • HIRE A PERSONAL ORGANIZER • FIND
EAT BIRTHDAY PRESENT FOR UNDER $10 • SELECT GOOD CHAMPAGNE • BUY A DIAMOND • BUY JEWELRY MADE OF PRECIOUS METALS
DESMAIDS' DRESSES • HIRE AN EVENT COORDINATOR • HIRE A BARTENDER FOR A PARTY • HIRE A PHOTOGRAPHER • HIRE A CATERER •
Y AN ANNIVERSARY GIFT • ARRANGE ENTERTAINMENT FOR A PARTY • COMMISSION A FIREWORKS SHOW • BUY A MOTHER'S DAY GIFT •
T • SELECT A THANKSGIVING TURKEY • BUY A HOUSEWARMING GIFT • PURCHASE HOLIDAY CARDS • BUY CHRISTMAS STOCKING STUFF
E HIGH ROLLERS ROOM IN VEGAS, BABY • BUY SOMEONE A STAR • PAY A RANSOM • GET HOT TICKETS • HIRE A LIMOUSINE • BUY A CR
M • BUY A PERSONAL JET • ACQUIRE A TELEVISION NETWORK • ACQUIRE A BODY GUARD • BOOK A LUXURY CRUISE AROUND THE WO
DROUGHBRED RACEHORSE • BUY A VILLA IN TUSCANY • HIRE A PERSONAL CHEF • PURCHASE CUBAN CIGARS • HIRE A GHOSTWRITER
NESS • MAKE BAIL • DONATE YOUR BODY TO SCIENCE • HIRE YOURSELF OUT AS A MEDICAL GUINEA PIG • SELL PLASMA • SELL YOUR
LLEGE EDUCATION • BUY AND SELL STOCKS • CHOOSE A STOCKBROKER • DAY-TRADE (OR NOT) • BUY ANNUITIES • BUY AND SELL MUT
Y PERSONAL FINANCE SOFTWARE • CHOOSE A TAX PREPARER • SET UP A LEMONADE STAND • SELL YOUR PRODUCT ON TV • HIRE A CA
SINESS IDEA • BUY A SMALL BUSINESS • BUY A FRANCHISE • LEASE RETAIL SPACE • LEASE INDUSTRIAL SPACE • LEASE OFFICE SPACE
B SITE • BUY ADVERTISING ON THE WEB • SELL YOUR ART • HIRE A PERSONAL COACH • SELL ON THE CRAFT CIRCUIT • HIRE A LITERAR
LING BUSINESS • BUY A HOT DOG STAND • SHOP FOR A MORTGAGE • REFINANCE YOUR HOME • SAVE BIG BUCKS ON YOUR MORTGAG
L A FIXER-UPPER • SELL THE FARM • SELL MINERAL RIGHTS • SELL A HOUSE • SELL A HOUSE WITHOUT A REAL ESTATE AGENT • OBTAI
OK A VACATION RENTAL • BUY A CONDOMINIUM • RENT AN APARTMENT OR HOUSE • OBTAIN RENTER'S INSURANCE • BUY A LOFT IN M
RNISH YOUR STUDIO APARTMENT • BUY USED FURNITURE • BUY DOOR AND WINDOW LOCKS • CHOOSE AN ORIENTAL CARPET • BUY LA
RRANTIES ON APPLIANCES • FIND PERIOD FIXTURES • BUY A BED AND MATTRESS • HIRE AN INTERIOR DESIGNER • HIRE A FENG SHUI C
I • BUY A WHIRLPOOL TUB • BUY A SHOWERHEAD • BUY A TOILET • CHOOSE A FAUCET • BUY GLUES AND ADHESIVES • CHOOSE WIND
CHEN CABINETS • CHOOSE A KITCHEN COUNTERTOP • BUY GREEN HOUSEHOLD CLEANERS • STOCK YOUR HOME TOOL KIT • BUY A V
ENTRY DOOR • BUY A GARAGE-DOOR OPENER • BUY LUMBER FOR A DIY PROJECT • HOW TO SELECT ROOFING • HIRE A CONTRACTOF
OWERS FOR YOUR GARDEN • SELECT PEST CONTROLS • BUY SOIL AMENDMENTS • BUY MULCH • BUY A COMPOSTER • BUY FERTILIZE
Y KOI FOR YOUR FISH POND • BUY A STORAGE SHED • HIRE AN ARBORIST • BUY BASIC GARDEN TOOLS • BUY SHRUBS AND TREES • B
LECT KITCHEN KNIVES • DECIPHER FOOD LABELS • SELECT HERBS AND SPICES • STOCK YOUR KITCHEN WITH STAPLES • EQUIP A KITC
UNTAIN OYSTERS • PURCHASE LOCAL HONEY • CHOOSE POULTRY • SELECT FRESH FISH AND SHELLFISH • SELECT RICE • PURCHASE
EADS • BUY ARTISAN CHEESES • PURCHASE KOSHER FOOD • BUY FOOD IN BULK • CHOOSE COOKING OILS • SELECT OLIVE OIL • SELI
FFEEMAKER OR ESPRESSO MACHINE • PURCHASE A KEG OF BEER • BUY ALCOHOL IN A DRY COUNTY • CHOOSE A MICROBREW • ORE
ULATION PREDICTOR KIT • PICK A PREGNANCY TEST KIT • CHOOSE BIRTH CONTROL • FIND THE RIGHT OB-GYN • HIRE A MIDWIFE OR D
OOSE DIAPERS • BUY OR RENT A BREAST PUMP • CHOOSE A CAR SEAT • BUY CHILD-PROOFING SUPPLIES • FIND FABULOUS CHILDCA
CKYARD PLAY STRUCTURE • FIND A GREAT SUMMER CAMP • SELL GIRL SCOUT COOKIES • BUY BRACES FOR YOUR KID • BUY TOYS •
A MODEL • SELL USED BABY GEAR, TOYS, CLOTHES AND BOOKS • FIND A COUPLES COUNSELOR • HIRE A FAMILY LAWYER • BUY PRO
PENSES • GET VIAGRA ONLINE • PURCHASE A TOOTHBRUSH • BUY MOISTURIZERS AND ANTIWRINKLE CREAMS • SELECT PAIN RELIEF
PPLIES • SELECT HAIR-CARE PRODUCTS • BUY WAYS TO COUNTER HAIR LOSS • BUY A WIG OR HAIRPIECE • BUY A NEW BODY • GET A
NICURIST • GET WHITER TEETH • SELECT EYEGLASSES AND SUNGLASSES • HIRE A PERSONAL TRAINER • SIGN UP FOR A YOGA CLASS
EA MARKET • RENT SPACE AT AN ANTIQUE MALL • BUY AT AUCTION • KNOW WHAT YOUR COLLECTIBLES ARE WORTH • DICKER WITH D
COGNIZE THE REAL MCCOY • BUY COINS • BUY AN ANTIQUE AMERICAN QUILT • BUY AN ANTIQUE FLAG • LIQUIDATE YOUR BEANIE BA
WNSHOP • BUY AND SELL COMIC BOOKS • BUY AND SELL SPORTS MEMORABILIA • SELL YOUR BASEBALL-CARD COLLECTIONS • CHO
MPUTER • BUY PRINTER PAPER • BUY A PRINTER • BUY COMPUTER PERIPHERALS • CHOOSE AN INTERNET SERVICE PROVIDER • GET
Y BLANK CDS • BUY AN MP PLAYER • CHOOSE A DVD PLAYER • BUY A VCR • CHOOSE A PERSONAL DIGITAL ASSISTANT • CHOOSE MO
ITAL CAMCORDER • DECIDE ON A DIGITAL CAMERA • BUY A HOME AUTOMATION SYSTEM • BUY A STATE-OF-THE-ART SOUND SYSTEM
IVERSAL REMOTE • BUY A HOME THEATER SYSTEM • BUY VIRTUAL-REALITY FURNITURE • BUY TWO-WAY RADIOS • BUY A MOBILE ENT
NEY • GET TRAVEL INSURANCE • PICK THE IDEAL LUGGAGE • FLY FOR FREE • BID FOR A SLED RIDE ON THE ALASKAN IDITAROD TRAIL
REIGN OFFICIAL • GET A EURAIL PASS • TAKE AN ITALIAN BICYCLE VACATION • CHOOSE A CHEAP CRUISE • BOOK A HOTEL PACKAGE F
OTLAND • BUY A SAPPHIRE IN BANGKOK • HIRE A RICKSHA IN YANGON • TAKE SALSA LESSONS IN CUBA • BUY A CAMERA IN HONG K
ST BASEBALL GLOVE • ORDER UNIFORMS FOR A SOFTBALL TEAM • BUY ANKLE AND KNEE BRACES • BUY GOLF CLUBS • JOIN AN ELI
OWMOBILE • BUY A PERSONAL WATERCRAFT • HIRE A SCUBA INSTRUCTOR • BUY A SKATEBOARD AND PROTECTIVE GEAR • BUY SKA
ATHER ACTIVITIES • SELL USED SKIS • BUY A SNOWBOARD, BOOTS AND BINDINGS • BUY SKI BOOTS • BUY A BICYCLE • SELL YOUR E
Y A BACKPACK • BUY A BACKPACKING STOVE • BUY A KAYAK • BUY A PERSONAL FLOTATION DEVICE • BUY A WET SUIT • BUY A SURF
DER CUSTOM-MADE COWBOY BOOTS • BUY CLOTHES ONLINE • FIND SPECIALTY SIZES • BUY THE PERFECT COCKTAIL DRESS • BUY
Y A MAN'S SUIT • HIRE A TAILOR • BUY CUSTOM-TAILORED CLOTHES IN ASIA • BUY A BRIEFCASE • SHOP FOR A LEATHER JACKET • B
TE MONITOR • SELECT A WATCH • BUY KIDS' CLOTHES • CHOOSE CHILDREN'S SHOES • PURCHASE CLOTHES AT OUTLET SHOPS • BU

UQUET OF ROSES • BUY SOMEONE A DRINK • GET SOMEONE TO BUY YOU A DRINK • BUY YOUR WAY INTO HIGH SOCIETY • BUY YOUR
ORDER THE PERFECT BURRITO • ORDER TAKEOUT ASIAN FOOD • ORDER AT A SUSHI BAR • BUY DINNER AT A FANCY FRENCH RESTAURA
LOWERS FOR YOUR SWEETHEART • BUY MUSIC ONLINE • HIRE MUSICIANS • ORDER A GREAT BOTTLE OF WINE • BUY AN ERGONOMIC
USECLEANER • HIRE A BABY SITTER • BUY A GUITAR • BUY DUCT TAPE • GET A GOOD DEAL ON A MAGAZINE SUBSCRIPTION • GET SEN
ARIAN • BUY PET FOOD • BUY A PEDIGREED DOG OR CAT • BREED YOUR PET AND SELL THE LITTER • GET A COSTUME • BUY A PIÑATA •
RED GEMSTONES • CHOOSE THE PERFECT WEDDING DRESS • BUY OR RENT A TUXEDO • REGISTER FOR GIFTS • BUY WEDDING GIFTS
DEAL WEDDING OFFICIANT • OBTAIN A MARRIAGE LICENSE • ORDER CUSTOM INVITATIONS AND ANNOUNCEMENTS • SELL YOUR WEDDI
HER'S DAY GIFT • SELECT AN APPROPRIATE COMING-OF-AGE GIFT • GET A GIFT FOR THE PERSON WHO HAS EVERYTHING • BUY A GRAD
HANUKKAH GIFTS • PURCHASE A PERFECT CHRISTMAS TREE • BUY A PRIVATE ISLAND • HIRE A SKYWRITER • HIRE A BIG-NAME BAND •
MBER • RENT YOUR OWN BILLBOARD • TAKE OUT A FULL-PAGE AD IN *THE NEW YORK TIMES* • HIRE A BUTLER • ACQUIRE A PROFESSION
YOUR FUR COAT • BOOK A TRIP ON THE ORIENT-EXPRESS • BECOME A WINE MAKER • PURCHASE A PRIVATE/CUSTOM BOTTLING OF WIN
R MEMOIRS • COMMISSION ORIGINAL ARTWORK • IMMORTALIZE YOUR SPOUSE IN A SCULPTURE • GIVE AWAY YOUR FORTUNE • HIRE
E DEVIL • NEGOTIATE A BETTER CREDIT CARD DEAL • CHOOSE A FINANCIAL PLANNER • SAVE WITH A RETIREMENT PLAN • SAVE FOR YO
• BUY BONDS • SELL SHORT • INVEST IN PRECIOUS METALS • BUY DISABILITY INSURANCE • BUY LIFE INSURANCE • GET HEALTH INSU
SELOR • HIRE A HEADHUNTER • SELL YOUR... ...ENT • MARKET YOUR INVENTION • FINANCE YO
DATED OFFICE EQUIPMENT • HIRE SOMEONE... ...RE A GRAPHIC DESIGNER • ACQUIRE CONTENT
ITCH A MAGAZINE STORY • SELL A SCREEN... ...YOUR BOOK • START A BED-AND-BREAKFAST •
OME OWNER'S INSURANCE • OBTAIN DISAS... ...USE AT AUCTION • BUY A FORECLOSED HOME
QUITY LOAN • BUY A LOT • BUY HOUSE PLA... ...• PULL BUILDING PERMITS • BUY A VACATION H
BUY A TENANCY-IN-COMMON UNIT • BUY RE... ...A MOVIE OR CATALOG SHOOT • FURNISH YOUR
GHT FIXTURES • BUY A PROGRAMMABLE LIG... ...NCES • BUY FLOOR-CARE APPLIANCES • BUY E
INCORPORATE FLUID ARCHITECTURE INTO... ...ARNISH • CHOOSE DECORATIVE TILES • CHOOSE
NTS • GET SELF-CLEANING WINDOWS • CH... ...SELECT FLOORING • SELECT CARPETING • CHO
Y SYSTEM • BUY A HOME ALARM SYSTEM... ...OXIDE DETECTORS • BUY FIRE EXTINGUISHERS
PAINTER OR ELECTRICIAN • HIRE A GARDEN... ...PERFECT ROSEBUSH • BUY FLOWERING BULBS
EGETABLE GARDEN • HIRE A GARDEN PROF... ...R SYSTEM • START A NEW LAWN • BUY A LAWN
B • BUY AN OUTDOOR LIGHTING SYSTEM •... ...ECT PEACH • BUY AND SELL AT FARMERS' MAR
E FRESH PRODUCE • SELECT MEAT • STOC... ...ASE A HOLIDAY HAM • BUY NATURAL BEEF • BUY
T AND PEPPER • GET A CHEESESTEAK IN P... ...EATTLE • FIND CRAWDADS IN LOUISIANA • BUY
BUY ETHNIC INGREDIENTS • PURCHASE VIN... ...OFFEE • ORDER A GREAT CUP OF COFFEE • BUY
L • CHOOSE A RESTAURANT FOR A BUSINE... ...OCK YOUR BAR • BUY AND SELL SPERM • CHO
GOOD PEDIATRICIAN • HIRE A CHILD THER... ...NEW CRIB • CHOOSE A STROLLER • BUY BABY
EAT NANNY • FIND THE RIGHT PRIVATE SC... ...RAM • SIGN YOUR CHILD UP FOR LESSONS • BU
VIDEOS AND MUSIC FOR YOUR CHILDREN •... ...R • HIRE AN ADOPTION AGENCY • GET YOUR CH
TIREMENT COMMUNITY • CHOOSE AN ASS... ...IVING WILL • BUY A CEMETERY PLOT • PAY FOR
ICINES • SAVE MONEY ON PRESCRIPTION... ...ONAL • CHOOSE A WHEELCHAIR • BUY HOME-U
DY PIERCING • OBTAIN BREAST IMPLANTS... ...ALTERNATIVE AND HOLISTIC PRACTITIONERS •
SELF TO A DAY AT THE SPA • BOOK A MAS... ...Y AND SELL USED BOOKS • SHOP AT AN ANTIQU

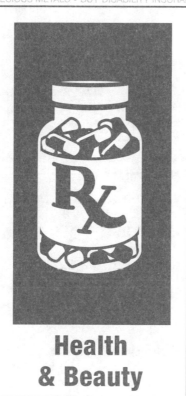

**Health
& Beauty**

AN ANTIQUE APPRAISED • BUY SILVERWARE • EVALUATE DEPRESSION-ERA GLASSWARE • BUY AND SELL STAMPS • BUY ANTIQUE FURI
• SCORE AUTOGRAPHS • TRADE YU-GI-OH CARDS • SNAG STAR WARS ACTION FIGURES • SELL YOUR VINYL RECORD COLLECTION •
COMPUTER • SHOP FOR A USED COMPUTER OR PERIPHERALS • CHOOSE A LAPTOP OR NOTEBOOK COMPUTER • SELL OR DONATE A
OMAIN NAME • BUY A HOME NETWORK • UPGRADE THE MEMORY IN YOUR COMPUTER • BUY COMPUTER SOFTWARE • CHOOSE A CD
RVICE • NEGOTIATE YOUR LONG-DISTANCE PHONE SERVICE • BUY VIDEO AND COMPUTER GAMES • CHOOSE A FILM CAMERA • CHOOS
D-VIDEO DISTRIBUTION SYSTEM • BUY A SERIOUS TV • CHOOSE BETWEEN CABLE AND SATELLITE TV • GET A DIGITAL VIDEO RECORDE
STEM • GET A PASSPORT, QUICK! • PURCHASE CHEAP AIRLINE TICKETS • FIND GREAT HOTEL DEALS • RENT THE BEST CAR FOR THE L
TY-FREE • SHIP FOREIGN PURCHASES TO THE UNITED STATES • TIP IN A FOREIGN COUNTRY • TIP PROPERLY IN NORTH AMERICA • BRI
SLANDS • RAFT THE GRAND CANYON • BOOK A CHEAP BUT AWESOME SAFARI • RENT A CAMEL IN CAIRO • GET SINGLE-MALT SCOTCH
R WAY ONTO A MOUNT EVEREST EXPEDITION • HIRE A TREKKING COMPANY IN NEPAL • RENT OR BUY A SATELLITE PHONE • BUY YOUR
SELL FOUND GOLF BALLS • BUY ATHLETIC SHOES • BUY A RACKET • BUY A GYM MEMBERSHIP • BUY AN AEROBIC FITNESS MACHINE
FISHING • GO SKYDIVING • BUY WEIGHTLIFTING EQUIPMENT • CHOOSE A CAR RACK OR CARRIER • BUY SKIS • BUY CLOTHES FOR CO
RAGE SALE • COMMISSION A CUSTOM-BUILT BICYCLE • BUY A PROPERLY FITTED HELMET • BUY THE OPTIMAL SLEEPING BAG • BUY A
Y-FISHING GEAR • BUY ROCK-CLIMBING EQUIPMENT • BUY A CASHMERE SWEATER • PURCHASE VINTAGE CLOTHING • SELL USED CL
HES AT A DISCOUNT • CHOOSE A BASIC WARDROBE FOR A MAN • BUY A MAN'S DRESS SHIRT • PICK OUT A NECKTIE • BUY A WOMAN
LOTHES • GET A GREAT-FITTING BRA • CHOOSE A HIGH-PERFORMANCE SWIM SUIT • HIGH PERFORMANCE WORKOUT CLOTHES • BUY
UY THE BASICS FOR YOUR CAR • BUY A USED CAR • BUY OR SELL A CAR ONLINE • BUY A HYBRID CAR • SELL A CAR • BUY A MOTOR

347 Get Viagra Online

All that stands between a man's impotence problems and revived virility is a credit card, an Internet pharmacy, and a subtly packaged delivery of those famous blue, diamond-shaped pills—right? Not so fast. If you buy Viagra online or by mail order without taking precautions, you could end up with fake pills that aren't effective—or safe.

Steps

1 See your doctor first to evaluate possible causes for impotency, check your overall health, assess Viagra's suitability in your case, rule out medication conflicts, and make sure you're fit for sex. The two of you will discuss possible side effects.

2 Go to a U.S.-based online pharmacy certified by the National Association of Boards of Pharmacy (NABP) program and bearing the Verified Internet Pharmacy Practice Sites (VIPPS) trademark. VIPPS-designated sites are safe because they won't diagnose online, honor the right to privacy, follow a quality assurance policy and let you talk directly with a pharmacist.

3 Get assurance of the drug's authenticity, precise dosage instructions and a list of possible side effects.

What to Look For

- Your doctor's supervision
- Online pharmacies with NABP and VIPPS approval
- Assurance of drug authenticity
- Precise dosage instructions

Warning

Avoid herbal products that claim to function like Viagra. They aren't subjected to quality control or scientific rigor like prescription drugs, so there's no way to know what (or how much of it) you're getting, or if it works.

348 Purchase a Toothbrush

A power toothbrush can make you feel as if it's whirring you straight toward smile nirvana. If you want to splurge on one of these plug-in or switch-on toothbrushes, check out the benefits you'll enjoy.

Steps

1 Ask your dentist to recommend a toothbrush. Depending on the state of your teeth and gums, she may give you a soft-bristled regular toothbrush or steer you toward an electric one. Always get soft-bristled brushes or heads to avoid pushing gums up.

2 Get a buzz with vibrational toothbrushes. They work better because people brush longer and more debris is loosened by the vibrations. Many dentists recommend the Philips Sonicare Elite with its curved head, great for getting around the back of the teeth and for powerful, gentle cleaning at the gumline.

3 Buy an electric toothbrush with a rotational oscillation design; although it costs more, it gives you tangibly better results. An example of this is the Braun Oral-B 3D Excel, which has bristles that spin in two directions.

4 Experiment with tufted, angled or rounded-end bristles and easy-grip, curved or flexible-grip handles to see which type of toothbrush best helps you reach the nooks and crannies.

What to Look For

- Rotating or vibrational bristles
- Head size
- Bristle softness

Tips

If you have proper brushing technique and do it for two to five minutes at least twice daily, you'll do just as well with a regular manual toothbrush as you would with a power toothbrush.

If your teeth have gaps or you wear braces or any kind of bridge, use Butler Gum's Proxabrush and/or floss threaders to get under wires.

349 Buy Moisturizers and Antiwrinkle Creams

Most basic moisturizers—both drugstore and high-end brands—contain the same key ingredients (water, propylene glycol, lanolin) to soften your skin and help with surface dryness. Wrinkles? That's another story. Here's the rub.

Steps

1 Choose moisturizers, makeup base and other daily-use beauty products with built-in sun protection factor (SPF) 30. Sunscreen really can prevent new wrinkles from forming. Look for at least one of these active ingredients: titanium dioxide, zinc oxide or avobenzone (aka Parsol 1789). These protect you from harmful UVA and UVB rays.

2 Mind your skin's moisture needs. Dry skin drinks up rich moisturizers, while oily or acne-prone skin does better with *noncomedogenic* or *nonacnegenic* products. (These are preferred over "oil-free" products, which often include pore-clogging oil imitators.)

3 Study the active ingredients, which are listed on labels in order of the amount contained. If soothing aloe vera or vitamin C is 15th on the list, you're not getting much of it.

4 Be skeptical of products that claim to augment your own natural collagen or elastin, whose job it is to keep skin plumped up and youthful. The molecules in these products are too big to actually penetrate the skin.

5 Ask your doctor about *tretinoins,* one of the few active ingredients shown to truly reverse sun damage, reduce fine lines and soften wrinkles. These medications, which include Retin-A and Renova, are available by prescription only. Because of their ability to actually change your skin's structure, they are designated as drugs rather than cosmetics.

6 Sample other weaker, nonprescription vitamin A relatives like alpha hydroxy acids (AHAs) and beta hydroxy acids (BHAs). You need at least 8 percent AHA for any visible results, though, which is just as likely to be present in a cheap drugstore product as in an expensive brand.

7 Experiment with antioxidant ingredients like coenzyme Q10, vitamin C and alpha lipoic acid. Some dermatologists make great claims for them (with promising research), while others are skeptical about visible results given the low concentrations used.

What to Look For

- SPF 30 sunscreen
- Active ingredients
- Right ingredients for your skin type
- Prescription treatments
- AHAs and BHAs
- Antioxidant ingredients

Tip

Reduce long-term risks of skin aging, skin cancer, and other harmful effects of the sun by limiting sun exposure, wearing protective clothing, and using sunscreen. While it's true that genes play a large part in how you age, with care, your skin will appear younger—for free.

Warnings

Never use tretinoin or AHA products on the sensitive skin around your eyes. Because these are mildly exfoliating, they can cause redness or flaking en route to revealing fresh new skin. They also make your skin more photosensitive.

Hypoallergenic products should be free of fragrance and other common irritants like preservatives, but can still aggravate your skin.

350 Select Pain Relief and Cold Medicines

If your congested head is occupied by a sadist pounding a jackhammer, you need the right relief, right away. The main thing you need to look at in over-the-counter (OTC) products are the active ingredients and what they do. Then zero in on the one that's tailor-made for your symptoms without extra ingredients you don't need. The following information is for adults only.

ACTIVE INGREDIENTS	BRAND NAME	WHAT IT'S USED FOR	POSSIBLE SIDE EFFECTS
Acetylsalicylic Acid or Aspirin	Alka-Seltzer, Bayer, Bufferin, Ecotrin	Nonsteroidal anti-inflammatory drug (NSAID). Reduces inflammation, fever, minor aches and pains, and headaches.	Don't take with ibuprofen, especially regularly. Never give to young children or teens due to a link to Reye's syndrome. Can be harsh on the stomach.
Ibuprofen	Motrin, Advil, Nuprin	An NSAID. Reduces inflammation (swelling), fever, headaches, minor aches and pains, including sprains, arthritis and muscle pains.	Gentler on stomach than aspirin. Maximum adult dosage is 1,600 mg in 24 hours to avoid hurting stomach.
Naproxen Sodium	Aleve	An NSAID. Alleviates minor pain from headache, colds, toothache, muscle ache, backache, arthritis and menstrual cramps. Reduces fever. Works for 12 hours.	Works slowly. Can cause indigestion, nausea, heartburn and diarrhea; irritate stomach; and cause gastrointestinal bleeding. Available in prescription and nonprescription strength.
Ketoprofen	Orudis	An NSAID. Relieves the pain, tenderness, inflammation (swelling), and stiffness caused by arthritis, muscle and menstrual pain, and pain after surgery, dental work or childbirth.	Can cause drowsiness, indigestion, nausea, heartburn and diarrhea; can irritate the stomach; and cause gastrointestinal bleeding. Avoid if you have a history of gastrointestinal problems or ulcers.
Acetaminophen	Tylenol, Excedrin	Works well for many headaches, menstrual pain or muscle aches. Good choice for fevers and sore throats.	Ideal for those who can't tolerate NSAIDs' side effects, although less effective at reducing inflammation. Used in allergy, cough and sinus medications. May be mixed with caffeine (as in Excedrin) to increase effectiveness. No adverse effects on stomach.
Guaifenesin	Robitussin	Cough expectorant designed to liquefy phlegm. Relieves coughs of colds, bronchitis, and other lung infections.	Doesn't help congested nose.

ACTIVE INGREDIENTS	BRAND NAME	WHAT IT'S USED FOR	POSSIBLE SIDE EFFECTS
Dextromethorphan	Robitussin, Sucrets	Cough suppressant	May not be beneficial if chest is congested; may prolong cough. Can be useful at night, as sleep aid.
Chlorpheniramine, Diphenhydramine, Pheniramine, Clemastine, Tripolidine	Benadryl, Chlor-Trimeton, Tavist, Dimetapp	Antihistamines relieve hay fever and allergy symptoms, including sneezing; runny nose; and red, itchy, tearing eyes. Common in cold and flu medications.	Can cause drowsiness, sluggishness and dry mouth. Don't take with antidepressants or other medications without doctor supervision.
Loratadine	Claritin	Nonsedating antihistamine (doesn't cause as much drowsiness).	May be less effective than sedating antihistamines.
Phenylephrine, Pseudoephedrine	Sudafed, Neo-Synephrine	Relieves nasal or sinus congestion due to colds, sinusitis, hay fever and other respiratory allergies. Relieves ear congestion caused by inflammation or infection.	Doesn't help runny nose. Do not use if have high blood pressure, diabetes, heart problems, asthma and for other conditions.
Cromolyn	NasalCrom	Helps allergy symptoms with few side effects.	Burning, stinging or irritation inside of nose; flushing; increase in sneezing.
Nasal Saline	Afrin, Breathe Right	Nonmedicated. Thins nasal secretions and relieves congestion. May be advised following sinus or nasal surgery.	Multiuse containers are subject to bacterial growth over time unless antimicrobial preservatives are in the solutions. Using sprays for more than a few days can cause rebound congestion and may lead to severe dependency.

OTC terms you need to know:

- Enteric: Coated to be kinder on the stomach because the medication doesn't dissolve until it reaches the intestines.

- Buffered: Added antacid to help avoid upset stomach, but it's likely too little to be effective.

- Migraine-relieving: Ingredients same as in nonmigraine counterparts, just with tailor-made package instructions.

- PM: Indicates a pain-relief and sleep-aid combo. Often acetaminophen for pain and diphenhydramine for sleeplessness.

351 Save Money on Prescription Drugs

Thanks to skyrocketing prescription drug costs, it's getting tougher to get pricey brand-name drugs covered by insurance plans. Here are some savvy drug-shopping strategies.

Steps

1 Ask your doctor about good—and far cheaper—generic alternatives to name brands.

2 Find out if you qualify for discounts through Medicaid. Call your state's Agency on Aging if you are 55 years or older. Elderly consumers on Medicare may be eligible for the Together RX Card (togetherrx.com), a discount card that will let them save on more than 100 brand-name drugs.

3 Contact individual drug manufacturers for programs for people on limited incomes or who have no insurance. Also check out sources like NeedyMeds (needymeds.com), which has information about patient assistance programs and other programs designed to help those who can't afford their medicines.

4 Shop online, but only at Verified Internet Pharmacy Practice Sites (VIPPS)—approved Internet pharmacies (sanctioned by the National Association of Boards of Pharmacy) in the United States. Or try trusted drugstores' Web sites like Eckerd (eckerd.com) and Walgreens (walgreens.com).

5 Shop for bulk discounts with mail-order pharmacies. At Express Scripts Mail Service Pharmacy (express-scripts.com), for example, you may be able to get up to a three-month supply of your medication for the equivalent of a two-month co-pay at a retail pharmacy.

What to Look For

- Generic drugs
- Discount programs
- Discount prices
- Online pharmacies and drugstores
- Mail-order pharmacies

Tip

Price-shop locally; there can be a world of difference in cost for the same prescription drug from one local pharmacy to another.

352 Hire a Mental-Health Professional

If you've just experienced a traumatic event—the death of a loved one, loss of a job—or are at a transition point, you want a trusted professional with whom to talk through your feelings. Here are some ways to help you find the right therapist, psychologist or psychiatrist.

Steps

1 Find out if your insurance policy covers mental-health providers. If so, find out what kind of provider and how many sessions are covered. Ask if you must see a doctor to be reimbursed.

What to Look For

- Insurance coverage
- Professional credentials, License
- Appropriate therapy method
- Comfort, trust

2 Verify that the provider is licensed, which indicates they've undergone rigorous, standardized training. For more information, contact the National Coalition of Mental Health Professionals and Consumers (nomanagedcare.org/resources).

3 Book a consultation. Ask the provider to explain his or her predominant theoretical orientation and discuss favored methods. Expect to talk frankly about any issues and how they affect your ability to work, sleep, eat, concentrate, relate to family and so on. Establishing a good rapport is essential to effective therapy.

4 Ask the provider to explain any proposed treatment.

Tips

Find out if your state considers mental-health care to be medical care. If so, therapy should be covered by your insurance policy.

See 315 Hire a Child Therapist.

DEMYSTIFYING THE CREDENTIALS

Psychotherapist	Not licensed. Catchall label; anyone can claim to be one. Many are well trained and highly skilled, but there's no way to identify them by the title alone.
Clinical Social Worker	Licensed clinical social workers (LCSWs) and certified social workers (ACSWs) generally have a master's degree plus two years of supervised experience, and passed a state exam.
Marriage, Family and Child Therapists (MFTC)	Specialize in helping clients deal with major life changes or transitions, such as marriage, divorce, job change and death in the family. Can also help when communication is an issue for families, couples or individuals. In most states, a license signals a professional with similar training to that of a CSW. Ask if member of American Association for Marriage and Family Therapy.
Counselor	Another catchall label. Often has a master's degree, but not always. If your state has licensed counselors, training level is similar to that of social worker. Often treat substance abuse, short-term crises and stress-related disorders. Not normally chosen for more serious disorders.
Clinical Psychologist	Specialists in testing and assessing mental-health problems. Licensed, generally with a doctorate or master's degree plus at least two years of supervised clinical experience and advanced specialized training. Does all of what an MFTC does and more.
Psychiatrist	MDs trained in diagnosing and treating severe mental illness with one to two years of additional training in psychiatry. Can write prescriptions for antidepressants, antianxiety drugs and other psychiatric medications.

353 Choose a Wheelchair

The fanciest wheelchairs cost more than some automobiles, but competition has brought down the cost of basic manual models. It's an intensely personal choice, with many features to think about.

Steps

1 Seek a physical therapist or nurse's advice on special features that would enhance your quality of life.

2 Check your insurance coverage. Medicare covers electric wheelchairs nowadays, but don't assume any insurer does. Factor in what you can spend out of your own pocket and decide what your budget is. Keep in mind that popular powered models go from $5,000 to nearly $30,000.

3 Determine how you will control a motorized chair. For example, if you have C-7 tetraplegia, you may use a joystick as the input device, but the top of the joystick may need to be modified to accommodate for your lack of grip.

4 Decide what kind of back height and support you require. Criteria include head control, trunk control, upper extremity function and propulsion, as well as personal preference. Therapists generally recommend that people with little or no upper body strength need a chair that tilts back 45 degrees to avoid bedsores. A range of cushion options are available such as visco-elastic memory foam which provides unparalleled relief from seat pressure as well as great back support. Air cushions are equally effective for other people. Take a test drive before you decide.

5 Research different foot and leg supports, as well as armrests and attachments such as trays. The style you want or need might determine the specific wheelchair frame that you will order. For instance, a fixed tapered front-end cannot be ordered on a lightweight wheelchair frame.

6 Obtain measurements of potential environment obstacles, such as doorframes, hallways, and desk clearance, and compare these to the chair's overall width, overall length, turning radius and seat height from the floor. There's nothing worse than buying a new chair and finding out the hard way that it can't make the tight turn into your bedroom.

7 Find a local supplier that lets you put a range of models through their paces and sit in them long enough to make sure you'll really be comfortable. The largest manufacturers are Invacare, Everest & Jennings, Sunrise/Quickie and Permobil.

8 Compare weights. Manual chairs range from 4 to 30 lbs. (1.8 to 13.6 kg), so the strength of the wheelchair wrangler—be it you or an aide—is a big consideration. Motorized chairs can top out at 250 lbs.

What to Look For

- Professional advice
- Insurance coverage
- Suitability to lifestyle and ability
- Maneuverability
- Lightweight
- Easy transfer to vehicle

Tips

You can buy your wheelchair through a hospital or nursing home, or from a medical-equipment chain store that gives you the option to rent or buy (there are thousands of such stores).

Wheelchair manufacturers unveil new models annually and, more important, consult wheelchair users during the design process. As with cars or computers, you pay more for the very latest model.

9 Test how easy it is to smoothly move from the chair to your car and back again, and to fold and pack (manual) chairs into your vehicle. (Motorized wheelchairs do not fold.) If you have a van, make sure the chair fits both the ramp and the vehicle's interior.

10 If you'll only need help getting around or are fatigued easily, give a scooter, or personal mobility vehicle, a test-drive. Three- and four-wheel models are available depending on mobility requirements and terrain.

11 Look into a custom-made chair. Some models have a dozen different seat widths and even more colors.

12 Research performance wheelchairs if you are active in competitive sports or marathons at such sites as Sportaid.com and SpinLife.com..

354 **Buy Home-Use Medical Supplies**

Whether your need is permanent or temporary, here's how to shop for home-use medical supplies like trapezes, walkers, bathroom aids and adjustable beds. With health maintenance organizations pressing for more home care and recuperation, manufacturers are pursuing this expanding market very aggressively, so smart shopping really pays.

Steps

1 Ask your doctor, rehabilitation therapist, occupational therapist or caregiver what specific pieces of equipment are necessary.

2 Discuss your options with your insurance provider so you know what's covered.

3 Test products from a showroom or exhibition with many choices. The Abilities Expo (abilitlesexpo.com) is the largest.

4 Have a professional rehabilitation expert visit your home. They can advise on constructing a wheelchair ramp, for example, or the positioning of a bathtub grab bar or trapeze over the bed.

5 Zero in on details. Something as simple as crutches can be made much more comfortable (and safe) when correctly adjusted for height. Or, if you lack upper body strength, you may opt for crutches with an adjustable flexible cuff that goes around the forearm just below the elbow and minimizes arm strain.

6 Rent what you need, particularly if your disability is short-term. Or, find bargains on items like hospital beds, patient-lifting equipment, walkers and canes at medical-equipment exchange programs. Some organizations pass donated used equipment on to people with inadequate health insurance coverage.

What to Look For

- Informed expert advice
- Insurance coverage specifics
- Suitable, reasonably priced equipment
- Good selection

Tip

Check out disabilityinfo.gov, a gold mine of information with helpful leads on all kinds of medical equipment. Also, AbleData.com, which is sponsored by the National Institute on Disability and Rehabilitation Research, has the lowdown on almost 20,000 assistive technology products.

355 Select Hair-Care Products

Are you finding your bad-hair days outnumber the good ones? It could be due to your hair-care products. You may be using one made for hair that's a different texture than yours. Consult this chart, then head to the salon or drugstore. Soon your tresses will go from terrible to terrific.

PRODUCT	FEATURES
Moisturizing Shampoos and Conditioners	Good for very dry hair. Restore moisture lost in blow-drying. Products containing aloe, seed oils or shea butter are especially rich. Generally too heavy for oily or fine hair, though can be used just on the ends.
Clarifying Shampoos or Conditioners; Buildup Removers	Clean hair that's dulled by too much build-up. Help greasy hair if used periodically. Can be drying; limited use recommended. Special antidandruff shampoos are far more effective for flaking or itchy scalp.
Color-fading Shampoos and Conditioners	Gentle, moisturizing; won't strip color or natural oils from hair. Easy to confuse color-protecting products with color-boosting or color-enhancing products. The latter two deposit color (and can stain highlights) and thus might be more than you bargained for, especially on dry or processed hair.
Regular Conditioners	Panthenol is a cosmetic coverup found in most grocery store products. Look for dimethicone, a mineral emollient, which helps smooth and straighten a mop of thick hair before blow-drying. A light conditioner tames static and detangles normal to oily hair. Deep, rich conditioners resuscitate dry or damaged hair. Using too much can flatten thin, fine or oily hair, so use on midshaft and ends. If hair is very fine, use very little to create shine and smoothness.
Leave-in Conditioners and Reconstructive Detanglers	A light leave-in conditioner is great for creating shine and body to straight hair and for taming. Also tames frizz and defines curls in wavy hair.
Hair Masks, Hot Oil Treatments, Deep-conditioning Protein Packs	Restore softness and shine by penetrating into the hair shaft and filling in "pockets" of missing protein. Indulge yourself and your hair with a 20-minute treatment that rejuvenates and replenishes lost moisture, protein and shine.

PRODUCT	FEATURES
Volume-enhancing Sprays and Root-lifting Products	Apply to damp roots, then again when dry to add volume to flat, limp, thin or very straight hair. Not for bushy or thick curly hair.
Hair Gels and Cremes	Add texture and shape. Good for defining curls; holding styles. Cremes can be softer and lighter; gels are harder and stiffer. Use sparingly and experiment with different effects.
Styling Cremes or Pomades	Stop staticky, flyaway hair. Tames frizz when worked into dry curls with fingers. Can be too greasy and weigh down hair. Best to start with coffee bean–size amount and add more later if needed.
Shine-enhancing Gels or Sprays; Glossing Cremes	Calm curls and fix frizzies on dry, processed (colored or permed) or curly hair. Add shine. Look for silicone in ingredient list to help hair reflect light and look shinier. Too much product weighs down oily hair. Use very lightly or just on ends. Sprays are the least oily; spray on hands and smooth over hair.
Hair Balms	Handy to carry around for touchups on frizzies or flyaways. Is a cosmetic coverup and doesn't restore moisture, but gives a healthier look to hair.
Straighteners, Spray Relaxers, Relaxing Cremes	Straighten all hair types for people of all skin colors. Can transform curls into waves. Temporary products often contain moisturizing ingredients like glycerin, coconut oil and plant extracts. Permanent straighteners and relaxers are serious business and should always be applied by professionals. Use at-home products sparingly and monitor how they affect your hair.
Hair Sprays	Tame flyaways, add volume, seal coiffure. Try spraying on brush, then brush through hair. Use light varieties for natural-looking hold. Firm-hold sprays can give a bulletproof, rigid look.

356 Buy Ways to Counter Hair Loss

The loss of one's hair can be a grievous blow to self-image and confidence. Medications, illness, heredity, pregnancy, menopause, changing hormone levels and stress can all contribute to hair loss. Other culprits are chemotherapy, hereditary baldness or alopecia.

Steps

1 Consult your doctor, dermatologist or an endocrinologist to eliminate medical causes such as thyroid issues or alopecia. Rule out any dietary contributors by making sure you're getting all the vitamins, protein and calories you need.

2 Apply over-the-counter minoxidil (Rogaine) to thinning or balding patches twice a day. The exact way this medicine works is not known, but it is thought to cause dilation of the blood vessels in the scalp. If you stop treatment once you've started, hair loss will resume within a few months.

3 Try prescription-only Propecia or Proscar, which have been found to work rather well for women. The active ingredient finasteride blocks the formation of active testosterone and allows those hairs predisposed to inactivity to become active again and make new hairs. The two brands have different dosages of finasteride.

4 Explore hair-replacement surgery options. Mini- or micrografting may offer the most natural results. A strip of scalp with hair is divided into a few hundred tiny grafts with just a few strands apiece, then inserted into minuscule slits in the scalp. Skilled surgeons ensure all hair is growing in the same direction. Make sure to see live examples of the surgeon's work before proceeding.

5 Discuss treatment options with your doctor for alopecia. While very little is known about the disorder, there is evidence of a genetic component as well as a link to autoimmune problems. Depending on the variety (*areata:* spots on the head; *totalis:* the entire head; or *universalis:* all body hair), there's a good chance that cortisone injections on the head and eyebrows will spur hair growth. Injections can be painful but may offer a huge morale boost for people who would do just about anything to look the way they used to.

What to Look For

- Underlying cause
- Your doctor's opinion
- Topical treatments
- Hair-replacement surgery

Tip

Talking to other people who've lost their hair can be enormously helpful, as are supportive friends and family. Contact the National Alopecia Areata Foundation at alopeciaareata.com for information and to subscribe to their newsletter.

Warning

Be aware that 5 percent minoxidil is not recommended for use by women, due to the potential for greater drug penetration. Women using this percentage in clinical trials were inclined to grow hair in areas where minoxidil was not applied.

357 Buy a Wig or Hairpiece

Bald might be beautiful in the eyes of some people, but not for those with gradual or drastic hair loss who just want to look like their old self again. With a wide range of colors and styles, wigs have never looked more fabulous, darling.

Steps

1 Talk to your doctor and insurance provider and find out what's covered. Ask for a prescription for a cranial hair prosthesis.

2 Find a hairstylist experienced in working with wigs and ask about style and shape. They can take your measurements and order your wig, as well as cut and style it after it's delivered. Ask about each wig's scalp and hairline. A bad hairline is the biggest give-away, so ask to see and try on samples.

3 Price out various kinds of wigs. Prices reflect whether the wig was made by hand or by a machine.

   • Synthetic wigs are affordable and easy to style, and cost from $100 to $500. They're not quite as durable, and frizz more, but are ideal if you're experiencing temporary hair loss due to chemotherapy.

   • Human hair, of course, has the most lifelike look and bounce. You'll pay around $1,000 for a net-based wig, and up to $6,000 or more for a custom-molded polyurethane vacuum base. These top-quality cranial hair prostheses adhere securely to the head and, since hairs are injected through the base one at a time, look the most natural.

4 Consider a partial wig if you have a few bald or very thin spots (common with alopecia). They can be custom-made to blend in with and bulk up your own remaining hair.

5 Feel confident your wig won't take flight with different anchoring options. Many wigs have adjustable fasteners or straps in the back; tape tabs at the hairline and ears also provide security. A nonirritating head band such as the Comfy Grip ($29) is helpful if you've lost all your hair. Custom-fit caps help smooth any remaining hair underneath (stretch lace costs around $22).

6 Ask if extra hair can be added to the wig later if it thins in places. While a quality wig starts showing wear at two or three years, spot repairs can extend its life to four or five years.

7 Ask for tips on care and styling. Depending on how dirty it gets, you might need to wash it every 10 to 14 days. Store on a wig block when it's not in use, and wipe down the inside of polyurethane-based models with rubbing alcohol each day.

8 Find out if the hairstylist can revitalize color later if the wig fades.

What to Look For

• Insurance coverage
• Hairstylist with wig experience
• Synthetic or human-hair
• Custom-molded base
• Secure fasteners
• Wig care and maintenance

Tips

For help in getting your wig paid for, chemotherapy patients can contact the Susan G. Komen Foundation's national help line at susangkomen.com. Alopecia sufferers can contact the National Alopecia Areata Foundation (alopeci-aareata.com) for advice on dealing with insurers.

The American Cancer Society's "Look Good, Feel Better" program is available to women countrywide through chapters and outreach programs. It offers free expert advice from volunteer cosmetologists on selecting wigs and scarves, and on choosing makeup to help build confidence and self-esteem.

358 Buy a New Body

Had it with those bags and sags? Buy yourself a head-to-toe body transformation. Courtesy of recent advances in cosmetic surgery, almost anything is possible. A new you won't be cheap, though, and there are other important considerations to weigh.

Steps

1 Interview several surgeons and ask how many procedures similar to yours each has performed, which is particularly important with new treatments. Identify a top-notch plastic surgeon via referrals from your physician and satisfied friends.

2 Make sure prospective surgeons are certified by the American Board of Plastic Surgery and is a member of the American Society of Plastic Surgeons (plasticsurgery.org). The ABPS requires a five-year surgical residency plus two years of specialized training. Ask if doctors have surgical privileges at a hospital; if not, it's possible their credentials fell short, so tread carefully.

3 Ask to see living examples of the surgeon's work, not just photographs in a book. Ask to be introduced to satisfied patients, but frank talk with all former patients is valuable.

4 Consider a rushed consultation a red flag. If a surgeon doesn't thoroughly advise you on possible side effects, potential problems and how much discomfort or disability you can expect, you aren't getting what you need to give informed consent to surgery, which is your right.

5 Confirm exactly what the quoted prices cover, since some plastic surgeons' offices quote the surgeon's fee separately. You might need to factor in other costly items like the consultation, anesthesia, supplies, medication, facility fees, hospitalization, compression garments and blood testing.

What to Look For

- Personal referrals
- Surgeon's expertise and credentials
- Testimonials from patients
- Living examples of surgeon's work
- Clear explanation of prices

Tip

See 352 Hire a Mental Health Professional.

PROCEDURE	DESCRIPTION	PROS AND CONS	COST
Face-lift (Rhytidectomy)	Heredity, personal habits, the pull of gravity, and sun exposure contribute to the aging of the face. The skin is raised outward before the surgeon repositions and tightens the underlying muscle and connective tissue. Some fat, as well as excess skin, may be removed.	A face-lift cannot stop aging, nor can it turn back the clock. What it can do is help your face look its best and give you a healthier and more youthful appearance. Recovery usually takes two to three weeks. Insurance does not generally cover surgery that is done purely for cosmetic reasons.	$5,000 to $15,000

PROCEDURE	DESCRIPTION	PROS AND CONS	COST
Nose Job (Rhinoplasty)	Reshapes nose by reducing or increasing size, removing hump, changing shape of tip or bridge, narrowing span of nostrils, or changing angle between nose and upper lip. May also relieve some breathing problems.	One- to two-hour outpatient procedure. Patients are back to work in one to two weeks. Must avoid strenuous activities for two to three weeks. Side effects: temporary swelling, bruising around eyes and nose, headaches, some bleeding and stiffness. Risks include infection.	$4,000 to $5,000
Eye Lift (Blepharoplasty)	Correct drooping upper eyelids and puffy bags below the eyes by removing excess fat, skin and muscle.	One- to three-hour outpatient procedure. Patients are back to work in 7 to 10 days. Can cause temporary discomfort, tightness of lids, swelling, bruising; dryness, burning or itching of eyes; tearing, sensitivity to light. Risks include temporary blurred or double vision; infection, bleeding; swelling at the corners of the eyelids.	$3,000 for upper and lower lids, plus $700 for anesthesiologist, $800 for operating room
Neck Lift	Endoscopic surgery, performed under local anaesthetic, gets rid of neck sag. Good for those prone to fat deposits and drooping under chin.	Minimal scarring. Back to normal life in two or three days. Endoscopic neck surgery is relatively new, so look for an expert.	$8,000 to $9,000
Breast Reduction or Breast Lift (Mastopexy)	Nipple and areola can be repositioned and reduced for balance and aesthetic purposes. Can also rebalance breasts after one has been reconstructed after a mastectomy. (For breast enlargement, see 360 Obtain Breast Implants.)	Can be huge relief for women with large, heavy breasts, which can be truly uncomfortable and cause years of backache and neck pain. Surgery may be covered by insurance. Hospitalization after breast-reduction surgery, four to six weeks to return to normal activity. Risk of infection, bleeding, loss of feeling in the breast, and permanent visible scars.	$3,000 to $5,000 for breast lifts; $5,000 to $6,000 for reductions.
Upper-arm Lift (Brachioplasty)	Lifts skin that is drooping below tricep from aging or weight loss.	Reduces circumference of upper arm; contours and tightens. Visible scars. Ask about how much scarring to expect. Nerve injury, change in sensation and swelling are possible complications. Requires a couple of weeks to recover.	$3,000 for surgeon's fees alone

PROCEDURE	DESCRIPTION	PROS AND CONS	COST
Liposuction (Suction-assisted Lipectomy)	Contours the fat layer beneath the skin. Removes excessive fat when exercise doesn't help. New ultrasound-assisted liposuction can liquefy fat deposits first, making them easier to remove. The power-assisted lipoplasty method is less traumatic for the body and lets these few surgeons experienced in using it sculpt the body more easily.	New fat can build up afterward in untreated areas. Expect bruising and swelling after surgery. May need to wear supportive garments. Removing too much fat can cause dangerous blood loss. Serious nerve damage, although rare, can occur. Can result in lumps and bumps or even sagging.	$1,000 to $2,000 surgeon's fee, plus at least $800 per site
Tummy Tuck (Abdominoplasty)	Spot-shaping treatment that slims and trims, removing excess fat and skin that hasn't responded to dieting and exercising. Doctors can be adamant about requiring patients to make a serious effort to lose weight before surgery. Incisions don't show much as they're just above or within pubic area. New shape lasts for years barring substantial weight gain.	Removing excess sagging skin is a major undertaking. Support garment must be worn for a few weeks. Benefits take several months to become fully apparent. Not for the overweight. Won't remove cellulite.	$4,000 for surgeon's fees alone
Buttock Implants	Add curve to flat derriere by inserting silicone implants.	A little more shape, a little more lift. Risk of thrombosis (a blood clot).	$3,000 to $10,000 a pair

359 Get a Tattoo or Body Piercing

Body piercings and tattoos, ancient forms of adornment and beautification, are now found on all sorts of bodies. Few states have laws governing piercing and tattoo establishments or their practitioners. Before you let a stranger puncture your skin, shop around and find out how to mutilate your body safely.

Steps

1 Think hard about what designs you want. Collect art, leaf through books, and make sketches. A qualified tattoo artist will take what you bring in and transform it into beautiful art.

2 Place temporary tattoos on different parts of your body until you're clear where you want yours: Tattoos on your back or shoulder may look incredible, but you'll never see them without a mirror. Designs on your arms may be appealing, but you may tire of always having something there.

3 Consider long-term social or professional fallout for visible piercings and tattoos. While a particular style of body art may be appealing right now, ask yourself: Will you love it for the rest of your life? Will the indulgence of a moment eliminate certain career options down the road?

4 Evaluate your ability to handle pain. Does a tattoo hurt? Not as much as childbirth, but pain is considered part of the experience. Piercings are briefer. Location also determines pain levels—anything near major nerves (down the side of the leg, for example, or on or near bones) can be excruciating; the bigger the tattoo, the longer your agony lasts.

5 Ask about hygiene practices: In the age of AIDS, cleanliness is taken very seriously. Artists should wear gloves, sterilize their tools and work space, and use packaged, single-use needles.

6 Take your time and review lots of portfolios when choosing a tattoo artist. When you see a great tattoo, ask who did it. Look for clean, smooth outlines, and excellent use of color.

7 Be prepared to pay for an experienced, reputable piercer or tattoo artist. Tattoo artists charge by the hour and usually have a minimum (about $50), but designs can run into the thousands for large, intricate work. Common piercings (including jewelry) range from $50 to $75.

8 Insist on surgical-grade stainless, niobium, platinum or titanium steel jewelry, or solid 14-karat or 18-karat gold for all piercings until they're healed.

9 Review all procedures and risks ahead of time. Be clear on the after-care regime.

What to Look For

- True artistry
- Surgery-standard hygiene
- Experienced practitioner

Tips

Check the Association of Professional Piercers' Web site (safepiercing.com) for studio recommendations.

Professional tattoo artists will not work on a client who is under the influence of judgment- or pain-altering substances, legal or otherwise.

Warnings

Piercing in particular, but also tattooing, damages the body's natural infection barrier. Serious problems can include viral hepatitis, nerve and vein damage, and sexually transmitted diseases (most commonly with genital piercing). Tongue piercings are particularly prone to complications. If a piercing site looks infected, don't touch the jewelry, just get to a doctor.

A new tattoo is dressed with a bandage and takes up to two weeks to scab and heal. One medical journal reported people with tattoos are nine times more likely to be infected with hepatitis C. However, you can avoid many problems by choosing a sterile establishment.

360 Obtain Breast Implants

Breast augmentation can be a powerful morale booster, but it's not something to take lightly. Whether you've opted for implants for cosmetic reasons alone or as a part of breast reconstruction surgery after a mastectomy, here's how to go about it safely.

Steps

1 Read up on implants at the FDA Web site (fda.gov), where the information comes from unbiased sources. Do your visual homework at ImplantInfo.com, where you can see scores of before and after photographs.

2 Locate a surgeon who is certified by the American Board of Plastic Surgery and is a member of the American Society of Plastic Surgeons (plasticsurgery.org).

3 Consult with several surgeons, taking along photographs of breast sizes and shapes you like. Ask if your body type is suited to implants; very thin women aren't always good candidates, as wrinkling in the implant can show through the skin.

4 Ask surgeons for patient referrals before you go under the knife. Also check out the doctor with medical societies in your state to find out if there have been any complaints or malpractice lawsuits filed against him or her.

5 Inquire about the incision: Will the surgeon go in under the breast or armpit, through the belly button or the nipple? Most implants go in beneath the chest muscle for more natural-looking results and easier mammograms, but this method takes longer to heal.

6 Ask what kind of implants are used. Saline-filled sacs are really the only type available at this time. The American Society of Plastic Surgeons does not recommend silicon implants.

7 Wear a bra in your desired cup size to the doctor's and ask to try it with an implant. Although most women go up two cup sizes, many later wish they'd gone bigger. Discuss this with the doctor.

8 Make sure you receive comprehensive advice about potential complications and all aspects of the surgery and recovery.

9 Prepare to pay about $1,300 for saline implants or about $1,800 for silicone, with an additional $3,000 for surgeon's fees.

10 Expect scarring. Ask about possible future problems such as difficulty with breast-feeding. Complications can range from ruptures and leakage to infections and tightening of the scar tissue around the implant. The implants themselves can wrinkle, deflate, harden and develop an unnatural feel.

What to Look For

- Accredited surgeon
- Thorough consultation
- Clear explanations
- Implant costs and surgeon's fees

Tip

Although breast reconstruction can do so much for cancer patients after a mastectomy, up to one-third of doctors never refer their patients for this surgery. However, women can explore this option on their own and safely benefit from the surgery right after their mastectomy.

Warnings

Implants make diagnostic mammograms less effective because they literally cloud the picture.

Implants aren't forever; they often need to be replaced within 15 years. Patients sometimes return years earlier to have them removed, change their shape and size, or have repair or maintenance work done. One study found more than a quarter of the women receiving saline implants underwent more surgery within five years—about two-thirds for corrective work, the remainder to get a different shape or size.

361 Get Wrinkle-Filler Injections

If you're not squeamish about needles and don't mind the cost, a few tiny injections of Botox, collagen or even your own fat can temporarily turn back the clock. Watch frown lines, crow's-feet and lip creases all but disappear. But first, weigh these safety concerns and be sure to put your face in the right hands.

Steps

1 Find a skilled cosmetic surgeon or dermatologist who injects Botox, collagen or fat as a part of his or her daily practice. A medical qualification alone isn't enough; it's a specialized, aesthetic field. Ask to see living examples of the doctor's work. (See 358 Buy a New Body.)

2 Ask your doctor which substance will work best for you given the location and severity of your facial lines.

  • Botox is a diluted form of a powerful nerve toxin. Minuscule amounts are injected to temporarily paralyze or relax facial muscles so they don't—and can't—contract into wrinkles.

  • Collagen injections fill out lines from underneath—smile lines, lipstick bleed lines, crow's-feet, acne scars, even wrinkling on lips and hands. This synthetic filling agent derived from cows requires an allergy patch test before treatment.

  • Your own body's fat is good for filling in deep lines and poses no allergy problems. It can be removed from hips or buttocks then stored. The results can last longer than with Botox or collagen.

3 Factor in the cost of upkeep. With Botox and collagen, you'll need to repeat the injections every three to six months. Depending on the number of injections, Botox can cost $300 to $1,000 each time, and collagen $300 to $700.

4 Expect some irritation or redness afterward, and perhaps a little bruising with collagen, but nothing that makeup can't cover. You'll notice collagen's benefits right away. Botox's effects can take a few days or even up to three weeks to peak, then the effects gradually disappear as nerves regenerate. Getting injections may be a little uncomfortable, but it isn't painful because the needle is so fine.

What to Look For

• Doctor's expertise
• Right type for you
• Funds for upkeep

Tips

Look out for a new treatment called Artefill—bovine collagen coupled with microscopic plastic spheres. Although it has some risks (it can turn lumpy or cause rashes), expect to hear more about it, as its results can be permanent. All the more reason to have a great surgeon do the treatment.

Botox and collagen injections work best on people under 65 because the skin has more natural elasticity. Sun-damage wrinkles in older people don't always respond as well. Ask for a realistic assessment of expected improvement, given your age and skin.

Warning

Botox is FDA-approved and there's no known allergy problem, but short-term problems can occur, such as a drooping eyelids or eyebrows, a frozen expression, and even drooling if it's used near the mouth. The usual cause for such problems is off-target placement.

362 Find Alternative and Holistic Practitioners

Government and medical research institutions have poured millions of dollars into studies on promising complementary and alternative medicine (CAM). You'll still need to check with your doctor, but here's how to find legitimate CAM professionals.

Steps

1 Ask your doctor for a referral. You may face possibly well-warranted skepticism. Also ask friends, family, nutritionists or physical therapists for recommendations. Some alternative-medicine professional organizations have CAM referral services.

2 Find out what your health plan covers; many costly CAM treatments are not. While more insurers include chiropractic treatments in their plan, far fewer cover acupuncture, let alone Ayurvedic medicine or homeopathy.

3 Do some detective work at state and local departments of health and consumer affairs, which increasingly have licensing and accreditation requirements for alternative practitioners. Ask about practitioners' educational background and training, and if any formal complaints have ever been filed against them. Inquire if any scientific research supports specific treatments you may be considering. Search for existing study results at the National Institutes of Health Web site (clinicaltrials.gov).

4 Check qualifications if possible, despite the patchy regulations on CAM. For example, acupuncturists must be licensed in more than 35 states, but might also be called registered or certified, or doctors of acupuncture or Oriental medicine.

5 Consider applying to be part of a clinical trial or study if money is an issue. The National Center for Complementary and Alternative Medicine (NCCAM) is the federal government's lead agency devoted to supporting research; learn about trial participation at www.nccam.nih.gov/clinicaltrials.

What to Look For

- Medical doctor's referral
- Additional recommendations
- Health insurance coverage
- Local and state requirements
- Clinical trial or study

Tips

Look to studies underway—like the massive clinical trials testing the supplements glucosamine and chondroitin sulfate, separately and together, against Celebrex and a placebo on osteoarthritis sufferers—for clues to remedies with the best potential. Check with your doctor first; these supplements might cause elevated blood sugar, for instance.

Keep your general physician informed about your treatment plans.

363 Choose a Manicurist

Have you been going sans-trowel in the garden? Using your nails to tighten screws and scratch off labels? Regain your glamour and pamper yourself with a soothing manicure or pedicure. Choose the salon wisely, though, or you may end up with sore cuticles—or worse.

Steps

1 Make sure the manicurist's license is current and displayed.

2 Study how the manicurists work at a prospective salon. Metal tools should go straight into disinfectant after use, and nail files and buffing blocks should be brand-new for each client. Ask how their tools are cleaned. Since dirty nail-care equipment can harbor and pass on tenacious fungal infections, consider taking your own tools and polish for your manicurist to use. They can be kept at the salon for you.

3 Observe how the foot baths are cleaned and if fresh hand towels are used for each customer. Is the salon clean in general?

4 Stop any snip-happy manicurist who tries to clip your cuticles. They tear more easily as they grow back, can look ugly and are more vulnerable to infections and fungus. A manicurist should use cuticle softening oil after a warm soak, then gently ease them back with an orangewood stick. Too many manicurists try to remove the cuticle, which only brings on infection.

5 Discuss the length and shape you like—oval, squared-off, rounded. A good manicurist has the eye and artistry to shape nails uniformly. Don't file them down at the sides because that weakens nails and can cause splitting.

6 Go glam and get acrylic nail tips for $20 to $40, but bear in mind that you'll need to return regularly for fills as the nail grows out. Or get a silk wrap to strengthen existing nails. Tips soften and weaken nails, but can cure chronic nail-biting.

What to Look For

- Current manicurist's license
- Disinfected tools
- Excellent hygiene
- Pristine tubs, shop

Tip

Nail-polish remover can be drying. Moisturizing and protecting cuticles makes them less likely to split or crack; use cuticle cream, facial moisturizer, hand and body lotion—whatever's handy. Cuticles are near the nail growth center and also protect the proximal nail groove, which, if exposed, is vulnerable to bacteria, fungus and paronychia, a common nail infection.

Warning

If your nails ever look discolored, see your doctor. Onychomycosis (nail fungus) is serious and can lead to deformed nails or even loss of nails.

364 Get Whiter Teeth

If your pearly whites, well, aren't—blame it on caffeine, candy, prescription drugs or aging, all of which dull the gleam. Whiten and brighten dingy teeth with high-tech treatments in your dentist's office or over-the-counter bleaches you use at home. Here's how to bring that sparkle back.

Steps

1 Ask your dentist if you're a good candidate for whitening, since results can vary. Yellowed teeth generally lighten well; darkened grayish or brownish teeth may not.

2 Try over-the-counter products, which have low concentrations of hydrogen peroxide. A dental tray and gel kit can be used for a short time each day to lighten teeth one to two shades in two weeks, at best. Whitening strips cover the six front teeth—which must be even—for similar results, and keep peroxide on teeth and off gums. Paint-on gels get similar results and cover more teeth, but can be messy to use. Hydrogen peroxide works faster than carbamide (see Step 3), but takes longer to get results and deactivates faster. These are the least-expensive treatments to use when staining reoccurs due to beverages and smoking.

3 Use a dentist-made tray at home twice daily for an hour for a couple of weeks, or wear it overnight. The gel's active ingredient is 10, 15 or 20 percent carbamide peroxide, which is gentler than hydrogen peroxide. Teeth could lighten several shades depending on the strength of the gel used. Higher percentages work faster but also increase the chance of teeth sensitivity. Ask your dentist for whitening products that include fluoride to reduce sensitivity. Cost: $300 to $450.

4 Whiten your teeth by up to 10 shades in one 60- to 90-minute session with a potent, light-activated bleaching formula of 35 percent hydrogen peroxide. Cost: $500 to $1,100.

5 Consider porcelain veneers or bonding if you have conditions where bleaching isn't effective, such as tetracycline or intrinsic staining. Bonding is a resin that's contoured over teeth. Veneers are thin porcelain manufactured in a laboratory. Cost: $500 to $1,500 per tooth for porcelain veneers, $150 to $300 for bonding.

6 Keep in mind that two to three weeks of whitening by over-the-counter products equals one week of overnight tray treatment from the dentist—and may well equal one hour of the light-activated treatments.

What to Look For

- Dentist's options
- Over-the-counter kits
- Percentage of active ingredient

Tips

See 348 Purchase a Toothbrush.

The results of whitening treatments, even the costly ones, aren't permanent. Touch-ups may be required every six to 24 months.

Warnings

If you experience severe sensitivity after using a product, let your dentist know.

Since whitening treatments have no effect on artificial materials such as crowns, fillings or veneers, monitor your progress closely to keep color uniform with your natural enamel.

Avoid restaining brightened teeth with red wine, sodas, tea, coffee or tobacco. Bonded teeth can be affected but to a lesser degree. Veneers will not be affected at all.

"Whitening" toothpastes contain polishing agents that improve tooth appearance by removing surface stains. This can take months to see results, if any.

365 **Select Eyeglasses and Sunglasses**

Prescription glasses and sunglasses have to be functional but also look good. Fortunately, there are so many styles that it's easy to find the right pair. Learn the technical details first, then shop around.

Steps

Prescription eyewear

1 Consider frame materials. Aluminum and titanium frames are very durable and offer custom fitting options. Plastic frames are light and durable but usually can't be bent to offer a custom fit.

2 Assess overall weight. Glasses need to be comfortable. Large lenses and thick frames add up to heavy glasses, something most people find uncomfortable. If you need thick lenses, get the smallest diameter lens that looks good on you.

3 Understand lens materials. Glass lenses resist scratching but are heavy and have lower shatter resistance. Polycarbonate (plastic) lenses are light and shatter resistant but demand care to prevent scratches. Custom options for lenses include an antireflective coating to cut glare, enhanced thinness for light weight and good looks, and photoreactive tinting that gets darker in bright light. Beware: These options can easily double your total cost.

4 Shop for metal frames that can withstand vigorous bending without damage. Opt for a separate set of specialized sports glasses with an impact-resistant frame and lenses secured by a strap.

Sunglasses

1 Read the label carefully. You want 100 percent UV (ultraviolet light) protection from both UVA and UVB rays. Some lenses are labeled as UV400, which means the same thing.

2 Own several pair of sunglasses since one pair can't do everything. Leave a pair in the car for driving—cheap ones if you tend to sit on them. A slim stylish pair will not protect your eyes from debris while riding your bike. Expensive, sporty wrap-arounds will make you look like a yahoo at work.

3 Look for shatter-resistant polycarbonate lenses for water and snow sports, which require protection against strong reflected rays. Glass lenses, with their increased scratch resistance and fine optical quality, are a good choice for pricey, dress-up glasses. Polarized lenses, which reduce glare, are always a good idea.

4 Choose lens color carefully. Sensitive eyes need dark lenses. Gray or gray-green are good for general use. Brown works well for daytime driving or golf. Yellow and amber provide depth perception in low-light conditions. Avoid light blue and pink for driving or sports as they distort color. Some models have interchangeable lenses.

What to Look For

- Durability
- Comfort
- UV protection
- Lens color
- Style

Tips

Talk to your optometrist and get prescription sunglasses if you need them. Or get clip-ons that attach to your regular glasses.

You don't have to spend a lot to get good protection. Moderately priced sunglasses, around $20, frequently offer good eye protection. Designer sunglasses can cost $100 to $300. Ask about a warranty.

Take a Polaroid camera along when you shop for glasses. If you're undecided, get a picture of you wearing them to bring home.

If you're under age 20, your eyes let in more UV rays. Since children spend a lot of time outside, protect their little eyes from UV exposure and glare.

Warning

Too much UV radiation can lead to blindness. Not all tinted glasses—even very dark ones—protect against UV radiation, so be sure to check the label.

Health & Beauty

366 Hire a Personal Trainer

Whether you want to become the next Demi or Arnold, or just get back in shape, working with a personal trainer will do the job. Trainers' expertise and workout styles vary enormously: Here's how to find the best person for you—and that six-pack just waiting to be discovered.

Steps

1 Determine which fitness activities are most likely to keep you feeling happy, enthused and committed: Kickboxing, spinning, free weights, Pilates, walking, step aerobics, dance, rock climbing, gospel aerobics, circuit training or cardio-focused training. Doing what you love will keep you doing it.

2 Get a referral from a satisfied (and buffed) friend or call nearby fitness centers, gyms or studios and find out what programs are offered by their personal trainers.

3 Find out if the trainer is certified by a nationally recognized body such as the American Council on Exercise (acefitness.org) or the American College of Sports Medicine (which requires a health-related academic degree). Check if dance or martial arts teachers have had proper training as well.

4 Schedule a trial workout to see if a trainer is suited to your personality and shows a genuine interest in you and your goals.

5 Choose a trainer or teacher with a good grasp on your workout level—and limitations. You want someone who motivates and challenges you without setting impossible goals or pushing you too fast or too hard. Creative workout planning will help avoid burnout.

6 Some gyms employ trainers who only have a college degree in physiology or kinesiology. However, there are lots of graduates of weekend programs or, worse, home-based or Internet classes, out there claiming to be qualified. Standardized fitness certification guidelines for the industry are imminent; meanwhile, check credentials carefully.

What to Look For

- Favorite workout activities
- Referrals
- Qualifications
- Motivating personality
- Good pacing

Tips

Check on your trainer's cancellation policy to avoid wasting money on classes you can't make.

Look into mobile gyms if you've got more money than time. Some personal trainers can drive a gym on wheels straight to your house, but it will cost you.

367 **Sign Up for a Yoga Class**

With its allure of peace, enlightenment, physical flexibility and fitness, interest in yoga has exploded. Choose between the many different schools and find a yogi with the wisdom and advanced training to help you best. Also check with the nonprofit Yoga Alliance (yogaalliance.org).

TYPE	DESCRIPTION
Iyengar	Developed by Yogacharya B.K.S. Iyengar, this type of yoga focuses on an in-depth study of asanas (posture) and pranayama (breath control). Helps increase flexibility, strength and connection of mind, body and spirit.
Kundalini	Brought to the West in 1969 by Yogi Bhajan, kundalini focuses on unleashing spiritual (and sexual) energy, and is used to increase strength, movement and balance. It can promote greater physical well-being and awareness, while also helping the participant feel more relaxed.
Hatha	Hatha is the most widely practiced form of yoga in the world, and is used to promote flexibility and relaxation. Combining postures and stretches with proper breathing techniques, it encourages strength and proper body alignment while decreasing stress. There are many styles of hatha yoga, some of which use props such as blocks or belts to assist the postures.
Mantra	A mantra is a sound or word, and mantra yoga is a meditation practice that helps quiet the mind. The goal is to focus on a single thought (your mantra) until the mind and emotions are transcended and the superconscious is revealed.
Bikram	Taught in a grueling 90-minute session and a 100 degrees F (38 C) room, this form of yoga developed by Yogiraj Bikram Choudhury is for those wanting to combine yoga with an intense workout. The sweltering heat so loosens the muscles and ligaments that they stretch much farther than they normally would. Beginners should work slowly to avoid strains and other injuries.
Ashtanga	An ancient form of hatha yoga composed of a series of postures, connecting movements, and rhythmic deep breathing. One of the purposes of ashtanga is to rid the body of toxins through vigorous movements that create sweat. It is a challenging practice, but enhances mental focus and relaxation, while developing strength and flexibility.
TIPS	• Most yoga classes provide the props that are used in class, such as blocks and belts, but it is a good idea to bring your own mat and towel. Bring a water bottle as well, especially if participating in "hot" yoga such as Bikram or Ashtanga. • Videos are widely available, but it is best to learn the techniques in a class first, to avoid injury. • Specialized classes are available at many yoga studios including pre- and postnatal, restorative, seniors and children.

368 Treat Yourself to a Day at the Spa

Need to rejuvenate but don't have the time or money for a weekend getaway? A day spa could be the perfect solution. Popping up in cities across the country, day spas offer a variety of treatments and pampering techniques that are sure to leave you feeling refreshed.

Steps

1 Get personal referrals, worth their weight in gold, since there are so many levels on which to assess the day spa experience.

2 Take a tour of the spa before you commit to spending a day there. Look for beautiful, clean surroundings and ample plush towels. Do you like the atmosphere? It can vary from alluring and relaxing with candlelights, flowers and water fountains, to more spartan and natural with soft music.

3 Scan the treatment menu. Full packages can be more economical than several à la carte treatments.

4 Ask about the qualifications of aestheticians, massage therapists and spa personnel: Where were they trained? What methods or styles do they use? How long have they worked there?

5 Decide how lush you want to go and what your body is really crying out for. Is it a deep-tissue massage and a facial? Or a stimulating salt rub and then a pedicure? Choose your treatments accordingly. Throw in at least one exotic-sounding full-body treat, the kind that sounds like a dessert-cart delicacy with tasty ingredients like pineapple, chocolate or papaya.

What to Look For

- Personal referrals
- Clean, attractive environment
- Staff expertise
- Relaxing, get-away-from-it-all ambience
- Menu of treatments

Tip

Inquire if robes, slippers and towels are provided. And although many spas have lockers that lock, it is best to leave valuables at home.

Warning

Don't drive yourself home. If you're truly as relaxed as a limp noodle, as prescribed, you'll be a road hazard—and rallying to negotiate traffic will kill the mood.

TREATMENT	DESCRIPTION AND PRICE
Facial	Types include anti-aging, stress-reducing and therapeutic. Includes thorough cleansing as well as product application and generally a mini massage of the head and neck. $75 to $125 for 60 minutes.
Reflexology	Using the foot as a map of the entire body, apply pressure to different areas of the foot to reduce stress, improve circulation and cleanse the body of toxins. $70 for 60 minutes.
Aromatherapy	Uses therapeutic, essential oils to soothe or regenerate the body. May be used in conjunction with other treatments like massages and facials. $85 to $150.
Body Wrap	Using mud, paraffin, seaweed or aromatherapy-infused cloth to cover the body, these treatments stimulate the circulation, release muscle tension and promote general relaxation. $90 to $150 for 60 minutes.

369 Book a Massage

Massage has enormous potential to do a body good if you're in the right hands. But the way people like to get rid of knots and tension is highly personal. Get the lowdown on the rubdown.

TYPE	TRADEMARK TOUCH	BENEFITS
Swedish	Technique includes kneading, shaking, tapping, long sweeping strokes and circular pressure. Oil is generally used.	Energizes, eases sore muscles and joints, improves blood flow.
Deep-tissue	Strokes are intentionally firm and can be painful as therapist gradually breaks through muscle spasms and layers of tension and goes deeper to slowly release it. Oil is generally used.	Can give remarkable relief. Should never be horribly painful; if it is, the therapist isn't tuning into your body, so ask for a lighter touch.
Acupressure	For the faint of heart who can't face acupuncture's needles. Finger pressure is applied to the same spots and pathways. Acupressure points that are initially painful to the touch hold more pain, stress and tension.	Puts the body into balance, rejuvenates and relaxes. Gives sense of well-being. During the massage, pain gradually ebbs away.
Shiatsu	A Japanese art; widely available variation on acupressure.	Puts the body into balance, rejuvenates and relaxes. Gives sense of well-being. During the massage, pain gradually ebbs away.
Thai	Therapist uses his or her hands, arms, feet, legs and whole body to ease you into yoga poses. Fully clothed. Involves rhythmic stretching and pulling, plus pressing key energy points for total relaxation.	Makes you feel loose and limber. Gives feeling of peace and well-being followed by rush of energy. Can help chronic pain.
Reflexology	Stimulation of specific points on feet and hands believed to connect to specific internal organs.	Can remove energy blockages and improve overall health. Finds tender spots you didn't know you had.
TIPS	Let your massage therapist know about any injuries or tender spots you'd prefer to avoid. Check that your massage therapist is certified. Ask to see evidence of special training in methods like Thai or Swedish massage. Contact local massage schools for less expensive services.	

REHOUSE STORES • BUY WHOLESALE • GET OUT OF DEBT • BUY NOTHING • BUY HAPPINESS • BUY A BETTER MOUSETRAP • BUY TIME
MEONE'S FAVOR • BUY POSTAGE STAMPS WITHOUT GOING TO THE POST OFFICE • TIP PROPERLY • BUY HEALTHY FAST FOOD • BUY SU
TING SERVICE • SELL YOURSELF ON AN ONLINE DATING SERVICE • SELL YOURSELF TO YOUR GIRLFRIEND/BOYFRIEND'S FAMILY • BUY D
HOOSE FILM FOR YOUR CAMERA • BUY RECHARGEABLE BATTERIES • DONATE TO A GOOD CAUSE • HOLD A PROFITABLE GARAGE SALE
STUDENT DISCOUNTS • BUY FLOWERS WHOLESALE • GET A PICTURE FRAMED • HIRE A MOVER • HIRE A PERSONAL ORGANIZER • FIND
REAT BIRTHDAY PRESENT FOR UNDER $10 • SELECT GOOD CHAMPAGNE • BUY A DIAMOND • BUY JEWELRY MADE OF PRECIOUS METALS
IDESMAIDS' DRESSES • HIRE AN EVENT COORDINATOR • HIRE A BARTENDER FOR A PARTY • HIRE A PHOTOGRAPHER • HIRE A CATERER
Y AN ANNIVERSARY GIFT • ARRANGE ENTERTAINMENT FOR A PARTY • COMMISSION A FIREWORKS SHOW • BUY A MOTHER'S DAY GIFT •
FT • SELECT A THANKSGIVING TURKEY • BUY A HOUSEWARMING GIFT • PURCHASE HOLIDAY CARDS • BUY CHRISTMAS STOCKING STUF
E HIGH ROLLERS ROOM IN VEGAS, BABY • BUY SOMEONE A STAR • PAY A RANSOM • GET HOT TICKETS • HIRE A LIMOUSINE • BUY A CP
AM • BUY A PERSONAL JET • ACQUIRE A TELEVISION NETWORK • ACQUIRE A BODY GUARD • BOOK A LUXURY CRUISE AROUND THE WO
OROUGHBRED RACEHORSE • BUY A VILLA IN TUSCANY • HIRE A PERSONAL CHEF • PURCHASE CUBAN CIGARS • HIRE A GHOSTWRITER
TNESS • MAKE BAIL • DONATE YOUR BODY TO SCIENCE • HIRE YOURSELF OUT AS A MEDICAL GUINEA PIG • SELL PLASMA • SELL YOUR
OLLEGE EDUCATION • BUY AND SELL STOCKS • CHOOSE A STOCKBROKER • DAY-TRADE (OR NOT) • BUY ANNUITIES • BUY AND SELL MU
Y PERSONAL FINANCE SOFTWARE • CHOOSE A TAX PREPARER • SET UP A LEMONADE STAND • SELL YOUR PRODUCT ON TV • HIRE A C
SINESS IDEA • BUY A SMALL BUSINESS • BUY A FRANCHISE • LEASE RETAIL SPACE • LEASE INDUSTRIAL SPACE • LEASE OFFICE SPACE
EB SITE • BUY ADVERTISING ON THE WEB • SELL YOUR ART • HIRE A PERSONAL COACH • SELL ON THE CRAFT CIRCUIT • HIRE A LITERA
LING BUSINESS • BUY A HOT DOG STAND • SHOP FOR A MORTGAGE • REFINANCE YOUR HOME • SAVE BIG BUCKS ON YOUR MORTGAC
LL A FIXER-UPPER • SELL THE FARM • SELL MINERAL RIGHTS • SELL A HOUSE • SELL A HOUSE WITHOUT A REAL ESTATE AGENT • OBTA
OOK A VACATION RENTAL • BUY A CONDOMINIUM • RENT AN APARTMENT OR HOUSE • OBTAIN RENTER'S INSURANCE • BUY A LOFT IN M
RNISH YOUR STUDIO APARTMENT • BUY USED FURNITURE • BUY DOOR AND WINDOW LOCKS • CHOOSE AN ORIENTAL CARPET • BUY L
ARRANTIES ON APPLIANCES • FIND PERIOD FIXTURES • BUY A BED AND MATTRESS • HIRE AN INTERIOR DESIGNER • HIRE A FENG SHUI
N • BUY A WHIRLPOOL TUB • BUY A SHOWERHEAD • BUY A TOILET • CHOOSE A FAUCET • BUY GLUES AND ADHESIVES • CHOOSE WIN
TCHEN CABINETS • CHOOSE A KITCHEN COUNTERTOP • BUY GREEN HOUSEHOLD CLEANERS • STOCK YOUR HOME TOOL KIT • BUY A V
ENTRY DOOR • BUY A GARAGE-DOOR OPENER • BUY LUMBER FOR A DIY PROJECT • HOW TO SELECT ROOFING • HIRE A CONTRACTO
OWERS FOR YOUR GARDEN • SELECT PEST CONTROLS • BUY SOIL AMENDMENTS • BUY MULCH • BUY A COMPOSTER • BUY FERTILIZE
Y KOI FOR YOUR FISH POND • BUY A STORAGE SHED • HIRE AN ARBORIST • BUY BASIC GARDEN TOOLS • BUY SHRUBS AND TREES •
LECT KITCHEN KNIVES • DECIPHER FOOD LABELS • SELECT HERBS AND SPICES • STOCK YOUR KITCHEN WITH STAPLES • EQUIP A KIT
OUNTAIN OYSTERS • PURCHASE LOCAL HONEY • CHOOSE POULTRY • SELECT FRESH FISH AND SHELLFISH • SELECT RICE • PURCHASE
READS • BUY ARTISAN CHEESES • PURCHASE KOSHER FOOD • BUY FOOD IN BULK • CHOOSE COOKING OILS • SELECT OLIVE OIL • SEL
OFFEEMAKER OR ESPRESSO MACHINE • PURCHASE A KEG OF BEER • BUY ALCOHOL IN A DRY COUNTY • CHOOSE A MICROBREW • OR
ULATION PREDICTOR KIT • PICK A PREGNANCY TEST KIT • CHOOSE BIRTH CONTROL • FIND THE RIGHT OB-GYN • HIRE A MIDWIFE OR
HOOSE DIAPERS • BUY OR RENT A BREAST PUMP • CHOOSE A CAR SEAT • BUY CHILD-PROOFING SUPPLIES • FIND FABULOUS CHILDCA
CKYARD PLAY STRUCTURE • FIND A GREAT SUMMER CAMP • SELL GIRL SCOUT COOKIES • BUY BRACES FOR YOUR KID • BUY TOYS
A MODEL • SELL USED BABY GEAR, TOYS, CLOTHES AND BOOKS • FIND A COUPLES COUNSELOR • HIRE A FAMILY LAWYER • BUY PRO
PENSES • GET VIAGRA ONLINE • PURCHASE A TOOTHBRUSH • BUY MOISTURIZERS AND ANTIWRINKLE CREAMS • SELECT PAIN RELIEF
IPPLIES • SELECT HAIR-CARE PRODUCTS • BUY WAYS TO COUNTER HAIR LOSS • BUY A WIG OR HAIRPIECE • BUY A NEW BODY • GET
ANICURIST • GET WHITER TEETH • SELECT EYEGLASSES AND SUNGLASSES • HIRE A PERSONAL TRAINER • SIGN UP FOR A YOGA CLAS
EA MARKET • RENT SPACE AT AN ANTIQUE MALL • BUY AT AUCTION • KNOW WHAT YOUR COLLECTIBLES ARE WORTH • DICKER WITH I
ECOGNIZE THE REAL MCCOY • BUY COINS • BUY AN ANTIQUE AMERICAN QUILT • BUY AN ANTIQUE FLAG • LIQUIDATE YOUR BEANIE BA
WNSHOP • BUY AND SELL COMIC BOOKS • BUY AND SELL SPORTS MEMORABILIA • SELL YOUR BASEBALL-CARD COLLECTIONS • CHO
OMPUTER • BUY PRINTER PAPER • BUY A PRINTER • BUY COMPUTER PERIPHERALS • CHOOSE AN INTERNET SERVICE PROVIDER • GET
JY BLANK CDS • BUY AN MP PLAYER • CHOOSE A DVD PLAYER • BUY A VCR • CHOOSE A PERSONAL DIGITAL ASSISTANT • CHOOSE MO
GITAL CAMCORDER • DECIDE ON A DIGITAL CAMERA • BUY A HOME AUTOMATION SYSTEM • BUY A STATE-OF-THE-ART SOUND SYSTEM
NIVERSAL REMOTE • BUY A HOME THEATER SYSTEM • BUY VIRTUAL-REALITY FURNITURE • BUY TWO-WAY RADIOS • BUY A MOBILE EN
ONEY • GET TRAVEL INSURANCE • PICK THE IDEAL LUGGAGE • FLY FOR FREE • BID FOR A SLED RIDE ON THE ALASKAN IDITAROD TRAI
OREIGN OFFICIAL • GET A EURAIL PASS • TAKE AN ITALIAN BICYCLE VACATION • CHOOSE A CHEAP CRUISE • BOOK A HOTEL PACKAGE
COTLAND • BUY A SAPPHIRE IN BANGKOK • HIRE A RICKSHA IN YANGON • TAKE SALSA LESSONS IN CUBA • BUY A CAMERA IN HONG K
RST BASEBALL GLOVE • ORDER UNIFORMS FOR A SOFTBALL TEAM • BUY ANKLE AND KNEE BRACES • BUY GOLF CLUBS • JOIN AN EL
NOWMOBILE • BUY A PERSONAL WATERCRAFT • HIRE A SCUBA INSTRUCTOR • BUY A SKATEBOARD AND PROTECTIVE GEAR • BUY SKA
EATHER ACTIVITIES • SELL USED SKIS • BUY A SNOWBOARD, BOOTS AND BINDINGS • BUY SKI BOOTS • BUY A BICYCLE • SELL YOUR
JY A BACKPACK • BUY A BACKPACKING STOVE • BUY A KAYAK • BUY A PERSONAL FLOTATION DEVICE • BUY A WET SUIT • BUY A SUR
RDER CUSTOM-MADE COWBOY BOOTS • BUY CLOTHES ONLINE • FIND SPECIALTY SIZES • BUY THE PERFECT COCKTAIL DRESS • BUY
JY A MAN'S SUIT • HIRE A TAILOR • BUY CUSTOM-TAILORED CLOTHES IN ASIA • BUY A BRIEFCASE • SHOP FOR A LEATHER JACKET • E
ATE MONITOR • SELECT A WATCH • BUY KIDS' CLOTHES • CHOOSE CHILDREN'S SHOES • PURCHASE CLOTHES AT OUTLET SHOPS • BL

Collectibles

370 Get on Antiques Roadshow

This wildly popular PBS program started in 1990 and has been largely responsible for the growing awareness of antiques. If the Roadshow comes to your town, don't miss a chance for a free appraisal—and a chance to be on national television.

Steps

1 Check for tour stops on PBS.org. Each year the Roadshow visits a number of major cities.

2 Send a postcard with your name and address to enter a random drawing for tickets. If your postcard is one of the 3,000 drawn (per city), you'll receive two tickets to the event—for free.

3 Choose your antique wisely. There's no sure-fire item that will land you an on-air appraisal. Unusual and older items tend to receive more attention.

4 Weigh your options. If you decide to bring along a large hutch, you'll have to figure out how to get it safely from home to the show and home again. You and your back might be happier toting a nice piece of jewelry instead.

5 Wear an outfit that's suitable for TV, but also dress comfortably, especially when it comes to shoes. You'll spend a lot of time on your feet.

6 Get in line early. The Roadshow suggests you arrive no earlier than 30 minutes prior to the doors opening, but expect the crowd to be there then anyway. When you reach the head of the line, general appraisers will listen as you tell what you know about your antique. Then they will point you toward the right table for an appraisal.

7 Be a star. If appraisers see something rare or unusual in what you've brought, they might film your appraisal. You won't receive any information until the cameras roll; the show is looking for a genuine reaction. If you're chosen, don't assume you'll receive good news. Some treasure hunters learn the hard way that they spent too much.

What to Look For

- Tour stops
- Tickets
- Chance at stardom, riches

Tip

Share everything you know about your antique, such as how long it's been in your family, who the previous owners were or what it was used for. It not only helps the appraiser put the right price on something, it's good TV.

Warning

If you're worried about damaging an item while you wait in line, or transporting your antique to the show site, don't bring it.

371 Buy and Sell Used Books

In the real-estate game, the mantra is location, location, location. In the book trade, it's condition, condition, condition. Even the dust jacket figures into a book's value.

Steps

Buying

1 Determine what kind of collector you are. Will you collect by author? Subject? First editions only? Answering these questions will set your course.

2 Do your homework. Yes, there are books about books. They tell you who published the book first and when, as well as how to approximate a book's value.

3 Surf for pricing information on the Internet. Be aware that some of the listings are asking prices, not actual selling prices.

4 Visit a few used bookstores and introduce yourself to the owners. Let them know what kinds of materials interest you. Bookstore owners frequent many more auctions and shows than you will.

5 Buy only the best. Once you've established what you're looking for, get the best example you can find.

6 Keep your books in good condition by storing them upright on bookshelves. If you must pack them away in boxes, lay them one on top of another, keep weight evenly distributed, and pack them tightly so they don't rub against one another. Don't put any weight on top of the books that might cause the binding to bend or the top to wear.

Selling

1 Lower your expectations—most sellers tend to place a value on books far above what they are really worth. Finding a rare gem among a pile of books you inherited is highly unlikely. Invite a local book dealer to see what you've got and ask for an off-the-cuff appraisal.

2 Sort paperbacks in one pile, hardcovers in another. Only in rare cases do paperbacks possess more than just word value. Sell them at a garage sale or trade them in at a used bookstore.

3 Find out what you can about any hardcover books you have in good condition. Check the library for reference books and search the Internet for used-book sales venues.

4 Sell your rare examples on an Internet auction site or at an auction house. If you're selling online, set a reserve (a price that must be met for a sale to take place) so you will get what you expect. See 374 Buy at Auction and 10 Use Online Auction Sites.

What to Look For

- Pricing info
- Used bookstores
- Best quality
- Library
- Internet auction sites

Tips

First editions are to book collectors what rookie cards are to sports-card collectors. Look for the words *first edition* and *first printing* in the front of the book (often just after the title page) on a page that also lists copyright date, publisher, printing location and reference numbers.

Not all first editions are marked as such. You may have to determine age by points of issue, such as spelling corrections or changes in illustrations made between printings.

Warning

Books made especially for a book-club distributor have little worth, except for folks who collect only book-club editions. To identify a book-club edition, look for a small circle, square, maple leaf, dot or star blind-stamped at the bottom right of the outside back cover. (A blind stamp is a slight indentation in the cover.)

372 Shop at an Antique Fair or Flea Market

These fairs and exhibitions offer the opportunity to view the wares of hundreds of dealers from all across the country in one location. Go with a partner and a plan.

Steps

1 Make a list. It's easy to get distracted by all the wonderful antiques and collectibles on display. Set some priorities so you won't waste precious time.

2 Decide how much you're willing to pay for items on your wish list. A quick Internet search will reveal what similar items are selling for. Figure at least one splurge item into your budget, to award yourself for being in the right place at the right time.

3 Get there early, because the best items are snatched up quickly. The serious shoppers will be waiting at the gate when it opens. Find out if the event offers a preview party. You will pay to get in, but you'll see the best material.

4 Be prepared. Take a bag or a rolling cart to put purchases in so you can keep shopping. If you're buying furniture, bring blankets, ropes and a vehicle that will enable you to transport the item safely home. Take a partner. Two people can cover more ground than one. Some high-tech shoppers use two-way radios to stay in touch.

5 Bring your own bottled water and munchies. Even though concession stands may be available, you don't want to have to fight the crowd or spend precious shopping minutes standing in line.

6 Wear comfortable walking shoes so you can be on your feet all day and navigate uneven ground. If the market is held outdoors, bring a hat to protect yourself from the sun.

7 Bring cash, credit cards and your checkbook. Different dealers accept different forms of payment. Dealing in cash can sometimes land a better price for an item.

8 Ask for what you want. If a dealer has items similar to but not exactly like the ones you're looking for, there's a chance he or she may have just what you want back home in the shop.

9 Make quick decisions. Few dealers will hold an item while you take time to think about it. They're at the fair to sell, sell, sell.

10 Ask dealers if they are open to trading or purchasing the items you bring to the show. Grab a business card for later contact.

11 Ask if a dealer will take less for a blemished or flawed item. The worst that can happen is that he or she will say no.

What to Look For

- Shopping list
- Budget
- Partner
- Cash
- Dealers who trade

Tips

Search antiquing newspapers and magazines for listings of antique fairs in your area and beyond.

One of the largest antique fairs is Nashville's Heart of Country Antiques Show (heartofcountry.com), which is held each February and October.

Most large shows offer a map of exhibitors and the types of merchandise they sell. Get one to help focus your shopping efforts.

These are some hot items to look for: vintage cookbooks and '50s kitchenware, and anything for the garden.

Warning

Big shows bring out large numbers of shoppers. Find a landmark that will help you remember where you parked, or tie a ribbon to your car antenna so you can find it in the lot.

373 Rent Space at an Antique Mall

If you've been toying with the idea of opening your own antique shop, take that notion for a test drive by setting up shop at a local antique mall. Here, many different dealers rent space to display their wares, creating a one-stop shopping bonanza for collectors.

Steps

1 Take inventory to see if you have enough merchandise to fill up the space you rent. Remember, the more diverse your inventory, the more shoppers you'll entice.

2 Choose a mall with good foot traffic and a friendly staff. Ask yourself, "Would I shop here?"

3 Weigh your commitment. You will pay the mall owner rent for the space you choose, plus a portion of your sales income—10 percent is common.

4 Choose a space. A display case may be all you need if you're selling sports cards or jewelry. Some malls even rent single open shelves. If you have furniture, you'll want a booth. Prices vary from state to state.

5 Know the local market and what appeals to the mall's clientele. If you have a lot of diverse items but not what shoppers want, the merchandise won't move.

6 Display your wares in a way that makes it easy for passersby to see what you have for sale. Don't stack items on top of or in front of each other.

7 Give customers room to shop. Don't pack your booth so full of merchandise that people can't get close to items they want to look at. Collectors are hands-on shoppers.

8 Price your goods appropriately and fairly. Consult price guides and compare your merchandise to that of other sellers in the mall when pricing items. If something doesn't sell, mark it down. Discounted tickets will attract attention.

9 Keep your booth or display case looking fresh by bringing out new merchandise. If it appears the same from week to week, repeat shoppers will walk by without a second glance.

10 Let mall employees handle the sales for you. One of the advantages of showing merchandise in an antique mall is that you don't have to deal with customer questions and requests.

11 Review your progress, keeping a close eye on profits. Contracts for mall space tend to be short-term, and either party can terminate them, which is to your advantage if you find the antique-mall route isn't for you.

What to Look For

- Diverse inventory
- Good location
- Friendly staff
- Rent rates
- Mall owner's commission
- Contract terms

Tips

Think like a business owner. Keep items dusted and looking their best. Faded price tags indicate to shoppers that no one is minding the booth.

Label items with as many facts as you have, including the date an item was made, its rarity, and any information on its provenance. All those factors will help make a sale.

Warning

Make sure your insurance is sufficient and up to date. If merchandise is stolen, broken or lost in a fire, the owner of the items, not the owner of the mall, is responsible for their loss.

374 **Buy at Auction**

Auctions put your antiques and collectibles in front of the greatest amount of serious buyers at one time. If you're in the mood to buy rather than sell, auctions offer an exhilaration you can't get from just walking into an antiques store. See also 10 Use Online Auction Sites.

Steps

1 Find the type of auction that works for you. Online auctions are the most time-consuming option and the riskiest for buyers, since you never get to see the merchandise in person. Auction houses like Sotheby's and Christie's feature high-end items you won't find anyplace else. Country auctions offer the best chance for finding a diamond in the rough. When it comes to pace, an auction house event is a golf tournament, and a country auction is a NASCAR race.

2 Know the purchasing rules of the auction house. Sellers pay a commission to the house for their services, from 5 to 15 percent, depending on the value of the piece. Similarly, buyers may be required to pay a premium to auction owners for high-end sales.

3 Get the timing down. Country auctions and auction house events will last from just a few hours to a day. Online auctions are timed; items are usually posted for a week or so. Bidding really heats up as the deadline approaches.

4 Ask questions about the provenance (ownership history) of a piece. It's especially important to find out from online sellers if anything was left out of their description of the piece. As a seller, you need to be able to provide this type of feedback.

5 Decide on a bid limit for yourself, after inspecting merchandise. It's easy to get swept up in the excitement of a live auction and overbid.

6 Register so you can be identified as a bidder. No matter what type of auction you participate in, you'll need to do this— by name on the Internet, by number in person. You may also be asked for proof of payment to show your seriousness as a bidder.

7 Get the auctioneer's attention if you enter late in the bidding on a particular item at an auction house. His or her assistants will be concentrating on bidders already in the fray.

8 Have fun. A live auction is pure entertainment, from fast-talking auctioneers to fast-spending collectors. Auctions are free and open to the public, and you don't have to bid if you don't want to. In fact, attend a few auctions without bidding to pick up on the rules of the game.

What to Look For

- The right auction
- Rules of engagement
- Auction fees
- Information
- Reasonable budget
- Registration
- Preview

Tips

When selling high-end pieces, set a reserve (a minimum price you will accept for sale) to guarantee that you either get the amount you're after or get to keep the item.

Many auctions, such as the Napa Valley Wine Auction, benefit charities so bids often exceed the item's worth. But your contribution is tax-deductible.

See 112 Buy a Thoroughbred Racehorse for livestock auction information.

Warnings

The hammer price (the final bid amount when the gavel closes bidding) is not all you'll pay as a buyer. The auction house receives a percentage of the hammer price, and you'll have to pay for shipment (unless you transport it yourself).

Shilling is the practice of fraudulently driving up bids on the seller's behalf and voids the sale if discovered.

TYPE	LOCATION	MERCHANDISE VALUE	HOW TO PLACE A BID	SCOPE	MARKETING MATERIALS
Auction House	Sale rooms sometimes at an estate	High end, usually from $500 up to millions	Bidding paddle, rub of nose	Inter-national	Glossy catalog with photos, descriptions, sometimes minimum bids
Country Auction	Backyard, farmyard	Midrange, from hun-dreds into the thousands	Wave of hand, tip of hat	Regional	Flyers listing highlights, newspaper advertisements
Online Auction	Internet	Wide range, from a few dollars to thousands	Click of mouse	Global	Online listing with photos, descriptions

375 Know What Your Collectibles Are Worth

When you start collecting, always buy things you love and you'll never regret your investment. It's important to do some research before buying and selling. Finding information you can trust is key.

Steps

1 Consult price guides, which list collectibles and their price ranges. General guides list a number of collecting categories in one book. You'll also find more-specific single-topic guides.

2 Visit shops or antique shows to see how items similar to yours are priced. Establishing a relationship with a dealer may get you a better price when you're ready to sell or buy.

3 Contact auction houses to obtain a report of the most recent sales. Look for items similar to yours and the price they fetched.

4 Scour the Internet for antiques and collectibles that are for sale through online auctions or stores.

5 Search newspapers and other publications devoted to antiquing to find collecting clubs.

6 Find an experienced mentor who can tell you if you're getting a fair offer. Some of these experts work as pickers (regional buyers) for antique dealers and see a lot of merchandise.

7 Get a verbal appraisal from a dealer for free. If you have an item you think is really valuable, you might want to contact a professional appraiser, who will charge for that service.

What to Look For

- Price guides
- Antique experts
- Auction houses
- Internet sources
- Other collectors
- Mentor
- Appraisals

Tips

If you're selling to a dealer, expect to get only 50 percent or less of the price listed in the price guides. Selling to another collector may bring a better price.

If you own a valuable collectible, such as a piece of fine art, always seek out a second opinion on its value before you sell or buy.

376 Dicker with Dealers

Part of the fun of going to antique and collectibles shows is feeling like you've made the deal of the century. Many dealers love to dicker and leave room for negotiating in their pricing. Brush up on the rules of the game.

Steps

1 Be serious about your offer. Know what you can pay for the merchandise and then be ready to follow through. While dickering can be fun for novice buyers, it's serious business for dealers.

2 Gather all the merchandise you're interested in from a particular booth before tallying your take. The more items you buy, the more room you have to negotiate.

3 Prioritize the merchandise. Decide what you can do without just in case you and the owner can't make a deal and you don't want to raise your price.

4 Make only one deal a day at any given booth. Don't come back a second time and try to make another deal. Dealers might not remember you from show to show, but they will remember someone who tried to dicker them down twice in one day.

5 Build a relationship with the dealer. If you bought from a dealer before, remind him or her of that fact. He or she may offer a better price even before you ask. Dealers like to know that they are getting repeat customers and sales they can count on.

6 Say, "What's your best price on these things?" or "Would you take X amount for this?" Don't say, "I saw something like this a couple booths down for only X amount." The dealer's reaction will probably be, "Then go buy that one."

7 Deal in cash or a check for more leverage. If you're paying by credit card, the dealer will have to figure credit card company charges into the bottom line.

8 Negotiate a compromise. If the merchandise adds up to $250 and you have $200 in your pocket, offer to buy it all for $200. Expect the dealer to ask for something between those two totals.

9 Show your hand. The last step is to pull the cash out of your pocket and say, "But $200 is all the cash I've got." The dealer doesn't want to repack merchandise after the show and might be willing to take cash on the barrelhead. If not, you might have to let something go to get your total down to an affordable amount.

What to Look For

- Serious offer
- Strength in numbers
- The right questions
- Compromise
- Cash offer

Tip

Keep your poker face on. If you're drooling slightly, the dealer will know he or she doesn't have to bother with a discount because you'll buy it at any price.

Warning

Don't insult the dealer with a ridiculously low price for merchandise or by calling into question the authenticity of what he or she is selling. That's a sure way to kill a deal and a potentially profitable relationship.

377 Get an Antique Appraised

An appraisal is just one person's opinion, whether it's free or for a fee. Get a second opinion (and even a third or fourth) if you have a lot of money on the line.

Steps

1 Find out what you have, but don't buy $200 worth of books to research an item that may bring only $100. Price guides and printed estimates of value are just guidelines. What someone's willing to pay dictates the real worth of an item, and for that you need an expert in the field.

2 Look in the Yellow Pages under "Appraisers." Often they will include their specialty in the listing. Check their standing with the Better Business Bureau (bbb.org).

3 Look for groups like the American Society of Appraisers and the International Society of Appraisers, which are self-governing organizations that provide consumers with information.

4 Show the item in its original condition. If you refinish furniture or polish your coin collection, you might actually diminish the item's value. (See 381 Buy Antique Furniture and 383 Buy Coins.)

5 Find out what a written appraisal is likely to cost before you give the OK. An appraiser's research time can add up quickly.

6 Try to get a free verbal appraisal as part of an antique show or exhibit. You can also ask an antique dealer to give you an idea what your piece may be worth.

7 Find an online appraiser. The drawback here, of course, is that the appraiser isn't in the same room with the item.

8 Beware of the appraiser who offers to buy your item after appraising it, especially if you've never conducted business together before. Unscrupulous people may lowball your estimate to get a better deal.

What to Look For

- Price guidelines
- Experts in the field
- Professional associations
- Estimates for written appraisals
- Verbal appraisals
- Online appraisals

Tips

When presenting your item, don't say that you don't know anything about it. Simply say, "Tell me what you think about this."

Check with your insurance agent to see what's required to insure an item. You might not need a professional appraisal; a detailed bill of sale might be enough.

378 Buy Silverware

Back when entertaining meant a formal meal rather than a backyard barbeque, people set ornate tables full of unusual pieces, a treasure trove for today's collector.

Steps

1 Select a conversation piece to collect, like a crumb knife (looks like a sugar scoop with a flat bottom and one open side; used to sweep up crumbs between courses) or a butter pick (looks like a mini corkscrew; used to grab individual curls or balls of butter).

2 Choose large serving pieces you can use at holiday time, or pick a silver pattern you like and try to collect a complete set. One fun collectible category is ladles. Our ancestors relied on ladles for serving (from smallest to largest) mustard, mayonnaise, sauce, gravy, bouillon, oysters, soup and punch.

3 Look for the word *sterling* on the back of the handle. If it's not there, it's silver-plated. Look for the name of the manufacturer as well. An 18th-century find may have the craftsman's initials.

4 Avoid badly worn pieces if you plan to use them at your own table. Over the years, the silver plate on the back of a spoon or along a fork's tines can wear off.

5 Collect flatware for an affordable hobby. You can find teaspoons for less than a dollar. Large serving forks and spoons in fine condition can be had for $20 or less. Harder-to-find patterns will cost more, of course.

What to Look For

- Usable pieces
- Complete set
- Sterling
- Flatware

Tip

Collecting silverware is not a labor-free hobby. Silverware needs to be polished to look its best. Buy products expressly meant for silver cleaning. Never substitute toothpaste, which may include abrasives like baking soda that will damage silver. Rub polish back and forth instead of in a circular motion for a uniform finish. Rinse immediately with warm water and pat dry with a cotton dish towel. Silverware used and washed frequently is less likely to tarnish.

379 Evaluate Depression-Era Glassware

That colorful, translucent vase collecting dust on Grandma's mantel might actually be now-valuable mass-produced glass from the 1920s. Here's how to determine if you've got a treasure.

Steps

1 Research the pieces you own. Since more than 200 patterns of Depression glass exist, rarity determines value. Most had little to no hand-finishing or treatments done to the glass once it was came out of the mold. Short-run colors like alexandrite (lavender) and tangerine now command hefty prices in the collector market.

2 Attend an antique show and look for Depression glass dealers. Remember that the prices you see at the show are retail; you'll get half that or less if you sell your wares to a dealer.

3 Search the Internet for Depression-glass collector clubs and enthusiasts. The National Depression Glass Association (ndga.net) has an annual convention.

What to Look For

- Rare pieces
- Antique dealers
- Collector clubs

Tip

Used as promotional items during the Depression, this glassware came in soap or cereal boxes, or was given away at movie theaters or gas stations to encourage patrons.

380 Buy and Sell Stamps

Stamps won't make the casual collector rich, but as a hobby they're almost unbeatable. They don't take up much room, and your postal carrier brings new opportunities every day—for free!

Steps

Buy

1 Decide what you want to collect. Topical collecting (looking for any stamp with a flag, train or other specific item on it) is the latest trend. For example, an extensive collection can be made from collecting the Christmas stamps of just one country, especially if you include all the varieties of each issue. Some people even collect postmarks.

2 Look in the Yellow Pages for a shop that specializes in stamps. The store owner will know of upcoming stamp shows in the area.

3 Ask the shop owner about auction houses that sell stamps. Order an auction catalog. Expect big-ticket items; most auction houses want their lots to sell for more than $100 to make it worth their while. Look in collector magazines for advertisements by mail-order stamp sources.

4 Search online. Some stamp dealers have opened shop online, and a few auctions feature stamps. The U.S. Postal Service (usps.gov) also has information on starting a collection.

5 Select stamps with a bright color—fading can be caused by sunlight, artificial light, dirt, pollution and natural skin oils. The stamp should not be torn or damaged, and all perforations should be complete. It should be centered inside the white border.

Sell

1 Look through your collection for pre-1940 stamps for investment-quality material. Many fewer stamps were printed in the old days, making good specimens more difficult to find. For the most part, today's stamps are not going to greatly appreciate in value over the years because so many are in circulation.

2 Join a stamp club—it's a great way to find fellow collectors looking to buy. Clubs often hold their own stamp shows for members.

3 Ask a stamp dealer to assess your collection if you want your money right away. Face-to-face interactions are best.

4 Keep in mind that auction houses won't even look at your collection if they don't think it will sell for hundreds of dollars, and it may take a month or more to receive the proceeds.

5 Sell your stamps online. This method can be time-consuming: You must submit a photo and description for each stamp or lot.

What to Look For

- Stamp shops
- Auction houses
- Mail-order sources
- Web sites
- Stamp clubs
- Stamp shows

Tips

Glue on the back of a stamp means it has never been circulated. Removing stamps from letters also removes the glue.

Don't bother trying to soak a stamp off a colored envelope. The ink in the envelope will bleed and ruin the stamp.

Store your stamps using hinges or mounts on acid-free paper, all available at hobby shops. You'll also need tongs, a magnifier, a watermark detector and a perforation gauge.

See 374 Buy at Auction.

Warnings

You can't buy just one collectible stamp at the post office—you have to buy a roll or a sheet. If you don't send many letters, you might prefer to pay double face value at a shop for just one stamp.

Since it's so easy to sell items online, keep in mind that the seller might not be an expert and could overstate the quality of the item.

381 Buy Antique Furniture

You can find antique furniture to fit any decor, from country to contemporary. Let the buyer beware: Reproductions abound in the furniture field. Do your homework to make sure you're purchasing the real deal.

Steps

1 Become familiar with terms like *cabriole legs* that you're going to come across in advertisements and auction catalogs. (By the way, cabriole legs curve out like a cowboy's after too long in the saddle.)

2 Study the names (there can be more than one) of the styles you like best. Sellers classify their furniture by style—Louis XV, Queen Anne, Chippendale and so on.

3 Check the antiques section of your local bookstore or library for reference guides. The Internet is another good source for information and photographs of different furniture styles.

4 Visit a local museum. Seeing antique furniture up close will help you identify it in the field. Ask the curator for the names of trustworthy local dealers.

5 Learn to spot features that could affect the value of a piece such as damaged finish or joints, or unauthentic hardware. (See chart, next page.)

6 Get to know the local antique dealers and show them your wish list. They'll have contacts in other cities and states who can further your search. They will also be able to help you recognize a reproduction.

7 Go to an auction. For top-quality, top-dollar furniture, choose an auction house that guarantees what it sells. If you're not looking for a museum-quality piece, try a country auction, where you could find a bargain. (See 374 Buy at Auction.)

8 Watch for estate sales. If you're lucky, a family member will be at the sale to tell you about the piece's provenance or history.

9 Look through antiquing newspapers and magazines for ads, or search the Internet for antique fairs specializing in furniture. (See 372 Shop at an Antique Fair or Flea Market.)

10 Curb your desire for perfection in a piece of furniture that might be more than 100 years old. It should show signs of wear in places where you'd expect it, like the bottoms of chair legs and underneath drawer runners.

What to Look For

- Style
- Reputable dealers
- Auctions
- Estate sales
- Furniture shows
- Wear and tear

Tips

Definitions vary, especially regarding more recent items, but generally speaking, an antique is at least 100 years old. Everything newer than that falls into the collectible category.

Buy pieces you can use. Few of us have extra rooms we can fill with an untouchable collection of antique furniture.

If you know how to date a piece of furniture, you won't fall for a reproduction. Read one of the many books on the subject.

WHAT TO LOOK FOR	WHERE TO LOOK	IS IT OLD?
Hand-planing	The bottom of a chair or drawer.	If a seat bottom shows signs of hand-planing, it was probably made before 1810.
Construction Joints	The joints between two pieces of wood.	18th-century furniture was often pegged and glued, not nailed. Look for irregularly shaped and spaced dovetails (notches cut in wood so pieces fit together like puzzle pieces). Until the last half of the 19th century, these were cut by hand and shouldn't be perfectly spaced or formed.
Size of Boards	Tabletops and backs of dressers, bureaus.	These should be built with one solid piece or different pieces of various widths if the piece is truly old. Perfectly sized and spaced boards indicate new construction.
Saw Marks	On the backs of chests and under tables.	Straight saw marks indicate the piece was made before the mid-18th century. Wavy lines (cut with a band saw) show it was made in the mid-18th to 19th century. Look for circular saw patterns in furniture made after that.
Secondary Wood	Inside drawers and on dresser backs.	The builders of old furniture used less-expensive wood in places where it wouldn't show. No secondary wood is a sure sign of new construction, and any plywood is a dead giveaway.
Original Paint Finish	Cracks or dents in painted furniture.	If the paint finish is original, exposed wood should appear in any cracks and gouges. If you spy paint down in the cracks and crevices, then it's been painted since the ding occurred.
Antique Glass	Mirrors.	Antique glass is very thin. Test by placing a coin on edge against the mirror. If the reflection is very close to the coin itself, almost touching it, the glass is old.
Wormholes	On the surface of any wood piece.	Stick a pin in the hole. If the pin goes straight through, the hole is manufactured. True wormholes are winding paths.

382 Recognize the Real McCoy

McCoy is a type of colorful American pottery that was made in Ohio from 1910 until the late 1990s. Its popularity has spawned a number of knockoffs. Here's how to tell if you're buying the real McCoy.

Steps

1 Check the bottom of the piece for a special McCoy marking: Early pieces feature a shield with a number inside a circle; pieces made during the 1940s have an overlapped *N* and *M;* those in later production show *McCoy USA.* And don't fret if there is no mark—it may still be McCoy.

2 Compare the size. Copies are made by creating a mold from an authentic McCoy. When fired, ceramic shrinks, so an imposter is smaller than an original piece. Reference books on McCoy pottery will often include dimensions of the originals.

3 Examine the raised designs that decorate the pottery. Copies won't have the same sharpness of detail as original McCoys. They also tend to weigh less. Get to know what true McCoy looks and feels like by finding a dealer who specializes in pottery.

4 Visit sites like McCoy Pottery Online (mccoypottery.com) and Mostly McCoy (mostlymccoy.com) for the latest news.

What to Look For

- Potter's mark
- Size
- Sharp details
- Weight

Tips

McCoy is one collectible where you can still stumble across a treasure. A $20 garage-sale vase could fetch thousands at auction.

Just because a piece is old doesn't necessarily mean it carries greater value. Rarity and condition play a major role. A flowerpot can go for $25, while a rare tugboat cookie jar is worth $5,000.

383 Buy Coins

When it comes to buying coins, buy the best example you can find. And if you get serious about coin collecting, you can call yourself a numismatist—it'll look great on your résumé!

Steps

1 Look for luster—the shine on a new coin. If you're collecting old coins, however, luster is less of a concern.

2 Get a lucky strike. The strike is the impression on the coin. Look for a design that's perfectly centered on the coin.

3 Examine a coin for sharp details. One that has been in circulation for years will show a wearing down of high points on the design.

4 Avoid coins with small scratches on their surface: hairlines decrease its value. Cleaning the coin can also create hairlines, so learn the correct cleaning method from an expert.

5 Check your collection for the famed Buffalo nickel, with the profile of an American Indian chief on one side. Believe it or not, they are not hard to find. A complete date and mintmark set (one of each nickel minted between 1913 to 1938) goes for between $500 and $600. In uncirculated condition, that coin set would fetch closer to $27,000.

What to Look For

- Luster
- High-quality strike
- Sharp details
- Absence of hairlines

Tips

The year 1964 marked the end of true silver coins in the United States. Coins made before that, no matter how worn, retain at least their value in silver.

The United States Mint (usmint.gov) has more information on collecting coins.

384 **Buy an Antique American Quilt**

When it comes to craftsmanship, handmade quilts can rival the best examples of antique furniture you'll find. Expect to pay hundreds, even thousands of dollars for quilts in very good condition. A quilt writes a history with every stitch. Here's how to read it.

Steps

1 Look at authentic antique quilts at living history museums, local quilt guilds or antique shops to train your eye. For example, old fabrics tend to have a tighter weave (more threads per inch) than new ones.

2 Ask to touch the quilts so you can learn how vintage material feels. Watch for old quilt tops that have been given new cotton-polyester backs. To spot new batting (material sandwiched between the quilt top and back), gently rub the batting between your fingers. Polyester batting feels slippery.

3 Turn the quilt over and look for a label attached by the quilter. These list occasions, such as birthdays, weddings or national events, or names and dates.

4 Inspect the entire quilt. If the composition looks wrong, it may have been altered. Look for signs of wear in the binding (the edging on the quilt). Sometimes consistency of stitching is easier to see on the back than on the front.

5 Revel in the beautiful colors and craftsmanship of Amish quilts, one of the most prized categories. Look for plain, solid-color fabrics in bold, geometric designs. Amish beliefs reject adornments, including floral and stripe patterns. Quilts made from the late 19th century to the first half of the 20th century, with brilliant contrasting colors on black backgrounds can command $2,500 to $10,000.

6 Find a quilt that tells a tale. One of the most stirring examples of quilt as folk art, and quilter as historian, are story quilts. Introduced by African Americans about the time of the Civil War, these quilts feature appliquéd figures (cloth cut in the shapes of animals, people and landmarks) sewn onto a background, often with biblical quotes. Story quilts pictured an historic event (like an inauguration) or special occasions of everyday life (such as a circus), which can provide clues to date the quilt.

What to Look For

- Authenticity
- Label
- Flaws
- Stories

Tip

In the 1950s to 1970s, borders were sometimes added to older quilts so they would fit on modern beds.

Warning

Learn to recognize fakes and Pacific Rim imports. As with any deal, if it sounds too good be true, it probably is.

385 Buy an Antique Flag

If your passion runs toward folk art, you'll love collecting American flags with their creative star configurations and patriotic symbols.

Steps

1 Look for antique shows advertising Americana or political memorabilia. You'll find American flags as well as state flags.

2 Be familiar with the two types of flags. Large sewn flags (19th-century versions are at least 8 feet or 2.4 m) were used for extended periods of time, whether outside government offices or on ships. These were usually made of wool, muslin, cotton or a blend. Cotton or silk parade flags are small (some fit in the palm of your hand) and had a short-term use for parades or rallies.

3 Check construction. If a flag is machine-sewn (look for perfectly uniform stitches), it is likely no older than 1850 (about the time the sewing machine arrived in homes). From 1850 to 1900, stripes were often machine-sewn, but stars were done by hand. After 1900, almost no hand-stitching is evident on flags.

4 Gaze at the stars. Before 1912, there were no rules for putting stars on the canton (top inner quarter of flag), so earlier versions sometimes have the stars in a circle or another pattern, or stars with the image of an eagle.

386 Liquidate Your Beanie Baby Collection

If you were swept up in the collecting craze of the 1990s, chances are you've got a few drawers heaped with bean-filled plush toys. Here's how you can reclaim that storage space.

Steps

1 Check the tag. If it doesn't say Ty, forget it. Ty made the original Beanie Babies. Look for the words *first generation;* these toys have the most value. Also, the value goes up for those sporting a clear plastic tag protector.

2 Don't let toy price guides fool you. They will list some Beanie Babies for hundreds of dollars, but finding someone willing to pay that much is almost impossible now that the craze is over.

3 Browse the Internet for your best chance of finding a Beanie Baby lover who's trying to round out a collection. Otherwise, find a flea market seller who will give you a few dollars apiece for the items in your collection.

4 Give the toys to a local hospital or children's shelter. The pleasure you'll get from watching kids enjoy the toys is reward enough.

387 Score Autographs

You never know where your next brush with fame may be. Here are a few tips for adding to your collection of John Hancocks without relying on serendipity to put you in the right place at the right time.

Steps

1 Start a collection fast by purchasing autographs at memorabilia shows and auctions. Get proof of authenticity.

2 Stand in line. A sports show might book a Hall of Famer to sign autographs. An auto dealership might feature a NASCAR driver. Sometimes players or speakers sign autographs before or after an event. Bring the kids along for a chance to meet a hero. Stars are usually good about signing items for their younger fans.

3 Write letters to famous folks asking for signatures. Be sincere and include a self-addressed stamped envelope and blank cards.

4 Protect your investment by keeping autographs in their original state. Don't glue or tape an autographed paper onto cardboard or any other surface. Don't laminate. Hobby stores sell boxes or albums appropriate for storing autographs.

5 Don't give up your day job. While some autographs are very valuable (Ernest Hemingway, $1,000; JFK, $1,500), for the most part, this isn't a money-making hobby. Still, time will tell. Today's Brad Pitt ($25) could be tomorrow's Bruce Lee ($600).

What to Look For

- Memorabilia shows
- Promotional events
- Stars' addresses

Tips

You can find addresses for agents or representatives of famous people in Who's Who (whoswhoonline.com) or through fan clubs. Reach political bigwigs through their government offices.

Keep a supply of blank index cards and a permanent black marker with you at all times.

388 Trade Yu-Gi-Oh Cards

Two years ago, this item would have been titled "Trade Pokémon Cards." By the time you read this, there's sure to be a hot new card game for the preteen scene. A craze card by any other name trades the same.

Steps

1 Keep cards in top shape. Only those in mint condition (as they came out of the pack) will retain top value.

2 Know what your cards are worth so you can be sure to get a fair trade. You don't want to trade a $60 first-edition Gate Guardian straight up for a $25 Dark Magician.

3 Drop in at comic-book shops and card stores that allow kids to play the game and make trades. Also, the shop owner may take your extra cards in exchange for store credit.

4 Keep a poker face, no matter how badly you need the card. Some cards are necessary to play combinations. Everyone knows you can't play Great Moth without a Cocoon of Evolution.

What to Look For

- Card condition
- Fair value
- Fellow collectors
- Store credit
- Combinations

Tips

First-edition cards have more value—sometimes twice as much—than later versions of the same card. Check for the words *first edition* under the photo.

Once a deal is made, there's no going back.

389 Snag Star Wars Action Figures

Star Wars may seem like a galaxy far, far away, but to many collectors, the adventure is here and now. Stalking these hot sellers can turn into an epic quest. Your search will take you beyond your local toy store.

Steps

1 Focus your intergalactic collection. For example, narrow your search to just vintage (1977 to 1985) items, such as loose figures, vehicles or lightsabers. Or choose a favorite character, scene or ship. Internet auctions are your best bet for these items.

2 Watch for new-releases dates in collector magazines and on sites like GalacticHunter.com, and online forums. Visit SciFi gatherings to get an idea of what's hot and what's not.

3 Keep in mind future resale value. It's not always the hero who wins the day. Bad-guy Boba Fett may bring a bigger payoff to collectors than Luke Skywalker. As with any collectible, it all depends on rarity. More Lukes were made, another reason why this character goes for less.

4 Do not open, bend or damage the packaging. The best prices go to items in mint condition.

What to Look For

- New releases
- Resale value
- Packaging

Tips

Buy three of your favorite new figures—one for your kid, one for your own collection, and one to sell someday.

Store items out of direct sunlight, away from excessive heat or cold, and in a dry place. Moisture, including high humidity, can damage the packaging and reduce resale value.

390 Sell Your Vinyl Record Collection

With CDs on the scene, vinyl records seem to be going the way of cassettes and eight-track tapes. But there are still plenty of collectors out there interested in your Louis Armstrong albums.

Steps

1 Understand supply and demand of selling records. Owning a chart-topping Elvis record is like owning a first-edition Harry Potter book. Because there were so many printed, they're easy to find and the value goes down. That's why *Baby It's You* by the Beatles is listed in price guides at $5 while *Ragtime Cowboy Joe* by David Seville and the Chipmunks is $20.

2 Check for damage. To fetch top dollar, the record itself can't be scratched or warped. The album jacket should have sharp corners and few signs of wear.

3 Go to a local used-record store to find a buyer, or look in the back of price guides and collector magazines for advertisements.

4 Scrutinize the cover, which can often be even more valuable than the record inside. Collectors frame them as works of art. Especially popular are album covers with portraits of the singer like Frank Sinatra or Doris Day.

What to Look For

- Unusual artists
- Scratches
- Warping
- Buyer's advertisements

Tip

An out-of-town buyer may want to judge the condition of your collection. Send only a few albums or you might pay more in shipping than the whole collection is worth.

Warning

Don't stack your records— the weight leaves a ring on the album cover.

391 Sell at a Pawnshop

The repo man will be by tonight to take your new convertible unless you have cash in hand. When it comes to fast money, there's no place like the pawnshop. Sometimes, though, cashing in on an antique can be difficult.

Steps

1 Think small. Items like antique jewelry, a silver service piece, old guns or artwork are most likely to get a shop owner's attention. Fewer pawnshops are equipped to deal with big furniture pieces or rare pottery.

2 Put yourself in the shop owner's shoes to judge the sales appeal of your item. He or she is only going to buy what will easily resell. If you have an antique to pawn, finding a pawnshop in an antiques district may bring a better deal. That shop will have more customers looking to get a deal on an antique.

3 Lower your expectations. The shop owner may offer only about 30 percent of value for your item. The offer will be lower yet if the shop owner is not familiar with the piece.

4 Ask the owner how long he or she is legally required to hold onto an item before offering it for resale, in the off chance you come down with a case of seller's remorse or your mom finds out.

What to Look For

- Small items
- Sales appeal
- Low return
- Seller's rights

Tips

If your need for cash is short-term, ask the pawn-shop owner for a loan on the item. Keep in mind that the 4 to 6 percent interest rate is per month, not per year. Fees could get out of control fast if you took a year or more to pay back the loan.

Check if the broker is a member of the National Pawnbrokers Association (nationalpawnbrokers.org).

392 Buy and Sell Comic Books

Collecting comic books isn't just kid stuff anymore. A copy of *Action Comics #1,* the first appearance of Superman, sold for 10 cents in 1938. Today it could bring $1 million. Windfalls like that are extremely rare, but who knows what you might find in your parents' attic.

Steps

1 If you're looking to sell your old collection for a bundle, it'll help to have some #1s (the first comic in a series) or issues that intro-duce popular characters.

2 Condition is key whether you're buying or selling; the cover is especially critical. Keep comics in top condition by sliding them into plastic sleeves with a piece of acid-free cardboard. Store protected comics upright on bookshelves in a cool, dry place.

3 Internet auctions offer the best access to other buyers and sell-ers of older comic books. Another good place to make a deal on older material is at one of the many comic book conventions.

4 If you're looking to unload more recent comics (5 or 6 years old), try a local comic book shop. That's also the place to look if you need just a couple of comics to fill out a series.

What to Look For

- Superheroes
- Condition
- Internet auctions
- Conventions
- Local sources

Tip

As a rule, the older the comic book, the more value it has. Before the 1970s, people treated comic books like magazines; many ended up in the trash. Today, collectors treat them more like books, coveting creative storylines and colorful artwork.

393 Buy and Sell Sports Memorabilia

In the past 25 years, the value of sports memorabilia has only gone up. Because of that, this collecting category offers some good investments. It can also quickly become a very costly hobby.

Steps

Buy

1 Pick a category to collect: Sports cards? Which sport? One team only? One player only? The options are endless.

2 Look in price guides such as *Beckett*, periodicals and Internet sources to find out what items sell for. Expect to spend thousands on Babe Ruth–signed baseballs and Derek Jeter bats.

3 Go to a sports memorabilia show to get a feel for the variety and quality of items for sale.

4 Get to know the owners of local baseball-card shops. They will have other memorabilia besides cards, and will also have contacts for national sources of sports collectibles.

5 Take in an auction. Some auction houses specialize in sports memorabilia; order one of their catalogs for an upcoming sale. Mail in a bid or hire a proxy if you can't be there in person. Of course, check out Internet auction sites like eBay.com.

6 Ask about the item's authenticity—proof of its provenance is essential to making a good investment. Buying from a reputable dealer will give you some level of assurance.

7 As with every collecting category, a lot of fakes circulate in the marketplace, including reprinted baseball cards and cardboard advertising-display pieces. There are businesses that specialize in authenticating sports memorabilia. You might want to get some off-the-cuff, free opinions from dealers first. You don't want to pay $200 to authenticate an object that's only worth $50.

Sell

1 Find someone qualified to give you an appraisal if you're not sure about the value of what you own. Start at a local sports-card shop, but don't stop there. You'll want more than one opinion, and you might have to pay for it. Collectors' magazines are filled with ads for authentication services.

2 Sell it yourself. If your collection doesn't contain any high-ticket items, you can try to sell them one at a time or in small lots on the Internet. A local dealer might be interested in your collection.

3 Take any really high-quality items among your sports collectibles to an auction house for the best return on your investment.

4 Bring any documentation you have to help you get the best price. If you have a Jerry Rice jersey, that's good; if you have a photo of Rice handing it to you after a game, that's better.

What to Look For

- Price guides
- Local outlets
- National outlets
- Authenticity

Tips

Prices vary from year to year and month to month on articles related to current players. The smart money is in retired players, who won't have any more scoring slumps or legal woes to affect their status. Hall of Famers are always a good investment.

"Older is better" doesn't hold true in all collecting categories, but it's a good rule of thumb in sports memorabilia. Materials from the 1940s and 1950s are relatively rare and therefore more valuable.

Baseball dominates the category, but all sports memorabilia are collectible, from tennis to auto racing, boxing to bowling.

Warning

When selling sports memorabilia to a dealer, expect to get about half the wholesale price listed in popular price guides.

ITEM	COLLECTOR TIPS
Baseball Cards	Condition is key. Look for sharp corners and no creases. Rookie cards are the most valuable cards for star players. You can still find famous players' cards for $30 or even less sometimes.
Signed Baseballs	Look for baseballs that are clean and white, and that have a very clear auto-graph. Value depends on availability. The best find is a ball from the athlete's playing days. Many players hit the memorabilia circuit after retirement.
Team Jerseys	This is one of the few collecting categories in which sweat stains are a plus. Jerseys worn in games are the only way to go. Ask for authentication; don't be fooled by a new jersey that's been passed off as the real thing.
Equipment	Shoes, golf balls, gloves, bats, hockey pucks and sticks, and tennis rackets; again, it's key that the items were used in a game. Even a cracked bat will sell for hundreds (sometimes thousands) of dollars if a famous player used it.
Stadium Items	Seats, signs and even turnstiles are available to collectors. Especially valu-able are those from old stadiums that have been renovated or that hosted a historic sports moment, like a milestone Hank Aaron home run.
Ticket Stubs and Programs	World Series' items are especially coveted because so few are available. A ticket stub from the 1955 World Series lists at $110.
Bobble Heads	These ceramic dolls have a bobbing, oversize head on a spring. Early exam-ples represented an entire team; newer examples depict a particular player.

394 Sell Your Baseball-Card Collection

Are those old boxes full of baseball cards taking up precious space? Don't toss them; you might have a Sammy Sosa rookie in there!

Steps

1 Sort your cards according to manufacturer (Topps, Fleer, Score, Donruss, and so on). Try to get a complete set, which is all the cards in one manufacturer's series for a particular year.

2 Look for names you recognize and put those cards aside. Cards of popular players sell well individually.

3 Search for rookies. A player's first major-league card (check for minor-league statistics on the back) sells best. The card's condi-tion will play a big part in its price.

4 Find a buyer at a local sports-card shop. Selling over the Internet is time-consuming, but you might find someone who will pay more. Sell rare and valuable cards at auction.

5 Check the *Beckett* price guide. Prices vary for cards of current players, but retired players' cards hold their value. A 1954 Ernie Banks rookie card might sell for $500, depending on condition.

What to Look For

- Full sets
- Rookie cards
- Mint condition

Tip

Wear is expected in old cards. If it's a rare card, it will have great value despite some flaws.

Warning

Expect to get less than half the listed price if you sell to a shop owner.

EHOUSE STORES • BUY WHOLESALE • GET OUT OF DEBT • BUY NOTHING • BUY HAPPINESS • BUY A BETTER MOUSETRAP • BUY TIME •
EONE'S FAVOR • BUY POSTAGE STAMPS WITHOUT GOING TO THE POST OFFICE • TIP PROPERLY • BUY HEALTHY FAST FOOD • BUY SUNS
NG SERVICE • SELL YOURSELF ON AN ONLINE DATING SERVICE • SELL YOURSELF TO YOUR GIRLFRIEND/BOYFRIEND'S FAMILY • BUY DO
OSE FILM FOR YOUR CAMERA • BUY RECHARGEABLE BATTERIES • DONATE TO A GOOD CAUSE • HOLD A PROFITABLE GARAGE SALE • H
DENT DISCOUNTS • BUY FLOWERS WHOLESALE • GET A PICTURE FRAMED • HIRE A MOVER • HIRE A PERSONAL ORGANIZER • FIND A VE
HDAY PRESENT FOR UNDER $10 • SELECT GOOD CHAMPAGNE • BUY A DIAMOND • BUY JEWELRY MADE OF PRECIOUS METALS • BUY CO
ESMAIDS' DRESSES • HIRE AN EVENT COORDINATOR • HIRE A BARTENDER FOR A PARTY • HIRE A PHOTOGRAPHER • HIRE A CATERER •
AN ANNIVERSARY GIFT • ARRANGE ENTERTAINMENT FOR A PARTY • COMMISSION A FIREWORKS SHOW • BUY A MOTHER'S DAY GIFT • E
LECT A THANKSGIVING TURKEY • BUY A HOUSEWARMING GIFT • PURCHASE HOLIDAY CARDS • BUY CHRISTMAS STOCKING STUFFERS •
I ROLLERS ROOM IN VEGAS, BABY • BUY SOMEONE A STAR • PAY A RANSOM • GET HOT TICKETS • HIRE A LIMOUSINE • BUY A CRYONIC
Y A PERSONAL JET • ACQUIRE A TELEVISION NETWORK • ACQUIRE A BODY GUARD • BOOK A LUXURY CRUISE AROUND THE WORLD • S
ROUGHBRED RACEHORSE • BUY A VILLA IN TUSCANY • HIRE A PERSONAL CHEF • PURCHASE CUBAN CIGARS • HIRE A GHOSTWRITER T
NESS • MAKE BAIL • DONATE YOUR BODY TO SCIENCE • HIRE YOURSELF OUT AS A MEDICAL GUINEA PIG • SELL PLASMA • SELL YOUR S
LEGE EDUCATION • BUY AND SELL STOCKS • CHOOSE A STOCKBROKER • DAY-TRADE (OR NOT) • BUY ANNUITIES • BUY AND SELL MUTU
SONAL FINANCE SOFTWARE • CHOOSE A TAX PREPARER • SET UP A LEMONADE STAND • SELL YOUR PRODUCT ON TV • HIRE A CAREER
Y A SMALL BUSINESS • BUY A FRANCHISE • LEASE RETAIL SPACE • LEASE INDUSTRIAL SPACE • LEASE OFFICE SPACE • BUY LIQUIDATE
ERTISING ON THE WEB • SELL YOUR ART • HIRE A PERSONAL COACH • SELL ON THE CRAFT CIRCUIT • HIRE A LITERARY AGENT • PITCH
A HOT DOG STAND • SHOP FOR A MORTGAGE • REFINANCE YOUR HOME • SAVE BIG BUCKS ON YOUR MORTGAGE • OBTAIN HOME OW
THE FARM • SELL MINERAL RIGHTS • SELL A HOUSE • SELL A HOUSE WITHOUT A REAL ESTATE AGENT • OBTAIN A HOME EQUITY LOAN
A CONDOMINIUM • RENT AN APARTMENT OR HOUSE • OBTAIN RENTER'S INSURANCE • BUY A LOFT IN MANHATTAN • BUY A TENANCY-I
RTMENT • BUY USED FURNITURE • BUY DOOR AND WINDOW LOCKS • CHOOSE AN ORIENTAL CARPET • BUY LAMPS AND LIGHT FIXTURE
LIANCES • FIND PERIOD FIXTURES • BUY A BED AND MATTRESS • HIRE AN INTERIOR DESIGNER • HIRE A FENG SHUI CONSULTANT • INC
RLPOOL TUB • BUY A SHOWERHEAD • BUY A TOILET • CHOOSE A FAUCET • BUY GLUES AND ADHESIVES • CHOOSE WINDOW TREATMEI
OSE A KITCHEN COUNTERTOP • BUY GREEN HOUSEHOLD CLEANERS • STOCK YOUR HOME TOOL KIT • BUY A VIDEO SECURITY SYSTEI
ARAGE-DOOR OPENER • BUY LUMBER FOR A DIY PROJECT • HOW TO SELECT ROOFING • HIRE A CONTRACTOR, PLUMBER, PAINTER OR
LECT PEST CONTROLS • BUY SOIL AMENDMENTS • BUY MULCH • BUY A COMPOSTER • BUY FERTILIZER • START A VEGETABLE GARDE
A STORAGE SHED • HIRE AN ARBORIST • BUY BASIC GARDEN TOOLS • BUY SHRUBS AND TREES • BUY A HOT TUB • BUY AN OUTDOO
D LABELS • SELECT HERBS AND SPICES • STOCK YOUR KITCHEN WITH STAPLES • EQUIP A KITCHEN • CHOOSE FRESH PRODUCE • SEL
EY • CHOOSE POULTRY • SELECT FRESH FISH AND SHELLFISH • SELECT RICE • PURCHASE PREMIUM SALT AND PEPPER • GET A CHEE
CHASE KOSHER FOOD • BUY FOOD IN BULK • CHOOSE COOKING OILS • SELECT OLIVE OIL • SELECT OLIVES • BUY ETHNIC INGREDIEN
CHASE A KEG OF BEER • BUY ALCOHOL IN A DRY COUNTY • CHOOSE A MICROBREW • ORDER A COCKTAIL • CHOOSE A RESTAURANT
GNANCY TEST KIT • CHOOSE BIRTH CONTROL • FIND THE RIGHT OB-GYN • HIRE A MIDWIFE OR DOULA • FIND A GOOD PEDIATRICIAN •
AST PUMP • CHOOSE A CAR SEAT • BUY CHILD-PROOFING SUPPLIES • FIND FABULOUS CHILDCARE • FIND A GREAT NANNY • FIND THE
IMER CAMP • SELL GIRL SCOUT COOKIES • BUY BRACES FOR YOUR KID • BUY TOYS • BUY BOOKS, VIDEOS AND MUSIC FOR YOUR C
THES AND BOOKS • FIND A COUPLES COUNSELOR • HIRE A FAMILY LAWYER • BUY PROPERTY IN A RETIREMENT COMMUNITY • CHOOS
THBRUSH • BUY MOISTURIZERS AND ANTIWRINKLE CREAMS • SELECT PAIN RELIEF AND COLD MEDICINES • SAVE MONEY ON PRESCR
'S TO COUNTER HAIR LOSS • BUY A WIG OR HAIRPIECE • BUY A NEW BODY • GET A TATTOO OR BODY PIERCING • OBTAIN BREAST IMP
GLASSES AND SUNGLASSES • HIRE A PERSONAL TRAINER • SIGN UP FOR A YOGA CLASS • TREAT YOURSELF TO A DAY AT THE SPA • B
L • BUY AT AUCTION • KNOW WHAT YOUR COLLECTIBLES ARE WORTH • DICKER WITH DEALERS • GET AN ANTIQUE APPRAISED • BUY
' AN ANTIQUE AMERICAN QUILT • BUY AN ANTIQUE FLAG • LIQUIDATE YOUR BEANIE BABY COLLECTION • SCORE AUTOGRAPHS • TRAD
' AND SELL SPORTS MEMORABILIA • SELL YOUR BASEBALL-CARD COLLECTIONS • CHOOSE A DESKTOP COMPUTER • SHOP FOR A USE
' COMPUTER PERIPHERALS • CHOOSE AN INTERNET SERVICE PROVIDER • GET AN INTERNET DOMAIN NAME • BUY A HOME NETWORK
YER • BUY A VCR • CHOOSE A PERSONAL DIGITAL ASSISTANT • CHOOSE MOBILE PHONE SERVICE • NEGOTIATE YOUR LONG-DISTANCE
ME AUTOMATION SYSTEM • BUY A STATE-OF-THE-ART SOUND SYSTEM • BUY AN AUDIO-VIDEO DISTRIBUTION SYSTEM • BUY A SERIOU
TUAL-REALITY FURNITURE • BUY TWO-WAY RADIOS • BUY A MOBILE ENTERTAINMENT SYSTEM • GET A PASSPORT, QUICK! • PURCHASE
FREE • BID FOR A SLED RIDE ON THE ALASKAN IDITAROD TRAIL RACE • BUY DUTY-FREE • SHIP FOREIGN PURCHASES TO THE UNITED
ATION • CHOOSE A CHEAP CRUISE • BOOK A HOTEL PACKAGE FOR THE GREEK ISLANDS • RAFT THE GRAND CANYON • BOOK A CHEA
E SALSA LESSONS IN CUBA • BUY A CAMERA IN HONG KONG • BUY YOUR WAY ONTO A MOUNT EVEREST EXPEDITION • HIRE A TREKK
LE AND KNEE BRACES • BUY GOLF CLUBS • JOIN AN ELITE GOLF CLUB • SELL FOUND GOLF BALLS • BUY ATHLETIC SHOES • BUY A R
JY A SKATEBOARD AND PROTECTIVE GEAR • BUY SKATES • GO SPORT FISHING • GO SKYDIVING • BUY WEIGHTLIFTING EQUIPMENT • C
SKI BOOTS • BUY A BICYCLE • SELL YOUR BICYCLE AT A GARAGE SALE • COMMISSION A CUSTOM-BUILT BICYCLE • BUY A PROPERL
TATION DEVICE • BUY A WET SUIT • BUY A SURFBOARD • BUY FLY-FISHING GEAR • BUY ROCK-CLIMBING EQUIPMENT • BUY A CASHM
ES • BUY THE PERFECT COCKTAIL DRESS • BUY DESIGNER CLOTHES AT A DISCOUNT • CHOOSE A BASIC WARDROBE FOR A MAN • BU
EFCASE • SHOP FOR A LEATHER JACKET • BUY MATERNITY CLOTHES • GET A GREAT-FITTING BRA • CHOOSE A HIGH-PERFORMANCE S
RCHASE CLOTHES AT OUTLET SHOPS • BUY A NEW CAR • BUY THE BASICS FOR YOUR CAR • BUY A USED CAR • BUY OR SELL A CAR O

QUET OF ROSES • BUY SOMEONE A DRINK • GET SOMEONE TO BUY YOU A DRINK • BUY YOUR WAY INTO HIGH SOCIETY • BUY YOUR W
RDER THE PERFECT BURRITO • ORDER TAKEOUT ASIAN FOOD • ORDER AT A SUSHI BAR • BUY DINNER AT A FANCY FRENCH RESTAURAN
OWERS FOR YOUR SWEETHEART • BUY MUSIC ONLINE • HIRE MUSICIANS • ORDER A GREAT BOTTLE OF WINE • BUY AN ERGONOMIC DE
ECLEANER • HIRE A BABY SITTER • BUY A GUITAR • BUY DUCT TAPE • GET A GOOD DEAL ON A MAGAZINE SUBSCRIPTION • GET SENIOR
• BUY PET FOOD • BUY A PEDIGREED DOG OR CAT • BREED YOUR PET AND SELL THE LITTER • GET A COSTUME • BUY A PIÑATA • BUY A
ISTONES • CHOOSE THE PERFECT WEDDING DRESS • BUY OR RENT A TUXEDO • REGISTER FOR GIFTS • BUY WEDDING GIFTS • SELECT
EAL WEDDING OFFICIANT • OBTAIN A MARRIAGE LICENSE • ORDER CUSTOM INVITATIONS AND ANNOUNCEMENTS • SELL YOUR WEDDING
R'S DAY GIFT • SELECT AN APPROPRIATE COMING-OF-AGE GIFT • GET A GIFT FOR THE PERSON WHO HAS EVERYTHING • BUY A GRADUA
'KAH GIFTS • PURCHASE A PERFECT CHRISTMAS TREE • BUY A PRIVATE ISLAND • HIRE A SKYWRITER • HIRE A BIG-NAME BAND • GET IN
RENT YOUR OWN BILLBOARD • TAKE OUT A FULL-PAGE AD IN *THE NEW YORK TIMES* • HIRE A BUTLER • ACQUIRE A PROFESSIONAL SPC
JR COAT • BOOK A TRIP ON THE ORIENT-EXPRESS • BECOME A WINE MAKER • PURCHASE A PRIVATE/CUSTOM BOTTLING OF WINE • BUY
MEMOIRS • COMMISSION ORIGINAL ARTWORK • IMMORTALIZE YOUR SPOUSE IN A SCULPTURE • GIVE AWAY YOUR FORTUNE • HIRE AN
DEVIL • NEGOTIATE A BETTER CREDIT CARD DEAL • CHOOSE A FINANCIAL PLANNER • SAVE WITH A RETIREMENT PLAN • SAVE FOR YOUR
BUY BONDS • SELL SHORT • INVEST IN PRECIOUS METALS • BUY DISABILITY INSURANCE • BUY LIFE INSURANCE • GET HEALTH INSURA
• HIRE A HEADHUNTER • SELL YOURSELF   MARKET YOUR INVENTION • FINANCE YOUR BUS
IPMENT • HIRE SOMEONE TO DESIGN AND   ESIGNER • ACQUIRE CONTENT FOR YOUR WEB S
STORY • SELL A SCREENPLAY • SELL YOUR   RT A BED-AND-BREAKFAST • SELL A FAILING BUS
NCE • OBTAIN DISASTER INSURANCE • BUY   JY A FORECLOSED HOME • BUY AND SELL A FIXE
• BUY HOUSE PLANS • HIRE AN ARCHITECT   TS • BUY A VACATION HOME • BOOK A VACATION
NIT • BUY RENTAL PROPERTY • RENT YOUR   FURNISH YOUR HOME • FURNISH YOUR STUDIO
OGRAMMABLE LIGHTING SYSTEM • BUY HO   APPLIANCES • BUY EXTENDED WARRANTIES ON
JID ARCHITECTURE INTO YOUR HOME • SEL   DECORATIVE TILES • CHOOSE A CEILING FAN • BI
F-CLEANING WINDOWS • CHOOSE WALLPA   NG • SELECT CARPETING • CHOOSE KITCHEN C
ME ALARM SYSTEM • BUY SMOKE ALARMS   JY FIRE EXTINGUISHERS • CHOOSE AN ENTRY DC
• HIRE A GARDENER • BUY OUTDOOR FURI   JY FLOWERING BULBS • BUY FLOWERS FOR YOU
DEN PROFESSIONAL • BUY AN AUTOMATIC   • BUY A LAWN MOWER • BUY KOI FOR YOUR FIS
STEM • BUY ORGANIC PRODUCE • CHOOS   RMERS' MARKETS • SELECT KITCHEN KNIVES • D
OCK UP FOR THE PERFECT BURGER • PUR   EF • BUY ROCKY MOUNTAIN OYSTERS • PURCHA
ILADELPHIA • ORDER FRESH SALMON IN S   JY ARTISAN BREADS • BUY ARTISAN CHEESES •
E VINEGAR • CHOOSE PASTA • BUY TEA • B   FEE • BUY A COFFEEMAKER OR ESPRESSO MACH
S FUNCTION • STOCK A WINE CELLAR • ST   CHOOSE AN OVULATION PREDICTOR KIT • PICK A
HERAPIST • GEAR UP FOR A NEW BABY •   JY BABY CLOTHES • CHOOSE DIAPERS • BUY OI
SCHOOL • FIND A GOOD AFTER-SCHOOL   SONS • BUY A BACKYARD PLAY STRUCTURE • FIN
A VIDEO GAME SYSTEM • HIRE A TUTOR •   HILD HIRED AS A MODEL • SELL USED BABY GEAF
CARE OR NURSING HOME • WRITE A LIVIN   FUNERAL EXPENSES • GET VIAGRA ONLINE • PU
HIRE A MENTAL-HEALTH PROFESSIONAL   MEDICAL SUPPLIES • SELECT HAIR-CARE PRODL
RINKLE-FILLER INJECTIONS • FIND ALTERN   OSE A MANICURIST • GET WHITER TEETH • SELEC
E • GET ON ANTIQUES ROADSHOW • BUY   QUE FAIR OR FLEA MARKET • RENT SPACE AT AN
VALUATE DEPRESSION-ERA GLASSWARE • BUY AND SELL STAMPS • BUY ANTIQUE FURNITURE • RECOGNIZE THE REAL MCCOY • BUY C
DS • SNAG STAR WARS ACTION FIGURES • SELL YOUR VINYL RECORD COLLECTION • SELL AT A PAWNSHOP • BUY AND SELL COMIC B
R PERIPHERALS • CHOOSE A LAPTOP OR NOTEBOOK COMPUTER • SELL OR DONATE A COMPUTER • BUY PRINTER PAPER • BUY A PRI
MEMORY IN YOUR COMPUTER • BUY COMPUTER SOFTWARE • CHOOSE A CD PLAYER • BUY BLANK CDS • BUY AN MP PLAYER • CHOC
• BUY VIDEO AND COMPUTER GAMES • CHOOSE A FILM CAMERA • CHOOSE A DIGITAL CAMCORDER • DECIDE ON A DIGITAL CAMERA
BETWEEN CABLE AND SATELLITE TV • GET A DIGITAL VIDEO RECORDER • GET A UNIVERSAL REMOTE • BUY A HOME THEATER SYSTEM •
TICKETS • FIND GREAT HOTEL DEALS • RENT THE BEST CAR FOR THE LEAST MONEY • GET TRAVEL INSURANCE • PICK THE IDEAL LUG
A FOREIGN COUNTRY • TIP PROPERLY IN NORTH AMERICA • BRIBE A FOREIGN OFFICIAL • GET A EURAIL PASS • TAKE AN ITALIAN BICYC
SAFARI • RENT A CAMEL IN CAIRO • GET SINGLE-MALT SCOTCH IN SCOTLAND • BUY A SAPPHIRE IN BANGKOK • HIRE A RICKSHA IN Y
NEPAL • RENT OR BUY A SATELLITE PHONE • BUY YOUR CHILD'S FIRST BASEBALL GLOVE • ORDER UNIFORMS FOR A SOFTBALL TEAM
YM MEMBERSHIP • BUY AN AEROBIC FITNESS MACHINE • BUY A SNOWMOBILE • BUY A PERSONAL WATERCRAFT • HIRE A SCUBA INS
ACK OR CARRIER • BUY SKIS • BUY CLOTHES FOR COLD-WEATHER ACTIVITIES • SELL USED SKIS • BUY A SNOWBOARD, BOOTS AND B
• BUY THE OPTIMAL SLEEPING BAG • BUY A TENT • BUY A BACKPACK • BUY A BACKPACKING STOVE • BUY A KAYAK • BUY A PERSON
PURCHASE VINTAGE CLOTHING • SELL USED CLOTHING • ORDER CUSTOM-MADE COWBOY BOOTS • BUY CLOTHES ONLINE • FIND SPE
SHIRT • PICK OUT A NECKTIE • BUY A WOMAN'S SUIT • BUY A MAN'S SUIT • HIRE A TAILOR • BUY CUSTOM-TAILORED CLOTHES IN AS
PERFORMANCE WORKOUT CLOTHES • BUY A HEART-RATE MONITOR • SELECT A WATCH • BUY KIDS' CLOTHES • CHOOSE CHILDREN'S
'BRID CAR • SELL A CAR • BUY A MOTORCYCLE • LEASE A CAR WITH THE OPTION TO BUY • TRANSFER YOUR LEASED CAR • DONATE

**Computers &
Home Electronics**

395 Choose a Desktop Computer

Shopping for a computer doesn't need to be hard. First think about what you need. Are you looking for a computer to perform basic tasks or to meet special requirements? Then do a little homework, and finally go shopping armed with that knowledge. You'll get a computer you can be happy with, and you'll get the best value for your money.

Steps

Before you shop

1 Decide if you're better served by the PC/Windows platform or the Macintosh. You can generally get a faster computer for your money by choosing a Windows machine, but Macs come with more easy-to-use built-in software. Top brands are Dell, Hewlett-Packard, IBM, Gateway and Toshiba. Apple, of course, makes the Macintosh.

2 Think about whether this machine will need to work with your office or school server. Exchanging files between platforms is less of an issue than it used to be, but it's still worth noting.

3 Ask your friends and co-workers in similar lines of work what machines they have, where they bought them, if there were any problems, and whether they're happy with their choices.

4 Expect to spend $1,000 to $2,000 for a general-purpose machine, although you can find desktop computers for anywhere from $400 to $10,000.

The basics

1 Realize that if you buy a super cheap computer at a warehouse store or discounter, you're going to be on your own. Technical support from the major manufacturers tends to be a lot better.

2 Buy as much random-access memory (RAM), or system memory, as you can afford. At a bare minimum, get 128 megabytes (MB); 256 MB or 512 MB is preferable. (For a Macintosh, get at least 256 MB.) Memory is more critical than a faster processor.

3 Get at least two universal serial bus (USB) connections and a FireWire (also called IEEE 1394) connection. These will connect peripheral devices, such as a printer, PDA, digital cameras and camcorders, scanners and game controllers.

4 Get a CD burner so you can back up valuable data and make your own music CDs. Look into a DVD burner too if you're involved in film making or editing, but remember that there are multiple competing standards; computer-burned DVDs might not play in your home DVD player. Make sure your machine has a DVD drive if you want to watch movies on your computer. (See 408 Buy Blank CDs.) Also look for an internal modem.

5 Ask about upgradability if you intend to use this computer for a long time, which is considered three or more years.

What to Look For

- 128 MB RAM (minimum)
- USB and FireWire connections
- CD or DVD burner
- DVD drive
- Internal modem
- 3D graphics card
- 5.1 Surround sound
- 120 GB hard disk
- Video input/output

Tips

The term *desktop computer* is misleading. *Desktop* refers to computers that aren't laptop or notebook computers.

Computers continue to get faster and cheaper. Don't torture yourself by second-guessing your purchase, or by waiting for the next jump in power or drop in price.

Warnings

Don't toss your old computer in the trash (see 398 Sell or Donate a Computer). Like many other electronic devices, they contain toxic chemicals and need to be recycled.

6 Choose any current computer model from the major manufacturers with a high degree of confidence if you simply want to send e-mail, surf the Web and do word-processing.

Special considerations

1 Get high-quality graphics and sound if you plan to play games. Look for a system that has a graphics card with a coprocessor, and 5.1 Surround sound. You'll want a broadband Internet connection to play online games, and to improve your Internet experience overall. (See 402 Choose an Internet Service Provider.)

2 Buy the biggest hard drive you can afford—120 to 180 gigabytes (GB) is now commonplace. Get more than 200 GB if you're storing music and/or editing video. For video editing, you'll also need a video input/output card and a FireWire connection.

3 Add a TV capture card, and you can even have your computer function as a DVR. (See 424 Get a Digital Video Recorder.)

You might be able to use your current monitor, printer, and other peripherals with a new computer if you're happy with them. Write down their specifications and bring your notes to the store. But remember that many computers come packaged with hardware preconfigured to work together and with the latest operating systems.

396 Shop for a Used Computer or Peripherals

If you've got your computer and are looking for a usable one for your kids—or if the kids want a computer for you so they can keep the good one to themselves—save big and buy a used machine. Hundreds of computers go on sale daily on Internet auction sites.

Steps

1 Ask your most tech-savvy friend to shop with you.

2 Follow a half-dozen online auctions of used systems and note what people were willing to pay. Unfortunately, there's no unbiased, reputable source for used computer prices.

3 Give the computer a thorough physical inspection to ensure it's not damaged. Then turn it on and run it; be alert for obvious glitches. Insist on doing this yourself, rather than watching the seller do it.

4 Make sure that the sale includes the original operating system software discs and manuals. Get the manuals, discs and licenses for any software applications and fonts on the computer.

5 Be careful not to overpay, since older computers depreciate fast as lightning. It doesn't matter how much the seller paid for it; the important thing is how much it's worth now. Be brutal.

6 Don't buy used printers, scanners or disk drives unless you know exactly what you're doing. These peripherals have moving parts that inevitably wear out or break down.

What to Look For

- Intact hardware
- Bug-free operating
- System and program software

Tip

Refurbished computers from major manufacturers can be a good alternative. They're cheaper than new but generally carry a full warranty.

Warning

Hundreds of thousands of laptops are stolen every year. Use common sense to avoid buying a hot machine.

397 Choose a Laptop or Notebook Computer

Today's laptops are much more powerful than even the hottest desktop computers of yesterday. They're also lighter and much more stylish. Many people are opting out of desktop computers altogether and use a laptop for all their computer needs. If you're thinking of going this route, check out these shopping tips.

Steps

1 Read through 395 Choose a Desktop Computer. The "Before you shop" points and most of "The basics" also apply when shopping for a laptop.

2 Pick up the laptops at the store. (Ask to have them unlocked if necessary.) Choose one that feels sturdy, solid and not too heavy.

3 Try the keyboard. Since you can't replace it (except with the exact same item), make sure you're comfortable with its touch and responsiveness. Test it on a desk and on your lap.

4 Test the pointing device, track pad or track ball, the laptop alternatives to a mouse. Some of these can be hard to master. You'll be able to connect an external mouse, but the built-in device is more handy when you're mobile.

5 Check if the computer's bottom gets uncomfortably hot when it's running—a problem if you actually use the laptop on your lap.

6 Pay attention to screen size and resolution. Current liquid-crystal display (LCD) screens on laptops measure from 12 to 17 inches (30 to 43 cm) diagonally. Screen resolution may be as low as 800 x 600 pixels or as high as 1600 x 1200. The more pixels, the crisper the screen image. View the screen in a variety of settings: A screen that looks great in normal room lighting can look terrible in bright or dim light.

7 Choose a laptop with at least two USB connections. A FireWire (IEEE 1394) connection is also handy for high-speed peripherals such as CD burners.

8 Consider buying an internal wireless card and a Bluetooth adapter if you really plan to be mobile. A wireless network card (also called Wi-Fi or 802.11) will free you from having to be wired to your Internet connection (see 404 Network Your Computers). Bluetooth capability will let you share information wirelessly with other Bluetooth-equipped devices, such as your cell phone or personal digital assistant.

9 Get an internal DVD player so you can watch movies on the road.

10 Get an antitheft device. Hundreds of thousands of laptops are stolen every year. Look for cables that secure the laptop to a desk. Install software that disables a stolen laptop, or better yet, reports the laptop's location when it connects to the Internet.

What to Look For

- Overall sturdiness and solidness
- Weight
- Keyboard
- Pointing device
- Temperature while in use
- Screen size and resolution
- USB, FireWire connections
- Wireless networking
- DVD player
- Antitheft device

Tips

Be skeptical of claims about battery life. In the real world, battery life is almost always less than what the manufacturer advertises.

What's the difference between a laptop and a notebook? Nothing. Use the two terms interchangeably.

398 Sell or Donate a Computer

We've all been there. The computer you spent thousands on a year or two ago is now a dinosaur worth pennies on the dollar. Don't toss it in the trash—it contains toxic materials that shouldn't go in landfills. Here's how to recycle, donate or sell it to recoup some of your cash.

Steps

1 Uninstall any applications you plan to use on your next computer. (Make sure you have the installation disks and serial numbers.)

2 Purge the computer of all personal information. It's not enough to drag documents to the Trash. Use a utility program to permanently delete or overwrite sensitive documents, then reformat the hard drive and reinstall the operating system. Professional data-recovery firms can also do this.

3 Collect the original software disks and manuals for the operating system that came with the computer.

4 Find out what your computer is worth by following online auctions, then put it up for auction too, or go through the classifieds. Don't expect to rake it in; old computers aren't worth much.

5 Donate the computer to a school, charity or recycling center. Recyclers may charge a fee. Get a receipt for tax purposes.

What to Look For

- Original software disks and manuals
- Delete-overwrite utility software
- Receipt for tax purposes

Tip

Experts recently found credit card numbers, medical records, and financial data on random hard drives bought at online auctions. To truly purge your hard drive of sensitive information, destroy it with a hammer. This will decrease your computer's resale value, but increase your peace of mind.

399 Buy Printer Paper

How do you choose the right paper? Answer just two questions: What type of printer do you have, and what do you want to print?

Steps

1 Determine what type of printer you have. Most people own ink-jet printers, but some have laser printers.

2 Decide what weight of paper you want. Everyday paper is 20 lb. and works with any printer. The higher the number, the heavier the paper. Card stocks are 60 to 100 lb. or more.

3 Pick ink-jet stock for important projects. The printing is crisper because the paper is smoother and less absorbent.

4 Select photo paper to print pictures on an ink-jet printer. This coated stock is very smooth and somewhat stiff, so the finished prints feel like photographs. Matte photo paper is less shiny than glossy. Buy special archival paper and ink if you're printing photographs that you'll want to last a long time without fading.

5 Choose color laser printer paper only if you have a color laser printer. It's not good for ink-jet printing. Laser prints are more permanent than ink-jet prints, and less likely to run and bleed because they use toner rather than water-based ink.

What to Look For

- General-purpose paper
- Ink-jet paper
- Photo paper (matte or glossy)
- Color laser printer paper

Tips

Ink-jet prints will always run or bleed when wet, no matter what sort of paper you use.

Make sure that transparencies, labels, stickers, and other specialty media work with your type of printer.

400 Buy a Printer

With printers costing from zero to thousands of dollars, how do you choose the machine that's right for you? Comparing your needs with the features of different printers will make your decision an easy one.

Steps

1 Consider the various sizes, shapes, and capabilities. They range from portable printers to printer/copier/scanner/fax combinations the size of a small filing cabinet. Combination units (called all-in-one or multifunction printers) are great if you're short on space, but be sure to test the features that are most important to you.

2 Decide between ink-jet and laser printers. How you'll use the printer will guide your decision.

   • Choose ink-jet if you print infrequently, or if you're going to print color pictures. Ink-jet printers are less expensive, but can cost more per printed page because of expensive inks.

   • Go for a laser printer if you mainly print text (and lots of it), and you want fast, permanent printing. They cost more up front, but less in the long run due to cheaper supplies. Longer lasting laser printers can be repaired more easily and less expensively.

3 Buy a brand name to help ensure that you'll be able to get service, software, support and supplies in the future. Brother, Canon, Epson, Hewlett-Packard and Lexmark are the leading brands.

4 Confirm your computer's operating system, especially with older machines, supports the printer. Printer drivers come with the printer, but you can also download them from the manufacturer's Web site. (Search for the driver to confirm that the printer will work with your computer.)

What to Look For

- Size and shape
- Capabilities
- Ink-jet versus laser
- Brand names
- Operating system support

Tips

By law, the printer's warranty remains in effect even if you use toner or ink produced by a company other than the original manufacturer.

It's probably not worth having an inexpensive ink-jet printer repaired if it breaks.

ANY PRINTER FEATURES	
Quality of Text Printing	• Test print to see quality of text.
Cost of Supplies	• How much are ink or toner cartridges, and how long do they last? Divide cost of cartridge by number of pages it can print. Add the cost of premium or photo paper to determine the real lifetime cost.
Connectivity	• Most new printers have USB connections. If you have an older computer, look for a printer with a parallel port or, better yet, add USB to your computer. Some high-end printers have network connections. This is handy if you have a home network and will share the printer among several machines. (See 404 Network Your Computers)
Warranty	• If you rely on your printer for business, look for a warranty that supplies you with an immediate loaner machine if yours goes in for repairs.
Paper Handling	• Look for a large paper tray to handle multiple-page jobs. Look for manual feed trays, multiple trays and envelope handling if you print a variety of materials or large formats.

ANY PRINTER FEATURES (continued)

Straight Paper Path	• If you print on card stock, labels or envelopes, look for printer with a straight paper-path option (sometimes called a bypass). Paper path should not have any 90-degree or tighter bends.
Image Resolution	• Measured in dots per inch (dpi). How dots are formed—a function of printer and computer software—can be as important as number of dots, so use resolution as only one indicator.
Speed	• Measured in pages per minute (ppm). Take manufacturer's speed claim with a grain of salt. It indicates how quickly printer can send paper through its mechanism, not how quickly machine will actually print. If speed is important, bring a variety of documents when you shop, and test print them on several printers from the same computer.

LASER PRINTER FEATURES

Expandable Memory	• Get at least 8 megabytes (MB); 64 MB or more is better, especially if you're printing graphics or pages with lots of fonts.
PostScript Capability	• A printer description language used to produce high-quality images and fonts. Vital for Macintoshes or working with complex graphics.
Resolution	• Resolution of 600 dpi is usually sufficient for most uses.
Economy Mode	• Extends life of toner cartridges without sacrificing print quality.
Energy-saving Features	• Energy Star designation means the unit uses less electricity when idle.
Color	• Color laser printers are considerably more expensive than noncolor ones.
Price	• Black-and-white laser printers cost $200 and up with many good deals around $500. Color laser prices are dropping, but they're still expensive (starting at around $1,000) compared with ink-jets.

INK-JET PRINTER FEATURES

Photo Quality	• How do prints of pictures look? Bring your own images to print, rather than relying on test prints.
Ink Cartridges	• Look for separate ink cartridges (sometimes called tanks) for each color (blue, yellow and red) plus black, so you'll only need to replace the one that's empty.
Color Print Speed	• Some printers slow down dramatically if there's just a little color on the page.
Water-resistant Inks	• This is valuable if you know printouts will be exposed to the weather.
Removable Memory Media	• On new models, memory cards from a digital camera plug directly into the printer, bypassing the computer altogether. Make sure the printer works with your camera's media type.
Price	• Prices for ink-jet printers can range from free (included with purchase of new computer) to $1,500, with most models costing under $500. Combination units with scanner and copier functions cost $100 and up; fax capability always costs more.

WARNING	Some manufacturers void a printer's warranty if you use refilled ink cartridges.

401 Buy Computer Peripherals

Although computers are getting more complicated, buying peripherals is actually getting easier because most modern devices connect with either universal serial bus (USB) or FireWire (also called IEEE 1394). Both high-speed connections work easily and almost automatically. If your computer is relatively new (Windows 98 or Mac OS 9 or newer), you should be in good shape. Windows XP users will probably have very few problems, especially with big-brand peripherals.

DEVICE	FEATURES TO CONSIDER
Monitor	• Video connector.
	• Flat-panel liquid-crystal display (LCD) monitors cost more, but are easier on the eyes and use less energy than cathode-ray tube (CRT) monitors.
	• Flat shadow mask and flat aperture grille CRT monitors have sharper pictures than regular CRTs.
	• CRT monitors can operate at multiple resolutions, but LCD monitors operate optimally only at maximum resolution. Before you buy an LCD monitor, make sure your computer can handle it. Resolution information should be in the computer manual.
	• The higher the refresh rate of a CRT monitor, the less the screen will flicker. Look for a refresh rate of 85 hertz (Hz) or higher.
	• USB or FireWire.
Scanner	• Scanner resolution is measured in dots per inch (dpi) and typically appears as two numbers, such as 2400 x 1200. Higher resolution results in better-quality scans.
	• Bit depth tells you how many colors a scanner can recognize. Choose at least 24-bit; 48-bit is preferable.
	• Get a scanner with a transparency adapter or lid if you plan to scan slides or film negatives.
	• A good-quality scanner includes photo-editing software.
	• Use optical character recognition (OCR) software to convert scanned printed pages to editable word-processing documents.
Speakers	• Audio-out (sound card) or headphone jack.
	• For Surround sound, you need a sound card that supports multiple speakers. Check your manual.
	• Computer speakers need to be shielded, or they will hum when set next to a CRT monitor. Regular stereo speakers are OK as long as they aren't right next to the monitor or drive.
CD Burner	• USB or FireWire.
	• Three numbers give the maximum write, rewrite and read speed of a CD burner in kilobytes per second (Kbps). A 24 x 12 x 24 CD burner can create CD-Rs at 24 Kbps, create CD-RWs at 12 Kbps, and read CDs at 24 Kbps. The first number is most important, so get the unit with the highest write speed you can afford.
	• CD-RW burners can use both CD-R and CD-RW disks. CD-RWs can be used again and again. (See 408 Buy Blank CDs.)
	• Don't use your CD burner to read CDs if your computer also has a CD drive.

For more USB connections, buy a USB hub, which plugs into a single USB connection and provides two, four or even eight more connections. Choose a powered hub for better performance. If you have a choice between choosing FireWire and USB 1.1, go for the faster FireWire. For USB 2.0 to operate at full speed, all three elements—computer, cable and peripheral—must support it. Check packages carefully. USB 1.1 peripherals can plug into USB 2.0 jacks.

DEVICE	FEATURES TO CONSIDER
Keyboard	• USB or PS/2.
	• For flexibility, choose a USB keyboard rather than a PS/2 model.
	• Never buy a keyboard without typing on it. If store doesn't have display models available, ask for models to test.
	• Special controls on keyboard (for Internet access or speaker volume) require special software (included) on your computer.
	• Wireless keyboards are available. Infrared (IR) models require a small receiver on your desk and a line-of-sight connection between keyboard and receiver. Radio frequency (RF) or Bluetooth models allow receiver to be out of sight.
Mouse	• USB or PS/2. Choose a USB mouse rather than a PS/2 model.
	• Feel how the mouse fits in your hand; see how it responds on screen.
	• Opt for an optical mouse, which works on many surfaces and won't be affected by dirt and lint.
	• If you go wireless, get a rechargeable mouse. Mice eat batteries like cheese.
	• Some mice with extra buttons and scroll wheels require installation of software (included) to use all features.
Media Reader	• USB or FireWire.
	• Popular with people who own digital cameras, MP3 players, and PDAs. Remove memory product (Compact Flash, Smart Media, Memory Stick, SecureDigital/MMC) from device and plug it into media reader for quick access to data.
	• Some are multiple-media readers. Check your electronic devices to see what products they use.
Game Controller	• USB or game port.
	• Computer games may use joysticks, game pads and steering wheels instead of (or in addition to) keyboard and mouse.
	• Look for a model that feels right in your hands and makes sense for your needs.
	• Most game controllers require special software (included).
	• Most computers lack game ports, so look for controller with USB connector.
	• Wireless game controllers also available.
WARNING	If you want to install an internal CD burner or media reader, be sure you know how to safely open your computer and connect devices to its internal circuitry.

402 Choose an Internet Service Provider

These days, a computer without Internet access is like a car with flat tires—it works, but it won't get you very far. To get online, you need an Internet service provider (ISP). You have two general choices: dial-up service, which is cheap but slow; and broadband service, which is more expensive and much faster.

Steps

1 Determine your needs. Do you want to send and receive e-mail and occasionally surf the Web? An inexpensive dial-up account, which uses regular telephone lines, is probably enough. If you want to connect to your office network, play online games, or download and exchange music and video files, you'll want a speedy broadband connection, such as DSL or cable.

2 Find out what hardware is needed. For a dial-up account, a modem is required. Broadband service uses a network interface card (NIC), sometimes called an Ethernet connection. Both are standard equipment on newer computers.

3 Ask your friends and neighbors what Internet service they use and whether they're satisfied with it. Customer service varies from region to region, especially with broadband providers, so seek out a local recommendation.

4 Dial-up users should make sure an ISP has local access numbers (telephone numbers) in your area to avoid long-distance charges.

5 Check for DSL and cable broadband providers in your area. (DSL ISPs use telephone wiring, while cable ISPs use cable TV wiring.) For technical reasons, DSL is sometimes not available in rural or suburban areas.

6 Ask potential broadband providers about package deals. Cable companies may discount Internet access if you buy cable TV service, and phone companies sometimes offer DSL-telephone packages.

7 Consider other broadband options. Try satellite broadband if you live in a rural area. People in some urban areas can get broadband access from a fixed wireless ISP, which use flat, square antennae mounted on your roof to send and receive Internet traffic via radio waves. Some brand-new housing developments have built-in fiber-optic Internet access.

8 Get a T-1 line only if you have heavy use and serious business needs, as this service can cost $500 or more per month.

9 Choose AOL if you want to take advantage of some of its special features, such as content from Time Inc. magazines like *Sports Illustrated* or *People*. If you have a broadband connection, you can still use AOL with a "bring your own access" account that costs a little more than half of the usual $24-per-month AOL dial-up price. AOL is useful if you travel a lot with a laptop because you can use its toll-free number almost anywhere.

What to Look For

- Broadband versus dial-up service
- Appropriate hardware connections
- Recommendations
- Local access numbers
- Package deals with telephone or TV service
- Satellite, fixed wireless, or fiber-optic connections

Tips

A broadband connection can be shared by several computers. See 404 Network Your Computers.

Some experts recommend choosing an ISP that does not require you to install its own specialized software on your computer.

Warnings

With a broadband connection, your computer is always connected to the Internet. Get firewall software to protect against potential snoopers. See 406 Buy Computer Software.

In the fast and furious internet world, even big name ISPs go out of business. This means you'll have to find a new service, and possibly a new email address. See 403 Get an Internet Domain Name for an easier solution.

403 Get an Internet Domain Name

Tired of changing e-mail addresses when you change Internet service providers? Want to put up a Web site but don't want an address that's a yard long and full of slashes and squiggles? Then claim a piece of Internet real estate by registering your own domain name.

Steps

1 Go to InterNIC.net and click "Whois."

2 Enter the name you want to register (don't forget the part after the dot) and click on Submit.

3 Read the search results on the screen. If the name you want is available, it'll read "No match for domain."

4 If the name you want is taken, try variations, such as adding a middle initial, a city name, or trying ".net" instead of ".com."

5 When you find a name you like, return to InterNIC.net and click on the link to the Accredited Registrar Directory. You'll see a list of more than 150 registrars, or companies that can register your domain name for you.

6 Survey these companies for services. Most people want e-mail forwarding (automatically sending e-mail from john@*yourown- name*.com to jsmith2424@*yourISP*.com) and Web site forwarding (sending people who go to www.*yourownname*.com directly to www.members.*yourISP.com/* jsmith2424/index.html).

7 Shop for price among the registrars who provide the services you want. Most registrars offer reduced rates for registering multiple domains or for registering domain names for several years.

8 The company that registers your name doesn't have to host your Web site. If your monthly ISP fee includes Web hosting, you can save money by using Web site forwarding. Most ISPs can register a domain name for you, but they don't always offer the best prices or service.

9 Provide your chosen registrar with contact and credit card information. Now you need a Web site: For the lowdown, see 157 Hire Someone to Design and Build Your Web Site.

What to Look For

- Available domain name
- E-mail forwarding
- Web site forwarding
- Web site hosting

Tip

There's no single, objective, authoritative place to check the reputation of a registrar. But typing the registrar's name and *complaint* into a search engine might give you some clues about how happy its customers are.

Warning

"Cybersquatting," or registering a domain name trademarked by another company, is illegal.

404 Network Your Computers

It's not surprising that home networking is hot: Nearly 70 percent of U.S. households with broadband connections have more than one computer. If you want all your computers to share one Internet connection, this information will help you make the right choices.

Steps

Learn the jargon

1 A *router* relays data between your broadband Internet connection and your individual computers.

2 A *network adapter* connects to each computer. It sends data from the computer to the router.

3 An *Internet protocol (IP) address* is your computer's unique identification on the Internet. When you have a home network, all your computers share one IP address.

4 A *print server* is a special network adapter that's used to connect a printer to a network. With a print server, several computers can share one printer.

Choose a network type

1 Network your computers wirelessly over radio waves using a special type of router called an *access point*. One access point can serve most average-sized homes. The trade name for this technology is Wi-Fi or 802.11b, or its faster cousin, 802.11g. Wi-Fi products should be compatible with each other regardless of brand. Wireless networks work for people who move from room to room with their laptops, or want to use them in cafés, airports and other places with wireless service.

2 Use your home's electrical wiring to connect the router to each computer with a *powerline network*. The trade name for this technology is HomePlug. HomePlug networks are more secure than Wi-Fi networks and don't require special wiring. However, it's the newest technology and tends to be the most expensive.

3 Hook up with the most secure home network, a *wired network*, sometimes called Ethernet, 10-Base-T or 100-Base-T. If your broadband connection, router and all computers are in one room, it's the best choice. But because of its special wiring, it's also the least flexible if your needs change.

Buy the equipment

1 Get one router. If you're going wireless, this router is called an access point or base station.

2 Get a network adapter for each computer. The simplest ones plug into the computer's universal serial bus (USB) port. If you're using a wired network, your computer probably already has an Ethernet network interface card (NIC) in it.

What to Look For

- Router or access point
- Network adapter
- Print server
- Ethernet cable
- Technical support

Tips

Hybrid networks are very popular. For example, you can have wired Ethernet going to a desktop computer and printer in your home office, and a wireless access point for a roaming laptop and a desktop in a bedroom.

Microwave ovens and some cordless phones can interfere with wireless networks. If you have problems, move the access point and experiment with different channels.

Competing network technologies brag about their speed differences, but if you're sharing a broadband Internet connection, the claims are probably irrelevant. Most broadband connections to homes run considerably slower than any home network's rated speed.

3 Purchase extra-long Ethernet cables (also called Category 5 or Cat5 cables) if you're using a wired network.

4 Buy a print server if you want to put a printer on your network. Make sure the connectors on your print server and printer match.

Set it up

1 Start reading and experimenting. Many products have surprisingly good manuals and online support, and many Web sites are packed with good advice, such as HomeNetHelp.com, PracticallyNetworked.com and compnetworking.about.com. Many manufacturers offer online advice. Good technical support can make a huge difference in your installation, especially if you're not particularly patient or computer savvy.

2 If you're putting in a wired network, run cables to your stereo or home theater. Many new home entertainment components including digital video recorders and game systems are Internet-enabled.

Warning

When you first fire up a router, change its password. Every hacker and mischief-maker on the Internet knows default passwords. Wireless network owners should also enable wireless encryption protocol (WEP) to keep information private.

405 Upgrade the Memory in Your Computer

The best way to improve your computer's performance is to add random-access memory (RAM). Unless you're confident of your abilities, have a store technician do the work.

Steps

1 Find out how much memory your computer has. Here's how:

- In Windows XP, click on Start, then Control Panel, then Performance and Maintenance, then System. In other versions of Windows, double-click on My Computer, then double-click on Control Panel, then double-click on System.

- In Mac OS X, find the Applications folder, double-click on the Utilities folder, and double-click on Apple System Profiler. In Mac OS 9 or earlier, select the Apple System Profiler (usually found in the Apple menu).

2 Check your manual or manufacturer's Web site to determine whether there are open memory slots on the motherboard. Also see what the maximum amount of memory your computer can take, as well as the type, category and speed of memory it uses. For example, PC2100 DDR 133 MHz RAM means PC2100 is the type, DDR is the category, and 133 MHz is the speed in megahertz.

3 Compare your current memory with the maximum. You have two choices: Add new memory in open slots; or, if all slots are full, replace the existing memory with new, greater-capacity modules.

What to Look For

- Current memory
- Maximum allowable memory
- Type, category and speed of memory
- Open slots

Tip

Good tools for choosing memory are available online, including Crucial.com (you don't need to purchase from them to use the selector tool). You can also check the shopper sections of most computer magazines.

406 Buy Computer Software

These days, almost all new major-brand computers come with a software bundle that can handle most people's basic needs. If you buy a bare-bones machine, you may find yourself spending a lot of time and money to properly equip it. Here's how you can get started.

Steps

1 Collect your computer's vital statistics. You should know the operating system, the amount of random-access memory (RAM), and the available hard-disk space before you shop. Knowing whether it's Windows or Mac OS isn't enough; you need the operating system version number (Windows 98, 2000, Me or XP; Mac OS 8.*x*, 9.*x* or OS X). To locate this information:

   • In Windows XP, click on Start, then Control Panel, then Performance and Maintenance, then System.

   • In other versions of Windows, double-click on My Computer, then double-click on Control Panel, then double-click on System. You may need to click on the Performance tab.

   • In Mac OS X, open the Applications folder, double-click on the Utilities folder, then double-click on Apple System Profiler.

   • In Mac OS 9 or earlier, select the Apple System Profiler (usually found in the Apple menu).

2 Think about what kind of work you want to do. Software applications are organized into broad categories by retailers:

   • Office applications (sometimes called productivity software) are for word processing, spreadsheets, databases, and presentations. Most new computers come with some sort of office software. Whatever you choose, make sure it works with industry standards Microsoft Word and Excel.

   • Internet applications include Web browsers and e-mail, and come with most computers. E-mail software is sometimes called "communications."

   • Personal finance software includes money-management and tax-preparation tools. Make sure these will work with your financial institution's online banking systems.

   • Utilities include virus protection, Internet firewall, backup and recovery, and disk-management software. Every computer should have current virus protection, and computers on a broadband Internet connection should have a firewall.

   • Graphics and multimedia applications include digital photo manipulation, drawing, video editing and sound. These often demand huge amounts of available disk space and memory.

   • Entertainment software refers to games. Most run best with graphics or sound cards; some require external controllers such as joysticks. See 415 Buy Video and Computer Games.

What to Look For

- System requirements
- Software categories
- Reviews
- Version number
- Support options
- Trial versions
- Packaged versus downloaded
- Freeware
- Shareware

Tips

Students can get discounts on many software products at their college bookstore.

Wondering what the difference is between software programs, and applications? Some tech-industry people say that the *software* includes operating systems, but *applications* do not.

Note that some software programs can cause conflicts with others; ask manufacturers or read online reviews to learn if you have these.

Some companies create "home" and "professional" versions of the same software. Find out what the difference is, and whether you need the more expensive pro version.

- Educational software includes typing tutors, language instruction, and math and reading learning programs for children.

- Reference software includes atlases, dictionaries and encyclopedias.

- Development applications are for advanced users and programmers who want to create their own software.

3 Learn about which specific software will best serve your needs by talking with friends and colleagues, and reading reviews. Read software reviews on ZDNet.com and Cnet.com and in *Macworld* and *PC World*.

4 As you narrow your choices, compare the system requirements of the software with the information you collected in Step 1. In stores, look for the system requirements on the package. Catalogs and online stores list requirements with the product description. Make sure your system can handle the application.

5 Find out what the current version of the software is. If a newer version exists (or is expected soon), make sure that the version you buy can be upgraded to the most current version for free. Updates and patches can be costly.

6 Find out what technical support comes with the software. The options vary greatly, from free lifetime support to per-minute charges for telephone help. Most software companies are moving toward self-service Web-based support, so visit the manufacturer's Web site to see if it seems helpful and complete.

7 Look for a free trial version, found at the software company's Web site, if you can't decide between two products. Some trial versions quit working after a set time period; others lack some basic functionality (such as the ability to save or print work). Most can be upgraded to full versions online for a fee. Many computers come loaded with trial versions of popular software.

8 Purchase packaged software if you like having a printed manual and an installer disc you can file away. (Make sure that the package actually contains a printed manual; they're often on the disc.) Buy software online and download it if you have a broadband Internet connection and need to use the software right away. This can be done from manufacturers' Web sites.

9 Spend little or nothing on freeware (no-cost software) and shareware (low-cost software purchased on the honor system). Many of these products, as well as trial versions of commercial software, are available at Tucows.com, VersionTracker.com and Download.com.

407 Choose a CD Player

CD players are the hardest-working piece of equipment in most home music systems. When you're out shopping, look for the features you use most. Very good machines can be found for well under $300.

Steps

1 Think about how you listen to music. Do you routinely drop in several CDs and hit Shuffle, or listen to one at a time? Do you burn your own CDs? Your habits should drive your choice.

2 Check the CD connection on your current stereo. If it accepts digital optical inputs (which provide better sound quality than normal wire jacks), find a CD player with digital optical output.

3 Bring some home-burned CDs when you go shopping to play on any unit you're considering. Some CD players can't play CD-RWs, and many can't play MP3s.

4 Consider a CD jukebox or a carousel that holds dozens (or hundreds) of discs if you have lots of CDs and rarely take them out of the house. A cataloging feature uses disc and track names encoded on newer CDs to help you find songs.

5 Serious listeners can look at high-definition compatible digital (HDCD), DVD-Audio, or super-audio CD (SACD) players. These new (but incompatible) formats provide better sound quality. All will play traditional CDs, as well, but only HDCDs will play on a regular CD player.

What to Look For

- Shuffle/random/programmable playback
- Digital optical output
- CD-RW capability
- MP3 capability
- Carousel or jukebox
- Cataloging feature
- HDCD capability
- DVD-Audio
- SACD capability

Tips

Manufacturers use the terms *shuffle* and *random* differently. If a CD player has both features, find out what they mean.

Broken CD players can sometimes be repaired, but repairs can be expensive and often don't last.

408 Buy Blank CDs

Blank CDs cost anywhere from 10 cents to more than $1 apiece. The kind you buy depends on your equipment and what you want to do.

Steps

1 Check your computer manual to see if your CD burner is a CD-R (recordable) or a CD-RW (rewritable). Recordable discs can be used only once, but rewritable discs can be used over and over.

2 Keep in mind that blank CD-Rs will work in a CD-RW burner, but CD-RWs won't work in a CD-R burner.

3 Buy blank CDs with gold-tone on the bottom to record archival material, such as family photographs or financial records.

4 Get less-expensive green-toned CDs if you're making everyday copies of documents, photos, and music.

5 Buy CD-Rs (not CD-RWs) if you're recording music to be played on a portable or car stereo. Choose blank CDs labeled "Music," "Digital Audio" or "DA" if your CD burner is part of your system.

What to Look For

- CD burner (CD-R or CD-RW)
- Gold-tone CDs
- Green-tone CDs
- Music CDs

Tip

Blank CDs labeled "Music" cost more, as a portion of the price goes to recording artists as royalties. They are the only CDs that work in stereo-component CD burners.

409 Buy an MP3 Player

The digital revolution has caught up with the venerable Walkthing. An MP3 player is the perfect tool for people on the go who have moved their music collections onto their computers. Because they're digital—some with absolutely no moving parts—MP3 players don't skip or warble if you're running, skiing or biking.

Steps

1 Shop for price. MP3 players range from $60 for a bare-bones RCA Lyra to $500 for the top-of-the-line Apple iPod. Other popular brands are Creative Labs, SonicBlue, Archos, Samsung, Sony and Panasonic.

2 Get a player with as much storage as you can afford. The more storage, the more music it can hold. One minute of MP3 music takes up about 1 megabyte (MB) of memory, so a 128 MB MP3 player can hold about two hours of tunes. Unlike computers, memory and storage are sometimes used synonymously in MP3 players, since the storage in smaller devices (under 128 MB) is usually made of Flash memory chips.

3 Make sure any potential purchase works with your computer. Many MP3 players don't work with Macintosh computers, though that's improving.

4 Try the controls. Less-expensive players often have control panels that can charitably be described as "minimalist." Make sure they make sense to you.

5 Pick up the unit to gauge its size and weight. Would it be comfortable in your pocket or on your belt? How about when you're moving around?

6 Check out the player's advertised battery life. Manufacturers' claims aren't exact, but they can be used for comparison.

7 Choose a unit with USB or FireWire, rather than a parallel connection to your computer. USB and FireWire are fast and flexible.

8 Look for a player with an FM radio receiver. Some models can record music from the radio, and will identify the artist and title the next time you connect the player to your computer. Some also double as digital voice recorders.

9 Look for expandable storage, especially on units without much built-in memory. CompactFlash, MemoryStick and SecureDigital media are common choices. Newer models with more storage have internal hard disks that can store computer data.

10 Have a listen. MP3 players use standard stereo headphones. If you don't like the headphones that come with a player, there are a variety of styles you can purchase.

What to Look For

- Maximum storage
- Computer connectivity
- Easy-to-use controls
- Size and weight
- Battery life
- USB or FireWire
- FM receiver
- Expandable storage
- Headphones

Tips

A few high-end MP3 players have built-in FM transmitters to send music wirelessly to a car stereo. You can do the same with a pocket-sized FM transmitter; if you don't mind wires, use a cassette-on-a-cable device from a portable CD player car kit.

Some MP3 players double as portable CD players, so you can burn your MP3 files to a CD and pop it in the player.

Warning

The legalities of MP3 music-swapping are constantly changing, but please respect the work of the artists: Make sure they get compensated for their work. See 35 Buy Music Online.

410 Choose a DVD Player

The thing that convinces some people to move up to a DVD player is the great picture quality. Or, maybe it's just being able to click to hear Tony Soprano speak French. Prices for DVD players are all over the map, but even the cheapest ones have features galore.

Steps

1 Inspect your TV and home theater connections. You'll want your DVD player to take advantage of the best-quality inputs available: For audio, look for coaxial or optical inputs. For video, look for component-video, S-Video, or composite-video inputs. At the store, look for DVD players with corresponding outputs.

2 Bring a homemade DVD with you when you shop. There are three competing, incompatible formats: DVD-R, DVD-RW and DVD-RAM. Even if a player says it takes your format, test it.

3 Get a progressive-scan player if you have an HDTV. These deliver higher resolution for more natural-looking output. Better yet, purchase a DVD player with 3:2 pulldown, if you can afford it, for even better picture quality. See 422 Buy a Serious TV.

4 Remember that the audio encoding—Dolby Digital or digital theater system (DTS)—on the DVD itself is critical. Proprietary audio features on some DVD players aren't as important as having a good home theater receiver and speakers. See 426 Buy a Home Theater System.

What to Look For

- Digital audio output: coaxial or optical
- Component-video output
- S-Video output
- Composite-video output
- Progressive scan
- 3:2 pulldown
- Good receiver and speakers

Tips

If your home theater system includes DTS and/or Dolby Digital decoding, you don't need these features in your DVD player.

DVD players can also play audio CDs. If you burn CDs on your computer, bring along a homemade disc to test it.

411 Buy a VCR

Have you shopped for a VCR lately? Models that are comparable to units that cost hundreds of dollars a few years ago now are available for as little as $50. Maybe you don't have to replace all of those VHS movies with DVDs right away after all.

Steps

1 Check the connections on your television set or home theater receiver. You'll want a VCR with the best possible connectors— in descending order of quality, they're S-Video, composite-video, and antenna/cable inputs.

2 Choose a VCR with S-VHS (super VHS), high-fidelity MTS stereo audio, and four or six heads for best recording and playback.

3 Pick a model with audio-video connectors on the front panel if you plan to transfer movies from a video camcorder to tape.

4 Expect a raft of standard features. Even on low-priced models you should find auto clock set, commercial skip, fast rewind speed, and VCR+ (for easy programming).

What to Look For

- S-VHS
- Four or six heads
- Audio-video connectors in front
- Auto clock set
- Commercial skip
- Fast rewind
- VCR+

Tip

Avoid combo VCR/DVDs unless you don't have room for both. You get more for your money with stand-alone components, and one invariably breaks before the other.

412 **Choose a Personal Digital Assistant**

Tired of lugging around an address book, a calendar, a pad of paper, a photo album, your journal, a game machine, the newspaper, and a calculator? With today's handhelds—sometimes called personal digital assistants (PDAs) or pocket computers—you can consolidate them all into one handy device. All your information is readily available and searchable. And prices for PDAs have dropped out of the geeks-only realm into that of everyday folks.

Steps

1 Think about how you might use a handheld. What would you like to do on it? (If you're not sure what PDAs can do, read up on them in specialty magazines or on the Web.)

2 Look at your computer. What operating system (Windows or Macintosh) does it have, and what sort of connectors (USB 1.1, USB 2.0, FireWire) does it have? Make sure that any handheld you consider is compatible with your computer. You don't need a computer to use a handheld, but it helps. Your computer can back up the information on your handheld (this is called "synchronization"), give you another way to enter information, and act as a bridge between your handheld and the Internet.

3 Compare the two leading handheld operating systems: Palm OS and Pocket PC. They serve the same basic functions (calendar, address book, notebook, calculator), but they differ in features and approach. Try out a few models in the store.

4 Focus on screen display; quality is vital. Is text on the screen easy to read in a variety of settings? If you'll be viewing photographs, look at color screens. Utilitarian black-and-white screens might be acceptable for text-based tasks.

5 Pick up the handheld and get a feel for its weight, sturdiness and comfort.

6 Learn how you'll enter text on your handheld. If the handwriting-recognition method isn't comfortable for you (it takes some practice), look for a model with a built-in thumb-operated keyboard. Add-on keyboards are available but have drawbacks.

7 Look at the battery type. Rechargeable handhelds usually need recharging every week or two, while those with disposable batteries need replacements monthly. (Your mileage may vary.)

8 Get as much memory as you can afford, especially if you plan to load lots of pictures, games or documents from your computer.

9 Look for handhelds with slots for expanding memory and adding functions. Popular add-ons include MP3 players, Global Positioning System (GPS) receivers, modems and wireless network adapters (Wi-Fi).

What to Look For

- Compatibility with your computer
- USB or FireWire connectors
- Palm OS or Pocket PC
- Screen display
- Weight, sturdiness, overall feel
- Text-entry method
- Battery type
- Memory
- Expansion slots

Tips

You don't need a Microsoft-based Pocket PC just because you run Windows on your computer. Palm OS devices are reportedly better at handling Word and Excel documents.

Avoid cheap address book–only devices. Palm OS and Pocket PC handhelds are generally much more useful, for not much more money.

Warning

If you are upgrading from an older Palm OS device to a new handheld with Palm OS 5, make sure the programs you use are enhanced for, or at least compatible with, the new operating system.

413 Choose a Mobile Phone Service

What genius said competition makes everything better? If you've shopped for mobile phone service lately, you know that the variety of service plans and phones is overwhelming. Carriers entice customers with hot new phones, but that's the last item you should think about. First choose a carrier, then a service plan, then your hardware.

Steps

Compare competing carriers' coverage

1 Make sure a prospective carrier's service works where you do. Carriers provide maps of their service areas. If you travel a lot, look for national coverage.

2 Ask friends and colleagues which carrier they use and how satisfied they are with its service. Then ask them to check reception by making some calls in your home and office—there's nothing worse than a dead spot where you spend all your time.

3 Check where data services—such as e-mail, Internet access, games and pictures—are available if you want these services.

Compare service plans

1 Look at your needs. If you stay close to home, a plan with unlimited local or regional calling may suit you. But if you travel a lot, a national plan can save you money. Roaming charges can add up in a hurry.

2 Watch the clock. If you use your phone throughout the day, more "anytime" minutes can be a better deal (since day rates are higher) than lots of "night and weekend" minutes.

3 Remember where you call. Mobile phone plans can include free long distance—a big money-saver if you frequently make long-distance calls.

4 Ask that standard features such as call waiting, voice mail and caller ID be included in your plan at no extra charge.

5 Look for a plan with rollover minutes that don't expire at the end of the month if your calling pattern varies over time.

6 Watch for rounding up. Most carriers round phone time up to the nearest minute.

7 Check into package plans for data services if you plan to use their services heavily. They can add an extra charge per month—often at a cost per kilobyte of data.

8 Look for a plan with a low cancellation fee if you think your needs might change. But before you pay such a fee, ask your carrier to switch you at no cost to a plan that makes better sense for you in the future.

What to Look For

- Coverage
- Service plan
- Phone

Tips

You can compare mobile phone service offers on two unbiased Web sites: MyRatePlan.com and TeleBright.com.

If you know you'll use data services heavily, the right phone may be even more important for you than the right service plan.

Mobile phone companies are supposed to give you the ability to take your mobile phone number with you when you move to a new carrier by late 2003. However, this mandate has already been postponed several times.

Select a telephone

1 Ask about free phones. You can get some great full-featured phones when you sign a one- or two-year contract.

2 Make sure the phone's basic features work simply and well: an easy-to-use keypad, clear sound, long battery life, voice dialing, a minute counter, and voice mail are important for most people.

3 Insist on a hands-free headset with your phone.

4 Consider advanced features, like color screens, speaker-phone operation, built-in cameras, address books that synchronize with your computer, or custom ring tones.

5 Look for Global Positioning System (GPS) location capability on high-end phones, good if you need to be found in an emergency.

6 Consider a combination mobile phone and PDA if you rely on these services heavily. They are costly, but can reduce the load in your briefcase or purse.

Most mobile phone companies (including all nationwide carriers) let you terminate a contract without paying a cancellation fee if you do so within a set time, usually 14 to 30 days.

414 Negotiate Your Long-Distance Phone Service

Americans spent almost $100 billion on long-distance telephone calls in 2002—and some estimates say one-fifth of that was wasted on excessive charges. Picking a smart plan can shave wasted cash.

Steps

1 Review several months of phone bills to understand your long-distance calling patterns. How might they change in the near future? Is a friend or family member planning to move out of the area?

2 Separate your in-state and interstate charges, usually billed at different rates. Shop for a plan that has low per-minute interstate rates if most of your calls are made to other states. Find a plan with low in-state rates if that's where you're calling. Regional plans from a local carrier might be your best bet.

3 Seek out a plan with small—or no—monthly fees if you make less than 100 minutes of long-distance calls per month.

4 See what advantages you gain by using the same carrier for both local and long-distance service. Make sure the promised savings are based on the plan you currently have, rather than on a competing carrier's most expensive plan.

5 Ask a new carrier to pay all the costs associated with switching you over. Get the promises in writing.

What to Look For

- Calling patterns
- In-state versus interstate rates
- Regional plans
- No fee long-distance
- Single carrier versus multiple carriers
- Switching costs

Tips

Many mobile phone service plans include free long distance—a good deal if the minutes and times fit your calling patterns. See 413 Choose a Mobile Phone Service.

Check your plan every few months to make sure you're still getting the best deal.

415 Buy Video and Computer Games

Fun and games aren't just kid stuff anymore. Video games—both computer-based and console games—are mainstream entertainment for adults, too. Indeed, experts talk about the "battle for the living room," with game consoles rivaling digital video recorders (DVRs) and DVD players in power and features.

Steps

1 Always start your shopping with the games you want to play. Not all games are available on all platforms. Game genres include action/adventure, educational, puzzle, role-playing/strategy, simulation and sports, but there is some overlap among them.

2 See what platform the games you want are on. Some games are exclusive to one platform. Games fall into two general categories: computer games and console games (usually played on a Microsoft XBox or Sony PlayStation2).

3 Look for these features in a computer game.

- System requirements: Make sure your computer's processor, memory and video card meet the minimum requirements. Also be alert for special hardware, such as game pads or joysticks. (See 401 Buy Computer Peripherals.)

- Multiplayer Internet capability: This allows you to play computer games online against other people. Some games don't even have a single-player mode. A broadband Internet connection will improve game performance.

- Free demonstration versions: Demos are available for many computer games from manufacturer Web sites. You can upgrade them to full versions later.

4 Look for these features in a console game.

- Compatibility: XBox games won't play on a PlayStation2 and vice versa.

- Special controller needs: Most games will play with the standard console controls, but some work better with other types.

- Internet connectivity: Many new console games are made to play online against other people. Manufacturers sometimes make extra features available to Internet-connected consoles.

- High-end video or audio needs: Newer game consoles and games can handle HDTV and 5.1 Surround sound, but the consoles might require additional hardware.

5 Understand the rating system established by the Entertainment Software Rating Board (ESRB.org). Ratings are based on violence; sexual content; language; depiction of drug, alcohol or tobacco use; gambling; and other factors. Ratings are especially important for people who are buying games for children. (See 335 Buy a Video Game System.)

What to Look For

- Computer versus console
- System requirements
- Multiplayer capability
- Demo versions
- Special controllers
- Internet connectivity requirements
- Audio-video needs
- ESRB ratings

Tips

Most game consoles can double as DVD and music CD players. Game consoles with built-in DVRs are on the horizon.

The hottest games—especially the so-called first-person shooters—are released as computer games before they come out on consoles. If you want to be first on your block to play, stick to computer games. They also go on sale much more often than console-based games.

Nintendo GameCubes are solid systems for kids 13 years old and younger. But they are waning in popularity among adult gamers, because these systems lack expandability and Internet connectivity.

416 Choose a Film Camera

The boom in digital photography hasn't killed the market for film cameras. More than 80 percent of people with digital cameras still use film cameras occasionally, and great choices are available in all price ranges. There are a couple of big issues to consider when shopping for a film camera, and lots of features to choose from.

Steps

1 Get the picture—decide what you're shooting. If you want great vacation and family snapshots, you'll do fine with a point-and-shoot camera. Don't underestimate the quality you can find in these easy-to-operate cameras—many are full-featured with good optics. If serious photography is your bag, look for a single lens–reflex (SLR) camera, which gives you manual control over a number of features.

2 Consider your film choices. For most uses, you'll choose between 35 mm and Advanced Photo System (APS) film. The former is easier to find, cheaper to buy and process, and easier to develop, while the latter (in the proper camera) lets you shoot panoramic and wide-angle shots on the same roll as normal pictures. See 39 Choose Film for Your Camera.

What to Look For

- Point-and-shoot versus SLR
- 35 mm versus APS
- Special features

Tips

The majority of SLR cameras use 35 mm film, not APS.

You can find good deals on SLRs and lenses at reputable used-camera shops.

Some film cameras have LCDs like digital cameras so you can see the photo you just took (although you won't be able to erase it).

POINT-AND-SHOOT CAMERA FEATURES	SLR CAMERA FEATURES
Flash: Look for red-eye reduction and fill-in modes. The farther the flash is from the lens, the less likely you are to get red-eye in your pictures.	• Interchangeable lenses.
Timer and/or remote control: These let you appear in your own photos.	• Manual exposure control: You'll want to be able to adjust both the shutter speed and aperture.
Date stamp: This marks the photo with the date you took it.	• Automatic exposure control: Look for both shutter speed and aperture priority.
Automatic film loading, winding and rewinding.	• Automatic and manual focus: Some cameras will even track your eye movements in the viewfinder and focus on the element you're looking at.
Zoom lens.	• Film handling features: Look for autoloading, autowind, autorewind and DX sensing. With DX sensing, the camera reads a bar code on the film can and adjusts itself accordingly.
Panorama mode (in APS cameras).	• Flash capability: Some SLRs have a built-in flash. Make sure the camera also has a hot shoe, which lets you connect an external flash.
Price: $30 and up, with many very good cameras under $200.	• Price: $150 and up, with very good cameras around $400.

Choose a Digital Camcorder

Now that everybody in America has written a screenplay (see 166 Sell a Screenplay), it's time to start shooting. Digital camcorders, many selling for under $1,000, capture remarkably high-quality images and are just plain fun to use. Combine one with editing software on your computer, and capture your family's favorite moments in style.

Steps

1 Walk right by those analog camcorders. When it comes to image quality, even the worst digital camcorders are on a par with the very best analog models. Still waffling? Analogs can't connect to your computer so forget about editing your home movies.

2 Choose a digital recording format: MiniDV (the most popular format, with easy-to-find blank tapes), Digital 8 or MicroMV.

3 Pick a model with a liquid-crystal display (LCD) screen that's at least 2.5 inches (6 cm) diagonally. The bigger and brighter the screen, the easier the camera will be to focus and use. Ask to view it outside, in bright daylight. (Many cameras have a black-and-white viewfinder in addition to the LCD.)

4 Look for a front-mounted microphone rather than a top-mounted one. For the best sound, get a jack for an external mike.

5 Pay attention to the optical zoom. The higher the numbers, the closer your camera will bring you to the action. Digital zoom, on the other hand, simply reduces the resolution of the recorded image.

6 Try the controls and the on-screen menus. See if you're comfortable using them and they make sense to you.

7 Picture-stabilizing circuitry and low-light operation can be useful. Ask to see what they do and how well they work.

8 Weigh—pun intended—the features of the camera against its bulkiness, weight and price tag. A large, heavy camera won't be comfortable for you to use. Tiny, palm-sized camcorders can be had, but at a hefty price.

9 Make sure to get a camcorder with a FireWire (IEEE 1394) or USB 2.0 jack if you're planning to edit your movies on your computer. (Check that it has the appropriate connection.)

10 Have a ball with video-editing software and turn your raw digital footage into entertaining movies complete with professional looking cuts, transitions, and sound tracks. Basic editing programs come with some computers and digital camcorders. For example, new Macs come standard with easy-to-learn iMovie.

What to Look For

- Digital format
- LCD screen at least 2.5 inches (6 cm) in size
- Front-mounted microphone
- Optical zoom
- Easy-to-use controls
- Picture-stabilizing circuitry
- Low-light operation
- FireWire or USB 2.0 connection

Tip

As you shop you may see the term *i.LINK*. It's another name for FireWire and is used mostly with digital camcorders.

418 Decide on a Digital Camera

The price of digital cameras is falling as quickly as their quality is soaring. That means great opportunities for shoppers. Remember that while they seem expensive compared with film cameras, digital cameras never need film. And you can create photo-quality prints using your home computer and a good-quality ink-jet printer. The only downside is the dizzying array of choices. Here's some help.

Steps

1 Decide what you want to get out of your camera. Are you shooting family snapshots, professional portraits or something in between? A good basic digital camera costs under $400, while professional models are upwards of $2,000. Spend what you need to get a camera that covers the high end of projected uses.

2 Enlarge your knowledge of image resolution, which is measured in megapixels, or mg (1 million pixels, or picture elements). The more megapixels, the higher resolution the final image. How large you want to blow your images up should be your guide: A 1-mg camera can create a 3-by-5-inch (7.5 by 13 cm) photo-quality print; a 2-mg camera will make a 5-by-7-inch (13 by 18 cm) print; a 3-mg camera will make an 8-by-10-inch (20 by 25 cm) print, and a 6-mg camera will make a 9-by-13-inch (23 by 33 cm) print.

3 Find out if the camera includes a cable for your computer (USB or FireWire). If it doesn't, it's not the end of the world. (See 401 Buy Computer Peripherals: "Media Reader.")

4 See if a camera comes with image-editing software that works with your computer (Windows or Mac OS). Adobe Photoshop Elements and ULead PhotoImpact (ulead.com) are two to look for.

5 Choose a camera with removable memory in addition to built-in memory. The most popular formats are CompactFlash, MemoryStick, SmartMedia and MultiMedia/Secure Digital (MMC/SD). (The differences between formats are irrelevant for most uses.) They cost about the same, as little as 40 cents per megabyte, with 128-MB cards usually being the best value.

6 Expect an LCD screen for viewing pictures, a built-in flash, a timer, and a time/date stamp on even the most basic camera. Some models let you record short snippets of video.

7 Insist on optical zoom, not digital, if you need zoom capability. Midrange cameras should have high-quality optical zoom lenses.

8 Get manual exposure control—a feature on midrange cameras— if you plan to shoot in low-light conditions or otherwise need to override automatic settings.

9 Expect features equivalent to those of the best single lens–reflex (SLR) cameras on the best digital models. Features include removable lenses, full exposure control, a hot-shoe mount for an external flash, and through-the-lens focusing.

What to Look For

- Image resolution
- Battery life
- Cable and software
- Removable memory
- LCD screen
- Built-in flash
- Timer
- Time/date stamp
- Video recording
- Optical zoom lens
- Manual exposure control

Tips

Ignore claims of digital zoom. When you use digital zoom, the image resolution drops accordingly. For example, 2X digital zoom will reduce the resolution of your finished pictures by half.

Digital cameras eat batteries, especially to power an LCD screen. For longer life, avoid using the LCD and use lithium batteries—but always carry extras. Be skeptical of manufacturers' claims of projected battery life. See 40 Buy Rechargeable Batteries.

Look for software that helps you organize and manage your digital photos, such as Jasc Paint Shop Photo Album, Apple iPhoto, and Adobe PhotoAlbum.

Take lots of pictures and trash the unwanted shots later, at your computer.

Most digital cameras, especially inexpensive ones, have a slight delay between tripping the trigger and actually exposing the picture. This can cause you to miss shots, especially when you're first learning to use the camera.

419 Buy a Home Automation System

If you've seen so-called smart houses with remote controls for lights, heating and cooling, security, home theater, and even window shades, you've probably been amazed—and they're not just available for high-end homes. Here's how to put automation into your home.

Steps

1 Start fantasizing. Pore through *Electronic House, Home Automation* and *Popular Home Automation* magazines or go online to see what's available. Look at Home-Automation.org or in Yellow Pages under "Home Theater and Automation Systems." (See 242 Hire a Contractor, Plumber, Painter or Electrician.)

2 Think about what you'd like to automate. If you plan to start small—with just lights, perhaps—get a system that can be expanded when you want to add other functions.

3 Calculate your budget. Prices can range from a few hundred dollars for basic systems to many thousands of dollars for whole-house automation systems

4 Make sure that any system you're considering installing will work with your current furnace and air conditioner, security system, and home entertainment equipment. You may need to replace light switches, alarm controllers and thermostats.

5 Place the master control panel, also known as the headend, in a convenient, central spot. This is where home automation systems come together.

6 Consider a powerline or radio frequency (RF) controls if you're installing home automation in an existing house. These don't require extra wiring for controls, but tend to be less useful or flexible than systems that operate with low-voltage wiring.

7 Get a system with external remote control capabilities so you can turn on your home's system as you approach, check its status when you're away, and shut down the house as you leave. Remote controls include telephone and Internet-based controls.

8 Look for a system with a vacation mode. This tracks your lighting patterns while you're home, and re-creates them when you're gone so your house appears occupied. Separate programs for weekdays and weekends should be standard.

9 Check out the wireless touch-screen controllers to be sure they are programmable, make sense, and work anywhere in the house.

What to Look For

- Pie-in-the-sky ideas
- Plan that fits your budget
- Compatability with existing systems
- Remote access
- Vacation mode
- Programmable touch-screen controllers
- Uninterruptible power supply
- Compatibility among products
- Maximum flexibility

Tips

Each individual system (lights, security, heating and cooling, media) is a subsystem in an overall home automation system.

The best time to install a home automation system is when you're in the building or remodeling process.

10 Install an uninterruptible power supply with your system to maintain service even if the power goes off.

11 If you're looking to combine top-of-the-line products from a variety of vendors, make sure they're compatible with each other.

12 Shop for a system that gives you maximum flexibility. The more preset options, the better.

SYSTEM	FACTS AND FEATURES
Lighting Control	• Look for timer that adjusts to seasons. Lights can turn on automatically later in summer than in winter.
	• An All Off command is useful if you tend to leave lights on.
	• An All On setting can quickly illuminate the whole house in emergencies.
	• Scene or Event controls let you create multiroom lighting schemes (for small dinner parties or large-group entertaining) with a single command.
	• "Light paths" lead from one room to another and can be turned on with one command.
	• See 206 Buy a Programmable Lighting System.
Heating and Cooling	• Automating your climate control can save money on energy costs.
	• Combined with remote controls, climate control makes sense for vacation homes that get very hot or cold when unoccupied.
	• It should be easy to switch between home and away settings.
Security	• System should let you monitor and control security cameras and motion detectors remotely, within the house, by telephone or via the Internet.
	• Look for ability to arm or disarm alarm by zones, rather than the whole house.
	• Remote control–powered curtains or blinds are good for home security, privacy and home theater rooms.
Audio-video	• See 421 Buy an Audio-Video Distribution System.
Other Controls	• Systems can control appliances. For example, you can preheat the oven as you leave work.
	• Pools, spas and saunas can be tied into the system.
	• Temperature sensors can control drapes and ceiling fans to save energy and maintain comfortable rooms.
	• See 214 Incorporate Fluid Architecture Into Your Home.

420 Buy a State-of-the-Art Sound System

If music is important to you—indeed, if you find that your daily life *requires* a soundtrack—then having the best-quality sound may be your top priority. Forget those department-store all-in-one-systems. There's a whole world of high-end, high-priced audio equipment just waiting for your discriminating ears (and discretionary income).

Steps

1 Let your listening habits and desires be your guide. You should assemble a system that sounds great to you, not a salesperson.

2 Assess your living and work spaces. A system that sounds incredible in a small demonstration room might sound crummy in a large, high-ceilinged living room.

3 Bring your own music when you shop. You'll know the nuances of that music better than demo CDs designed to highlight an audio system's strengths.

4 Listen to systems without regard to price range, at least at first. You want to *hear*—if it's perceptible—why prices vary so much. Try to listen to various components in isolation. If you're comparing two amplifiers, use the same CD player, CD and speakers during your test.

5 Select a system with separate components (including amplifiers and preamps). Each component should have its own power supply to reduce electrical interference between components. Get a power conditioner to further reduce interference.

6 Splurge on speakers, if you're making budget trade-offs. Crank up the music as loud as you're likely to play at home.

7 Shop for a digital audio receiver if you want your stereo to play Internet-based music or MP3s from your computer. Digital audio receivers are a new and varied breed of component. Some connect directly to the Internet via your broadband connection; others connect via your computer and can access MP3s on your hard drive. They require a network connection in addition to stereo cables. (See 404 Network Your Computers.)

8 Buy high-quality cables. It makes little sense to connect top-end audio components with dime-store cables.

9 Link your high-end audio system into whole-house media and control systems. (See 426 Buy a Home Theater System, 419 Buy a Home Automation System, and 421 Buy an Audio-Video Distribution System.)

What to Look For

- Separate components
- Power conditioner
- Good-sounding speakers
- Digital audio receiver
- High-quality cables

Tip

See 407 Choose a CD Player to learn about high-definition compatible digital, super-audio CD and DVD-Audio.

421 Buy an Audio-Video Distribution System

You've sprung for the home theater setup and the stereo with the 300-CD changer. Now what happens when you're downstairs and want to listen to a CD that's trapped in the player upstairs, or when you're watching a pay-per-view movie in the home theater but need to go cook dinner? You need a whole-house audio-video distribution system.

Steps

1 Count the number of audio and video sources (DVD player, CD player, cable or satellite box, FM receiver) in your current setup.

2 Determine the number of outputs (rooms or zones in your house) where you want to listen or view.

3 Shop for a controller—the central brain of the system—that can serve your entire home. The cost of the controller varies depending on how many inputs and outputs it has. Most controllers can be linked: If one controller handles six outputs but you have nine zones, you can chain together two six-output controllers.

4 Look for control panels that are sensible and easy to operate. Most systems employ touch-screen pads in each room to control the audio and video, and come with handheld remotes.

5 Look for an Internet-enabled system if you listen to Internet radio and streaming media. Some systems can work with dial-up connections, but they work much better with broadband. Some have a built-in hard disk for storing MP3s.

6 Get a system with a built-in intercom if you have a large house. Some systems can alert you when the doorbell rings.

7 Remember that these systems require wiring to each room, so it's easiest to install one while you're building or remodeling. If you're installing one in an existing house, hire an experienced contractor (see 242 Hire a Contractor, Plumber, Painter or Electrician). Audio-video systems can also be tied in to home automation systems (see 419 Buy a Home Automation System).

What to Look For

- Input/output controller
- Sensible control panels
- Internet radio connectivity
- Hard disk for MP3s
- Intercom
- Extras

Tips

Because of their complexity, audio-video distribution systems are sold mostly by dealers/installers. If you want to buy and install your own, you'll probably have to shop online.

Some systems have flashy extras. For example, you can have cover art for the CD or DVD that's playing be displayed on an LCD keypad in individual rooms. You can decide if that's worth the money.

422 Buy a Serious TV

Today's mind-numbing array of serious, big-screen TVs can intimidate the uninitiated. But one fact will help you decide whether to get an expensive TV: The FCC has mandated that high-definition television (HDTV) will be broadcast by 2007. If you're investing in a big set, get HDTV. You'll get better performance from DVDs and digital satellite or cable systems, and when 2007 hits, you'll be ready.

Steps

1 Look at the size of your TV room. The bigger the screen, the farther away you need to sit for the picture to look good. One simple formula suggests that you multiply the diagonal size of an HDTV screen by 2.5 to 4 to get viewing distance. That means you'd watch a 30-inch (75 cm) TV from a distance of 70 to 120 inches (5¾ to 10 feet, 178 to 305 cm). Conventional (analog) TVs should be watched at twice that distance.

2 Get a widescreen TV if you can afford it. Widescreen DVDs and much HDTV programming are made for widescreen TVs.

3 Learn the difference between flat screens and flat panels. Flat-screen TVs have a heavy glass picture tube just like regular TVs, but are flat rather than curved on the front. Flat panels—which include plasma and liquid-crystal displays (LCD)—can be as thin as 3.5 inches (9 cm) and can hang on the wall like a picture.

4 Keep in mind that some flat panels don't have a TV tuner in them, requiring a home theater tuner, a satellite or cable box, or a VCR to tune in TV stations. Also, some flat-panel TVs can't handle HDTV.

5 Buy a rear-projection TV to get the best bang for your buck. Look at the TV from different angles to judge picture quality.

6 Shop for the best-quality video inputs. In descending order of quality, they are component-video, S-Video, composite-video and antenna/cable inputs.

7 Make sure that your TV has enough audio and video connections for your DVD, digital video recorder, cable, satellite, VCR and other devices. If you're going to connect your TV to a home theater system, don't worry about the sound quality from the TV's built-in speakers. (See 426 Buy a Home Theater System.)

8 Future-proof your purchase. If you really can't afford an HDTV now, get one that's HD-ready or HD-upgradable. You can purchase an HDTV tuner in a few years when prices drop.

9 Shop for good prices. They vary by the size of the screen, but here are some ranges: Flat screens: $1,000 to $3,000; flat-panel LCDs: $1,000 to $2,500; rear-projection: $1,500 to $3,000; flat-panel plasma: $3,500 to $10,000.

What to Look For

- HDTV or HD-ready
- Screen size
- Widescreen (16:9 aspect ratio)
- Flat-screen versus flat-panel
- Rear-projection
- Component-video, S-video, or composite-video inputs
- Sufficient audio and video connections

Tips

Nothing ruins the effect of a cool-looking flat-panel TV like a tangle of wires and cables. If you're going to spend a wad on a high-end plasma model, run cables and wires inside your walls.

Many projectors made for computer-based presentations also have S-video or component-video inputs. With a home theater system and a blank wall, you've got a big-screen TV.

Spring for a plasma TV if your home theater is the center of your entertainment universe. These are the most stylish, the best-viewing and not coincidentally the most expensive. Make absolute certain that the plasma TV can handle HDTV, or you'll have to learn an expensive, painful lesson in a few years when all television signals are HD.

423 Choose Between Cable and Satellite TV

Cable providers used to have a monopoly on expanded TV service, but satellite companies have brought competition to the marketplace. Now, dishes are sprouting like mushrooms on chimneys, balconies and roofs everywhere. Ask lots of questions before you choose a provider.

Steps

1 Contact local cable companies and satellite providers for their price lists. They'll range from $15 for the most basic cable service (just local channels) to $100 and more for premium packages. Be aware that companies may have separate costs for hardware—control boxes and/or satellite dishes—and programming. Ask about all the costs, including contract commitments.

2 Check out the channel packages each provider offers. Decide what combination of TV channels, movies and sports is best for your household.

3 Ask satellite companies if they carry your local channels, especially if you live in a small town. Of the 210 Nielsen designated market areas in the United States, fewer than half can get local channels via satellite. And competing satellite providers don't necessarily provide local channels in the same markets.

4 Keep in mind that satellite TV generally has better broadcast quality than cable, but is more prone to interference from heavy snow or rain. Also, satellite service requires a south-facing surface on which to mount the dish.

5 Ask if high-definition (HD) programming is available—especially if you have an HDTV—and what it costs.

6 Check installation and per-room charges. If you have multiple televisions, you may need a cable or satellite box for each one.

7 Inquire about package deals. Cable companies sometimes offer broadband Internet service and cable TV packages at reduced prices (see 402 Choose an Internet Service Provider), and satellite TV companies have packages with digital video recorder (DVR) companies (see 424 Get a Digital Video Recorder).

What to Look For

- Hardware versus programming
- Channel packages
- Local channels
- Broadcast quality
- Per-room charges
- Broadband Internet packages
- Digital video recorder packages

Tips

The two major satellite TV providers in the United States use incompatible equipment. If you change services, you'll need to change the dish and box.

Apartment and condominium dwellers should check with their property manager about mounting satellite dishes on the building roof. You don't need the approval to mount a dish on a private balcony or patio.

424 Get a Digital Video Recorder

Digital video recorders (DVRs)—those mysterious black boxes with names such as TiVo, DirecTV DVR with TiVo, Sony Digital Network Recorder, UltimateTV and ReplayTV—have a devoted following for a reason: They let the viewer take control of the viewing. DVRs record TV programs onto a hard disk, rather than tape, so you can store, start, stop and erase them at the touch of a button.

Steps

1 Decide if you want a generic or subscription-based DVR. Generic models are programmed like a VCR: You choose the channel and the viewing time after looking up a show in the newspaper. Sub-scription-based DVRs have a user-friendly onscreen program guide, but you must pay a monthly or lifetime fee to use the services.

2 Choose between a monthly fee and a onetime charge if you decide on a subscription-based DVR. The onetime charge is a better deal in the long run; the service can be transferred to the new owner if you sell or give away the DVR.

3 Compare the features of each subscription-based DVR's program guide. With an interactive list of upcoming programs, it selects the shows you want to record by title, genre, actor or other fea-tures. Try the program guide at a store or a friend's house to see if it makes sense for your TV viewing.

4 Compare prices. Subscription-based DVRs run from $250 up to $1,000, depending on the size of the machine's hard disk. The subscription service can cost $200 to $400 (a onetime fee) or $6 to $15 per month. The lowest prices are available through pack-age deals with satellite or cable companies; see Step 8.

5 Decipher the remote. Pausing live TV, doing instant replays, fast-forwarding, or creating the David Hasselhoff Channel is fun only if you know how to work the remote.

6 Make sure you have a phone line available: Subscription-based DVRs regularly connect to their service provider to update their software and programming information. Some newer DVRs con-nect via the Internet if you have a broadband connection (the DVR uses your home network; see 404 Network Your Computers).

7 Get the most recording time you can afford. A gigabyte of disk space will store about an hour of programming at the lowest-quality recording; that same hour recorded at the highest quality will use about 4 gigabytes of storage. Most DVRs have four recording quality settings. The listed capacity (usually 40 and 80 hours but some go up to 160 hours) on a DVR is most likely at the lowest-quality setting.

8 Look into package deals. Some satellite and cable TV companies sell bundled TV service with DVRs at reduced subscription fees (see 423 Choose Between Cable and Satellite TV).

What to Look For

- Generic or subscription-based
- Monthly fee versus one-time charge
- Onscreen program guide
- Remote control
- Phone or broadband Internet connection
- Disk size
- Package deals with cable or satellite TV

Tips

DVRs are fast becoming Internet-enabled. On some models you can adjust your programming choices online; others let you share recorded videos over the Net.

You can copy programs from DVR to videotape—handy when your disk fills up (and it will).

If your entertainment center is tight for space, you can find combination DVR-DVD players on the market.

425 Get a Universal Remote

If the remote control for your TV has croaked—or if your collection of remotes is getting so big and confusing that only an 8-year-old can sort it out—it's time to shop for a universal remote. Chances are good that one device can handle all of your video and audio equipment and reduce the clutter on your coffee table.

Steps

1 List all the remote-control devices in your home. Note the type of device (CD player, TV, VCR) and the manufacturer.

2 Shop at a discount store if you want just a basic unit. These can cost as little as $10. Special universal remotes with large, colorful buttons are good choices for seniors, people with limited vision or other disabilities.

3 Go to an electronics store or shop online if you want something more powerful. Some remotes have LCD screens that change depending on the device you're controlling. Others are voice-activated. Prices can go as high as $500.

4 Consult your list to make sure the remote you choose will control all your components. The remote's package should have a chart specifying what brands and types of devices it will control.

5 Look for a device that lets you program macros if you want to simplify lots of complicated gear. Macros can perform several functions in sequence with the press of a single button. For example, a home-theater user might create a macro that turns on the TV, sets it to DVD, turns on the DVD player, turns on the amplifier, sets the volume to level 5, and opens the DVD tray. (See 426 Buy a Home Theater System.)

6 Home remote-control systems can also handle some functions of universal remotes. (See 419 Buy a Home Automation System.)

What to Look For

- Discount store
- Electronics store
- Online store
- Compatibility with your home-entertainment components
- Macro capability

Tips

If your needs are simple, see if the remote that came with your most recent audio or video purchase can be programmed to support multiple devices. You might save yourself a shopping trip.

Very high-end remotes can attach to a computer for programming.

426 Buy a Home Theater System

So now you've got a CD player, a DVD and digital video recorders (DVR), a plasma-screen TV, and a satellite dish. The perfect way to tie all these media components together is with a state-of-the-art home theater. Everything from low-end theaters-in-a-box to custom systems costing thousands of dollars is available. Here's how to create the ultimate private screening room.

Steps

1 Take stock of your current components. A home theater system connects video sources (DVD, VCR, DVR, and cable or satellite boxes), a TV or monitor, and a set of five or six speakers through a home theater receiver. Many people also plug audio components (CD and MP3 players) into their receiver. It may be that all you need is a receiver and speakers.

2 Look at your space. If you have a dedicated room for the home theater, get a more powerful system (measured in watts per channel). For a bedroom, 40 watts is plenty; 40 to 80 watts is good for an average-sized living room. Get at least an 80-watt receiver if you have a large room with high ceilings.

3 Buy a receiver with at minimum Digital Theater System (DTS) or Dolby Digital. (Dolby Digital and DTS are competing, incompatible formats for home theater sound. Check your DVDs—they're more likely to have Dolby Digital sound.) Avoid receivers with Dolby Surround or Dolby ProLogic unless they also have Dolby Digital. Dolby Digital EX and DTS-ES are the next step up; THX is the top of the line.

4 Check out the universal remote that comes with the receiver. You'll want to operate several components with this remote, so make sure it's easy to use and makes sense.

5 Listen carefully to the speakers when you shop. Six speakers make up the ideal home theater: left and right front-channel speakers, left and right surround speakers, a subwoofer, and a center-channel speaker. The center-channel speaker is probably the most important, since most movie dialogue comes from it. If you're watching the bottom line, forgo the subwoofer.

6 Consider theater-in-a-box systems if your space is average to small or you're technically challenged. Combining receiver, speakers and cables (and often a DVD player), these systems offer easy setup and operation as well as a smaller price tag. Read up on these systems online or in specialty magazines, since their quality ranges from surprisingly good to very bad.

What to Look For

- Home theater receiver
- DTS or Dolby Digital
- Universal remote
- Speakers, especially center channel
- Theater-in-a-box system

Tips

Got kids? Dolby Digital includes a feature for late-night viewing that plays dialogue and quiet scenes a little louder, and noisy scenes a little quieter.

Always hook up components by the connectors that provide the highest-quality signal. For video components, they are (in descending order) component-video, S-Video, composite-video, and antenna/cable inputs. For audio components, they are digital optical, coaxial, and RCA connectors.

427 Buy Virtual-Reality Furniture

You've got the biggest home theater, the best video screen, and the fastest game system out there. Take the leap and immerse yourself in the action with a virtual-reality chair or motion simulator. These systems employ a motion track electronically keyed to the movie's sound track and literally move you, giving new meaning to poetry in motion.

Steps

1 Get a handle on your budget. Choices range from $50 for seat cushions, to digitally controlled platforms (like that of Odyssee Motion Simulator) that cost in excess of $20,000 and rock the entire sofa.

2 Find out how the furniture connects to the entertainment system. Most virtual-reality chairs are made for video games but will also connect to the speaker jacks of home theater systems. Just make sure that the person in the chair isn't the only one who can hear the sound.

3 Choose a chair system if you play a lot of video games. Most of these look like high-tech office chairs. They contain an array of speakers to surround you with sound and shake your innards in sync with the game. (If that doesn't sound like fun, you may want to skip virtual-reality furniture all together.)

4 Rock your world with a sofa-shifting system. Consult with a home theater specialist, as these require lots of space, extra components for the home theater, and actuators that generate the motion under your furniture.

5 Use the system for a good hour before you buy—watch an entire movie or play your favorite game. This way, the initial surprise of the effect will wear off, and you can decide if it truly enhances your experience.

What to Look For

- Connections to entertainment system
- Virtual-reality chair systems
- Motion-generator sofa systems

Tips

Most virtual-reality furniture isn't available to try out at your local electronics store. That's unfortunate, since this is a product you want to try before you buy. If you buy online, make sure the seller has a good return policy.

Check out sites such as HighTechHomeTV.com for information on more impossibly cool equipment.

428 Buy Two-Way Radios

Taking the family to a playground, amusement park or campground and want to stay in contact? Look at Family Radio Service (FRS) or General Mobile Radio Service (GMRS) two-way radios. Boasting clearer sound, better range and more channels, these tough little units are a far cry from old walkie-talkies.

Steps

1 Look at your budget. If you want to save money and expect to use the radios over short range (less than two miles), choose FRS radios.

2 Choose GMRS radios—a newer type—if you need range up to five miles.

3 Apply for a Federal Communications Commission (FCC) license, which you'll need to use a GMRS radio. You'll need to complete FCC Forms 605 and 159 (Form 605 can be filed electronically at wireless.fcc.gov/uls/applications/).

4 Purchase multiple radios from the same manufacturer. Although all FRS and GMRS radios use the same frequencies, their other features (such as so-called privacy codes) don't always work between brands. GMRS radios share some channels with FRS radios. If you're replacing an FRS radio, buy a GMRS unit.

5 Take the range claims of two-way radios with a grain of salt. FRS purports to reach two miles and GMRS up to seven miles, but walls, hills, trees, people and almost anything else will reduce that range.

6 Look for a scanning function if you like to listen in on other people's conversations. A scanning radio will search across its channels for activity.

7 Pick units with a vibrating call feature if you need to remain quiet while you use them (during your clan's paintball war, for instance).

What to Look For

- FRS radios
- GMRS radios
- FCC license
- Scanning
- Vibrating call

Tip

You can add an external antenna to a GMRS radio, but not to an FRS radio.

Warnings

You can use FRS and GMRS radios in the United States, Mexico and Canada, but they're illegal in Europe.

Never say anything on a two-way radio that you wouldn't say in public. They're not secure lines.

429 Buy a Mobile Entertainment System

For better or worse, it seems that nowadays kids want to do more than count cows or play license-plate bingo on road trips. Fantastic mobile entertainment systems have high-quality video and Surround sound. Forget drive-ins—now movies are on the go.

Steps

1 Look at what you can afford. Mobile entertainment gear ranges from simple, portable units that sit between the seats and plug into the cigarette lighter, to full-blown in-car theater systems (from $100 to $3,000 and more).

2 Decide between videocassette or DVD units. Most people will want to future-proof their purchase by choosing DVD players.

3 Buy an all-in-one unit or individual components if your budget is small (under $250) and your needs are simple. An all-in-one unit includes a videocassette player (VCP) or a DVD player, speaker and screen. Many electronics retailers carry them.

4 Choose a component system ($400 and up) where a single video source can run several screens, usually liquid-crystal displays (LCDs). The screens can pop out of the dashboard, drop down from the car's ceiling or mount in headrests. Component systems tap into your vehicle's stereo and pipe sound directly to headphones for quiet viewing. Most high-end car stereo retailers carry these systems.

5 Make sure any component system is expandable, so you can add more or different screens and input devices in the future.

6 Get a double-antenna system, known as a *diversity antenna*, for better TV reception when the car is moving.

7 Make sure your vehicle's electrical system can handle the demands of a mobile entertainment system. You may need a professional installer to determine this.

8 Large SUVs, vans and recreational vehicles can incorporate a backup camera into the mobile video setup.

What to Look For

- Videocassette versus DVD
- All-in-one versus components
- LCD screens
- Audio connections
- Expandability
- Diversity antenna
- Backup camera

Tips

A laptop computer with a DVD drive can serve as an entertainment system for smaller cars with one viewer.

Mobile entertainment systems are theft targets. Invest in a good car alarm. (See 546 Buy a Theft-Prevention Device.)

Warning

In most areas, front-seat viewing is illegal, not to mention idiotic, while a car is in motion.

REHOUSE STORES • BUY WHOLESALE • GET OUT OF DEBT • BUY NOTHING • BUY HAPPINESS • BUY A BETTER MOUSETRAP • BUY TIME
MEONE'S FAVOR • BUY POSTAGE STAMPS WITHOUT GOING TO THE POST OFFICE • TIP PROPERLY • BUY HEALTHY FAST FOOD • BUY SUN
'ING SERVICE • SELL YOURSELF ON AN ONLINE DATING SERVICE • SELL YOURSELF TO YOUR GIRLFRIEND/BOYFRIEND'S FAMILY • BUY DC
OOSE FILM FOR YOUR CAMERA • BUY RECHARGEABLE BATTERIES • DONATE TO A GOOD CAUSE • HOLD A PROFITABLE GARAGE SALE •
JDENT DISCOUNTS • BUY FLOWERS WHOLESALE • GET A PICTURE FRAMED • HIRE A MOVER • HIRE A PERSONAL ORGANIZER • FIND A VI
THDAY PRESENT FOR UNDER $10 • SELECT GOOD CHAMPAGNE • BUY A DIAMOND • BUY JEWELRY MADE OF PRECIOUS METALS • BUY C
DESMAIDS' DRESSES • HIRE AN EVENT COORDINATOR • HIRE A BARTENDER FOR A PARTY • HIRE A PHOTOGRAPHER • HIRE A CATERER •
Y AN ANNIVERSARY GIFT • ARRANGE ENTERTAINMENT FOR A PARTY • COMMISSION A FIREWORKS SHOW • BUY A MOTHER'S DAY GIFT •
ELECT A THANKSGIVING TURKEY • BUY A HOUSEWARMING GIFT • PURCHASE HOLIDAY CARDS • BUY CHRISTMAS STOCKING STUFFERS
5H ROLLERS ROOM IN VEGAS, BABY • BUY SOMEONE A STAR • PAY A RANSOM • GET HOT TICKETS • HIRE A LIMOUSINE • BUY A CRYONI
UY A PERSONAL JET • ACQUIRE A TELEVISION NETWORK • ACQUIRE A BODY GUARD • BOOK A LUXURY CRUISE AROUND THE WORLD • 5
OROUGHBRED RACEHORSE • BUY A VILLA IN TUSCANY • HIRE A PERSONAL CHEF • PURCHASE CUBAN CIGARS • HIRE A GHOSTWRITER
'NESS • MAKE BAIL • DONATE YOUR BODY TO SCIENCE • HIRE YOURSELF OUT AS A MEDICAL GUINEA PIG • SELL PLASMA • SELL YOUR
LLEGE EDUCATION • BUY AND SELL STOCKS • CHOOSE A STOCKBROKER • DAY-TRADE (OR NOT) • BUY ANNUITIES • BUY AND SELL MUT
RSONAL FINANCE SOFTWARE • CHOOSE A TAX PREPARER • SET UP A LEMONADE STAND • SELL YOUR PRODUCT ON TV • HIRE A CAREE
UY A SMALL BUSINESS • BUY A FRANCHISE • LEASE RETAIL SPACE • LEASE INDUSTRIAL SPACE • LEASE OFFICE SPACE • BUY LIQUIDATE
VERTISING ON THE WEB • SELL YOUR ART • HIRE A PERSONAL COACH • SELL ON THE CRAFT CIRCUIT • HIRE A LITERARY AGENT • PITCH
Y A HOT DOG STAND • SHOP FOR A MORTGAGE • REFINANCE YOUR HOME • SAVE BIG BUCKS ON YOUR MORTGAGE • OBTAIN HOME OV
LL THE FARM • SELL MINERAL RIGHTS • SELL A HOUSE • SELL A HOUSE WITHOUT A REAL ESTATE AGENT • OBTAIN A HOME EQUITY LOA
Y A CONDOMINIUM • RENT AN APARTMENT OR HOUSE • OBTAIN RENTER'S INSURANCE • BUY A LOFT IN MANHATTAN • BUY A TENANCY
ARTMENT • BUY USED FURNITURE • BUY DOOR AND WINDOW LOCKS • CHOOSE AN ORIENTAL CARPET • BUY LAMPS AND LIGHT FIXTUR
PLIANCES • FIND PERIOD FIXTURES • BUY A BED AND MATTRESS • HIRE AN INTERIOR DESIGNER • HIRE A FENG SHUI CONSULTANT • INC
HIRLPOOL TUB • BUY A SHOWERHEAD • BUY A TOILET • CHOOSE A FAUCET • BUY GLUES AND ADHESIVES • CHOOSE WINDOW TREATME
OOSE A KITCHEN COUNTERTOP • BUY GREEN HOUSEHOLD CLEANERS • STOCK YOUR HOME TOOL KIT • BUY A VIDEO SECURITY SYSTE
GARAGE-DOOR OPENER • BUY LUMBER FOR A DIY PROJECT • HOW TO SELECT ROOFING • HIRE A CONTRACTOR, PLUMBER, PAINTER O
ELECT PEST CONTROLS • BUY SOIL AMENDMENTS • BUY MULCH • BUY A COMPOSTER • BUY FERTILIZER • START A VEGETABLE GARDE
Y A STORAGE SHED • HIRE AN ARBORIST • BUY BASIC GARDEN TOOLS • BUY SHRUBS AND TREES • BUY A HOT TUB • BUY AN OUTDO
OD LABELS • SELECT HERBS AND SPICES • STOCK YOUR KITCHEN WITH STAPLES • EQUIP A KITCHEN • CHOOSE FRESH PRODUCE • SE
NEY • CHOOSE POULTRY • SELECT FRESH FISH AND SHELLFISH • SELECT RICE • PURCHASE PREMIUM SALT AND PEPPER • GET A CHE
RCHASE KOSHER FOOD • BUY FOOD IN BULK • CHOOSE COOKING OILS • SELECT OLIVE OIL • SELECT OLIVES • BUY ETHNIC INGREDIE
RCHASE A KEG OF BEER • BUY ALCOHOL IN A DRY COUNTY • CHOOSE A MICROBREW • ORDER A COCKTAIL • CHOOSE A RESTAURANT
EGNANCY TEST KIT • CHOOSE BIRTH CONTROL • FIND THE RIGHT OB-GYN • HIRE A MIDWIFE OR DOULA • FIND A GOOD PEDIATRICIAN
EAST PUMP • CHOOSE A CAR SEAT • BUY CHILD-PROOFING SUPPLIES • FIND FABULOUS CHILDCARE • FIND A GREAT NANNY • FIND TH
MMER CAMP • SELL GIRL SCOUT COOKIES • BUY BRACES FOR YOUR KID • BUY TOYS • BUY BOOKS, VIDEOS AND MUSIC FOR YOUR
OTHES AND BOOKS • FIND A COUPLES COUNSELOR • HIRE A FAMILY LAWYER • BUY PROPERTY IN A RETIREMENT COMMUNITY • CHOO
OTHBRUSH • BUY MOISTURIZERS AND ANTIWRINKLE CREAMS • SELECT PAIN RELIEF AND COLD MEDICINES • SAVE MONEY ON PRESC
AYS TO COUNTER HAIR LOSS • BUY A WIG OR HAIRPIECE • BUY A NEW BODY • GET A TATTOO OR BODY PIERCING • OBTAIN BREAST IM
EGLASSES AND SUNGLASSES • HIRE A PERSONAL TRAINER • SIGN UP FOR A YOGA CLASS • TREAT YOURSELF TO A DAY AT THE SPA •
ALL • BUY AT AUCTION • KNOW WHAT YOUR COLLECTIBLES ARE WORTH • DICKER WITH DEALERS • GET AN ANTIQUE APPRAISED • BUY
IY AN ANTIQUE AMERICAN QUILT • BUY AN ANTIQUE FLAG • LIQUIDATE YOUR BEANIE BABY COLLECTION • SCORE AUTOGRAPHS • TRA
IY AND SELL SPORTS MEMORABILIA • SELL YOUR BASEBALL-CARD COLLECTIONS • CHOOSE A DESKTOP COMPUTER • SHOP FOR A US
IY COMPUTER PERIPHERALS • CHOOSE AN INTERNET SERVICE PROVIDER • GET AN INTERNET DOMAIN NAME • BUY A HOME NETWORK
AYER • BUY A VCR • CHOOSE A PERSONAL DIGITAL ASSISTANT • CHOOSE MOBILE PHONE SERVICE • NEGOTIATE YOUR LONG-DISTANC
OME AUTOMATION SYSTEM • BUY A STATE-OF-THE-ART SOUND SYSTEM • BUY AN AUDIO-VIDEO DISTRIBUTION SYSTEM • BUY A SERIO
RTUAL-REALITY FURNITURE • BUY TWO-WAY RADIOS • BUY A MOBILE ENTERTAINMENT SYSTEM • GET A PASSPORT, QUICK! • PURCHAS
OR FREE • BID FOR A SLED RIDE ON THE ALASKAN IDITAROD TRAIL RACE • BUY DUTY-FREE • SHIP FOREIGN PURCHASES TO THE UNITE
CATION • CHOOSE A CHEAP CRUISE • BOOK A HOTEL PACKAGE FOR THE GREEK ISLANDS • RAFT THE GRAND CANYON • BOOK A CHE
KE SALSA LESSONS IN CUBA • BUY A CAMERA IN HONG KONG • BUY YOUR WAY ONTO A MOUNT EVEREST EXPEDITION • HIRE A TREK
JKLE AND KNEE BRACES • BUY GOLF CLUBS • JOIN AN ELITE GOLF CLUB • SELL FOUND GOLF BALLS • BUY ATHLETIC SHOES • BUY A
BUY A SKATEBOARD AND PROTECTIVE GEAR • BUY SKATES • GO SPORT FISHING • GO SKYDIVING • BUY WEIGHTLIFTING EQUIPMENT •
JY SKI BOOTS • BUY A BICYCLE • SELL YOUR BICYCLE AT A GARAGE SALE • COMMISSION A CUSTOM-BUILT BICYCLE • BUY A PROPEP
OTATION DEVICE • BUY A WET SUIT • BUY A SURFBOARD • BUY FLY-FISHING GEAR • BUY ROCK-CLIMBING EQUIPMENT • BUY A CASH
ZES • BUY THE PERFECT COCKTAIL DRESS • BUY DESIGNER CLOTHES AT A DISCOUNT • CHOOSE A BASIC WARDROBE FOR A MAN • B
RIEFCASE • SHOP FOR A LEATHER JACKET • BUY MATERNITY CLOTHES • GET A GREAT-FITTING BRA • CHOOSE A HIGH-PERFORMANCE
JRCHASE CLOTHES AT OUTLET SHOPS • BUY A NEW CAR • BUY THE BASICS FOR YOUR CAR • BUY A USED CAR • BUY OR SELL A CAF

Travel

430 Get a Passport, Quick!

You've just been invited on an all-expenses-paid trip to Europe, but the departure date is next week and your passport expired last year. Egad! What to do?

Steps

1 Get two identical 2-by-2-inch (5-by-5-cm) passport photos. Look under "Passport Photos" in the Yellow Pages for the nearest instant-photo service.

2 Locate the nearest passport office. Look under "Passports" in the "U.S. Government Offices" section of your phone book. You can also call the National Passport Information Center at (900) 225-5674 or log onto the U.S. State Department's passport Web site (travel.state.gov/passport_services.html) and click on "Where to Apply for a Passport Nationwide." To save even more time, download a passport application from the site.

3 Make a special appointment by calling the passport office if you're leaving in less than 14 days. If you're leaving within six business days, skip the appointment and head to the nearest passport office immediately and take along your airline tickets or airline-generated itinerary to prove your need for speed. Bring the photos and your old passport—or, if you don't have one, your birth certificate and valid driver's license. For each application, in addition to the standard fee (see travel.state.gov/newfees.html), you will need to pay a $60 fee for expedited service plus fees for two-way overnight mail.

4 Go to one of the 5,000 passport acceptance facilities nationwide if your departure is within 7 to 10 business days. Such facilities include federal, state and probate courts; post offices; libraries; and county and municipal offices. Pay the extra $60 expedited-service fee and provide a self-addressed, prepaid, two-way overnight delivery envelope that's clearly marked "Expedited." If you're departing in less than seven days, drive to the nearest passport office and get in line.

5 Make a copy of your passport's identification page along with two passport-size photos and bring them with you, in case you need to apply for an emergency passport replacement while traveling abroad. If you lose your passport, visit the nearest U.S. consulate as soon as possible for a replacement.

What to Look For

- Passport photos
- Nearest passport office
- Airline tickets or itinerary
- Expired passport
- Additional fees

Tips

You can get passport forms from any passport agency or acceptance facility. Many travel agents stock application forms as well.

Always include your departure date and travel plans on your passport application.

Some countries require that your passport be valid at least six months beyond the dates of your trip.

The U.S. State Department (travel.state.gov/foreignentry reqs.html) has a country-by-country listing of visa and passport requirements.

Warning

You must always apply in person if (1) you are 13 years or older and applying for a U.S. passport for the first time; (2) your passport was lost or stolen; or (3) your previous passport has expired and was issued more than 12 years ago.

431 Purchase Cheap Airline Tickets

Passengers on the same flight rarely pay the same price for their tickets. Numerous factors determine ticket prices, but the surest way to get the best deal is to be thorough, be flexible and know where to shop.

Steps

1 Be thorough. Don't rely just on travel Web sites for the best deal; call airlines and travel agents, and ask about promotional or special fares. Look for Internet specials on Web sites of smaller airlines such as Southwest Airlines (southwest.com), JetBlue Airways (jetblue.com), Ryanair (ryanair.com), AirTran Airways (airtran.com) and WestJet (westjet.com). Also browse your local Sunday newspaper's travel section and major travel magazines.

2 Be flexible. Avoid peak vacation months and holidays, buy as far in advance as possible, fly midweek and off-hours, and stay over Saturday night. Better yet, put your vacation on stand by until a fare war erupts.

3 Research all the major online travel agencies such as Orbitz.com, Expedia.com, Travelocity.com and lastminute.com. Each has a unique arrangement with the airlines and may offer different fares on the same flights. Each site also offers numerous package deals and last-minute bargains that change daily.

4 Book your flight as part of a travel package that includes car rental and hotel accommodations. Such deals are sold in bulk to tour operators who resell them to the public at prices that are usually far less than standard à la carte rates. Most major airlines offer their own vacation packages, such as United Vacations (unitedvacations.com).

5 Consider the name-your-own-price ticket providers such as priceline.com and Hotwire.com. You can save up to 40 percent over the lowest published airfares, but it's not without risk: The exact airline, flight times and routes are not disclosed to you until after you've purchased your tickets: think red-eye and layovers.

6 Purchase from a consolidator—a wholesaler that buys discount tickets in bulk. It's an excellent resource for cheap international tickets. The Sunday travel section of the *New York Times* and *Los Angeles Times* are the best sources for consolidator fares, but they're often nonrefundable or have brutal cancellation penalties.

7 Look into courier flights, where companies hire a courier (you) and use your excess baggage allowance for their time-sensitive business cargo (see 436 Fly for Free).

What to Look For

- Promotional discount fares
- Small and regional airlines
- Fare wars
- Package deals
- Last-minute bargains
- Vacation packages
- Internet rates
- Consolidators
- Courier flights

Tips

Many charter operators sell their discount vacation packages only through travel agents, so don't rely solely on Web-based fares.

Last-minute airfare specials are often available through free weekly e-mail announcements from airlines. They're usually announced on Tuesday or Wednesday for travel that Saturday, and tickets must be purchased online.

Try to book a ticket in its country of origin. For instance, if you're planning a one-way flight from Paris to Rome, a France-based travel agency will probably offer the lowest fares.

Warning

Lowest-price fares often require one to three weeks' advance purchase, are non-refundable, require a certain length of stay, and carry stiff penalties for changing dates and destinations.

432 **Find Great Hotel Deals**

To find a deal on a hotel room, be thorough, be flexible, and know where to look and what to ask. The steepest price a hotel charges for a room is the *rack rate* (the hotel's standard price for a room sans discounts), and your goal is to get well below that inflated figure with package deals, off-season rates and savvy bargaining.

Steps

1 Plan your vacation well in advance and during the off-season, or midweek when hotel rates are far cheaper—up to 50 percent—due to less demand. Call the hotel and ask for the exact day its off-season rates start. Timing is everything.

2 Call the hotel and ask about package deals, promotions and special discounts for seniors, military, students, corporations or American Automobile Association (aaa.com) members. When you're quoted a rate, ask if less expensive rooms are available.

3 Book your room via the Web: Many hotels offer discounts for commission-free online transactions. Major online agencies, such as HotelDiscounts.com, Hotels.com, Orbitz.com, Expedia.com and Travelocity.com, have special arrangements with thousands of hotels, offering room rates you can't get on your own.

4 Ask if kids stay free if you're traveling with your family. Find out if the rooms have kitchens or kitchenettes—you'll save a bundle by preparing your own meals.

5 If you're very flexible about the type and location of a hotel, let name-your-own-price online travel agencies such as Priceline.com and Hotwire.com do the haggling for you. You save up to 40 percent on published room rates, but there's a catch: The hotel, room, neighborhood and rate are not disclosed to you until after your room is already charged to your credit card (however, they usually come pretty close to meeting your requests).

What to Look For

- Off-season rates
- Package deals
- Special discounts
- Internet rates
- Family rates
- Online travel agencies

Tip

If you're staying at a hotel longer than seven days, haggle for one free night per week or ask about weekly rates.

Warning

Beware of hidden costs. Taxes, surcharges, resort fees and "incidental" fees tacked on to your bill are common and rarely mentioned until you check out, so be sure to ask if there are *any* extras charges on the agreed room rate. If they are tacked on without your prior approval, refuse to pay them.

433 **Rent the Best Car for the Least Money**

Nearly 100,000 rental cars in the United States go unused every day—a good reason to drive a hard bargain. Car reservation agents rarely volunteer money-saving suggestions, but if you follow this advice, you could save hundreds on your next car rental.

Steps

1 Make a reservation online through one of the major car rental companies. It's by far the easiest and cheapest way to rent a car either locally or internationally. Just about every car rental Web site offers Internet-only discounts (about 10 percent) and upgrades as well as various special offers.

What to Look For

- Internet discounts
- Upgrades
- Online travel agencies
- Package deals
- Special discounts

2 Rent through a name-your-own-price online travel agency such as priceline.com or Hotwire.com, particularly if you're not choosy about the car. These agencies will get the best deals with the car rental companies for you, including upgrades and unlimited mileage. Note: Once your request is accepted, you can't cancel or change your reservation or get a refund.

3 Search for package deals. Fly-drive-stay vacation packages offer huge discounts on car rentals. Many online travel agencies also offer fly-drive discounts as well. Avoid reserving a rental car through an airline. It's convenient, but you rarely get the best deal.

4 Ask for more discounts that may apply to you, even when you think you've scored the best deal: AAA, AARP, frequent-flier programs and military service are just a few of the many special discounts that car rental companies may honor.

Tip

Always fill the gas tank before you return a car or you'll get tagged with a service charge to have the rental company fill it for you—at an inflated price per gallon.

Warning

If you don't have auto insurance, you'll need to buy it from the rental company.

434 Get Travel Insurance

Travel insurance is a combination of trip-cancellation insurance and 24-hour emergency assistance. It helps you get your money back if, for example, you have to cancel your vacation or go home early. It's a smart purchase if you've planned a major vacation well in advance, but the trick is knowing which policy to buy, if any.

Steps

1 Check your existing insurance policies and credit card coverage before you buy travel insurance. You may already be covered for medical expenses, canceled tickets or lost luggage.

2 Decide which type of travel insurance is best suited for your destination (for example, terrorism insurance for your trip to Egypt, or emergency medical transportation insurance during your ocean cruise). Keep in mind that the cost varies widely, depending on your age, your health, and the cost and length of your trip.

3 Determine whether the following is included in your policy: international medical insurance, emergency medical evacuation (including helicopter transport), accidental death and dismemberment, repatriation of remains, and family travel benefits.

4 Have your travel agent purchase an insurance plan for you or shop commission-free online. You'll find a wide selection of reputable insurance companies on the Web, including TravelGuard.com and AccessAmerica.com, that can get you a policy within 24 hours.

5 Make sure your travel insurance provider offers 24-hour hotline service. Don't buy trip-cancellation insurance from the tour operator that may be responsible for the cancellation, and don't over-buy—you won't be reimbursed for more than the cost of your trip.

What to Look For

- Baggage loss/delay insurance
- International medical insurance
- Emergency medical evacuation
- Accidental death and dismemberment
- Repatriation of remains
- Family travel benefits
- 24-hour hotline service

Tip

Many travel-related injuries and thefts are not fully covered by your credit card company, home owners or medical insurance.

Warning

Read the fine print to make sure your cruise line or airline is on the list of carriers covered in case of bankruptcy.

435 Pick the Ideal Luggage

Few things are more worthless and frustrating than a cheap piece of luggage that falls apart during your vacation. Ergo, it's crucial to invest in quality luggage that can withstand a baggage handler's bad day. Somewhere out there is your dream luggage set.

Steps

1 Consider where you're going and what you're packing before you shop for new luggage. This will determine the quantity and size of luggage you'll need.

2 Determine your budget before you shop. This will help steer you in the direction of quality luggage brands you can afford. A reputable luggage store that specializes in all types of luggage will give you advice based on your budget and travel needs.

4 Decide whether you want soft or hard-case luggage. Heavier, hard-sided suitcases offer far better protection for fragile items (if packed properly). Soft luggage is lighter.

5 If you choose a roller model, look for heavy-duty wheels (some have durable in-line skate wheels) and a sturdy base.

6 When buying soft luggage, check the *denier* of a fabric, a measurement that refers to the fineness of the yarn. Generally speaking, the higher the denier the more durable the fabric.

7 Look for a quality zipper that's heavy-duty enough to support the weight the bag was designed to hold. (Top of the line zippers are YKKs.) Critical seams and attachment points for webbing should be bar-tacked.

8 Make sure the bags fits airlines' approved carry-on size. Most bags within the 24 x 14 x 9–inch (61 x 35.5 x 23–cm) size restriction is considered legal on all planes.

9 Choose a size that's appropriate for the length of your trip. Keep in mind the possibility of needing to accommodate unexpected items or expand for a longer trip.

What to Look For

- Prices in your budget
- Reputable luggage store
- Soft case or hard case
- Heavy-duty wheels
- Expandability
- Denier of fabric
- Appropriate sizes

Tips

Look for luggage that isn't too heavy to carry long distances. For larger suitcases, a difference of 5 lbs. (1.9 kg) or less doesn't matter much in the overall weight of a fully packed bag.

Consider a color other than black. Brightly colored luggage stands out better on the airport carousel.

The majority of airlines allow bags up to 40 lbs. (14.9 kg).

Warnings

Is the pullout handle protected? It won't work if the shaft gets bent.

If you unintentionally buy a knockoff, the warranty is also fake.

LENGTH OF TRIP	SUGGESTED LUGGAGE SIZE
1 to 3 days	22-inch (56-cm) upright-wheeled carry-on
3 to 7 days	24-inch (6l-cm) upright case
7 to 14 days	26- to 27-inch (66- to 69-cm) upright case
14 to 21 days or longer	29- to 30-inch (74- to 76-cm) upright case

436 Fly for Free

Aching for an exotic vacation but short on funds? Drastically discounted or free fares can be yours if you're willing to pack light, travel solo and work for a courier. Complete a few simple tasks, save yourself hundreds of dollars—and collect frequent-flier miles to boot!

Steps

1 Decide where and when you'd like to go, but be sure to choose a destination outside of North America. There are no courier flights within North America.

2 Find a courier company by looking in the Yellow Pages under "Air Courier Services," "Air Transportation" or "Courier, Air Travel."

3 Be prepared to offer a $500 deposit that will be returned to you a couple of weeks after the completion of the trip.

4 Make your reservation through the courier company's travel agent. Call the airline a few days in advance of your flight to verify your reservation and request a seat assignment.

5 Pack sparingly. You can only take carry-on baggage since your check-in space will be used for the company parcel.

6 Upon arrival, carry out your agreed-upon responsibilities, such as delivering a manifest to a representative at the destination and completing paperwork.

What to Look For

- Destinations beyond North America
- Reputable courier companies
- Carry-on bag

Tips

Couriers must join a courier organization such as the International Association of Air Travel Couriers. You can contact other couriers for referrals via Courier.org.

Ask about earning frequent-flier miles.

There is only one courier seat per flight.

437 Bid for a Sled Ride on the Alaskan Iditarod Trail Race

If you don't have what it takes to single-handedly race 16 dogs across 1,000-plus miles of frozen tundra for almost two weeks, you can enter the Iditarod as an Idita-Rider. Each year the race committee auctions off an exclusive ride in the sled basket of an Iditarod musher for the first 11 miles (17.7 km) through the snowy streets of Anchorage.

Steps

1 Log onto the official Iditarod Web site (iditarod.com), read the Idita-Rider rules on bidding, and mail or fax your completed form to the Iditarod headquarters. Bidding typically starts on November 1 and ends on January 24.

2 Place a bid in the general pool for better odds. All initial bids must be at least $500, and the minimum amount by which an existing bid may be increased is $100.

3 Attend the mandatory Idita-Rider meeting at the Millennium Alaska Hotel, usually the day before the race. The 30-minute session with a dog team will teach you how to get in and out of the sled—and how to hang on for dear life.

What to Look For

- Bid form at Iditarod Web site
- $500 minimum bid
- Mandatory Idita-Rider meeting
- White-knuckle ride

Warning

The uber-hyper and powerful sled dogs are difficult to control on the narrow city course—it's not uncommon for a musher to lose control of his or her sled.

438 Buy Duty-free

Duty-free goods are sold wherever international travel takes place: in airports, in-flight between two countries, aboard ships at sea, at international land border crossings—even on the Internet. It's easy to save on the world's most common vices: alcohol and tobacco.

DESTINATION	LIQUOR LIMIT	TOBACCO LIMIT
Argentina	2 liters	2 cartons and 25 cigars
Australia	1 liter	1 carton or 50 cigars
Belgium	1 liter	1 carton or 50 cigars
Brazil	2 liters	Goods up to $500
Canada	1 liter	1 carton or 50 cigars
Chile	2.5 liters	2 cartons and 50 cigars
China	2 bottles	2 cartons or 100 cigars
France	1 liter	1 carton or 50 cigars
Germany	1 liter	1 carton or 50 cigars
Greece	1 liter	2 cartons or 100 cigars*
Hong Kong	1 liter	1 carton or 50 cigars**
India	1 liter	1 carton or 50 cigars
Italy	1 liter	2 cartons or 100 cigars*
Japan	3 bottles	2 cartons and 100 cigars***
New Zealand	1 liter	1 carton or 50 cigars
Philippines	2 liters	1 carton or 50 cigars****
Singapore	1 liter	Not applicable
South Korea	1 liter	1 carton or 50 cigars
Spain	1 liter	1 carton or 50 cigars
Switzerland	1 liter	2 cartons or 100 cigars*
Taiwan	1 bottle	1 carton or 25 cigars
Thailand	1 liter	1 carton or 50 cigars
United Kingdom	1 liter	1 carton or 50 cigars
United States	1 liter (33.8 oz.)	1 carton or 50 cigars*****
Venezuela	2 liters	1 carton or 25 cigars
WARNING	Be sure to stay within the allowance limits set by the country you're heading to next and keep a lid on your purchases—or you might have some explaining to do at customs.	

*   For residents of Europe, half this amount.

**   For residents of Hong Kong, 100 cigarettes or 25 cigars.

***   For residents of Japan, 1 carton of foreign cigarettes or 50 cigars and 1 carton of Japanese cigarettes.

****   For residents of the Philippines, 100 cigarettes.

*****   For residents of the United States, goods up to $800.

439 Ship Foreign Purchases to the United States

Byzantine might be the best word to describe the process of shipping purchases to the United States. Every country has its own confusing set of shipping regulations, and then you have to factor in U.S. duty, taxes and customs fees. Cramming that sucker in your luggage is your best bet; otherwise, follow these steps and hope for the best.

Steps

1 Wrap your purchase as carefully as possible to avoid breakage. Next, along with the mailing address (don't forget to write *U.S.A.* below the ZIP code), mark the outer wrapping with (1) the contents' identity, (2) the fair retail value and (3) whether the package is for personal use or a gift (this determines the exemption limit).

2 Ship the purchase via the nearest postal exchange. International shipping companies such as Federal Express (gofedex.com) and UPS (ups.com) are available in most countries (check before you leave the States), but you pay a steep premium for their services. Be sure to inquire about insurance for valuable items.

3 Be prepared to pay a duty fee for your package when you return home. The U.S. Postal Service (USPS.gov) sends all foreign mail shipments to the U.S. Customs Service for examination. Customs then returns packages that don't require duty to the USPS, which sends them back to the post office for delivery without any additional fees.

4 If the package does require duty fees, a customs agent attaches a *mail entry* form (Form CF-3419A, which shows how much duty is owed) and charges a processing fee. The USPS then delivers the package to you, charging both the customs fees and a separate handling fee.

5 Keep all receipts for items you buy overseas: You might need them to solve potential problems with customs. If you feel you've been charged too much duty on a package mailed from abroad, you may file a protest with the U.S. Customs Service.

6 Be aware that items mailed to the United States are not included in your personal U.S. Customs exemption. Express mail companies usually take care of clearing your merchandise through U.S. Customs but charge a fee for that service.

What to Look For

- Duty exemption limits
- Postal exchange or shipping company
- Insurance
- Duty fees upon return
- Additional taxes

Tips

American embassies and consulates abroad cannot forward, accept or hold mail for U.S. citizens abroad.

Some European countries waive the Value Added Tax (VAT) on items that you ship home.

Warnings

Be especially careful when shipping wildlife souvenirs (possibly illegal), and antiques that could be construed as national treasures. At best you could be detained and fined; at worst, arrested.

Beware: No matter what a foreign postal employee or store owner may tell you, you cannot prepay duty fees.

440 Tip in a Foreign Country

When you're abroad, tipping can be a perplexing experience: In some countries it's expected, in others it's an insult—and the rules are constantly changing. As corporate mentality replaces traditional ideology (that the honor of providing hospitality is reward itself), tipping etiquette has become more mainstream.

COUNTRY	GRATUITY PROTOCOL
Australia and New Zealand	Round up taxi fares and restaurant bills to nearest dollar.
Austria	Service charges generally included in bill.
Britain and Ireland	Service charges usually included in restaurant bills; otherwise, standard U.S. tipping rules apply.
China and North Korea	Tipping is illegal.
Czech Republic	Round up the bill to nearest koruna.
France and Germany	Service charges generally applied to bills; customary to add 5 percent extra.
Hong Kong	Tipping is common—about 10 percent in most situations—even when a service charge has already been applied.
Hungary	10 percent tip is customary.
Indonesia	Service charges are usually included in bill.
Israel	Restaurants and hotels typically add 10 percent service charge to bills; otherwise, tipping not expected.
Italy	Tipping is customary, about 10 percent, even when a service charge is already included.
Japan	Tips are usually included in hotel and restaurant bills; otherwise, tipping is not expected.
Malaysia	Tipping is expected for porters and room service.
Mexico	Tipping is customary, about 10 to 15 percent. Service charges rarely applied.
Philippines	10 percent tip is common for most services.
South Korea	Tipping is not expected.
Spain	Offer a 10 to 15 percent tip even when service charges have been added.
WARNING	Double-check the tipping protocol at South Pacific and Asian hotels. Many prohibit tipping to prevent staff from hustling guests for money.

441 Tip Properly in North America

One of the most common questions asked by vacationers is "How much should I tip?" The answer is complex when you consider various protocols around the world, but general rules do apply here at home. Commit these tipping tips to memory to avoid getting fleeced or forgotten.

Steps

1 Don't tip if it's not deserved. You're essentially buying good service, and if it's not earned it shouldn't be rewarded. You're only promoting poor service habits and wasting money.

2 Tip above the norm for two reasons: if service is exceptional, and if you plan on returning to the hotel or restaurant in the future. Big tippers are rarely forgotten by the staff.

3 Tip discreetly. There's an art to passing money: Fold the bill three times, cup it in your palm with your thumb, and hand it to the staff member with a casual handshake while saying, "Thank you."

4 Tip big when first checking into a hotel to assure better service throughout your stay.

Tips

When in doubt, tip. Failure to tip—or not tipping enough—can have dire consequences to your vacation, from lost luggage to molasses-slow restaurant and room service.

See 24 Tip Properly, and 440 Tip in a Foreign Country.

SERVICE	TIPPING CONVENTION
Airport Porters	$1 per bag for normal sizes, $2 per bag for large or heavy items.
Chauffeurs	10 to 15 percent of fare.
Coat Check	$2 to $5 upon retrieval.
Concierges or Guest Services Representatives	$10 to $20 depending on the complexity of the service—theater tickets, restaurant reservations, tour bookings, last-minute arrangements.
Hotel Door Persons	$2 for summoning a taxi by phone, $1 for hailing from street, $2 to $5 if they opened the door for you each time you entered and left the hotel.
Hotel Porters	$1 to $2 per bag, $5 minimum.
Housekeeping Staff	$2 to $5 per night, paid daily or as a sum at checkout.
Parking Valets	$2 to $5 for parking and delivery.
Restaurant and Bar Service	15 to 20 percent of the total tab.
Room Service	$5 minimum.
Taxicabs and Hotel Courtesy Cars	10 percent of fare, $2 to $5 minimum depending on service. Add $1 per bag placed in trunk.

442 Bribe a Foreign Official

Take a shortcut through a minefield, and you'll either get where you're headed sooner or end up wishing you'd never left home. Bribing an official is a lot like that. In many third-world countries an unofficial travel "tax" is de rigueur. Although every bribery situation is unique, there are a few universal rules you'll want to follow to successfully negotiate a mutual agreement.

Steps

1 Verify that bribery is customary in the country you'll be traveling through. The X-rated magazine you proffered up to get you past a Mexican army checkpoint would get you imprisoned in a communist country. Travel guidebooks are typically good sources of information about dealing with foreign officials.

2 Determine who is in charge before offering a bribe. If you deal with anyone other than the superior, you may offend him and create a face-losing confrontation. Be extremely careful not to insult or upset anyone.

3 Identify exactly what the problem is. If you're in violation of some law, ask to pay the fine on the spot. If you're carrying something they want, offer some of it. Your ultimate goal is to agree with the official on both the problem and a mutually beneficial solution.

4 Offer a legitimate explanation for the bribery to put a veneer of legality to the situation. For example, say that you're afraid the fine will get lost in the mail and that you'd rather pay the proper authorities right now. The way in which you offer a bribe is sometimes more important than the bribe itself.

What to Look For

- Local bribery traditions
- The official in charge
- Exact problem
- Speedy solution
- Legitimate explanation

Tip

Carry small amounts of U.S. currency to offer as bribes. Offer cash first, then other items.

Warning

Only reveal the amount of money you're willing to part with. If you show the official $500, the fine will most likely be $500. Hide the bulk of your money along with all valuable personal items.

443 Get a Eurail Pass

A Eurail Pass lets you travel like a local to almost every corner of Europe—17 countries, to be exact. The problem is figuring out which of dozens of Eurail Pass options best suits your travel plans.

Steps

1 Decide which countries you want to visit and how long you plan to be in Europe, then choose which type of Eurail Pass best complements your itinerary. For example, a Eurail Selectpass gives you the choice of travel to any three bordering countries, a savings of nearly $250 over the Europe-wide Eurailpass.

2 Determine if you will be on the train overnight or be needing to get somewhere quickly. A Eurail Pass does not include sleeper cars or high-speed rail (TGV). An additional payment and reservation is required in most cases.

What to Look For

- Multiple-country deals
- Sleeping arrangements
- RailEurope.com
- Special fares

Tip

Travel must begin no later than six months after the issuing date of the Eurail Pass.

3 Log onto the Web site of Rail Europe (RailEurope.com), the official North American representative for 60 European railroads. This is by far the best Web site for researching, choosing and purchasing a Eurail Pass. Everything you could possibly want to know about Eurail Passes is explained here.

4 Ask about special fares for seniors, youths and families. For example, if you are under age 26, take advantage of the Eurail Youth Pass.

5 Purchase your pass online using a credit card. Allow two or three business days for standard delivery. Passes can also be shipped overnight for an additional fee. Have a nice trip!

444 Take an Italian Bicycle Vacation

If sweating your way through *la bella Italia* is your idea of a good time, you're in luck: Dozens of companies offer packaged bicycle tours throughout Italy. But to pick the one that best fits your interests, you'll need to do your homework.

Steps

1 Start by asking yourself these questions: Where in Italy do I want to ride? During what season? In what type of terrain? What distance, pace and level of difficulty am I comfortable with? How much am I willing to spend?

2 Make an honest assessment of your riding skills and endurance. Most trips cater to the out-of-shape tourist (hence the full-time van support); this means a lot of waiting around. If you're a strong rider, a more challenging tour operator such as La Corsa Tours would be a better match.

3 Cruise the Web. Type "Italian bicycle vacation" in a search engine and spend a few hours shopping for the tour outfits that best suit your requirements.

4 Call and ask these questions: What's the typical riding day like in terms of duration and difficulty? What are the accommodations? How much experience does the tour leader have? Is transportation from the airport provided? What's the leader-to-client ratio? What's not covered (for example, meals, bikes and helmets)? Is there a maximum number of people? Will the trip be canceled if not enough riders sign up? Will there be van support? Are marked maps and written route instructions included? How many days do riders actually ride?

5 Budget in tips for your guides along with other trip expenses. Ten percent is standard; 15 percent will reward superior service.

6 *Pedala forte, mangia bene.* (Ride hard, eat well.)

Warning

There are myriad quirky rules and limitations that apply to each type of Eurail Pass. Be sure to carry a list of all the rules that apply to your pass at all times.

What to Look For

- Suitable level of challenge
- Experienced leader
- Bike rental/transportation costs
- Extra costs
- Full-time van support
- Desired accommodations

Tips

The more challenging itineraries—45 to 85 miles (72 to 137 km) per day on varied terrain—tend to be the most scenic and least crowded.

Call or visit a local bike club for tour company recommendations.

Warning

Check the daily itinerary for the word *transfer*, a euphemism for a requisite van, bus or train ride to your next destination. Make sure these transfers are few and brief.

445 Choose a Cheap Cruise

Cruising is one of the fastest-growing segments of today's suffering travel industry. Hard times for the travel trade spell lower prices for the budget-minded passenger seeking a great deal. Packages offering a wide range of activities and destinations are now easy to find.

Steps

1 Inquire about theme packages that are tailored for your lifestyle (single, golden years, gay and lesbian). If it's going to be a family affair, ask about money-saving family discount packages. Most cruise lines offer something for everyone.

2 Look for departures close to home. Many cruise line companies are adding departures from new ports to drum up more business, which cuts airfare expenses for you.

3 Book early—or late. Cruise lines are eager to make bookings far in advance and to fill up last-minute cancellations. If your schedule is flexible, you may find even hotter deals at the last minute.

4 Use a cruise-only travel agent. These agents have access to the best deals on the lines they do the most business with. A good agent will also recheck prices close to the departure date and refund part of your money if the rate has gone down. Some fares (often called *fax specials*) are so low that the agents aren't allowed to publicize them; you have to ask if they're available.

5 Budget for gratuities to shipboard waiters and service personnel. Ships often have suggested amounts depending on cruise length.

6 If you've got some time on your hands, book a slow boat to China—on one of 150 freighters worldwide that accept passengers. Voyages last for 21, 45, even 90 days, cost $50 to $100 per day, and offer many amenities. Visit FreighterWorld.com.

What to Look For

- Theme trips
- Family discount packages
- Departures nearest you
- Last-minute bargains
- Reputable cruise-only agent
- Freighters

Tips

It's wise to purchase cruise insurance to protect you and traveling companions. (See 434 Get Travel Insurance.)

Stick with your favorite lines; many offer special discounts for repeat customers.

Review sites such as CruiseCritic.com and CruiseMates.com.

Warning

Port fees are often not included in advertised prices and can add significantly to your cruise cost.

446 Book a Hotel Package for the Greek Islands

There are a multitude of gorgeous Greek isles to choose from when planning an Aegean island-hopping excursion, not to mention the many hotels and resorts on each. With the right amount of research, you'll be swilling ouzo and yelling "Opa!" in no time.

Steps

1 Figure out when you want to go and how long you'd like to stay. Factors such as climate, European holidays and political crises (skip a Greek garbage strike) are important considerations.

2 Choose which islands you'd like to explore on your trip by researching what each island has to offer. If you've never been to

What to Look For

- Optimum travel periods
- Reputable travel agent
- Web-based discount packages

Greece before, spend at least a few days touring the glories of Athens before you hit the islands.

3 Shop the Internet for package options or hire a reputable travel agent who specializes in trips to Greece to book your package.

4 Contact the hotel(s) directly before you arrive to be sure that all of your arrangements are in correct order, especially if you've booked your trip through a travel agent, no matter how reputable.

Tip

It's wise to purchase travel insurance for international vacations (see 434 Get Travel Insurance).

447 Raft the Grand Canyon

Rafting the Colorado River through the Grand Canyon is one of North America's greatest adventures. The wet 'n' wild ride is an expensive thrill, however, so be sure to choose wisely when hiring a rafting outfitter. Here's what you need to know.

Steps

1 Plan the trip at least a year in advance. Most of the rafting trips through the Grand Canyon book quickly—National Park regulations allow a limited number of boats through the canyon each season—and require a down payment. If you can't plan that far in advance, go standby and ask the rafting outfitters to call you if there's an opening. The Colorado's water releases are controlled, so the best rafting conditions are typically in the spring (April) and fall (September and October).

2 Review your budget—you may be draining more than your raft every day. Costs run a minimum of $250 per person per river day. (All food and nonalcoholic beverages are included.) Add more for travel to and from, gratuities, hotels and alcohol.

3 Choose from four types of watercraft: oar rafts (the guide does all the work), paddle rafts (you paddle and the guide steers), motorized rafts (long raftlike boats with a specialized outboard motor), and traditional dories (charming 17-foot/5.2-m wood boats that carry three passengers and a guide). Hybrid trips, where you paddle one day and rest the next, are also available.

4 Scrutinize potential outfitters. Visit the Web sites of commercial rafting companies licensed to run the Grand Canyon, then call the toll-free numbers, ask for brochures and grill the staff. Where possible, try contacting previous clients via e-mail or phone numbers provided by rafting companies.

5 Expect to spend six to 16 days: six to seven days for Upper Canyon trips, nine days for Lower Canyon trips, and 13 to 16 days for full-canyon trips. Rapids range from class I to V; however, Grand Canyon water levels are based on the water being released from Lake Powell through the Glen Canyon Dam.

What to Look For

- Advance planning
- Advance deposit policy
- Last-minute cancellations
- Unexpected costs
- Boat types
- Web sites and brochures

Tips

You don't need to know how to swim to take a rafting trip, but you do need to let your guide know if you can't swim.

Include in your budget tips for you guides. They're doing the work because they love it, certainly not for the pay. Ten percent is standard; 15 percent will reward superior service.

Warning

If you get tossed from the raft, *never* attempt to stand up: If your foot gets wedged between rocks, you could drown.

448 Book a Cheap but Awesome Safari

There are hundreds of safari companies competing for your business, which means incredible deals await the savvy safari hunter armed with a computer. Be aware of the political climate in any destination country before booking your trip.

Steps

1 Get a clear idea of the type of safari you'd like to experience, from viewing Egypt from camelback to camping in Australia's famed Outback to touring a Kenyan wild game preserve. Begin by researching safari companies on the Internet.

2 Settle on where and when you'd like to go based on the type of safari you've chosen. Be sure to take the regional climate into account. High-season prices vary dramatically from low-season rates, which correspond with seasonal weather conditions.

3 Figure out whether you'd like to be part of an organized tour or if you'd prefer a custom tour. Money-saving packages are often available depending on how you book your safari.

4 Decide on the type of accommodations, services, transportation and food you'd like to experience on your safari. Consider how much roughing it you're willing to do before you plan your adventure. If the lodge sounds like your cup of tea, check the amenities.

5 Determine what you can realistically afford, and keep in mind that you will get what you pay for. Generally speaking, a budget safari runs from as little as $75 to as much as $125 per person per day.

6 Consult with travel agents who specialize in adventure travel. They can find the deals you're looking for and offer more specific safari information than a general travel agent would.

What to Look For

- Locations and climate
- Package deals
- Organized versus custom safaris
- Adventure-travel agents

Tips

Staying at a hotel or a beach resort is often less expensive than a safari camp.

If you really want to splurge on location, transportation, accommodations and food, safaris can add up to thousands of dollars.

Travel insurance is often mandatory for safaris. (See 434 Get Travel Insurance.)

Warning

Before traveling to Africa and Asia, contact the National Center for Infectious Diseases (cdc.gov/travel) for recommended vaccines and immunizations.

449 Rent a Camel in Cairo

Planning to visit Egypt's capital and Great Pyramid of Giza? The absolute best way to soak in this wonder of the ancient world is on the back of a camel—a truly Egyptian experience. But there are a few rules you should follow when hiring a camel and guide.

Steps

1 Rent your camel just outside the entrance to the Giza Plateau. Alternatively, you can pick up a camel behind the Sphinx once you're inside the Plateau.

2 Expect to pay about 25 Egyptian pounds (US$4.40) per person plus tip for a camel. It's customary to pay after you return with the camel.

What to Look For

- Healthy-looking camels
- Clean stables
- Recommended guide

Tip

Choose a calm, clear day for a camel ride. Desert sunsets behind the pyramids are breathtaking.

3 Check out the condition of the camels before you rent one. Sadly, it's normal for the camels to appear undernourished, but they should not have sores or look beaten. Also, the stables in which they are kept should appear clean. If you're not satisfied, move on to the next spot.

4 Tip your guide between 5 and 10 pounds (US90 cents to US$1.75). The only people who get out of tipping are those who ride on their own camels.

Warning

Hire a recommended guide in advance. Dubious guides have a tendency to hassle unaccompanied travelers.

450 Get Single-Malt Scotch in Scotland

Since there's not much more to do in Scotland than golf, get rained on and listen to bagpipes, you might as well delve into the fine art of single-malt Scotch tasting while you're there. What wine tasting is to Napa Valley, whiskey sipping is to Scotland—so much so that an entire tourism industry is built around Scottish whiskey tours.

Steps

1 Plan a tour of Scotland's distilleries. If you just want to buy single-malt scotch, save the airfare. Because of Britain's ultrahigh liquor taxes (about 70 percent of the retail price), quality Scotch is far cheaper in the States or a duty-free shop. (See 438 Buy Duty Free.)

2 Purchase these two books: *Michael Jackson's Complete Guide to Single Malt Scotch: The Connoisseur's Guide to the Single Malt Whiskies of Scotland* (Running Press, 1999) and *The Whisky Trails: A Traveller's Guide to Scotch Whisky,* by Gordon Brown (Trafalgar Square, 2000). Also order the *Collins Whisky Map of Scotland* (William Collins & Sons Ltd., 1999).

3 Using the books and map, plot a course among the dozens of distilleries open to the public throughout Scotland, particularly Islay and the regions of Speyside, Scotland's famed malt whiskey country.

4 Look into one of the many organized tours of Scotland's distilleries that include lodging, meals and transportation. Taking such a tour is often the only way to get a real behind-the-scenes look into traditional distillery techniques and sample rare Scotches.

5 Join the Scotch Malt Whisky Society. If you're a die-hard Scotch lover, fork over the membership fee and join the worldwide fraternity of single-malt Scotch whiskey connoisseurs. Privileges include access to The Vaults, a 19th-century members-only whiskey lounge in Leith, the historical port of Edinburgh.

What to Look For

- Scotland distillery guidebooks
- Organized distillery tours
- Private whiskey clubs

Tips

In Scotland you have to pay a 17.5 percent Value Added Tax (VAT) on your liquor purchases, but non-British citizens can claim much of this back when you leave the country. When you arrive, check with the customs authority for details, and save all your receipts when you shop. See 439 Ship Foreign Purchases to the United States.

Plan your trip to coincide with one of Scotland's many whiskey festivals, such as the Spirit of Speyside Walking Festival held each May.

451 Buy a Sapphire in Bangkok

Gem scams have ruined the holidays of many a visitor to Thailand. Before you set out shopping, read 63 Buy Colored Gemstones. Then consult the Thai Gem and Jewelry Traders Association's information booklet (thaigemjewelry.or.th), which lists reputable stores and members of the association.

Steps

1 Determine your budget before you shop—it will give you a good foundation for your shopping negotiations.

2 Explore the wholesale jewelry market on Mahesak Road just off Silom (similar to New York's West 47th Street). Here you'll find Thai, Chinese, Iranian, Israeli and Indian dealers who import and export cut stones.

3 Comparison shop at several stores before you buy, and never feel rushed in your decision. The educated buyer gets the best deals, especially in a place where negotiation is critical.

4 Pay a fair price by negotiating with the knowledge you've gained from comparison shopping. Nearly all jewelry shops negotiate, so always ask for a "special discount" on the quoted price.

5 Know what you're buying and purchase your sapphire with a credit card so that you can cancel payment if you've been defrauded. Gem receipts should always be marked "Subject to identification and appraisal by a registered gemologist."

6 Carry your sapphire home with you rather than having it shipped.

What to Look For

- Wholesale market
- Competitive prices
- Quality stones
- Credit card protection

Tip

If you intend to make a sizable purchase, ask the jeweler to accompany you to a facility for an independent appraisal.

Warning

For every reputable gem dealer, there are hundreds of crooks waiting to snare you. The Tourism Authority of Thailand receives more than 1,000 complaints a year about fake jewelry.

452 Hire a Ricksha in Yangon

Whether you call it a ricksha, trishaw or pedicab, a ride on one of these historic cycles offers much more than just transportation. Travel in a virtual time machine that adds an exotic element to your trip to Yangon (formerly Rangoon), the ricksha capital of the world.

Steps

1 Decide where you're going and for how long. Ricksha drivers can go the distance, but a bus may be more comfortable for long trips.

2 Find your ricksha along the outer edge of the city. You can hail one just as you would a taxi. Otherwise, step up to a ricksha stand and put your order in.

3 Bargain for your fare in advance. You can charter a ricksha for a full day for about 400 to 500 kyat (US$65 to $80) and less for shorter trips around town, but you must bargain.

What To Look For

- City perimeter
- Ricksha stands
- Good deal

Tip

Rickshas are not allowed in the central area of Yangon during the daytime.

453 Take Salsa Lessons in Cuba

Anyone can take salsa lessons at the local dance hall, but only the truly inspired make the pilgrimage to the Mecca of salsa—Cuba. Although direct travel from the States to Cuba is still prohibited, the ardent salsa afficionado can easily book dance lessons from Hackensack and land in Havana a few days later.

Steps

1 Evaluate your salsa skills before arranging your trip. This will help you enroll in the most appropriate class for your level. If you don't know salsa from the macarena, take a few lessons before you go to be one step ahead when you arrive.

2 Book an "educational" excursion to Cuba through a travel agent who features salsa dancing. Several travel companies offer packages designed exclusively for those in search of salsa lessons during their visit.

3 Get to Cuba. If the U.S. government denies your educational pretext for a visa, arrive there as most *Americanos* do—under the radar on a short flight from Cancun, Mexico.

4 Ask your hotel concierge for the best discotheque that offers salsa lessons. Arrive early to catch a few expert tips before the crowds arrive to show off their moves.

What to Look For

- Educational excursions
- Cancun connection
- Salsa lessons at discotheques

Tip

Although travel restrictions in Cuba are relaxing, virtually all visitors require a Cuban visa or tourist card, which is available through the Cuban government.

Warning

U.S. citizens entering Cuba require permission from the U.S. Department of the Treasury.

454 Buy a Camera in Hong Kong

Cameras may be a bit cheaper in Hong Kong, but if you don't shop wisely, you may end up paying the difference in headaches. Visit the Hong Kong Tourist Association office in Tsim Sha Tsui at the Star Ferry Pier and ask for its brochure. The Hong Kong Tourism Board Web site (hkta.org) lists recommended shopping areas and stores.

Steps

1 Make specific decisions about what brand and model camera you want to buy. Researching on the Internet is a fast and effective way to make informed decisions.

2 Check the prices among different shops in the United States as well as Hong Kong to know whether you're getting a good deal.

3 Shop at Hong Kong's reputable establishments. To help discern which retailers are reputable, look for the Quality Tourism Services Scheme symbol of quality on shop display windows.

4 Visit Stanley Street in the Central District. This is where local professional photographers shop.

5 Get a proper receipt. If you're not satisfied with your camera, you'll have an easier time returning it with a receipt than without.

What to Look For

- Specific brands and models
- Reputable stores
- Stanley Street
- Receipt

Tip

Shop early for the best prices. Chinese merchants consider the first sale of the day to be very important and will offer special prices just to make that first sale.

455 Buy Your Way onto a Mount Everest Expedition

So you want to climb the world's highest mountain? It's just spooky how easy it is to sign on with an Everest expedition. In fact, you can join an expedition in minutes via the Web. Essentially all you need is a lot of cash and rudimentary mountaineering experience. It's prudent to get your affairs in order: Many climbers—even experienced ones—die on Everest each year.

Steps

1 Pony up at least $60,000 in cash, most of which has to be wired to the expedition company's bank account before you start the 62-day journey. Might as well write your will while you're at it.

2 Get in the best shape of your life and join as many serious mountaineering climbs as possible. There are numerous U.S. companies offering mountaineering clinics. Whether a climbing team will take you on depends on your skills and value as a team member.

3 Choose an ascent route. Everest's southeast ridge on the Nepal side is the classic first ascent route. Less technical and dangerous than the northern Tibetan route, it's usually more expensive.

4 Make sure the expedition's guides are highly trained and have serious Everest experience. Numerous companies will take your money and your word that you have the skills and stamina to summit. Just fill out an online trip application form (scary, eh?).

5 Watch out for hidden costs such garbage deposit ($4,000 per team), entry visa, oxygen and regulator, Sherpa and porter gratuities, extra yaks and customs duty for all your gear.

6 Buy at least $50,000 in emergency medical evacuation insurance in case you need to be helicoptered out.

What to Look For

- Large cash reserves
- Mountaineering experience
- Physical stamina
- Highly experienced guides
- Hidden costs

Tips

Purchase accident insurance before you depart, particularly for helicopter evacuation and rescue. Travel and trip cancellation insurance is highly recommended as well (see 434 Get Travel Insurance).

Check with your physician what shots are needed before you go.

Everest summit expeditions typically depart in late March and late August.

See 344 Write a Living Will.

456 Hire a Trekking Company in Nepal

OK, so summitting Everest is out of the question, but trekking to Base Camp (17,388 feet or 5,300 m)? Now you're talking. If you don't book a trip with an adventure travel company and instead choose to do it all yourself, here's what's involved.

Steps

1 Figure out exactly where in Nepal you'd like to explore and with whom you will be trekking. The person in your group with the least mountaineering skills and weakest physical condition determines which regions everyone can safely explore together.

2 Determine how many days you want—and can afford—to trek. You can find trekking packages that offer short or longer treks based on your interests and financial commitment.

What to Look For

- Physical limitations
- Online trekking companies
- Prebooked space
- Insurance and liability

Tips

In high-season base camp can be packed; consider less-traveled regions.

3 Get recommendations from personal contacts. Talk to people who have been there, ask if they enjoyed the trip, what route they took and how the food was. Find out which companies ran the trip. Browse some of the many books on the topic.

4 Plan your trek with the size, fitness level, and interests of trip members in mind as well as the size of the crew, number of porters and desired comfort level. Trail accommodations range from tents to comfy tea house lodgings.

5 If just one or two of you need reservations in a prebooked group trek, inquire about cancellations. In the high season—October through December—this may be the only way openings are available in Nepal.

6 Be sure to buy travel insurance that includes at least $50,000 in emergency medical evacuation insurance. Then if you need to be helicoptered out of the mountains (the only other way out is to get carried on someone's back), you can repay the trekking company (about $10,000) by credit card, then place a claim with your insurance (see 434 Get Travel Insurance).

A trekking permit is required for all Himalayan destinations and may be obtained only in Nepal. Pick one up at the Immigration Offices in Kathmandu or Pokhara.

Budget in tips for your crew. Ten percent is standard.

Warning

Get into shape well before your trek starts. Flat trails are rare in Nepal: the mountains are steep and require strong legs and good lungs.

457 Rent or Buy a Satellite Phone

Purchasing a satellite phone is very much like shopping for the best cell phone plan, just much more expensive—sky high, you might say. First choose a satellite phone, then a provider, then a plan. Or the smarter move may be just to rent one for your off-the-grid odyssey.

Steps

1 Choose between buying a new or used satellite phone or just renting one. For example, a high-end Motorola 9505 handheld unit is about $1,500 new, $1,000 used, and $20 a day to rent. Less fancy units sell for as little as $300 used or $45 a week to rent. If you're heading to an ultraremote location, be sure to bring along a solar-powered battery charger (about $40).

2 Choose a provider. Satellite telecommunications companies such as Globalstar USA and Iridium Satellite offer competitive plans and varied coverage zones.

3 Make sure the provider you choose offers service to wherever you're headed.

4 Choose a plan that best suits your needs. Like cell phone plans, satellite phone companies offer package deals, prepaid calling cards and free e-mail and text messaging.

5 Shop online for the best price. There are dozens of satellite phone retailers offering very competitive package deals.

What to Look For

- Buying versus renting
- Noncoverage zones
- Calling card plan
- Package deals

Tips

Don't confuse Global System for Mobile Communications (GSM) cellular phones with satellite phones that offer cellular service. GSM phones don't use a satellite network.

Most satellite phone companies require a one-week minimum rental period and a large deposit.

Satellite airtime rates range from about 99 cents to $2 per minute depending on the calling plan.

QUET OF ROSES • BUY SOMEONE A DRINK • GET SOMEONE TO BUY YOU A DRINK • BUY YOUR WAY INTO HIGH SOCIETY • BUY YOUR W
ORDER THE PERFECT BURRITO • ORDER TAKEOUT ASIAN FOOD • ORDER AT A SUSHI BAR • BUY DINNER AT A FANCY FRENCH RESTAURAN
LOWERS FOR YOUR SWEETHEART • BUY MUSIC ONLINE • HIRE MUSICIANS • ORDER A GREAT BOTTLE OF WINE • BUY AN ERGONOMIC DE
USECLEANER • HIRE A BABY SITTER • BUY A GUITAR • BUY DUCT TAPE • GET A GOOD DEAL ON A MAGAZINE SUBSCRIPTION • GET SENIO
RIAN • BUY PET FOOD • BUY A PEDIGREED DOG OR CAT • BREED YOUR PET AND SELL THE LITTER • GET A COSTUME • BUY A PIÑATA • B
RED GEMSTONES • CHOOSE THE PERFECT WEDDING DRESS • BUY OR RENT A TUXEDO • REGISTER FOR GIFTS • BUY WEDDING GIFTS •
DEAL WEDDING OFFICIANT • OBTAIN A MARRIAGE LICENSE • ORDER CUSTOM INVITATIONS AND ANNOUNCEMENTS • SELL YOUR WEDDIN
ER'S DAY GIFT • SELECT AN APPROPRIATE COMING-OF-AGE GIFT • GET A GIFT FOR THE PERSON WHO HAS EVERYTHING • BUY A GRADU
KKAH GIFTS • PURCHASE A PERFECT CHRISTMAS TREE • BUY A PRIVATE ISLAND • HIRE A SKYWRITER • HIRE A BIG-NAME BAND • GET IN
• RENT YOUR OWN BILLBOARD • TAKE OUT A FULL-PAGE AD IN *THE NEW YORK TIMES* • HIRE A BUTLER • ACQUIRE A PROFESSIONAL SP
UR COAT • BOOK A TRIP ON THE ORIENT-EXPRESS • BECOME A WINE MAKER • PURCHASE A PRIVATE/CUSTOM BOTTLING OF WINE • BUY
R MEMOIRS • COMMISSION ORIGINAL ARTWORK • IMMORTALIZE YOUR SPOUSE IN A SCULPTURE • GIVE AWAY YOUR FORTUNE • HIRE AN
E DEVIL • NEGOTIATE A BETTER CREDIT CARD DEAL • CHOOSE A FINANCIAL PLANNER • SAVE WITH A RETIREMENT PLAN • SAVE FOR YOU
BUY BONDS • SELL SHORT • INVEST IN PRECIOUS METALS • BUY DISABILITY INSURANCE • BUY LIFE INSURANCE • GET HEALTH INSURA
R • HIRE A HEADHUNTER • SELL YOURSELF ... MARKET YOUR INVENTION • FINANCE YOUR BUS
E EQUIPMENT • HIRE SOMEONE TO DESIGN ... HIC DESIGNER • ACQUIRE CONTENT FOR YOUR W
AZINE STORY • SELL A SCREENPLAY • SELL ... START A BED-AND-BREAKFAST • SELL A FAILIN
NER'S INSURANCE • OBTAIN DISASTER INSU ... AUCTION • BUY A FORECLOSED HOME • BUY AN
AN • BUY A LOT • BUY HOUSE PLANS • HIR ... BUILDING PERMITS • BUY A VACATION HOME • BO
NANCY-IN-COMMON UNIT • BUY RENTAL PRO ... R CATALOG SHOOT • FURNISH YOUR HOME • FU
RES • BUY A PROGRAMMABLE LIGHTING SY ... Y FLOOR-CARE APPLIANCES • BUY EXTENDED W
E FLUID ARCHITECTURE INTO YOUR HOME ... OSE DECORATIVE TILES • CHOOSE A CEILING FAN
LF-CLEANING WINDOWS • CHOOSE WALLPA ... RING • SELECT CARPETING • CHOOSE KITCHEN C
ME ALARM SYSTEM • BUY SMOKE ALARMS ... UY FIRE EXTINGUISHERS • CHOOSE AN ENTRY D
• HIRE A GARDENER • BUY OUTDOOR FUR ... UY FLOWERING BULBS • BUY FLOWERS FOR YO
HIRE A GARDEN PROFESSIONAL • BUY AN A ... EW LAWN • BUY A LAWN MOWER • BUY KOI FOR
HTING SYSTEM • BUY ORGANIC PRODUCE ... LL AT FARMERS' MARKETS • SELECT KITCHEN KN
T MEAT • STOCK UP FOR THE PERFECT BU ... ATURAL BEEF • BUY ROCKY MOUNTAIN OYSTER
CHEESESTEAK IN PHILADELPHIA • ORDER F ... DS IN LOUISIANA • BUY ARTISAN BREADS • BUY A
• PURCHASE VINEGAR • CHOOSE PASTA • ... CUP OF COFFEE • BUY A COFFEEMAKER OR ESPI
R A BUSINESS FUNCTION • STOCK A WINE ... L SPERM • CHOOSE AN OVULATION PREDICTOR
D THERAPIST • GEAR UP FOR A NEW BABY ... • BUY BABY CLOTHES • CHOOSE DIAPERS • BUY
ATE SCHOOL • FIND A GOOD AFTER-SCHO ... ESSONS • BUY A BACKYARD PLAY STRUCTURE •
N • BUY A VIDEO GAME SYSTEM • HIRE A T ... YOUR CHILD HIRED AS A MODEL • SELL USED BA
SSISTED CARE OR NURSING HOME • WRITE ... AY FOR FUNERAL EXPENSES • GET VIAGRA ONLI

Sports & Outdoor Recreation

PTION DRUGS • HIRE A MENTAL-HEALTH PR ... UY HOME-USE MEDICAL SUPPLIES • SELECT HAI
MPLANTS • GET WRINKLE-FILLER INJECTIO ... CTITIONERS • CHOOSE A MANICURIST • GET WH
A MASSAGE • GET ON ANTIQUES ROADSH ... T AN ANTIQUE FAIR OR FLEA MARKET • RENT SP
RWARE • EVALUATE DEPRESSION-ERA GLASSWARE • BUY AND SELL STAMPS • BUY ANTIQUE FURNITURE • RECOGNIZE THE REAL MCCO
RI-OH CARDS • SNAG STAR WARS ACTION FIGURES • SELL YOUR VINYL RECORD COLLECTION • SELL AT A PAWNSHOP • BUY AND SELL
MPUTER OR PERIPHERALS • CHOOSE A LAPTOP OR NOTEBOOK COMPUTER • SELL OR DONATE A COMPUTER • BUY PRINTER PAPER •
GRADE THE MEMORY IN YOUR COMPUTER • BUY COMPUTER SOFTWARE • CHOOSE A CD PLAYER • BUY BLANK CDS • BUY AN MP PLA
E PHONE SERVICE • BUY VIDEO AND COMPUTER GAMES • CHOOSE A FILM CAMERA • CHOOSE A DIGITAL CAMCORDER • DECIDE ON A
US TV • CHOOSE BETWEEN CABLE AND SATELLITE TV • GET A DIGITAL VIDEO RECORDER • GET A UNIVERSAL REMOTE • BUY A HOME T
CHEAP AIRLINE TICKETS • FIND GREAT HOTEL DEALS • RENT THE BEST CAR FOR THE LEAST MONEY • GET TRAVEL INSURANCE • PICK
STATES • TIP IN A FOREIGN COUNTRY • TIP PROPERLY IN NORTH AMERICA • BRIBE A FOREIGN OFFICIAL • GET A EURAIL PASS • TAKE
AWESOME SAFARI • RENT A CAMEL IN CAIRO • GET SINGLE-MALT SCOTCH IN SCOTLAND • BUY A SAPPHIRE IN BANGKOK • HIRE A RIC
OMPANY IN NEPAL • RENT OR BUY A SATELLITE PHONE • BUY YOUR CHILD'S FIRST BASEBALL GLOVE • ORDER UNIFORMS FOR A SOF
KET • BUY A GYM MEMBERSHIP • BUY AN AEROBIC FITNESS MACHINE • BUY A SNOWMOBILE • BUY A PERSONAL WATERCRAFT • HIRE
OOSE A CAR RACK OR CARRIER • BUY SKIS • BUY CLOTHES FOR COLD-WEATHER ACTIVITIES • SELL USED SKIS • BUY A SNOWBOARD
Y FITTED HELMET • BUY THE OPTIMAL SLEEPING BAG • BUY A TENT • BUY A BACKPACK • BUY A BACKPACKING STOVE • BUY A KAYA
SWEATER • PURCHASE VINTAGE CLOTHING • SELL USED CLOTHING • ORDER CUSTOM-MADE COWBOY BOOTS • BUY CLOTHES ONLIN
AN'S DRESS SHIRT • PICK OUT A NECKTIE • BUY A WOMAN'S SUIT • BUY A MAN'S SUIT • HIRE A TAILOR • BUY CUSTOM-TAILORED CL
M SUIT • HIGH PERFORMANCE WORKOUT CLOTHES • BUY A HEART-RATE MONITOR • SELECT A WATCH • BUY KIDS' CLOTHES • CHOO
CAR ONLINE • BUY A HYBRID CAR • SELL A CAR • BUY A MOTORCYCLE • LEASE A CAR WITH THE OPTION TO BUY • TRANSFER YOUR

458 Buy Your Child's First Baseball Glove

A mistake here could turn your potential Big Leaguer into a literature professor. Scary. Better to do a little research and get the correct glove. Gloves made from synthetic material are cheaper than leather ones and, although not as durable, can be a good starter mitt.

Steps

1 Ask your child's coach or manager for advice, if possible. Don't be shy about specifying your budget. Sports expenses add up quickly, and parents need to be careful.

2 Buy the smallest glove on the rack for a very young player (under 7 years old). These gloves usually measure 9 inches (23 cm) from the bottom of the palm to the tip of the longest finger and cost about $20. Softer gloves are also preferable for youngsters. Keep in mind that many kids resist using child-size equipment because they want to look like adult players. Avoid drawing attention to the fact that your child is using a smaller glove.

3 Go up to the next size increment, an 11-inch (28-cm) glove, for larger kids. If yours is a serious player, the glove will likely see several years of use if maintained well. Consider paying more for a higher-quality leather glove. It's best to take your child with you when selecting it. The glove should feel good and your child should like it. A basic 11-inch glove is about $45. Higher-end gloves can cost $100 or more.

4 Avoid buying a specialized glove such as a catcher's mitt unless the coach requires it. Your child will probably play a variety of positions, and an all-around glove will be the most useful.

What to Look For

- Reasonable price
- Right size

Tips

If you want to surprise your child with a special gift, look for a suitable glove endorsed by a favorite player.

The best way to break in a glove is to use it a lot. To speed things up, try putting a ball in the pocket and wrapping a strong rubber band around the outside of the glove. Let it sit overnight.

Glove oil can extend the life of a glove.

459 Order Uniforms for a Softball Team

If you're picked for this job, either you have an outstanding fashion sense or you were absent when team duties were handed out. Choose carefully, because your efforts will be on display all season.

Steps

1 Select a supplier. Sporting-goods stores frequently provide uniform services. If not, search the Internet for suppliers. Make sure the supplier can arrange an appropriate delivery deadline prior to the start of your season. Ask for a price guarantee and any bulk-order discounts that apply.

2 Bring a sample of the team's colors to your supplier, if you have them. Make sure the supplier can match the colors. Know the colors of all other teams in your league to avoid conflicts.

3 Inform all team members of your assigned task. Let them know that you need and expect their input.

What to Look For

- Delivery-date guarantee
- Price guarantee
- Large-order discounts
- Team colors

4 Create a form (your supplier may be able to provide one that lists the player's name and number, shirt and pant sizes, and style preferences. Include color choices if you haven't picked them already. Distribute to all team members to fill out.

5 Set a deadline for returning both form and money. You'll need to make final decisions on colors and styles, subject to availability.

6 Get out on the field and practice so those uniforms look good!

Tips

Expect suppliers to be very busy at the start of the season and order early.

Ask if you can get a bulk rate if you buy home *and* away jerseys.

460 Buy Ankle and Knee Braces

Preventing knee and ankle injuries is simple—never leave your armchair. For most of us, that's not an option, nor is it good for our health. But you can stay active and protect yourself with a few precautions. Modern braces provide an impressive amount of lightweight support.

Steps

1 Determine what type of brace you need. The following can be purchased at sporting goods stores, orthopedic supply houses and drugstores.

- Knee braces provide lateral support while allowing full flexion and extension. They also protect against hyperextension, which is a common cause of major knee ligament injuries. Those with a hole for the kneecap can supply some pain relief. Hinged neoprene braces ($100 to $300) with extension stops offer compression and are best for protecting previously injured knees. Knee straps ($20 and up) relieve pain and pressure caused by an irritated kneecap by helping the kneecap track correctly.

- The best types of braces for stabilizing the ankle provide good lateral support. Most sports ankle injuries occur when the ankle is rolled inward. Lace-up ankle supports slip on like a sock with laces to provide rigid side-to-side support while allowing freedom of motion. The Aircast brace is a rigid, plastic ankle brace with air-filled bladders that can be adjusted to provide varying degrees of support. The sport version (under $50) has a figure-8–type elastic that wraps around the ankle and is designed to fit into sports shoes and provide excellent support and free range of motion.

2 Get a custom-built brace. Usually requiring a referral from an orthopedist, these braces are given to postoperative or injured patients. Using a plaster mold of your knee or ankle, a rigid brace is constructed allowing the maximum safe range of motion while preventing unwanted lateral movement. It is covered by some health-insurance plans and must be fitted by a physician.

What to Look For

- Fit
- Lightweight or rigid
- Custom built

Tips

By itself, a brace is a second-best solution. The best idea is to strengthen the problem area through appropriate exercises, which in the long run may eliminate the need for a brace entirely.

Be sure to see your doctor about any injuries.

Verify that your sport allows participants to wear braces. Some sports do not allow certain kinds of braces.

461 Buy Golf Clubs

There are two schools of thought about golf clubs. You can buy a cheap set and then blame the clubs when you miss, or buy an expensive set and look great while you miss. Kidding aside, even a beginner will benefit from the right clubs. Golf is a demanding game, and if you're going to make the effort, give yourself every advantage.

Steps

1 Experiment with different clubs before you buy by renting, borrowing or demo-ing a set from a reputable golf store.

2 Find the right shaft length. Shaft length affects the feel of the club, but most players will fit an off-the-shelf club. If you have questions or are exceptionally short or tall, find a knowledgeable shop willing to match you to a shaft length. If necessary, ask if they have clubs made specifically for children.

3 Know the various clubs and how they are sold. Because it is important that they match, irons are sold as sets, usually consisting of the 3, 4, 5, 6, 7, 8 and 9 irons and a pitching wedge. A basic set costs about $200. Woods may be sold individually or in sets. A set, consisting of a driver, a 3 wood and a 5 wood, starts at about $250. Woods do not need to match. Some novices buy only a 3 wood instead of a full set of woods.

4 Select a putter based on what feels good to you. You can get one for about $25, but spend what it takes for a putter that makes you feel confident.

5 Understand the differences in club design. Most new clubs are perimeter weighted, with a larger hitting area to reduce the chances of an errant shot. Experts prefer bladed clubs, which demand great precision but deliver more power in skilled hands.

6 Wait to buy expensive clubs until your game has developed. There are many design options available; eventually, your style of play and preferences will determine the clubs you'll want to own.

What to Look For

- Knowledgeable shop
- Comfortable putter
- Perimeter-weighted or bladed clubs

Tips

Do not buy expensive balls at first. You'll lose many of them.

Unless you're planning to always ride in a cart, look for a lightweight golf bag with a stand.

A wire brush and towel for cleaning clubs are handy items to keep in your golf bag.

462 Join an Elite Golf Club

You're a benevolent man (or woman) of the people, filled with charity and good will. Your respect for the common golfer is boundless. You just don't want to share your fairways with the public every day. There's only one solution. Get yourself into the most exclusive golf club and savor the solitude of the well-heeled.

Steps

1 Prepare to pay a premium. You get what you pay for sometimes, and this is one of those times.

What to Look For

- Sponsor
- Membership tiers
- Member benefits

2 Take golf lessons. Do not underestimate the need to impress people with your ability. Solid skills can make up for any negative qualities that others (mistakenly) may believe you possess.

3 Find a sponsor. Unless you recently appeared on the cover of *BusinessWeek*, you probably need to have an existing member pass your application to the membership committee.

4 Review the different tiers of membership. Equity members own the facilities and usually make club decisions. Social members pay lower dues but have restricted access to facilities.

5 Decide what else you want to do besides play golf and investigate the facilities at various clubs. Some also have spas, tennis courts, swimming pools and gyms.

6 Look into member benefits, primarily reserved tee times during peak periods. Also consider access to club buildings for private events such as parties and weddings.

463 Sell Found Golf Balls

Living next to a golf course brings many benefits. For one, you get to regularly replace your old, worn-out windows with fresh new ones. Also, you get a large supply of golf balls delivered to your yard. Serious scroungers stroll the course and comb through the rough for lost balls. The question is, how do you turn these freebies into cash?

Steps

1 Clean the balls thoroughly. No one will buy grubby golf balls.

2 Sort the balls. Place the shiniest ones into one bucket, the moderately shiny ones into another, and old-looking balls into a third. Driving-range balls (identified by a solid color stripe around the middle) go into their own bucket. Balls with cuts go into another or possibly into the trash. If they sell at all, damaged balls will go for a very low price.

3 If you have a large supply of balls, consider sorting them by brand. Many golfers prefer a specific brand.

4 Pick a spot on or near the course where you're visible but not in the way. Make a sign that says "Golf Balls $1." This, of course, is the price for the oldest balls. Experiment with prices for better balls until you have a feel for what the market will bear.

5 Encourage haggling. This can be fun and also allows you to move more balls. If the customer says "Five bucks? No way, I'll give you two," you say, "Great, two bucks each, but you have to buy five of them."

What to Look For

- Golf balls
- Good spot to sell

Tips

Dress respectably and act friendly to reduce the likelihood that course management will chase you away.

Try to avoid offering a customer the very same ball he or she hit into the stream 10 minutes ago.

464 Buy Athletic Shoes

The choices in athletic footwear are overwhelming. Basketball alone spawns dozens of new designs every year, some changes purely cosmetic and others representing real technical advances. Avoid buying shoes that pinch your toes, which should have room to move and never touch the tip of the shoe. For longevity, wear your athletic shoes only when needed. Get another pair of sneakers for everyday.

ACTIVITY	SHOE DESCRIPTION
Running	● Get fitted correctly with shoes designed for your foot. The salesperson at a quality store will be able to offer you specific models that correct pronation or supination (where your foot turns inward or outward), or aid flat feet or high arches. Decide if you prefer more stability or more cushioning. Replace your shoes at least once a year: Even with infrequent use, running shoes wear out as the sole pad hardens. If you run every day, check the cushioning often and replace the shoe as soon as it feels stiff.
	● You can purchase adequate running shoes for $40 or $50. But if you're running more than a few miles per week, spend what it takes to get the right fit. Great deals can be found with shoe clubs or in catalogs; once you've been fitted properly and know what type shoe you need, shop by mail or online.
	● Track runners use different shoes for competition. Racing is done in flats, which have almost all padding removed to reduce weight. While some people use flats for road running, the lack of cushioning can cause injury.
	● Sprinters wear spikes—flats with small cleats attached. Different track surfaces require specific cleat types; check with your coach or other runners to make sure you have the proper cleat for the track. Racing shoes are intended to fit snugly and not provide long-wearing comfort or durability.
Walking	● Walking shoes often have a sole with an upward-curving toe to allow the walker to roll through the gait. With less cushioning than running shoes, high-mileage walkers training on pavement might want to stay with a good running shoe.
	● Florsheim, Mephisto and Ecco make high-quality walking shoes. They are expensive but can be worn with a wide range of clothing styles for people who don't want to look like a Nike ad. Costs range from $50 to $200.
Golf	● Most courses no longer allow metal golf spikes. Modern golf shoes have short plastic prongs on the sole for traction. Some models have replaceable prongs.
	● Look for soft leather uppers that require little or no break-in time. Your toes should have room to move, and the arch should be adequately supported.
	● If you play in a wet climate or in the early morning when the grass is damp, consider paying more for a waterproof model. Many golf shoes are now designed in a casual sneaker look, as well as traditional styles. Costs range from $50 to $250.
Baseball	● Baseball cleats used to have sharp metal spikes. Now they're removable and made from plastic, which is lighter and safer. For children, consider molded soles to which the cleats are permanently attached. These are cheaper and require no maintenance. Most players use lighter low-top cleats, especially players in speed positions, although high-tops with additional ankle support are available. Expect to pay $40 to $100.

ACTIVITY	SHOE DESCRIPTION
Basketball	• Whether you usually play indoors or outdoors will dictate the type of shoe you buy. Indoor shoes have a softer outsole (the very bottom of the shoe). For outdoor play on asphalt, get a shoe with a harder, more durable outsole. • Powerful or aggressive players usually choose a slightly heavier shoe for more support and durability. Faster players prefer lighter weight at the expense of durability. Expect to pay $75 to $200, although less-fashionable shoes cost less.
Hiking	• Shop for a boot that matches your intended use. Unless you're on a serious trek, the days of the heavy, all-leather hiking boot are over. Modern lightweight designs offer comfort, good protection and durability. • Many models are not water resistant: If this is an issue, look for a model with a higher top, a water-resistant upper, and a waterproof welt (the connection between the sole and the upper). A bellows tongue, attached to the upper at its edges, keeps out water and dirt. • Avoid wide, soft, running-shoe–type soles which are very unstable on rough terrain. Boots should not fit tightly anywhere, but when fully laced with a medium-weight pair of socks, should hold your heel firmly in place. (Consider sock liners for blister prevention.) You can also find boots built specifically for women's feet. High-quality, long-lasting models cost about $80 to $150.
Cross-training	• Advances in shoe construction have ushered in lightweight but sturdy shoes suitable for a variety of sports, such as a tennis shoe you can use for short running sessions. Look for a light-colored sole for use on various courts without marking the surface. If you are primarily a runner, get a model with maximum cushioning. If you're mostly playing tennis or basketball, opt for more lateral support. Prices range from about $50 to $100.
Aerobics	• Resembling a lightweight basketball shoe, aerobics shoes feature ankle support and durable soles. Look for complete freedom of movement with a secure fit. If you already own a cross-trainer shoe, you probably don't need to buy a separate pair for aerobics. Prices range from $50 to $150.
Soccer	• Basic cleats use molded plastic soles, a good choice for growing children. Better models have removable cleats, which you can change to suit different field surfaces. Experienced players prefer a thin, supple leather shoe with a very tight fit and narrow toe box for maximum feel and ball control. If you want the tightest possible fit, bring your soccer socks when buying. Do not buy football cleats for soccer; they have a different cleat pattern. Prices run from $40 to $150.
Tennis	• A secure feel and lateral stability should be your primary concern. Shoes not specifically designed for tennis' side-to-side action can be unstable and may lead to ankle injuries. • The shoe should be reinforced on high-wear areas, such as the top of the toe for quick stopping. Competitive players may prefer lightweight shoes, while those purchased for recreation or practice may be heavier and more durable. You can also find tennis shoes tailored specifically for grass, clay or hard courts. A good-quality pair costs between $50 and $100.

Eliminate your romantic notions about that old wooden racket in your basement. It won't help your game, whether you play tennis, squash or racquetball. Today's rackets are lighter, larger and stiffer. Popular brands including Wilson, Head, Prince and Dunlop offer a range of design options; test as many as possible. And with a price tag to fit any game ($20 to $90), you're sure to keep your eye on the ball.

TYPE	FEATURES	WHAT TO LOOK FOR
Tennis	Grip Size	• Too small a grip is hard to hold securely. Too large a grip tires your hand and arm. To test, grasp the racket and place your thumb along the shaft, pointing away from you. You should see a space about the width of your index finger between your fingertips and palm.
	Frame Material	• Heavier frames generate more power and less vibration. Aluminum rackets are inexpensive but may cause excessive vibration. Carbon, graphite and titanium composite rackets are more expensive and offer increased durability and stiffness. As you move up in price, rackets generally become stiffer, an advantage for advanced players who want more power.
	Head Size	• Rackets are frequently identified by the size of the head, measured in square inches. A smaller head appeals to experienced players seeking more control, while larger racquets appeal to beginning and intermediate players seeking more power and a larger "sweet spot." Larger rackets may weigh more. A common head size is from 95 to 110 square inches.
Squash	Grip Size	• Grip size is the same for all squash rackets, but different manufacturers have slightly varied shapes. Sample brands to find what feels best. You can increase the size with a grip wrap, if necessary.
	Frame Material	• The majority of rackets are composites of carbon, graphite or fiberglass. Inexpensive rackets are heavier. Experienced players prefer stiffer, lighter-weight rackets for increased control of the ball and better vibration dampening. Squash rackets break frequently from court contact. Check for a replacement guarantee.
	Head Size	• Head sizes are usually measured in square centimeters. Most rackets are around 500 square cm, although some beginner rackets are larger and advanced rackets are smaller. Larger rackets offer a larger hitting area, but are harder to swing quickly. Advanced players are more likely to choose a small racket to minimize weight.
Racquetball	Grip Size	• Grip sizes are coded like clothing, using letters—for example, S for small and XS for extra small. A racquetball grip is much smaller than a tennis racket grip. Select a grip that gives you maximum flexibility of movement.
	Frame Material	• Advanced players prefer lighter rackets, which offer superb control but are more likely to break from contact with the court. A novice can ignore weight in favor of durability. Most rackets are made from composites of carbon fiber, fiberglass or graphite.
	Head Size	• These rackets vary less in head size than tennis rackets. Most are 100 to 110 square inches. The racket's weight and feel are likely to be more important than its head size and shape.

466 Buy a Gym Membership

This may seem simple, but many subtle factors can affect your ultimate satisfaction with a gym membership. By making a fully informed choice, you have the best chance of achieving your fitness goals.

Steps

1 Proceed slowly. Many people join a gym on impulse, then never follow through. True fitness is based on your total lifestyle, not on a short-lived training program.

2 Research prospective gyms. Buy a guest pass that allows several visits. Go during peak periods or when you're most likely to use the gym, and check the availability of equipment. Check out the clientele. Are they people you feel comfortable around?

3 Weigh any opposing factors. Are you more likely to utilize a large, well-appointed gym located across town, or a small gym in your neighborhood? For many people, convenience is the most important factor—and that is determined by when you're most likely to go.

4 Review the facilities. Are they clean and in good working order? Are there activities geared toward your entire family, from kids to teens to seniors? Some gyms have hot tubs, saunas, swimming pools, lockers, and basketball and tennis courts. They may also offer child care, physical therapy and massage services.

5 Sample classes you're interested in. Are they easy to get into, or do you have come early and reserve a spot? Are they geared just for experts or are they suitable for newcomers?

6 Talk to current members. What do they like and dislike? Talk to the staff. Are the trainers full-time employees or freelancers? Is there a rapid turnover or will you be able to stick with a trainer?

7 Examine the contract. If the gym has a high initiation fee, you will be reluctant to change gyms, and the gym may hit you with frequent fee increases. Is it easy to get out of the contract?

8 If you travel frequently, a gym with nationwide affiliates (such as 24-Hour Fitness or the YMCA) may be a good deal. Check to see that you have full access to all locations.

What to Look For

- Convenient location
- Comfortable with clientele
- Activities, services and classes
- Cleanliness
- Helpful staff
- Flexible contract

Tips

Some health insurers offer discounts to health-club members. Employees of large corporations may also get discounts at some gyms.

See 367 Sign Up for a Yoga Class.

467 Buy an Aerobic Fitness Machine

Aerobic conditioning is the foundation of fitness. The ability to take in and utilize oxygen allows your body to perform; the more oxygen you can process, the more you can do. That's why aerobic workout machines are so popular. One major benefit of buying one is that it's in your house, not at the gym. However, it provides a less varied workout.

GENERAL ISSUES	SPECIFICATIONS
Price	• All types of machines have several quality and accessory levels. The least expensive aerobic machines sell for $100 or so, while the most expensive cost $4,000 or more. Expensive models are usually identical to those found in fitness clubs. Used machines, especially factory refurbished ones, may be a great deal. Be sure to ask about the warranty and maintenance records.
Quality	• Inexpensive machines don't provide the smooth operation of elaborate machines, and they may not maintain consistent resistance during a workout. Seats may not be as comfortable, and the machine itself may not be as stable. On the other hand, inexpensive machines tend to be small and easy to store, an important consideration for those with limited space.
Construction	• Many aerobic machines provide resistance by applying pressure to a flywheel, set spinning by the user's muscle power. The heavier the flywheel, the smoother the operation. Look for a large metal flywheel and a smooth, precise, sturdy resistance mechanism with a wide range of adjustment. Make sure your body weight does not exceed the machine's weight rating.
	• Inexpensive machines frequently use a system of hydraulic pistons (oil-filled cylinders) to control resistance. These can be subject to fading (lessening resistance) or leaking, which may render the machine useless.
	• High-quality machines have well-padded handrails. Any place where your body comes into contact with the machine (seat, pedals, rail and footrest) should be wide, secure and sturdy. Beware of wobbly connections and flimsy materials. Look for adjustable positioning for a wide range of body sizes.
Features	• Many machines have snazzy features like computerized workout displays. Basic machines may have no such functions, while most midlevel machines have a timer and an electronic display of your energy output, distance traveled or strides per minute. Look for preprogrammed workouts and the ability to store data on past workouts.
Maintenance	• Most machines require little or no maintenance. However, don't expect inexpensive machines to last more than a few years before numerous parts wear out. Many expensive machines are designed specifically for frequent use in fitness clubs, with the expectation of periodic professional servicing. Ask the seller about maintenance requirements before making a purchase.
Size	• All professional-quality machines are large. Check that you have sufficient space before buying one. Many exercise bicycles and rowing machines are designed for small spaces. If you have space restrictions, these may be your best choice.
Noise	• How noisy is the machine? It may need separate quarters.

MACHINE TYPE	FUNCTION	FEATURES
Stair-climbing	Provides vigorous and intense workouts with minimal impact.	Look for a stable machine—if it feels wobbly, it may be unsafe and you won't feel comfortable or secure using it. Secure handrails are mandatory. StairMaster (stairmaster.com) and Lifestep (lifestep.com) are recognized leaders in professional stair-stepping machines.
Rowing	The ultimate total-body workout that can accurately simulate rowing on water (without freezing weather and barge traffic).	For occasional use, a small, collapsible machine is fine. Larger units offer variable resistance, longer life and smoother operation. Test any machine for several minutes to assess seat comfort and pulling motion. The Concept II (concept2.com) is favored by collegiate, club and Olympic rowers worldwide. The WaterRower (waterrower.com) employs a water-resistance system mounted on an attractive wooden frame. Both models feature impact-free resistance and a motion that accurately simulates rowing on water; the handle pulls straight out, allowing for better technique and stronger body positioning.
Treadmill	Good for runners and walkers wanting weather-proof convenience and a killer aerobic workout. Set it up with a VCR and you're ready to roll.	While inexpensive machines do the job, they tend to be noisy and have a rough action. If you have the space and the budget, a high-quality machine will probably maintain your interest longer and provide more enjoyable workouts. Look for variable speed control, adjustable incline, sturdy pad and roller construction, and quiet operation. Life Fitness (lifefitness.com), Magnum Fitness Systems (magnumfitness.com), and Trimline (trimlinefitness.com) are all makers of top-quality treadmills.
Stationary Bike	Convenient, often compact units offer great aerobic workout—while you read or watch TV.	Get the model that feels best. It should have a comfortable, adjustable seat, secure feet attachment and smooth action. Excel (FitnessQuest.com) and Weslo (weslo.com) are makers of affordable exercise bikes, Tunturi (tunturi.com) offers mid-range machines, and Life Fitness is a recognized maker of top-end bikes.
Elliptical Machine	Provides a nonjarring workout with a smooth, elliptical motion that mimics the natural running stride.	A good choice when low impact is your main concern. Weslo and Stamina (staminaproducts.com) produce moderately priced machines, while Life Fitness, NordicTrack (nordictrack.com) and many others produce higher-end units.
WARNING	Make sure you are using any aerobic machine correctly. Incorrect body mechanics and bad posture may cause serious injury, particularly on rowing machines. Ask a salesperson or trainer for tips on technique.	

468 Buy a Snowmobile

Almost all snowmobiles are currently equipped with two-stroke engines that are noisy and pollute heavily. This may change dramatically in the next few years, with quieter, cleaner engines becoming the norm. If you're shopping for a new machine, ask your dealer what you can expect in the near future before you shell out $5,000 to $11,000.

Steps

1 Decide what you'll be doing most often. There are snowmobiles designed for deep snow, for racing, and for comfortable touring.

2 Review the various engine sizes, rated in cubic centimeters. Midsize machines usually have 500- to 600-cc engines. Large machines have 700- to 900-cc engines.

3 Understand that larger engines usually mean more horsepower and speed but also more weight and difficulty. A novice probably won't have the skills necessary to operate a large machine.

4 Explore the trade-offs of various models. A touring machine with a reverse gear is comfortable and easy to use, whereas a high-performance model is exciting but demanding to operate.

5 Ask about modification options. For example, it may be possible to change the machine's skis for better handling in deep snow.

What to Look For

- Snowmobile type
- Engine size
- Modification options

Tips

Test-ride your friends' sleds if possible and ask why they chose a certain model.

Snowmobile trailers can be purchased at most dealerships. Expect to pay $1,300 to $3,000 for a new two-sled trailer; be sure you have an adequate tow-vehicle and hitch. See 551 Buy a Trailer.

469 Buy a Personal Watercraft

Many people refer to personal watercraft (PWC) as Jet Skis, although this trade name applies only to one model made by Kawasaki. No matter what you call them, PWC range from small single-seaters to huge models that seat up to four. Costs range from $6,000 to $10,000.

Steps

1 Determine if you want a sit-down or stand-up PWC. Also decide if you want a craft powerful enough to pull a water-skier or tuber.

2 Examine the various size classes. This includes both engine sizes and hull sizes. Most manufacturers make a variety of both. Engine sizes are rated in cubic centimeters. Larger engines produce more horsepower and more speed, although the hull design has a big influence on performance.

3 Look at how performance and hull design are related. Short, narrow machines are maneuverable and very rewarding for skilled riders but may be difficult for beginners. Wider, longer designs are more stable, carry more people, and deflect spray better, but have reduced maneuverability.

4 See 551 Buy a Trailer to transport your new PWC from home to the beach.

What to Look For

- Sit-down or stand-up PWC
- Engine size
- Hull size
- Performance

Tips

Many waterways are restricting the use of two-stroke engines due to noise and pollution. New models with four-stroke or direct-injection two-stroke engines satisfy most emissions standards.

Life-preservers are required by law (see 491 Buy a Personal Flotation Device).

470 Hire a Scuba Instructor

To hire a scuba instructor, you need to establish his or her technical credentials. You need to be comfortable with your teacher's style of instruction and be able to trust his or her communication skills in an underwater setting. If this isn't the case, that person's not right for you, regardless of expertise.

Steps

1 Locate potential instructors. Get a referral from a qualified dive shop; most work with or recommend particular instructors. Ask the shop why it chooses an instructor. Your best bet could be an instructor that is affiliated with a reputable dive shop.

2 Ask about the instructor's credentials. Numerous U.S. and international training organizations certify instructors. One of the largest is the Professional Association of Diving Instructors (PADI.com). There are no federal regulations for U.S. diving instructors, but some states have regulations. A knowledgeable instructor should be familiar with these rules, if they are applicable, and should have up-to-date certification.

3 Inquire about the classes. What is the student-to-instructor ratio? Ask where the pool is located. If it's not easy to get to, you may find it difficult to complete the program.

4 Find out how long the certification program runs and how the sessions are scheduled. A responsible instructor gives classroom lectures before taking to the water. The schedule should allow sufficient time for personal attention from the instructor and questions from the students. Find out how to make up missed classes if necessary.

5 Review the equipment provided to students. While it is not always possible to tell if equipment is worn out just by looking at it, it shouldn't be obviously old or faulty. Check for dry, cracked rubber on suits, fins and hoses. Check for condensation inside gauges.

6 Inquire about open-water dive locations. Instruction should take place in an area where rescue personnel and medical facilities are available. If you will be transported to a dive site by boat, verify that the boat is seaworthy and equipped with a radio, fire extinguisher and life jackets for all passengers.

What to Look For

- Qualifications
- Up-to-date certification
- Appropriate class size
- Safety equipment

Tips

If you feel an additional check is required, contact the instructor's certifying organization to verify his or her standing.

Rent scuba gear until you become committed enough to buy your own equipment.

471 Buy a Skateboard and Protective Gear

The skateboard industry is extremely dynamic. Fashions change rapidly and new products are constantly hitting the shelves. If you're buying gear for children, understand what they want and are willing to use. The best helmet in the world will not provide much safety if it's thrown into the bushes.

Steps

1 Shop for safety gear, now required by many skate parks. Gloves, wrist guards, elbow pads and knee pads are labeled simply "youth" or S, M, L and XL. These should fit comfortably but must be snug enough to stay in place when you hit the ground.

2 Check the helmet fit. It should fit snugly and have a secure chin strap. Make sure the helmet can't rotate backward, exposing your forehead. The farther the helmet extends over the ears, forehead and back of the skull, the more protection it offers. See 485 Buy a Properly Fitted Helmet.

3 Determine whether you need a skateboard package or separate components. Inexpensive skateboards are usually sold as a complete package. These can be great for small children but probably won't bear the weight of an adult or teenager. Good-quality gear is usually sold as separate components, consisting of the deck, the wheels and the trucks (the metal devices that hold the wheels to the deck).

4 Decide on a skateboard deck. The most common deck type is around 31 to 32 inches (79 to 81 cm) long, with a slight upturn at each end. They are designed for maneuverability and cost around $50. Longer decks, called *longboards*, are anywhere from 35 to 50 inches (89 to 127 cm) long and are for speed riding. Decks vary slightly in width. Smaller riders should look at narrower decks.

5 Examine your wheel choices. Small wheels, up to about 55 mm in diameter, are for tricks, general street use and skate parks. Larger wheels are for carving long, fast turns on a longboard. A set of wheels costs about $25.

6 Choose a wheel hardness, which is rated using the durometer scale. The hardest wheels have a rating of 100. A wheel with a durometer rating of less than 90 is considered soft and is generally used on a longboard. A rating of 95 is about average for street and park use. A harder wheel can be better for tricks, while a softer wheel grips better.

7 Choose a truck width. Most trucks designed for a common 32-inch (81-cm) board are about 5 inches (13 cm) wide. A wider truck offers more stability, while a narrower one makes tricks easier. Many longboard riders prefer wider trucks. Truck costs range from $45 to $50.

What to Look For

- Snug safety gear
- Skateboard package versus components
- Appropriate deck size
- Wheel diameter and hardness
- Proper truck width

Tips

Take your time, and find a deck and wheel combination that fits your needs and also appeals to your sense of style, rather than buying the first board you see.

Ask plenty of questions in a shop. Any responsible shop will welcome you as a new customer.

See 140 Get Health Insurance.

Warning

If your new board doesn't have nonslip tape on the deck, buy a roll. Cut it into any pattern you wish and apply for traction and grip.

Skating used to be restricted to just a few people in the frozen North. Now people play ice hockey in Florida, in-line skates are everywhere, and every little girl is training to be the next Olympic skating champion. Before you commit to a purchase, know what you need in a pair of skates.

SPORT	HOW TO BUY
General	• For maximum performance, skates should fit snugly. Many experienced players opt for skates that are a size or more smaller than their regular shoes. Try on several different skates. Make sure your heel, ankle and instep are securely held in place but you don't feel any pressure points; toes should be able to move for balance.
	• Buy blade guards for hockey and figure skates for under $10.
	• Other accessories including sticks, shin guards and helmets can be found online at sites such as WorldWideSports.com, Hockey.com and Skatewell.com.
Ice Hockey	• For children, it probably doesn't make sense to buy snugly fitting skates, but they shouldn't be too large either. Too large a skate provides insufficient ankle support and leads to lack of control and security.
	• Higher-priced models offer improved ankle support, fit and protection from stiffer and more-sophisticated materials. Stainless-steel blades offer increased durability. Expect to pay about $90 for basic skates and up to $500 for top-quality skates.
In-line Skating	• More-expensive skates feature higher-quality wheel bearings, which roll faster and last longer than those of less-expensive skates.
	• The unique feature of in-line skates is their wheels. Choose wheels that suit your skating style and the type of surface you're most likely to skate on. Hard wheels last longer, but lose traction on slick indoor surfaces. Soft wheels wear down quickly on abrasive surfaces like asphalt. Smaller-diameter wheels allow you to change direction quicker, and larger-diameter wheels roll faster. In-line skates run from $100 to $250.
Figure Skating	• Figure skates should have stiff leather boots to provide adequate ankle support. The more advanced your skating, the stiffer boot you need.
	• Inexpensive figure skates lack ankle support and have poor-quality blades. If you're serious about pursuing figure skating, get good equipment.
	• Talk to other skaters or a coach about where to get skates. Expect to pay $75 for basic skates and hundreds for custom-fit skates.

473 **Go Sport Fishing**

Your number one concern here should not be catching fish, but coming home alive—anybody with a boat can say he or she is a charter captain. Spend a little time weeding out the amateurs from the pros, and you'll have a much safer and more relaxing voyage.

Steps

1 Hang around the fishing dock and see who comes in with the best fish. You can spot the most experienced charter captains by the happy crowds around their boats. Look for locals willing to give recommendations.

2 Make sure the boat in question is going after the type of fish you want. Ask what the captains have caught over the past few days. Also see how far out from shore they go, which also determines the type of fish they are likely to catch. If you hope to catch tuna, for example, make that clear to your prospective captain.

3 Check the captain's safety record, experience and knowledge of local waters. Inquire about the condition of the engine and the boat in general. Ask to see safety gear, including sufficient life preservers for everyone on board, a radio and a life raft. If the captain meets your concerns with anything less than forthright answers, look elsewhere.

4 Understand what the charter service provides and what you need to bring. Most charter tours provide all necessary fishing gear (and bait) but be sure to ask. You don't want to be 10 miles out when you discover that water, lunch and sunblock are your responsibility, nor do you want to have to pay unexpected extra charges.

5 Research costs carefully, since they vary considerably. Some boats offer private charters to small groups at a flat rate. Others offer per-person rates. The boat size, body of water, half- or full-day trip and time of year also affect rates. A basic multihour trip costs about $50 per person.

What to Look For

- Type of fish being caught
- Captain's safety record and experience
- Professional demeanor
- Knowledge of local waters
- Clear cost breakdown

Tips

It is unlikely that the charter operation will offer any sort of guarantee about catching fish, but it won't hurt to ask.

Inquire about help with cleaning and storing fish. Some charter operations will pack and ship to your home address.

Warnings

Pack motion sickness medication if you are the least bit prone to nausea.

Tell someone on shore your expected return time. A responsible operation will also have a contact on shore.

474 Go Skydiving

You know what they say about skydivers, right? There are old sky-divers and bold skydivers, but there are no old, bold skydivers. Picking a reliable instructor is therefore paramount.

Steps

1 Assemble a group to go with you. You need witnesses to your bravery.

2 Call the skydiving operations in your area and interview them. You want to establish that they are certified by an independent oversight agency, such as the U.S. Parachute Association (USPA.org); that they will take the time to answer your questions; and that they present a professional demeanor.

3 Verify their safety records. Ask if they have had any accidents. Call their certification agency to check.

4 Decide on a type of jump. Doing a jump by yourself (a *solo jump)* requires that you complete an instruction course, then jump using a static line. This line automatically opens your chute as you exit the plane, eliminating free fall. A *tandem jump* requires less instruction and allows you to experience a free fall since you are strapped to an instructor who does all the work, pulls the chute and controls the jump.

5 Make certain that you understand every element of the instruc-tion. Do not allow yourself to be rushed through it. If the instruc-tor is not answering your questions to a degree that makes you feel secure and confident, do not proceed.

6 Enroll in a certification course if you wish to pursue skydiving further. These instructor-led, multijump courses take several weeks or months and cost upwards of $1,500. As a certified skydiver, you'll be allowed to perform jumps at will.

What to Look For

- Certification
- Professional demeanor
- Good safety record
- Type of jump

Tip

Inquire about options for photographing or videotap-ing your jump. Some sky-diving operations provide this service.

The WWF might be on to something. Weight training benefits people of all ages by increasing bone density (preventing osteoporosis) and muscle endurance—it even lifts your spirits.

TYPE	FEATURE	WHAT TO LOOK FOR
Weight Machines	Basic Set	A weight machine has stacks of iron plates fixed in a frame. A range of exercises are performed at different stations on the machine with adjustable weight loads. Costs run from $500 into the thousands.
	Size	Allow enough room to set up the machine properly. If you have limited space, consider smaller individual machines. With one machine to work the arms and back and one for the lower body, you can get a complete workout. Universal and Nautilus are longtime manufacturers of professional-grade machines. You'll pay several thousand dollars, but get a setup that would satisfy an NFL team.
	Construction	Check that the machine is sturdy and that the framework remains immobile even during heavy lifting. Any point where your body contacts the machine will get lots of wear and tear; they should be padded with dense foam and covered by thick plastic or vinyl.
	Weight	Check that the machine has sufficient weight for the type of lifting you plan to do, and that you can add more weight in the future.
	Exercises	Test all the workout stations on the machine to make sure it performs the exercises you want. Read instructions for proper use. Investigate your options for adding stations.
	Alternative Designs	Some machines replicate the weight resistance through springs or elastic bands. These systems are lighter and more compact but still provide a good workout and range of motions. Bowflex ($1,000) makes a popular machine. However, some people miss the satisfying feel and sound that comes from moving a serious stack of iron.
Free Weights	Basic Set	Free weights provide a variety of strength-training exercises. Dumbbells are handheld weights. Barbells consist of a long steel bar with cast-iron plates that slide on and are secured. Weights are added or removed for various exercises. Choose a simple system with compatible parts for expandability and buy additional components as your training progresses. Verify that newly purchased plates fit your bar, but don't worry about mixing brands or types.
	Bench	The first accessory most people add is a bench, which allows you to lie on your back and work your chest, shoulders and triceps. The bench should have a rack at one end for holding the weight bar, and you should be able to set it flat or at an incline.
	Squat Rack	An upright rack that holds a bar and heavy plates at about shoulder height. Lifters add weight while the bar is secured in the rack, then move it onto their shoulders and squat, increasing explosive strength in the back, legs and glutes. A squat rack needs to be extremely strong and should be bolted securely to the floor, wall or ceiling.
WARNING		Free weights are more likely to cause injury than weight machines. To prevent injuries, emphasize proper technique and develop a warm-up and stretching routine before lifting.

Between the cup holders, the DVD player and the car seats, there isn't much room left in the car for equipment. That's where the rack comes in. Your needs and preferences, along with the type of vehicle you drive, will dictate your choice, but start by identifying models built to fit your specific car. Thule.com and Yakima.com offer expandable, comprehensive rack systems. Expect to pay slightly more for these brands, but know that you are getting good quality. Many other brands exist, particularly for hitch-mount racks. Word to the wise: Make sure you only need one key to operate all locks.

RACK TYPE	SET UP	FEATURES	PRICE
General Purpose	Basic roof rack consists of mounted stanchions and horizontal poles. Serves as the base unit for additional carriers, such as those for bikes, kayaks, skis or boards.	Check the rack's weight rating to make sure it can carry all your gear. Some people buy a basic rack and fashion their own systems to carry specific items. Quality racks can be locked.	$100 to $250
Trailer Hitch	For vehicles already equipped with a square tube-receiver hitch (a removable ball), get an equipment rack that utilizes the hitch mount.	This system is easier to load than a roof rack due to its lower height. However, this also means other cars can more easily damage your gear, and the gear collects more road grime. Look for hitch-mounted boxes.	$150
Spare-tire Hitch	Works like a trailer-hitch rack to carry up to three bicycles.	Some SUVs with a rear-mounted spare tire accept a hitch attached to the tire bracket. Make sure to keep bike tires away from car exhaust (to prevent warping).	$100
Roof Box	Considered by some an essential car complement, roof boxes are very slick, weather-proof luggage compartments.	Advantages over roof racks include security, watertightness, ease of loading, and improved aerodynamics. If you plan to carry bicycles, you still need a separate bike rack.	$300 to $600
Ski and Snowboard Rack	Simple to store when you don't need it; usually easy to install and remove.	A major disadvantage is that if later on you want to carry a bicycle, you'll have to buy a whole new rack. If you're buying a rack with individual slots, make sure the slots are compatible with newer, wider skis. Check out magnetic systems.	$100 and up
Side-mount Rack	Designed for smaller cars, hatchbacks or cars with rounded roofs.	If considering a side-mount rack, do not exceed its weight rating, as this puts excessive stress on the door windows. Otherwise comparable to any roof rack in terms of use. Use caution while loading skis so you don't chip the paint.	$50

477 Buy Skis

Ski technology advanced dramatically during the 1990s when new materials and designs came together in easy-to-use, high-performance skis. Ski design used to be race-driven, so everyone skied on slalom or giant slalom skis. Today it's largely driven by free-skiers who favor all kinds of terrain, including chutes and bowls, and skis now commonly defy categorization. When buying skis of any variety,

ALPINE	FEATURES
General	• Specialized for traveling downhill, with your boot rigidly fixed to the ski. For getting back uphill, most skiers rely on chairlifts.
Shopping for Deals	• Beginner and intermediate skis sell for $450 to $700. Advanced equipment sells for $600 to $900.
	• Some national sporting good stores have great deals. Buying any of the recognized brands—SalomonSports.com, Rossignol.com, K2Sports.com and AtomicSki.com—generally gets you a good ski for a good price.
	• Many ski shops sell demo skis in the early spring. Shop early, they go fast.
All-mountain Skis	• Where skis used to be 200 cm or longer, that much length isn't needed anymore. A versatile, do-everything ski for an average-height adult runs between 160 and 180 cm in length. For cruising groomed runs and making occasional forays into other terrain, look for a ski up to about 75 mm in width under the foot for versatile performance across most terrain. If you're a powder hound, consider a ski in the fat or midfat category. If you frequently ski icy snow, stick to a narrower design.
Midfat and Fat Skis	• Shorter skis, from 75 to 100 mm in width under the foot, excel in deep powder and soft snow. If you have always struggled in powder, this is your ticket to the next level. Many of these skis are stiff and demanding, and are designed for accomplished skiers. If you're a beginner, make sure you aren't purchasing too stiff a ski, as you will not be able to turn it properly.
Slalom Racing Skis	• Racing skis have become incredibly short. The fastest racers in the world commonly use skis of about 160 cm, while a few years ago they would consider nothing less than 205 cm. Flexible and responsive, they offer incredibly quick turning on firm snow, but are not a great choice for deep snow and ungroomed terrain.
Parabolic Skis	• This is an outdated term referring to the first generation of shorter, wider skis. All current skis reflect some elements of this design, but none use the original parabolic shape. For convenience (if not total accuracy), old-style skis are referred to as *straight*, and new, wider skis are referred to as *shaped*.
Twin-tip Skis	• Favored by skiers who enjoy the challenges presented by half pipes and terrain parks, twin-tips are very soft and forgiving with a turned-up tail to land jumps backward. Bindings are mounted farther forward than normal. Make sure to demo a pair to see if that's what you're after. Twin-tips can be skied in the same length as all-mountain skis, or slightly shorter, depending on preference.

seasonality matters. Start looking in early spring and plan to purchase that year's models by late spring. If you wait to buy until the snow starts to fly in the fall, you'll pay a premium for the new models. Give the new gear a try—you might be surprised by how much your skiing improves. Talk to the experts at ski shops and sporting goods stores to help you narrow down your choices in each category.

CROSS-COUNTRY	FEATURES
General	• Cross-country skis differ from alpine skis in that they're lightweight and designed for self-propelled travel over a wide variety of terrain, not just down hills. The bindings let your heels lift off the ski, allowing a normal striding motion, which is why cross-country skis are also referred to as free-heel skis. Waxless skis are far easier to use and preferred by many. They achieve grip for forward movement by means of a texture set into the skis' base. Waxable skis require different wax for different snow conditions.
Shopping for Deals	• An inexpensive set of cross-country touring skis sells for about $150. Racing and telemark skis cost $250 to $500. Ski shops are your best source for equipment. Shop early in spring for the best deals.
Racing Skis	• Fast, narrow skis intended strictly for use on groomed cross-country trails, racing skis are not for exploring untracked areas. Each of the two racing styles—skating and the traditional diagonal stride—have specialized skis. Your skiing style, weight and the local snow conditions will determine what ski is best for you. Only a local shop can evaluate all of these factors.
Touring Skis	• Offered in a variety of widths and styles. Wider models, especially ones with metal edges, are designed for touring rugged terrain or ski camping. Narrower, lighter-weight models are for gentler terrain and for use on groomed trails.
Telemark Skis	• A telemark skier turns by sliding one ski forward, bending deeply at the knees, and arcing both skis into a turn as though using one long ski.
	• Unless you are a skilled, high-speed skier, a forgiving, easy-turning model will work best. Stiff or long skis are very challenging for a beginning telemark skier. For backcountry travel and deep snow where weight matters, look for lighter-weight skis at least 70 mm wide under the foot. If you are an aggressive skier, avoid very lightweight skis; durability is far more important than a few extra ounces.
Accessories	• Backcountry skiers will need a pair of skins to make ascents. These attach to ski bottoms for uphill traction.
	• Different types of skiing require different types of poles. Ask a ski shop for suggestions, but know that some poles run for $120 and more. Unless you're racing, a $35 pair is just fine.
	• Bindings also differ for different ski types. Talk to a ski shop for advice.
	• See 481 Buy Ski Boots.

478 Buy Clothes for Cold-Weather Activities

Many people invite disaster when selecting winter clothes: Not wearing a hat is the number one mistake. If you use fashion as your guide instead of function, rest assured you'll be miserable when that first icy blast hits.

Steps

1 Conduct research if possible. If you've just arrived in a resort town, check out what the locals are wearing. In bad weather, they'll be dressed more like mountaineers than fashion models.

2 Layer clothing for maximum warmth and convenience. Layers allow you to add and remove items as your body temperature rises and falls. Begin with a base layer of polypropylene underwear, top and bottom. You can purchase these inexpensively at many outdoor stores. Brand-name items don't always deliver better quality, despite their higher costs.

3 Add one or more fleece layers as dictated by your comfort range. Again, these needn't be expensive to provide effective warmth. A vest is a good option, paired with a long-sleeved layer.

4 Add an outer waterproof, breathable shell. This layer does not need heavy insulation unless you expect to encounter below-zero temperatures. For jackets, get something that extends below your waist and has a hood. Pants should be loose fitting and should rise above your waist to keep out snow. Look for sealed seams and elastic or drawstrings at cuffs and hems.

5 If you need an insulated top layer, decide on either synthetic or goose-down filling. Synthetic filling will perform better if it gets wet, while down loses its warmth when wet. If weight is your primary consideration, however, buy goose down. It is warmer for its weight than any synthetic insulator.

6 Inspect the seams of insulated clothing. High-quality items have baffled seams. This means the stitching on the outside and inside layers doesn't meet, creating cold spots. Clothes without baffled seams are sewn straight through the two layers, and allow cold air to enter. (See 486 Buy the Optimal Sleeping Bag.)

7 Wear a hat that completely covers your head, or even one that has earflaps, to prevent a potentially life-endangering loss of body heat. Look for itch-free fleece headbands on warm wool hats.

8 Waterproof, gauntlet-type gloves that extend over your jacket's sleeves provide the most protection from snow and water. Some people's fingers stay warmer in mittens.

9 Boots present the biggest challenge for the novice winter recreationist. The most successful boot design incorporates a rubber lower boot with a leather top and removable felt liner. Boot temperature ratings are particularly important if you will be outside for long periods of time and need your feet to stay warm.

What to Look For

- Layers
- Materials
- Baffled seams
- Waterproof gloves
- Winter boots

Tips

Many outdoor clothing retailers sell both online and through catalogs. REI.com has a tremendous variety of merchandise. SierraTradingPost.com offers cut-rate deals on overstocks from many name-brand manufacturers.

Check Schnees.com and Sorel.com for good boots. Be sure to select a pair designed for your anticipated needs, paying particular attention to temperature ratings.

Remember that with outer layers, more money usually does buy better quality.

See 516 Buy Performance Workout Clothes for more information on fabrics.

Warning

Be careful of drying your clothes too close to the fire or other heat source. Synthetic fabrics and insulators may not be able to withstand high temperatures.

MATERIAL	CHARACTERISTICS
Cotton	Avoid cotton, because once it gets wet, it stays wet and heavy. Snow country survival experts have a saying: Cotton kills.
Goose Down	Lightweight down is a great insulator for extreme cold, but can be too warm for active sports, and loses its ability to insulate when wet. Not all down provides the same warmth: the higher the fill power, the warmer it is. (Fill power is the volume filled by 1 oz. (31.1 g) of down, and is the standard measure of down quality and performance.) Look for a rating on the tag—650 fill power is good quality, 850 fill power is top quality. Items that don't specify the fill power are generally lower quality. (See 486 Buy the Optimal Sleeping Bag.)
Synthetic Insulation	Clothing with high-quality synthetic insulation usually lists the brand name. Hollowfill and Thinsulate are the most popular types. They are slightly heavier than down, but stand up to wetness better and dry quickly.
Gore-Tex	The first truly breathable waterproof fabric, Gore-Tex (gore-tex.com) remains the best and is unbeatable for strenuous activity in wet weather. This is an outer shell layer, not an insulator. Expect to pay more for Gore-Tex clothing, which features sealed seams, watertight pockets and covered zippers.
DuPont Cordura	This is a brand name for a tough nylon fabric used to reinforce clothing. Durable gear frequently includes Cordura (cordura.com) patches on heavy-wear areas like knees, cuffs and seat.

479 **Sell Used Skis**

Skis are expensive, so you'll want to sell your old pair before you get new ones. Unfortunately, they depreciate quickly. Leave the bindings in place because most buyers will want them.

Steps

1 Estimate their worth. Skis one season old in good shape might sell for about half what you paid. After two seasons, with light use, expect to get 30 to 40 percent of their original price. Between three and five seasons old, expect about $100 to $200. If they're more than five years old, consider them a permanent part of the house or sell for the price of a casual dinner for two.

2 Run a classified ad only if you reside in a ski town or your local paper frequently has a lot of these listings.

3 Bring your equipment to a ski shop and ask for ideas. Suggest that your next purchase be contingent upon selling your old gear.

4 Consider keeping your old skis. They are great for perfecting your waxing and repair skills, and can be useful during early season conditions when you're likely to run into exposed rocks.

What to Look For

- Skis less than five seasons old
- Ski shop

Tips

Many winter towns have ski-swap events, resembling a community garage sale.

Sell your old skis to shops on consignment, if possible.

Buy a Snowboard, Boots and Bindings

Snowboarding used to be simple—youngsters mysteriously possessed the necessary skills and old people stayed away. But now that everyone's doing it, things have become more complicated. Unless you plan to specialize in one type of riding (slalom racing, for example), get a versatile freeride setup.

Steps

1 Rent equipment or borrow a friend's before you buy. You need to know what's right for you, not what's right for someone else.

2 Consider the type of snow you encounter most often. For hard snow and ice, you want a stiffer board. For powder, a softer board rides better.

3 Choose board length. For example, a 5-foot 8-inch (1.7-m) novice will ride something in the range of 150 to 160 cm. More length provides stability and flotation in powder, while shorter boards are more maneuverable.

4 Look for a board that matches your needs rather than a particular brand. For research purposes, popular brands' sites include Burton.com, K2Snowboarding.com, MLY.com, M-Three.com, Rossignol.com, SCSnowboards.com and RideSnowboards.com.

5 Expect to pay $260 to $400 for a board. There is a range of materials for different riding preferences and abilities.

6 Take your snowboarding style into account when choosing a board. Young or adventurous riders develop an array of techniques for destroying their board. This is normal and expected. Stick to boards in the lower price ranges if you plan to trash yours. More-conservative riders can buy higher-priced models that will last them many years.

7 Select a binding system. Strap bindings hold your feet in place with overlapping straps. These can be slow to put on and remove, but many people prefer the support they provide. Step-in bindings are convenient, but have limited foot support. Step-ins can also clog up with snow, making them a chore to use in deep powder. Bindings range from $90 to $120.

8 Make sure the boots fit the bindings and that you can attach the bindings to the board. Not all gear is compatible.

9 Buy the boot that provides the best fit, even if it means moving to a different binding system. Look for boots that fit snugly in the calf and heel but do not crush your toes; get the smallest boot that is comfortable when you're wearing one medium-weight sock. If you require very large boots, consider purchasing a wider-than-average board to prevent your toes from dragging in the snow. Boots range from $80 to $160.

What to Look For

- Board, binding and boot compatibility
- Appropriate board length and stiffness
- Proper boot fit

Tips

A secondhand board can be a good deal. Check to see that it isn't bent or warped and that the edges are intact.

Long jackets and waterproof pants with a reinforced seat will keep you dry and protected. Even experienced snowboarders spend considerable time on the ground.

See 478 Buy Clothes for Cold-Weather Activities.

Warning

Even the most accomplished snowboarders can encounter the random tree or, worse, another body moving at high speed. Always wear a helmet (see 485 Buy a Properly Fitted Helmet).

481 Buy Ski Boots

Even if you ski only a few days per year, there's no substitute for good boots. Proper fit, appropriate level of stiffness, and comfort are essential for a great day of skiing. If you've been renting ski equipment, at least consider buying boots. Although the initial purchase price can be high, they last for years and provide a consistent foundation for improving your skills. Spending the time to find a skilled boot fitter will pay off every day you enjoy fun, pain-free skiing.

BOOT TYPE	FUNCTION, FIT AND PRICE
Downhill Ski (Alpine)	• Have a stiff plastic shell designed to hold your foot and ankle firmly in place. For the best performance, buy the smallest boot you can comfortably wear and use only one thin synthetic sock. All boots expand in size slightly after you have worn them several times.
	• Plan on spending at least an hour with a skilled boot fitter, and try on many different boots. A bargain boot that doesn't fit is no bargain. As you move up in ability, you generally want a stiffer (and more expensive) boot designed for faster, more aggressive skiing. If you're a beginner or an intermediate, you don't need this stiffness unless you're of above-average size.
	• Boot prices range from $250 to $400 for beginner and intermediate boots, to $450 to $750 for advanced boots. If your foot is very difficult to fit or you simply want the best fit possible, inquire about custom fitting. Some manufacturers recommend special molding systems that make the boot conform exactly to your foot. All downhill boots are compatible with all downhill bindings. Expect to pay $200 or more on top of the standard price.
Cross-country	• Cross-country boots need to provide ankle and heel support but still allow your toes some freedom of movement. Because you will be lifting your heel as you ski, the boot needs to be comfortable as you bend your foot. Check to see that the sole is laterally stiff, meaning that you can't wring the boot like a dishrag. Plan on wearing one pair of medium-weight socks. For racing, weight matters, and lightweight boots cost more.
	• If you already own skis, check that new boots are compatible with your current bindings (not all are).
	• Prices range from $100 to $300.
Telemark	• A telemark boot used to be just a heavy-duty cross-country boot. Now it looks more like a downhill boot, with some important differences. First, decide where you will spend most of your telemarking time. If you only go to downhill areas, get a tall, stiff boot. If you prefer touring the backcountry, get a shorter, lighter boot for easier and faster ascents.
	• As with alpine boots, spend time with a qualified boot fitter and experiment with different boots. A properly fitting boot holds your heel firmly yet allows your toes to move around even with the sole flexed. It should fit snugly around your calf without crushing your foot. All telemark boots expand in size slightly after you wear them several times. Your toes should never hit the end of the boot. A standard telemark boot measures 75 mm across the front of the sole, and all 75-mm boots fit all 75-mm bindings.
	• Prices range from $300 to $600.

482 **Buy a Bicycle**

There are so many different types of bicycles that making a decision can be difficult. The primary consideration is to get a bike that matches your needs and fits properly; after that, it's a matter of test-driving to see what you and your budget like.

Steps

Any bike

1 Examine the $150 bikes at a discount store. This is what junk looks like; do not buy these bikes, because they will never work well. Prepare to spend more at a reputable bike shop.

2 Test-ride before buying. Sizing systems are confusing, as some refer to wheel sizes while others refer to frame sizes. Additionally, frames are not always sized using the same measuring system. One company's 17-inch mountain-bike frame, for example, probably won't be the same size as another's. Look for smooth shifting and good handling.

3 Know what the bikes' components are: wheels, tires, brakes, pedals, derailleurs and anything that attaches. The more familiar you are with these individual items, the more information you can absorb from a salesperson.

4 Understand what benefits are provided by different frame materials. Aluminum alloys are stiff and good for short rides, while chromoly and titanium frames absorb more road vibration, making longer rides more comfortable.

5 Choose pedals depending on your need. Your options are a basic flat pedal; a basic pedal with a cage around it (called a *toe clip*); and clipless pedals for which you have to buy special shoes that attach directly to the pedal.

Mountain bike

Mountain bikes are designed to tolerate rough treatment and abuse. They also give comfort and stability over rough terrain, on a bona fide mountain or over curbs and potholes. A lot of this ruggedness comes from the fat tires, which don't roll as effortlessly as road tires.

1 Decide what you can afford. A $400 mountain bike works great for general cruising and trail rides. For aggressive riding with hard climbs and descents, plan on spending $700 or more.

2 Stand over the top tube of a prospective bike and make sure your feet touch the ground comfortably. This is very important on a mountain bike—you may need to bail to avoid a wipeout.

3 Look for a frame that allows a comfortable, upright riding position. A cramped frame with too short a distance between handlebar and seat will not allow you to stand up and pedal, and will tend to tip backward on steep climbs.

What to Look For

- Good handling
- Smooth shifting
- Smooth suspension
- Strong wheels
- Tire width

Tips

The more you know about bicycle components, the more likely you will be to spot good deals. Expensive bikes have top-shelf component packages that you would be hard-pressed to equal in price if you tried to purchase individually. Cheap bikes have cheap components, and midrange bikes have a mixture. As a buyer, it's your job to spot the differences.

Unless you are, in fact, a racer, extremely lightweight frames and wheels are not the best choice. They're designed to win races, not to provide stability and durability, and won't always tolerate riders who weigh over 180 lbs. (67 k).

4 Decide if you want front suspension, full suspension or neither. Most mountain bikes include front suspension, as the majority of riders consider it essential. Full suspension is fun for fast downhills but adds weight, cost and a decrease in pedaling efficiency.

5 Do a subjective assessment of how the bike feels. You'll usually achieve a proper fit by feel more than by numbers. How does the bike climb? Can you stand up and steer easily?

Road bike

Most road bike designs are race-driven, designed for lightweight and aerodynamic efficiency at the expense of comfort. Touring bikes may have upright handlebars, fenders, carrying racks and other amenities. A $300 bicycle is fine for moderate riding. A $500 bicycle will last longer, have better brakes and shift more smoothly. For serious workouts, racing or high-mileage riding, plan to spend $900 or more.

1 Decide on your comfort needs. Don't let the salesperson talk you into a racing-style bike if you don't want one. Instead look for one with higher handlebars to take the strain off your back.

2 Change the seat (also called a *saddle*) to suit your bottom line. Larger, well-cushioned seats are available. Both men and women can buy seats with a gel insert or concave area to reduce pressure on sensitive parts (check them out at sites such as REI.com and TerryBicycles.com).

3 Examine wheel and tire widths. Wider tires are comfortable and more secure but slower. Racing bikes are equipped with narrow, high-pressure tires, which are fast but require more skill and concentration.

4 Consider the bike's weight. It does matter, but not as much as most people think. A 40-lb. (15-kg) bike is not as pleasant to ride as a 22-lb. (8-kg) bike, but most of us can't tell a 20-lb. (7.5-kg) bike from a 22-lb. one.

5 Visit several shops and ask about frame sizing and composition. You are likely to get different answers. Listen to the staff, but use your own judgment and go for many test rides.

6 Pay attention to the top tube's length. This is the bar that forms the top of the bike frame and is the primary determinate of the distance between the seat and the handlebar. Too long a top tube and you will be uncomfortably stretched out. Too short and you will be cramped. Look for a frame length that allows you to move your hands to different positions on the handlebars and doesn't force you to place too much weight on them.

There's no need to spend a lot on children's bicycles because they're quickly outgrown. Spend enough to get important safety features like good brakes.

You can replace handlebars with a shape that suits your grip comfort needs and riding style.

483 Sell Your Bicycle at a Garage Sale

The only valid reason to ever sell a bicycle is to make room for a new one. With that understanding, here's the best way to send your old mount to a good home and simultaneously prep the garage for a sleek new centerpiece.

Steps

1 Know your market. If you're likely to sell to college students, don't underestimate the appeal of dorky, unique or nostalgic machines. Your Schwinn Stingray may look like, ride like and actually be junk, but lots of people like this model.

2 Check the prices at a local shop that deals in used bikes. If your bike is not too old and is in very good shape, you should be able to get a similar price.

3 Spray everything that moves with lightweight oil. Keep spraying until each part moves freely. Wipe off any excess oil with a rag. Then wipe down the entire bike, spending extra time on any parts that you can shine up nicely.

4 Pump up the tires. Repeat as needed when no one is looking.

5 If the bike has any Italian words on it, park it almost out of sight and act disinclined to sell. Buyers will find you. Otherwise, park it out front with a big sign.

What to Look For

- Right price
- Lubricated moving parts
- Presentable appearance
- Airtight tires

Tip

If your bike's tires won't hold air and you know how to replace an inner tube, go ahead and do so. Tubes are cheap and the bike is more likely to sell if it can be ridden.

484 Commission a Custom-Built Bicycle

You had a BMX in elementary school, a 10-speed in high school, and something you found in the trash during college. Now it's time for a machine designed and built just for you.

Steps

1 Go for a ride on your current bike. Consider its performance. How does it steer? Is it stable on downhills? How does your body feel after riding it for an hour? Take notes if necessary so you can discuss your needs with a builder.

2 Decide on a budget. The most inexpensive custom frames (not a complete bicycle) are about $1,500. Exotic materials and special paint jobs can raise this price to over $5,000.

3 Decide what you want from your custom bike. Your goals will be a big factor in selecting a builder. Concentrate on the elements of design that truly matter to you.

4 Locate prospective builders through a bike magazine, a local shop or the Internet. Ask questions. There's no need to pretend you know everything, but the more research you do about the basics of frame design, the more readily you will understand their

What to Look For

- Design philosophy and passion
- High-quality materials
- Skilled craftsmanship
- Attention to detail

answers. Ask about their design philosophy, what materials they use and why, and their fitting system. How do they transform your subjective statements into actual frame measurements? Will they build a complete bike, ready to ride, or will you need to supply your own components?

5 Make sure you are in love with your bike's final appearance. You will enjoy riding more if you smile every time you look at it.

485 Buy a Properly Fitted Helmet

Ah, the good old days, before seat belts, bike helmets and car seats. But were they really that good? Probably the crew down at the emergency room has an opinion about that. We seem to be moving faster, jumping higher and falling harder than ever before, so helmets just make sense.

TYPE	FEATURES	PRICE
Motorcycle	Look only at helmets that carry Department of Transportation and Snell approvals. A helmet with a chin bar and visor offers the most protection and blocks the most noise, but some riders prefer open-face helmets. Bright colors increase visibility to car drivers. Buy a snug-fitting helmet with no pressure points that will cause pain and headaches. They loosen up slightly with use, so don't buy one that is too big.	You can get complete protection from a $120 helmet.
Ski or Snowboard	A winter sports helmet must meet many conflicting demands. It needs to keep out snow but allow ventilation. It should keep you warm on cold days but not stifle you on warm ones. Look for ventilation points that you can seal up on cold days and removable insulation around the ears. Make sure the helmet fits snugly but allows you to hear. Buckle the chin strap and test the fit by trying to rotate the helmet forward off your head—you shouldn't be able to. Then rotate the helmet back until your forehead is exposed. If you can do this, you need a smaller helmet.	Most models cost $80 to $150.
Bicycle	Look for a helmet that provides plenty of ventilation. Some brands have pads you can add to or remove from the helmet for better fit. Fasten the chin strap: If you can rotate the helmet back until your forehead shows, it doesn't fit properly. Find an experienced salesperson when shopping for your child's helmet. Some pediatricians recommend against kids under age 2 wearing a helmet, as their neck muscles aren't strong enough yet.	$30 helmets are fine; more expensive ones are available.
WARNING	A helmet that has been in a crash or one that's been dropped on a hard surface may no longer protect your head. If you suspect it's damaged, replace it.	

For many people, crawling into a snuggly sleeping bag is the best (and perhaps only) reason to go camping. Getting a bag that best fits your body means you don't carry excess weight or spend a lot of time trying to heat up one that's too big for you. Know your options before heading for the hills.

FEATURE	DESCRIPTION
Goose Down	Down is the most efficient insulator available, with the highest warmth-to-weight ratio. Cared for properly, it will last a lifetime. Down does not perform well when wet but is perfect for very cold climates where moisture is less of a concern, and anytime weight concerns are paramount. Not all down is the same: The higher the fill power, the warmer it is. Two bags rated for 20 degrees F (–7 C), one with 650 fill and the other with 850, will keep you equally warm. The key is that it takes less 850 fill down to reach that degree rating, making it a lighter, more compressible bag than the 650.
Synthetic Insulation	Synthetics are cheaper than down but slightly heavier for the same warmth rating. They retain their warmth when wet because they dry better, retaining their loft. Polarguard, Hollowfill and Thinsulate are popular brands.
Outer Material	Most bags use polyester or nylon fabric for both the shell and lining. The shell is coated with a lightweight durable water repellent to allow small amounts of water to bead up but not penetrate to the insulation. Higher-priced bags are made with waterproof, breathable laminates that allow body vapor to escape to the surface of the bag while prohibiting moisture from coming in. These bags are used exclusively in high-altitude mountaineering.
Construction	Check the stitching: If it runs directly through the inner and outer layers of the bag, it's a low-quality bag good only for temperatures above 45 degrees F (7 C). This quilted construction creates cold spots along the seams. High-quality baffled construction has inner and outer stitches that do not meet.
Shape	Bags come in either rectangular or mummy shapes. The reduced volume of a mummy means it insulates better and compresses to a smaller size. Rectangular bags are bulkier and heavier but can open flat to act as a comforter. Some models are made in large or tall sizes for people over 6 feet (1.8 m) tall, or in short sizes for children. Better-quality bags are offered in men's and women's versions, wider at the shoulders or hips, respectively, and insulated in different patterns, which take into account anatomical and sleep differences.
Temperature Rating	Most bags list the lowest temperature at which the bag will be comfortable. An average backpacking bag, for example, might be rated for 20 degrees F (–7 C). These ratings are a handy way to compare bags, but they don't mean you'll always be comfortable at that temperature—you still need a secure tent, an insulated sleeping pad and proper clothing.
Hood	Cold-weather performance requires a hooded bag. Climb into the bag to test the hood; you should be able to seal it snugly around your face. Make sure your feet don't push against the bottom of the bag when the hood is fastened.
Price	The better a bag's warmth rating, the more it costs. A good down bag, rated to 20 degrees F (–7 C), costs $200 to $300. A synthetic bag with the same rating runs about $100 to $200.

487 **Buy a Tent**

Some claim to have fond memories of sleeping out in old canvas Army tents. When pressed for details, they're likely to confess the tents were drafty, musty, leaky and heavy. Modern tents, lightweight and simple to set up, come in a variety of designs to fit your precise needs.

Steps

1 Decide what type of tent you need. For warm-weather or low-elevation use, a car-camping tent from Costco or a sporting goods store will work fine. For general backpacking and moderate elevations, a three-season tent is best. For mountaineering and winter use, you need a four-season or high-elevation tent.

2 Step up to a specialty brand if weight, durability, speedy setup, and resistance to wind noise (tautness) are issues. For a variety of tent options, check out these sites: MarmotMountain.com, Kelty.com, MountainHardware.com, TheNorthFace.com and SierraDesigns.com. Added money buys a lighter-weight tent that lasts a lifetime (if well cared for), pitches easily, resists crumpling in wind (so you don't wake up and find your tent collapsed across your face) and keeps out rain.

3 Investigate prices. Three-season tents cost more than car-camping tents. The larger and/or better built the tent, the more it will cost. An average two-person, three-season tent costs $150 to $250. A two-person, four-season tent can cost up to $700.

4 Assess usable space. Some small two-person tents are fine in good weather, but can feel cramped if two people plus equipment and a dog are waiting out a storm. On the other hand, two hikers don't want to carry a heavier tent designed for four.

5 Shop for tents in person, then buy online if you find a better deal. Crawl in and stretch out. Make sure your feet and head are well clear of the ends. Imagine spending 24 hours in there during a storm. Cozy or torture? Keep looking until you find a cozy one.

6 Consider design trade-offs. Taller tents are comfortable but more subject to wind buffeting. A shorter tent is more secure in high winds and is likely to be warmer, but may feel claustrophobic. Vestibules offer a "porch" to stash your gear or to cook in during rough weather. Some tents need staking to stay upright, while others don't. All backpacking tents, even free-standing ones, perform better when staked out. Unless you have a single wall tent, you'll need a rain fly for protection from bad weather.

7 Practice pitching different tents. Most are erected using a system of collapsible poles. Some are easier to set up than others. The simplest tents have two interchangeable poles; more-complex designs have noninterchangeable poles. If tent assembly seems like a mysterious art to you, go for the simplest design.

8 Buy a single-wall tent, with one waterproof layer for high-elevation mountaineering when weight and wind-resistance are crucial.

What to Look For

- Appropriate size
- Sufficient weather protection
- Add-on features
- Ease of assembly

Tips

Practice setting up your tent at home. You don't want to be learning how it works in the field.

Tents are generally sold by how many seasons they can be used. *Three-season* tents are designed for all seasons except heavy snow. Choose a *four-season* tent if snow camping is your thing. *Car camping* designates lower-cost models.

Interior space is designated by how many people the tent can comfortably accommodate, ranging from two to five. This, of course, depends on the size of the people and their comfort level. Also take into account the need to tuck in small children and dogs when looking at sizes.

Better-quality tents come with a lifetime warranty. Keep your receipt in a safe place.

488 Buy a Backpack

Almost any backpack will carry your stuff. The trick is to find one that's comfortable, durable, versatile and convenient.

Steps

1 Define the primary use of your pack. Any one pack is unlikely to be ideal for both short day trips to the beach and carrying all your gear on an overnight camping trip.

2 Look at various sizes. Packs are rated by capacity with internal volume in cubic inches. Small packs, called *daypacks*, are 1,000 to 2,000 cubic inches. Medium packs are 2,000 to 4,000 cubic inches. Large packs are 4,000 cubic inches and more.

3 Examine pack construction. The simplest packs consist of a nylon bag with straps—fine for short hikes and light loads. Select better-built packs for backpacking and serious use. The pack should have dense padding anywhere the pack touches your body, including the straps, the waist belt and along your back. Make sure the straps are securely sewn to the bag and bartacked.

4 Try on the pack. The thick part of the shoulder straps should rest on top of your shoulders. The waist belt, if any, should rest on top of your hip bones. If possible, place a load in the pack while testing. Medium and large packs often have a mechanism for torso length; make sure it is adjusted properly.

5 Examine the pack's other features. Is the material sturdy and rip-resistant? Are the zippers durable? Is it water-repellent? Are the outside pockets easy to access and large enough for your needs? Is there a pocket for a water container? If the pack is for winter use, can it carry skis, ice axes or snowshoes? Packs that consist of one compartment without many pockets carry large gear well, but fishing around for small items can be annoying.

6 Understand the frame structure, if any. Large packs used to incorporate an external metal frame to support the load. Most now have a smaller, internal frame, allowing greater freedom of movement and easier maneuvering in tight places. Some people prefer the additional support of an external frame.

7 Test-drive a pack specifically created for the legions of female backcountry enthusiasts. Frames are designed to fit shorter torsos; hip belts are anatomically constructed to effectively transfer weight without crushing the hip bones; shoulder harnesses and sternum straps fit womens bodies more comfortably. Shop sites such as OspreyPacks.com, SierraDesigns.com and TheNorthFace.com.

8 Consider costs. Simple nylon packs can be had for $30 or $40. A high-quality daypack costs between $50 and $150. A medium-size pack, suitable for backpacking and technical climbing, costs $100 to $300. Large packs range from $150 to $500.

What to Look For

- Total volume
- Comfortable straps and waist belt
- Heavyweight material
- Durable zippers
- Water resistance
- Pockets
- Frame structure

Tips

Carrying books is very hard on a pack. Buy a basic daypack for books and save your outdoor gear for adventures. Single-strap bags or packs, while not recommended for serious hiking or load carrying, might be a good way to carry everyday items.

If your pack hits part of your body wrong or feels uncomfortable, it might just need readjusting.

Make sure a pack loaded for an extended trip has the heavy items on the bottom to keep the center of gravity low.

489 **Buy a Backpacking Stove**

Stoves come in a variety of styles and sizes, but most follow the same basic design of a single burner attached to a separate fuel source. Your intended uses and destinations will determine which stove and fuel type is the best choice for you.

Steps

1 Think of the most likely type of use for your stove. If you do lots of car camping with kids, a sturdy camp stove is your best bet. The most popular model is made by Coleman (coleman.com), has two burners, and uses either propane or white gas. For backpacking, explore the many lightweight stoves that are available (see REI.com for ideas and prices).

2 Understand the pros and cons of fuel types, primarily liquid fuel or pressurized gas canisters. The most popular fuel source is white gas, which performs well in cold weather. Costing only $5 per gallon, it can be purchased in large cans and poured into the stove's fuel bottle. White gas is readily available all over North America but may not be in other parts of the world. White gas stoves come in many models, ranging in price from $75 to $200.

3 Choose pressurized gas canisters, the next most popular fuel source, if simplicity of use is your main concern. These canisters are usually a blend of butane and other gases. Some but not all gas mixtures perform well in cold weather. There are many inexpensive stoves that use pressurized gas, starting as low as $35. These are small and easy to pack but not always highly durable. Gas canisters cost a few dollars each.

4 Consider other trade-offs. Gas canisters are not refillable and must be thrown away when empty. It is impossible to determine exactly how much fuel remains in a canister. With a stove using white gas, it is easy to check remaining fuel. White gas can spill but a canister can't.

5 Buy a stove that can use a variety of fuels for global travel. These are usually referred to as multifuel stoves and can be operated on white gas, kerosene, automobile gasoline or even jet fuel.

6 Set up a prospective stove and examine it. Is it easy to assemble and use? Pressurized gas stoves can be lit as soon as the fuel canister is in place. Liquid fuel stoves must be manually pumped then primed by preheating the burner. Make sure you understand the instructions before buying the stove, and learn how to use it at home instead of out in the field.

7 Check stability. Will the stove hold a large pot of water securely? This is a major consideration in the field, where a tip-over might be truly disastrous.

8 Be sure your stove or cook set includes a windscreen that shields the burner. This is helpful anytime but an absolute necessity in cold or windy weather.

What to Look For

- Appropriate fuel source
- Easy to assemble
- Ease of use
- Stability

Tips

Look for stove manufacturers that also make cookware. A cook set and stove that are designed to complement each other will pack neatly together.

Some liquid fuel stoves come with cleaning and repair kits. Don't be scared off by this. Cleaning is only likely to be an issue if you're traveling in parts of the world where kerosene of variable purity is the primary fuel source.

Some stoves have a built-in starter mechanism. These can be handy but unreliable. Always carry a lighter.

Warnings

Never use a stove in an enclosed area, such as a tent. In addition to the fire hazard, you can die from carbon monoxide poisoning.

For long trips, or those where your life depends on your stove's performance, be sure to pack more than one.

490 Buy a Kayak

Many modern kayaks barely resemble the long, narrow traditional crafts of a few years ago. These days you can choose between sea kayaks, tandems, sit-on-tops and white-water kayaks.

Steps

General

1 Look at boats designed for the type of water you are most likely to encounter. Do not expect a single model of kayak to excel in all bodies of water. A touring kayak, for example, would be downright dangerous on river rapids.

2 Understand kayak design. White-water kayaks tend to be less than 9 feet (2.7 m) long and are intended for tight maneuvering. Sea kayaks range from 10 to 22 feet (3 to 6.7 m) long, with shorter boats more appropriate for beginners. Longer boats are less maneuverable but are favored by more experienced paddlers for speed, paddling ease and improved tracking.

3 Spend time inspecting and paddling kayaks before you buy. Make sure you're comfortable sitting in the boat. Check the footrest, seat and backrest adjustments. Bring a paddle you're comfortable with to isolate differences between boats. Take several boats out for a paddle.

4 Bring any kayak equipment you already own. Check that your spray skirt is compatible with any new boat you're trying out.

Sea kayaks

1 Analyze hull advantages: Shorter molded plastic hulls are a good choice for beginning sea kayakers. This material, while not indestructible, is extremely durable and will tolerate scrapes and bumps. Inexpensive molded plastic may not be rigid enough to satisfy some users. Fiberglass hulls are more rigid but won't tolerate a lot of bumping and scraping. Wooden hulls, while very beautiful, require extra care and frequent maintenance.

2 Move up to faster, lighter and longer hulls of Kevlar or Kevlar-fiberglass combinations as you gain expertise and can handle a less-stable sea kayak. Experts savor the even longer ultralight, super-fast hulls made of Kevlar and carbon fiber.

3 Consider the kayak's aesthetic qualities. Many people find a high-quality fiberglass boat better looking than a molded plastic one. If this is important to you, get a fiberglass boat, but understand that it may require more care and attention.

4 Buy a boat with a rudder if you're a long-distance paddler. Rudders help the boat track, which means less work for you.

5 Perception and Old Town (OTCanoe.com) are popular brands of touring boats with a wide range of models. Expect to pay $1,500 and up.

What to Look For

- Boat to match water
- Hull options
- Boat material
- Watertight

Tip

Some kayaks have a rigid frame covered with waterproof material. Designed to come apart for storage and travel, they are lightweight and convenient, but don't paddle as well as a rigid boat and won't carry gear either.

Warning

Inspect the watertight compartments. If you can test the boat in the water, check for leaks. If not, check to see that it has been tested and guaranteed. Examine the compartment seals; they need to fit very securely.

OTHER KAYAKS	FUNCTION, FEATURES AND PRICE
White-water	Shorter boats are more maneuverable: Some are designed for spins and rolls, others for slalom. White-water boats can be good for riding ocean waves. You should be concerned primarily with durability and performance, not aesthetics. Get advice from a shop to match a boat to your preferred use. There are numerous brands of white-water kayaks, although the most popular are Dagger.com and Perception.co.uk. Expect to pay $650 to $1,200.
Inflatable	Inflatables can be convenient and easy to store, but they don't paddle as well as a rigid boat. Some can be used successfully in white water. Cheap boats for use on flat water cost $200 to $300. More sophisticated models are $400 to $700.
Sit-on-top	Paddlers sit directly on the exposed hull, in molded seats. Sit-on-tops are reassuring to beginners who are not confined in the boat. Basic models start at $400. Higher-performance models, designed for white water or wave riding, are $500 to $600. Ocean Kayak (oceankayak.com) is the most popular brand of this type.

491 Buy a Personal Flotation Device

Many people used to risk death rather than wear a bulky life preserver. Now called a personal flotation device (PFD), they are slick and comfortable. Most water sports have a variety of PFDs designed specifically for the needs of that sport.

Steps

1 Select a PFD that meets minimum U.S. Coast Guard safety requirements. Type I PFDs provide the most buoyancy and are suitable for offshore boating. Type IIs offer slightly less buoyancy but are smaller and allow easier movement. Type II and III PFDs assume either that the user will be conscious and able to rescue themselves or that nearby rescue options exist. Most canoe and kayak PFDs are Type III. Type I PFDs are designed to keep even unconscious people upright in the water for an extended time.

2 Spend more for a tough, durable model if you're going to use your PFD constantly. If you use it only occasionally, a moderately priced model will last many years. For the higher price, you get more comfort and durability, but not necessarily more safety.

3 Make sure it fits correctly. With the PFD on and all fasteners closed, you should be able to move your arms freely, and should not be able to pull it off over your head. Ask someone to give a good tug on the PDF while you raise your arms. If it moves more than an inch (2.5 cm) or so, your vest could be swimming up around your ears just when you need it most.

What to Look For

- Correct type
- Correct size
- Heavyweight material
- Secure fit

Tips

Children use the identical PDF type, but in appropriate sizes. Check the label for size and USCG ratings.

For warm-weather sailing, the most comfortable PFDs contain a CO2 cartridge, which inflates only when needed. These are lightweight and don't add unwanted insulation. For rough-water sailing, a regular PFD can provide valuable padding around your body.

492 Buy a Wet Suit

There are many types of wet suits, but surf-style suits are perfect for swimming and many water sports. They offer freedom of movement and span a range of water temperatures. Suits designed for scuba diving are vastly different—talk to an instructor before buying one.

Steps

1 Understand the relationship between suit thickness, designated in millimeters, and body warmth. A 4-3 full suit is 4 mm thick in the body and 3 mm thick in the arms and legs, and is the best choice for water that's 50 to 60 degrees F (10 to 16 C). For even colder water, get a 5-mm hooded suit. If you rarely see temperatures this low, consider one that's 1 or 2 mm thick.

2 Decide what kind you need. A suit with cut-off arms and legs is called a *shorty* and is good whenever maximum freedom of movement is needed. A *full suit* extends to your wrists and ankles, and is necessary for colder water. A *farmer john* has full legs and no arms. It's favored by paddlers and is the bottom layer for scuba divers.

3 Inspect the seams. The better the construction, the warmer the suit. In a high-quality seam, the edges of the material meet flush, are glued and sewn into place, and are then covered by a strip of cloth. Cheaper seams can leave a small hump and exposed stitching.

4 Try on different brands. You want a snug fit that doesn't constrict your movement or breathing. All suits enlarge slightly with use. Avoid suits that bag around your waist or ankles.

5 Set your budget according to how often you'll use your wet suit. An inexpensive shorty costs about $60, while a better-quality one may be $100. An inexpensive full suit is about $150 to $200. A top-quality full suit is $250 to $350.

6 Choose a wet suit for children based on the same criteria. Pint-sized wet suits range from $50 to $100. Keep in mind that kids often grow out of a wet suit before they wear it out, which makes finding a good used one a smart move. As they grow, kids want to spend more time in the water, which requires buying a better suit.

What to Look For

- Appropriate thickness
- Suitable type
- Glued and taped seams
- Snug fit

Tips

The zipper on a surf suit runs up your back. Avoid embarrassment in the shop by remembering this. All zippered wet suits are hard to get on and off; you just have to practice.

Rinse out suits used in saltwater after every use.

Warning

Adults should not buy used wet suits unless they like being cold. Even the best suits wear out rapidly, begin to leak and lose their suppleness.

493 **Buy a Surfboard**

Most accomplished surfers are unemployed for a reason. Surfing requires total commitment. Even buying a board is tough. However, surfboard selection is surprisingly nontechnical. Experienced surfers choose boards based on feel, intuition and experience as much as on any hard data. So quit your job, select a board and get in the water.

Steps

1 Find a comfortable spot and watch some surfers. Study the boards. Big boards glide easily but turn slowly. Small boards turn quickly but glide poorly.

2 Decide on a type of board. Small boards—less than about 7 feet in length, with pointed noses—are called *shortboards*. These are ideal for aggressive, rapid maneuvers. Larger boards—usually between 9 and 10 feet, with rounded noses—are called *longboards*, and excel at graceful, smooth turns.

3 If you're a beginner, get a cheap used board that you can knock around while learning, not an expensive and stylish board. Check that the fins are securely in place and that there are no holes in the fiberglass. Small repairs are fine, but avoid boards that have been broken in half and repaired.

4 Inspect the dimensions, usually written on the bottom. For beginners, concern yourself with the length, width and thickness. Ignore the nose and tail dimensions. Width ranges from about 18 to 21 inches. Most thicknesses fall between 2 and 3 inches.

5 Larger surfers need larger boards. A 220-lb. (82-kg) person might choose a 7-foot shortboard, 21 inches wide and 3 inches thick. An 80-lb. (30-kg) kid will surf better on a 5-foot board, 18 inches wide and 2 inches thick. For longboards, most people choose 9-foot boards. People of above-average size should consider slightly longer boards, such as 9-foot-6 inches.

6 Avoid very old boards; they just won't surf very well. Old longboards are easy to identify because they weigh over 20 lbs.(7.5 kg). If it's hard to lift, it will be hard to surf with. Also avoid shortboards with only one fin. A modern shortboard has three or more fins.

7 Expect to pay at least $100 for a serviceable used shortboard. New shortboards range from $350 to $500. A good used longboard will cost at least $300. New longboards cost $450 to $700.

What to Look For

- Appropriate type
- Correct dimensions
- Age
- Condition

Tips

Most shops make their own boards. Ask about having a board custom-made. The shop will have ideas about what will work for you, based on your experience and size, and the local waves.

Wax is applied to the top of a surfboard for grip. If you buy your board from a surf shop, it will usually throw in a few bars of wax for free.

Surfboards around the world are sold in feet and inches, not metrics.

494 Buy Fly-Fishing Gear

For some, shopping for fly-fishing gear resembles the quest for the Holy Grail. Tradition, lore, family bonding—it all comes together to make for a gripping experience. Some advice for the newcomer: Spend as little as possible until you're committed, then reward yourself with the best gear you can afford.

Steps

1 Establish a relationship with a knowledgeable shop. In addition to getting help with gear, you will also gain access to important fishing information and news.

2 Buy only equipment you want. A shop that is willing to work with you should understand this immediately and shouldn't push you into making unnecessary purchases. Some people enjoy owning every bit of gear they can carry. This is fine if you enjoy it, but not essential.

3 Start by purchasing a rod-and-reel combination. Basic sets can be had for $50. You needn't concern yourself with rod materials and characteristics at first—you want an inexpensive set with which you can learn the basics. Later, get a high-quality rod with a lifetime guarantee. Materials range from wood-laminates to carbon fiber and fiberglass.

4 Buy a good pair of waders, which allow you to stay dry while entering the water and are mandatory for comfort in cold water. Comfortable, bib-overall types have attached boots that need to fit securely to provide stability on wet rocks. Inexpensive waders for about $75 are fine for occasional use. For frequent use, spend more to get a longer-lasting pair.

5 Save money on expendable items. Some of your stock of flies, line and leaders will end up decorating the bushes at your favorite fishing spot. There's no need to waste money on top-quality items at first.

6 Befriend an old pro, or buy an instruction book and video, and start tying those flies. Fly-fishing requires knowledge of specific knots—practice at home before you go fishing.

7 Embrace two competing concepts when buying flies. First, seek and listen to advice. Don't expect the old-timers to share all their secrets, but most will be happy to set you on the right path. Second, experiment with your own ideas.

8 Experiment with different rods as you develop your casting style. Your technique will determine the rod length and stiffness that works best for you.

What to Look For

- Knowledgeable shop
- Basic rod-and-reel set for beginners
- Accessories
- Pair of waders
- Fly-tying book and video

Tip

Try out new flies and fishing spots. In addition to an adventure, you may also get some stories to tell back at the shop.

495 Buy Rock-Climbing Equipment

Aspiring rock climbers may find the equipment intimidating at first—but if you ask lots of questions and buy over time, it can be fun. Quality gear is labeled by Independent testing agencies. Only buy new equipment, and only from a reputable shop. Treat your gear as if your life depends on it, because it does.

ITEM	WHAT TO LOOK FOR
Rope	Various rope systems are in use today, but for the majority of climbing needs, a single rope, 10 or 11 mm in diameter and 50 to 60 m long, will do. Make sure you buy a true climbing rope, not a static rope intended only for rappelling. $120 to $150.
Harness	An inexpensive harness is fine for most climbing. More money will add neat features but not necessarily be safer. Spend more for a harness that is easy to get into. It should be comfortable but able to be tightened until it is very snug. From $40.
Climbing Shoes	Fit is the most important consideration, and the only way to find that perfect fit is to try on different models. Buy the smallest shoe you can comfortably wear for long periods of time. $90 to $150.
Carabiners	These metal links attach ropes to harnesses and webbing. They come in two major styles—locking and nonlocking. Locking 'biners are more secure but can sometimes be cumbersome. All types are strong enough for general use, so don't worry about strength ratings unless you really enjoy engineering trivia or are doing some specialized climbing. An introductory climbing set should include four locking ($15 to $20 each) and four nonlocking ($8 to $12 each) carabiners.
Webbing	Webbing is a strong, flat, ribbonlike material with numerous climbing applications used to secure a climber or carabiner to the rock. While webbing is now made from a variety of materials, the most common and affordable type is nylon. For starters, buy four 10-foot (3-m) sections of 1-inch–wide (2.5-cm–wide) tubular webbing. Consider buying different colors for ease of identification. About 50 cents per foot.
Pitons	Steel pegs hammered into the rock to secure a climber. State-of-the-art equipment for decades, they have been supplanted by newer, easier-to-use tools that do not scar the rock. An introductory climbing set does not require pitons, but it may be fun to own one for practice or as a paperweight. Understand that it is considered bad form to hammer pitons indiscriminately into the rock at popular climbing spots.
Chocks (Nuts)	A small metal block with cable or webbing attached, which can be inserted into a crack in the rock, creating a secure anchor. Well-equipped climbers on extended climbs carry a large selection of chocks in different sizes. Again, an introductory climbing set does not require these, but eventually you will want to become skilled in their use. Consider buying a few small chocks for practice. $10 to $15 each.
Cams	A cam is essentially a chock that can expand or contract to fit a variety of crack widths. They perform the same function as chocks, although they are much more sophisticated and offer great flexibility of use. Not required in a basic setup, but aspiring climbers should practice with them as soon as possible. $50 to $120 each.
Instruction Book	There's no substitute for climbing instruction from a qualified guide, but you can learn a lot while sitting on your couch. Purchase a book that covers the basics, including a section on climbing terminology and etiquette. Most important, make sure the book has a section on rock-climbing knots, and practice whenever you can.

HOUSE STORES • BUY WHOLESALE • GET OUT OF DEBT • BUY NOTHING • BUY HAPPINESS • BUY A BETTER MOUSETRAP • BUY TIME •
EONE'S FAVOR • BUY POSTAGE STAMPS WITHOUT GOING TO THE POST OFFICE • TIP PROPERLY • BUY HEALTHY FAST FOOD • BUY SUNS
NG SERVICE • SELL YOURSELF ON AN ONLINE DATING SERVICE • SELL YOURSELF TO YOUR GIRLFRIEND/BOYFRIEND'S FAMILY • BUY DOG
OSE FILM FOR YOUR CAMERA • BUY RECHARGEABLE BATTERIES • DONATE TO A GOOD CAUSE • HOLD A PROFITABLE GARAGE SALE • HI
ENT DISCOUNTS • BUY FLOWERS WHOLESALE • GET A PICTURE FRAMED • HIRE A MOVER • HIRE A PERSONAL ORGANIZER • FIND A VET
HDAY PRESENT FOR UNDER $10 • SELECT GOOD CHAMPAGNE • BUY A DIAMOND • BUY JEWELRY MADE OF PRECIOUS METALS • BUY CO
ESMAIDS' DRESSES • HIRE AN EVENT COORDINATOR • HIRE A BARTENDER FOR A PARTY • HIRE A PHOTOGRAPHER • HIRE A CATERER •
AN ANNIVERSARY GIFT • ARRANGE ENTERTAINMENT FOR A PARTY • COMMISSION A FIREWORKS SHOW • BUY A MOTHER'S DAY GIFT • B
LECT A THANKSGIVING TURKEY • BUY A HOUSEWARMING GIFT • PURCHASE HOLIDAY CARDS • BUY CHRISTMAS STOCKING STUFFERS •
ROLLERS ROOM IN VEGAS, BABY • BUY SOMEONE A STAR • PAY A RANSOM • GET HOT TICKETS • HIRE A LIMOUSINE • BUY A CRYONIC
Y A PERSONAL JET • ACQUIRE A TELEVISION NETWORK • ACQUIRE A BODY GUARD • BOOK A LUXURY CRUISE AROUND THE WORLD • SE
ROUGHBRED RACEHORSE • BUY A VILLA IN TUSCANY • HIRE A PERSONAL CHEF • PURCHASE CUBAN CIGARS • HIRE A GHOSTWRITER TO
ESS • MAKE BAIL • DONATE YOUR BODY TO SCIENCE • HIRE YOURSELF OUT AS A MEDICAL GUINEA PIG • SELL PLASMA • SELL YOUR SO
LEGE EDUCATION • BUY AND SELL STOCKS • CHOOSE A STOCKBROKER • DAY-TRADE (OR NOT) • BUY ANNUITIES • BUY AND SELL MUTU
SONAL FINANCE SOFTWARE • CHOOSE A TAX PREPARER • SET UP A LEMONADE STAND • SELL YOUR PRODUCT ON TV • HIRE A CAREER
Y A SMALL BUSINESS • BUY A FRANCHISE • LEASE RETAIL SPACE • LEASE INDUSTRIAL SPACE • LEASE OFFICE SPACE • BUY LIQUIDATED
ERTISING ON THE WEB • SELL YOUR ART • HIRE A PERSONAL COACH • SELL ON THE CRAFT CIRCUIT • HIRE A LITERARY AGENT • PITCH
A HOT DOG STAND • SHOP FOR A MORTGAGE • REFINANCE YOUR HOME • SAVE BIG BUCKS ON YOUR MORTGAGE • OBTAIN HOME OWN
THE FARM • SELL MINERAL RIGHTS • SELL A HOUSE • SELL A HOUSE WITHOUT A REAL ESTATE AGENT • OBTAIN A HOME EQUITY LOAN
A CONDOMINIUM • RENT AN APARTMENT OR HOUSE • OBTAIN RENTER'S INSURANCE • BUY A LOFT IN MANHATTAN • BUY A TENANCY-IN
RTMENT • BUY USED FURNITURE • BUY DOOR AND WINDOW LOCKS • CHOOSE AN ORIENTAL CARPET • BUY LAMPS AND LIGHT FIXTURE
LIANCES • FIND PERIOD FIXTURES • BUY A BED AND MATTRESS • HIRE AN INTERIOR DESIGNER • HIRE A FENG SHUI CONSULTANT • INCO
RLPOOL TUB • BUY A SHOWERHEAD • BUY A TOILET • CHOOSE A FAUCET • BUY GLUES AND ADHESIVES • CHOOSE WINDOW TREATMEN
OSE A KITCHEN COUNTERTOP • BUY GREEN HOUSEHOLD CLEANERS • STOCK YOUR HOME TOOL KIT • BUY A VIDEO SECURITY SYSTEM
RAGE-DOOR OPENER • BUY LUMBER FOR A DIY PROJECT • HOW TO SELECT ROOFING • HIRE A CONTRACTOR, PLUMBER, PAINTER OR
LECT PEST CONTROLS • BUY SOIL AMENDMENTS • BUY MULCH • BUY A COMPOSTER • BUY FERTILIZER • START A VEGETABLE GARDEN
A STORAGE SHED • HIRE AN ARBORIST • BUY BASIC GARDEN TOOLS • BUY SHRUBS AND TREES • BUY A HOT TUB • BUY AN OUTDOOR
D LABELS • SELECT HERBS AND SPICES • STOCK YOUR KITCHEN WITH STAPLES • EQUIP A KITCHEN • CHOOSE FRESH PRODUCE • SEL
EY • CHOOSE POULTRY • SELECT FRESH FISH AND SHELLFISH • SELECT RICE • PURCHASE PREMIUM SALT AND PEPPER • GET A CHEES
CHASE KOSHER FOOD • BUY FOOD IN BULK • CHOOSE COOKING OILS • SELECT OLIVE OIL • SELECT OLIVES • BUY ETHNIC INGREDIENT
CHASE A KEG OF BEER • BUY ALCOHOL IN A DRY COUNTY • CHOOSE A MICROBREW • ORDER A COCKTAIL • CHOOSE A RESTAURANT F
GNANCY TEST KIT • CHOOSE BIRTH CONTROL • FIND THE RIGHT OB-GYN • HIRE A MIDWIFE OR DOULA • FIND A GOOD PEDIATRICIAN •
AST PUMP • CHOOSE A CAR SEAT • BUY CHILD-PROOFING SUPPLIES • FIND FABULOUS CHILDCARE • FIND A GREAT NANNY • FIND THE
MMER CAMP • SELL GIRL SCOUT COOKIES • BUY BRACES FOR YOUR KID • BUY TOYS • BUY BOOKS, VIDEOS AND MUSIC FOR YOUR CH
THES AND BOOKS • FIND A COUPLES COUNSELOR • HIRE A FAMILY LAWYER • BUY PROPERTY IN A RETIREMENT COMMUNITY • CHOOS
THBRUSH • BUY MOISTURIZERS AND ANTIWRINKLE CREAMS • SELECT PAIN RELIEF AND COLD MEDICINES • SAVE MONEY ON PRESCRI
S TO COUNTER HAIR LOSS • BUY A WIG OR HAIRPIECE • BUY A NEW BODY • GET A TATTOO OR BODY PIERCING • OBTAIN BREAST IMPL
GLASSES AND SUNGLASSES • HIRE A PERSONAL TRAINER • SIGN UP FOR A YOGA CLASS • TREAT YOURSELF TO A DAY AT THE SPA • B
L • BUY AT AUCTION • KNOW WHAT YOUR COLLECTIBLES ARE WORTH • DICKER WITH DEALERS • GET AN ANTIQUE APPRAISED • BUY S
AN ANTIQUE AMERICAN QUILT • BUY AN ANTIQUE FLAG • LIQUIDATE YOUR BEANIE BABY COLLECTION • SCORE AUTOGRAPHS • TRADE
AND SELL SPORTS MEMORABILIA • SELL YOUR BASEBALL-CARD COLLECTIONS • CHOOSE A DESKTOP COMPUTER • SHOP FOR A USE
COMPUTER PERIPHERALS • CHOOSE AN INTERNET SERVICE PROVIDER • GET AN INTERNET DOMAIN NAME • BUY A HOME NETWORK
YER • BUY A VCR • CHOOSE A PERSONAL DIGITAL ASSISTANT • CHOOSE MOBILE PHONE SERVICE • NEGOTIATE YOUR LONG-DISTANCE
ME AUTOMATION SYSTEM • BUY A STATE-OF-THE-ART SOUND SYSTEM • BUY AN AUDIO-VIDEO DISTRIBUTION SYSTEM • BUY A SERIOUS
UAL-REALITY FURNITURE • BUY TWO-WAY RADIOS • BUY A MOBILE ENTERTAINMENT SYSTEM • GET A PASSPORT, QUICK! • PURCHASE
FREE • BID FOR A SLED RIDE ON THE ALASKAN IDITAROD TRAIL RACE • BUY DUTY-FREE • SHIP FOREIGN PURCHASES TO THE UNITED
ATION • CHOOSE A CHEAP CRUISE • BOOK A HOTEL PACKAGE FOR THE GREEK ISLANDS • RAFT THE GRAND CANYON • BOOK A CHEAP
E SALSA LESSONS IN CUBA • BUY A CAMERA IN HONG KONG • BUY YOUR WAY ONTO A MOUNT EVEREST EXPEDITION • HIRE A TREKKI
LE AND KNEE BRACES • BUY GOLF CLUBS • JOIN AN ELITE GOLF CLUB • SELL FOUND GOLF BALLS • BUY ATHLETIC SHOES • BUY A R
JY A SKATEBOARD AND PROTECTIVE GEAR • BUY SKATES • GO SPORT FISHING • GO SKYDIVING • BUY WEIGHTLIFTING EQUIPMENT • C
 SKI BOOTS • BUY A BICYCLE • SELL YOUR BICYCLE AT A GARAGE SALE • COMMISSION A CUSTOM-BUILT BICYCLE • BUY A PROPERLY
TATION DEVICE • BUY A WET SUIT • BUY A SURFBOARD • BUY FLY-FISHING GEAR • BUY ROCK-CLIMBING EQUIPMENT • BUY A CASHM
ES • BUY THE PERFECT COCKTAIL DRESS • BUY DESIGNER CLOTHES AT A DISCOUNT • CHOOSE A BASIC WARDROBE FOR A MAN • BUY
EFCASE • SHOP FOR A LEATHER JACKET • BUY MATERNITY CLOTHES • GET A GREAT-FITTING BRA • CHOOSE A HIGH-PERFORMANCE S
RCHASE CLOTHES AT OUTLET SHOPS • BUY A NEW CAR • BUY THE BASICS FOR YOUR CAR • BUY A USED CAR • BUY OR SELL A CAR O

QUET OF ROSES • BUY SOMEONE A DRINK • GET SOMEONE TO BUY YOU A DRINK • BUY YOUR WAY INTO HIGH SOCIETY • BUY YOUR W
RDER THE PERFECT BURRITO • ORDER TAKEOUT ASIAN FOOD • ORDER AT A SUSHI BAR • BUY DINNER AT A FANCY FRENCH RESTAURAN
OWERS FOR YOUR SWEETHEART • BUY MUSIC ONLINE • HIRE MUSICIANS • ORDER A GREAT BOTTLE OF WINE • BUY AN ERGONOMIC DE
ECLEANER • HIRE A BABY SITTER • BUY A GUITAR • BUY DUCT TAPE • GET A GOOD DEAL ON A MAGAZINE SUBSCRIPTION • GET SENIOR
J • BUY PET FOOD • BUY A PEDIGREED DOG OR CAT • BREED YOUR PET AND SELL THE LITTER • GET A COSTUME • BUY A PIÑATA • BUY A
MSTONES • CHOOSE THE PERFECT WEDDING DRESS • BUY OR RENT A TUXEDO • REGISTER FOR GIFTS • BUY WEDDING GIFTS • SELECT
FAL WEDDING OFFICIANT • OBTAIN A MARRIAGE LICENSE • ORDER CUSTOM INVITATIONS AND ANNOUNCEMENTS • SELL YOUR WEDDINC
ER'S DAY GIFT • SELECT AN APPROPRIATE COMING-OF-AGE GIFT • GET A GIFT FOR THE PERSON WHO HAS EVERYTHING • BUY A GRADU/
KKAH GIFTS • PURCHASE A PERFECT CHRISTMAS TREE • BUY A PRIVATE ISLAND • HIRE A SKYWRITER • HIRE A BIG-NAME BAND • GET IN
RENT YOUR OWN BILLBOARD • TAKE OUT A FULL-PAGE AD IN *THE NEW YORK TIMES* • HIRE A BUTLER • ACQUIRE A PROFESSIONAL SPO
JR COAT • BOOK A TRIP ON THE ORIENT-EXPRESS • BECOME A WINE MAKER • PURCHASE A PRIVATE/CUSTOM BOTTLING OF WINE • BUY
R MEMOIRS • COMMISSION ORIGINAL ARTWORK • IMMORTALIZE YOUR SPOUSE IN A SCULPTURE • GIVE AWAY YOUR FORTUNE • HIRE AN
DEVIL • NEGOTIATE A BETTER CREDIT CARD DEAL • CHOOSE A FINANCIAL PLANNER • SAVE WITH A RETIREMENT PLAN • SAVE FOR YOU
BUY BONDS • SELL SHORT • INVEST IN PRECIOUS METALS • BUY DISABILITY INSURANCE • BUY LIFE INSURANCE • GET HEALTH INSURA
• HIRE A HEADHUNTER • SELL YOURSELF   MARKET YOUR INVENTION • FINANCE YOUR BUS
JIPMENT • HIRE SOMEONE TO DESIGN AND   ESIGNER • ACQUIRE CONTENT FOR YOUR WEB S
STORY • SELL A SCREENPLAY • SELL YOUR   RT A BED-AND-BREAKFAST • SELL A FAILING BUS
ANCE • OBTAIN DISASTER INSURANCE • BUY   Y A FORECLOSED HOME • BUY AND SELL A FIXE
• BUY HOUSE PLANS • HIRE AN ARCHITECT   S • BUY A VACATION HOME • BOOK A VACATION
JNIT • BUY RENTAL PROPERTY • RENT YOUR   FURNISH YOUR HOME • FURNISH YOUR STUDIO
OGRAMMABLE LIGHTING SYSTEM • BUY HO   APPLIANCES • BUY EXTENDED WARRANTIES ON
JID ARCHITECTURE INTO YOUR HOME • SE   DECORATIVE TILES • CHOOSE A CEILING FAN • B
F-CLEANING WINDOWS • CHOOSE WALLPA   NG • SELECT CARPETING • CHOOSE KITCHEN C
ME ALARM SYSTEM • BUY SMOKE ALARMS   Y FIRE EXTINGUISHERS • CHOOSE AN ENTRY DO
• HIRE A GARDENER • BUY OUTDOOR FURI   Y FLOWERING BULBS • BUY FLOWERS FOR YOL
RDEN PROFESSIONAL • BUY AN AUTOMATIC   • BUY A LAWN MOWER • BUY KOI FOR YOUR FIS
STEM • BUY ORGANIC PRODUCE • CHOOS   RMERS' MARKETS • SELECT KITCHEN KNIVES • D
OCK UP FOR THE PERFECT BURGER • PUF   FF • BUY ROCKY MOUNTAIN OYSTERS • PURCHA
HILADELPHIA • ORDER FRESH SALMON IN S   UY ARTISAN BREADS • BUY ARTISAN CHEESES •
E VINEGAR • CHOOSE PASTA • BUY TEA • B   EE • BUY A COFFEEMAKER OR ESPRESSO MACH
S FUNCTION • STOCK A WINE CELLAR • ST   HOOSE AN OVULATION PREDICTOR KIT • PICK A
HERAPIST • GEAR UP FOR A NEW BABY •   UY BABY CLOTHES • CHOOSE DIAPERS • BUY DI
E SCHOOL • FIND A GOOD AFTER-SCHOOL   SONS • BUY A BACKYARD PLAY STRUCTURE • FIN
A VIDEO GAME SYSTEM • HIRE A TUTOR •   HILD HIRED AS A MODEL • SELL USED BABY GEAF
CARE OR NURSING HOME • WRITE A LIVIN   FUNERAL EXPENSES • GET VIAGRA ONLINE • PU

**Clothing &
Accessories**

HIRE A MENTAL-HEALTH PROFESSIONAL   MEDICAL SUPPLIES • SELECT HAIR-CARE PRODU
RINKLE-FILLER INJECTIONS • FIND ALTERN   OSE A MANICURIST • GET WHITER TEETH • SELEC
E • GET ON ANTIQUES ROADSHOW • BUY   QUE FAIR OR FLEA MARKET • RENT SPACE AT AN
VALUATE DEPRESSION-ERA GLASSWARE • BUY AND SELL STAMPS • BUY ANTIQUE FURNITURE • RECOGNIZE THE REAL MCCOY • BUY C
DS • SNAG STAR WARS ACTION FIGURES • SELL YOUR VINYL RECORD COLLECTION • SELL AT A PAWNSHOP • BUY AND SELL COMIC B
R PERIPHERALS • CHOOSE A LAPTOP OR NOTEBOOK COMPUTER • SELL OR DONATE A COMPUTER • BUY PRINTER PAPER • BUY A PRIN
MEMORY IN YOUR COMPUTER • BUY COMPUTER SOFTWARE • CHOOSE A CD PLAYER • BUY BLANK CDS • BUY AN MP PLAYER • CHOO
E • BUY VIDEO AND COMPUTER GAMES • CHOOSE A FILM CAMERA • CHOOSE A DIGITAL CAMCORDER • DECIDE ON A DIGITAL CAMERA
BETWEEN CABLE AND SATELLITE TV • GET A DIGITAL VIDEO RECORDER • GET A UNIVERSAL REMOTE • BUY A HOME THEATER SYSTEM •
TICKETS • FIND GREAT HOTEL DEALS • RENT THE BEST CAR FOR THE LEAST MONEY • GET TRAVEL INSURANCE • PICK THE IDEAL LUGG
A FOREIGN COUNTRY • TIP PROPERLY IN NORTH AMERICA • BRIBE A FOREIGN OFFICIAL • GET A EURAIL PASS • TAKE AN ITALIAN BICYC
SAFARI • RENT A CAMEL IN CAIRO • GET SINGLE-MALT SCOTCH IN SCOTLAND • BUY A SAPPHIRE IN BANGKOK • HIRE A RICKSHA IN YA
NEPAL • RENT OR BUY A SATELLITE PHONE • BUY YOUR CHILD'S FIRST BASEBALL GLOVE • ORDER UNIFORMS FOR A SOFTBALL TEAM
YM MEMBERSHIP • BUY AN AEROBIC FITNESS MACHINE • BUY A SNOWMOBILE • BUY A PERSONAL WATERCRAFT • HIRE A SCUBA INS
ACK OR CARRIER • BUY SKIS • BUY CLOTHES FOR COLD-WEATHER ACTIVITIES • SELL USED SKIS • BUY A SNOWBOARD, BOOTS AND B
• BUY THE OPTIMAL SLEEPING BAG • BUY A TENT • BUY A BACKPACK • BUY A BACKPACKING STOVE • BUY A KAYAK • BUY A PERSON.
PURCHASE VINTAGE CLOTHING • SELL USED CLOTHING • ORDER CUSTOM-MADE COWBOY BOOTS • BUY CLOTHES ONLINE • FIND SPE
SHIRT • PICK OUT A NECKTIE • BUY A WOMAN'S SUIT • BUY A MAN'S SUIT • HIRE A TAILOR • BUY CUSTOM-TAILORED CLOTHES IN ASI
PERFORMANCE WORKOUT CLOTHES • BUY A HEART-RATE MONITOR • SELECT A WATCH • BUY KIDS' CLOTHES • CHOOSE CHILDREN'
YBRID CAR • SELL A CAR • BUY A MOTORCYCLE • LEASE A CAR WITH THE OPTION TO BUY • TRANSFER YOUR LEASED CAR • DONATE

496 Buy a Cashmere Sweater

Cashmere is synonymous with softness and luxury, and the finest garments are still manufactured in Scotland. Quality counts, though, so be a savvy shopper. After all, it took four years for a goat to grow enough wool for your sweater, and if taken care of well, it will last a lifetime.

Steps

1 Prepare to part with some cash: This high-quality, soft wool is an investment, averaging $200 for a 100 percent cashmere sweater.

2 Pull gently and release the sides of the sweater. A high-quality garment returns to its proper shape; a loosely knit one doesn't.

3 Feel the fabric: If it feels coarse or fuzzy, it's a sign of poor quality. In the world of cashmere, softer is better. Lighter-colored garments are softer since darker dyes are harsher on the yarn.

4 Check if the sweater is two-ply knit, which is sturdier than one-ply but still lightweight. Ply refers to weight, not quality.

5 Beware of bargains and mislabeling. In recent years, cashmere and sheep wool blends have been sold as 100 percent cashmere. If the price seems too good to be true, it probably is.

What to Look For

- Quality weave
- Soft texture
- At least two-ply knit
- Pure cashmere

Tips

Many cashmere items can be hand washed safely. Use baby shampoo or gentle-wash detergent and rinse well. Washing actually makes cashmere softer, allowing the yarns to bloom.

Use a lint brush to remove pills, which should be minimal on a good-quality garment.

497 Purchase Vintage Clothing

Whether your style is a 1970s Adidas jogging suit or a 1950s Chanel suit, an authentic disco shirt or a period zoot suit, going retro is a way to stand apart from the crowd.

Steps

1 Scout out local and online sources that specialize in high-quality vintage clothes from a particular era or style.

2 Scour thrift stores, garage sales and flea markets for bargain-priced treasures, from gasoline station jackets and bowling shirts to wedding gowns and embroidered aprons.

3 Plan to shop frequently because the availability of vintage clothing is, by its nature, hit or miss.

4 Consider having a quality item altered if it's too big. Some damage can be repaired: It's easy to sew up a split seam but not a moth hole. Odors and stains are often permanent. Factor in the complexity and cost of alterations. For example, it's far easier and cheaper to take up a pant hem than to take in a lined jacket.

5 Examine the garment's quality and condition. Check stress points such as under the arms for wear, and make sure zippers work.

What to Look For

- Correct size and flattering fit
- Garment condition

Tips

Vintage fabrics can be fragile. A cleaner can advise you on whether to dry-clean or hand wash the garment.

Don't go by the size on the label: Sizes varied before they were regulated.

498 **Sell Used Clothing**

If your closet is bursting at the seams with clothing you've barely worn, turn your clutter into cash—and make room for that next purchase you can't live without—by selling your clothes online or at resale stores.

Steps

1 Clean out your closet. Toss worn-out or stained clothes in the ragbag. Pull out clothes, shoes and accessories that are in good shape, still in fashion and will be in season for the next few months. Sort kids' clothes by size and gender.

2 Clean and iron the clothes. All stores want clothes that look as new as possible; many require you to bring them on hangers.

3 Visit resale stores that sell clothes similar to yours and browse the racks to become familiar with what they carry. Ask what they're looking for and about their buying policies. For example, some stores that sell jeans are interested in only Levi's 501s; other stores want only designer kids' clothes. Don't waste your time trying to sell to the wrong store.

4 Consider a consignment store for selling gently worn designer-label clothes that are two seasons to two years old. Consignment shops usually display clothes for 30 to 90 days (often with periodic markdowns). You are paid a portion of the sales price (usually 40 to 50 percent, excluding tax) for any items that sell. Some consignment stores have two seasons—spring/summer and fall/winter—so batch your clothes accordingly.

5 Find out what hours a buyer will be on the job. If necessary, make an appointment to take in your clothes. Check to see if there is a maximum number of garments that you can bring in.

6 Hold on to your receipt, and contact the shop when the consignment period is over. Most stores will mail you a check for any items that sold. If you don't pick up your unsold clothes promptly, they may be donated to charity.

7 Walk away with cash—or more clothes—by selling casual styles to second-hand shops. They normally pay about 30 to 40 percent of the price that they intend to charge for your items—more if you take store credit instead.

8 Be your own retailer by selling your clothes, especially designer or vintage items, on your own Web site or auction sites like eBay.com. To get top dollar, write clear, accurate descriptions, give specific dimensions and include quality color photos.

What to Look For

- Clothes clean and in season
- Store policies
- Appropriate shop for your clothing

Tips

Donate your unsold clothing to a local charity that collects used clothing. Get a receipt for tax purposes.

Think a season ahead or target the very beginning of seasons with weather-sensitive items such as winter coats and boots, and shorts and sandals.

Listen when buyers explain why they don't take certain clothes or what else they're looking for. And don't take it personally if a store passes on your clothes or your items don't sell on consignment.

499 Order Custom-made Cowboy Boots

Not just for cowboys—or cowgirls—these boots are classy and timeless and, in some places, the ultimate fashion statement. Exquisitely comfortable and intricately tooled, custom boots are an investment that can run from $200 to $2,500 or more.

Steps

1 Find a custom bootmaker. If you live in ranch country, seek out a local artisan. Go to a rodeo and ask the cowboys for a recommendation. If you live elsewhere, ask a Western-wear shop if it custom-orders boots, or shop online.

2 Choose the leather or skin. Cowhide is common, tough and cheap, but if you're willing to pony up a little more for dress boots and aren't squeamish, choose from the exotics—eel, ostrich, lizard, elk, shark, kangaroo, goat, deer, bison, python or alligator. Get a feel for the texture and ask about a particular material's durability. A range of color options are available.

3 Select a boot style and height. Western boots go all the way up the calf. Stockman, packers and work-style boots are a few inches shorter. Others come up a few inches above or hit right at the ankle.

4 Look at heels and soles. There are riding heels, walking heels and combinations. The standard height is 1¾ inches (4½ cm), just right to hook around the bar of a stirrup. Soles are made from leather, thick crepe and rubber. What you plan to be kicking while wearing the boots will determine the type of heel height you need.

5 Specify a toe shape. Western boots have a very pointy toe. Ropers and work boots are more rounded. There are many other options including French toes and square-cut hog noses.

6 Indulge your wildest fantasies with decorative options. Bootmakers pride themselves on exquisite stitching, wingtips, inlay patterns, silver or gold toe and heel plates, and intricate custom designs. For the ultimate gift, have your sweetheart's name inlaid in green lizard.

7 Measure your feet according to the instructions provided by the bootmaker. Unlike shoes or boots that lace, a cowboy boot is held snug to the foot by the instep alone. Proper fit is critical: Make sure you take accurate measurements.

8 Get all design options, costs and the delivery date in writing. Ask what recourse you have if you're unhappy with the finished results. Most artisans proudly guarantee both the work and your satisfaction; many have repeat customers who come back again and again over the years.

9 Pull on your boots, kick up your heels and enjoy.

What to Look For

- Local artisan or online store
- Type of leather
- Style and height
- Heel, sole and toe
- Decorative details
- Foot measurements
- Guarantee
- Delivery date

Tips

Cowboyoutfitters.com, Cowboybootsbygeorge.com, and Caboots.zoovy.com are some of the many bootmakers you can find online.

If you're unsure about measuring your feet yourself, visit a local boot store and ask a salesperson to do it for you.

A bootmaker can take a few months to over a year to finish a pair of boots.

Scallops—the shape of the top of the boot—vary from a straight cut to a deep scallop cut, plus more decorative shapes.

500 Buy Clothes Online

Although you can't finger the fabric or try on the item, the payoff in convenience and an almost unlimited selection may make you a convert once you master the basics of buying clothes online.

Steps

1 Ask a friend, a tailor or a clothing store salesperson to help you measure your chest, waist, hips, arm length and inseam (the distance from your crotch to where you want the hem of your pants to fall). Another way to get your inseam is to measure a pair of pants that fit perfectly.

2 Look for sites that provide you with lots of information about their clothes via high-quality photos and detailed descriptions, dimensions and sizing information.

3 Check out one of the coolest aspects of buying online: virtual model technology at sites like MyVirtualModel.com. You can see clothes you're interested in on a generic model or on one that you customize with your weight, height and body shape, so you can virtually try before you buy.

4 Find jeans that were literally made for you. Sites like IC3D.com, LandsEnd.com and AmericanFitClothing.com give you options to design your own pants, from $54 to $125. Customize lengths, colors, waistlines, leg styles and more.

5 Contact customer service by phone or e-mail with any questions not addressed by the site's frequently asked questions (FAQ) area. Representatives often have additional notes about the fit or care of items. Some sites let you converse with customer service reps by typing in questions and receiving instant answers.

6 Buy several items at the same time to avoid paying individual shipping charges. Look for retailers that offer free shipping when you spend a certain amount.

7 Understand the return policy. Some online retailers let you return clothes to their local store, which saves you shipping charges. Be sure to bring your shipping invoice. Some stores provide a prepaid shipping label for returns, which reduces the hassle of returns. Many stores don't charge additional shipping when exchanging an item for a different size. See 4 Make Returns.

8 Read the fine print before you click the button to finalize your order. Reputable retailers have secure sites to keep your credit card and personal information safe and private, but you may have to check a specific box to prevent your name from being sold to other mailing lists or to avoid receiving additional catalogs.

What to Look For

- Accurate body measurements
- Detailed product information
- Customer service
- Shipping charges
- Return policies
- Fine print

Tips

If you have a favorite Web retailer, sign up to be notified about upcoming sales via e-mail.

Online clothing sites are often packed with images, which can make Web pages load slowly. Save time and frustration by browsing through a retailer's catalog before you go online.

Check out sites such as DealCatcher.com that gather discounts. Or search the Web for the retailer's name plus "coupon" or "discount." Web sites that aggregate retailers such as Yahoo Shopping and credit card company Web sites sometimes feature exclusive merchant discounts.

See 65 Buy or Rent a Tuxedo.

501 Find Specialty Sizes

Do you have trouble buying clothes or shoes off the rack? You're not alone if you fall outside the limits of what the fashion industry considers standard sizes. Here are some resources for finding clothes and shoes that actually fit.

Steps

1 Start with local retailers, especially department stores and specialty stores, such as Rochester Big and Tall for men's clothes. Nordstrom is known for its wide range of shoe sizes and extra-long ties, and its willingness to search for the size you need.

2 Ask stores if they will custom order items for you from the manufacturer. Salespeople may also recommend other sources.

3 Take advantage of online and catalog shopping. EddieBauer.com, LandsEnd.com, JCrew.com and JJill.com, for example, offer clothes in tall sizes, but sometimes in their catalog or Web site only. Take advantage of search engines, chat rooms and newsgroups to find retailers that carry your size. Sites that let you search multiple merchants at one time, such as Yahoo Shopping, are also good resources. Check out ShoesOnTheNet.com, a portal for online shoe sites.

4 Find brands that cater to your size. For example, New Balance athletic shoes come in varying widths, and Birkenstock has a mismatched and single-shoe service. Liz Claiborne makes lines of petite and plus-sized women's clothing. JCPenney's, Sears and Lands' End also carry clothing in a wide range of sizes.

5 Consider having shoes or clothes custom-made if you have difficulty finding your size. There are several sources for reasonably priced custom-made jeans, including Levi's and Lands' End (see 500 Buy Clothes Online). Some higher-end stores will tailor custom clothing, especially suits. Working one-on-one with a tailor gives you more options and control over the design (see 509 Hire a Tailor).

What to Look For

- Helpful salespeople
- Department stores
- Informative Web sites
- Brands that cater to special sizes
- Custom-made shoes or clothing

Tip

Understand the return policies, especially on custom orders. Just because an item is the right size doesn't mean it's going to be comfortable or fit well.

502 Buy the Perfect Cocktail Dress

Picture Audrey Hepburn in *Breakfast at Tiffany's.* Elegant, timeless and tasteful, a stylish cocktail dress has long been a must-have item for any woman's closet.

Steps

1 Shop at stores such as Talbot's and Ann Taylor, and many department stores to find options in the $100 to $150 range. If you intend to spend more or want something unusual, head to a boutique.

2 Buy an all-season fabric, such as lightweight wool or silk. Linen and cotton are also options, but their color may fade faster. Test how easily the fabric wrinkles: Grab and release a handful.

3 Ignore hemline fads and select a flattering length just above or around the middle of the knee. Shorten a dress that's too long.

4 Look for a versatile style that you can dress up or down with different shoes, jewelry and other accessories. A sleeveless or short-sleeved dress works year-round, either alone or with a jacket, sweater or wrap.

What to Look For

- All-season fabric
- Flattering fit and cut
- Timeless lines
- Versatile style

Tips

When you try the dress on, walk, sit and dance around to make sure it's comfortable.

Go from day to night in a flash: replace a canvas tote, denim jacket and sandals with a beaded bag, pashmina shawl and stilettos.

503 Buy Designer Clothes at a Discount

So you're a believer that it's better to have fewer high-quality items than a closet packed with cheap clothes? The sales racks at department stores and boutiques aren't the only way to scout out a bargain.

Steps

1 Remember the cardinal rule: Everything eventually goes on sale. When new clothes arrive, stores have to clear out anything that's been on the racks too long. Keep checking back to find out if the price of your designer treasure has been reduced.

2 Shop at upscale off-price stores like Loehmann's to find seasonal overstock from designers and lots of specially made merchandise at deep price cuts.

3 Visit resale, vintage and thrift stores. You never know when you might spot a designer bargain.

4 Check the Web. Sites like Bluefly.com often sell designer clothes at heavily discounted prices.

5 Ask salespeople to put you on mailing lists for back-room and sample sales, which are a great way to acquire discounted designer clothes. Sites like DailyCandy.com send out fashion e-mail alerts for sample sales in major U.S. cities.

What to Look For

- Sales
- Resale, vintage and thrift stores
- Discount designer Web sites
- Mailing lists

Tip

January and July are big end-of-season sale months when you may find heavy markdowns.

Choose a Basic Wardrobe for a Man

A man's wardrobe—and his ability to coordinate that wardrobe—expresses his personal style and taste. But comfort and care also play a big part. This chart demonstrates the basic furnishings for a stylish wardrobe, plus some suggestions for injecting more personality.

ITEM	QUANTITY	COLOR	STYLE	FABRIC	FOR FLAIR
Sport Coat (blazer)	1	Navy blue or tan camel hair	Proper fit	100 percent wool	Nubuck suede in chocolate brown
Button-down shirts	2 or 3, more if worn daily	Basic white, then light or French blue, or ecru	Tab collars or straight collars	100 percent cotton or cotton-polyester blend (depending on ironing skills)	French cuffs with cuff links
Casual Shirts	1	White, black or other solid neutral	Polos, T-shirts, turtlenecks	Cotton knit or cotton-spandex blend	European fit; retro '50s style
Sweater	1	Neutral	V-neck, crewneck or mock neck	Cotton, wool or cashmere	Silk; deeper colors
Dress Slacks	1	Navy, mid-gray, tan or charcoal	Pleats	100 percent wool	Lightweight wool; pinstripe; flat front
Khakis (chinos)	1	Tan, stone or olive	Pleats	100 percent cotton	Corduroys; flat front
Jeans	1	Medium wash	Not too baggy, not too tight	Denim, of course!	Black; carpenter style
Ties	2 or 3, more if worn daily	Red, burgundy or patterns	Width and length according to current fashion	Silk	Graphic prints, vibrant colors
Belt	2	Black and/or brown; should match shoes	One for casual pants, one for dress slacks	Leather	Suede with contrast stitching
Dress Shoes	1	Black or cordovan (reddish-black)	Cap-toe or wing tip	Leather	Square toe; tassel
Casual Shoes	1	Brown or black	Loafers or oxfords	Leather	Low-rise boots
TIPS	To save time, take advantage of free personal shoppers at department stores. Read care tags. Don't buy a garment that requires hand washing or dry-cleaning if you throw everything in the washer.				

505 Buy a Man's Dress Shirt

Men are no longer limited to the standard white dress shirt. While it remains a classic choice, options have expanded to include many more colors and styles. Prices start at about $40 and go up to hundreds of dollars for a hand-stitched shirt.

Steps

1 Buy all-cotton, which breathes and offers the greatest comfort. Look for cottons that have been treated to resist wrinkles.

2 Examine the collar. Though styles differ, every collar should be aligned, lay flat and fit snugly but comfortably around the neck. The best shirts have removable stays, which hold the collar's points and keep them in place. Never wear a button-down collar with a suit; instead opt for a spread collar.

3 Inspect the shirt's stitching. A higher-quality shirt has single-needle stitching and 22 stitches per inch, and cross-stitched buttons for durability. The design on any patterned shirt should meet perfectly at the seams.

4 Select a cut to accommodate your build. Dress shirts come in either a fitted cut or a standard cut, which is looser.

What to Look For

- All cotton
- Collar details
- Stitching and seams
- Standard versus fitted cut

Tips

Have the salesperson measure your neck size and sleeve length, if you are not sure of your correct size or if your weight has fluctuated since your last shopping trip.

French cuffs with cuff links add a dash of style.

Ceramic buttons are nearly indestructible.

506 Pick Out a Necktie

Ties allow for a bit of creativity in what might otherwise be a straight-forward ensemble. While color and pattern depend on personal preference, the right tie should have excellent construction.

Steps

1 Inspect the tie's lining, also called *pocket tipping*. It should extend from the bottom of the tie to its narrowest point. A fully lined tie costs more; most ties these days are not.

2 Check the stitching along the back of the tie, which helps maintain the shape. Slip stitching runs vertically, while bar tacking runs horizontally across the bottom and top ends. A high-end tie has bar tacking on the top and bottom.

3 Get a feel for the fabric. Silk is the most popular because it holds its shape, and it's lightweight and durable. Polyester blends also hold their shape, but don't take dye as well as natural fabrics do. Excessive wrinkling can be a problem with cotton ties.

4 Expect to pay at least $50 to $100 for a nice tie. Prices can exceed $300 for a designer or a handmade tie.

5 Find extra-long ties—for taller or not-so-thin men—at some department stores.

What to Look For

- Lining
- Inner facing
- Stitching
- Fabric
- Handmade ties

Tips

Wear a white dress shirt to serve as a backdrop for viewing ties.

"Hand-finished" does not mean that a tie is handmade, only that the last few steps were performed by hand.

The background color of the tie should match or complement your shirt or suit.

507 Buy a Woman's Suit

Whether you want a formal suit for an interview, a pantsuit for a wedding shower or a classic Armani, look for a suit that's stylish, well-made and fits like a dream.

Steps

1 Consider where you will wear the suit and how dressy your attire needs to be. Options include a formal skirt suit, a casual pantsuit or an interchangeable set with a jacket, skirt and pants. If you wear different sizes on top and on bottom, your best bet is to buy matching separates.

2 Head to a store, whether Brooks Brothers or Banana Republic, that matches your style and budget. Because fit is so important with a suit, buying online is riskier, but possible if you're familiar with a retailer or designer's fit and have a good tailor.

3 Anticipate spending at least $300 to $400. (Prices range from $200 to $2,000 or more.) Keep in mind that a higher price doesn't necessarily mean a better suit. Some manufacturers are coming out with stylish yet less-expensive suits.

4 Get a high-quality, all-season fabric such as 100 percent worsted wool, which looks and wears better better than polyester blends. If you're expanding your suit collection, you might consider more seasonal fabrics such as cotton twill, linen or silk.

5 Find a color that fits your needs. Start with a neutral like navy, black or gray before adding other colors.

6 Find a jacket style that suits you. Choose from single- or less popular double-breasted jackets; with a lapel and collar (or neither); and a cut and length that flatters your figure. Once you've found a style you like, inspect the construction and fit in more detail.

7 Try the jacket on. You should be able to move your arms freely. The shoulders should be about an inch (2½ cm) wider than your shoulder bone, and the sleeves should extend to about the wrist bone. Button the jacket to test for comfort and to make sure the buttons don't gap across the chest or pull over the hips.

8 Choose a flattering style for the skirt or pants. Flat-front pants tend to be more slimming. Straight skirts aren't very forgiving but can be slimming when they fit just right. An A-line, pleated or slit skirt makes walking easier. You should be able to insert two fingers into the waistband. Choose a length that's appropriate for its intended use.

9 Examine the construction of each piece. They should be fully lined with straight hems, flat-lying collars and buttons that are even. Zippers, buttons and other fasteners should lie flat. Pockets shouldn't gap, and the hem should hang straight.

What to Look For

- Appropriate style
- Wool fabric
- Color, style
- Quality construction
- Comfortable fit

Tips

Investing in alterations can make an enormous difference in how the suit feels and looks.

Wear a blouse, dress shoes and hosiery, or try on matching garments with the suit.

Plastic buttons can be replaced with higher-quality ones of pearl or bone.

Make sure your freedom of movement is unrestricted — sit, walk and pick something up off the floor to test.

10 Have a knowledgeable salesperson or, better yet, a tailor check the suit's fit before you buy it. Spend the money to have your suit altered to fit.

508 Buy a Man's Suit

Whether you need another suit for the office or want to dress to impress at an upcoming special occasion, a sharp suit is a wardrobe essential. The trick is to buy the best quality you can afford in an all-season fabric, and a style that won't look dated too soon.

Steps

1 Expect to pay at least $300 to $400. Suits can cost from $200 to $2,000 or more. The best values come from finding originally expensive ones on sale. Watch for sales and get on the mailing lists of your favorite stores. But remember, even an expensive suit will lose its charm if it doesn't fit you well.

2 Get measured for your correct size pants and jacket. Sizes include a number (for example, even numbers between 36 and 56) plus a *short, regular, long* or *extra-long* designation.

3 Look for an all-season fabric. All-wool fabric wears longer and looks better than wool-polyester blends, but blends typically wrinkle less. Other options are twill, linen and wool crepe. If you choose a pattern, such as pinstripe, opt for a flattering, versatile color such as navy or charcoal.

4 Select a jacket style. The three-button jacket is a classic look, but some men prefer a two-button or double-breasted jacket, which is better for thin men. Make sure the jacket buttons easily and doesn't pull on either side, whether you're standing up or sitting down. Make sure you can move your arms freely. The lapels should lie flat and show a ½-inch (1 cm) rim of shirt collar. Shoulders cannot be altered, so make sure they aren't bulging or too boxy. The sleeves should extend to about the wrist bone. The jacket should be fully lined with no puckering seams.

5 Select a pants style. Flat-front pants tend to be more slimming, while pleats and cuffs can make the pants dressier. (Shorter men, however, should avoid cuffs.) Go for lined pants that rest comfortably on your waist. When they're hemmed, they should break at the laces of your shoes and hit just above your heel.

What to Look For

- Wool fabric
- Flattering style
- Comfortable fit
- Quality construction

Tips

Wear a button down shirt and dress shoes when you shop for a suit, or plan to try them all on at the store.

Once you know your size, consider ordering online then have a tailor do any alterations.

If you put your hands in the pockets of your pants while wearing a coat with a central vent, you expose your rear. You can decide if that's a good thing—or ask a friend.

Warning

Don't buy a suit without having a knowledgeable salesperson or tailor check the fit. Some fitting problems, such as shoulder pads, cannot be fixed.

509 Hire a Tailor

If you can't find the clothes you're looking for at a store, consider having them made. Good tailors can create garments that reflect your personal style and fit your figure impeccably. They also can perform minor miracles when you need an item updated or altered.

Steps

1 Ask friends or your favorite salespeople for recommendations. A local fabric store is another possible source for referrals. Otherwise, look up "Tailors" in the Yellow Pages.

2 Talk to tailors about their skills and experience. Do they specialize in a certain sort of work, such as bridal gowns or suits? Women's or men's clothing?

3 Check availability and turnaround time. If possible, give the tailor a deadline that's a few weeks before you need an item, in case of an unexpected delay.

4 Inquire about their rates. Although tailors should be able to give you a ballpark estimate, they'll need specifics before they will give you a firm price.

5 For custom designs, ask to see examples of their work and get the names of some of their former clients. Call the clients to see if they were happy with the work and if it was delivered on time.

6 Bring any garments or pictures that would help illustrate what you'd like done. If a tailor is reluctant to try something, ask why; his or her expert opinion might change your mind.

7 Take advantage of what tailors can do to update or alter existing garments. Generally, it's far easier to take in or shorten clothes than to let them out or lengthen them. Adding cuffs, narrowing pants legs and changing necklines are all possible. Complexity adds to the price, and some alterations aren't worth it unless the piece is very high-quality, or a beloved, irreplaceable garment.

8 Once the tailor has a firm idea of what you expect, get a description of the work, the price and the delivery date in writing.

What to Look For

- Personal recommendation
- Skills, experience, and specialization
- Availability and price

Tips

Make sure the tailor measures both legs and arms for symmetry.

The more complex the job, the more often you may have to visit the tailor for fittings.

See 510 Buy Custom-Tailored Clothes in Asia.

Warning

Try on the tailored clothes when you pick them up to make sure they fit.

510 Buy Custom-Tailored Clothes in Asia

Vietnam, South Korea, Thailand and other Asian countries are known for having tailors and seamstresses who make exquisitely crafted custom-tailored clothes in a few days (or even a few hours) for unbelievable prices. An evening dress can be as cheap as $15, while suits start as low as $20.

Steps

1 Pack any item of clothing that you want copied and bring magazines and clothing catalogs that show designs you want made. A talented tailor can copy many garments swiftly and skillfully.

2 Ask other travelers, locals, longtime foreign residents or the hotel concierge to recommend a tailor. A good recommendation will save you time and money.

3 Browse fabrics, either at the tailor's shop or in fabric stores. In addition to the variety of silks in Asia—such as raw silk, print silk, patterned silk and brocade—you can buy cotton and other fabrics. Flip through swatches in the store and show them the fabrics and patterns. A tailor will charge for any fabric or trims you do not supply.

4 Give the tailor adequate guidance. If you're using a picture for reference or duplicating an article of clothing, explain any modifications you want to the piece. For example, perhaps you like a dress shirt in a photo, but you don't want the chest pocket, or you may want a slit up both sides of a skirt, not just the left side.

5 Discuss price in advance. Expect to pay a flat rate that includes measurement and fittings. Prices drop when you select a tailor who designs the garment but contracts out for cutting and sewing. Be aware that Hong Kong is not a bargain for custom-made clothing; an upscale tailor may charge $500 to $800 to design and sew a man's suit.

6 Get the agreed-upon price in writing with a description of all design options and any additional charges, to eliminate any unpleasant surprises when you pick up your clothes later. Typically, you don't have to pay anything upfront, although some shops require a 50 percent deposit.

7 Find out when the clothes will be ready. Remarkably, clothes are sometimes ready the same day or the following day. However, make sure you allow enough time. It may take three or more visits to order, be fitted and pick up your garment.

8 Try on the finished garment and check both construction and fit. Allow sufficient time to correct any problems.

What to Look For

- Clothing you want copied
- Magazines and catalogs
- Trusted referrals
- Quality fabrics
- Adequate guidance
- Upfront price agreement

Tips

The Vietnamese cities of Hanoi, Ho Chi Minh City and especially Hoi An are known for beautiful tailor-made clothing at bargain prices.

You can have clothes custom-made for friends and family if you have their measurements. Ask if the tailor will continue the relationship via mail, if you want future garments created. Inquire about having shoes copied, too.

Warning

Often what is called "silk" in Asian countries is actually a synthetic. That said, this replacement looks just as good, doesn't wrinkle and wears better than the real thing.

511 Buy a Briefcase

In many circles, over-the-shoulder leather cases and padded computer bags have replaced the hard-sided briefcase that once was considered the standard of the business world. First determine your budget.

Steps

1 Think big. You may intend to travel light when heading to and from the office, but look for expandable compartments and outside pockets for stashing extra items.

2 Hoist the case or bag. Leather is strong and classic, but can be heavy. Consider lighter-weight alternatives like canvas and Cordura. If you routinely carry heavy books and files, a case with wheels and a retractable handle might work well for you.

3 Look for features that fit your needs: a padded laptop compartment, pockets for a phone and PDA; a back sleeve that allows the briefcase to slip over the handle of wheeled luggage; backpack straps or chest strap, and lockable zippers.

What to Look For

- Large size
- Lightweight but durable material
- Useful features

Tip

Bicycle courier style bags sell for $100 or less, while you can pay $500 and more for high-end leather cases from Dooney & Bourke, Atlas of Boston, Coach and Hartmann.

512 Shop for a Leather Jacket

A leather jacket is a wardrobe staple and great way to express your personal style. Warm and durable, but also timeless and classic, leather is an investment that pays off over and over through the years.

Steps

1 Be prepared to spend at least $250. A good leather jacket costs $500 or more—not unreasonable when you consider how often and how long you'll wear this garment.

2 Slip into one of the classic styles, which include bomber, blazer and zip-up jackets. A medium-length jacket hits the top of your thigh. Waist or hip-length jackets are versatile. A trench coat can be sleek and slimming on the right figure.

3 Choose color and texture. Although black is the most popular choice, with brown not too far behind, there are a wide range of colors to choose from. Textures vary from buttery soft, thin leather to thicker, more durable jackets. Suede (which requires a little more care) is another option.

4 Inspect the jacket's construction. Seams should be strong and perfect and the bottom hem straight. The collar and pockets should lie flat. Check the lining for strong seams, especially in the pockets where they get a lot of wear and tear. Motorcycle jackets should have vents, a padded kidney panel, and tough leather—all crucial for safe and comfortable riding.

What to Look For

- Style and length
- Softness
- Color
- Detailing
- Quality construction

Tips

Store your leather jacket either flat or on a wide, sturdy, padded hanger to prevent stretch marks. Never use plastic covers.

Take care of stains pronto. When in doubt, take it to a dry cleaner.

513 Buy Maternity Clothes

When your belly expands beyond your baggiest waistbands, it's time to shop for maternity clothes. You don't need to spend a lot of money to get through your pregnancy in style. A few well-chosen pieces let you look professional and keep you comfortable.

Steps

1 Shop for maternity clothes labeled in your pre-pregnancy size. Maternity clothes are designed to give you extra room only where you need it—primarily in the belly and the bust. If you're having twins or have a history of having big babies, you may need a larger size and might outgrow even maternity clothes. If necessary, plus-size shirts and dresses can get you through the last few weeks (don't even bother with pants).

2 Buy basic items in stretch fabrics. Cotton jersey is good, and a little spandex is even better. Many department stores sell the Belly Basics Pregnancy Survival Kit (bellybasics.com), which has a black skirt, dress, tunic, and pants in this easy-care fabric for around $150. You can duplicate this idea for less money by buying similar separates at Target.com or OldNavy.com. Motherhood Maternity (motherhood.oom) sells a wide range of inexpensive cotton clothes that aren't too fussy or cute, as well as good options for the office.

3 Buy only one or two bras at a time because you may grow several sizes over the course of your pregnancy, and wait to buy nursing bras until the last two months. Some women swear by the Bravada bra, available at many maternity shops. These can be expensive, but the correct fit is crucial. Maternity stores are a good place to get expert advice on fitting, even if you end up buying elsewhere.

4 Splurge on at least one outfit that makes you feel great. Whether it's a slinky dress that shows off your shapely belly or a funky pair of pants, find something to wear when you want to look fabulous. Japanese Weekend (japaneseweekend.com) and A Pea in the Pod (apeainthepod.com) offer many elegant styles for special occasions.

5 Remember, no one leaves the hospital in her pre-pregnancy size. You may need to wear your maternity clothes for a while after the baby is born. Remember to pack a nursing nightgown for the hospital.

What to Look For

- Pre-pregnancy size
- Stretchy fabrics
- Comfortable basic items
- Undergarments that fit well
- Splurge outfit

Tips

Save money by borrowing from other recent moms or shopping in second-hand shops.

As your feet swell in the third trimester, you might need new shoes as well as clothes. Comfortable slip-on thongs, clogs or low-heeled mules or slides are a good choice, especially since you don't have to bend over to put them on. Make sure they fit well so you don't turn an ankle and take a spill.

Two-piece maternity swimsuits provide the most flexible fit. JCPenney and maternity stores are your best options for swimwear but if you can, borrow one unless you'll be in it frequently.

514 Get a Great-Fitting Bra

A badly fitting bra is not only a fashion faux pas, it can be extremely uncomfortable. Yet, many women unwittingly wear the wrong size. Getting properly fit is the first step to finding a bra that makes you look and feel your best.

Steps

Everyday bras

1 Go to a lingerie or department store and suss out an experienced salesperson to measure you.

2 Try on a variety of styles. Underwires increase support, push-up bras enhance cleavage, and thicker padding adds inches.

3 Lean forward at the waist and pull the bra away from your breasts by the straps so that your breasts fall naturally into the cups. The band should fit snugly but not dig into your flesh. If it's too tight, go to the looser hook or try a larger size. If the bra doesn't feel comfortably snug or it feels like your breasts might fall out below, tighten the hooks or go to a smaller band size.

4 Adjust the shoulder straps so that they feel snug but don't dig into your shoulders.

5 Walk around, jump up and down, and swing your arms around to test comfort and support.

Sports bras

1 Shop at a store where you feel comfortable. The staff should be helpful and able to answer your questions knowledgeably. Or shop online at a merchant such as Title9Sports.com, which has a vast selection of sports bras including one that holds up to size 40DDDs, as well as a nursing sports bra.

2 Put the bra on. You'll have three choices: pulling it on over your head, fastening it in front, and closing it in the back. It should feel comfortable when you put it on. Large-breasted women should check that there's no pressure on the shoulders.

3 Inspect how the bra is built. There should be no exposed metal or hardware, which will irritate by the end of your workout. Quality bras have plush lining surrounding all metal pieces.

4 Jump up and down to gauge movement. Women up to an average D cup are best off with a compression bra, while full Ds need an encapsulation bra to minimize movement. Ask if you can test-drive the bra and take a run around the block.

5 Read the label to find out what the fabric content is. Virtually every sports bra has a coolmax/lycra lining for wicking. The outer fabric, aside from looking great, lends support and maintains shape. Pure cotton won't wick, but a cotton/polyester/lycra blend is very supportive. Skin that chafes easily will be happiest in a

What to Look For

- Correct band and cup size
- Right bra for the purpose
- Comfortable fit

Tips

If you've never had one, get a professional fitting, even if you've been wearing the same size for years. Recheck your size if your weight changes appreciably.

One manufacturer's 32B may fit like another's 34C, so beware of buying a bra based only on the size.

When you find a bra you like, buy several. Styles get discontinued often.

poly/lycra blend. Many bras use a supplex/lycra/cotton mix for superior wicking. See 516 Buy Performance Workout Clothing for more information on high-tech fabrics and blends.

6 Pick a fabric blend that maximizes performance. Women with A and B cups can choose almost any fabric and still maintain their shape. Cs and Ds need to look for more supportive blends.

7 Live well and sweat hard even if you wear a prosthesis. Several bras accommodate prostheses, such as The Grace Bra by Moving Comfort (movingcomfort.com).

First bras

1 Be supportive and buy your daughter a bra, even if you think she doesn't need one. If all her friends have bras, she'll want to fit in.

2 Take her to a department or specialty store where an experienced, professional sales woman can properly fit her.

3 Skip the fitting if it's just too excruciating and select a sport-style bra that fits snugly but not tightly around her rib cage.

Wash your bras by hand or in a lingerie bag in the washer and allow them to air-dry.

When you purchase a bra online, make sure you can return it without penalty before you click that last send button.

515 Choose a High-Performance Swim Suit

Since the 1996 Atlanta Olympic Games, a new breed of performance swimwear has helped swimmers shave off more time than a Gillette Mach 3. Introduced to the mass market in 2000, these suits cover more of the body, and are revolutionizing competitive racing.

Steps

1 Understand how the suits work. By enclosing the body with a fabric that is smoother than skin, they make the swimmer more streamlined in the water. These suits actually change the way water flows around the body to create less drag. They also compress the body, which reduces vibration.

2 Check out the Aquablade and Fastskin suits on Speedo.com. TYR Sport (tyr.com) offers Aquapel, a coated fabric with a water-repellent, hydrophobic finish in the Powerflow performance suit. Nike (nike.com) has a comparable suit called the Liftsuit.

3 Make sure you get fitted correctly, which means skin-tight and wrinkle-free. It should not be so tight as to limit your range of motion, which will reduce your effectiveness. Wrinkles cause added drag, which defeats the whole purpose of the suit.

4 Spend the money only if you're seriously hard core. These suits cost considerably more than traditional racing suits. Prices range from $68 for a men's brief up to nearly $600 for some full-body suits.

What to Look For

- Speedo, TYR Sport and Nike brands
- Correct fit

Tip

Performance may decline as the suit gets older.

516 Buy Performance Workout Clothing

The old T-shirt and sweats workout combo is only comfy until you get sweaty. Newer synthetic products offer the same freedom of movement while looking better and keeping you drier. Most modern athletic wear starts with some form of nylon or polyester, combined with other materials, to achieve the desired qualities. See 478 Buy Clothes for Cold-Weather Activities for more discussion of synthetic clothing.

MATERIAL	WHAT IT IS	WHAT IT'S GOOD FOR
CoolMax	A DuPont product, designed to enhance evaporation and cooling.	Gym workouts, running wear, base layer under warm clothes.
Lycra	Another DuPont product, Lycra is designed to be close-fitting and stretchy, yet retains its shape well.	Swimwear and stylish workout wear. Lycra is frequently added to other fabrics to add stretchiness and durability.
Fleece	A soft, lightweight material designed to provide maximum insulation with a minimum of weight and bulk. Quick drying and water resistant.	Fleece is everywhere, from jacket linings to gloves and underwear. Fleece has replaced wool as the all-purpose performance material.
Phase Change Materials	Fabrics that absorb and release body heat. Changes as skin temperature fluctuates to keep body temperature constant and increase comfort.	Outerwear constructed with these materials already exists (see Outlast.com). Look for increased use of phase change fabrics in workout wear.
Supplex	Supplex, yet another DuPont product, is soft and comfortable. It recreates the comfort of cotton in a durable, quick-drying fabric.	Supplex is frequently combined with other synthetics to make stretchy, durable fabrics, suitable for everything from lightweight workout wear to jackets.

517 Buy a Heart Rate Monitor

Monitoring your heart rate is easy: If you're living, you've got one. A heart rate monitor allows you to effectively train at your target heart rate for optimal results during competition.

What to Look For

- Easy to use
- Comfortable chest strap
- Knowledgeable shop

Steps

1 Understand how monitors work. Most look like wristwatches and combine timekeeping functions with heart monitoring. For constant heart rate readout, purchase one with a chest strap transmitter that sends heart data to the wrist unit. Devices without a chest strap provide heart rate data but only when you are touching the unit with your hand.

2 Basic units cost about $75, more sophisticated units about $120. Popular brands include Polar, Reebok and Lifesource. You can buy online, but a knowledgeable shop can better educate you about the devices. Read the instructions.

Tips

Get a unit with an audible signal if your heart rate falls above or below your specified range.

Some monitors can store data and download it to a computer to chart your progress.

518 Select a Watch

Watches serve a variety of functions, from workout aid to fashion accessory. Some people even use them for telling time. Before making a purchase, it's worth understanding the basics of watch construction. World-renowned designer models can cost many thousands, while fun disposable watches can be had for a few dollars.

Steps

1 Find out about the true origin. Switzerland has long been associated with fine watch making, and many manufacturers try to take advantage of that cachet. Watches identified as a "Swiss Watch" must meet certain requirements as to where production and assembly took place. Before making a major purchase, be sure to get a full explanation from the seller about the watch's origin.

2 Understand what keeps 'em ticking. Most modern watches use a battery-powered quartz crystal to keep time. Mechanical watches use gears and springs, which are charming and beautiful but require periodic servicing. A few companies, including ETA and Valjoux, make good mechanisms that are found in many popular brands. The very best watch makers build their own mechanisms.

3 Examine the watch case. Any top-quality watch has a screw-on back and screw-down crown (the winding knob) for the most protection from water and dirt. Some watches feature a display back that allows you to see the mechanism. Common case materials include stainless steel, gold, silver, platinum and titanium. All of these are highly durable (except gold, which is fairly soft) and provide a distinctive, classy look.

4 Check the crystal, which is the transparent face that covers the watch (not to be confused with quartz crystal mechanisms). Acrylic crystals are the least expensive and offer good shatter resistance. Sapphire crystals are the choice for top watches, due to their clarity and scratch resistance.

5 Consider other features. Some models combine both digital and analog faces on one watch. A water-resistant watch is fine for swimming and general use. For diving, be sure to check the depth rating. A chronograph (stopwatch) function is essential for a sports watch. For travel, an alarm is handy, as is the ability to track time in other cities. Gemstones are an elegant if expensive addition to high-end fashion watches.

6 Be sure the band is comfortable and secure. Segmented steel bands with their clean look and smooth feel are popular. Leather bands provide a timeless, understated look. Strong, secure, and quick-drying nylon bands are the best choice for sports watches.

7 Expect top-quality movements, materials (including gemstones) and construction from premium watches that run several thousand dollars. Prestigious watchmakers include Rolex, Tag Heuer, Omega, Bulova, Cartier and Jaeger, with many others worldwide.

What to Look For

- Mechanism type
- Extra features
- Casual, sporty or dressy

Tips

While you will spend more on a designer watch, you won't necessarily get increased accuracy. Even moderately priced watches can keep accurate time.

Self-winding watches use the movement of your body to wind themselves; if you don't wear the watch for a few days, it has to be reset.

Warning

Do not be misled by a watch listing a large number of jewels. Tiny, low-value jewels are frequently employed within watch mechanisms, as a way to reduce friction and provide long wear. But overall workmanship is more important than the number of jewels. In other words, jewels by themselves do not guarantee quality and accuracy, and more jewels are not necessarily better.

519 Buy Kids' Clothes

Buying kids' clothes can go from being a delight with your first baby to a challenge with your preteen. Whether you're shopping for a child who's growing like a weed or locked into a battle of wills with your toddler or preteen, planning before you shop is the key to saving time, money and sanity—all valued commodities for busy parents. Borrow as many infant clothes as possible, especially undershirts, onesies and sleepers. It's hard to have too many.

Steps

Shopping for infants and toddlers

1 Keep in mind that babies grow fast and have the next size ready to go. Many new parents and gift givers don't realize that some babies never fit, or fit only for a few days, in clothes sized zero to three months. If you receive a lot of gifts in this size, exchange most for sizes six to nine, or nine to 12 months.

2 Shop at a local used clothing store that specializes in children's clothes, and check out auction Web sites such as eBay.com. Used clothes for infants and toddlers are a great deal because they outgrow clothes before they wear them out.

3 Shop when and where you can. Cruise the clothes department at Target for deals when you're there buying diapers. Shop online anytime at sites such as Babycenter.com and Babystyle.com and keep your eyes peeled for frequent sales.

4 Remember that toddlers need clothes that pull on and off easily when they're in the "I can do it myself" and potty-training stages.

Shopping for older kids

1 Take inventory. At the start of each season, pull out and sort all the kids' clothes. Box any outgrown items for selling, donating to charity or storing. (See 339 Sell Used Baby Gear, Toys, Clothes and Books.)

2 Make a season-specific shopping list that includes categories such as basics, school clothes, outerwear, and athletic and extracurricular attire. When considering quantities, consider how frequently laundry gets done in your house.

3 Keep kids' preferences and ages in mind, and ask for their input. Many kids will reach for sweats before khakis. By second or third grade, expect them to have firm opinions about what's cool and what's not. Look at Web sites and catalogs together at home to see what they like before venturing out to the mall. Explain any limits you have regarding styles you're willing to purchase, but use your veto power sparingly.

What to Look For

- Resale stores
- Online shopping
- Easy-to-use fasteners
- Season-specific list
- Budget
- Bulk socks in one color
- Frequent-shopper programs
- Durable basics

Tips

Make sure you understand return policies, which have gotten stricter in many stores, and file your receipts, which are also important for any items with a wear-out warranty. See 4 Make Returns.

4 Set a budget and use it as a teaching tool. As soon as your kids are old enough to understand, tell them how much you plan to spend and let them help decide where to spend it. If the name-brand wardrobe your daughter must have costs too much, a compromise might be a few T-shirts from her favorite store and less expensive jeans from a discount store.

5 Buy socks and underwear to fit, in bulk and in the same color, style and/or brand for each child. These items wear out fast and are uncomfortable if they're too big. You don't want to have to throw out a good sock just because its mate got lost. If you have more than one child, assigning a color or brand to each also decreases laundry mix-ups. Limiting styles to one choice also eliminates fussiness on busy mornings.

6 Take a child shopping if you have a question about size or an exceptionally picky child. Make sure everyone is well rested and fed to cut down on short tempers. Consider shopping without the kids for expediency. Just make sure you can return anything that doesn't work out.

7 Shop Sears or JCPenney for a large selection of children's plus and husky sizes. Lands' End and Limited Too also offer some styles in larger sizes through their catalogs and Web sites.

Shopping for all kids

1 Purchase seasonal outerwear large to leave room for growth spurts.

2 Find the retailers that work best for you. Outlets can have great prices but can be hit-or-miss for busy parents. Catalogs and Web sites, such as Hanna Andersson, Gymboree, Gap and Old Navy, let you shop from home and often have online specials. Land's End overstocks, for example, are a great source for bargains.

3 Join frequent-buyer programs and sign up for mailing lists for your favorite retailers. For example, Limited Too offers a discount coupon when you spend a certain amount. Check out wear-out warranty programs. Sears and ShopKo will replace certain items if they wear out before kids outgrow them.

4 Focus on buying durable basics such as jeans that will hold up after many washings. Inspect items for quality construction. Feel the fabric to see if it seems sufficiently heavy to withstand wear and tear. Check that buttons and zippers fasten securely.

Warning

Don't waste your money buying clothes your children won't wear. You might think it's the bees knees, but your rascal might not agree.

520 **Choose Children's Shoes**

Kids go through enough shoes that you may want to consider a 401(k) plan just for their feet. Toddler's feet can grow an entire size or more every three months, and rough-and-tumble play takes its toll. Shopping for kids' shoes, though, doesn't need to be daunting. The key is to keep up with growth spurts by having your child's feet properly measured on a regular basis.

Steps

Shopping for the first pair

1 Wait to buy shoes until your child starts to walk. Research suggests that children develop healthy, well-developed feet when they learn to walk barefoot. Keep their feet toasty and unrestricted with soft booties or warm skid-free socks. Robeez (robeez.com) makes thin but warm leather moccasins in a range of colors and sizes that actually stay on little crawlers' feet.

2 When it's time for your baby's first pair of shoes, take your well-rested, recently fed child to a quality children's shoe store that stock brands such as Stride Rite and Elefanten. The best stores have patient and knowledgeable salespeople who are expert at fitting children's feet.

3 Have the salesperson measure the length and width of both of the child's feet. Many babies have an extra wide foot and may need a special size.

4 Make sure the shoes aren't too big, which can cause a baby to trip. First shoes should be soft and pliable to let new walkers feel the ground.

As they grow

1 Have your child's feet measured on a regular basis at a shoe store that specializes in children's shoes. Kids grow fast, and shoe sizes can change from month to month. Really good salespeople can spot evasive maneuvers like scrunched up toes, and know how to woo a reluctant tot out of a parent's lap. Toys and play areas are added bonuses.

2 Head to discount stores, such as Payless ShoeSource, Target and Kmart, which are also great sources for shoes that get limited wear, such as dress shoes. If you're clear about your child's shoe size, you can save a bundle at these discounters. However, many of these stores don't carry wide or narrow shoes.

What to Look For

- Precise measurements
- Proper fit
- Shoe quality

Tips

Some shoe stores such as Stride Rite offer warranties. If the shoes wear out before your kids outgrow them, they will replace them. Be sure to keep receipts.

Shoes with lights are a huge hit with little kids and are found on both quality and discount brands.

Outlets and discounters like Marshall's, Ross and T.J. Maxx often sell brand-name shoes. The selection of sizes and styles may be limited, though.

If your child wears orthotics, bring them with you when trying on shoes.

3 Have your child try both shoes on. Shoes vary in fit, even within the same brand. Toes should have a ½-inch (1-cm) clearance, but not much more. Getting one size larger than their foot is typical. Watch your child walk and make sure that the heels don't slip out. If a heel is too wide but the rest of the shoe fits, try heel pads (available at some shoe stores and drugstores).

4 Invest in a good pair of sneakers that your child can wear every day. This pair will take a pounding, so look for quality. Leather holds up better than vinyl, and stitching lasts longer than glue.

5 Take advantage of Velcro fasteners. At some point, though, all kids need to learn to tie shoelaces, so get your preschool-age child at least one pair that ties.

6 For summer months or warm climates, purchase cheap canvas sneakers for playing in the sand box, jumping in puddles or going in the creek. Velcro-strapped sandals are great for tender feet that want to have wet summertime fun.

7 Buy rain and winter boots a size or two bigger. Kids can wear heavier or even doubled socks. Most retailers won't restock boots, even if they sell out of a size, until the following year's season. Be aware that most rain boots don't come in wide sizes; you may have to go up in size to get them wide enough.

521 Purchase Clothes at Outlet Shops

When a clothing manufacturer can't sell items for full price, its loss is your gain. Outlet shops stock slow-sellers and slightly flawed products, typically at 25 to 75 percent off the retail price.

Steps

1 Call the outlets you want to visit and ask about upcoming sales where already-reduced prices are sometimes slashed even more.

2 Use the Web to familiarize yourself with the retail prices of the items you'd like to buy, so you'll know what kind of bargain you're getting at the outlet. Set priorities.

3 Examine garments carefully for flaws. If you find a flaw in an item that isn't marked as a second, ask for an additional discount.

4 Ask about the store's return policy. You may be looking at a long drive back to the store, and many outlet purchases are nonreturnable. Find out if you can return clothes to a store's non-outlet location near you, and get the answer in writing.

What to Look For

- Upcoming sales
- Retail price comparison
- Prioritized shopping list
- Flaws
- Return policy

Tip

While most retail shops sell clothes for the following season, outlet shops usually offer the current season.

Autos & Other Vehicles

522 Buy a New Car

As exciting as it is to own a new car, many people dread shopping for one. Do your research before you head out, and the experience can be fairly painless. You can avoid haggling altogether by shopping online via a car broker (see 525 Buy or Sell a Car Online). Or go to a "no haggle" dealership such as Saturn where the price isn't negotiated.

Steps

1 Take a hard look at your bottom line and consider these factors: who will drive the car and where; how many passengers does it need to carry; how much are you willing to pay; will you finance it and if so, what kind of monthly payment can you afford; and how much will it cost to insure?

2 Learn as much as you can about which safe, well-built cars in the class you're considering retain their value longer than others. Test-drive your top choices to help you decide on one model and to learn about prices and options.

3 Before you commit to a model, research its safety and cost-of-maintenance history through consumer reporting agencies, auto magazines, newspaper stories, and Web site reviews of the vehicle. Contact the National Highway Traffic Safety Administration (nhtsa.gov) to see if there has been a recall on the model.

4 Once you've picked an option package, trim level and possible colors, you're ready to shop. Research the vehicle's pricing through auto sales Web sites, dealers' newspaper ads and consumer advocacy sites such as consumerreports.org that compare prices and list rebate information.

5 Get a copy of your credit report from a free service, such as Experian.com. (See also 532 Obtain Auto Insurance.) Make sure there are no issues that might cost you a decent financing rate or sink the deal altogether.

6 Investigate other financing options besides the dealer's—you might get a better rate at a credit union or bank.

7 Work the phone and the Internet to find a dealer with the car you want, then bring your research on pricing and rebates with you. Ask lots of questions and show that while you're not in a hurry, you are serious about getting a fair deal. Be rested and well-fed before you negotiate for your car. You want to be alert, comfortable and in your element. Be ready to walk if you don't get the price you're looking for.

8 Ask the dealer about special ordering the exact options and color for the vehicle if you don't see what you want on the lot. It may take a month or so for your car to be delivered, but if you're not in a rush, this could be the way to go. Also ask about dealer cars, which may have a few miles on them, and thus are cheaper.

What to Look For

- Pricing comparisons
- Safety, cost of maintenance
- Credit report
- Financing options
- Manufacturing irregularities

Tips

No-haggling dealerships may not offer the lowest price, so if you're not afraid to wheel and deal, go elsewhere.

If you bring along a friend or a family member to help you shop and negotiate, make it clear who the dealer should be selling to.

If negotiations stall, don't be afraid to go to another dealer. Savvy shoppers play dealers against each other to get the best price.

Shop at certain times of the year for a better deal. Late December is busy for nearly everyone except car dealers, so they'll welcome your business. Annual clearances are held in late summer and early fall, when the old models are sold off.

Avoid high-priced extras like rust-proofing and road safety kits.

9 If you're satisfied with the price and vehicle, it's time to get down to the nitty-gritty and sign the contract. Read it carefully: It should spell out sale price, down payment, trade-in value of your previous car (if applicable), destination charge, sales tax, total cost and loans. Make sure no extra costs were added that you didn't discuss. Manufacturers pay the dealer to get a car ready for its new owner, so try talking your dealer out of dealer-prep fees.

11 Discuss warranties thoroughly, and understand what they cover. Compare warranties on vehicles using the manufacturers' Web sites and on others such as Cars.com.

12 Sign the contract, write your check and show proof of insurance to fill out the paperwork for the Department of Motor Vehicles.

13 Inspect the car before you take possession. It's your chance to catch any manufacturing irregularities as well as damage to the body, which the dealer should fix at no cost.

Warning

Unless it's in writing on your bill of sale, don't assume there's a three-day grace period to change your mind.

523 Buy the Basics for Your Car

Whether you like to baby your car on the weekends or need to top off fluids before a trip, it's good to have supplies on hand. Your owner's manual has the specifics of what your car needs.

LOCATION	PARTS, FLUIDS AND SUPPLIES	
Under the Hood	• Air filter • Automatic transmission fluid • Brake fluid • Clutch fluid • Engine coolant • Engine oil	• Fuses (for cooling fan, fuel injector and other circuits) • Oil filter • Power-steering fluid • Spark plugs • Windshield-washer fluid
Interior	• Waterproof floor mats • Fuses • Gauges	• Oil for hinges • Light bulbs (overhead, dashboard, visor vanity)
Exterior	• Battery for car alarm fob • Car polish • Car wash soap • Car wax • Headlamps • Leather/vinyl cleaner and conditioner	• Light bulbs (trunk, parking, license plate and indicator lights) • Matching paint for touch-ups • Rear axle oil • Tires • Windshield wipers and blades
WARNINGS	Many car fluids are flammable, so store all automotive basics with care. Keep away from temperature extremes, and throw out greasy rags that were used on your car. Keep all fluids out of reach of both pets and children.	

524 **Buy a Used Car**

The hot car that was out of your price range just a few years ago may be much more affordable today—preowned. Here's how to buy a used car from a dealership or a private party.

Steps

1 Follow Steps 1 through 3 in 522 Buy a New Car. Browse the Kelley Blue Book (kbb.com) for used-car pricing.

2 Search car ads from as many sources as possible, including dealer ads in newspapers and private ads in print and online classifieds to find out what's available in your area. Many dealers offer manufacturer-certified preowned cars; they generally charge more, but may offer a limited warranty.

3 Make a list of the features you want, along with acceptable mileage limits and condition of the car you're willing to buy.

4 Set up appointments to see your top choices in person, and bring your most car-savvy friend. Take notes.

5 Ask for maintenance records and inspect cars closely. Fear rust. Cars.com and AutoWeb.com have used-car buyer's checklists that can be helpful.

6 Ask the seller questions in order to rule out lemons (see 538 Avoid Buying a Lemon). Check the car's history using a service such as Carfax.com, which can list a car's actual mileage, number of title changes and if it's been wrecked or salvaged.

7 Test-drive the car: Does it feel good? Take it on the freeway to check for alignment issues. Accelerate from zero to 60 mph (97 kph) to see how punchy it is. Brake sharply and see if the car pulls. Turn everything on at some point and have your friend walk around and see that they're all working: brake lights, headlights, tail lights, hazards, turn signals, dome light, wipers, fluid lights, radio, heater and AC/fan. Test all the doors, windows and the horn. Check that the tires have good tread since new tires can put you out hundreds of dollars (See 543 Choose the Right Tires).

8 When you've found the car you want, take it to your mechanic and have it checked out for about $60.

9 When you've agreed upon a price with a dealer, you'll get the necessary forms, including a bill of sale and the car title (pink slip). If you're financing, you won't get the actual title until the car is paid for. Some dealers handle all the paperwork, including tax.

10 When you've agreed upon a price from a private seller, you may not get a bill of sale, but you can find samples in car-buying books or online at Edmunds.com. Or agree to meet the seller at the DMV to fill out sales forms there.

What to Look For

- Pricing
- Acceptable mileage
- Maintenance and repair records
- No recalls
- Clean title
- Good running condition
- Good appearance

Tips

A private-party sale doesn't include sales tax: That's paid to the DMV.

Walk away from sellers who try to close the deal too quickly. There's the hard sell and then there's the "unload it before they know what hit 'em" sell.

You'll need proof of insurance to register your new car at the DMV, along with the bill of sale and title. States have different time frames that this must happen in and different emissions requirements as well.

Warnings

Check that the vehicle identification number (VIN) on the dashboard matches VINs printed elsewhere on the car (on the frame under the hood or in the door frame) and the bill of sale. Mismatched VINs could indicate stolen parts or a hot vehicle.

If the seller doesn't have the car's title to sign over to you, this means it's not paid off and you need to get the title from the seller's bank. You need a title to register a car.

525 Buy or Sell a Car Online

The Web supplies a hassle-free way to reach lots of hungry shoppers for sellers. If you know exactly what new car you want, buying it online is as easy as pie.

Steps

Buy a new car online

1 Follow Steps 1 through 3 in 522 Buy a New Car.

2 Research various option packages and trim levels. Write down exactly what you're looking for and the price you're willing to pay.

3 Go to a secure, reliable Web site that sells cars online. Two examples are AutoByTel.com and CarsDirect.com. Select your desired make and model of car, or browse by price range.

4 Conduct the entire transaction online: Order the car via the site, perhaps pay the Web site's sales price without negotiating, and have it delivered to the nearest dealer in its network.

5 Initiate contact with a dealer to get the buying process started. After finding a local dealership online, work with the dealer in person to negotiate the deal and sign the paperwork.

6 Pick up your new car at a nearby dealership. Some dealerships will even deliver it to you.

Sell a used car online

1 Find a Web site that accepts online advertising. Newspaper, auto sales sites and local community sites all run ads for used cars.

2 Take some good digital pictures of your car.

3 Take advantage of online ads' ability to convey more facts about your car than print ads can, to reach more people and to feature multiple pictures of the car. To post your ad, sign up by entering your contact information and a description of your car, and pay a small fee (if required) with a credit card.

4 Post a Web page with a simple design and good-quality images of your car. Include any other details you weren't able to fit in your online ad (such as a scanned copy of the vehicle's history report). You might be able to link it to your ad.

5 Wait for the offers to roll in. (See 527 Sell a Car.)

What to Look For

- Secure Web sites
- Reliable service
- Clear communication
- Concise online advertising

Tips

Research an auto sales Web site as you would any company you're making a major purchase from.

Talk to anyone you know who's bought a car online about their experience.

Warning

Don't buy a used car online—not directly, anyway. You need to inspect it for rust and other potential problems. (See 524 Buy a Used Car.)

526 Buy a Hybrid Car

A hybrid electric vehicle (HEV) has two engines: electric and combustion. The car generally runs on one or the other until the driver needs more power or faster acceleration than either of the two small engines can deliver alone. At that point they operate in concert. HEVs are low emission, fuel efficient and downright slick.

Steps

1 Learn the lingo. A Super Ultra Low-Emission Vehicle is 90 percent cleaner than the average new 2002 model year car, according to the California Air Resources Board. An Ultra Low-Emission Vehicle is about 50 percent cleaner than the average new 2001 model year car. There are zero-emission cars on the road now, but they are electric vehicles, not HEVs.

2 Evaluate how and where you drive your current vehicle to decide whether an HEV is right for you. Hybrid vehicles are terrific for urban and suburban driving: The short trips and stop-and-go traffic make for impressive fuel savings, if your car runs on an electric engine at low RPMs. Highway and interstate commuters who drive these cars won't see the same great gas mileage as their city cousins. Cars that run on combustion engines with an electrical assist, such as the Honda Civic Hybrid, will see less difference between highway and city driving gas usage.

3 Decide whether you can live with the limited choice of HEVs on the market. There are currently very few models to choose from, although many manufacturers have hybrid concept cars in development or demonstration stages. If you're not satisfied with the current choices, more will come on the market eventually.

4 Be prepared to spend several thousand dollars more on an HEV than a comparable gas-powered vehicle, due to low production numbers and mechanical complexity. HEVs also have low resale value.

5 Research the availability of the car where you live and check the manufacturer's Web site to see where you can have repairs made. Auto shopping sites list the typical cost of ownership on available models.

6 Follow the steps in 522 Buy a New Car.

What to Look For

- Super Ultra Low- and Ultra Low-Emission vehicles
- Availability of HEVs
- Local repair shops
- Cost of ownership

Tips

Any car shopper who purchases a new hybrid through 2003 is eligible for a one-time federal tax deduction of $2,000. A smaller deduction will be available through 2006. Check your state tax department for more possible deductions.

Some cities are offering free parking as an incentive to drive low-emissions vehicles.

Hybrids, unlike electric cars, recharge their batteries as you drive and brake, so you never have to plug your car into the wall socket.

527 Sell a Car

When selling a car, private transactions almost always generate more money than selling to a dealer. Make the process smoother by putting yourself in the buyer's shoes (see 524 Buy a Used Car) and sell your car quickly, and possibly for more money.

Steps

1 Clear out your car, then wash, vacuum and wax it. Fix minor problems, or prepare to come down substantially in your asking price. Have a mechanic look at your car before you sell to help appraise its value. This will keep some buyers from telling you to lower the price by claiming the car needs significant work.

2 Research the vehicle's value in the Kelley Blue Book (kbb.com), and compare with other sellers' asking prices for the same vintage model. This will give you the basis for a realistic price (add a little more so you can comfortably bargain).

3 Post an ad in the newspaper, online, in the window of your car, on community bulletin boards—wherever you can get the word out. Create a Web site to display additional photos and descriptions of the vehicle. (See 525 Buy or Sell a Car Online.) Be sure to highlight selling points such as low mileage, great condition, option packages, aftermarket additions (new hardtop or car alarm), number of owners (if it's very low), nonsmoking owner(s), and complete maintenance records.

4 Run a car history report on your vehicle through a service such as Carfax.com, then print it to show prospective buyers.

5 If you're selling a specialty car whose appeal is seasonal, sell when it's most in demand. Spring and summer are when convertible sales are hot, while fall weather sells all-wheel-drive vehicles.

6 Make sure you have in your possession: the title, no outstanding tickets, a bill of sale or vehicle transfer form (available from the DMV), up-to-date emissions certification, registration and a release of liability form.

7 Confirm that anyone wanting to test-drive your car has a current driver's license. Be prepared for potential buyers to ask if their mechanic can check out the car. If you've had a mechanic look at your car recently, you can show the receipt or work order.

8 After you've agreed on a price, ask for cash or a certified check. Do not accept personal checks or payment in installments.

9 Fill out the bill of sale, which buyer and seller both sign, and make copies for you both. Sign over the title and fill out a release of liability form (available at the DMV). Cancel your insurance for the car, so if anything happens to it you won't be responsible. Unless you have arranged otherwise, it's a good idea to add "Car is sold in 'as is' condition without any guarantee or warranty" to the bill of sale.

What to Look For

- Realistic price
- Advertisements
- Registration
- Emissions certificate registration
- Cash or cashier's check
- Bill of sale
- Release of liability
- Transfer of title

Tips

To sell a car you're still making payments on, have the buyer either pay the bank directly, or pay you so you can pay off the loan.

If the car has a lien, the original title will be mailed from the bank to whoever paid them for the car. Buyers of cars with liens can get temporary operating permits from the DMV, using the bill of sale.

The DMV will determine whether to leave the license plates on the car after the sale.

Warning

Avoid using the expression "or best offer." You'll get the *worst* offers.

528 Buy a Motorcycle

Everyone loves motorcycles. Some people will tell you they're scary and dangerous, and they may be right, but they're lying when they say they don't like them. While many bikes look similar, they may behave in completely different ways, based primarily on their engine size, configuration and intended use. Before deciding on a bike, be sure you understand these basic differences.

ENGINE CHARACTERISTICS	DESCRIPTION
Size	• Motorcycles are frequently identified by their engine size. For example, a Honda CBR600 has an engine with a cylinder volume of 600 cubic cm (cc). • If you're not sure of the engine size, look for an identifying sticker on the frame, below the handlebars.
Power	• So, the larger the cylinder volume (cc) the more power, right? Not always. Engine configuration and design matter too. A highly tuned, four-cylinder 600 cc machine has much more power than a single-cylinder 600 cc machine. The four-cylinder bike is also wider and heavier—important considerations for a novice looking for a stable ride.
Straight-four	• Most bikes that use a straight-four engine (four cylinders arranged in a straight line) are sport bikes. Japanese manufacturers have been associated with these engines since the '70s and have been spectacularly successful in producing reliable, affordable machines with true racetrack performance.
V-twin	• This configuration is favored by Harley-Davidson, a motorcycle that is as much a lifestyle as it is transportation. Harley V-twins are big, macho and heavy. Other manufacturers have produced their own successful V-twin lines to compete with Harley. Bikes using these engines are usually not designed for sportiness and quick handling, but for cruising and looking relaxed. • As an alternative to the straight-four, some sport bikes use a V-twin configuration although in a much more highly tuned format than in a Harley. V-twin sport riders claim their bikes are smoother, easier to ride and sound better than four-cylinder machines.
Single-cylinder	• Many bikes designed for both on and off the road use a single-cylinder engine. This keeps the overall weight of the bike relatively low but also reduces horsepower. • If simplicity, lightweight and ruggedness are important to you, these bikes are a great choice.
Two-stroke	• In the United States, these are reserved strictly for off-road use because they don't meet emissions requirements for on-road use. Two-strokes are simple and lightweight, making them popular with dirt-bike riders. They are also maintenance intensive, loud and smoky.

MOTORCYCLE TYPES

Sport Bike

If you want more performance than a Ferrari will give you for one-tenth the price, this is for you. Sport bikes typically have a fairing to cut the wind, a very racy look and limited passenger room. They provide unmatched handling and acceleration but have few concessions to comfort. The most popular classes of these bikes are the 600 cc and 1,000 cc machines. Extremely few riders have the skill to truly utilize a 1,000 cc machine, even on a racetrack. (ER doctors sometimes refer to them as "donor cycles.") If you're buying a used sport bike beware of race bikes, as they will have had hard use. Small sport bikes cost about $5,500, large ones about $10,000 to $15,000.

Standard Street Bike

If you don't want the manic speed of a sport bike but need more performance than a cruiser, there are many fine standard motorcycles available. Standard street bikes may have a small fairing or none at all. They frequently use engines derived from those of sport bikes, but are built in a more user-friendly format. Performance is usually good enough to satisfy all but the neediest for speed. Comfort, particularly for passengers, is much higher than on a sport bike, while insurance costs are likely to be lower. BMW and Triumph are major makers of standard-style bikes, as are all the Japanese manufacturers. Prices span a wide range, from about $4,000 to $15,000.

Motocross Bike

Motocross bikes are intended exclusively for off-road use and are usually powered by a two-stroke engine, although four-strokes are becoming popular. There are many different sizes available, but the majority of full-size motocross bikes are 125 cc, 250 cc or 500 cc. Unless you live near a riding area, you will need a trailer or a truck to transport your bike.

Touring

Built for long-distance travel, touring bikes have a windscreen, comfortable seating for two, and lots of storage. The Honda Goldwing is the recognized leader in the touring category, although BMW and Harley also make popular models. Average cost is about $18,000. A wide range of accessories are available to increase comfort on long rides.

Cruiser

Long, low and built for style, many cruisers utilize V-twin engines designed to have a retro look. Owners frequently add accessories to suit their taste. Harley-Davidson is the recognized trendsetter in cruiser bikes, although many manufacturers produce quality machines. The average price for a Harley is about $17,000. Japanese cruisers average about $9,000.

Vintage

Bikes from the '60s and earlier can be very beautiful and rewarding, but they can also be fragile and temperamental. Don't buy a vintage bike on a whim. Bargains are rare, and a cheap vintage bike is probably missing a lot of key parts. Do plenty of research and be honest about your abilities and enthusiasm for upkeep. Don't get a vintage bike with the expectation of using it for daily commuting, unless you're a highly skilled mechanic.

Dual-purpose

Street legal but designed to handle off-road use, dual-purpose motorcycles are usually powered by a single-cylinder, four-stroke engine of 600 cc or less.

Scooter

Low cost and ease of use are the primary attractions of a scooter, but they don't have the power to let you drive safely in anything but low-traffic city driving.

529 Lease a Car with the Option to Buy

Leasing a car is a little like long-term renting. It's a great option if you want a new car but have little capital, or if you want a fancier car than you can afford to buy. Monthly payments are significantly lower than when you buy outright, but the number of miles you can put on the car is restricted. Is leasing the right choice for you? Read on.

Steps

1 Assess your needs: For people who drive many miles each year, or who want to keep a car for many years and want the option to sell later, leasing a car is not the way to go.

2 Determine how many miles you drive annually. Different manufacturers have different yearly allowances on mileage, which helps determine which car you choose. Many leases now are for only 10,000 miles per year, whereas they used to be 15,000. The extra charge for mileage can be substantial, often 20 cents per mile over the allowance, and when you're driving to work every day, that adds up quick. Often you can purchase extra miles up front, but this cost changes the lease expense.

3 Decide how long you'll want the car, keeping in mind that a longer lease makes for smaller payments.

4 Calculate how large a deposit you can put down up front and how much you can afford to pay monthly. Bankrate.com and other sites offer auto lease payment calculators so you can find out how much you'll have to pay. Factors include manufacturers suggested retail price (MSRP), final negotiated price, down payment, usage tax, length of lease, and new car lending rate.

5 Find a reutable dealership that leases the kind of car you want, in your price range. Take a test drive. Have the dealer explain warranties offered on the car, servicing and fees for overmileage, wear and tear, and early-out for quitting the lease. Always ask if taxes are included in the quoted fee. Make sure you understand everything you can be charged for before you sign the contract.

6 Ask how a buyout at the end of the lease works. You don't have to decide just yet whether or not you will buy out.

7 Negotiate the lowest possible lease price (capitalized cost) to keep payments low. Cars with higher residual values have lower lease costs.

8 Consider getting gap coverage insurance, which is usually included but may not be on your policy. If you don't have it and the car gets stolen, it can cost more than the price of your lease.

What to Look For

- Reputable dealership
- Warranty period
- Extra charges
- High residual value
- Gap coverage insurance

Tips

For peace of mind, keep your lease's length within the car's warranty period.

Ask if you can transfer the lease to someone else at some point. This is not legal in some states. See 530 Transfer Your Leased Car.

Warning

If you plan to buy the car at the end of the lease, you often pay more than if you had bought the car in the first place.

530 Transfer Your Leased Car

You can't sell a leased car, since you don't hold the title to it. If you need to end a lease, you can transfer it to another person and avoid paying the termination penalty or remaining payments.

Steps

1 Contact your lessor to make sure it allows lease transfers or lease assumptions. The lessor probably doesn't advertise the fact, but may allow it after a certain period of time.

2 Find someone willing to take on your lease. Ask acquaintances, friends and relatives. Advertise. There are Web sites that facilitate lease transfer for a fee, such as LeaseTrading.com, LeaseTrader.com and SwapALease.com.

3 Have the buyer complete a credit application. When the leasing company approves the application, it will issue transfer documents for you and the lessee-to-be to sign.

4 Hand over your former leased car to the new lessee, who begins making the remaining payments. At the end of the lease, the new lessee returns the vehicle to the leasing company (or might have the option to buy, depending on the company).

What to Look For

- Permission for lease transfer
- Someone to take on lease

Warning

Lease transfer isn't the same as a sublease. Subleasing a car is not legal in some states.

531 Donate Your Car

Donating to charity is a relatively painless way to get rid of a car when you don't have the time to sell it or don't think you can get what it's worth. While not every car is acceptable, donating to a charity lets you deduct its fair market value from your taxable income.

Steps

1 Find a charity that accepts cars without charging a large removal fee. Make sure the organization is a registered 501(c)(3) charity or qualified religious organization that can lawfully accept your donation and from which you can lawfully claim a deduction.

2 Determine the fair market value of your car. According to the IRS, you are responsible for determining this; use the Kelley Blue Book or IRS Publications 526 ("Charitable Deductions") and 561 ("Determining the Value of Donated Property"). If it's worth $5,000 or more, have the car appraised by a certified professional.

3 Get a tax receipt with the charity's name and federal tax ID number, donor's name, date of donation, as well as the year, make and model of the donated car.

4 Notify the DMV and your insurance company that you no longer own or insure the vehicle. Follow state regulations on what to do with the title and plates. Keep your receipt and completed IRS Form 8283 for tax time.

What to Look For

- No or low removal fee
- 501(c)(3)-classified charity
- Fair market value of car
- Tax receipt from charity
- Completed forms

Tips

Religious organizations aren't required to apply for an IRS tax exemption in order to be qualified.

The tax break or refund could be the same amount as if you'd sold the car, but without the bother. IRS Publication 78 (at irs.gov) can verify if an organization is qualified to receive deductible contributions.

532 Obtain Auto Insurance

Car insurance can be ridiculously expensive, but by avoiding excessive coverage and perhaps paying a higher deductible, you can get affordable insurance that actually protects you. Before you shop, however, make sure there are no errors on your driving record or your credit record. A surprise on either can jack up your rates.

Steps

1 Contact the DMV to find out about any unaddressed violations you might have on your driving record and straighten them out. Order a free credit report from a company like Experian.com to make sure it's clean.

2 Find out how much coverage you're required to carry according to your state's department of insurance and determine which types of coverage you'll need. This requires balancing how much you can afford to pay with how much you can afford to lose (see chart on the following page). You should carry enough liability to cover your assets if you cause a very expensive accident; otherwise the claimant might go after your house and possessions.

3 Shop around for quotes based on what you've determined you need, instead of asking agencies what they think you need. Independent insurance agents and Web sites like esurance.com, Insweb.com and AllQuotesInsurance.com will compare rates for you. Are you willing to pay more for a well-known company?

4 See what you can get discounts for. Here are some of the things you may already have that can save you money: air bags, antilock brakes, automatic seat belts, antitheft devices, safe driving record, safe car, age, marital status and multiple insured vehicles.

5 Ask the carrier if filing a claim raises premiums, and under which circumstances it cancels insurance.

6 Research prospective insurers. To learn how the company's service is regarded, talk to other customers and repair shops who have worked with the insurer. Check out the company's rating with your state's department of insurance, the Better Business Bureau (bbb.org) and national consumer surveys. The company should be in good standing so you can collect when there's a claim.

7 Read your policy before signing. Make sure it includes the coverage you're requesting and no surprise clauses. Avoid arbitration clauses that keep you from suing your insurer if it doesn't pay a claim by asking the insurer to delete it from the contract or going to another insurer.

8 Keep the policy in a safe place, and keep proof of insurance in the car with your registration.

What to Look For

- Cost
- Types of coverage
- Size of deductible
- Competitive quote
- Insurance company's rating
- Consumer complaints
- Discounts

Tips

Pay six months in full, twice a year, rather than financing the premiums.

If you lease a car, find out if your insurance pays for original parts or aftermarket parts. Some lessors make repairs to a leased car with aftermarket parts. See 529 Lease a Car with the Option to Buy.

Warning

If you've had an accident, this information will follow you, much like bad credit will.

TYPE OF INSURANCE	EXTENT OF COVERAGE
Bodily Injury Liability	Pays whomever you injure.
Car Rental	Pays toward a rental car while car is in the shop.
Collision	Pays for car repairs after crashing into a vehicle or inanimate object. Good drivers may want less coverage or higher deductibles.
Comprehensive	Covers non-traffic–related damage like a fire.
Full Coverage	Meets state's minimum requirements for insurance, but may not be enough for individual needs.
No-fault	No one has to be at fault for the accident in order for claim to be paid.
Liability	Pays for repairs if you hit someone's car or other property.
Personal Injury or Medical	Pays for injuries to you and your passengers.
Towing	Pays for a tow truck or roadside assistance If your car breaks down.
Underinsured or Uninsured Motorist	Pays you when some uninsured goon smashes into you (may include hit-and-run drivers). Bodily injury liability pays whomever you injure.

533 Spring for a New Paint Job

No matter where you live, acid rain, UV rays, tree sap, falling leaves and bird droppings can all conspire to make your car look old, dull and pitted. A paint job runs from $200 to $4,000 and enhances the value of a car as it protects against rust and corrosion.

Steps

1 Compare written estimates from several auto-body shops. Before you sign on the dotted line, inquire if the auto-body technicians have been certified by the paint company to apply its paint, and if paint and workmanship warranties exist.

2 Choose a color, then decide from single-stage finish to multiple layers (primer, base, clear/tint and final coat). More layers result in a deeper shine, a more durable paint job—and a larger bill.

3 Save money by repainting your car the same color, so sills and internal frame parts (such as the trunk) don't have to be repainted to match. Special paint and designs add to the price.

4 Ask your body shop exactly how to care for and clean your new finish, as some paint jobs take weeks to cure. During that time, stay away from commercial car washes and don't use an ice scraper or spill gasoline on the finish.

What to Look For

- Written estimates
- Paint company certification
- Warranties
- Matching color
- Care instructions

Tips

Some car experts swear by a good wax job; some say new paints don't need wax. Ask your technician what's best for your paint job.

Unless your car's paint is damaged or is an old acrylic lacquer finish, you don't generally need to strip old paint before repainting.

534 Buy a Radar Detector

The obvious way to avoid a speeding ticket, of course, is not to speed. But where's the fun in that? Crafty manufacturers, such as Escort, Valentine, Bel-tronics and Cobra, have developed sophisticated radar detectors to keep those flashing red lights out of your rear-view mirror.

Steps

1 Understand that radar used by law-enforcement officers works by shining microwave searchlights down the road. When your car comes into range, the beam bounces off of it. The radar antenna calculates your speed from the reflections it receives.

2 Decide where you'll mount the radar detector—to the windshield, the dash or the visor, for $50 to $100—or have it custom installed for upwards of $1,000. Where the unit is mounted significantly affects signal detection—the higher the better. Consider, too, whether you'll use it in one particular vehicle or in multiple vehicles (in which case you'll need a mount that's easy to remove).

3 Shop for a radar detector that's most appropriate for your driving habits. The greater the detector's sensitivity, the more effective it'll be. An experienced salesperson can help you determine the best detector and placement for you.

4 Look for a unit that detects a wide range of frequencies, or bands, including laser (sometimes called *Lidar*). Police radar guns use a variety of frequencies to clock speeders. If you want to be stealthy, look for VG-2 alert, which protects your vehicle from VG-2 radar detection and makes your detector undetectable. Check with a salesperson for the frequency in your area.

What to Look For

- Installation position
- Sensitivity of detector
- Wide range of frequencies detected
- Laser detection

Tip

Radar detectors aren't fool-proof. You can get false positives or be alerted too late to that radar gun behind a hill or around a bend.

Warnings

Radar detectors are illegal to use in some states and Canadian provinces, and on certain vehicles. Obey the laws wherever you drive.

Avoid radar jammers: They're illegal and don't work.

535 Purchase the Right Gasoline

Different brands of gas—even those with the same octane rating—can cause a vehicle to behave very differently. Your car may act sluggish or misfire (knock) on one oil company's fuel but not another's. Since different refineries offer different formulations of oxygenates, detergents and even octanes, changing brands will often perk up sluggish performance.

Steps

1 Check your car's owner manual for the recommended fuel (unleaded gasoline versus diesel) and octane rating or antiknock index (on the yellow sticker affixed to the pump).

2 Try another gasoline brand if your car isn't running smoothly on the manufacturer's required minimum octane. Each refinery mixes its own blends with additives to encourage cleaner burning. Your

What to Look For

- Manufacturer's fuel recommendation
- Octane rating
- No knocking sound
- Improved engine power

Tips

If your car is running smoothly and getting top gas mileage, there's no need to use a higher-octane fuel.

car may simply need a higher-quality fuel with more scrubbing power to clean out its fuel system and run better. If switching fuels doesn't solve the problem, it may be time to have your mechanic search for a different cause.

3 Get the skinny on octane numbers. Octane ratings are based on a scale of relative burn resistance: Higher-octane gas will not combust prematurely and cause your engine to knock.

4 If your vehicle makes a knocking sound on acceleration, try a higher-octane gasoline. Most cars can optimize their own performance to the gas they're fed, but only up to a certain point: Gas with too low an antiknock index causes an engine to fire prematurely and lose power. Gas with an antiknock index well above the required octane level doesn't increase performance or power, just your fuel costs.

5 Try changing brands again if your engine runs rougher in winter, since fuel blends change seasonally.

Engine knock is very damaging to cars. Simply increasing the octane level can save your car from expensive engine wear and tear.

MTBE is an oxygenate added to fuel to increase its octane rating and clean up emissions. It has proven to be an environmental disaster, leaking into the groundwater supply. As of 2000, the EPA Is reducing the use of MTBE.

536 Buy Fuel Treatments

Fuel treatments or additives are fluids you put directly in your gas tank. They're designed to reduce wear on your engine and deposits on intake valves and manifolds, carburetors and fuel injectors. Additives lubricate engine parts and generally enhance performance.

Steps

1 Check your car owner's manual to see what fuel treatments are recommended, or if the manufacturer recommends against using any at all. Don't gum up your engine with the wrong additive.

2 Figure out which problem with your engine's performance you need to correct. As with cold medicines, you want the specific treatment that addresses your engine's issues.

3 Find treatments for sale at auto-supply stores, at mass-market or discount stores in the auto section, or from your mechanic (16-oz. bottles sell for less than $5).

4 Add the treatment at your next fill-up (usually a full bottle per tank) to the empty tank, then pump gas as usual. Use treatments regularly for maximum effectiveness.

What to Look For

- Manufacturer's recommendation
- Treatment for specific problem
- Regular use

Tip

Fuel treatment may be a simple solution for knocking or hesitating on acceleration. Higher-octane gas, however, is often a cheaper solution. See 535 Purchase the Right Gasoline.

537 Hire a Reliable Mechanic

It's not that hard to find a trustworthy mechanic—until you're desperate. It's worth taking the time to look for one before you're in dire straits. Have a good mechanic regularly maintain your car to help keep surprise breakdowns to a minimum.

Steps

1 Ask friends who have your make or model car if they would recommend their mechanic.

2 Get a recommendation of certified mechanics from an auto club like AAA, if you're a member. You can also find mechanics with valuable certification from the National Institute for Auto Service Excellence (ASEcert.org).

3 If you have a specialty vehicle or sports car, try to get a recommendation from a local auto club—the Miata Club, for example.

4 Find a dealer that has the most service awards from the manufacturer. Those mechanics have been manufacturer certified.

5 Check with the Better Business Bureau (bbb.org) to learn whether a garage has any strikes against it. Ask how the shop charges before you have any work done.

What to Look For

- Recommendations
- Auto club referrals
- ASE-certified technician
- Manufacturer-certified mechanic
- Approval from the BBB

Tip

If you can't decide between mechanics, call each with a problem and ask how much repairs would be. Get a friend to do the same the next day, and compare the pricing you got from each. Some mechanics have random pricing policies.

538 Avoid Buying a Lemon

A lemon is any new or warrantied vehicle with a major problem that can't be fixed in a reasonable amount of time or number of attempts. Every state has a lemon law to give consumers rights and redress.

Steps

New vehicles

1 Find out from the manufacturer or the National Highway Traffic Safety Administration if there's been a recall on your model.

2 Research the model's safety recall and maintenance history through consumer safety and protection agencies such as the Center for Auto Safety (CAS), auto magazines, newspaper articles and Web site reviews of the vehicle.

3 Ask your mechanic how often this model shows up in his shop for repairs (and how many children he put through college based on those repairs).

4 Talk to other owners of this model: Are they satisfied?

Used vehicles

1 Follow the steps under "New vehicles."

What to Look For

New cars
- No recalls
- Safety, maintenance, and repair history
- Positive recommendations

Used cars
- All of the above
- Vehicle history report
- Best possible condition
- No frame damage
- Seller not too hasty

Tip

Call the NHTSA hotline at (800) 424-9393. You can also look up recalls by make and model on nhtsa.gov or check www.lemonflower.com/ lemon_ law/lemon_law.shtml.

2 Get a vehicle history report to make sure the car you're considering is clean—no salvage title issued, and no major wrecks or any illegal activity in its history. Several commercial agencies, such as Carfax.com, sell this service.

3 If you're buying from an owner, have a trusted mechanic inspect the car (it takes an hour and costs about $60). Avoid vehicles that have been in an accident or have frame damage.

4 Be wary of a model that's often offered for sale below Kelley Blue Book (kbb.com) price. Ask the seller why he or she is selling. Be wary of sellers who try to close the deal too quickly.

539 Sell Your Clunker

Should you pay someone to haul away that beast in your driveway? Perhaps not: You might find someone willing to buy it. Before you advertise, though, take time to discover the inner beauty of the vehicle. The more selling points you can cite, the better the pitch. Then scrub the heck out of it to reveal any outer beauty it may still have.

Steps

1 Read 527 Sell a Car.

2 Clear out the interior, then wash, vacuum and wax the vehicle. Cleanliness impresses buyers and makes any clunker look like less of a project.

3 Fix whatever's broken if it's inexpensive to repair. The more working parts it has, the more selling points you've got.

4 Research the vehicle's used-car value as well as other sellers' asking prices for the same "vintage" model in your area. It'll help you determine a realistic asking price (leave yourself room to comfortably drop the price when bargaining).

5 Bedazzle prospective buyers with whatever advantages you can find in writing: great crash-test results, clean title history.

6 Have the title ready, and registration and smog test updated. Missing paperwork or hassle for the buyer can kill a deal.

7 Include "free with car" aftermarket parts or accessories you bought, such as the hammer you use to start it with. Maintenance records, too, indicate you had at least a little love for this vehicle.

8 Avoid volunteering bad news during bargaining (needs new tires and a tune-up). Pitch the high points (has new brakes, is the same car Steve McQueen drove in *The Heist*), but don't lie; it'll catch up with you.

What to Look For

- Cleanliness
- Inexpensive repairs
- Used-car value
- Positive points
- Accessories
- Maintenance records

Tips

Find ads for comparable cars to learn which selling points are hyped, and possibly how to downplay a clunker's character flaws.

The bill of sale should include the phrase "as is," meaning you're not responsible for further repairs.

In a worst-case scenario, look into donating the car for a tax write-off. (See 531 Donate Your Car.)

Warning

You must disclose a legal lemon (with recalls) to prospective buyers.

540 Buy, Restore and Sell a Vintage Car

It might look like an aging heap of rusted metal to some, but you know with a little elbow grease you can bring that beauty back to life. Nearly everyone who restores cars will tell you that they're in the business for the love of it, not the money—it's hard to beat the feeling of pride when new life has been given to an old classic.

Steps

Buying

1 Look in the mirror and tell yourself that in all likelihood you won't turn a profit on this. Don't be bitter if it doesn't turn out to be a money maker.

2 Be realistic when calculating the expenses of restoring a vintage vehicle to sell for profit. Get to know the car's market well. How much time and expertise you have to devote to the project will determine which cars you can restore. Find and talk to other people who have worked on the same car; members of car clubs and books are good sources of information. If you're starting from scratch, be prepared to spend a lot of money on tools and equipment in addition to parts for the car.

3 Follow the steps in 524 Buy a Used Car, except be prepared to buy your car one piece at a time. The perfect frame could be in someone's garage, while the seats may have to be remanufactured in Canada. Go to car shows, scan the ads in collector and car parts magazines, check salvage yards, scour the Internet, and ask friends if they have any auto parts lying around.

4 Beware of cars that are heavily rusted. Some rust may be unavoidable, but make sure it's not corroding structural parts.

5 See in person any advertised car or parts you're considering buying. If this is not an option, ask for detailed photos. A third alternative is to arrange to have the vehicle inspected for a fee by a national group like Automobile Inspections (automobile-inspections.com), which can provide you with a comprehensive condition report within 72 hours.

Restoring

1 Make sure you have enough room. A dismantled car takes up a considerable amount of space. Ideally, you need the equivalent of two adjacent garages: one to dismantle the car and keep the parts, and the other to build the car up again. Alternatively, store parts like the engine, gear-box, doors and bonnet in a dry basement or shed while you are working on the chassis and body.

2 Expect the unexpected: You'll always find that aspects of the restoration are more involved than anticipated. If you're not sure you can do some of the work correctly or if it's dangerous (as is

What to Look For

Buying
● Car shows
● Salvage yards

Restoring
● Ample space
● Original equipment
● Vintage magazines

Selling
● Mint condition
● Complete sales package
● Vintage collectibles
● Car shows
● Museums

Tips

Pay attention to details that sell cars. A catchy license plate or an antique bud vase make car buffs squeal with delight.

It's not a good idea to try selling the car based on how much money was sunk into its restoration.

With the revamped VW Beetles and Mini Coopers now out on the streets, their forefathers are in hot demand. There's always a market for muscle cars like Camaros and Mustangs.

working with springs), call in a professional. In the end it will save time and money, if not your pride.

3 Use as much original equipment as you can get your hands on (hood ornaments, old mirrors, original radios) to enhance the value and raise the asking price. A successfully restored car is a trip back in time for car buffs.

4 Take your restoration cues (paint color and more) from publications of the same era that show your vehicle. Magazines like these are great to back up the work you've done when selling the car.

Selling

1 Clean the car extremely well. Steam-clean under the hood (car detailers can do this). Try to make sure its details are as complete and mint-looking as possible. Change the oil and service the car—the fact that the car doesn't require servicing right away may encourage some buyers.

2 Put together a complete sales package to market your car. Does it have its full set of chrome, for example?

3 Collect any artifacts or knowledge related to the car's history that might increase its allure and value. Was it a race car at some point? Car buffs love log books and proof of races won. Collect manufacturer medallions, racing badges, maintenance records, and original options and sales brochures as well as the manual.

4 Determine your asking price. Compare your car's make, model, year and condition to others listed in advertisements. Ask a fellow enthusiast for a valuation.

5 Choose advertising venues carefully, to get reasonable offers. A college campus bulletin board is a waste of time, but the catalogs where you found parts for your car, magazines and automobile clubs devoted to your model, and online mailing lists of car buffs all might turn up eager buyers willing to pony up.

6 Try not to limit the car's advertising to one geographic region. Different regions have different demands for the same vehicles, and buyers in another state may pay thousands more than local buyers would.

7 Take it to car shows and museums, and park it prominently near the venue's entrance or exit. Car nuts will appreciate this vehicle, so wave it under their noses. If you're going to a car show far away, trailer your car to eliminate road wear or damage.

8 Remind yourself as you sign the bill of sale that you weren't planning to make a profit, and focus instead on that next fixer-upper.

Warnings

Lift with your knees, not your back.

Be realistic about how much you can afford to spend on restoration. Costs can mount quickly.

541 Locate Hard-to-Find Parts

The only thing your beloved 1972 Dodge Dart is missing is the Swinger logo. Never fear: New, original and reproduction parts—even the most obscure—can be found with some detective work.

Steps

1 Know the exact specifications of the part you are searching for. Ask yourself what kind of shape the part needs to be in for you to buy it, and how much you're willing to spend. If you can't find original parts, rebuilt or remanufactured parts could save you money and may also be the only replacement parts you can find.

2 Assuming you've already checked with your local auto-parts store, browse the classified sections in both paid and free local newspapers. Some sellers (who advertise in the papers but aren't listed in the phone directory) offer cars for parts—a good source if you have a popular, hard-to-shop-for car.

3 Root around a local scrap yard for a forgotten gem (look under "Salvage" in the Yellow Pages).

4 Check with local shops that work on your model car and that might be able to recommend a source for the elusive part.

5 Speak to local dealers who sell your car's make and model, if it's a new car.

6 Swap stories with auto-club members who own your model. Read the classifieds in specialty magazines.

7 Scour Internet auction sites, online search services and bulletin boards. Check back often, as new items are listed frequently. An Internet auto parts locator service will put you in contact with dealers and private sellers for a fee.

8 Find out if you can use parts from another model car on yours. Companies like Hollander Interchange (hollander-auto-parts.com) have manuals ($25 to more than $100) that identify interchangeable mechanical and body parts on foreign and domestic vehicles—including trucks—dating back to the 1920s.

What to Look For

- Acceptable condition and price
- Classified ads
- Scrap yards
- Garages
- Dealers
- Auto clubs
- Internet auctions
- Interchangeable parts

Tip

Original parts (commonly known as OEs) from car aficionados or dealers probably cost more, but are in better shape and guaranteed to work.

Warning

Saving money shouldn't be your goal for every replacement-part purchase. Some parts are vital to the safe operation of a vehicle, like rims, tires and brake parts.

542 **Buy Basic Automotive Tools**

Every car owner should have basic tools at home for keeping a car running or for doing minor repairs. Tools should have insulated grips (rubber or plastic-coated) for extra protection. Keep tools in a box where they can stay dry, and clean off grease, dirt and especially water after using them. You'll find many of these tools at hardware stores and auto supply stores.

ITEM	USES	PRICE RANGE
Adjustable Wrenches	Loosening and tightening everything properly.	$10 to $40
Continuity Tester	Testing electrical circuits.	$3 to $20
Funnels	Adding oil or other fluids. Clean after each use; designate a funnel for each fluid type.	$1.50
Hand Degreaser	Works better than regular hand soap.	$1.50 to $3
Jack	Lifting car to change tires.	$19
Jumper Cables	Jump-starting a car.	$8 to $30
Lug Wrench	Removing tires.	$9 to $22
Oil-filter Wrench	Removing and securing filters.	$7 to $13
Pliers	Loosening and tightening everything improperly.	$5 to $20
Rags and Paper Towels	Checking oil and other fluids. The more the better.	Free to $2
Rubber Gloves	Keeping hands grease-free.	$4 to $8
Rubber Mallet	Tapping open stuck parts into position.	$4 to $16
Screwdrivers	Unscrewing screws, prying lids off cans.	$3
Socket Set	Tightening nuts and bolts; available in English and Metric.	$9 to $15
Spark-plug Wrench	Removing and tightening spark plugs.	$2
Stiff, Nonwire Brush	Cleaning battery contacts.	$10
Tire Pressure Gauge	Checking air pressure.	$5 to $35
Utility Knife	Slicing rubber belts, tubes, etc.	$3 and up
Work Gloves	Keeping hands intact and blister-free.	$4 and up
WARNING	Never work underneath a jacked-up car. Jacks are not very stable and are meant for changing tires only. Use a proper automotive lift or wheel ramps (along with tire chocks and a set parking brake) designed for working under a car.	

543 Choose the Right Tires

Wonder what all those letters and numbers on your tire's sidewall mean? This chart will set you straight. If you like your current tires, buy more of the same. A tire with a different rating but the same size and type may give you a smoother ride or better handling in bad weather.

TIRE TALK	IN PLAIN ENGLISH
Typical Tire Label: P185/60R 14 82H	• P indicates passenger car tire. LT stands for light truck, and T for temporary (spare). • 185 is the section width of tire in millimeters. Shorter or narrower tires have lower numbers. • 60 indicates tire's aspect ratio (section height as percentage of section width); this tire's height is 60 percent of its width. Performance tires (with short sidewalls) have smaller numbers. • R stands for tire's type—in this case, radial. 14 is the wheel rim diameter in inches. • 82 is this tire's load index, according to the industry standard Maximum Load-Carrying Capacity chart. This tire will safely bear 1,047 lbs. (475 kg). Four of these tires can carry a fully loaded car weighing a maximum of 4,188 lbs. (1,900 kg). • Last letter (H in this example) is the speed rating: Q (99 mph/159 km per hour), S (112 mph/180 kph), T (118 mph/190 kph), U (124 mph/200 kph), H (130 mph/209 kph), V (up to 149 mph/240 kph), Z (more than 149 mph/240 kph), W (168 mph/270 kph), Y (186 mph/299 kph). • Speed-rating letters indicate the maximum safe speed the tire is capable of carrying under ideal conditions, for an extended period of driving. You might not feel a difference between riding on T-rated tires and H-rated tires, but you'll save money on the former. • Higher-performance tires have softer, grippier rubber with shorter tread life. They're not only more expensive up front, but need to be replaced more frequently.
Temperature Resistance	Grades tires' resistance to overheating over long distances at high speeds. Grade A is better than a B, which is better than a C.
UTQG Tread Life Number	Uniform Tire Quality Grading is a comparative rating of wear on a tire, when tested under controlled conditions on a government test course. Tires are rated against a standard, designated 100. For example, a tire rated 150 will wear 50 percent longer than the 100-grade tire.
DOT Number	The Department of Transportation uses this number to track tire sales. When a particular tire is recalled, the DOT can locate and inform the unlucky buyers.
Traction Rating (AA, A, B or C)	Indicates tire's grip on the road during straight-line braking on wet surface. AA-rated tires have the best traction.

TIRE TALK	IN PLAIN ENGLISH
Size, Type and Tread	The three most important things to know about your car when you're tire shopping. Your owner's manual or the label on the driver's-side doorpost shows correct tire size and type for your car. Tires generally come in radial, bias ply and bias belted types. Tires are sold with treads designed to handle standard highway driving or mud and snow (called *all-season tires*). If you're unsure, ask the tire dealer which tread best suits your driving conditions.
Ride Quality	The aspect-ratio number; indicates how hard a tire will ride. One reason sports cars ride so bumpy is their 40 to 50 aspect ratio is great for handling but offers a stiff ride. For a cushier ride, go up to 60 or so.
WARNING	Check your tire pressure once a month. Improperly inflated tires can cause low gas mileage, a hard ride or even dangerous blowouts.

544 Select Wheel Rims

For some drivers, the biggest concern with their car's tire rims (or wheels) is appearance. But an owner's choice of rims really affects the car's performance, too. New wheels run upwards of $100 apiece. If you're replacing a damaged rim, consider buying a used one.

Steps

1 Think about buying alloy wheels if you do a lot of driving in the mountains or in stop-and-go traffic. Some alloy wheels are designed to encourage cool air flow over the brakes to prevent overheating. The alloy itself can help dissipate heat, too.

2 "Plus-size" your rims if you want to improve performance and add a sportier look. With a larger inner diameter, you'll find steering is more responsive and your car holds the road better. Purchasing rims that are one or two sizes larger than what you have means you'll have to buy new tires as well. While the outside diameter of the tire your car uses should remain the same, the inner diameter—wrapped around the rim—needs to be bigger to fit a bigger rim.

3 Look for rims that aren't too heavy for your vehicle. Big, steel rims on a small car can decrease handling ability. Heavy wheels are *unsprung* weight—not supported by your car's suspension— and therefore useless for smoothing out the ride or improving balance in driving maneuvers.

What to Look For

- Alloy wheels
- Appropriate size and weight

Tips

Rims come in a staggering array of designs. For something spectacular, skip the tire store and check out custom-tuned car shows and specialty catalogs.

Be sure any wheels you buy have a maximum-load rating compatible with your vehicle.

Make sure your car's bolt pattern matches the new rims you're purchasing.

545 Outfit Your Car for Emergencies

Emergencies strike unannounced, so be prepared and carry an emergency kit in your car. They're commercially available, or you can easily put together your own. Go to FEMA.gov.prepare.org for more information on developing an emergency plan for your family.

ROADSIDE KIT	FIRST AID KIT	EARTHQUAKE KIT	SNOW COUNTRY KIT
• Cell phone, CB radio, *RoadStar* check	• Pain relievers	• Thermal blanket or sleeping bag	• Thermal blanket or sleeping bag
• Global positioning system (GPS) navigating device	• Medium-size adhesive-strip bandages	• Nonperishable food	• Additional warm clothing
• Spare tire (inflated!)	• Small roll of sterile gauze	• 3-day supply of water	• Wool socks
• Jack and lug wrench	• Bandage tape	• First aid kit (see left)	• Waterproof jacket and pants
• Jumper cables	• Alcohol (isopropyl) or antimicrobial wipes	• Change of clothes for each family member	• Snow boots, hat, gloves
• 1 gallon (about 4 liters) of water for radiator, drinking or squirters	• Saline or eye wash solution (to wash out eyes or wounds)	• At least $100 cash	• Hand warmers (instant snap-and-break kind)
• First aid kit (see right)	• Antibiotic ointment	• Medications	• Water
• Rechargeable NiCad flashlight with car recharger	• Quick-reference first aid card or book	• Baby food, formula, bottles	• Emergency food, energy bars
• Mini fire extinguisher	• Scissors	• Diapers in the next size	• Tire chains
• Screwdrivers (one Phillips, one flathead)	• Antihistamines (to relieve itch and possibly limit severe allergic reactions)	• Wipes	• Salt or sand
• Adjustable wrench		• Dog and cat food	• Snow shovel
• Utility knife	• Commercially available snake-bite kit	• Heavy-duty gloves	• Ice scraper
• Flares/hazard signs	• Disposable rubber gloves	• Shovel	• Matches or lighter
• Transmission/clutch fluid	• Plastic baggies	• Flashlight	
• Can of oil	• Tissue pack	• Photos, names of family members, descriptions (for rescue and recovery)	
• Brake fluid	• Tick removal kit	• Goggles, dust masks	
• Empty gas can		• Bottle and can openers	
• Rain coat and/or umbrella		• Water purification tablets	
• Spare fuses		• Whistle	
• Rags and/or paper towels		• Backpack	
• Waterproof hose tape		• Knife	
		• Nylon rope	
		• Personal hygiene items	
		• Matches or lighter	

WARNINGS

Not all medications are appropriate for all people. Before breaking out the first aid kit, consider the patient's age, special conditions (such as pregnancy), and health issues.

Read your first aid quick-reference card before you put it in your automobile. It takes only minutes and may keep you from doing something foolish or harmful.

546 Buy a Theft-Prevention Device

Antitheft devices for vehicles run the gamut from low-tech to fancy and expensive. Electronic engine immobilizers, for example, are very effective at keeping a car safe. They allow your car's engine to start only in the presence of a special key or device carried by the owner. But even a hunk of steel locked onto the steering wheel can deter opportunistic thieves.

Steps

1 Lock your car doors regularly, and close the windows and sunroof. Take your keys with you. A ridiculous number of cars are stolen simply because owners forget the basics.

2 Contact your insurance company to ask if antitheft device discounts are offered on premiums.

3 Consider where you typically park your car: Would you be able to hear the alarm? Would it be ignored if it went off?

4 Deter thieves with indicator lights, window decals ($2 to $5), and/or large and heavy-gauge steel objects such as steering wheel or tire locks ($80 to $200).

5 Know how effective any theft-prevention measures you're considering actually are. A determined thief can cut through certain steering immobilizers or shut off a simple alarm.

6 Look at the range of antitheft devices. They include audible alarms, a concierge system or cellular alarms that notify police, or locking steering-wheel cover, steering-column covers, locking steering-wheel bars, electronic immobilizers (kill switches, secret switches), engine or fuel-system locks, tracking devices and delay devices.

7 Evaluate what level of protection you'd like. (Car ugliness is not a deterrent to car thieves.) Some alarms ($150 to $1,000) arm automatically, as do tracking devices ($400 to $1,500) for locating the car after it's stolen. Steering-wheel ($25 to $100) and column ($100 to $200 installed) locking devices must be manually put into place each time.

8 Budget for ongoing expenses. Low-tech solutions like mechanical immobilizers ($10 to $125) don't have to be professionally installed, nor are there monitoring fees attached.

9 Purchase your antitheft device. Low-tech devices are often available at auto-supply stores or the automotive section of general retail stores. Your local car dealer might install car alarms and immobilizers. Otherwise, companies that sell and install car electronics (radar detectors, sound systems) often install car alarms and immobilizers.

What to Look For

- Common-sense safety measures
- Insurance discount
- Convenience and cost
- Environment and visibility
- Effectiveness
- Installation

Tips

If you use a steering-wheel immobilizer, attach it so the lock faces the dashboard, making it even harder for thieves to remove.

Some manufacturers etch their cars' parts with the vehicle Identification number (VIN). You can have any car etched ($20 to $100), which helps you recover a stolen car or parts. The National Highway Traffic Safety Administration site (nhtsa.gov) has a list of manufacturer-etched vehicles.

Warning

Have any ignition immobilizer installed by a professional with lots of experience and who guarantees the work. Since these link to the car's electrical system, shoddy work can harm the system or the immobilizer.

547 Bring a Car in From Europe

Importing a car from Europe can be complicated. Generally speaking, imports must meet the requirements of the U.S. Department of Transportation and the Environmental Protection Agency. Many foreign models don't and must be modified. Paying for these modifications on top of duties and taxes can become alarmingly expensive, so check the NHTSA's list of conforming cars.

Steps

1 Before importing a vehicle, ask your DMV about state-specific requirements, including emissions, temporary plates or special documentation from customs.

2 Make sure your sales contract verifies that the car has been built to U.S. standards. The manufacturer's certification label is attached to the vehicle (near the driver's door).

3 Before exporting your car, steam or thoroughly clean it to remove foreign soil (particularly on tires and the undercarriage). The U.S. Department of Agriculture doesn't want harmful pests sailing over with your car.

4 Show the U.S. Customs Service the shipper's original bill of lading, your bill of sale, foreign registration, and whatever vehicle documents you have, including original certificate of title or a certified copy of the original.

5 Complete the EPA's Form 3520-1 and the DOT's Form HS-7. Vehicles meeting U.S. emission requirements carry a manufacturer's label (in English) certifying this, in the engine compartment.

6 Verify that you need to pay duty on imported, foreign-made vehicles; generally, you do. You may be able to apply your $400 customs exemption (and accompanying family members' exemptions) toward its value. But be prepared: If your car's combined fuel-economy rating is under 22.5 miles per gallon—you might pay a gas-guzzler tax.

7 Get more information from the following sources: Environmental Protection Agency (epa.gov); Department of Transportation Office of Vehicle Safety Compliance NHTSA (nhtsa.gov); U.S. Customs Service (www.customs.ustreas.gov).

What to Look For

- Complies with state requirements
- Complies with U.S. standards
- Thorough cleaning
- Title and bill of sale showing ownership
- Foreign registration and other vehicle documents
- Completed EPA and DOT forms
- Duty payment

Tip

If you import a passenger vehicle on the condition that it'll be modified, it must be made compliant, or it could be exported or destroyed.

Warning

The U.S. government recommends against using your imported car as a shipping container, since some shippers don't allow it. Otherwise, everything in the car must be declared through customs and you might have to pay duties on the contents.

548 Buy Then Sell a Car Impounded by the Police

A police auction can be a viable place to pick up a car for a fraction of its worth to rehabilitate and sell for profit. You get a real mix of cars at these auctions, from old heaps left by the side of the road to functional, decent cars seized due to driver infractions.

Steps

1 Find out from your local police when the next auction is. Some departments hold auctions every month, running advertisements in newspapers or posting notices on their Internet site.

2 Arrive early for the inspection period to look over the vehicles up for bid. Auctions are frequently held at a commercial towing facility contracted by the police or at the police storage lot. You're allowed a few hours for inspection before cars go on the block.

3 Bring cash. Most sales are final, and the auction house may only accept cash or certified checks.

4 Bring a valid driver's license and proof of insurance, in case you make a winning bid and you need to pick up a temporary permit to drive the car home (permit regulations vary by locality).

5 Pay the nominal bidder registration fee, and save your bidder number to show the auctioneer when you make a bid. Bids are accepted only from registered bidders. (See 374 Buy at Auction.)

6 Look for clues that the car was moving under its own power recently. Some police stickers, such as "driving with license suspended" (DWLS), may indicate it probably runs OK. Also be aware that impounded vehicles could have been sitting for a year or longer with no maintenance whatsoever.

7 Whip out a used-car price guide (like Kelley Blue Book) once you've seen the cars, and look up trade-in values of the vehicles up for bid. If you own a PDA with wireless Internet connection, get the vehicle identification number (VIN) and run a Carfax.com vehicle history report before you even think about bidding. (See 412 Choose a Personal Digital Assistant.)

8 Familiarize yourself with the rules of the auction before the bidding starts, so you don't miss out on a great car. Read 374 Buy at Auction and learn the lingo. For example, an *absolute auction* means there's no reserve (minimum) price, in which case a car might be picked up for an extremely low bid. Also, some auction houses charge a 5 to 15 percent buyer's premium on top of the bidding price.

9 Remember that when you bid for these cars, you're not likely to get any warranties or guarantees. In fact, the car you buy may not even start.

What to Look For

- Monthly auctions
- Inspection period
- Used-car prices
- Auction rules

Tip

An "as is, where is" sales clause basically means the auction can't be held responsible for misrepresentation or defect: You're knowingly bidding on potential junk.

Warnings

Some auctions don't allow bidders to start up cars during inspection. Since you won't know if a vehicle runs, these auctions are a crap shoot.

Some auctions don't allow owners to try to recover their own impounded cars by bidding on them instead of paying all the fines, towing and storage fees they owe.

549 Get a High-Performance Car Audio System

Buying a car audio system can be more complex than buying the car. Audio components come with their own set of technical specifications, which may be unintelligible unless you're an electrical engineer. Find a salesperson who will help you cut through the marketing talk and evaluate what's really important to you.

Steps

1 Conduct enough research so that you're conversant with the basic terminology of audio systems. Audio and car magazines, knowledgeable friends and the Internet are your best sources.

2 Set a budget. Complete systems range from $500 to many thousands of dollars, but you can find choices within any budget.

3 Determine what *high performance* means to you. If you like rock and rap, maximum power output is important. If you like classical music, you want moderate power and exceptional sound quality.

4 Avoid buying a system one piece at a time. Every component, regardless of quality, has its own sound characteristics. If you buy everything separately, you won't have a chance to preview the whole system before you own it.

5 Understand speaker options. Most speakers are two-way, with a low-range driver *(woofer)* and a high-range driver *(tweeter)*. Three-way speakers include a midrange driver, which provides precise sound quality. Small car owners may opt to mount individual drivers, with the tweeters up front, and woofers and midrange drivers in back. Such systems require an *external crossover* device to synchronize the individual drivers. An audio shop will know the speaker limitations for your vehicle.

6 Research *head units,* also called *receivers,* which typically include a radio, an amplifier, and a CD or tape player. Head units list a power output figure in watts. Find a knowledgeable salesperson willing to explain the true power output. Higher-quality units usually have more power. Expect to pay $200 and up.

7 Check the *preouts,* plugs that allow for additional components on the head unit. If you plan on installing an equalizer (for improved sound tuning) and an additional amplifier (for more volume), be sure enough preouts exist. If you're connecting the head unit to existing components, be sure the preouts are compatible.

8 Make sure the head unit is compatible with satellite radio, MP3 and home-recorded CDs. Even if you don't use these now, you might in the future.

9 Select speakers and a head unit that are compatible in terms of power. Don't use speakers with a lower power rating than the head unit. In fact, it's a good idea to get speakers with a slightly greater rating, allowing for the addition of an amplifier later. Expect to pay $200 or more for top-quality speakers.

What to Look For

- Quality of sound
- Room for speakers
- Adequate power
- Preouts for more components
- Head unit compatibility

Tips

Budget for installation costs. High-power systems require professional installation. The pros will also know how to protect the appearance of your car.

Bring along some of your own CDs when you're shopping. You want to test a system using familiar music.

Any system will sound different in your car than it does in the showroom. The best you can do is preview the entire system as a unit, prior to installation.

If you're worried about your flashy new audio system prompting a break-in, a head unit with a detachable face is a very good idea. (See 546 Buy a Theft-Prevention Device.)

Warning

Wattage figures have become a marketing tool and are thus subject to misrepresentation.

550 Buy an RV

Buying an RV can be as complicated as buying a home. Start with the basics—running water, cooking and bathroom facilities, and a power source—then explore amenities such as entertainment systems, king-size beds and even hot tubs. Now you're ready to bust out the Willie Nelson and hit the road.

Steps

1 Understand that RVs are usually designated by length. The longer the RV, the more opulent and expensive. Height and width measurements do not vary significantly.

2 Remember that you need to drive the RV. What size vehicle can you handle confidently? Are you comfortable backing up? Will your spouse be comfortable driving it? Do you need a special license in your state?

3 Decide on which class vehicle is right for you. Class A motorized models are the largest. Class B motorized models are modified and have expanded van conversion: They are smaller, with better mileage, but you may sacrifice some comfort and amenities. Class C motorized RVs are even smaller and have a bed over the cab. The largest towable RVs are travel trailers, up to 35 feet (10.7 m) long. Fold-out camper trailers are smaller. A truck camper, fit to the back of a pickup, is considered a towable RV. If you already own a truck, this type may make the most sense.

4 Class A motorized models start at about $100,000. Class B range from $42,000 to $68,000. Class C models are about $50,000 to $100,000. Folding camper trailers and truck campers start at about $4,000, while larger travel trailers start at $9,000.

5 Negotiate the purchase price as you would with a car; in fact, you may have even more room to bargain. There are far more RV manufacturers than car manufacturers; use this competition to your advantage. If you can't find the style and options you want at a price that you think is reasonable, keep looking.

6 Go to an RV show. These are frequently advertised in newspapers and on TV. Talk to owners, dealers and other shoppers.

7 Try before you buy. Two of the largest rental operations in the United States are El Monte RV (elmonte.com) and Cruise America (cruiseamerica.com). Prices run from $90 to $200 per day (depending on the model) and peak in the summer.

8 Ask for deals. Most manufacturers offer rebates and significant kickbacks to dealers, who will pass along some or all if they think it will make a deal. Late summer is the best time to shop, as dealers are looking to get rid of the previous year's stock.

What to Look For

- Appropriate class
- RV shows
- Size
- Options and amenities

Tips

If you're a novice, consider taking driving lessons with your RV to make sure that both you and your fellow drivers are safe.

Many RV fans suffer from what industry professionals call *2-foot-itis*—the urge to constantly get a larger RV. This can be fun if you have the money, but don't overlook the advantages of the RV you own.

Books on RV travel are available at many bookstores. Go online to GoRVing.com to order a free video about RV basics in exchange for filling out a survey.

Warning

Look into insurance specifically for RVs. Your auto insurance may not cover total loss replacement, emergency living expenses, and campsite liability.

551 Buy a Trailer

You've fallen in love with a horse, but you're reluctant to ride him down the freeway to your house. Now what? Time to get a trailer. Get the lowdown on general trailer options, then on issues specific to horse trailers.

Steps

Standard trailers

1 Research the maximum towing capacity of your vehicle. This data is on the driver's doorpost or in the owner's manual.

2 Calculate the maximum load that will be hauled (for horse trailers, that's based simply on the number of horses you'll carry) and check the unloaded weight of any trailer you are considering. This should be stamped on the trailer. The unloaded weight plus maximum load is the total weight that you will tow. If that load surpasses your vehicle's maximum towing capacity, you need to either adjust your plans or get a larger vehicle.

3 Understand trailer design. The smallest trailers have a single axle. Many of these are capable of hauling only small loads such as most recreational boats, snowmobiles and personal watercraft, although large single-axle trailers exist. Double-axle trailers usually have a higher load capacity than single-axle trailers and always ride more smoothly. The additional wheels also add stability when the trailer is unhitched. They're used for large sailboats and car haulers. Triple-axle trailers haul very large loads such as tractors, and are difficult to maneuver due to their long wheelbase.

4 Find out what's the hitch. Trailers that connect to the back of a vehicle are *tag-along* trailers. These are also referred to as *bumper hitch* trailers, although only a tiny trailer can connect solely to a bumper. Most tag-alongs require a hitch that mounts to the vehicle frame. Larger trailers use a *fifth-wheel* or *gooseneck* mount that can be used only with a pickup truck that has a permanent hitch mount installed. These trailers ride more smoothly than tag-alongs.

5 Expect to pay about $1,000 for the smallest single-axle trailer. A medium-capacity, double-axle trailer costs about $3,000. Fully enclosed trailers are more expensive.

Horse trailers

1 Decide on the number of horses you will transport. Few single-horse trailers exist anymore. A two-horse trailer is the smallest that is generally available.

2 Look for a double-axle trailer, which is preferred for horse transport because of the smoother ride. Hitch mechanisms are the same as for general trailers.

3 Decide between a *stock* trailer and a *show* trailer. Stock trailers

What to Look For

- Towing capacity
- Weight of load
- Weight of trailer
- Number of axles
- Hitch type

Tips

Check local laws regarding trailer specifications. Some states require auxiliary battery power on trailers to power the brakes and lights in case of problems with the tow vehicle.

Electric brakes are fine for most light trailers. Heavy-duty trailers should have air brakes.

Take a driving course to learn how to safely drive, turn and back up a loaded trailer.

See 112 Buy a Thoroughbred Racehorse.

contain few amenities and are designed to move horses and a small amount of feed or equipment. Show trailers are spiffier and incorporate storage room for clothes and tack, and some even have human living quarters.

4 Expect to pay $6,000 for a basic two-horse stock trailer. A large show trailer can cost $40,000 or more.

Warning

Avoid used horse trailers with any signs of damage, even to the top or sides, which may compromise the necessary structural rigidity.

552 Buy a Water-ski Boat

The changing nature of boat design reflects how the sport has evolved over time. Skiers prefer small, soft wakes. Wakeboarders, on the other hand, want big wakes from which to launch aerial maneuvers. But when mom and dad are die-hard skiers, and the kids want to wake-board—and with $25,000 and more at stake—then what?

Steps

1 Review your basic options. An inboard engine is the most powerful and is located in the boat's hull. Cheaper outboard engines clamp onto the transom. Inboard/outboard engines combine the power of an inboard with the maneuverability of an outboard.

2 Understand the trade-offs between inboard engine types:

- A direct-drive engine is located mid-boat and sends power directly from the engine to the drive shaft to the propeller. Direct drives with their flat bottoms are preferred by skiers because they produce small wakes, and handle and track better. The flat hull, however, makes riding on choppy water a bouncy ride; and the engine, smack dab in the middle of the boat, uses up prime seating.

- V-drive boats have rear-mounted engines and a deep V hull that cuts through chop without a blink, but produce a large wake. Some feature ballast tanks that can be filled for even bigger wakes, making wakeboarders ecstatic, then drained again for skiers. The engine location allows for quieter, more sociable seating. Tow lines attach from a tower high above the cockpit.

3 Meet in the middle. Recognizing the market's changing needs, boat builders have designed crossover boats. Mostly featuring direct-drive engines, these "all-event" boats have ballast tanks that hold up to 1,600 lbs (597 kg) with adjustable trim-plates. So fill it up and create monster wakes, or dial it back down for the skiers; one boat happily serves both camps.

4 Investigate available amenities. Swim platforms make it easier to climb into the boat after a hard run, and overhead racks stow gear safely away.

What to Look For

- Engine type
- Direct-drive or V-drive
- Crossover boats
- Amenities

Tip

Improved technology has boosted engines to over 300 horsepower. In the future, look for boats with new composite hull materials and engines that further reduce noise and water pollution.

Warnings

The hull ventilation system prevents the buildup of explosive gasoline fumes. Make sure it works before operating the boat.

If you're buying a used boat, hire a marine surveyor to perform an inspection. This service costs several hundred dollars but will reveal any potentially disastrous problems. You need to be sure the engine is functioning and the hull is sound.

553 Find a Classic Wooden Powerboat

You've seen the gleaming Chris-Crafts racing across Lake Tahoe in *The Godfather: Part II*. If you're a true fan, sooner or later you'll be forced to confront "wooden boat affliction." The classic good looks of a finely crafted wooden boat are seductive—but do you really want to own one? Before you decide, better do your homework. Hire the necessary help and proceed carefully.

Steps

1 Set a budget and stick to it. Sounds simple, but it isn't. The first person you talk to is likely to say, "For a few thousand more, you can get a . . . ." Include repairs and expenses in your budget. If your total budget is $15,000, look for boats with a $10,000 purchase price. Reserve $5,000 for transportation, repairs, insurance and docking fees. You'll also need a trailer (see 551 Buy a Trailer).

2 Research boats thoroughly, using the Internet and the phone. Attend one of the two largest wooden boat shows in the United States, held each summer in Lake Tahoe, California, and Clayton, New York.

3 Contact wooden boat dealers, restorers and owners' clubs. You'll find boats for sale as well as information about your favorites. Be flexible about the exact appearance or type of boat that you want. Most manufacturers made numerous changes to a given model over the years.

4 Be patient and wait for what you want, and quell the urge to make an impulse buy. Prices can range from a few thousand dollars to six figures, depending on condition, size and collector appeal. Popular classic boat makers include Chris-Craft, GarWood and Riva.

5 Tell boat brokers what you're looking for. They can arrange boats for you to view or suggest places to look. Fiberglass boat dealers will tell you about the complications of wooden boats. Listen well.

6 Understand the commitment required by wooden boats, which reward you with great beauty but require attention. Budget about $1,500 per year to have your boat professionally maintained if you're not prepared to do the work yourself.

7 Respond to classified ads, outside your area if necessary. Chase leads and ask lots of questions about the boat's condition: Has it been out of the water for many years? Are the engine, electrical systems and gauges all functioning? Is the hull intact? Any modifications, except structural improvements done by a professional, are likely to make the boat less desirable to collectors.

8 Hire a marine surveyor. This inspection costs several hundred dollars but will uncover any serious problems and may also enable you to negotiate price reductions for small issues. Be prepared to back out of the deal if the survey findings are bad.

What to Look For

- Wooden boat shows
- Dealers
- Restorers
- Owners' clubs
- Brokers
- Original condition
- Functioning engine
- Intact hull
- Marine surveyor

Tips

No matter how tempting, never buy a boat on impulse, especially an old one.

Ask boat brokers to recommend a transport operation that is experienced with boats. Research any necessary delivery costs.

Warnings

Don't expect to restore a boat, then sell it at a profit. Sales prices of classic boats are almost always lower than the cost of doing a restoration. For discouraging information, contact the Antique and Classic Boat Society (acbs.org).

Gasoline-powered inboard boats require proper bilge ventilation to avoid buildup of explosive gas fumes. Be sure your boat is properly equipped.

554 Rent an Aircraft

With a pilot's license, you're not at the mercy of the major airlines' timetables; you can rent yourself a plane at many airports across the country. Even if you don't have a license, fleet operators and charter groups can get you where you need to go.

Steps

Get checked out

1 Visit a fixed base operator (FBO), which manages and rents aircraft at an airport for training, charters and pleasure flights.

2 Go through the checkout with a certified flight instructor (CFI) to judge whether you can safely operate the aircraft. Unlike car rental companies, FBOs don't assume you know how to operate the plane just because you have a license. The checkout typically takes two to five hours or more, and includes basic flight maneuvers, emergency procedures, landings and stalls. For a single-engine, fixed-gear aircraft, the checkout is straightforward. Requiring a longer checkout are complex planes, which have retractable landing gear and variable pitch propellers, and include high-performance planes of 200 horsepower and above. Multi-engine aircraft have a different rating and require even more time.

3 Check into renters insurance, which determines the rules by which a visiting pilot can rent planes. Your experience and your rating will determine the type of plane you can fly.

4 Fly away. Rules vary by FBO, but once you're signed off by the CFI, you can fly aircraft in the same category as the one in which the test was conducted. The checkout is valid for 90 days to six months, but only at that FBO.

Join the club

1 Join a local flying club, which you can find in the phone book under "Aircraft Charter, Leasing and Rental," or check Landings.com for a flying club directory. These clubs may charge a membership fee plus regular dues and per-flight costs.

2 Go through the club's checkout to join. Once again, your experience will determine the type of plane you're allowed to fly.

Charter a flight

1 Look in the phone book under "Aircraft Charter, Leasing and Rental" for planning companies that make the arrangements, much like a concierge. The group will find you an appropriate-size plane, cater the in-flight meal when needed, and take care of any necessary fleet liaison. It contracts with a number of fleet operators to try to match its customers' requirements.

2 Charter a plane with a fleet operator. Choice and availability of planes may be limited, but the concierge services are comparable.

What to Look For

- Fixed base operators
- Local liability insurance
- Checkout with CFI
- Flying clubs
- Renters insurance
- Planning companies
- Fleet operators

Tips

The fastest way to board a plane (outside of commercial flying) is to hire a planning company to charter a plane for you.

Plane rental prices vary: *Wet* prices include gas and oil used; *Hobbs* billing charges are only for when the engine is running; *Air Hobbs* bills only for time when the plane is moving at flying speed.

555 Sell Your Sailboat

How do you make your beloved boat attractive to buyers and stand out from the crowd? Unfortunately, the answer is hard work. Many sailboats are neglected for years prior to the decision to sell. Don't force buyers to look past the dirt and mildew to see your beautiful yacht.

Steps

1 Survey the market for used sailboats. Sailing publications, boat dealers, marinas and sailing enthusiasts' Web sites all have lists of sailboats for sale. Compare prices for boats of a similar size, age and condition as yours.

2 Identify areas where your boat is commonly found, then advertise locally. Your boat will sell best where it is a known entity and already popular. Skip placing ads in regular newspapers unless your local paper routinely carries a lot of sailboat ads.

3 Include photos of your boat with any ad. A full or three-quarter profile shot is best. Some online bulletin boards let you include a variety of shots; take additional pictures of the interior and stern.

4 Be able to rattle off the facts about your boat. Know the overall length, year of construction, draft, sail area and displacement. Customers lose faith in sellers who can't answer basic questions.

5 Look for a racing fleet (a group of boats, identical in design, that get together to race) for your boat. Yacht clubs or boat dealers in the area know if a fleet exists and how to contact it. Your goal is to place an ad in the fleet organization's newsletter. Be sure to inquire about a national organization with additional advertising opportunities.

6 Boat prices vary widely, usually based on how well the boat is equipped, but also on appearance, recent overall maintenance, and condition of the sails. Be honest about how your boat ranks against others like it.

7 Empty everything off the boat, including seat cushions, anchor and fire extinguisher. Search all the compartments. Don't make a buyer dig through your junk.

8 Clean the boat. While everything is off, take a bucket of soapy water and a big sponge and go over the whole interior. Get rid of mildew, mold and rust stains. Clean the items that you removed from the boat. If you intend to sell them with the boat, return them to their proper storage compartment. Let everything dry completely before closing the boat back up.

9 Scrub the deck and cockpit with a stiff brush and soapy water. Oil any teak trim. Coil any loose lines. Check that the winches spin freely and all fittings operate. Oil any items that need it.

10 Check the lights and electrical systems. Be sure the engine runs and the batteries are fully charged. Repair any minor problems.

What to Look For

- Fair price
- Appropriate location
- Racing fleet
- Cleanliness
- Good condition
- Sails in good shape
- Clean hull
- Prospective buyers

Tips

A marine surveyor is likely to find the flaws in your boat. If you are aware of any problems, it's best to be up front about them early in the process.

11 Fold all the sails neatly and store them in sail bags, either on the boat or nearby where they can be examined.

12 If the boat is on land, be sure the bottom is clean. Scrub off any algae or barnacles. If the boat is in the water, use a long handled brush to remove any visible growth.

13 If the boat is in a marina, inform the harbor master that your boat is for sale. He or she may be able to direct potential buyers to your boat.

14 Be prepared to spend considerable time with prospective buyers. Some buyers will want to go for a test sail. You may also need to be present when a marine surveyor inspects the boat on behalf of a buyer.

Go to a boatyard and practice being a customer. Ask yourself these questions: What's effective about the presentation? What sort of information would be useful?

556 Purchase a Satellite Navigation System

A navigation system in your car—with the help of global positioning satellites (GPS) sending out synchronized signals to wandering souls all over the planet—pinpoints your location with great accuracy. When your position is compared with the GPS system's embedded maps, frustrating voyages of all kinds turn into precision-guided tours.

Steps

1 Take your budget into account. If you're lusting after a high-end GPS system for your car, buy a built-in unit from your car dealer. If cash outlay is a concern, good-quality dash-mount and hand-held systems are one-tenth to one-fifth the price of built-in ones.

2 Imagine where you want to use your navigation system—driving around city streets, hiking mountains or touring the Virgin Islands in your yacht? Each intended use has its unique needs, whether it's street maps and directions, topographical and altitude information or extra battery power.

3 Decide what kind of maps you'll need: general, what-state-am-I-in maps, or precise city-driving directions? This will determine the capabilities you'll need from your system. After you make your purchase, make sure all the appropriate maps are loaded.

4 Look for features such as audible alerts that warn you of upcoming intersections or turns, and scrolling maps to track your progress. Opt for units with a larger display to avoid zooming in and out repeatedly to read names and find intersections.

What to Look For

* Built-in system
* Dash-mount or handheld system
* Maps and directions capabilities
* Audible alert and scrolling map features

Warning

Don't try to read a tiny, moving map while driving. If no one's riding shotgun with you, pull over and figure out where you're going.

INDEX

CONTRIBUTORS

Sharon Beaulaurier is a writer who lives in the San Francisco Bay Area. She is the former managing editor of eHow.com and a former news producer. Her head is full of useful and useless how-to information, and she is frequently called upon by friends in need of how-to help.

Lori Blachford honed her collecting skills while working as managing editor of *Country Home* magazine. She now does a variety of freelance writing and editing from her home in Des Moines. Her current conquest: Yoda figures from the Star Wars series.

Laura Buller never met a thrift shop she didn't like. She spends so much time in them that her friends joke the movie *Good Will Hunting* is about her. To pay for those 1970s transistor radios, miniature buildings and lunchboxes, she writes and edits books for children. Her own family affair (Alice and Sean) takes place in Los Angeles.

Julie Jares spent several years in the dot-com fray as a writer and editor for various Web sites, including eHow.com, Sidewalk.com and Concierge.com. Currently a freelancer, her recent projects include *Out to Eat in San Francisco* and *Hawaii's Big Island* guide, both from Lonely Planet.

Kathie Kull specializes in writing about building and remodeling and is the former editor of *Better Homes and Gardens Home Products Guide* magazine. Her Maine house (circa 1800) generates endless "to fix" and "to buy" lists.

Matthew Richard Poole is a freelance travel writer who has authored more than two dozen guides to California, Hawaii and abroad. Before becoming a full-time writer and photographer, he worked as an English tutor in Prague, ski instructor in the Swiss Alps, and scuba instructor in Maui. Highly allergic to office buildings, he spends most of his time on the road doing research and avoiding commitments.

Elaine Rowland is a freelance editor and writer who has rediscovered the thrill of automobiles since leaving Manhattan. She contributes regularly to several car owner magazines, but spends the rest of her time driving her new black Miata, giggling.

Sue Russell is an internationally syndicated, veteran reporter with over 1,500 articles published in numerous magazines and newspapers, including *Redbook, Us* and *Good Housekeeping*. She has been a health and beauty editor at a major women's magazine and has written on countless diverse topics. She is also the author of several nonfiction books on subjects ranging from beauty to true crime.

Fred Sandsmark is a freelance writer in the San Francisco Bay Area who covers technology-related subjects. A self-described "gadget freak on a budget," his prized geek possession is a Wi-Fi wireless network interface, bought (cheap) on eBay.com, that works with his aging, beloved Handspring Visor.

Marcia Whyte Smart is a San Francisco food writer and editor who has contributed to *Cooking Light, Sunset*, Citysearch, and *Parenting*. She's the associate food editor of *7x7* magazine.

Derek Wilson has bought and sold more sporting goods than any normal person should and if you don't believe him you're welcome to visit his garage and count the bicycles. He lives in the Lake Tahoe area of California and divides his time between economic consulting and writing projects which include *Burritos: Hot on the Trial of the Little Burro*, and contributions to *How to Fix (Just About) Everything*.

Marty Wingate is an author and teacher. Her features appear every Thursday in the *Seattle Post-Intelligencer's* Northwest Gardens. She also writes for national gardening publications including *Horticulture* and *Fine Gardening*. Her first book is *Big Ideas for Northwest Small Gardens*.

Weldon Owen wishes to thank the following people for their generous assistance and unflagging support in the production of this book: Bruce Adair; Scot Adair; Mona Behan; Jayne Benton PA-C; Tom Benton; Michael J. Block, DDS; Eric Block, DDS; Bob Bredsteen; Carol Breuner; Chris Breuner; Clay Breuner; Dave Breuner; Kristen Best Breuner, Dr. Lisa Breuner; Patty Brink; Gretchen Brooks; Luna Calderon; Trisha Clayton; Sarah Clegg; Steve Crumley; Dave Cohen; Patty Curtin; Carolyn Walker Davis; Susan E. Davis; Anja DenOuden; Susan Eckart; Pat Spratlin Etem; Chad Furlong; Sioux Jennett; Devon Johnson; Daniel JouJou of Ketér Salon; Paul Kelly; Sierra Kelly; Jane Larson; Alice Lee; Hon. Robert L. Martin; Michelle Mason; Deirdre McLoughlin, MSPT; Liz Miles; Virginia Miller; John and Lilly Moriarty of 14 Karats; Greg Mortenson; Susan O'Hara; Missy Park; Past Perfect Antiques; Mark Pengelski; Laura Pilnick, MFCC; Mike Radke; Darlene Percoats Redmon; Dave Rees; Sabawun Kakar of The Bubble Lounge; Gayna Sanders; Mike Steger; Suzanne Steger; Chris Stevens; Katherine B. Stickley, ASLA; Sonya Tafoya; Stephen Thomas; Lisa Thompson; Dana Tillson; Ed Van; Melissa Washburn; Angela Williams; and the indomitable Riley Breuner.